AF333760

In the Courts of Religious Ladies

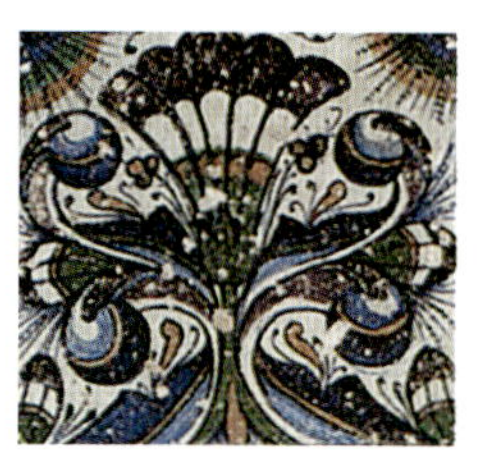

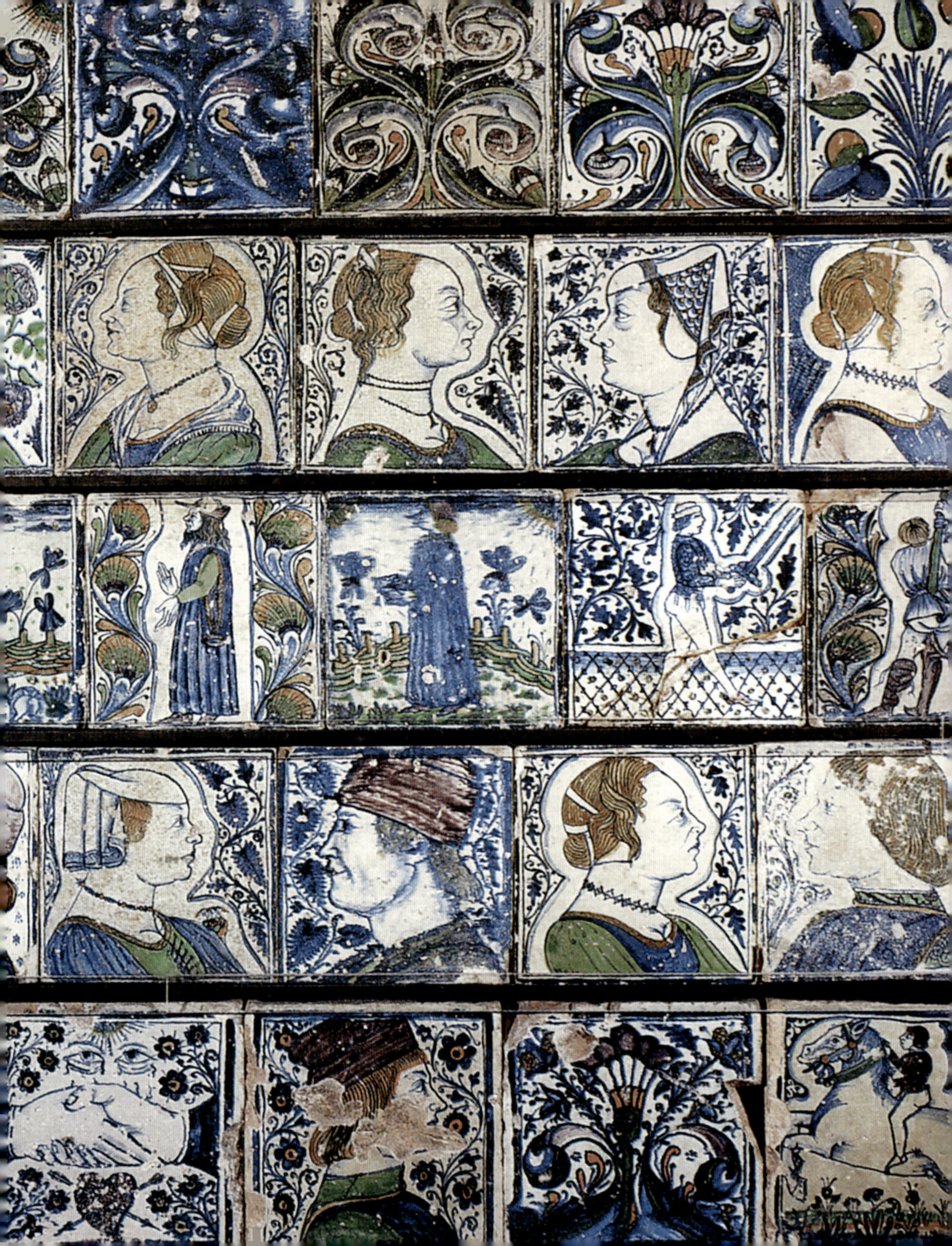

GIANCARLA PERITI

In the Courts of Religious Ladies

ART, VISION, AND PLEASURE IN ITALIAN RENAISSANCE CONVENTS

YALE UNIVERSITY PRESS NEW HAVEN AND LONDON

*Published with the assistance of the Lila Wallace –
Reader's Digest Publications Subsidy at Villa I Tatti*

Designed by Catherine Gaffney

Printed in China

Library of Congress Cataloging-in-Publication Data

Periti, Giancarla
   In the courts of religious ladies : art, vision, and pleasure in Italian
Renaissance convents /Giancarla Periti.
      pages cm
   Includes bibliographical references and index.
   ISBN 978-0-300-21423-9 (hardback)
   1. Art, Renaissance--Italy--Themes, motives. 2. Art, Italian--Themes, motives.
3. Women art patrons--Italy. 4. Monastic and religious life of women--Italy. 5.
Art and society--Italy. I. Title.
   N6915.P47 2016
   709.45--dc23
                                                    2015019377

A catalogue record for this book is available from The British Library

To *my parents*

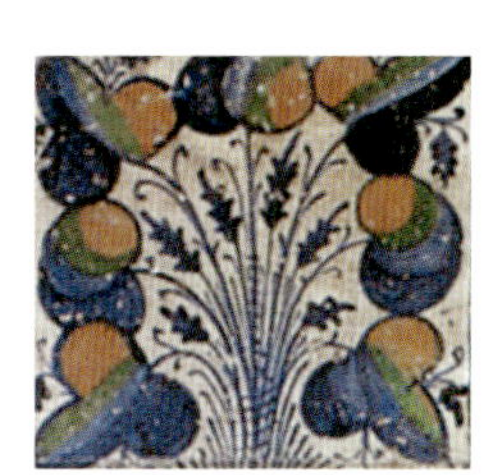

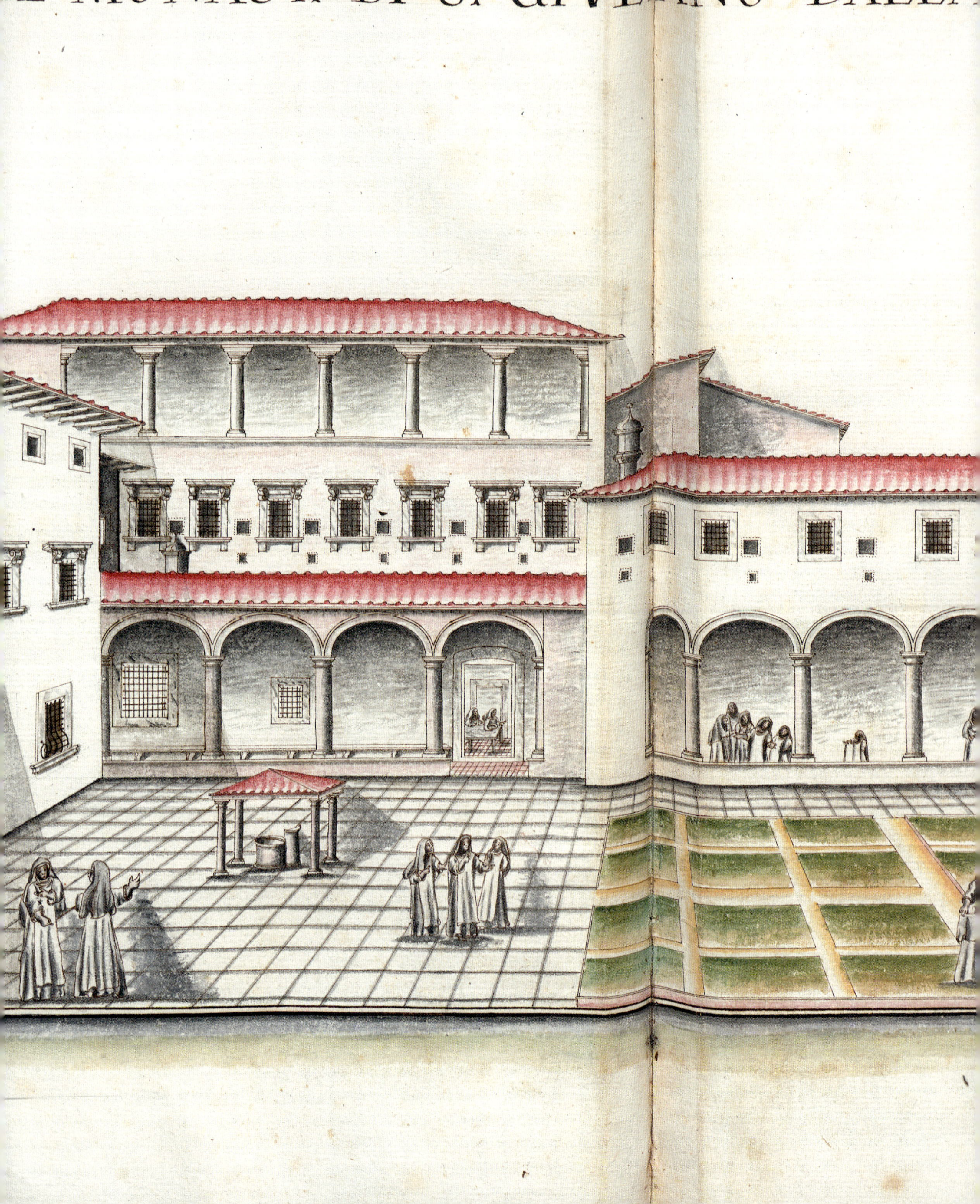

Contents

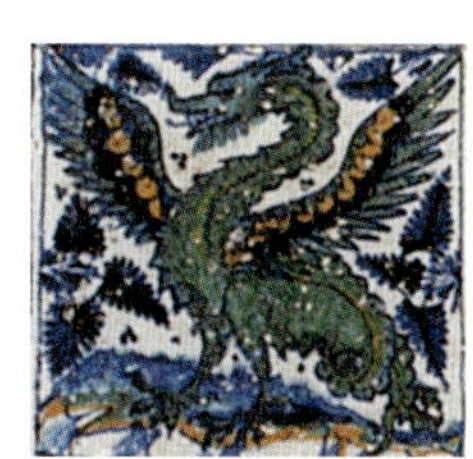

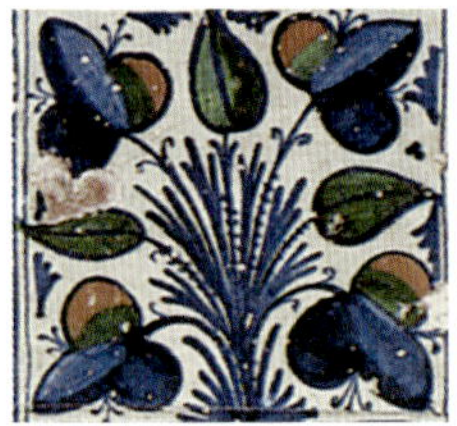

Acknowledgments

This book has had a long gestation. It gradually developed into a new project from my Ph.D. dissertation on the art of Correggio. As a book, it took shape while I moved between various institutions and countries and held different academic positions. Charles Dempsey, C. Jean Campbell, Ashley West, and Alessandra Talignani read earlier iterations of individual chapters and offered perceptive suggestions to improve and fine-tune my argumentations. To them I owe a great debt of gratitude. Jennifer Purtle, Ethan Matt Kavaler, and three anonymous reviewers read my entire manuscript, and their comments, both critical and encouraging, made this book stronger. I am grateful for their time and energy, and for the incisive feedback they all provided.

I could not have completed this book if I had not been supported by rich libraries and generous institutions, including the Center for Advanced Study in the Visual Arts, The Metropolitan Museum of Art, and The Harvard University Center for Italian Renaissance Studies at Villa I Tatti. A grant from the Lila Wallace-Reader's Digest Publications Subsidy at Villa I Tatti supplied funds to cover expenses that I accrued for photographs and permission fees. As I am writing these lines I am also conscious of how much I benefited from the seminars, symposia, and lectures that I attended at these institutions, as well as from conversations with fellow peers. I have especially profited from interactions with Diane Bodart, Flora Dennis, Sarah Guérin, Robert LaFrance, Paola Modesti, Shilpa Prasad, and Warren Woodfin.

Over the years portions of this book have been (or soon will be) published as independent articles. A segment of Chapter Two appeared as "Female Self-Commemoration, Spirituality and Lineage in Jacopo Loschi's Frescoes for the Convent of San Paolo in Parma," *I Tatti Studies* 13 (2010): 11–32, in a slightly different version from its present incarnation; "Correggio, Giovanna Piacenza and the Tradition of Monastic Interiors," *Artibus et Historiae*, forthcoming, comprises material from Chapter Four but the emphasis is different. I have also presented segments of what would become this book at the College Art Association and Renaissance Society of America conferences, at symposia and lectures held at the Galleria Nazionale in Parma, Rutgers University, Institute of Fine Arts, New York University, Tulane University, Wesleyan University, and The National Gallery of Art, Washington, D.C. All of these events brought me into contact with cordial hosts and engaged audiences who were generous in their suggestions.

I have benefited from conversations, advice and the expertise of several colleagues who have remained interested in my project over the years, especially Carmen Bambach, Andrea Bayer, Stephen J. Campbell, Keith Christiansen, Brian Curran, Paola D'Agostino, Charles Dempsey, Marzia

Faietti, Davide Gasparotto, Alessandra Galizzi Kroegel, Estelle Lingo, Stuart Lingo, Heather Hyde Minor, Vernon Hyde Minor, Alexander Nagel, Alessandro Nova, Giovanna Perini, Ulrich Pfisterer, Carl Brandon Strehlke, Michael B. Sullivan, Hérica Valladares, Timothy Wilson, and Christopher Wood. A special thanks is due to Elizabeth Cropper and Joseph Connors, who have been precious interlocutors at crucial junctures.

I would also like to acknowledge the assistance of Francesco Benelli, Stefano Calzolari and Raimondo Sassi, who intervened with practical help to solve problematic knots. Annarita Ziveri went beyond her call of duty to provide me with visual materials in the most rapid way. Mirna Bonazza also extended herself to smooth out problems with photographs from rare books for me. Tianna Uchacz redrew the plans of the convent of San Paolo in Parma. Julia C. Triolo made this book more readable and offered me sensible comments. To all of these individuals I owe a debt of gratitude.

Likewise, at the University of Toronto, I am grateful to all of my colleagues. Philip Sohm and Elizabeth Legge deserve special mention for their interest and support of my project. Extended conversations with Jennifer Purtle, in particular, served as a spur for rethinking and refining my argumentation. I cannot have found a more congenial intellectual atmosphere in which to push through the completion of my book.

At Yale University Press I am very thankful for Gillian Malpass's enthusiastic support of my book through its various stages. Katherine Ridler, my copy-editor, polished my manuscript with professionalism, and Jacquie Meredith revised the proofs with care. Catherine Gaffney is responsible for the beautiful design and layout of this book. It has been a pleasure to work with them.

Last but not least come those who have sustained me most. Throughout this long journey my family has been steadfast in its belief in me. My mother, Luigina Carella, is capable of uplifting me through a unique combination of strength and humor. My sister, Giovanna, and Johannes Zykoudis have often been piers to lean on. And my father, Gian Luigi Periti, saw nothing of this book, but he made sure early on that it would be a reality.

Toronto, October 2015

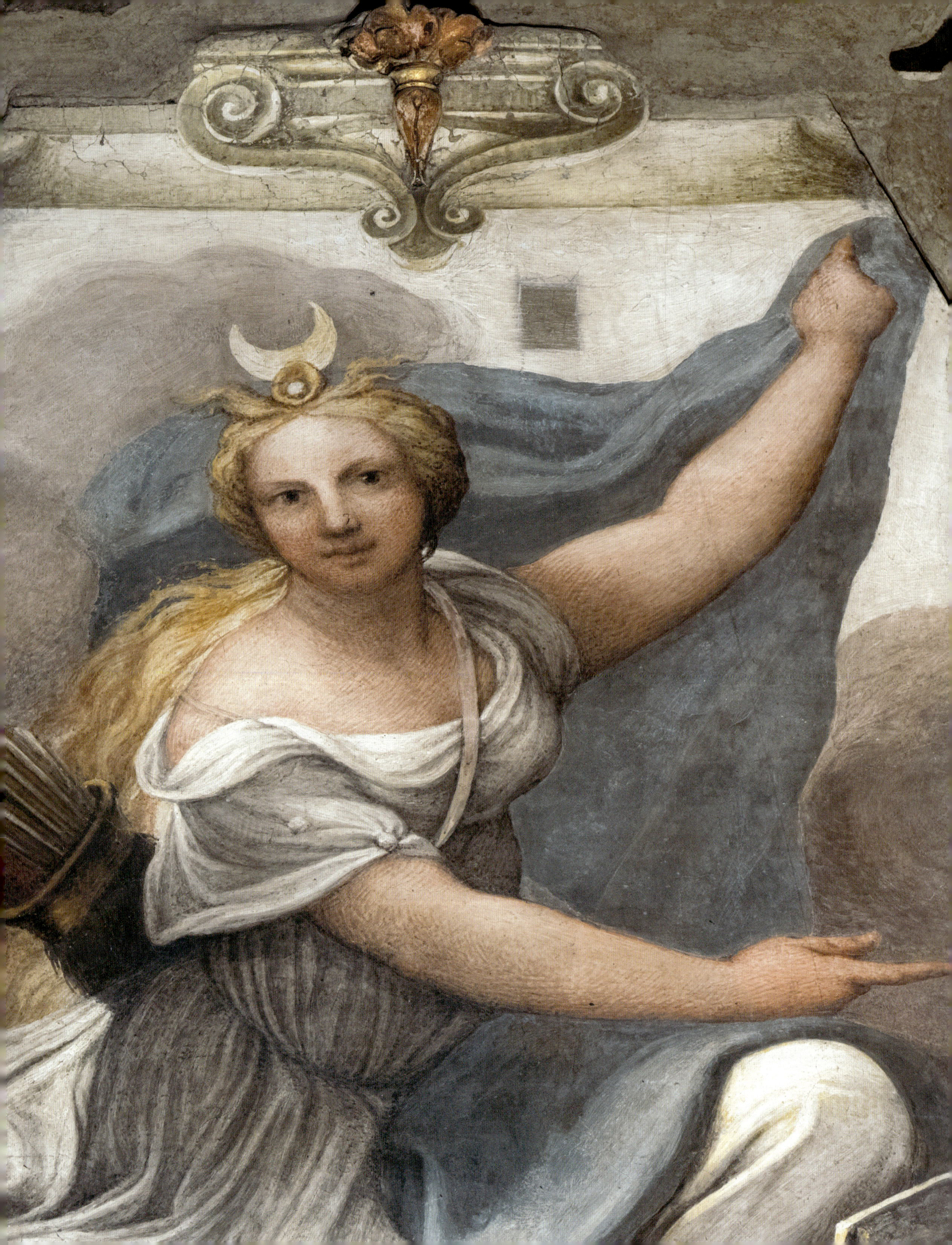

Introduction

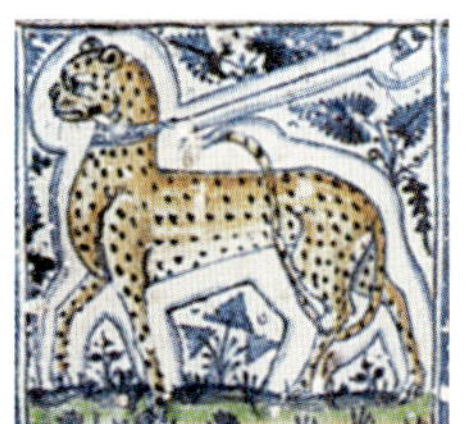

This book is about art and convents in Renaissance Italy. Elite abbesses had long sustained the distinction of their class and status by using personalized seals bearing female portraits and finely crafted crosiers as insignia of their office. Tapestries and frescoes of poetic subjects transformed conventual spaces into places of material splendor. Such artifacts appear to the modern spectator as manifestations of the power of noble consecrated women and as sites of productive exchange between religious and secular spheres. But Renaissance viewers, especially ecclesiastical authorities, perceived them in less neutral terms. Patrician consecrated women were seen as transcending the accepted discourses of social rank and role by surrounding themselves with precious and pleasing objects that dangerously transgressed the boundaries of monastic decorum. This study examines the multifaceted entanglements of art and religious obligation among the noble cloistered women of early modern Italy.

Conventual life was rigidly disciplined and cloistered individuals were expected to obey the rules of their orders. Rules were intended to regulate the inner and outer behavior of nuns, and their rituals and spaces, and to direct them toward the attainment of spiritual perfection. Monastic norms prescribed that consecrated women should shun contact with men, maintain their virginal status, separate themselves from worldliness, and deprive themselves of luxury, comfort, and earthly pleasure. Nuns were thus com-

pelled to inhabit a liminal zone between the sacred and the mundane, in which they prayed for the wellbeing of the laity, performed manual work, and dedicated their lives to the service of others. Secluded within the high walls of convents, however, religious women of noble extraction occupied a privileged zone "betwixt and between" the *seculum* (the secular world) and the *claustrum* (the cloister) that was often adorned with all manner of appealing art and furnishings. Elite cloistered women appointed their settings with fine objects that encouraged delight in the tactile and sensual, challenging the ideal of deprivation that was foundational to the religious life and subverting its routine organized around the daily cycle of prayers at fixed hours.

Italian Renaissance art made for patrician religious women in different media, dimensions, and genres is especially remarkable for its profane subjects and sensuous forms, as well as its inventive engagement with a wide range of concerns dear to its female audience. These works, not commonly expected in religious houses, turned conventual settings into courtly environments of material opulence and visual seduction. For its well-preserved body of work spanning almost half a century and the appeal of its frescoes by the eminent Italian painter Correggio (fig. 1), the Benedictine convent of San Paolo in Parma constitutes the culmination of this development of transforming monastic spaces into refined courtly sites. Up to now, the study of Correg-

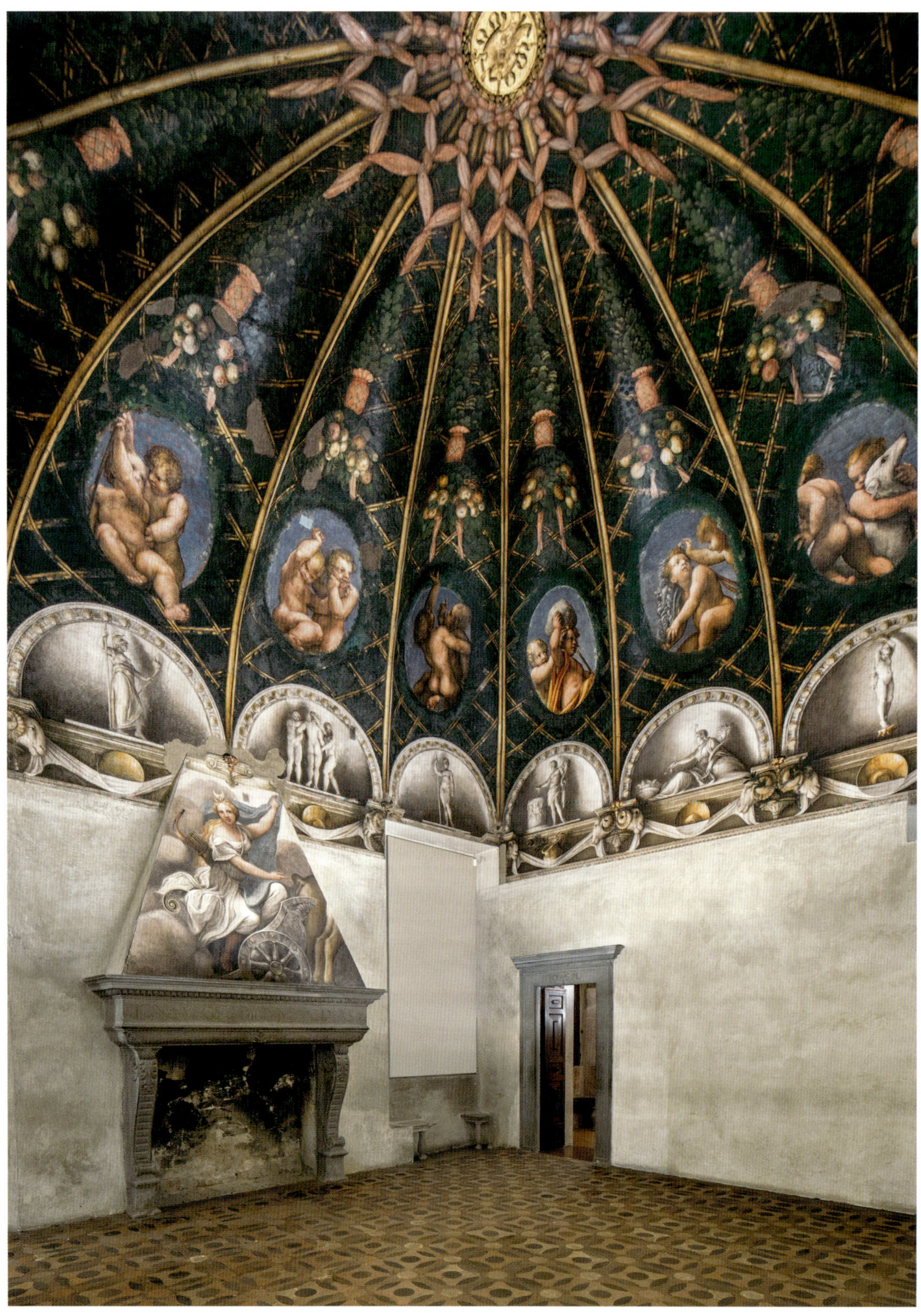

1   Correggio, frescoed room, ca. 1518–19, Parma, convent of San Paolo

gio's delightfully mischievous putti and mythological themes that ornament a room of the abbatial apartment (ca. 1518–19) has been subsumed either in monographs on the artist or under the rubrics of female patronage and iconography, neglecting the distinct phenomenology that they reflect as a whole. Such approaches have not provided persuasive answers to the most pressing questions that Correggio's frescoes pose: how should viewers understand his exquisite images that depict secular scenes for consecrated women? What was their purpose in such an environment, where the gaze was regulated and numerous signs warned against straying, "dishonest" eyes? What do these works say about the conventual culture they index, filter, and reproduce?

In general, modern scholarship has largely ignored this facet of monastic production that I define as courtly conventual art, in effect obscuring a tradition whose makers and beholders shared a code of values centered on notions of cultural attainment, Christian ethics, and magnificence. Such inattention is certainly rooted in the commonly perceived opposition between luxury and conventual life, but principally it stems from the covering, removal, and even destruction of fine monastic artifacts by ecclesiastical authorities in anticipation or in the wake of the convent reform promulgated by the Council of Trent in 1563.[1] This repressive Tridentine ideology has greatly shaped perception of the relations between art and female monasticism in the early modern period, contributing to the eclipse of the complex and contradictory world of elite religious communities and their visual culture. Decades of ground-breaking research on the role of art in religious institutions has begun, however, to pave the way for recovering this alternative conventual tradition in its historical and conceptual framework.

Studies have mainly concentrated on religious images seen as vectors of nuns' spiritual beliefs and dynamic mediators in encountering God. Although these contributions are tangential to my study, they remain relevant to the understanding of the courtly monastic art that flourished in Renaissance Italy. Jeffrey Hamburger's foundational scholarship on the "intelligence" of the medieval image and its liturgical and artistic performativity has much enhanced scholars' comprehension of the function of conventual art in joining human and divine spheres, and of the relationship between artists' imagination and their female religious viewers' response. In particular, Hamburger's writings on art objects made by German medieval nun-artists, with their manual labor turned into a form of monastic virtue, have begun to challenge standardized narratives of medieval art history. Currently, they are reorienting perceptions of the

relationship between images and sacred texts, the spiritual and the physical, the high and the low.[2]

Recent contributions by such historians as Kate Lowe, Gabriella Zarri, and Silvia Evangelisti have offered insights into the dense intersections of gender and religion, the social and economic history of Renaissance nuns, and the choreographed ceremonies that marked the stages of their advancement in the conventual life. Gabriella Zarri's exemplary studies since the 1970s have enriched knowledge of early modern women's spirituality, which embraced the body, senses, and mind. Her scholarship has addressed questions of monastic discipline, female conduct, and rituals, forging a renewed understanding of how nuns' devotional practices affected their assessment of the immanent world. Exploring convents' manuscript chronicles, Lowe's insightful book has considered processes of female education and writing, elaborating on the shifts that the Council of Trent's decree on convents brought to their inhabitants' lives and the interrelationship with the outside world. Silvia Evangelisti's valuable publications have done much to illuminate the tensions between clerics' repressive authority and nuns' resistance to their power. In general, this literature has covered questions of nuns' religiosity, learning, and behavioral customs from the late fifteenth century to the post-Tridentine periods. It does not disregard the turning point that rigid Tridentine regulations represented for convents' inhabitants but, rather, traces a *longue durée* that better articulates and nuances our understanding of pre- and post-Tridentine monastic culture.[3] Informed by feminist and social theories, this scholarship, which ultimately historicizes the lives of Italian Renaissance nuns, has many implications for the Renaissance reception of conventual art and architecture.

Equally helpful have been Helen Hills's illuminating studies on seventeenth-century Neapolitan conventual buildings, which have examined the dynamic intersections among patrician nuns, their secluded status, gendered identity and architectural patronage. Her work covers convents of different orders and with different historical profiles to define a post-Tridentine monastic architecture of enclosure that controlled nuns' bodies and gazes but simultaneously manifested consecrated women's presence in cities. Concerned with questions of vision and space, Hills has explored the tensions between religious women's obstructed views and the splendor of their confined sites, ultimately furthering comprehension of the spatial contexts in which elite nuns lived and the social and political values that their architecture negotiated and reproduced.[4] I have gratefully drawn on this literature in my research.

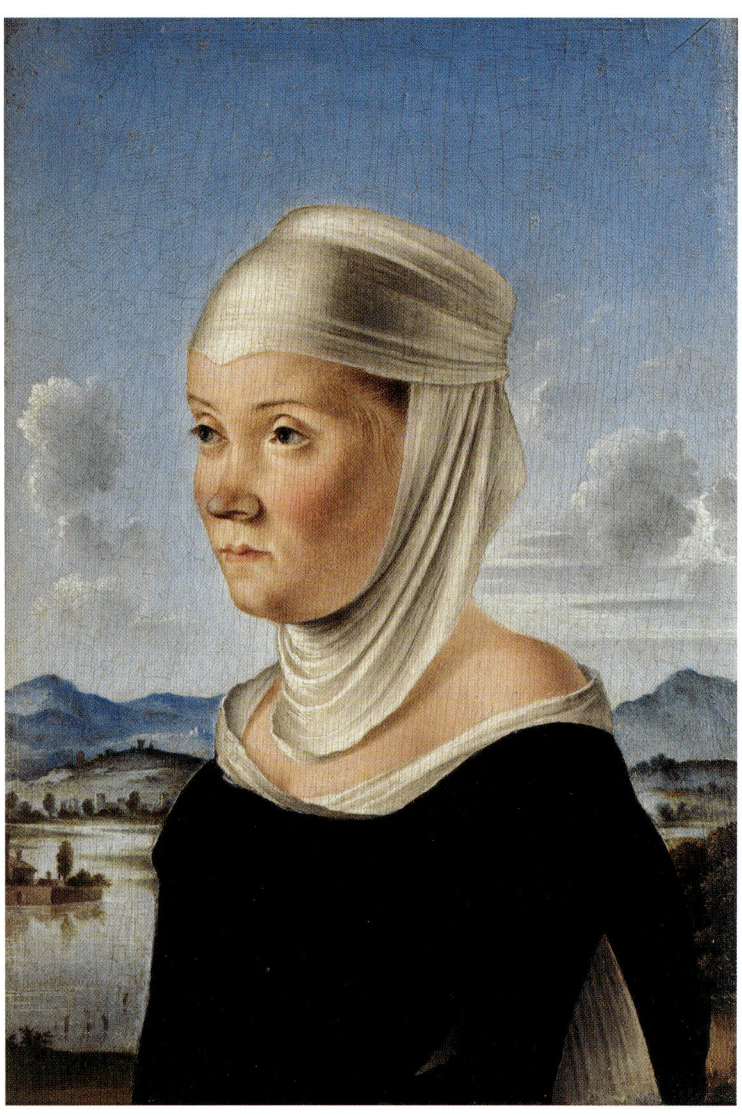

2   Jacometto Veneziano, *Portrait of a Nun from San Secondo* (recto), ca. 1485–95, oil on panel, 10.2 × 7 cm (4¹⁄₆₄ × 2¾ in), New York, Metropolitan Museum of Art

This book focuses on an unconventional monastic artistic corpus of poetic, mythological, and to a lesser extent Christian subjects inscribed with unusual markers of the female self, celebrating and memorializing the liminal subjectivity of upper-class cloistered women, and their yearning for knowledge and pleasure. Refined objects and seductive images, which monastic reformers had long censored, transformed convents into distinct courts with permeable and even volatile boundaries whose aesthetic and cultural implications are not fully apparent in the traditional narratives of the Renaissance. Here I contextualize and reconceptualize an eminent if atypical body of monastic works. My study considers both the so-called decorative artifacts such as maiolica floor tiles and wood intarsia passed over in the standard histories of Italian Renaissance art, and the celebrated frescoes by Correggio, among others, which have contributed greatly to the very definition of that art. At stake is not simply the recovery of a marginalized facet of early modern Italian conventual art. What matters more is the reconstruction of monastic spatial contexts and the historical modes of looking at images made for noble religious women, who used them to challenge concepts of female passivity, modesty, and deprivation. This study recaptures the messages projected by the images onto their audiences, revealing unanticipated hermeneutical registers, and the mediating role of that art.

Works from Parma's convent of San Paolo reflect this courtly conventual culture at its highest level, but its critical implications reach well beyond the confines of that institution. It is a paradigmatic corpus that does not merely mirror the convent's specific history and profile, its fractured relationships with local ecclesiastical authorities, or its nuns' disobedient behaviors and unreformed status. It also points to a larger reality, namely, that of noble women secluded in convents, which traversed the history of several female branches of religious orders (Benedictines, Cistercians, and Camaldoles). These elite nuns existed in a world of unresolved paradoxes and contradictions. They lived in religious communities without ever totally divorcing themselves from the wordly sphere; they embraced poverty but never gave up comfort, luxury, or decor; they were cloistered but enjoyed a certain freedom of movement. Their precariously confluential world enfolded opposite values, instances of seclusion and openness, sensuous delight and piety, obedient submission and disorderly discontent. Christians of inferior status according to the Church hierarchy, aristocratic nuns had long been admonished to conduct lives according to the morals and humility of religious life. Exasperated by their contrary behavior, ecclesiastical authorities often denounced them. For example, the Patriarch of Venice, Antonio Contarini, stated in 1509: "[local nuns] are accustomed to leaving convents and wandering about the city, in private houses, in St. Mark's and elsewhere, at leisure, dressed in secularized clothing causing scandal among the citizens and authorities alike."[5] Contemporary diarists and preachers even turned patrician nuns' profligate customs into the cause of the calamities that beset Italy, comparing elite nunneries to "whore houses" in urgent need of reform.[6] During his Christmas sermon in 1497, the Franciscan Fra Timoteo accused the nuns of Venice of sexual activity and thus of causing plague epidemics in the city. He continued: "Whenever a foreign lord comes to this country, you show them nunneries, [which are] not nunneries [but are really] public brothels."[7] And Fra Timoteo was not alone in his negative view of patrician nuns.

Their negotiation of sacred and profane values and ideals of both simplicity and sumptuousness are not only suggested in misogynist literature deploring the weak nature of female monastics, but are also prominently registered in works of art that capture this multifaceted world in its complexity. The images from San Paolo represent this conflicted and ambiguous culture of opposites, much as does Jacometto Veneziano's portrait of an attractive nun in décolletage (fig. 2), which has long perplexed scholars for its unusual representation of the female religious self. It is my aim to recover this still underground monastic visual tradition, and not merely to chart the significance of the San Paolo corpus. Such a study, a systematic reprocessing and reclaiming of the most impressive remains of this displaced corpus can help us to trace this aspect of Renaissance female monasticism and to reassess its rich intersections with local artists who promoted an active and sympathetic engagement with the values of that world.

The elite conventual art of the Renaissance was itself a development of a medieval tradition of monastic precious artifacts that religious reformers had strongly criticized and attempted to extinguish, but which resurfaced in self-consciously aestheticized forms and multiple media in early modern Italy, epitomizing the dialectic between the era of the cult image (*Bild*) and that of self-referential art (*Kunst*). For its representational concerns, aesthetic claims, and artistry, this alternative female monastic visual culture was first threatened by local pre-Tridentine movements of religious reform and then abruptly suppressed by Tridentine ecclesiastical authorities throughout the Italian peninsula. Yet it reappeared again in subsequent centuries and found expression in the New World as well, indicating that its study is fundamental to the elucidation of a long-lived tradition of material splendor, learning, and oppression within the history of female monasticism. This book specifically addresses one of its summits, thereby re-evaluating what can be defined as a kind of "counter-history" in Renaissance Italy. As Michel Foucault pointed out, forms of suppressed and alternative traditions regarding women and minorities often develop as counterparts of institutionalized history.[8]

By assembling and dissecting an unusual body of conventual images intended to please and provoke stimulations and that compensated for nuns' physical seclusion, I seek to show how this art interwove and filtered models of Renaissance courtly culture and Christian morality, introducing an unprecedented contamination between dominations of spirituality and carnality, beauty and sophistication, concealment and gendered perspectives. Developing notions of magnificence and luxury formulated in courtly literature and that had long been disparaged in monastic writings, this book suggests that appealing conventual images were designed to communicate ethical messages to elite audiences. This art addressed the values and possibilities of an irenic culture that combined sacred and humanist knowledge to foster instruction, spirituality, and pleasure. It was an art that presupposed and thematized the learning of noble religious women while presenting an original solution to the problem of decorating monastic environments, turning them into courts that proclaimed notions of female leadership, virtue, and independence.

Discussion of the ways cloistered women activated works distributed in their spaces is based on monastic comportment literature, documentation, and other contextual studies, compelling evidence that conveys the semiotic density and potentially subversive implications of this art, so integral to its original viewing modes. Indeed, the peculiarly ambiguous, liminal identity of the aristocratic nuns is an essential aspect of this dynamic. Defined as *dominae* (ladies), patrician religious women were well-educated, owned property, and were accustomed to a refined lifestyle. These ladies inhabited convents that fulfilled much-needed social functions in early modern Italy, serving as residences and educational centers for aristocratic women, widows, and abused wives. Civic, cultural, familial, and personal concerns were therefore much at stake in the genesis of this art, as was the desire of this female religious elite to articulate a culture distinct from that of their male peers. Deprived of any real power in the hierarchy of the Catholic Church but sharing the same insignia as bishops (the pastoral and the throne), abbesses of old, wealthy communities exerted considerable authority within the confines of their convents. Their embellished apartments could thus be seen as gendered responses to the residences reserved for bishops. As representatives of the Church in the local dioceses, they held court, received guests, and administered business in their ecclesiastical palaces, the spatial incarnation of male religious power.

In considering this alternative conventual art, I attempt to recover the function and meaning of decorated monastic settings. I concentrate on the embellished interiors of San Paolo in Parma, the best-preserved site, and to a lesser extent on highly ornate spaces in Benedictine convents in Milan, Brescia, and Ferrara, thus also contributing to the expansion of the artistic geography of Renaissance Italy that has concentrated on such canonical cities as Florence, Rome, and Venice. As has long been known, Benedictine houses were institutions of ancient, often royal or episcopal, foundation that enjoyed special privileges and were reserved for the daughters of local elites. This book looks at various impressively outfitted and ornamented spaces of Benedictine nunneries: parlors, abbatial apartments, nuns' cells, and choirs, among others. Designated as sites of contact with the outside world, these places were thresholds between the sacred and profane worlds, the loci where elite religious women's authority and virtue could be asserted, negotiated, and simulated through art.[9]

As a whole, these ornate spaces, which were characterized by specific access and rituals, are not wholly preserved in any extant institution, since most monastic buildings underwent major alterations during later centuries to adapt them to different uses. Even if this were not the case, a sustained art-historical account of this courtly monastic visual tradition requires consideration of decorated sites from more than one religious house. But this is not a comparative study; rather, its aim is to demonstrate how this female conventual visual culture participated in the larger trends of Renaissance art. In so doing, I hope to integrate this marginalized segment of monastic art with established accounts of the period and to nuance long-standing oppositions between religious and vernacular cultures, pagan and Christian mysteries, devotional and secular traditions.

Given these premises, the task of reconnecting works long divorced from their original monastic environments demands contextual analyses of the corpus and of its historical audiences' processes of activating meanings, both reframed in the light of recent critical rethinking of notions of space and vision. Elaborating on the scholarship on space advanced by Michel Foucault and others, one might see the lavishly fitted out conventual settings as "other" spaces that were neither private nor public, neither wholly domestic nor social. They were, rather, sites that facilitated sets of relations and associations bound up with the nuns' desire to follow, and yet in imagination to escape from, the institutional requirements forced on them.[10] Such dense intersections made possible provocations and disobedience against the spatial and visual restrictions imposed on religious women.

Modern scholarship on the modalities of vision, and its possibilities of penetration and exchange, has further made clear that the transmission of visual stimuli from objects to viewers' eyes and/or vice versa was not a neutral trajectory in the Renaissance. Sight had long been perceived as the noblest among the senses, because it was considered to provide the fullest knowledge of things, yet monastic writers maintained that vision was deceitful, with the power to mislead and distract from spiritual pursuit. Male authorities, aware that the eyes were especially porous and vulnerable to temptation, were constantly admonishing nuns not to look around to attempt to gain knowledge through vision. Michel de Certeau and Georges Didi-Huberman have refined the modern understanding of the density of perceptual experiences, advocating a phenomenology of the gaze and touch of perambulating individuals who cross spaces with an alert consciousness.[11] In particular, Certeau's rethinking of the relation between peripatetic bodies and enhanced forms of sensory perception permits us to theorize the viewing of art on walls, floors, and ceilings, which afforded the nuns and their guests who walked by these fields fresh mental and emotional sensations. These images and embellishments could reveal unexpected registers of humor, pleasure, and even the quiet subversion of regulations, modulating our understanding of how Renaissance individuals interacted with works in different art media. Each medium expanded the phenomenology of the nuns' vision and over time became more and more complex in its form, compositional strategies, and subjects, implying different levels of imagination and stimulation for its beheld subjects.

In evaluating this conventual art, I offer a sort of progression through the decorated spaces of a few Italian Renaissance Benedictine convents. A preliminary and general discussion of communal and private monastic spaces, and regulations about their use and viewing modes, introduces the nuns' routines and rituals. In the succeeding chapters dedicated to the nuns' choir, the parlor, and the chapter house, a nuanced comprehension will be gained of the plural message of artworks in differing media and scale, and simultaneously of the dangers of exalting refinement in conventual settings. These culminate in the frescoes in Giovanna Piacenza's abbatial apartment in San Paolo that do not merely decorate a courtly conventual world but actively create that world.

Drawing from monastic, artistic, and literary material, Chapter One provides an overview of elite convents in Italy, exploring their contradictions, paradoxes, and complexities, and noting how these patrician communities could become pockets of resistance to claustral rules. Particular attention is paid to the intersections between rules of monastic comportment and the architecture of seclusion, which both concurred to make nuns obedient and passive individuals subject to regulations that controlled the body and the gaze. Against the reality of the observant monastic community, I discuss how some aristocratic convents' inhabitants eluded strict obligations, creating the conditions for these nuns to assert their agency through investments in luxurious objects. Overall, the chapter contextualizes and historicizes the conditions for the rise of a conventual court visual tradition in early modern Italy.

Chapter Two engages with questions of vision and gaze by focusing on two marginalized artistic episodes in San Paolo: a set of frescoes by Jacopo Loschi from the 1460s, and a fine maiolica pavement from the late fifteenth century. Both works incorporate portraits of religious women who can be convincingly identified. These works memorialized confrontational moments in the history of the community and celebrated several of its members. In particular, the chapter explores the relationship between the prescription that nuns keep their eyes downcast while walking and the consequent activation of the poetic, mythological, and amorous subjects represented on the maiolica tiles underfoot. Such simultaneous engagement of sight and touch with the appealing tile scenes generated forms of intensified viewing and could be seen as constituting subtle forms of insubordination and/or even the opposite, of catharsis on the part of nuns treading on secular representations of the female self.

In Chapter Three I address the lavish furnishings in nuns' cells and the impressive frescoes by Girolamo Romanino and Bernardino Luini that turned the choirs of the reformed Benedictine communities in Brescia and Milan into sites of devotional splendor, reflecting on how the aesthetic value of religious art became a primary preoccupation of elite nuns in the early sixteenth century. The discussion concludes in a sustained engagement with the fine wood intarsia choirstalls of three rival elite religious communities in Parma, providing an account of the material opulence that enveloped religious institutions despite monastic strictures. Works in different media resonated with one another in choirs to create visually complex spatial environments, manifesting a tension between the rich materiality of the works, their artistry, and their devotional function.

Chapter Four takes up notions of gender, authority, and the cultivated female religious self that were projected in a set of witty inscriptions displayed in the rooms that Abbess Giovanna Piacenza (1507–24) commissioned for herself at San Paolo. These form a sequence of embellished chambers that served as the abbess's residence and the convent's guesthouse, a site for the gathering and the imagining of the convent's court, and the role and enjoyment of art. An examination of an additional fresco traditionally attributed to Alessandro Araldi, once located by the convent's gate and featuring St. Catherine defeating the philosophers, underscores the ideals of knowledge and excellence that pertained to the female sex at that crucial monastic interface between the sacred and the secular zone, the inside and the outside worlds.

Chapters Five and Six address the chambers painted in Giovanna Piacenza's residence by Araldi (ca. 1514–15) and Correggio. Giovanna's painted rooms are unique for their display of enigmatic images including hieroglyphs and other abstruse profane subjects. Araldi packed the vault of Giovanna's room with female hybrid figures set in dialectical and confrontational relationships with the wall lunettes, which depict deeds of ancient heroines and ideas of female virtue and Christian morality. It is suggested that the subject of this chamber is any viewer who is guided by examples of virtue and tools of visual enchantment in the search for nourishment through art, as promised by the psalm verses inscribed on the room's fireplace.

The enchanting room painted by Correggio, which has been much celebrated in twentieth-century historiography on Renaissance art, is the focus of Chapter Six. It is effectively the culminating instance of this art for cultivated consecrated ladies, strongly soliciting the onlooker to gaze upward to participate in its multiple games of interpretation, pleasure, and seduction. The image's aesthetic appeal also signals the rise of the artist's modern style that permitted Giovanna Piacenza and Correggio mutually to reinforce their agencies. Ecclesiastical authorities ultimately obscured this pinnacle of conventual art immediately after Giovanna's death in 1524. They closed off and sealed Correggio's chamber from the rest of the convent's building, hiding its significance until modern scholarship brought it to light.

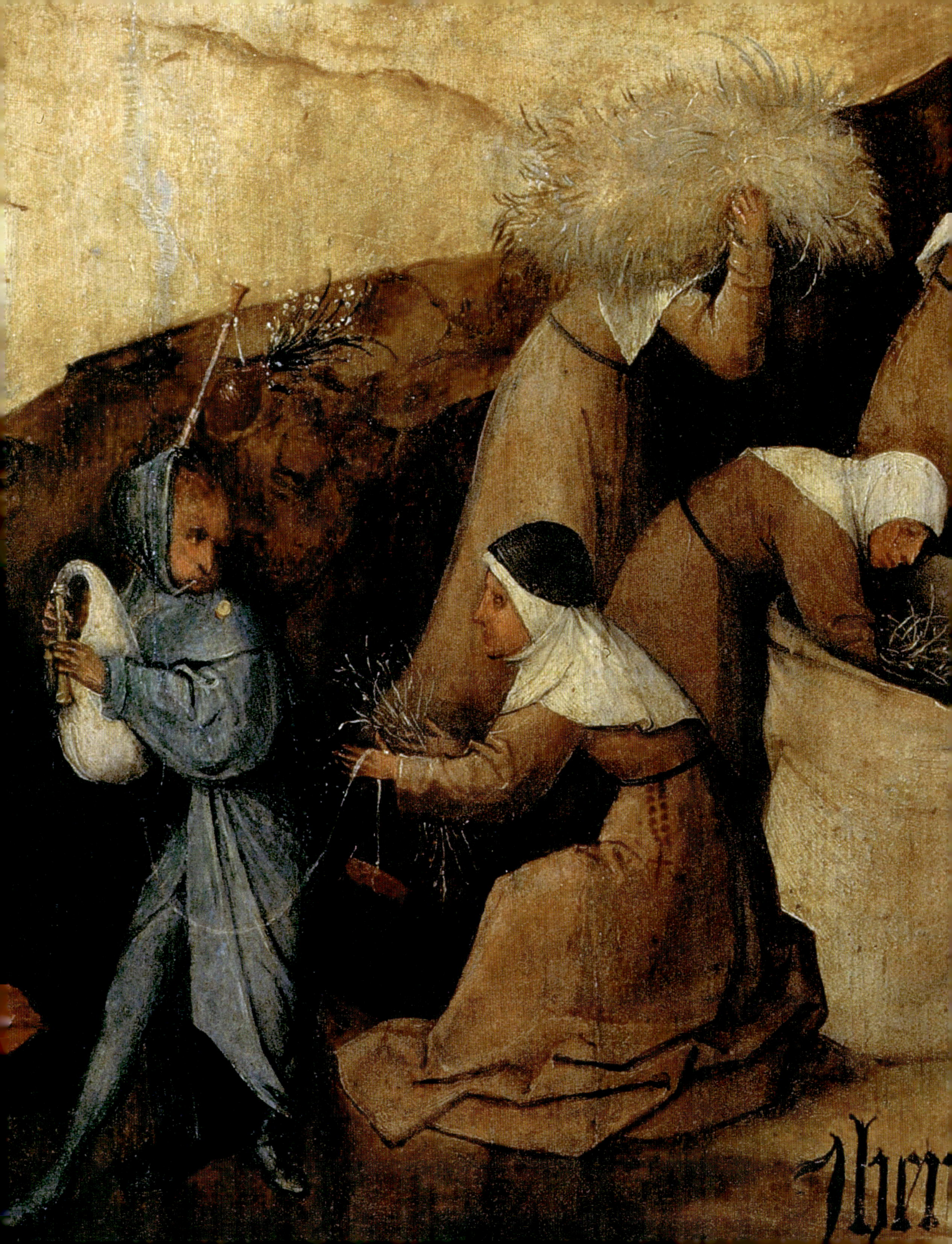

I

Courts of Elite Virgins

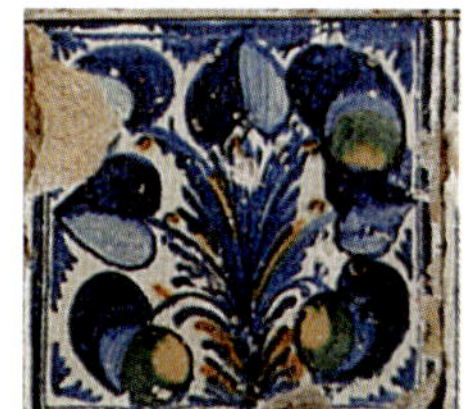

ENCLOSURE, CHRISTIAN MANNERS, AND THE FASHION OF LIMINALITY

There is no better way to begin my investigation on the intersections between Renaissance art and female monasticism than to compare two almost contemporary, but antithetical, depictions of nuns.[1] Cosimo Rosselli's *St. Catherine of Siena with Members of the Dominican Third Order* (1490s; fig. 3) presents a group of kneeling women enclosed in their sacred precinct, wearing the habit of their order. Together with a girl in lay dress, the nuns direct their prayers toward the central enthroned female saint, who hands down a volume of her devotional writings and a scroll of regulations to the women on either side of her throne. Three standing saints along with the Archangel Raphael and Tobias in the background witness the foundation of the female branch of the Dominican order staged at the center. Aside from this celebration of the Dominican third order, Rosselli's picture confirms a familiar perception of religious women, that is, their humility, obedience, and lives devoted to prayer. An opposite perspective is offered in the central panel of Hieronymus Bosch's *Haywain* triptych (ca. 1500–1506; fig. 4), where in the right foreground four nuns are portrayed not in a secluded space but in the open air, and they are engaged in activities suggesting their industrious participation in the universal struggle for wealth and carnal pleasure. Unmistakable in their full habits, they are laboring to fill a sack with hay on behalf of the stout friar comfortably drinking wine at a table. One of the nuns is even trying to

pay a musician with a handful of hay.[2] The two images propose wholly opposed profiles of nuns – devout and acquisitive, observant and disobedient – and reflect different artistic, religious, and cultural traditions, supplying as a result a binary view of Renaissance female monasticism. The reality, however, was far more articulated and nuanced than what is illustrated in these pictures. What did the world of Renaissance nuns encompass? When and under what conditions were nuns free to circulate outside their sacred precincts? How were women's lives structured in convents, and how was seclusion implemented in monastic spaces?

Such questions may sound simplistic, but the answers are not as obvious as they might first appear. Enclosed within high walls, convents were common features of early modern European cities. Citadels of virgins who secluded themselves from the world to experience a life in the service of God, nunneries were homes to inhabitants whose lives were organized around prayer, work, and the spiritual enjoyment of the fruits of their devotions and silent contemplation. Because of their status as virgins, nuns were believed to be by nature closer to God and their prayers were recognized as having a crucial intercessory force. Nuns acted as mediators between celestial and worldly spheres to win God's protection over cities and their inhabitants. At least, this was what Pope Gregory I (590–604) and subsequent ecclesiastical and lay authorities maintained as they promoted the

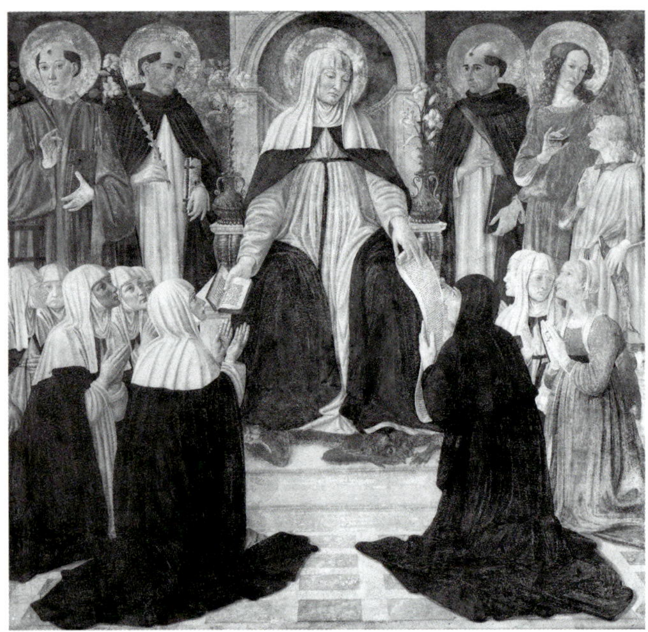

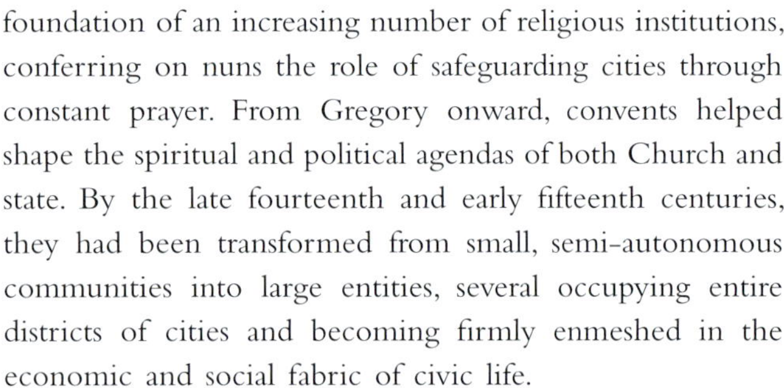

Above 3   Cosimo Rosselli, *St. Catherine of Siena with Members of the Dominican Third Order*, 1490s, tempera and gold on panel, 157.7 × 163.5 cm ($62^3/_{32}$ × $64^3/_8$ in), Edinburgh, National Gallery of Scotland

Right 4   Hieronymus Bosch, *The Haywain*, central panel, ca. 1500–06, oil on wood, 135 × 200 cm ($53^5/_{32}$ × $78^{47}/_{64}$ in), Madrid, Museo del Prado

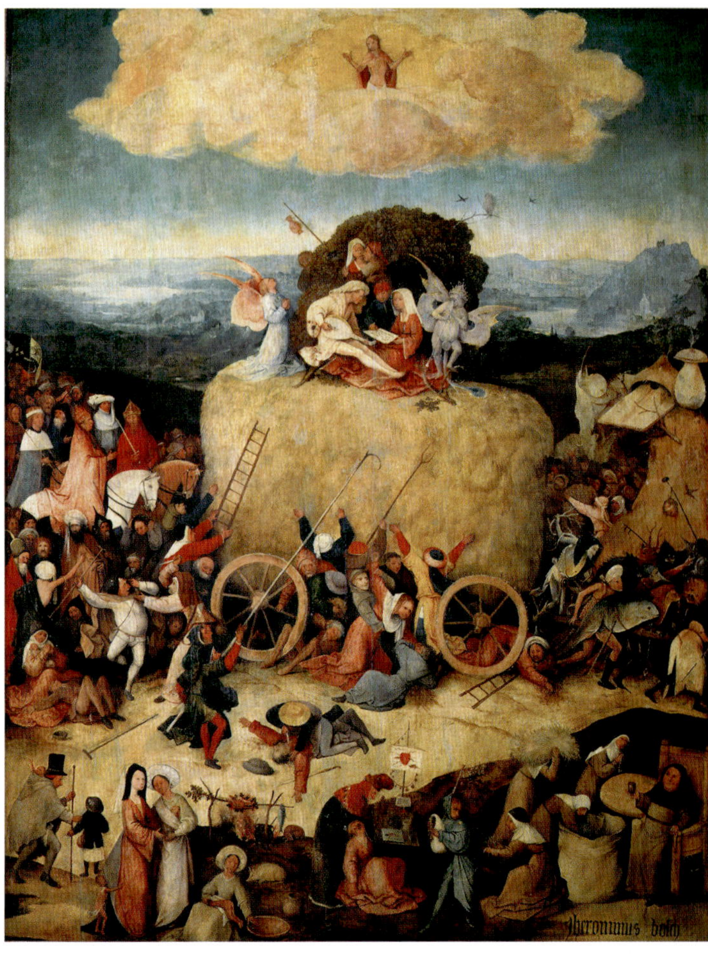

foundation of an increasing number of religious institutions, conferring on nuns the role of safeguarding cities through constant prayer. From Gregory onward, convents helped shape the spiritual and political agendas of both Church and state. By the late fourteenth and early fifteenth centuries, they had been transformed from small, semi-autonomous communities into large entities, several occupying entire districts of cities and becoming firmly enmeshed in the economic and social fabric of civic life.

Convents were open to women of different status, history, profile, and wealth who promised to live in claustration and to adhere to the rules of their order. In noble families the practice of limiting marriage to only a few members of each generation and of enclosing the others in religious houses had the effect of multiplying the number of inhabitants of early modern nunneries.[3] The Bolognese notary Giovanni Boccadiferro in his *Discorso sopra il governo delle monache* of the mid-sixteenth century perspicaciously refers to convents as "the sitting room of the women who could not be married off." He goes on to say that the cloistering of women may be necessary to prevent young girls from remaining in their paternal houses where they risk losing their chastity and honor.[4] Aristocratic nunneries, in particular, served a number of purposes in the Renaissance world, enabling families to maintain their patrimonies undivided, enhance political alliances, and possibly contain the troubles of marriage. These convents were entities necessary for sustaining the social and political status quo rather than, strictly speaking, fostering spirituality. Often their inhabitants were forced to profess vows less for reasons of religious vocation than for their subordination to economic, political, or social obligations.[5]

Little notice was taken of the girls' own desires and inclinations when they were secluded in convents as young as six or seven years old. Several involuntary nuns, including the seventeenth-century writer Arcangela Tarabotti, describe the convent as prison, hell, or a grave.[6] Such negative assessments, however, have obscured the fact that some noblewomen entered convents voluntarily either to escape their families' strategic machinations, or to pursue their studies. For example, in the *Paradise*, the third part of Dante's *Divine*

Comedy (1308–21), the poet meets Piccarda Donati, a historic figure who recounts having been a bride of Christ abducted from the convent and forced into a marriage by her relatives.[7] In 1511, Francesco Gonzaga and Isabella d'Este's daughter, Ippolita Gonzaga, then aged nine, defied her parents' wishes for a dynastic marriage and, in a bid for autonomy, withdrew to the convent of San Vincenzo in Mantua. Ippolita might have acted in imitation of her ancestor, the celebrated Cecilia Gonzaga, who after overcoming her father's opposition, had entered Mantua's convent of Poor Clares in 1445 to continue her education. In his letter to Cecilia, the humanist Gregorio Correr encourages her monachization, designing a specific program of study (reading the lives of the saints and patristic writings) and recommending strict adherence to the rules for reaching spiritual perfection.[8] Pisanello's portrait medal of Cecilia (fig. 5), dated 1447, celebrates her virginal condition, but there is nothing in Cecilia's posture, features, or elegant dress to remind viewers of her monastic status. Records attest that she entered the Poor Clares' convent wearing a fine white dress and a crown of juniper on her head, metaphors of her inner and outer beauty, purity, and learning. On the medal's reverse, the symbols of chastity, the unicorn (which could be tamed only by a virgin) and the adjacent seminude girl, are presented as the ornaments of Cecilia's persona. Chastity is embodied by Cecilia not as a passive attitude but as a virtue defining her pure being. With its elegant interplay of surface, relief, and symbols, Pisanello's portrait medal ultimately inscribes Cecilia's virtuous self in the perfection of his art.[9]

This chapter explicates and explores these facets of elite conventual culture from the mid-fifteenth century until well beyond the Tridentine decree on convents (1563), articulating the complexities of the aristocratic female cloistered self. It addresses questions related to nuns' secluded status and the mechanisms of enclosure that segregated religious women, limited their sight, and prescribed a specific use of monastic spaces. It reflects on rules that disciplined nuns' bodies and senses, as well as on the rituals that marked progression into the religious life, in order to define nuns' specific ways of seeing the world. In a further move that enriches this argument, the ways of living of early modern aristocratic nuns and their at times lax behaviours in conventual spaces are discussed and problematized. Noble virgins secluded in convents and living in liminal continuity with the secular sphere, these nuns contravened norms of proper religious comportment through free circulation, secular clothing, and forbidden forms of relaxation. The

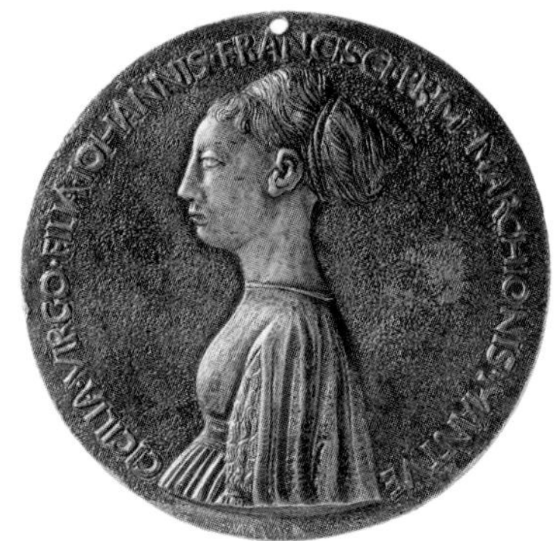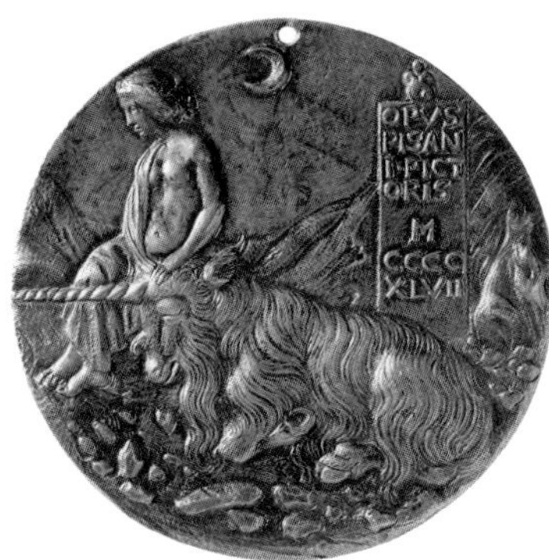

5   Pisanello, *Cecilia Gonzaga*, 1447, bronze portrait medal, (recto and verso), d. 8.4 cm (3⁵/₁₆ in), Paris, Musée du Louvre

contextualization of these defiant behaviors serves to illustrate two points: first, that patrician nuns' lax observation of obligations, resistance to strictures, and ambiguous, liminal status turned them into a special category of religious patrons and viewers of artworks even of secularized content; and second, it clarifies the circumstances in which the enjoyment of splendid artifacts became possible and meaningful. In tracing this aspect of elite female monasticism, this chapter ultimately recovers the nature and workings of the not yet fully unearthed conventual courtly visual culture that developed in Renaissance Italy, simultaneously historicizing the conditions that permitted this alternative female artistic tradition to arise.

ON CLAUSTRATION AND RELAXATION

Seclusion, confinement, and separation were the determinants of a religious woman's life. The segregation of consecrated individuals from the outside world, or their claustration, was a general precept recommended by all rules, but in the case of women the stakes were higher. Although monks and friars lived a life detached from worldly norms, they were allowed the freedom to come and go from their communities. For women, in contrast, strict seclusion became a rigid, coercive obligation linked to notions of virtue and honor. Originally devised to protect women and to provide them with inviolable environments in times of war and plague, the ideal of enclosing and safeguarding nuns eventually shifted into mechanisms to regulate their bodies and settings in response to the widespread misogynist belief that women were weak and inferior beings, and therefore in need of control and male supervision. In his *Periculoso* decree of 1298, Pope Boniface VIII prescribed perpetual and absolute claustration to be imposed on religious women of all orders. Sustained by the belief that women were more threatened than men by the temptation of worldly delights and that their bodies were dangerously "inflammable," the decree reinforced passive and active seclusion on nuns. In other words, nuns were forbidden to leave their convents, and outsiders were not permitted to enter monastic institutions. It is known, however, that the *Periculoso* had little effect on aristocratic religious communities, beyond empowering local authorities to intrude into convents' business.[10] Noble nuns continued to enjoy privileges that eased the routine of their daily lives devoted to the service of God, while ecclesiastical and civic officials lamented the decadent status of female monastic institutions.

Almost three centuries after Boniface's law, the Council of Trent promulgated a comprehensive religious reform (1563) that re-established strict seclusion over all consecrated individuals. Gradually enclosure was implemented throughout the monastic institutions of Catholic countries and its practical effects endured for centuries to come. The implementation and/or enforcement of cloister rules on female communities had been pursued in the Italian peninsula, however, well before the Tridentine decree.[11] From an art-historical perspective it is particularly instructive that the Tridentine decree and previous movements of religious reform brought about changes in monastic architecture. High walls, walled up doors, and grated windows were among the mechanisms used to contain and confine nuns within their sacred precincts, suppressing what authorities perceived as inadmissible interactions between religious women and laity, and simultaneously revealing the gendered nature of the monastic space. Nuns' enclosure through fortified architecture was a means both to exercise control and authority over consecrated women and to signal the dichotomy between the sacred and the mundane spheres. The structures and rituals of civic life governed the secular world, while architectural barriers isolated convents from their surroundings to guarantee their inhabitants' physical safety and assure the attainment of their spiritual mission.

Convents were not only sites that enforced nuns' separation from the outside world to support their perfected communication with God, however. They were also enclaves in which rituals and activities were bound to specific times and functions. Monastic complexes consisted of buildings that formed an ensemble of interconnected architectures related to the liturgical, administrative, and communitarian tasks performed on the inside. In his architectural treatise on the ideal city of Sforzinda (ca. 1460–64), Antonio Averlino, called Filarete, proposes to build convents for all religious orders, and offers a unified project for adaptation to the needs of each order (fig. 6). Filarete's convent plan shows a geometrical and rational arrangement of edifices, and supplies detailed instructions for building a crucial monastic space, the nuns' choir (or the inner church). He proposes it as an elevated gallery separated by gratings from the rest of church (the outer church) reserved to the laity. While the separation of nuns from the laity reflected the prescription of enclosure, Filarete's raised *matroneum* round the sides of the apse sets nuns apart without making them completely invisible, as in standard conventual double churches partitioned by a wall (see Chapter Three). Equally important, Filarete associates monastic architecture with notions of honesty and comfort, referring to convents as "convenient, beautiful, and decent" places. The architect's main concern seems to be to confer symmetry and beauty to convent buildings, as if these architectural features could extend to their inhabitants a certain moral authority and dignity.[12]

Despite Filarete's reflections on the language of monastic architecture beyond its mere functionality, ecclesiastical authorities routinely mandated that all sorts of physical boundaries be drawn between the enclosed and outside community. As argued by Helen Hills with reference to post-Tridentine Neapolitan convents, the view of a rigid distinction between the secluded and the exterior worlds nonetheless needs revising because convent architecture was composed of a unity of spaces that permitted certain degrees of communication between the sacred and the mundane.[13] Pre-Tridentine and post-Tridentine religious complexes were characterized by an increase in enclosure as one progressed from the outside to the inside. A good way into these questions of convents' viscous porosity and elite communities asserting their tangible presence in monastic settings is to consider the few places – parlors and cloisters included – where the sacred and profane realms intersected, and nuns had opportunities to pursue forms of relaxation beyond what was permitted by the rules. It will be further apparent that under certain conditions male outsiders were admitted not only to convents but also potentially into the most secluded zones in some of the "open" aristocratic religious communities of early modern Italy.

Serving as walkways for reading and meditation, cloisters were foundational locales, architectural *traits d'union* between communitarian and private zones of the convent.

6 Plan of a convent, from Filarete, *Trattato di Architettura*, ca. 1460–64, book x, fol. 78r, Florence, Biblioteca Nazionale Centrale

They were sites where certain services and rituals, including processions, commemorations, and burials, took place. In the monastic literature, the colonnaded cloister was often connected to heaven. Cloistered individuals gathering in their courtyards were supposed to be renewing the ritual of Christ's apostles meeting in the portico adjacent to Solomon's Temple in Jerusalem.[14] In his *De Re Aedificatoria* (1485), Leon Battista Alberti writes that monastic cloisters or porticoes "in winter receive the gentle sun, and in summer they offer whatever grateful shade or breeze there may be."[15] By the late fifteenth century the multistoried cloister had been substituted for the single-story model to accommodate better the nuns' needs for privacy, comfort, and intimate devotion. Around porticoes, as Alberti recognized, "cells, dining hall, council chamber and utility rooms" are arranged "as in a private house."[16] An effective visualization of the regulated conventual life organized around the centrally planned, square module of the colonnaded cloister is furnished by an early eighteenth-century hand-colored perspectival view of the Dominican convent of San Giuliano in Florence (fig. 7).[17] The refectory is visible through an open door within the left background portico, while working rooms occupy the wing shown in the left foreground. The adjacent lower room is that of the abbess, who is seated in her chair, attentively reading a document. In a second-story cell on the right a nun is seen praying before a crucifix and, in the corresponding room on the left, another nun is attending a laywoman holding a fan and a book. In the inner courtyard nuns are engaged in conversation, while another consecrated woman is at work in the adjacent garden. The cloister's symmetrical arms, where nuns read, walk, and congregate, convey simplicity and order as if the architecture itself incarnates the true spirit of religious life. As Georgia Clarke has observed, the simple, linear module of convent architecture ultimately provided a model for domestic buildings.[18]

Cloister walls were often decorated with religious scenes suitable to consecrated individuals' meditation and prayer. During Carnival and on other festive occasions, cloisters (or refectories and parlors) served as sites for theatrical perfor-

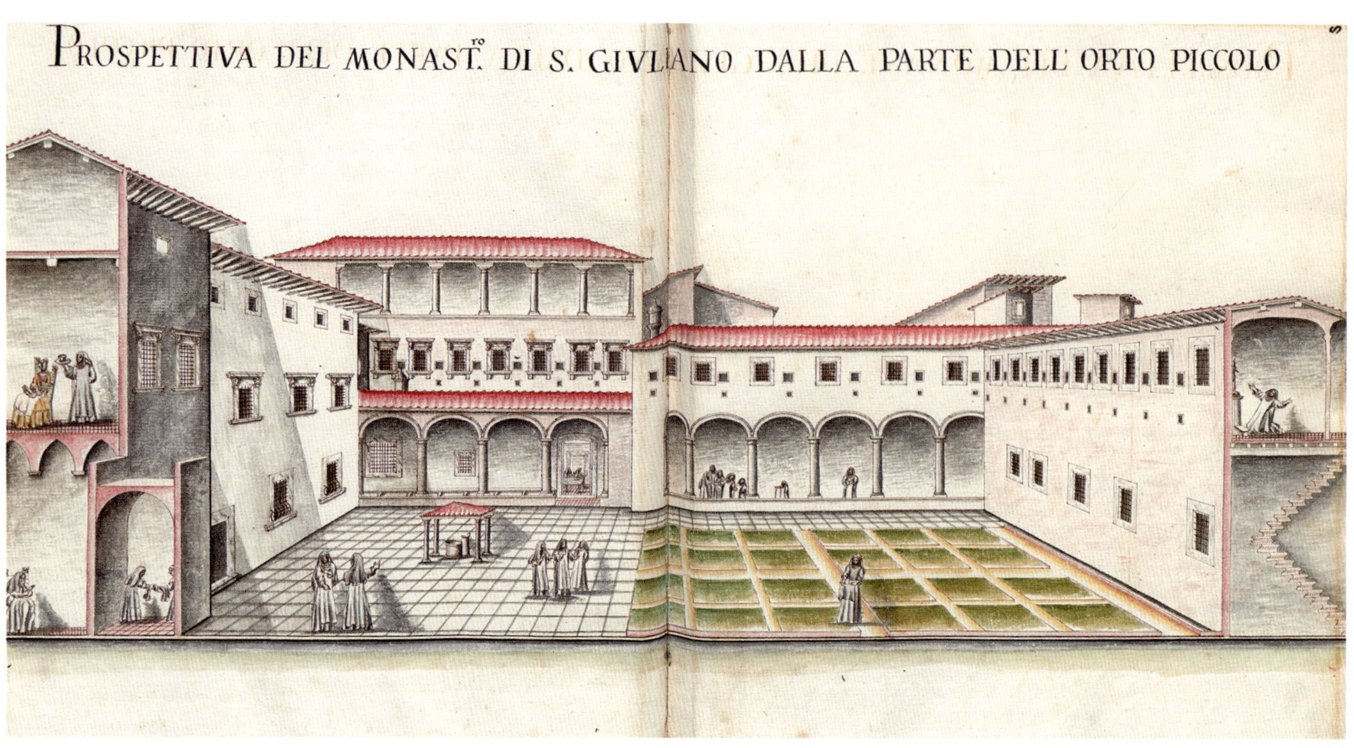

7 "Prospettiva del Monastero di San Giuliano dalla parte dell'orto piccolo," 1717, Florence, Archivio di Stato, Miscellanea di Piante 283, fols. 7v–8r

mances, including *sacre rappresentazioni*, tragedies, and comedies. Nuns staged plays that were in circulation or else new stories they composed themselves. According to Elissa Weaver, these performances were significant components of the education of boarding girls and novices as much as they were occasions of conviviality and "spiritual fun" (*spasso spirituale*) for nuns.[19] In general, ecclesiastical authorities gave approval for plays if they did not involve masquerades (*mascherate*) with the inevitable transvestism. Despite its being forbidden, crossdressing did occur in convents, as recorded in a list of nuns' "abuses" compiled by Bolognese ecclesiastical authorities in 1576.[20] The outside public was not admitted to nuns' performances, but relatives, sponsors, benefactors, and even the carpenters who constructed the stages attended.

Parlors were privileged spaces designed for meetings and conversations. Intended both to separate and connect the sacred and the secular communities, parlors functioned to limit and bridge distinctions between the two worlds. Large convents had two distinct parlors, one for conversations with outsiders coming to the convent (the outer parlor) and the other (the inner parlor) for meetings among members of the community itself.[21] Through meetings with visitors, nuns participated in the exterior world of their families, patrons, and sponsors. Although they were scrutinized sites, parlors

of aristocratic nunneries could also become places of recreation and merriment. Records attest, for example, that in 1509, several Venetian gentlemen were charged with having played horns and pipes and danced all night in the parlor of the Cistercian convent of Santa Maria Celeste (La Celestia), in celebration of the newly elected abbess.[22] Such entertainments are probably not dissimilar from those captured in eighteenth-century images, including a print by Petrus van der Aa featuring the parlor at San Lorenzo in Venice and Francesco Guardi's *Parlor of the Convent of San Zaccaria* (fig. 8). Dancing, eating, puppet shows, and conversations between gentlemen and nuns behind grates make the parlor a place of gallantry and convivial amusements. Likewise, Alessandro Magnasco's *Nuns in the Parlor* (fig. 9) proposes a close-up view of an ideal garden parlor, the stage of an intimate meeting between the nun and her beloved friend enlivened by music. Sites of sociability where enclosed women exchanged stories and gossip, and shared intimate feelings, parlors were liminal places of communication and traffic with the outside world. Preoccupied Tridentine authorities inspecting convents ordered that visitors be separated by gender, that parlor windows be made smaller, and that grills and thick curtains be added to the openings to prevent nuns from touching "whom they please," as a

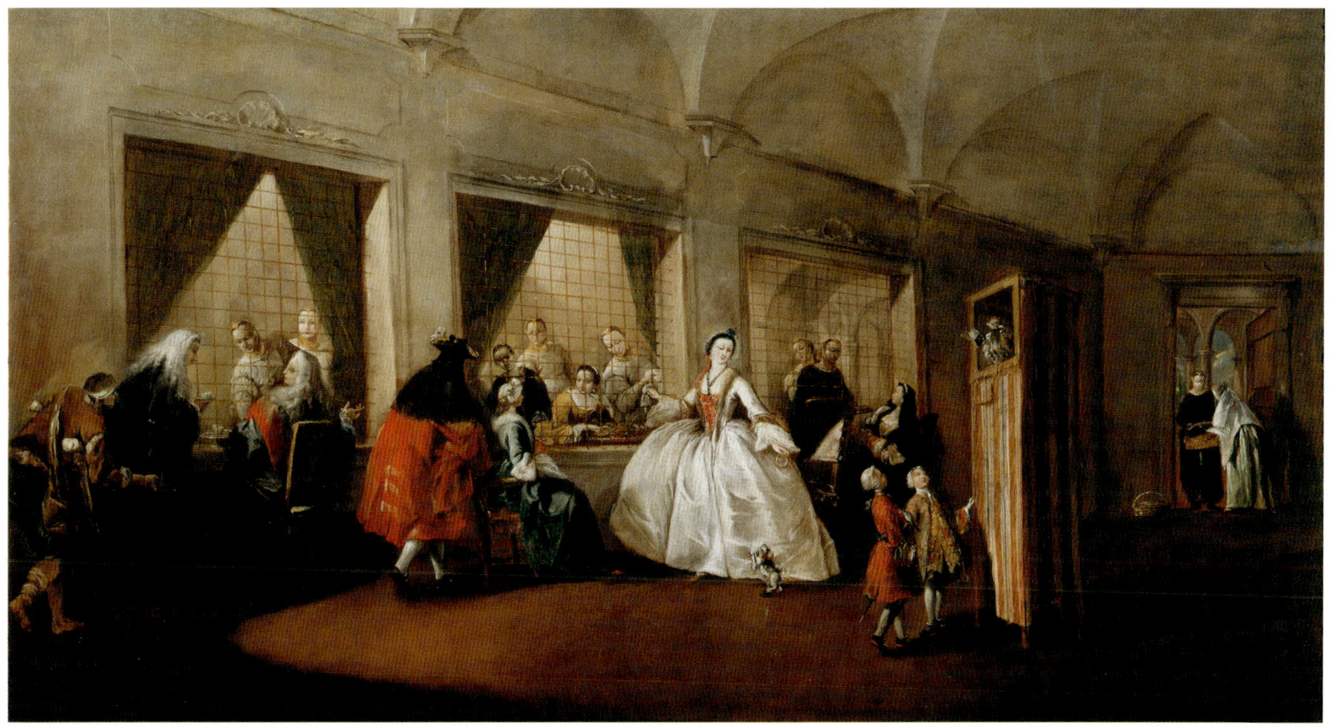

8   Francesco Guardi, *Parlor of the Convent of San Zaccaria*, 1746, oil on canvas, 108 × 208 cm (42½ × 81^{22}/$_{25}$ in), Venice, Ca' Rezzonico

Bolognese cleric put it.[23] In spite of Baldassar Castiglione's remark in his *Book of the Courtier* (1528) that a lover sometimes rejoices "to look upon a window, even if it is shuttered, because there it was that he once knew the bliss of gazing upon his lady love," authorities hastened to limit access drastically and to seal off all of a convent's possible openings.[24]

The more these mechanisms of seclusion were imposed to make convents impermeable and nuns invisible, however, the more they contributed to inflaming the desire of religious women for contact with the outside world. In reality, some Renaissance aristocratic nunneries were hardly the sealed entities for which the authorities hoped. It was indeed a necessity that male visitors be admitted to religious institutions, and their movements, albeit controlled, varied according to their rank and occupation. In general, the list of individuals permitted to enter monastic houses in their professional capacity included ecclesiastics, doctors, lawyers, notaries, procurators, and manual workers (for example, gardeners, merchants, artists, and servants).[25] And at least one female religious community is known to have petitioned to

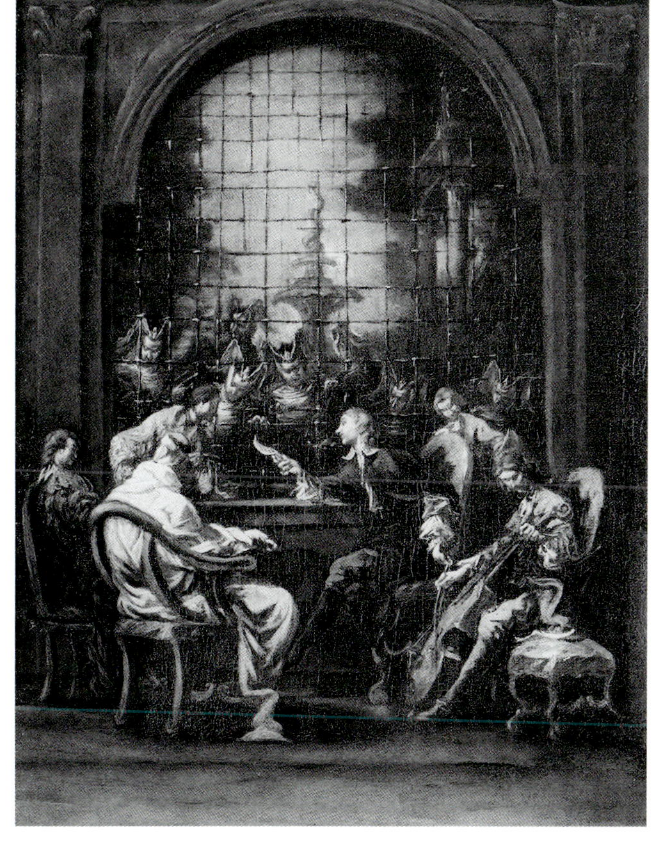

9   Alessandro Magnasco, *Nuns in the Parlor*, early 18th century, location unknown

end restrictions to its network of potential visitors. An unpublished record dating to 1509 states that the Benedictine nuns of San Ulderico in Parma asked the bishop vicar permission to admit to their house "benign and amicable" visitors.[26] The nuns' petition does not specify the sex of their guests but benevolence and friendship seem highly discretional requirements to meet. It is thus easily imaginable that "benign" guests could access even the most private monastic spaces. These nuns, it seems, were seeking an ecclesiastical sanction to welcome whomever they liked into their institution, and to be able to venture outside themselves.

In the same petition the nuns were granted permission to access a storage facility facing onto the public street and to visit local shrines to accept indulgences. Seclusion had never been strictly enforced on the San Ulderico community nor had its interactions with visitors been limited. Could San Ulderico be defined as an "open monastery" or was it more a court of elite nuns with relaxed, non-observant comportment? As Katherine Gill noted, there were several types of "open" religious houses in early modern Italy, that is, institutions in which the inhabitants eluded obligations.[27] In some institutions nuns were given license to live under a less strict form of enclosure, while still others housed *pinzochere*, beguines, and canonesses, that is, women who practiced a communitarian life but had not professed vows. In short, not every "open" convent housed nuns of noble birth, as did San Ulderico. But, most importantly in this and other elite communities, strict cloister rules tended to be eschewed and bypassed. Despite each convent's specific history, as a whole these institutions constitute a significant and still underexplored segment of the art-historical narrative of the Italian Renaissance, whose study can enrich comprehension of the vibrant works that decorated their secluded spaces. And, more critically, this "openness" enables scholars to affirm plausibly that little decoration within aristocratic nunneries was actually invisible to the outside world, and that its genesis intersected with secular realities in unexpected ways.

RULES AND CURIOSITY

Nuns took vows of poverty, chastity, and obedience that, along with the prescription of seclusion, were the keystones of the life of all members of the orders. Codifying behavioral customs and daily tasks, comportment in church, diet, and even the time for retiring to bed, religious rules convey a timeless picture of an ideal, disciplined life inside the convent that rarely corresponded to the real, lived experiences in any given institution. Rules for proper comportment and the design of monastic spaces converge to promote an ideal of nuns as modest, observant, and passive individuals. To confront this Christian comportment literature and pursue art-historical questions, it is instructive to explore how monastic rules impacted nuns' ways of seeing and approaching the world. What did the comportment regime mean for aristocratic nuns fashioning their identities as courtly religious ladies? To what degree did nuns actually experience a castigation of their senses through the required discipline of their bodies and behaviors?

At the outset of any discussion on monastic comportment and nuns' perceptions of such regulations, it should be stated that norms, and in particular the Benedictine Rule, the use of which increased from the tenth century onward, were formulated for male communities. In order for them to be implemented among their female peers, the regulations required adaptation and variation.[28] Several institutions had their own constitutions drawn up to provide norms that better suited their specific histories, while other houses adhered to customs that had long been in use. Kate Lowe has wondered, however, to what extent rules influenced women's lives if "convents in the same Italian city belonging to the same order could and did develop very different profiles."[29] This is a legitimate question to raise since it is undeniable that each institution had its own history, income, and network of sponsors. But I would argue that the basic rules of appropriate comportment were in any case imparted to nuns of all orders. While it remains vital to assess the specificities of each convent, such a model could be integrated with perspectives that acknowledge the comportment norms that early modern female consecrated individuals shared, and that shaped their ways of being and experiencing the world.

Nuns were all taught to aim only at perfecting their lives and not to question the authority of superiors (especially male officials), or to make improper enquiry. Rules present monastic life as a path leading to the sublimation of fleshly desires and of the foolish curiosity that prompts individuals to wonder about that which does not concern them. In monastic writing the genuine practice of religious life is often compared to a ladder with rungs consisting of prayer, humility, and obedience. Submission, moderation, discipline, and the abnegation of self-will are the means by which individuals progress on the ladder (*scala perfectionis*) to reach spiritual perfection, as illustrated in several didactic texts addressed to nuns. One of the earliest printed texts for nuns, entitled *Prologo de l'ordine del vivere neli monasteri de monache*, of 1497, endorses proper comportment, using a combination of vernacular language and instructive images. Bound together with the translation of St. Jerome's letters addressed to the nun-to-be Eustochium (see Chapter Four), some of the finest copies of the *Prologo* have hand-colored woodcuts clearly intended for an upper-class, cloistered audience.[30] Despite their crude quality and vignette format, the woodcuts visualize the most salient aspects of exemplary conventual life. Designed by an artist imitating the Pico Master, a late Quattrocento illuminator and printmaker from Venice, the woodcuts tend to represent a two-part narrative, stressing the message by juxtaposing the violation of the norm with its recommended pursuit. The obedient nun, covering her ears in order not to hear the gossiping laywomen behind the grate (fig. 10), is contrasted with the "bad" sisters who instead listen, and so misbehave, in a simplified, yet extremely evocative, picture. Several woodcuts present an image with a single scene, including the community in prayer before an altar, and of a shuttered convent portal with three persistent gentlemen standing before it (fig. 11). The sealed door is an unequivocal metaphor for the virginal status of the women kept inside. Texts on appropriate monastic comportment, such as the *Prologo*, capitalized on printing technology and on the assumption that, like courtly etiquette, good Christian manners could be taught to consecrated women for their pursuit of spiritual betterment.[31] Religious women sealed within their convents were expected to fortify and perfect their souls so as to be worthy of their heavenly spouse, and to act as modest and obedient members of their communities.

In general, modesty was considered a pivotal virtue for Renaissance women, but for nuns it was inextricably linked with the immaculate physical state of their bodies, underlying the ethical import of sexual abstinence.[32] By associating chastity with high moral value and the nobility of the soul, the fourth-century Church Fathers Augustine and Ambrose had characterized virgins' secluded life as the superior state of life for women. But in the early sixteenth century, the Dutch religious reformer Desiderius Erasmus (1466–1536) expressed reservations about this long-standing view, denouncing the metamorphosis of convents into secularized institutions, from sites of spiritual accomplishments into repositories of noblewomen with little spiritual vocation and who were, rather, concerned with power, social hierarchy, and careerism.[33] In one of Erasmus's *Colloquies*, his *The Girl with No Interest in Marriage* (1523), the male protagonist avers: "But just as I wouldn't want to argue that a girl who entered this kind of life should try to go out of it, so I wouldn't hesitate to warn all girls, particularly the talented

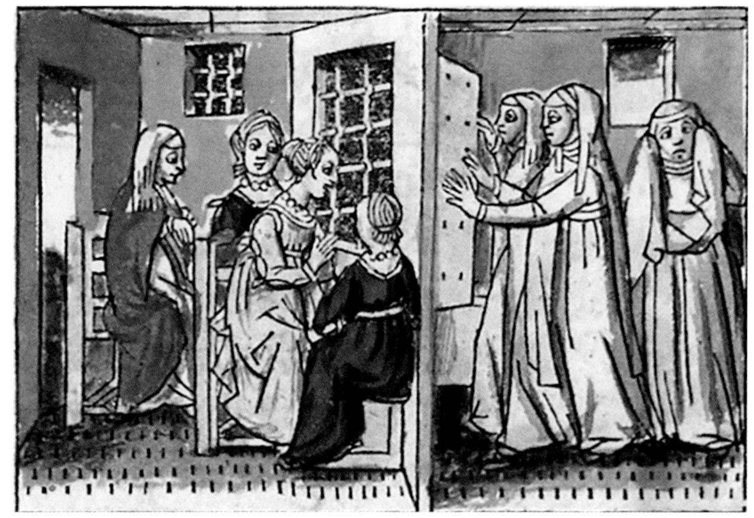

10   Nun covering her ears, from *Prologo de l'ordine del vivere neli monasteri de monache & temporale & spirituale. Excepta da diversi scripti de Hieronymo ad Eustochio sua Figliuola spirituale & ale sorelle*, chapter 23, 49 × 72 mm ($1^{59}/_{64}$ × $2^{53}/_{64}$ in) (Ferrara 1497), Ferrara, Biblioteca Ariostea, S.16.5.10

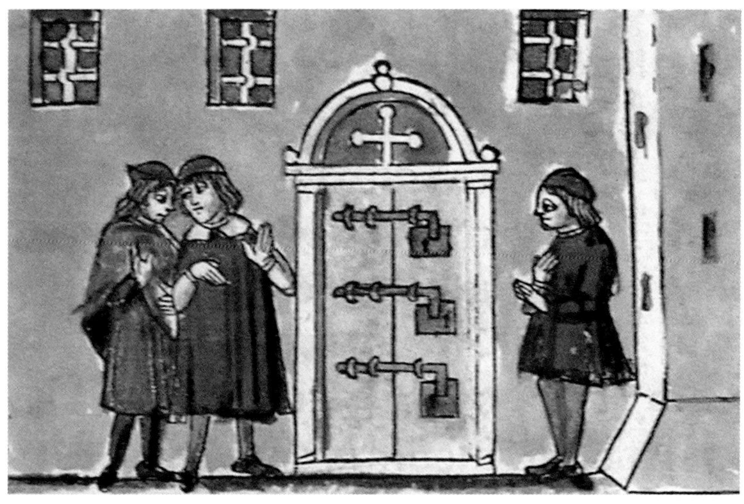

11   Men before the sealed door of a convent, from *Prologo de l'ordine del vivere neli monasteri de monache & temporale & spirituale. Excepta da diversi scripti de Hieronymo ad Eustochio sua Figliuola spirituale & ale sorelle*, chapter 27, 49 × 72 mm ($1^{59}/_{64}$ × $2^{53}/_{64}$ in) (Ferrara 1497), Ferrara, Biblioteca Ariostea, S.16.5.10

ones, against throwing themselves rashly into something there's no escape from afterwards, especially since in those very communities virginity is often in considerable danger."[34] Erasmus concluded that monastic life is not superior to others if the spiritual path is not accepted with genuine faith and motivation.

The traditional position regarding the higher value of the monastic status was, however, rehearsed and amplified in a series of popular texts published in the vernacular, including those of Fra' Cherubino da Spoleto and Fra' Bonaventura Gonzaga da Reggio. First printed in 1477 and reprinted several times, Fra' Cherubino's *Regole della Vita Spirituale e della Vita Matrimoniale* asserts that the religious condition is the highest calling for women, and dwells at length on virginity, in which body and senses are freed from the corruption of carnal desires. Virginity is viewed not only as a state of bodily purity through abstention from the sexual act, but also as an immaculate spiritual status that must be preserved by restraining one's inquisitive eyes and controlling the body. The enactment of chastity is discussed primarily in terms of spatial confinement and the repression of impulses, and is meant to be the focus of the nuns' lifelong project.[35]

In his instructions to nuns (published in 1568 and 1576) Fra' Bonaventura further encourages religious women to adopt outward behaviors, or what Marcel Mauss would call "techniques of the body," to signal their appropriate inward disposition. As Mauss put it, bodily acts seem to be natural, but they are instead learned and practiced. They are often modeled after those performed by figures of authority.[36] For nuns, authoritative figures whose actions were to be imitated included abbesses, venerated spiritual sisters, and female saints. Fra' Bonventura also insists on the strict control of the gaze and the "prudent" use of the eyes since the all-seeing eyes of God are constantly watching: "Never be so sure of not being seen that you do not proceed to look with prudence and touch with chastity . . . as if the entire world observes your actions. God himself . . . sees us. Equally our own conscience observes us."[37] The power of the all-seeing eyes is also stressed in various Scriptural passages to enhance a sense of control through the Divinity's omnipresence, as stated, for example, in the book of Proverbs: "The eyes of the Lord are in every place, beholding the evil and the good" (xv, 3). Helen Hills has perspicaciously commented on these statements that "not only does the expression of the eyes concern discipline, but the eyes of God enter into the disciplinary process as a controlling factor."[38] Elaborating on Michel Foucault's conceptualization of the gaze as a tool of power, Hills continues by observing that discipline and restraint were exercised in convents through the belief in a full-time, invisible watching gaze, meant to promote disciplined behaviors among individuals.

Fra' Bonaventura's insistence on the watchful eyes and the necessity of nuns' physical and psychological restrictions developed from the long-held belief that the eyes were the "windows" of the body, the mind, and the soul.[39] Yet, as such, the eyes could be easily distracted, drawing nuns away from the business of prayers and prescribed activities. Nuns are repeatedly warned to guard their fragile chastity by refraining from looking, and not to gaze about them in search of answers beyond the Christian interpretation of things. In other words, nuns are admonished not to indulge their natural curiosity. For centuries, monastic authors had linked finely crafted objects (which were also referred to as "curious") and their precious materials with the power to crowd and distract the mind, thereby becoming the engines of imaginative journeys, and motors for defiance of the rules. Sacred artworks were intended to serve as tools for controlling women's emotional spirituality, directing potentially divergent devotions into acceptable trajectories. In contrast, "curious," delightful images entangled the mind, propelling a circuit of restless motion and emotions, and a search for knowledge through viewing art.[40] Fine possessions stood in opposition to the vow of poverty and were considered signs of worldliness, but nonetheless ownership of such items is attested in numerous female religious communities. As shown by Sharon Strocchia's study on the economics of Florentine Renaissance convents, nuns enjoyed and managed pensions, income, and annuities. Some used their funds to pay for luxurious artifacts or even fashionable clothing, while others invested their resources to defray costs accrued by communitarian artistic commissions.[41]

Enclosed in convents for reasons other than spiritual vocation, patrician nuns can be seen as the curious individuals that Fra' Bonaventura admonished, eager to bypass strictures and to venture outside convents. Rules permitted women to leave their institutions only in cases of war, invasion, fire, and epidemic diseases, with penalties administered to transgressors. Noble nuns, however, were known to leave their houses on various occasions with or without papal or episcopal permission. Some resided for periods in their family homes or countryside villas, while others enjoyed free circulation in their cities. The free mobility of nuns became a major concern for ecclesiastical authorities from the mid-fifteenth century onward because of the scandal it aroused. Peripatetic nuns can be seen outside their sacred precincts as represented on a birth tray by the Florentine painter Masaccio or his circle (ca. 1427–8; fig. 12). Along with trumpeters and gentlemen carrying gifts, nuns and laywomen are shown passing through a private courtyard and entering a refined domestic setting to visit a mother and her newborn infant.[42] At first glance nothing seems particularly striking

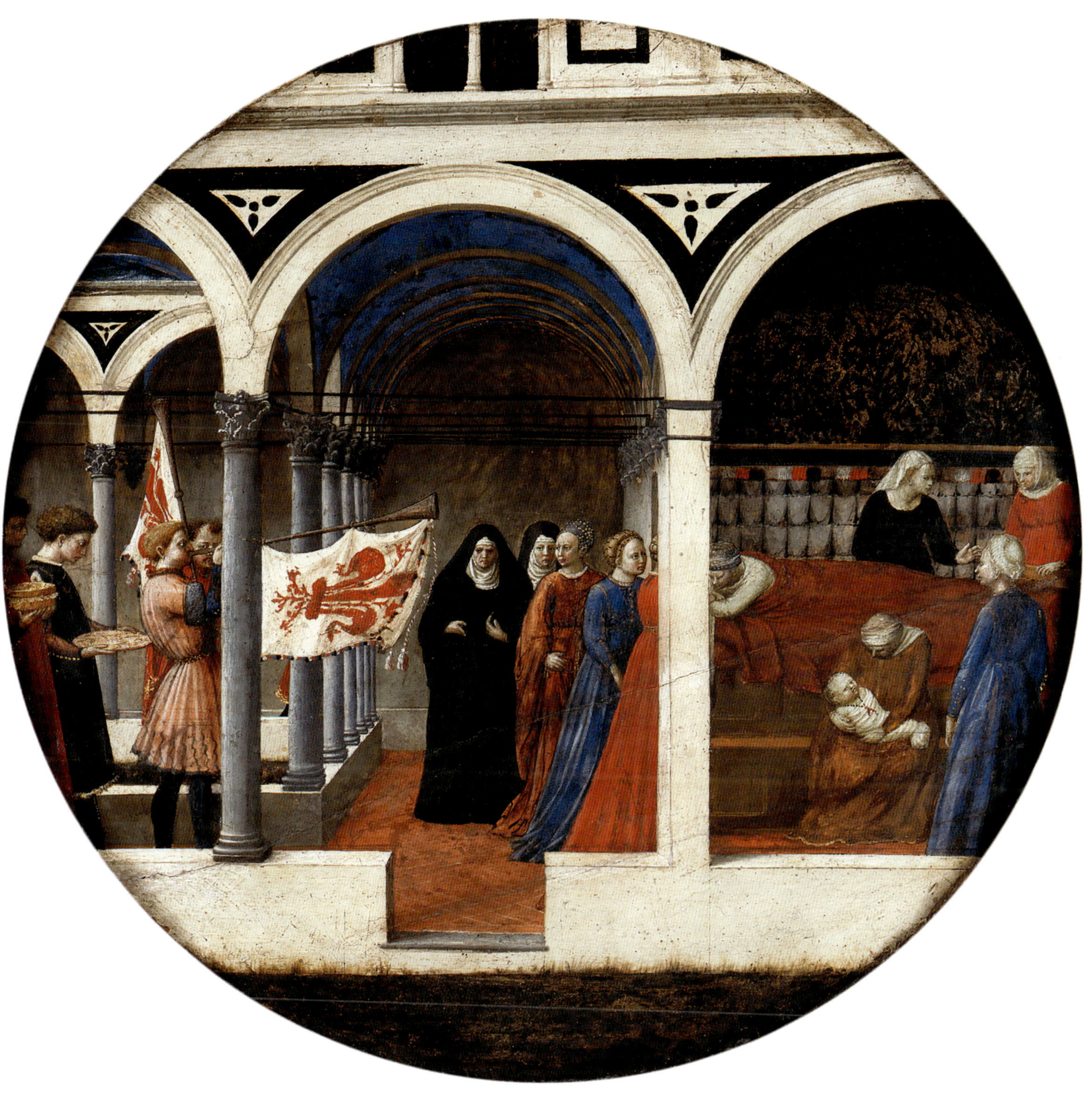

12   Masaccio or his circle, childbirth tray with a confinement room scene (recto), ca. 1427–8, tempera on wood, d. 56 cm (22 in), Gemäldegalerie, Staatliche Museen zu Berlin

about this image painted to honor a newly born heir. But the documented complaints by civic and ecclesiastical authorities in several Italian cities regarding "vagabond" nuns roaming about, and the improper intrusion of nuns into secular affairs, provide a context that problematizes the commemorative message of this depiction.

In his description of the city of Genoa (ca. 1450), Enea Silvio Piccolomini, the future Pope Pius II, links local nuns wandering about the city to its current deterioration, as if nuns' bad behavior was both a cause and symptom of Genoa's decline. Some forty years later, the Lateran canon Matteo Bossi again denounces the scandalous comportment of Genoese nuns in two letters addressed to Pope Sixtus IV, advising him to segregate such worldly women.[43] In 1501 the Venetian Senate asked Pope Alexander VI to annul exemptions granted to local "vagabond nuns" free to leave their convents. As the authorities put it, they "are roving around the city and countryside as they want, with great scandal and universal murmuring."[44] Again, in 1588, a Tridentine cleric reported to the ecclesiastical authorities in Rome that in the city of Aquileia nuns "live entirely as they please," venturing outside convents because they "have never deigned to obey the patriarch, nor to care about ecclesiastic censures."[45] Peripatetic nuns are considered as much a danger as a scandal in these records spanning more than a century, but Masaccio or his circle's image inscribes consecrated women in a family's celebration, ultimately suggesting that in early modern Italy the boundaries between the sacred and the profane, the enclosed and the outside worlds were permeable and fluid. As will be seen in the following chapters, patrician nuns shared a variety of experiences as well as luxury items with their female relatives living outside the cloister, but encountered or thought about them differently because of their status and enclosed contexts.

Much of what both pre-Tridentine and Tridentine authorities denounced as nuns' misbehavior and the decadent condition of convents had, however, constituted the standard life of patrician communities for centuries. The nuns of Santa Patrizia in Naples are a case in point, which can illustrate the social and political implications of their negotiation of religious strictures. These nuns, who were from the most prestigious Neapolitan families, had long been able to move freely about the city in fashionable dress, a compromise in the obligations represented by the cloister rules. When what they perceived as their "rights" were curbed in the 1570s, the nuns vigorously opposed the ecclesiastical authorities' attempts to reform them, pro-

claiming that they had simply adhered to long-practiced custom and that consequently their behavior had nothing to do with disobedience. Santa Patrizia was not an institution of vocational nuns or one in which the inhabitants had ever lived under strict claustration. A Basilian foundation converted by the Byzantine princess Patricia into a Benedictine house in the seventh century, the convent had been inhabited by canonesses in the thirteenth and fourteenth centuries. These women practiced a less restricted claustral life, including wearing fine apparel and making excursions outside the cloister, customs that ultimately shaped the comportment of the nuns for centuries to come. Their "unorthodox" conduct did not prevent donations from pouring into the community, presented as gifts to the nuns who, in return, agreed to pray for the institution's founders and its benefactors during their lifetime and beyond. Santa Patrizia's necrology records about 2,500 benefactors' names.[46]

The reactions of the court of elite virgins of Santa Patrizia to the enforcement of strict cloister rules varied, but all the nuns opposed them. A few went so far as to sue the institution for return of their admittance fees (or spiritual dowry, discussed in greater detail ahead) in order to reinvest the funds by entering religious houses where their "rights" would not be so limited. Relatives and sponsors of the nuns expected the convent to safeguard their daughters and preserve their virginity, but not to deprive them of all worldly pleasures. Furthermore, strict rules insisting on nuns' segregation, lack of contact with the outside, and the institution's placement under tight ecclesiastical control would have denied nuns' families the ability to manage the convent's vast patrimony. Families wanted to protect their daughters' (and their own) interests by continuing to administer the nunnery's property with profit and, at the same time, to assure their progeny a comfortable monastic existence appropriate to their noble birth. This nexus of political, social, and economic interests goes far to explain why the aristocratic nuns of Santa Patrizia, together with their families and sponsors opposed the religious reform, and why the convent required papal intervention to reduce it to an observant community.

Other elite communities protested about the implementation of strict regulations because they did not want their affairs placed under firm ecclesiastical watch, nor did they relish the loss of revenues from their services that would have ensued once they were cut off from the outside world. The Camaldolese nuns of Santa Cristina della Fondazza, the most renowned convent in Bologna

for its music, took extreme action to maintain its autonomy and status as a local center for excellence in music.
This unruly noble community had a long history of fractured relationships with authorities. In 1433 the Camaldolese prior general, Ambrogio Traversari, prohibited banquets
and music in the convent but his proscription went
unheeded.[47] Almost two centuries later the confrontation
took a dramatic turn. During a night in November 1628,
the nuns demolished a wall erected to close off their
parlor, and the following morning threw rocks at the
stonemasons who had come to wall up the entrance to
their cloister. On a later occasion, they assaulted the archbishop's notary who was bringing the seclusion paperwork
for the abbess to sign. As the documentation reports, asked
to approach a window the notary barely escaped a piece
of marble dropped by nuns who shouted: "Here is the
mother abbess!"[48] This life-threatening attack marked a
point of no return in the community's tumultuous relationships with the authorities. The nuns finally capitulated
in 1629 under conditions that included the threat of
excommunication, rejection by their families, and a
minimal food ration that had compelled them to resort to
eating grass.[49]

Certainly, the patrician nuns of Santa Cristina were
severely punished for not having been suitably humble and
obedient consecrated women who devoted their lives to
prayer and contemplative activities as prescribed. Normally,
prayer and the chanting of psalms at fixed hours marked
nuns' daily routine. Their prayer began as soon as they awoke
early in the morning; and the community was required to
congregate several times for the office of Mass. Prayer was
not limited, however, to the time spent kneeling in church.
Every moment of a nun's life was supposed to be dedicated
to prayer. A number of Renaissance images depict nuns
absorbed in ecstatic contemplation and interiorized meditation. One remarkable, albeit not well-known, representation
(fig. 13) is found in a finely illuminated antiphonary dating
to around 1507, recently attributed to the Maestro delle Ore
Barbazza.[50] It shows an observant Dominican nun, who has
been identified as the noble Bolognese Bernardina Isolani,
and a young lay woman kneeling in an uninhabited landscape with their hands clasped in prayer, while overhead
God the Father in a roundel imparts his benediction to
both. The women's silent, shared devotions are enveloped in
the serenity and beauty of the verdant landscape as if one
is the reflection of the other.

Through their prayer, good works, and also their skilled
art and artisanry, nuns contributed to the spiritual and eco-

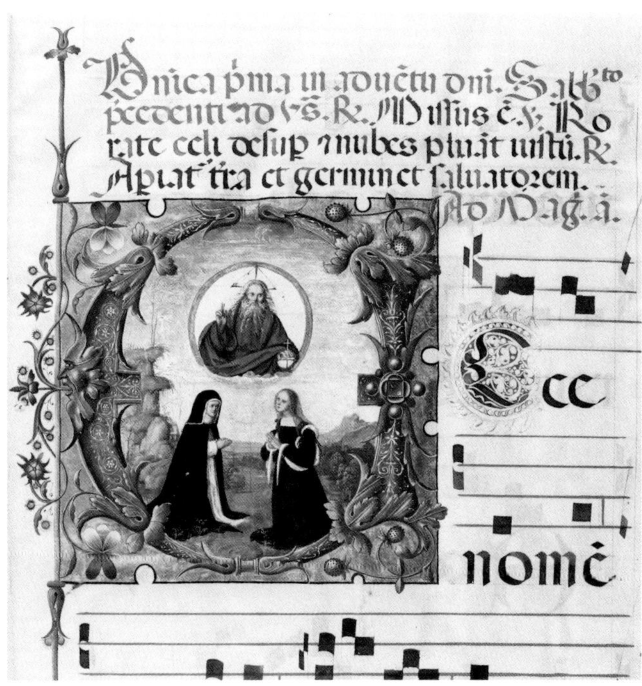

13   Maestro delle Ore Barbazza, antiphonary page showing
Bernardina Isolani and a relative, ca. 1507, pen, gold and pigments,
55 × 40 mm ($2^{11}/_{64}$ × $1^{37}/_{64}$ in), Modena, Biblioteca Estense

nomic wellbeing of their communities. Spinning, weaving,
sewing, and embroidering were the standard activities of the
obedient nun, activities that were shared in multifunctional
rooms, as a *Prologo* woodcut illustrates (fig. 14). Sharon Strocchia has demonstrated that nuns' cheap labor was, however,
widely exploited in early modern Italy. Textile production
was not merely a spiritual occupation, or a means of keeping
the hands of cloistered women fruitfully occupied, but was
also a source of revenue crucial to the economy of convents
and even to that of whole cities.[51] Engagement in productive
labor further comprised the copying and illuminating of
manuscripts, book printing, and the execution of large-scale
images, if, as the sixteenth-century nun-artist Plautilla Nelli
recorded in Giorgio Vasari's *Lives of the Most Eminent Painters,
Sculptors, and Architects* (1568), religious women had artistic
talent. In general, creative works were meant to spur contemplative practices, to be effective tools for spiritual enlight-
enment, and were primarily used for inculcating in women
the rudiments of devotion. The vast majority of nuns' handi-
work was left anonymous. But as a sign of her credited
artistic self, the Florentine Plautilla Nelli signed her *Last
Supper* scene (before 1568; Florence, Santa Maria Novella)
using the gender-declined version of a formula adopted by
male artists: "Pray for the Paintress" (*Orate pro Pictora*).[52]

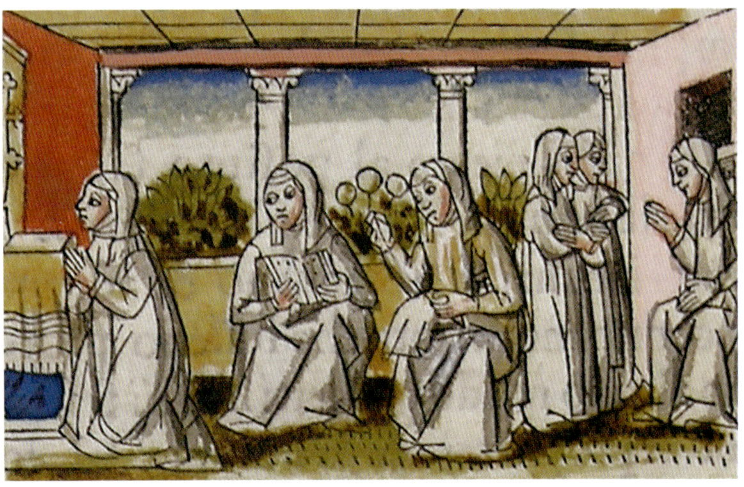

14   Nuns at work, from *Prologo de l'ordine del vivere neli monasteri de monache & temporale & spirituale. Excepta da diversi scripti de Hieronymo ad Eustochio sua Figliuola spirituale & ale sorelle*, chapter 13, 46 × 72 mm ($1^{13}/_{16}$ × $2^{53}/_{64}$ in) (Ferrara 1497), Ferrara, Biblioteca Ariostea, S.16.5.10

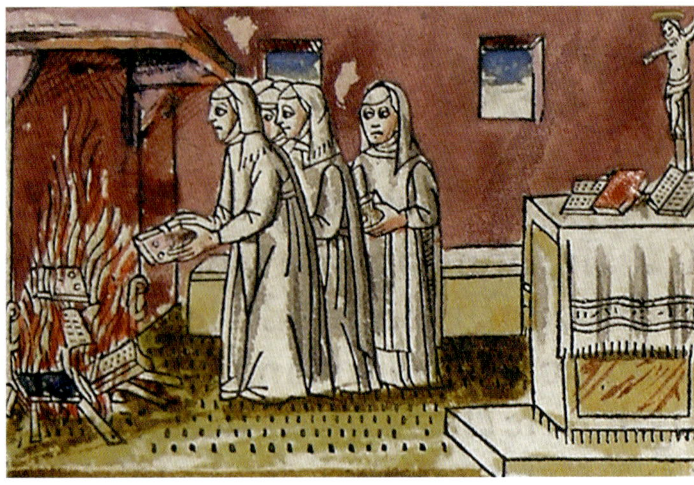

15   Nuns burning books, from *Prologo de l'ordine del vivere neli monasteri de monache & temporale & spirituale. Excepta da diversi scripti de Hieronymo ad Eustochio sua Figliuola spirituale & ale sorelle*, chapter 11, 49 × 73 mm ($1^{59}/_{64}$ × $2^{7}/_{8}$ in) (Ferrara 1497), Ferrara, Biblioteca Ariostea, S.16.5.10

LIMINALITY, RITES OF PASSAGE, AND FORBIDDEN CLOTHING

Early modern patrician nuns, in contrast, never fully engaged in manual labor. As noble religious women, they occupied an intermediate zone between the holy and the secular assigned to them by Church and society, a special realm of "institutionalized liminality," set apart from the outside world, yet also immersed in it. What were the implications of these nuns' privileged and ambiguously liminal status? As observed by Victor Turner, a liminal phase is a temporary state that ends when individuals are integrated into society through rites of passage. For those reinstated with an elevated spiritual status (nuns, friars, and monks), liminality then became a permanent state. Building on and departing from Turner's theory, Caroline Walker Bynum has provided a more historicized notion of liminality in relation to late medieval cloistered women.[53] Noting that Turner's theory was based on observations of the rites of male individuals rather than those of their female peers, Bynum argued that the early modern elite had a particular need to institutionalize female liminality in the form of structures for women not destined for marriage. When assigned to convents, patrician women were designated to live in liminal continuity with, and not in opposition to, the social status of their family of origin. The fitting out of their monastic spaces with fine objects could be seen as simply a manifestation of nuns' liminal status, and therefore an instance of institutionalized liminality. Yet, at the same time, the pleasure that fine artworks afforded and the reliance on the imagination that they demanded greatly complicates the understanding of nuns' liminal agency and their activation of painted subjects overhead and underfoot in their surroundings.

Patrician nuns often further exploited their status to make liminality central to their lives through the cultivation of learning. While the decision to enter a religious rather than a married life depended on their families, girls were assured better opportunities in convents to pursue an education, in addition to the attainment of virtue. Indispensable for the proper performance of offices and an understanding of Christian doctrine, a standard monastic education included acquiring Latin through the memorization of passages from the Gospels, psalms, and the lives of saints. Learning to read and write in Latin were some of the first skills novices were expected to master, with reading in Latin the norm rather than the exception in a nun's education. Judging from conventual library inventories, few nuns were exposed to Greek. Mythological tales of love and heroic epics were banned from convents, as shown in another *Prologo* woodcut (fig. 15) featuring the "wise" nuns burning their codices of pagan fables and mythologies, and vernacular poetry, in a fireplace. The monk Giovanni di Dio described these texts in 1471 as vehicles of intoxication, and the cause of the death of women's souls.[54]

In a few elite convents, the intellectual talents of the resident nuns were especially recognized and encouraged. The canonesses of Santa Maria delle Vergini in Venice were accomplished Latinists, as testified by their convent's chronicle. The Benedictine sisters of San Zaccaria, too, were known for their command of Latin.[55] Several nuns became notorious for their writings, which included record books, hymns, religious theatrical pieces, and devotional texts.[56] The Dominican sister Fiammetta Frescobaldi (1523–1586) from San Jacopo di Ripoli in Florence was praised for the excellence of her history writings. At the same time that convents fostered the intellectual life of their inhabitants, they served as pivotal centers for female education. Girls sent to religious houses for educational purposes (*in serbanza*), and for whom their fathers paid room and board, learned reading, needlework, and the so-called virtues, namely, the basic knowledge and comportment that were considered appropriate to their sex.[57]

To undertake lives as nuns, girls entered the convent by first passing through its gate. As thresholds to or from the outside world, gates delimited convents' outermost confines, symbolically and materially closing its residents off from the surrounding world. Gates were not the neutral spatial markers they may first appear to be. They were loci of social contact and communication, and also associated with emotion and anxiety. As liminal architectural borders, gates were stages for the first rite of monastic life, the girls' entry into the convent. Walking through these entries, girls left their families and the cities behind to join a religious community and be consigned to their heavenly groom. The act of walking through the gate signaled the girl's rite of passage from the lay to the spiritual life, and her separation from the secular world and initiation into conventual life. As Kate Lowe has outlined, ideally four stages marked the process of becoming a nun, each recognizing a perfected spiritual state: first, entry and acceptance into a convent; second, taking of the habit or the change from secular to monastic attire; third, profession of vows; and fourth, consecration or veiling. Often these rites were celebrated conjunctively, but in what follows the significance of each monastic ritual will be clarified through the examination of textual and visual materials that portray such rites.

The ritual of a girl's entry into a convent was literally her walk through the gateway, and this earliest crossing of that threshold symbolically signaled a new life. For patrician youth, in particular, this walk metamorphosed into a public event recorded in chronicles for its display of pomp and secularized flavor. Parents, civic authorities, and prominent sponsors escorted girls to the convent gates to celebrate their disengagement from society and new role in the service of their fellow citizenry. In 1481 the Ferrarese chronicler Bernardino Zambotti reports that such members of the ruling family as Eleonora d'Aragona and Sigismondo d'Este accompanied two noble girls "dressed as brides" to the local convent of Corpus Domini, stopping their carriage at the gate to participate in the ceremony of the girls' entrance.[58] The year before, a less grandiose but similar ceremony was recorded for Eufrosina Zambotti, the sister of the Ferrarese chronicler, who had entered the Augustinian convent wearing "a silver brocade dress with hair unbound on her shoulders, carrying a panel, an ornately dressed doll and a candle, as is usual for the brides."[59] A seventeenth-century French traveler provides additional details regarding the entrance rituals to the convent of Corpus Domini in Bologna. Dressed in white, with crowns of flowers on their heads, the girls were taken around "to see the city for the last time" and to bid farewell to their parents' house. After passing through the city streets, their adorned carriage drew up to the convent gate, where the ritual required that the girls declare "in a firm and modest way that the convent was to be their home."[60] At that point, they rang the bell and passed through the gateway to join their spiritual sisters, who greeted them from inside with the traditional chant of "Veni Sponsa Christi" (Come, Bride of Christ).[61]

Donning monastic clothing and being tonsured, or the sacrifice of physical beauty to the divine spouse, were subsequent rituals for the nuns-to-be. Usually within a year of admittance to a convent, girls took their vows, and this rite of passage to the full religious status was marked by another ceremony. The union of the girl's soul with Christ, the heavenly spouse, or the profession, was a ritual literally structured as a wedding celebration. In both the secular and the spiritual marriage, the same material signs — the ring and the crown — denoted this transformation of a woman's status. It is interesting to compare a few depictions of the ceremony in order to trace its implications from different perspectives. As shown in the richly illustrated *Pontificale Secundum Ritum Sacrosanctae Romanae Ecclesiae*, printed in 1520, the kneeling girl wearing the habit of her order is first veiled, after which she receives the "wedding" ring from the bishop (fig. 16) and ultimately the crown.[62] Manifesting the church's viewpoint, the colored woodcut declares that the ritual is governed by the ecclesiastical authorities. The kneeling, subservient nun is overshadowed by a dominant male churchman (the bishop) and his attendants, without the presence of any community at this initiation rite, which is presented simply as an ecclesiastical event.

The same consecration ceremony rendered in a slightly earlier illumination by a still unknown artist (fig. 17) proposes a different message. Probably the frontispiece of a manuscript that belonged to a certain Suor Antonia, a Cistercian nun of San Donato in Polverosa near Florence, this miniature depicts the event with both the religious community and the novice's family present to witness the rite.[63] On the upper wall of the chapel, a pair of escutcheons with the arms of the influential Florentine Albizzi and Vecchietti families assures viewers that they have gathered for the consecration of Cassandra Albizzi in 1501, who was given the name of Suor Antonia.[64] The right-hand side of the nave is occupied by the female audience, while the opposite side is reserved for the male public. Before the adorned altar the future nun kneels, dressed in a fine white garment with her hands clasped in prayer to receive the veil from the priest. At the bottom, near the lectern, her spiritual sisters participate in the ceremony being staged before them. As Kate Lowe has observed, these ceremonies were seen by patrician families as occasions for display and splendor and both values were rooted in the notion of honor "to be upheld in exactly the same way as it would have been in a secular wedding."[65]

Before they could make their profession, nuns were required to pay in full a spiritual dowry, or alms, consisting of cash given to the institution. Intended to cover the girls' living expenses, these funds were usually paid at the time of their admittance to convents. However, dowries were often treated as sources of income for the convent, to cover the costs of rebuilding, renovating, and embellishing its appurtenances, or for purchasing new properties.[66] Admittance dowries were therefore crucial sources of income for convents, guaranteeing both the nuns' standard of living and providing revenues to the institutions. A 1507 document attests that the fee required to become a nun in the elite convent of San Paolo in Parma was set at 100 gold *scudi*. It records that the dowry cash was placed in a purse and affixed to a white candle offered to the newly elected abbess Giovanna Piacenza at the altar following her election ceremony.[67] As was true for contemporary secular brides, finely carved and painted chests and even large paintings could be included in spiritual dowries. For example, in 1453 the admittance dowry of the nun Verde, the sister of the Ferrarese marquis Borso d'Este, comprised an image of the Virgin "with a triumph of angels" possibly by Andrea Vicenza and incorporating a donor portrait.[68] The admittance dowries also included goods and utensils. Unpublished documentation reports that the dowry "package" required to enter San Paolo included furniture for the nuns' cells, such as a bed, bedding, cabinets, and liturgical items. Supplementing the dowry were objects like copper and pewter cooking utensils, as well as maiolica tableware (dishes, pitchers, drinking vessels) and silverware for refectories or private dining in personal rooms.[69]

The fundamental difference between a marriage and a spiritual dowry was that convents had the right to retain the capital on a nun's death, whereas in such cases the dowries of wives were returned to their families. But all told, spiritual dowries were less onerous than their marital counterparts. For example, 100 gold *scudi* was the fee paid for admittance to San Paolo in 1507, whereas five years earlier a local patrician girl, Briseide Colla, brought her husband Ottaviano Bergonzi a dowry of 600 gold ducats, probably a sum typical for their social class.[70] For aristocratic families, admittance to honorable elite monastic settings like San Paolo represented a less expensive alternative for the placement of their female members. Nonetheless, it created a two-tiered system of upper-class girls who entered convents with paid dowries and girls of lower standing (*converse* or servant nuns) with minimal dowries.[71] Responsible for carrying out heavy work, *converse* performed tasks like assisting, feeding, and washing ill and aged nuns, and handling the dead. Given the hierarchical structure of aristocratic nunneries, the presence of *converse* and servants (women who worked for the nuns, chiefly performing errands outside the convent, without professing vows) is hardly

16   Profession of a nun, from *Pontificale Secundum Ritum Sacrosanctae Romanae Ecclesiae*, fol. 86v (Venice 1520)

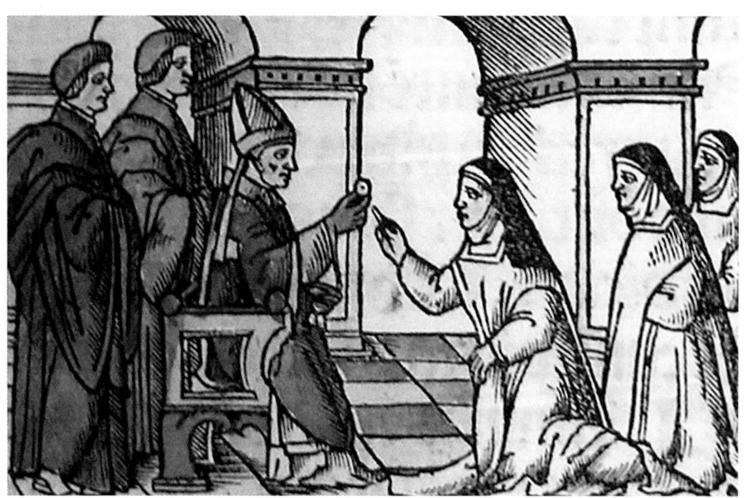

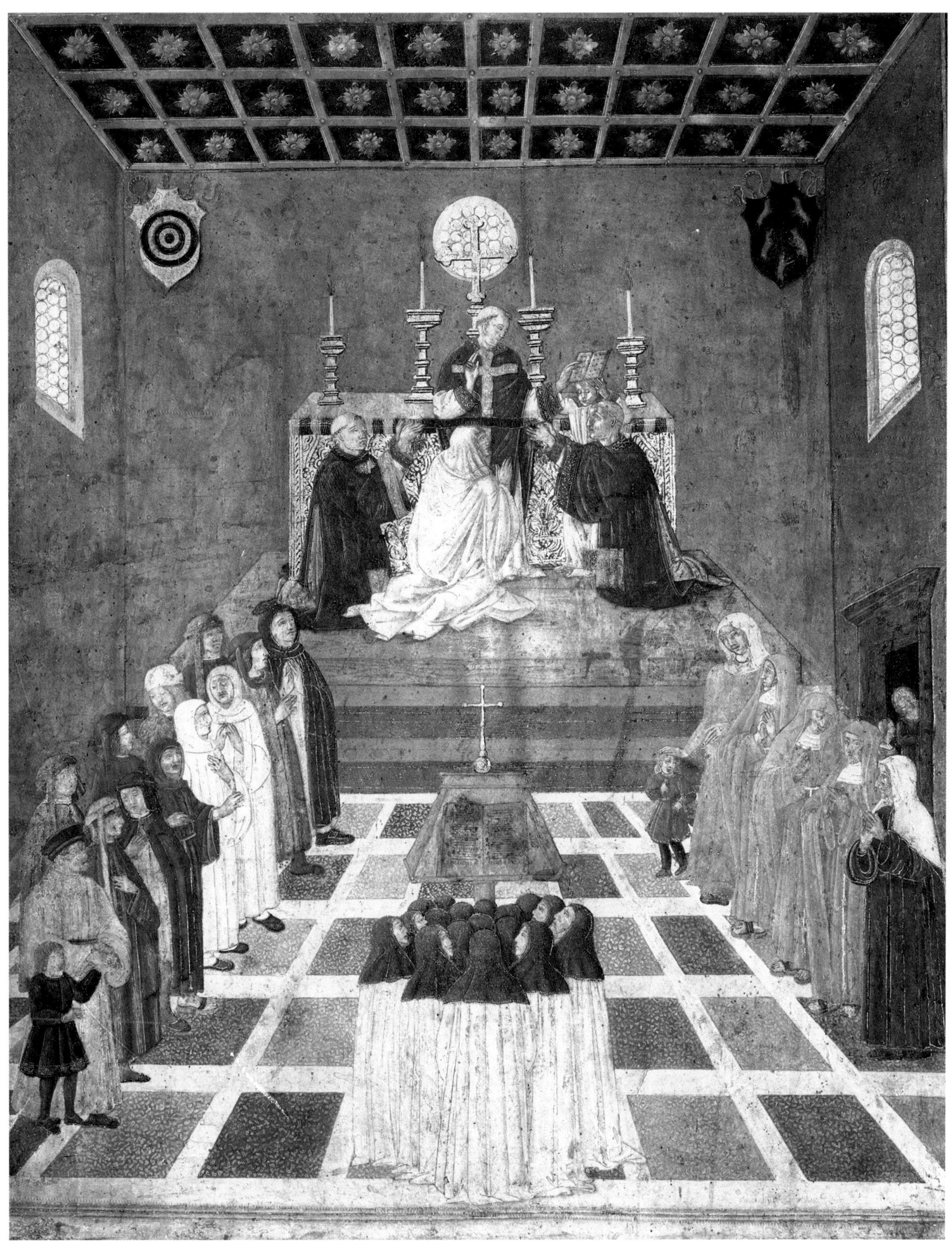

17   Anonymous, *Veiling Ceremony of a Florentine Nun*, ca. 1500, Florence, Polo Museale Fiorentino, Gabinetto Disegni e Stampe degli Uffizi

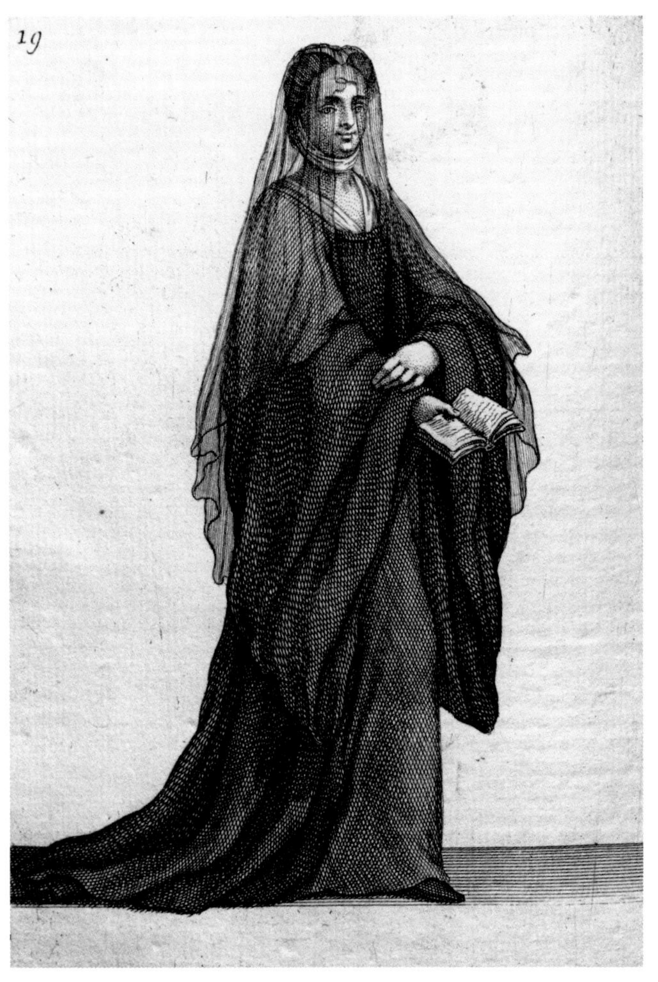

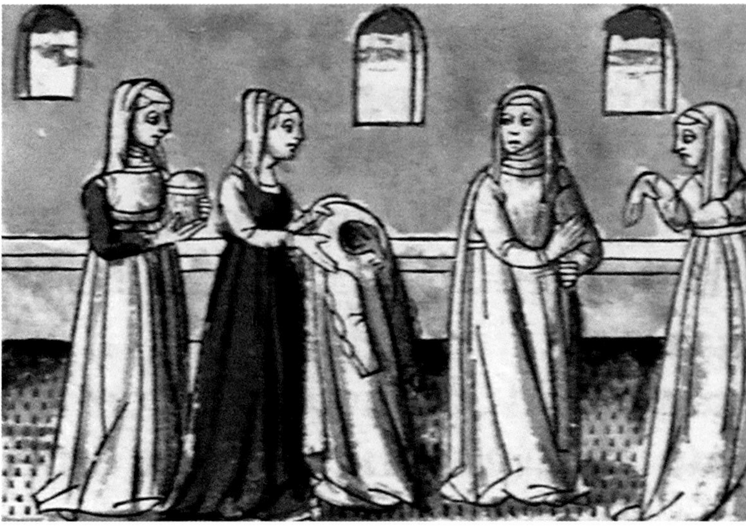

Left 18   Habit of a Venetian Benedictine nun from San Lorenzo, from Filippo Buonanni, *Ordinum Religiosorum in Ecclesia Militanti Catalogus*, plate 19 (Rome 1714)

Above 19   Nuns renouncing their attire, from *Prologo de l'ordine del vivere neli monasteri de monache & temporale & spirituale. Excepta da diversi scripti de Hieronymo ad Eustochio sua Figliuola spirituale & ale sorelle*, chapter 29, 49 × 73 mm ($1^{59}/_{64}$ × $2^{7}/_{8}$ in) (Ferrara 1497), Ferrara, Biblioteca Ariostea, S.16.5.10

surprising.[72] They allowed upper-class nuns to maintain a comfortable life similar to what they would have enjoyed in their homes, and to institutionalize their liminality in well-appointed monastic rooms. As Raffaella Sarti has put it, conventual life was a family life conducted in adorned, comfortable rooms, though not in secular settings.[73]

Patrician nuns usually retained their surnames. While a change of name was not mandatory for nuns, they were expected to change their surnames to signal their spiritual status. Retaining historical names thus marked patrician nuns' identification with their families rather than their monastic communities. The order's simple religious habit was another outward sign of a woman's spiritual initiation. For example, clothing for Benedictine nuns was relatively standardized by the Renaissance period, consisting of a white undertunic, black mantle, white wimple, and a black top veil. Tunics were to be made of the coarsest cloth, and veils were supposed to be worn lowered, to hide the nun's face. Sixteenth- and seventeenth-century inventories of patrician nuns' belongings, however, attest that they often possessed tailored garments decorated with elaborate embroidery, footwear enriched with pearl inlay, silk stockings, lace-trimmed handkerchiefs and gloves, and elegant dresses and accessories not dissimilar from those worn by their lay sisters. The alluring and ostentatious dress of a Venetian Benedictine nun from San Lorenzo illustrated in an early eighteenth-century print (fig. 18) reveals the forbidden fashion of generations of patrician nuns determined to maintain a secular identity at all cost. Her veil, transparent and fine, is short in front and long in the back, and the floor-length tunic of refined fabric has generous sleeves that seem all but tailor-made.[74]

Pre-Tridentine and Tridentine authorities urged nuns to dress modestly and to avoid self-adornment and cosmetics of any kind. A number of images in the *Prologo* depict the renunciation of worldly goods, especially of rich attire (fig. 19), all criticized as forms of personal vanity. As Isabella Campagnol has recently well documented, through their self-adornment, dyed hair, and fashionable clothing, elite cloistered women asserted their acquired right to live a more secularized life than the rules permitted, to exercise power through expenditure, and to resist ideals of poverty, deprivation, and humility.[75] Nuns were admonished to avoid attracting attention, but instead they brought attention to themselves by venturing outside convents often in fashionable dress and by living in adorned settings, a lifestyle that intersected the sacred and the profane in fluid ways. These and other forbidden experiences of elite cloistered women require additional qualification. Thus, in the following chapter I shall introduce related discourses around the viewing of two remarkable sets of late Quattrocento works of art from the convent of San Paolo in Parma, examining how frescoes on walls and a fine maiolica-tiled floor were challenges to the strictures placed on nuns' eyes and bodies.

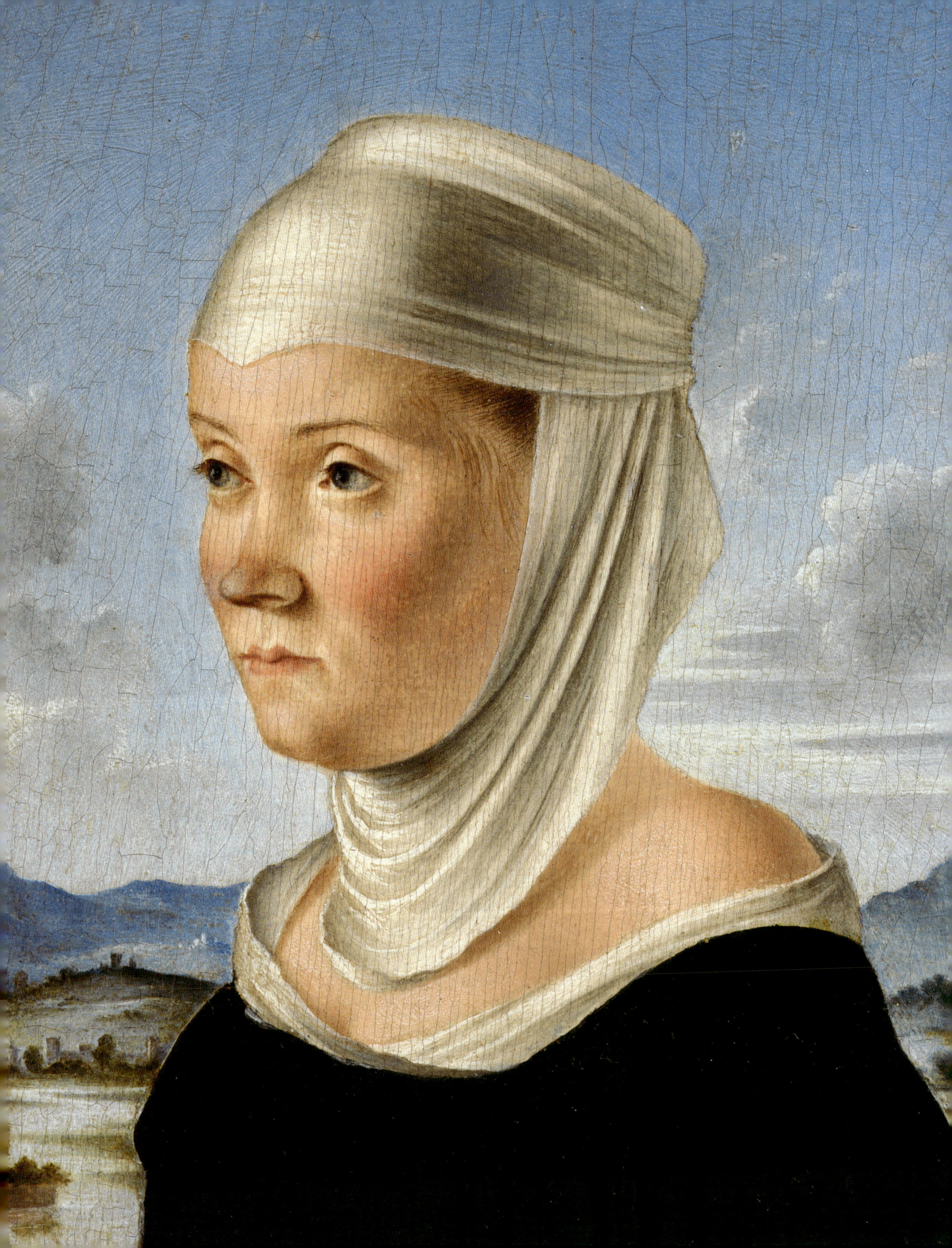

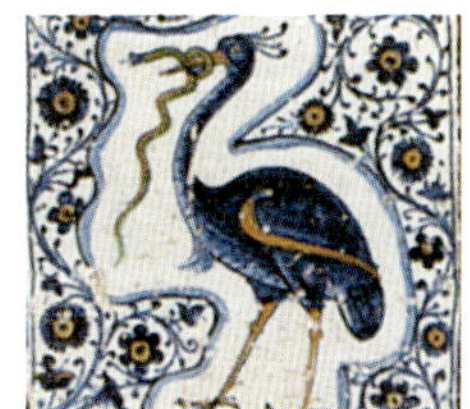

2

Art for Nuns

GAZE, TOUCH, AND PROVOCATION

A strict governance of the gaze had long been imposed on nuns. Late medieval and Renaissance religious writers were aware of the hazards to spirituality represented by the eyes, urging strict control of the faculty of vision. Visual stimuli were considered to be subject to interference on their passage from objects to the minds of individuals and vice versa, and it was believed that demons used visual illusions to distract cloistered women from their spiritual duties. Eyes were more than just entities registering impressions from the outside. They facilitated intuitive insights about things, and prompted emotions to come to the surface. Sight was disciplined in monastic spaces through mechanisms of physical and psychological repression, including warnings about the unwanted consequences of perceptive eyes. Cloistered women were constantly advised to have "honest" perceptual experiences, to keep their eyes downcast, and refrain from interrogating the eyes as a means to access the world.[1] This chapter reflects and expands on the implications of these proscriptions by exploring a paradigmatic yet still under studied corpus of late fifteenth-century works, namely, a set of murals by Jacopo Loschi and a polychrome maiolica pavement. Both works memorialize religious women's personae, and at the same time confirm that viewing was not a static action in convents. Nuns' experiences of the works embellishing their spaces were never merely occasions of patronage but, rather, were perceptual encounters implying participation and performance.

Loschi's murals, which are fairly large frescoes, are neither unconventional in terms of their sacred iconographies nor do they stand out particularly for their aesthetic values. Nonetheless, they display a remarkable combination of portraits of living female individuals set within religious narratives, redefining and reimagining a monastic community at a crucial moment in its history. In contrast, the maiolica floor tiles – featuring female and male heads, poetic and mythological subjects, and ornamental motifs are notable for their luminous quality, vibrant colorism, and their secular themes, inviting the beholder's bodily involvement in charming images underfoot. Beside their primary patrons and audience – the female community of San Paolo in Parma – the common link between these works is conceptual. Murals and maiolica tiles propose modes of viewing that presuppose distinct modalities of engagement and acts of looking. The beholder is asked to gaze across the wall to absorb Loschi's frescoes. Walking on the pavement and gazing down, the viewer instead activates the subjects of the tiles with feet anchored to the horizontal floor, becoming physically involved with the colorful surface underfoot. As a result, Loschi's frescoes and the maiolica floor tiles constructed distinct responses that expanded the phenomenol-

Facing page   detail of fig. 2

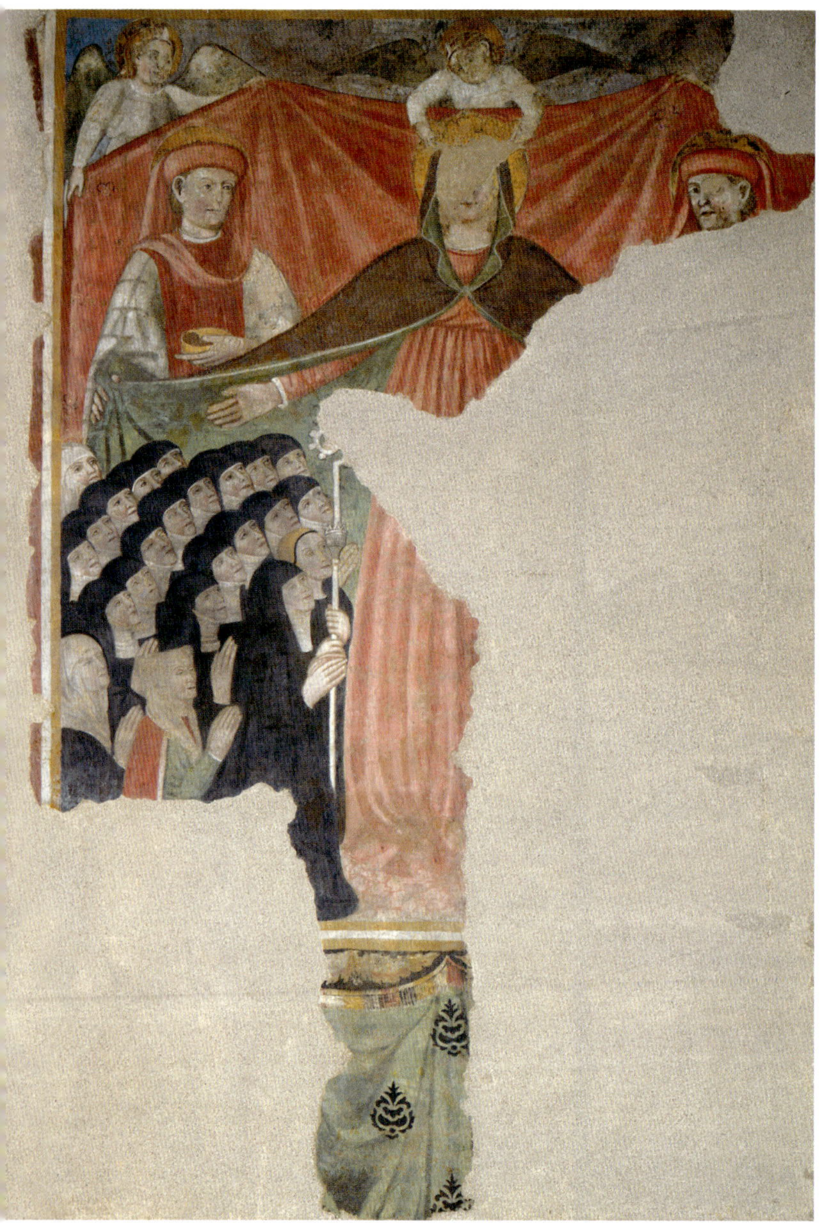

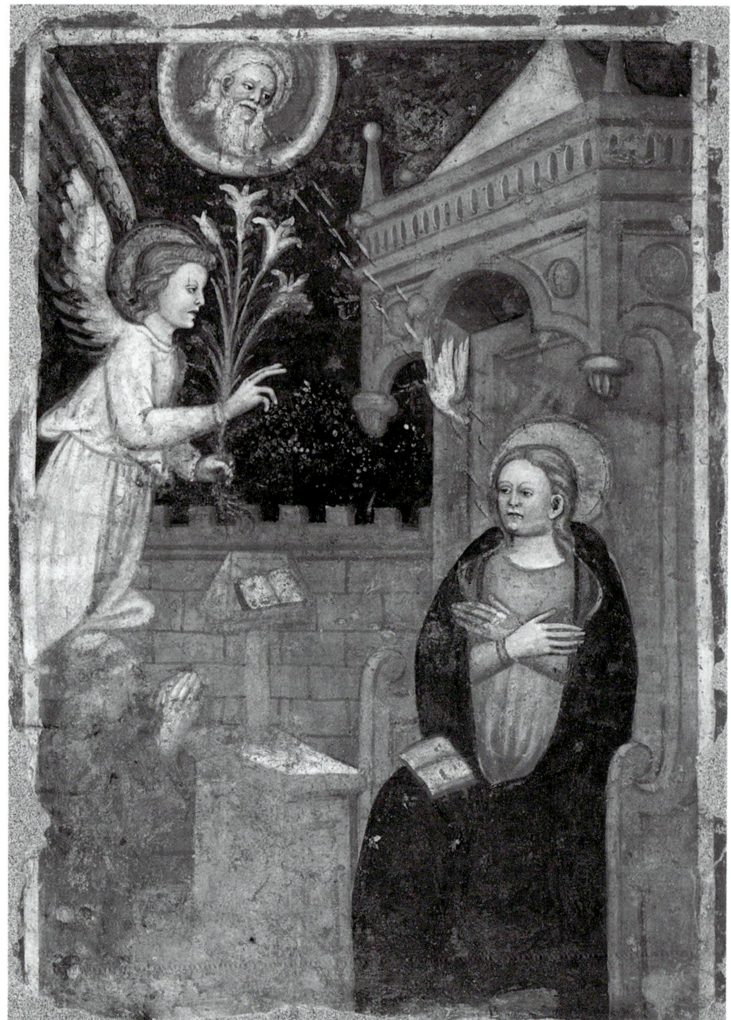

Left 20   Jacopo Loschi, *Madonna of Mercy*, 1460s, fresco,
301 × 230 cm (118½ × 90³⁵⁄₆₄ in), Parma, convent of San Paolo

Above 21   Jacopo Loschi, *Annunciation*, 1460s, fresco, 137 × 99 cm
(53¹⁵⁄₁₆ × 38³¹⁄₃₂ in), Parma, convent of San Paolo

ogy of gazes that the San Paolo community explored as it progressed along its own history in the Quattrocento. Simultaneously, they made claims of resistance, provocation, and disobeying monastic strictures.

To articulate these responses, I shall proceed by first offering a detailed reconstruction of the circumstances of the commissions, the function of the works in their original settings, and the perceptions pertaining to Loschi's frescoes and the maiolica tiled floor. Contextual research on these works is crucial since they have been relegated to the category of "second string" or "minor" art and have thus been marginalized in the history of Renaissance art. This is due to their poor condition (Loschi's murals) or status as mere decoration (the floor tiles). Contextual research further serves to identify the historical individuals who are portrayed in Loschi's murals and on the tiles, as well as to discern why and in which ways their representations mattered to the audiences beholding them. But most prominently it recovers nuns' modes of viewing and the sensorial experiences that each medium afforded, subsequently enabling me to expand on how the works are manifestations of the attitudes and the assumptions of those who made them and those who were shaped by the works themselves. Their materiality ultimately engages the senses, while their content touches on unexpected facets of the nuns' experience, from morality and insubordination, to humor. As the discussion unfolds, central to its argumentation will also be unconventional images of cloistered women in décolletage, including Jacometto Veneziano's *Portrait of a Nun from San Secondo* (see fig. 2). A miniature portrait such as this foregrounds a tension between appearance and reality, the mask and the face, that deserves probing. Accessible to both secluded and lay individuals, Loschi's murals, Jacometto's portrait, and the extraordinary ensemble of secular subjects displayed on the tiles are revealed as mediators of spiritual and worldly values, bearers of the interplay between real and reimagined identities, generative of the complex world of upper-class nuns, complicating the beholder's view of and insight into conventual courtly art.

JACOPO LOSCHI'S MURALS: SPIRITUALITY AND INDEPENDENCE

The frescoes by Jacopo Loschi depict the *Madonna of Mercy* (fig. 20), the *Annunciation* (fig. 21), *The Last Meeting between St. Benedict and St. Scholastica*, and *St. Scholastica's Soul Metamorphosed into a Dove* (fig. 22). They are all that remain of a lost cycle of fifteenth-century murals comprising episodes from the lives of the Virgin and St. Scholastica. Detached in 1968 from their original location in San Paolo and exhibiting extensive lacunae, at present they are displayed in a former nunnery space that has been transformed into a museum gallery. The large size (301 × 230 cm) and rectangularity of the imposing Madonna image contrast with the tympanum form of the somewhat smaller St. Scholastica narratives (235 × 230 cm), while the rectangular *Annunciation* picture is the smallest in scale (137 × 99 cm). Crowned by an angel whose two companions hold up a red curtain, the *Madonna of Mercy* is flanked by two male saints lifting her mantle beneath which extend her arms in a wide embrace. Given the saints' characteristic red gowns and round hats, they are identifiable as the physicians Cosmas and Damian. Below the picture, a fragment of the original *velarium* (curtain) survives. Distributed on two registers, the St. Scholastica scenes must have originally been set above the entrance to a chapel or other monastic space. The *Last Meeting* episode captures St. Benedict and St. Scholastica standing at a table, their identities confirmed by the names painted on the wall behind. St. Benedict touches the food on the table with one hand, raising the other in a gesture

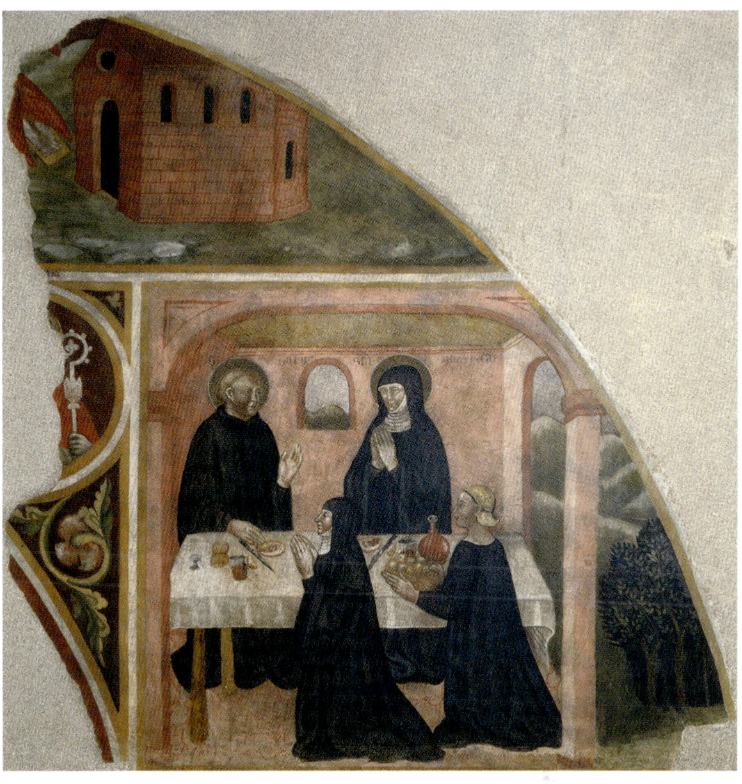

22   Jacopo Loschi, *The Last Meeting between St. Benedict and St. Scholastica* and *St. Scholastica's Soul Metamorphosed into a Dove*, 1460s, fresco, 235 × 230 cm (92$^{33}/_{64}$ × 90$^{35}/_{64}$ in), Parma, convent of San Paolo

of blessing, while his sister Scholastica joins her hands in a thanksgiving prayer. Two women shown in profile kneel in the foreground. The depiction in the upper register features St. Scholastica's soul transformed into a dove and escorted by angels to heaven, a scene set in front of a brick church. In the *Annunciation*, the angel Gabriel with lilies in hand appears from on high to the Virgin, who is seated on a wooden throne overhung with a baldachin, a book in her lap, while from the white-bearded head of God in a roundel above descends the dove of the Holy Spirit, and a robed figure kneels in prayer before the Virgin. This kneeling figure appears to be tonsured, but the gender is unclear, making additional observations virtually impossible.

Augusta Ghidiglia Quintavalle was the first to publish these frescoes in 1971, reporting in vague terms that they had been discovered "behind a wall in the church of San Paolo." According to Ghidiglia Quintavalle, they were produced around 1470 in Jacopo Loschi's workshop. The lack of documentation on the murals led Maria Chiara Cavazzoni to speculate that they had been whitewashed over as early as 1583, when the church was renovated in accordance to the Council of Trent's decrees, though she offers no corroborating evidence for her statement. Cavazzoni agreed with the attribution to Loschi but dated the frescoes slightly earlier, to the mid-1460s.[2] The following discussion on Loschi's murals proposes a new account of their original location, chronology, and the identity of the portrayed figures. Despite their poor quality, Loschi's images marked a significant moment in the convent's history, amounting to a declaration of the religious community's independence from local ecclesiastical authorities and to a celebration of its leading female personalities. The subjects of Loschi's images are hardly uncanonical, and the artist's uninventive approach is not the real issue. Their very existence and iconographies, however, proclaim strong messages challenging the power of local ecclesiastics over the nuns. Disregarding general prohibitions that required cloistered women not to be portrayed, the community of San Paolo instead felt it necessary to engage with the visual and have their effigies (regardless if ideal or real) represented in the murals. Therefore it is only the careful reconstruction of what this act meant, and the understanding of what the frescoes communicated to their audiences, that gives works of limited aesthetic impact major historical relevance.[3] As will be seen, they were more tied to the charming maiolica floor tiles than has hitherto been acknowledged.

A resident of the San Paolo neighborhood and trained by his father-in-law, Bartolino de' Grossi, Jacopo Loschi (ca. 1425–1504) was not only a painter accessible to the nuns living in the vicinity, but also the most credited master active in mid-Quattrocento Parma.[4] At the time, the city of Parma was not the site of a court, nor did it attract ambitious foreign artists, and the nuns were probably limited to choosing from among local artists. In general, cloistered women tended to commission works from local masters, and the community of San Paolo was apparently no exception.[5] What is noticeable in Loschi's murals are the portrayals of living individuals mingled with sacred iconographies. Under her benevolent right arm, the merciful Madonna shelters a female religious community that, given the fresco's provenance and despite the large area of loss, we can assume must be that of San Paolo. The women are characterized with specific clothing and facial features. Included are the abbess, professed nuns, and novices, but also laywomen who kneel to pray beseechingly to the Madonna. Dressed in the Benedictine habit, the abbess is absorbed in prayer and directs her gaze toward the Virgin. On her right hand she displays her ring as a sign of her status. A young woman

on her left holds the crosier, a symbol of the power of the abbess's office and of her claim to legitimate leadership. Unveiled, her blond hair is gathered in a net. The girl's proximity and the fact that she supports the crosier signal her ties to the *domina abbatissa*. At the head of the row behind the abbess, and dressed in lay costume, is a woman in a pale green gown and a red mantle, her head covered by a fashionable veil. Behind these three highly characterized figures kneel the professed nuns in the Benedictine uniform and the novices wearing the white veil. If cloistered women were supposed to remain faceless, the decision of this assembly of lay and religious women to have themselves portrayed with their own effigies held major implications and consequences. Who are these women, and how may one interpret the act of their praying together? In the *Last Meeting*, the same abbess and the lay girl reappear with the male founder and the female protector of the Benedictine order. Was the purpose of including living individuals in Loschi's scenes to communicate specific messages to the community before them? We might begin to answer these questions by revisiting the socio-political and religious context surrounding the images, considering particular events in which the nuns of San Paolo strongly opposed local ecclesiastical authorities in the mid-fifteenth century.

Founded as a female Benedictine abbey by the bishop of Parma, Sigifredo II, in 1005, the convent was secured from the first with a conspicuous endowment of lands, canals, and orchards.[6] Its first abbess, Liuda, shared with Sigifredo the credit for the convent's foundation and, like her successors Imilia and Berta, she was from the Attonidi family.[7] Sigifredo's episcopal successors upgraded the institution's endowment with privileges and benefices.[8] Pope Gregory VIII's bull of 1187 confirmed the convent's possessions and extended to its abbesses a form of temporal power over residences within its vast properties. The pope further subjected the community to papal authority, which meant that San Paolo was freed from local ecclesiastics' control.[9] As well as the episcopal and papal *magnanimitas* (munificence), the convent benefited from imperial and local government generosity.[10] In short, the nunnery was a site of wealth and privilege inhabited by upper-class women, with rights and benefits that the bishop of Parma, Delfino della Pergola (d. 1465), attempted drastically to curb.

The dispute commenced immediately after della Pergola took office as bishop in 1425, and began his interference in the convent's affairs.[11] Six years later he granted permission to the nun Agnese Benedetti – subsequently elected abbess in 1433 – to leave the *claustrum* and stay in her brother's household, after she had been excommunicated for having insulted and assaulted Abbess Caterina Castrobarco.[12] With the community's rights threatened, Abbess Castrobarco appealed to the pope, the only legitimate authority she recognized. Eugenius IV's privilege of December 4, 1431, exempted the nuns from obedience to Bishop della Pergola, reiterating that the "Abbess and the convent were under the protection of St. Peter and Apostolic authority."[13] A decree of excommunication issued by Delfino against the abbess and her nuns was thereby annulled. In its closing lines, the papal privilege even threatens that those who dare "to oppose the Pope's will" shall incur both "God's anger and that of his representatives on earth." Pope Eugenius's privilege empowered the nuns to resist the bishop's attack and conferred on them a strong sense of their identity, a reaffirmed agency that had a crucial impact on their investments in art and the representations of their personae. In addition, it marked a new phase of their interactions with Delfino and subsequent local bishops whose authority the community denied, establishing the convent as a center of power and complicating relationships with ecclesiastics for centuries to come.

This San Paolo–Delfino struggle lasted until the bishop was removed from office in 1463, and even involved the Sforza ruling dynasty. From 1450, Parma had been incorporated within the Duchy of Milan as its southern appendix, and when in 1456 Francesco Sforza granted San Paolo ecclesiastical benefits, Delfino challenged the duke, claiming that the benefits pertained to his diocese and were therefore under his jurisdiction. The bishop's aim in attempting to reform the nuns was, at the very least, to control the convent's patrimony in order to extend his own power and influence.[14] Supported by their families, the nuns held off reforms, keeping the institution an unreformed religious house. The broader goal was to maintain it as a nunnery where local patrician families could place their daughters in a comfortable environment and, at the same time, have opportunities to manage its properties as a way to enhance their social and political standing in the city.[15] More immediately, the aim was to maintain the abbess's office as one for life, and to secure the convent's privileges and its inhabitants' independence. Under these circumstances, the memorialization of the female religious self proposed in Loschi's paintings must have been felt as both desirable and necessary.

The controversy between the San Paolo community and Bishop della Pergola was manifested in several episodes pertinent here as background to the messages evoked in Loschi's images. Besides attesting the bishop's hostility and misogyny toward the nuns, these episodes shed light on the community's internal dynamics that led to the harsh episcopal attack against them. On November 3, 1459, two nuns of San Paolo, Giovanna Pallavicino and Masina Lalatta, obtained papal permission to leave their institution to enter a Franciscan house. In their petition to Pope Pius II, they claimed that Christian penitence and mortification appropriate to their religious status were not practiced in their convent, and they were therefore unable to serve God appropriately.[16] Bishop della Pergola could not but agree with their assertion, and in fact he was seen as their instigator and sponsor. While his real role remains difficult to ascertain, the nuns' request indicates that the institution's inhabitants were not paragons of strict monastic life. It would be mistaken, however, to assume that the principles of Benedictine life and spiritual exercises – the system of daily prayers and devotional activities undertaken to experience an enhanced relationship with the divine – were not exercised in San Paolo.

Aristocratic nuns attended Mass and recited prayers on a daily basis.[17] Yet, their spirituality coexisted with their involvement in family and political business, and, despite monastic prohibitions, they nourished their intellects through reading profane literature. In her petition to the pope for a review of the case, Abbess Selvaggia Arcimboldi (in office 1454–60) claimed that the request of her defecting nuns was generated by "an evil instigation and a feminine whim, rather than by genuine devotion."[18] She insisted that penitential exercises could be practiced by nuns in San Paolo through adherence to the prescriptions of the Benedictine Rule. At the papal court, the representatives of Duke Francesco Sforza supported Arcimboldi's petition and maneuvered for Pius II to cancel the previous concession made to the two nuns. The pope's final decision accorded with Abbess Arcimboldi's request, thus recognizing that her words, backed by male sponsors, were powerfully effective.

A few years earlier, Bishop della Pergola had attacked the community even more directly. According to Enrico Scarabelli Zunti's mid-nineteenth-century unpublished notes, a document was drawn up in 1457 to forbid lay men and women from being residents in San Paolo, requiring them to move out immediately because of the scandal such cohabitation caused among the citizenry.[19] If nothing else, the record proves that lay people of both sexes were lodged within the secluded zone of the nunnery. Men – for instance, legal representatives – were in charge of the institution's finances and could have had business or living spaces there. Likewise, *conversi* (lay brothers) either had easy access to or domestic quarters within the convent walls.[20] There is no doubt that their presence contravened regulations prescribing nuns' strict enclosure and their wholesale rejection of male company. The bishop's other major target was female secular living in the convent. But what is known about these residents?

Documents attest that the patrician Antonia Torelli had resided in San Paolo from 1455. Born into a local feudal family and well educated, Antonia had married Count Pier Maria Rossi, the lord of a small fiefdom outside Parma. Imposed by the families, their union was unsuccessful and the couple separated in the early 1450s. Pier Maria moved with his mistress Bianca Pellegrini d'Arluno to the castle in Torrechiara (a town on the outskirts of Parma).[21] Antonia was refunded her dowry (1,300 Venetian ducats), which she partly invested to enter San Paolo, and was assigned rooms to inhabit in the nunnery. She seems to have chosen the institution because she could conduct a comfortable, civilized life there, dedicating herself to both business and charitable activities.[22] Moreover, her relative Costanza Torelli had held the office of abbess a few decades earlier, and the convent was considered to be a "possession" of the Rossi family until 1477, when Pier Maria experienced a major political defeat.[23]

A series of contracts drawn up between 1455 and 1457 regulated Antonia Torelli's residence in the convent. The two parties were Abbess Arcimboldi and Torelli, who was defined as a laywoman (*mulier laica*).[24] One of the records states that Antonia rented and renovated *casamenti* (edifices) in ruinous conditions, including the infirmary and adjacent edifices to build her own *domus*.[25] Upon Torelli's death (which came in 1469), the *domus* was to return to the abbess's disposal. Antonia was granted permission to live with whomever she liked. Subverting the use of the space that the rules designated for the sick, Antonia created a house for herself. It must have been known that infirmaries were not necessarily locales reserved solely for the care of elderly, ill, or psychologically deranged nuns. They were spaces that could be adapted as lodgings for abbots and elite guests. In a document from the Benedictine Cassinese monastery of San Benedetto Po (Mantua) dating to 1521, the infirmary, the abbot's private rooms, and the guesthouse are described as a block on the eastern side of the cloister.[26] Frequently located in the southeast zone, infirmaries could be remodeled into abbots' houses, if needed. Given the blurred boundaries between infirmaries and abbatial chambers, the unusual definition of *valetudinarium* (infirmary) as a representational room proposed in the humanist Francesco Mario Grapaldo's

De Partibus Aedium (On the Parts of the House), first printed in Parma in 1494 and often reprinted, is not surprising. As a guest room in a private dwelling, the *valetudinarium* had its roots in monastic tradition, confirming the links between monastic and domestic architecture.[27] The proper place for sick nuns was the *hospitale*, of the kind documented near San Paolo as early as the thirteenth century, though its precise location is difficult to trace.[28]

The Arcimboldi–Torelli contract further specifies that the noblewoman's *domus* bordered a canal, which was in proximity to the eastern gate. It follows that the residence was located at the southeast, facing what the earliest plan of San Paolo indicates as the *chiostro vecchio* (old cloister) and near the church. Dating to the early seventeenth century and known through a late eighteenth-century copy attributed to Paolo Gozzi, this plan (fig. 23) is extremely useful, although potentially misleading with regard to the fifteenth-century convent setting. Visual information from Gozzi's plan when integrated with documentation suggests that in the mid-Quattrocento the convent's core block consisted only of structures on the southeastern side facing the old cloister. Key spaces such as the nuns' church and the chapter house formed a court zone at the eastern end. In general, chapter houses were connected with the church, sacristy, and the treasury on one side, and other rooms, including the parlor, on the other. Chapter houses are known to have generally been richly decorated spaces where the community gathered to pray, discuss, make decisions, admit failures, and receive punishments. Occasionally they also functioned as classrooms for instruction in grammar and basic theology.[29]

Serving as the parish church of the San Paolo neighborhood, the convent church certainly comprised a section reserved for the religious women (the nuns' choir; fig. 24) and separated from the space intended for the laity (the outer church).[30] Maria Benedetti, elected as abbess in 1460, is known to have rebuilt the monastic church "with solid and costly architecture," probably in the 1470s.[31] As discussed in Chapter Three, her successors Cecilia Bergonzi and Giovanna Piacenza refurbished and embellished the nuns' church, commissioning frescoes and wood intarsia stalls. Architecture and frescoes were lost when Marie-Louise of Austria remodeled the church in 1817, transforming half of the nuns' choir into the altar zone, shifting the façade to the east end (fig. 25), and placing an imposing funerary monument for her husband, the Count of Neipperg, in the chapel bordering the old monastic chapter house.[32] As a result, the nuns' choir and the outer church of San Paolo were dramatically and permanently altered.

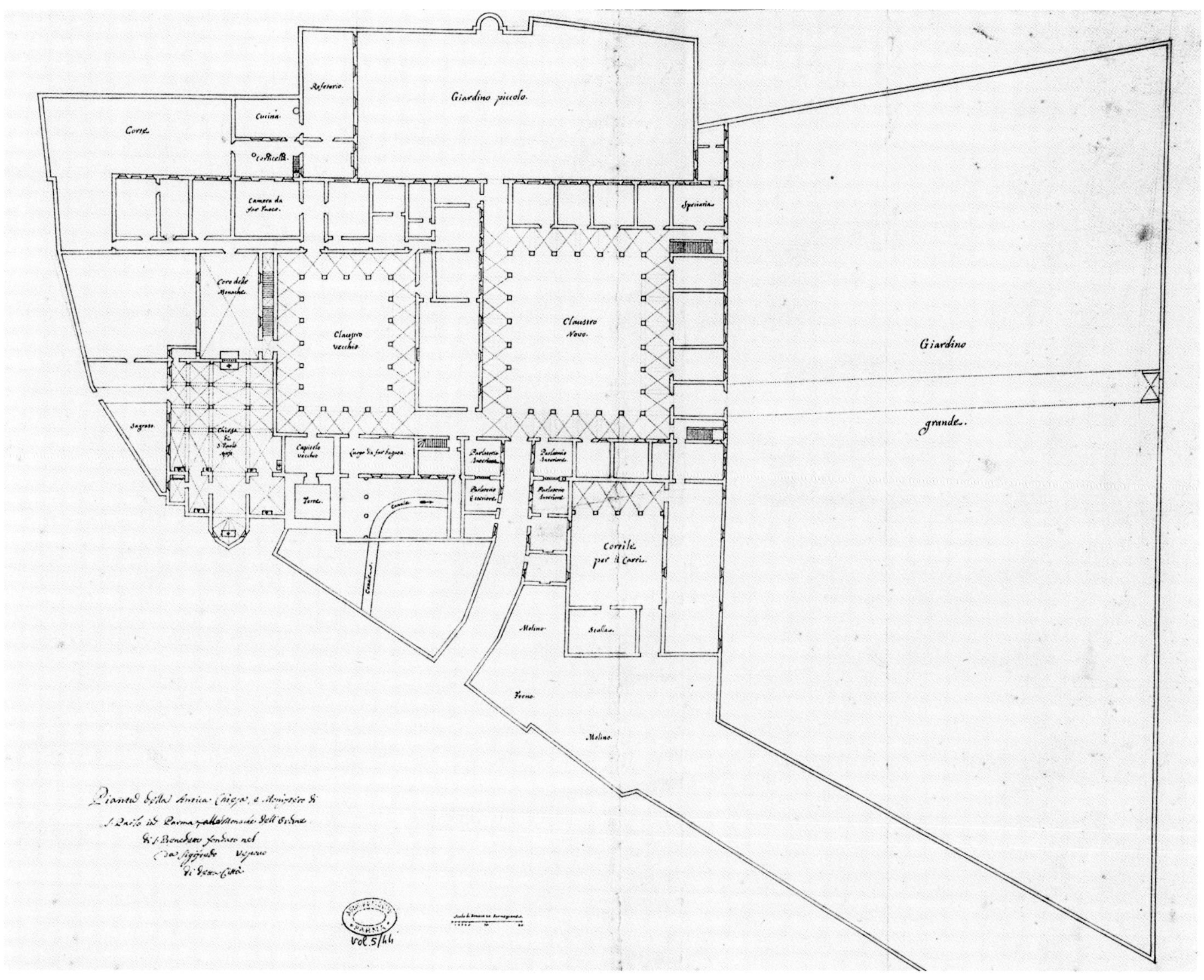

23　Paolo Gozzi, late eighteenth-century copy of a seventeenth-century plan of the convent of San Paolo, Parma, Archivio di Stato

Looking back at Loschi's murals with this understanding of the convent buildings, it should be remembered that Ghidiglia Quintavalle reported that they were found in the church of San Paolo. However, the frescoes are not mentioned in the report compiled by the Apostolic Visitor, Monsignor Giovanni Battista Castelli, in December 1578.[33] If Loschi's frescoes had been on the walls of the outer church, they would likely have been noticed. Clues as to their original location come from previously unconsidered pictorial fragments found on a wall that pertained to the old chapter house. Painted in a style similar to Loschi's murals, these fragments are in an area close to a *sacellum*, a brick-walled quadrangular site constructed in the seventh century and later transformed into a bell tower.[34] In short, visual and textual evidence suggests that Loschi's frescoes were probably originally in the chapter house (see fig. 24). An early nineteenth-century document describes it as a chapel dedicated to the Virgin.[35] The 1851 *Pianta icnografica* (sic) of San Paolo (fig. 25) refers to this space, numbered 17, as a "small oratory" with an altar.[36] It is likely that before Maria Benedetti's renovation of the nuns' choir in the 1470s, the chapter house served as a chapel, a multifunctional overlap that was not unusual in small communities. More importantly, the chapter house lay between the outer church and Torelli's *domus* on the east end, both facing onto the old cloister and constituting the core of the convent's litur-

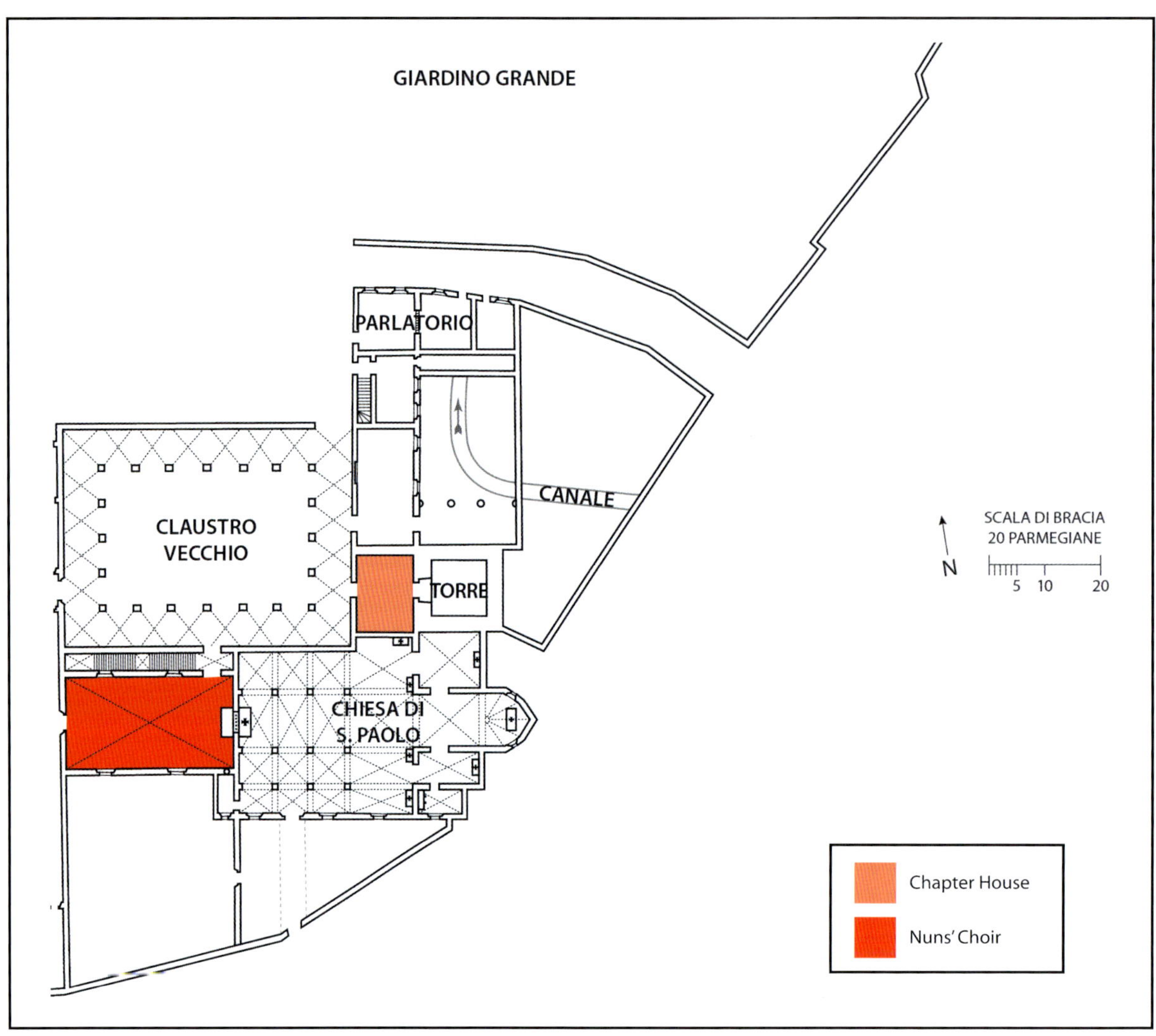

24   Convent of San Paolo, Parma, redrawn from Paolo Gozzi's late eighteenth-century plan

gical and administrative activities in the fifteenth century. Today, little survives of these buildings because of extensive alterations made over the centuries, particularly after the nineteenth-century dissolution of religious orders and the purchase of the San Paolo complex by the municipality of Parma in 1878.[37]

What, then, has survived? In terms of textual evidence, there is the contract between the nuns and Torelli. Among visual material, I would posit that Loschi's frescoes, which, as noted, probably ornamented the chapter house, are evidence of this lay noblewoman's residence in the convent, and also testify to what this meant to her and to the community at large. Loschi's stiff, frontal Virgin in the *Madonna of Mercy* (see fig. 20) shelters the San Paolo community under the right wing of her mantle. The contrast between the monumental, iconic Madonna and the tiny, profiled figures of the women portrayed could not be greater. Yet even in this latter group, a hierarchy has been observed. In the first rank, as remarked earlier, a young girl and an older woman in brightly colored, secular dress flank the abbess, whose right hand held forward in prayer touches the gown of the Virgin. In the Quattrocento, portraits of living individuals were introduced in religious scenes to give effective immediacy to the images, inscribing the timeless experience of the sacred into the historic present. In the *Madonna of Mercy* the foremost nuns under the crosier must be Abbess Maria Benedetti and the noblewoman behind her right, Antonia Torelli. The young, unveiled girl on Benedetti's left could be Maria's sister, Simona, who seems to have entered the convent temporarily (probably *in serbanza*)

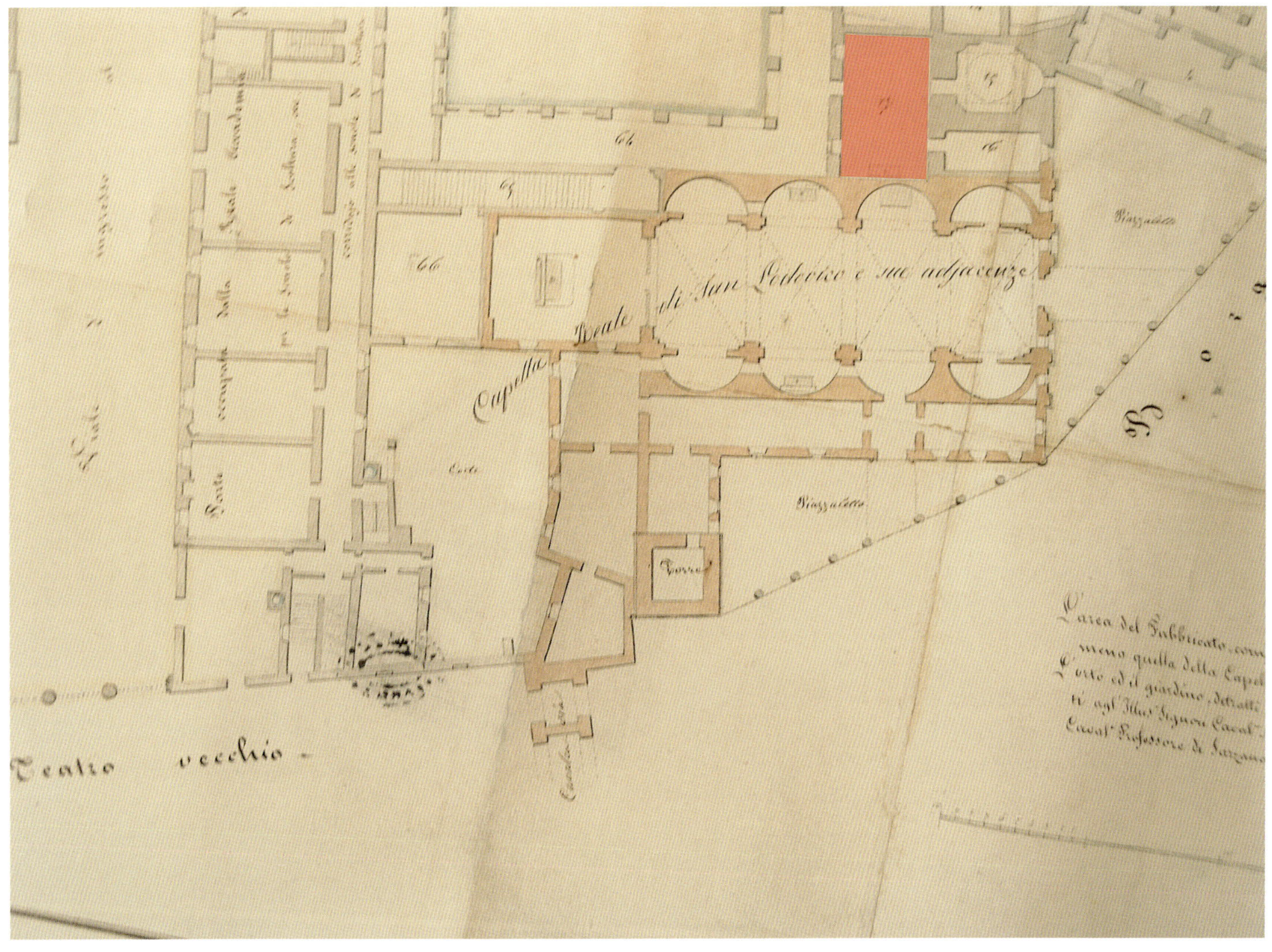

25 The church of San Ludovico and the oratory, from *Pianta icnografica* [sic] *dell'edificio di San Paolo*, detail, June 4, 1851, Parma, Archivio di Stato: room n. 17 highlighted

without taking vows.[38] If not Simona, Loschi's figure should be another member of the Benedetti family. Besides recording in a religious scene these historical individuals then present in the convent, what additional messages did Loschi's fresco suggest to the community of living women standing before it?

Abbess Maria Benedetti would have perceived Loschi's representation of herself at the helm of a united community protected by the Virgin Mary as a highly significant image made at a key juncture in the confrontation with Bishop della Pergola, when a corporate show of strength and resolve had become pressing and urgent. Born into a patrician family whose members had long held governmental and ecclesiastical offices in Parma, Maria Benedetti entered San Paolo as a young girl. Maria professed her vows in 1446,

when her aunt, Agnese Benedetti (in office 1433–54), was the abbess.[39] According to the regulations, nuns were eligible for abbatial office at the age of 30. In addition to the age bar, other requirements were birth from a legitimate marriage, no previous marital engagements, no mental illness, four years of monastic profession, and no professed sisters in the convent.[40] Possibly fulfilling this list of requirements, Maria was nominated as abbess of San Paolo in 1460 and not, as has been indicated in the past, in 1471.[41] Her office, which lasted probably until 1484, carried an annual income of 600 gold florins. Abbesses were expected to have a sufficient level of learning (*literatura*) for the office. The local chronicler Angelo Mario Edoari da Erba (ca. 1520–post 1590) recognizes Maria as one of Parma's most illustrious women.[42] Maria Benedetti's election was not an authentic expression of the nuns' will, however. The majority of them had voted for another nun, Caterina Bravi, but the Sforzas exerted pressure in Maria's favor. Their maneuvers were part of a strategy to gain the support and loyalty of urban patrician families like the Benedetti. During Maria's tenure, the Sforzas granted San Paolo privileges, tax exemptions, and benefits.[43]

The abbatial position was the highest office in a convent, and its achievement was the defining moment of a nun's career. Male members of abbesses' families assisted their relatives, serving the institution as procurators and representatives. Ludovico Benedetti had assisted his sister Agnese in this capacity. Likewise, his son Leonardo took charge of safeguarding his own sisters' interests.[44] On October 19, 1454, Leonardo denounced the theft of precious objects and fine clothing belonging to his sister Simona that were kept in the *domus* of Simona's sister, the nun Maria Benedetti.[45] Although the record fails to specify the stolen goods or other details of the theft, it nevertheless speaks to us today of a young girl living with her sister in a monastic *domus*, that is, an apartment, and of her (their) private possessions preserved there, as well as the vulnerability of a supposedly secured site and the eagerness of the convent's inhabitants to have goods at any cost (even that of breaking a commandment). Another unpublished document, drawn up on December 7, 1506, records the then widow Simona Benedetti living in the convent once again, along with her daughter, Palma Bajardi. Simona never took religious vows but married a goldsmith, Giberto Bajardi, by 1460.[46] Once widowed, she must have made some financial arrangements to return to San Paolo. The institution evidently offered an attractive alternative to the customarily solitary life of a widow. Simona probably managed to retire to rooms furnished with every comfort, in which she would have had contact with relatives and lived out her days in the convent where it is likely that she had been educated fifty years before.

This detailed account of personal and familial strategies, and social and political dynamics, in relation to the San Paolo's inhabitants supports an identification of the three women portrayed in the foreground of Loschi's *Madonna of Mercy* as Antonia Torelli, Abbess Maria Benedetti, and either her sister Simona or another member of her family. Assuming this is the case, then, their presence in the painting reflects their status, projecting to the contemporary and to later generations of nuns gazing at Loschi's image the sense of their community's corporate identity and agency. Along with Antonia and the young woman, the abbess is shown with eighteen of her nuns and two novices. On the right side of the Virgin, the community prays for its own wellbeing and, as was customary, for that of its fellow citizens, who may well have been represented by Loschi on the missing side of the work. The girl flanking the abbess holds the crosier, however, as if the abbatial title were a family business, passed from one generation to the next – as just noted, Maria was herself the "heir" of Abbess Agnese Benedetti. A sign of the abbess's power, the crosier signaled the equal authority of abbesses and bishops in their respective spheres. The fact that it is literally held by a relative had symbolic implications, ultimately revealing the intricate bonds between the power of Maria's office and that of her family in administering the convent's wealth.

The presence of Saints Cosmas and Damian raising the Virgin's mantle is another element in Loschi's image that must not have escaped notice. While they are unusual in representations of the *Madonna of Mercy*, the twin brothers and physician-saints are typical of painted cycles in infirmaries and hospitals. Loschi's images thus must be linked to Antonia Torelli's residence in the former infirmary of the convent, which had been remodeled as her apartment, and the commemoration of her persona. She is depicted wearing a red mantle, the same color as the curtain held up by angels behind the whole group. Red was the field color of the Torelli coat of arms, against which is emblazoned a bull (*toro*) alluding to the family name. The images of Cosmas and Damian and Torelli's portrait thus reinforce one another, pointing to Torelli's role within the monastic community during the San Paolo–della Pergola litigation, and suggesting that the Torelli and Benedetti women joined forces in defense of the institution's independence. Looking across the wall at Loschi's *Madonna of Mercy*, nuns would have found reassurance regarding the convent's corporate identity and divine protection, while also recognizing its message that the life of prayer was the keystone of its present and future members. Ranked by status, the convent's inhabitants, religious and lay alike, are portrayed in the fresco as an assembly that gained its strength through its unity.

Recounted in Chapter 36 of St. Gregory's *Dialogues* (593–4 CE), the last meeting of St. Benedict and his sister Scholastica was a popular subject for pictorial cycles in Benedictine complexes (see fig. 22).[47] Latin and vernacular editions of the *Dialogues* printed in the 1470s and 80s are not illustrated, but iconographic information must have circulated among Benedictine institutions.[48] Loschi's composition bears a close resemblance to a scene of the same subject in the right-hand transept wall of the Sacro Speco in Subiaco

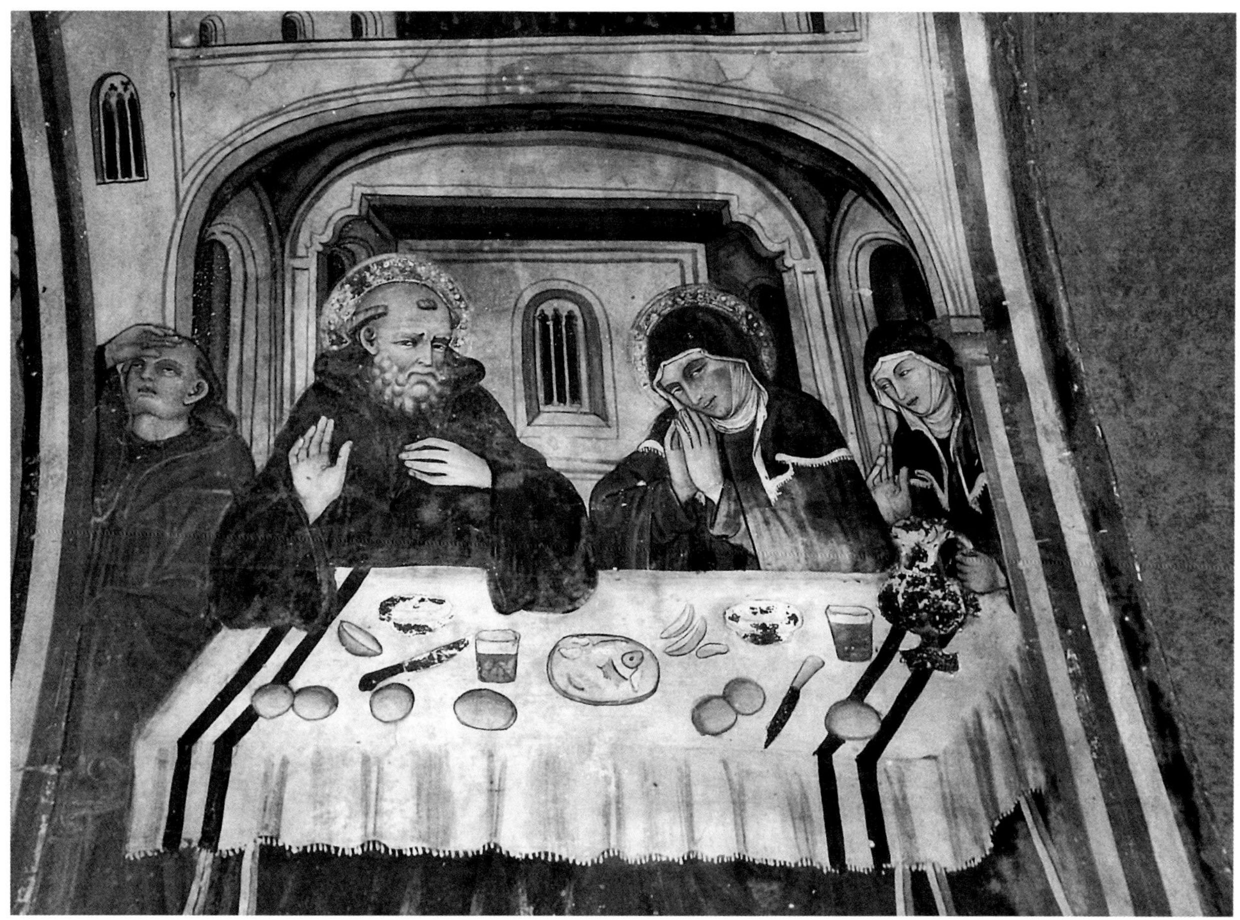

26 Anonymous early Quattrocento artist, *The Last Meeting between St. Benedict and St. Scholastica*, fresco, Subiaco, Sacro Speco, Superior Church

(fig. 26), a major center of Benedictine culture and spirituality in Western Europe.[49] This early fifteenth-century fresco shows the saints seated at the table, flanked by two companions. If Loschi had a record of this depiction at hand – perhaps a drawing, an illustrated manuscript, or a print – it was probably supplied to him by the abbess. Loschi eliminated secondary figures and inserted the Benedettis kneeling in the foreground. In Loschi's *Last Meeting*, St. Benedict is engaged in a food ritual while St. Scholastica joins her palms in prayer, their gestures emphasizing the dichotomy between the static, frontally painted saints and the living women kneeling and in profile. Appearing on the side of the table reserved for devotees, the Benedettis act as participants in the saints' ritual. They offer food and share with the Benedictine order's founding saints the spiritual fruits of the latters' final encounter. The abbess leads, folding her hands in prayer, preceded by the young woman who presents a basket of what appears to be bread or fruit. Their activities

and participation in the food ritual are also modes of replicating the message and generosity of Christ himself. As noticed by Caroline Walker Bynum, food preparation and distribution (but not eating) were considered the forms of asceticism appropriate to women. The control of food and its allocation were charitable and self-denying acts, expressions of the good works that the Benedettis were meant to carry out.[50] Like the *Madonna of Mercy*, Loschi's *Last Meeting* must have had a special significance for its female religious beholders. The Benedettis simultaneously assisted and participated in an episode centered on St. Scholastica, the founder of the lineage of all Benedictine nuns.[51] St. Gregory reports that St. Scholastica prayed fervently to God for the meeting between herself and Benedict. Her exemplum of devotion and perseverance long constituted a model for nuns. The Benedettis' identity as both the real and painted spectators produced and articulated their self-projection and self-reflectivity with the female Benedictine saint.

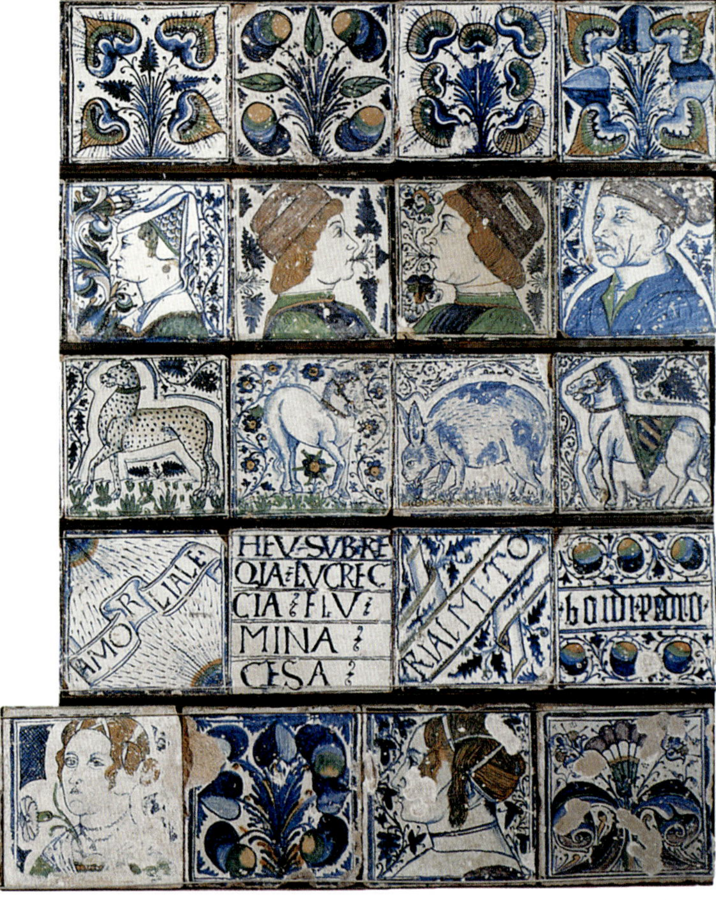

Above and facing page 27a, 27b and 27c Maiolica floor tiles, 1470s–after 1507, Parma, Galleria Nazionale

Over the cycle as a whole, Loschi's paintings celebrated Abbess Benedetti, her female genealogy, and her community, embodying the women's spirituality. The frescoes were well suited to a place like the chapter house, in which the entire community assembled to pray and make decisions. They would have been admired by the nuns and those outsiders (relatives, sponsors, and notaries) who were admitted to the room, but they must also have been visible, either through a grated window or screen, to the lay audience seated in the adjacent outer church, provided that the chapter house functioned as the nuns' choir in the 1460s. With their gendered model of devotion exemplified by St. Scholastica, Loschi's murals might have been a joint Benedetti-Torelli commission undertaken at the beginning of Maria Benedetti's abbatial office to declare the community's independence, corporate strength, and spirituality.[52] Gathered in the chapter house, the community that gazed across the wall at Loschi's frescoes recognized and honored the

Benedetti and Torelli women, whose resistance had kept San Paolo free from local ecclesiastical control. The frescoes can be dated to between 1463 and 1469, when Maria Benedetti's election was secured, Antonia Torelli was still alive, and the litigation with della Pergola had just been concluded. Loschi depicted conventional religious narratives in which historical particulars, temporal elements, and living individuals are interwoven. He simultaneously stressed the choral dimension of the female community and its leadership at a crucial historical moment in which it needed to be monumentalized and commemorated. By inscribing the Benedetti and Torelli personae within the sacred scenes, Loschi's otherwise canonical iconographies proclaim a defiant message to those aware of the convent–bishop litigation, thus shifting the emphasis of the communication toward the celebration of the female religious self rather than its devotions per se. It is only the identification of those depicted in Loschi's frescoes, and of what their presence meant, that suggests these unanticipated readings, as well as enabling viewers now to recognize the way the community presented and reimagined itself in the late Quattrocento. Loschi's murals magnify the community of San Paolo, stating that its female leadership had the authority and ability to run the convent independently of male ecclesiastical supervision, making a challenging claim of independence that parallels the nuns' assertions of their "rights" to conduct a noble way of living.

Building on this episode of self-affirmation in the medium of fresco, I now turn to the corpus of maiolica tiles formerly used to pave one or more floors in the convent, which with their ornate and figural motifs created intimate environments more typical of secular than of religious settings. As will be seen, the very horizontality of the floor decorations and the kinaesthetic relationships that spectators with lowered eyes established with the colorful scenes underfoot suggest discourses of pleasure, imagination, ethics, and the defiance of monastic strictures. But, before assessing the phenomenology of gaze and touch proposed by the tiles, it is necessary to confront fundamental questions concerning the genesis of the maiolica pavement (figs. 27a, 27b and 27c), its function, and the spaces that it recreated. I shall argue that what is now known as the San Paolo corpus is possibly the result of a dual campaign. First, in the late 1470s, Abbess Benedetti commissioned a set of tin-glazed tiles from Pesarese potters; then, after her election in 1507, Abbess Giovanna Piacenza may have ordered additional floor tiles. As architectural elements, floors were principally designated to perform struc-

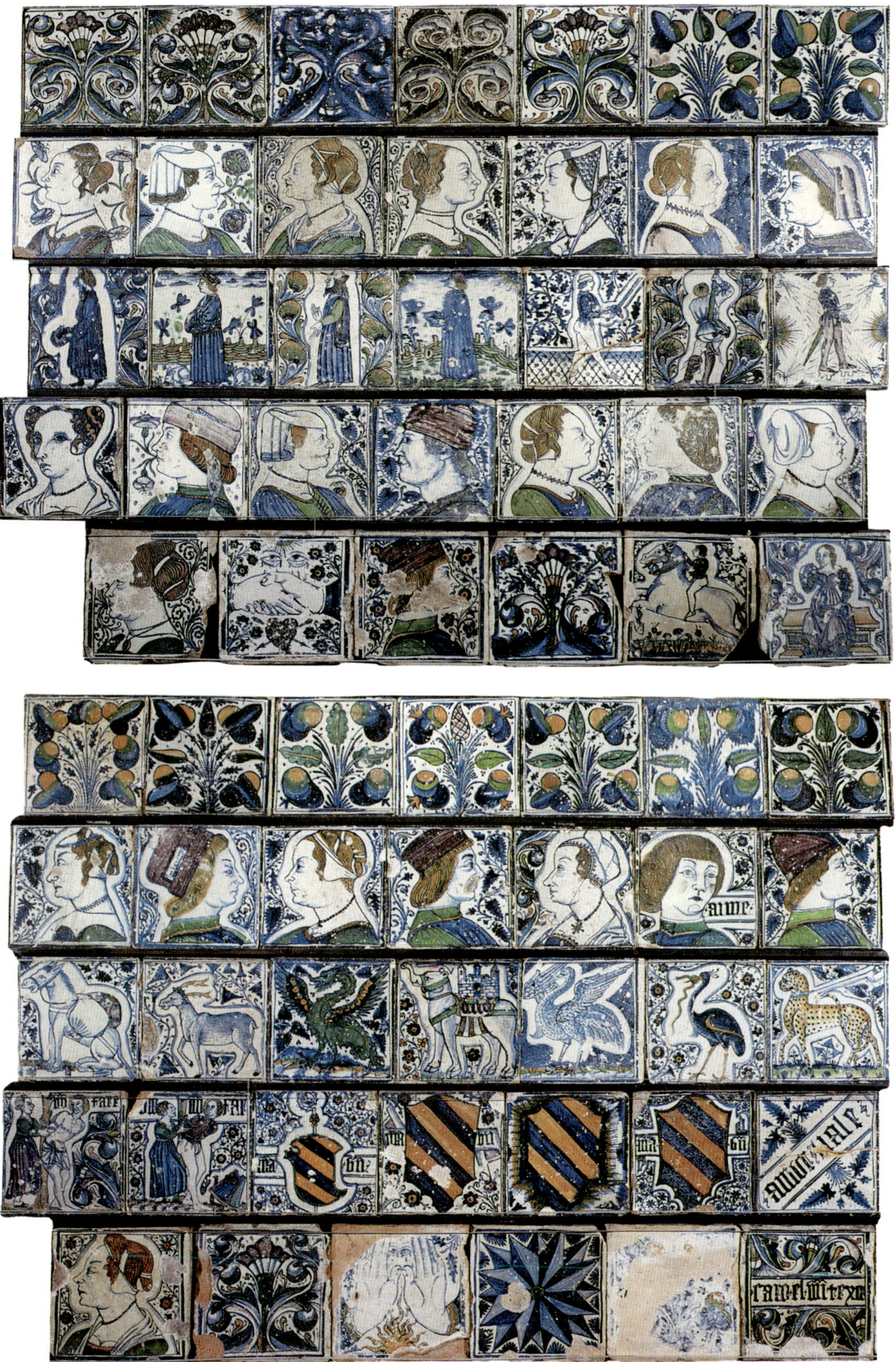

tural and hygienic functions, but in the sophisticated enclave of San Paolo they also became stages for the display of impressive artworks. As semiotically loaded items, the decorated tiles were designed to stimulate reflections, to shape behavioral customs, and to index potentially transgressive memories that could become a rallying point for upper-class nuns determined to maintain both their independence and a lifestyle they regarded as their birthright.

TIN-GLAZED PAVEMENTS IN CONVENTUAL SPACES

Tin-glazed wares were a relatively new commodity in fifteenth-century Italy, which registered a crucial technical evolution. On the basis of techniques that had evolved in Hispano-Moresque pottery, Italian ceramists developed and perfected tin-glazed pottery or maiolica, as it came to be called, a type of ceramic that astonished contemporaries for its clean white surface, lightness, and finesse. Richard Goldthwaite has connected the quantitative and qualitative rise of maiolica objects in the Renaissance to new patterns of consumer behaviors, indicating the diversification of the production, and its relatively economical costs to the buyer as factors in maiolica's success. Dora Thornton, Luke Syson, and Marta Ajmar have further suggested that the potters' ability to simulate other media (metalwork and paintings included) and to generate originality and freshness in their artifacts accounted for the rapid increase and development of the medium itself.[53] Counterbalancing a long historiographical tradition centered on a limited number of pottery centers, Timothy Wilson, John Mallet, and Carmen Ravanelli Guidotti, among others, have more recently shown that maiolica was widely manufactured in centers throughout the peninsula and especially in north-central Italy by the second half of the fifteenth century.[54] In particular, fine tin-glazed pottery made in the northeastern centers of the maiolica industry – chiefly Faenza, Urbino, and Pesaro – featuring a decorative repertoire of *all'antica* motifs, was considered an innovative and desirable addition to the credenze and household furnishings of sophisticated patrons and collectors like the Florentine Lorenzo de' Medici, the Marchioness Isabella d'Este, and many others in Italy and abroad.[55]

The aesthetic sensitivity that Abbesses Maria Benedetti and Giovanna Piacenza manifested for the maiolica medium was thus in perfect accord with the widespread appreciation of tin-glazed objects in the Renaissance.[56] Their decision to commission inventive tiled floors to walk on and to enjoy aligned them with other contemporary rulers who paved their *camere* and *camerini* with tin-glazed tiles. Documents show that the Marquis of Ferrara, Ercole d'Este, ordered maiolica floor tiles for two rooms in Villa Schifanoia in 1470–71, while in 1493–4 his daughter Isabella paved her own studiolo in Mantua's Gonzaga palace with tin-glazed tiles, and then commissioned a second set with her arms and *imprese*, carried out around 1510–25. In 1509 the ruler of Siena, Pandolfo Petrucci, had fine tin-glazed tiles decorated with grotesque motifs and other ornaments to pave a chamber of his palace.[57]

In practical terms, tiles were recommended as a clean, reflective, and impenetrable surface, but contemporary treatises also insist on the cultural values of polychrome floor revetments. Leon Battista Alberti's *De Re Aedificatoria* (published in 1485) states that figurative tiled floors promoted the cultivation of viewers' minds, while in his *Trattato di Architettura* (ca. 1460–64), Filarete (Antonio Averlino) advises the Milanese ruler Francesco Sforza to pave chambers with glass tesserae ornamented with inventive motifs.[58] Pioneers of the early Renaissance revival of antiquity, Alberti and Filarete had in mind Roman floor mosaics composed of thousands of small tesserae in marble and stone that display an infinite variety of subjects drawn from mythology and the natural world.[59]

Well before Giorgio Vasari's praise of colorful maiolica tiled floors in his *Vite* (1568), the new possibilities of this art form and its aesthetic values were registered in another significant text for the history of Renaissance art, Cristoforo Landino's vernacular translation (1476) of Pliny the Elder's *Natural History*. Describing the different types of Roman floor revetments, Pliny speaks of the small, colored tesserae that made up the pavement of the baths of Marcus Agrippa (63–12 BCE), tesserae which Landino translated as "le cose di terra dipinse a fuocho" (painted and fired clay things).[60] Niccolò Perotti reworked this passage in his *Cornucopiae* (1489 and 1513), asserting that the pavement of Agrippa's baths was made of earthenware tiles, heightened with colors and given a transparent glaze. In other words, he envisioned the ancient Roman mosaic floor of Agrippa's baths as a Renaissance maiolica pavement. With typical humanistic (mis)interpretation, anachronistic as it might be, Perotti blurred the distance between antique stone tessellated pavements and modern tin-glazed floor revetments, providing a classical pedigree for the contemporary trend of maiolica tiled floors, and an aura of art for splendid modern floorings that simulate paintings in their colors and figurative forms.

As Marco Collareta observed of Perotti, by ennobling the manufacture of maiolica floor tiles through his Latinized prose and by anchoring the Renaissance art form to an accredited ancient prototype, Perotti's reference to figurative tin-glazed tiled floors as a kind of brilliant, colored painting (*genus picturae encausticae*) historicized a new artistic medium, which fascinated viewers with its jewel-like surface and illusion of a shiny painting underfoot.[61]

In his *De Partibus Aedium*, Grapaldo borrowed Perotti's lines, speaking of maiolica floor tiles as glowing *picturae* that inexpensively replicated the beauty of ancient floorings, inflecting the horizontal spatial reality of a room with layers of signification for viewers' delectation.[62] The assertion by Perotti and Grapaldo that figurative tin-glazed pavements were species of paintings, thus likening maiolica to painting, considered the prime art in the Renaissance, was not a merely erudite philological claim, however. To confer a nobler status on maiolica works supported by horizontal floors and not displayed on vertical walls as frescoes and canvases could also be seen to signal an awareness of the specific condition of viewing this art form. Alberti's definition of painting (1436) as the representation of things seen as if through an open window according to a one-point perspective system resulted in images that presuppose a centrally placed viewer standing before them. A fixed onlooker activated images hung on vertical walls, and rendered as mimetically natural as possible, whose subjects are shaped according to principles of mimesis, decorum, and plausibility.[63] Leonardo da Vinci (1452–1519) enhanced the role of painting, theorizing its power and effects over the beholder, yet maintaining the vertical orientation as its primary condition, a privileged axis that, it has been argued, was only undermined in twentieth-century experimentations that subverted the image from its vertical axis.[64]

Renaissance ornamented maiolica floor tiles cannot quite be described as modern artistic experimentations comparable to what was being introduced in two-dimensional images on walls and ceilings, but with their dynamic and colorful imagery underfoot they shared in the creation of a relationship with the observers' perceptions. Floors were the support of maiolica figurative ensembles that Perotti and Grapaldo describe as simulating paintings, but it is only through the act of moving across pavements and simultaneously looking down that spectators acknowledge the dialectics of reality and ideality, and the empirical and transcendental values of this art form. In other words, maiolica pavements are embellished surfaces across which spectators walked, activating the painted stories and possibly becoming aware that the tiles' narratives would not unfold in the same way, and with the same emotional engagement of the senses, if they were seen on vertical walls. The act of moving and looking down projected observers onto the imaginative world displayed on the floor surface both literally and with renewed mental force, creating an environment that is discovered step by step in walking on it, at the same time connecting the feet to its horizontal, resplendent material reality. A passerby's feet remained in constant touch with the floor, while its colorful representations had the power to guide, suspend, or redirect bodily movements and also imaginatively and concretely to engage the eyes. The tiles are the individual elements of the pavements that act as tangible support for peripatetic viewers, and collectively form the stage of a painted illusion that propelled mental journeys. Perotti and Grapaldo's understanding of figurative tin-glazed tiles as glowing *picturae* signal their recognition of the maiolica medium as an art form that simulated painting in a less expensive medium. Its horizontal flatness afforded interactions and the transmission of meanings through viewers' movement across the decorated surface with their eyes lowered toward the ground. The act of crossing such floors ultimately produced sensorial experiences of a totally different order from those generated by gazing from a fixed point at paintings hanging on vertical walls.[65]

That said, it is impossible to ascertain the specific reaction of the abbesses Benedetti and Piacenza to Grapaldo's comment on tiled floors in his text, which must have circulated in Parma's elite circles even before its publication in 1494. But their acknowledgment of the links between the horizontality of the tiled floors and the monastic prescription regarding downcast eyes, on which more later, is unquestionable. Before conceptualizing this perceptual context and its multiple implications, it is necessary to address the genesis and the original location of the tiles, without which any theorization risks remaining vague.[66] Moreover, this corpus also requires better qualification in terms of its morphological features (dimensions and subjects included) and chronology, topics that will be treated in what follows.

MAKING MAIOLICA TILED FLOORS

Abbess Maria Benedetti's coat of arms and initials inscribed on several tiles (fig. 28) have been recognized as proofs of her patronage of the maiolica tiled corpus, but, while certainly important, do not resolve persistent uncertainties

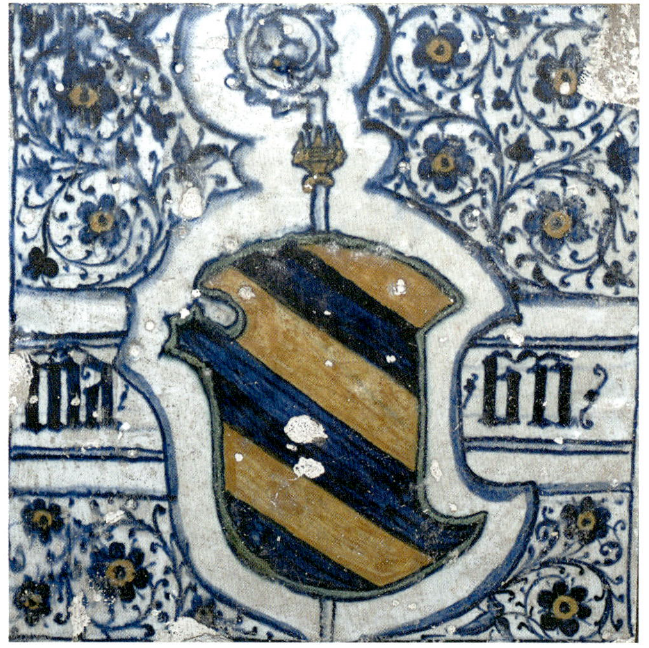

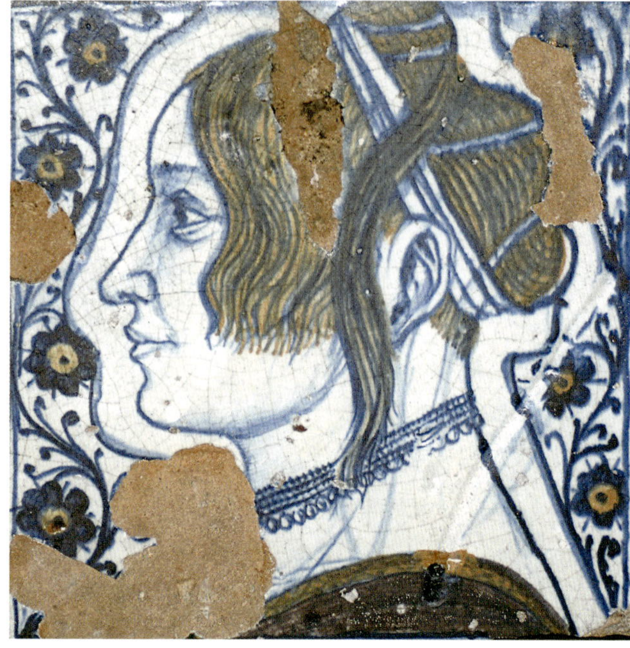

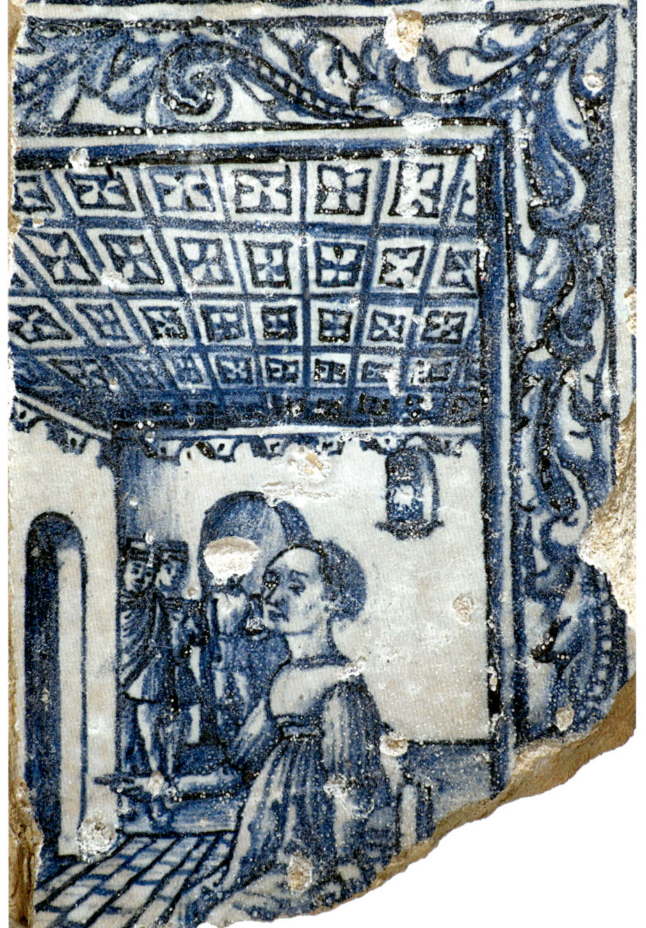

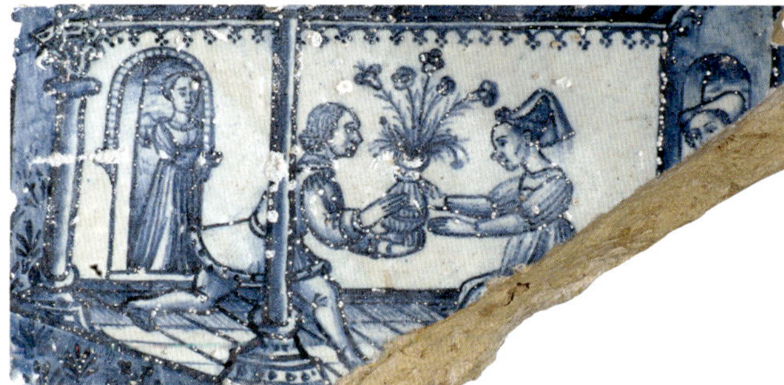

Top, left 28   Maria Benedetti's coat of arms, 1470s, maiolica floor tile, 19 × 19.2 cm (7¾ × 7⅝ in), Parma, Galleria Nazionale

Top, right 29   Female head, after 1507, maiolica floor tile, 20.5 × 20.5 cm ($8^5/_{64}$ × $8^5/_{64}$ in), Parma, Galleria Nazionale

Left and above 30   Fragments of a ceramic frieze, after 1507, 12.5 × 23.3 cm ($4^{59}/_{64}$ × $9^9/_{64}$ in), 19 × 13.2 cm ($7^{31}/_{64}$ × $5^{13}/_{64}$ in), Parma, Soprintendenza Belle Arti e Paesaggio per le Province di Parma e Piacenza

regarding its making and history. Transferred to the local Accademia in 1834 and from there to the Galleria Nazionale di Parma, the tiles have since been partially displayed in a vertical installation in a separate corridor of one of the museum galleries, a display that negates their original placement on a floor. Lucia Fornari Schianchi's illustrated catalogue (1988) documents an ensemble of 262 quadrangular tiles, which was augmented in 1997 by the discovery of 81 tiles painted with male and female heads (fig. 29), mytho-

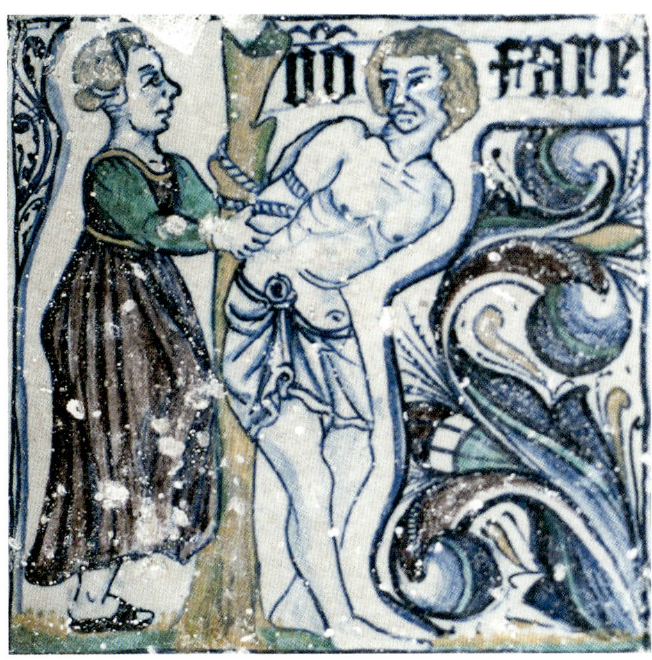

31   Cruelty of Love, 1470s, maiolica floor tile, 19 × 19.2 cm (7^{31}/$_{64}$ × 7^{5}/$_{8}$ in), Parma, Galleria Nazionale

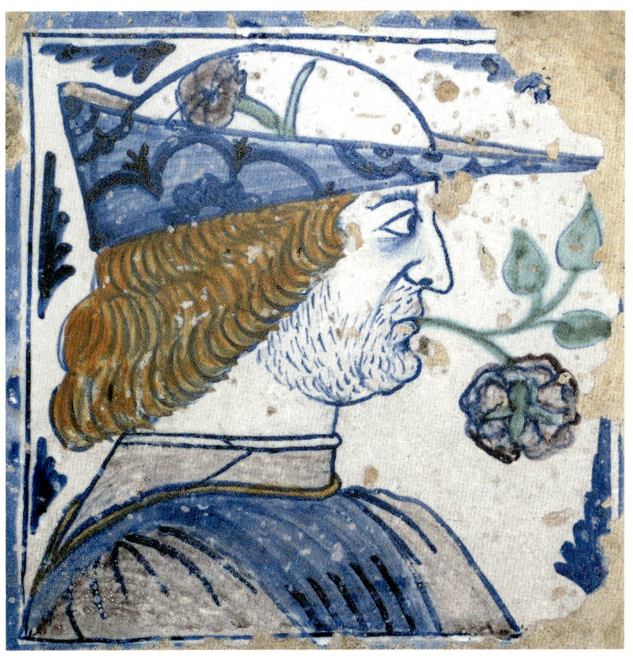

32   Male head, after 1507, maiolica floor tile, 21 × 21 cm (8¼ × 8¼ in), Parma, Galleria Nazionale

logical episodes, and fantastic animals.[67] Although the motifs on the newly found tiles are similar to those appearing on the previously known corpus, several of the rediscovered tiles show a compositional and formal refinement that is lacking in the others. In addition, three rectangular white and blue tin-glazed tiles featuring Petrarchan scenes of courtly love have been recovered (fig. 30). Despite the fragmentary condition of these latter tiles, the rendering of figures within three-dimensional domestic settings exchanging gifts and courtesies of love attests to an understanding of the surface field that cannot but date to the early sixteenth century. In short, there is now a body of 343 ornamented maiolica tiles, which feature a vast array of amatory scenes, allegorical and chivalric subjects, female and male figures, poetic motifs, animals (real and fantastic), inscriptions with mottoes, still-life objects, and geometrical, foliate, and heradic signs.[68]

One of the perhaps most puzzling aspects of this corpus is their variety of size: a large number of them measure around 19 × 19 centimeters (7½ × 7½ inches) and 4–5.5 centimeters in thickness (1⅝–2¼ inches), while a smaller group oscillates around 21 × 21 centimeters (8¼ × 8¼ inches), a clue that could signal that the tiles originally paved distinct sites.[69] Indeed, larger tiles were used in the borders of pavements.[70] But, if one compares an allegory of

the cruelty of love with its Gothic inscription (fig. 31) to a male sitter with a pointed hat with a flower tucked into the brim and holding the stem of a rose between his lips (fig. 32), notable differences are evident not only in scale but also in style and formal features. The episode of cruel love on the smaller tile surface, which represents only one of the lady's feet, is surrounded by arabesque filler motifs that accord with a date of the late 1470s. This chronology seems less applicable to the male sitter seen in profile with neatly trimmed, coiffed hair and stubbly beard, whose sculptural half-length bust is well adapted to the larger tile field, all of which suggests a command of the medium that is probably indicative of a later date rather than of particular artistic skills. Likewise, Gothic inscriptions (fig. 33) on the smaller tiles look quite rough and primitive in comparison to the elegant italics and the serpentine scroll shown on a wider tile surface (fig. 34). Many such examples could be cited, but the questions remain the same: what does this contrasting stylistic and dimensional evidence tell us? And what additional information is provided by the early sixteenth-century rectangular tiles?

Much of the scholarship on the tiles has focused on questions of attribution and patronage, foreclosing other lines of inquiry concerning their varied dimensions, potentially disjunctive chronology, and original location, none

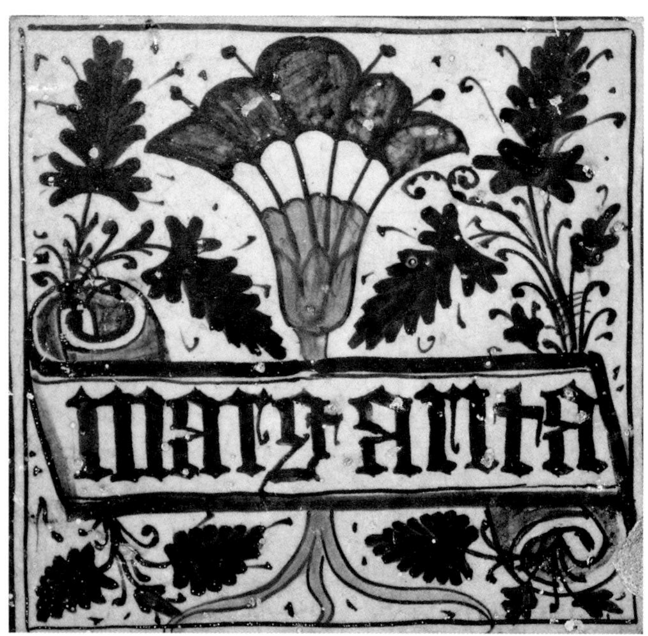

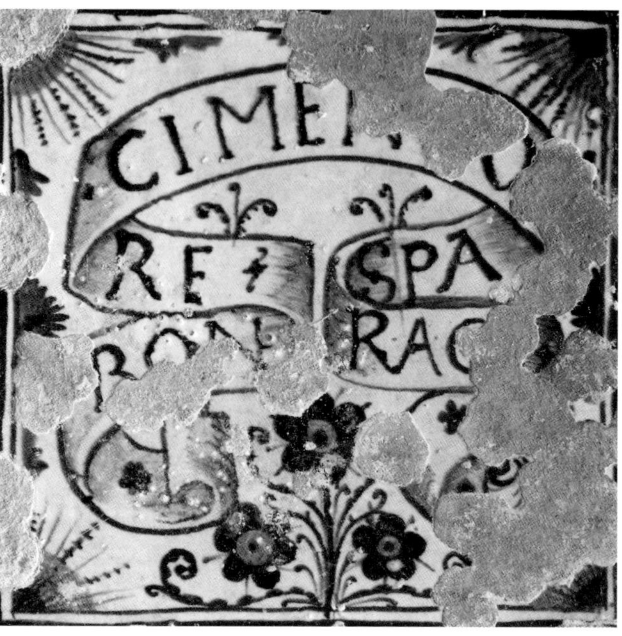

33 Gothic inscription "Margarita," 1470s, 19.1 × 19.3 cm (7⅓ × 7⅝ in), maiolica floor tile, Parma, Galleria Nazionale

34 Italics and serpentine scroll, after 1507, maiolica floor tile, 21 × 21 cm (8¼ × 8¼ in), Parma, Soprintendenza Belle Arti e Paesaggio per le Province di Parma e Piacenza

of which has been thoroughly investigated. On stylistic grounds, Fornari Schianchi argued for a Faentine origin for the tiles. Instead, citing analogies with Parma's clay pottery (*biscotto*), the colors and the ornamental repertoire of potters from Pesaro, Giuliana Gardelli has suggested that the tiles were manufactured in Parma but painted by itinerant Pesarese potters, an attribution with which Timothy Wilson has recently concurred.[71] A good way to substantiate this hypothesis (the tiles being made either in Pesaro or in Parma by Pesarese potters) is to assess the political and cultural implications of Maria Benedetti's choice of maiolica as the medium for the pavement of her floor. This discussion will address a peculiar subject displayed on one of the tiles, namely, the elephant bearing a castle on its back (see fig. 35), in order to set a chronological benchmark for the commission.

In 1445 Alessandro Sforza, a relative of the Milanese Duke Francesco, became the *de facto* ruler of Pesaro, bringing into the Sforza domain the cities of Milan and Pesaro. Alessandro and his son Costanzo, who succeeded his father in 1473, fostered antiquarianism at the court, which culminated in the production of a copy of Giovanni Marcanova's epigraphic sylloge.[72] In addition, the Sforzas were instrumental in the development of the local maiolica industry, promoting the dissemination and mobility of potters and pottery in the

other cities of the Sforza duchy, Parma included.[73] Maria Benedetti's appreciation of Pesarese maiolica undoubtedly aligned her to a widening group of discerning patrons, including rulers and nobility. Neutral as it might appear at first glance, her choice of manufactory did not stem from an aesthetically pure and disinterested enthusiasm, but was caught up in broad networks of political relations and alliances. As mentioned earlier, the San Paolo convent had long been a Rossi enclave and as such had suffered enormously after Pier Maria Rossi's military defeat in 1477, which brought in its wake political instability, violence, and several episodes of vendetta in Parma. The sacred precincts of the nunnery were even violated by armed troops in 1477. Despite warnings, Abbess Benedetti and her nuns did not leave the institution, and seem to have saved it from arson by handing over to the invaders the gold treasure that Pier Maria Rossi had stored there.[74] Amid this turbulent season for Parma and for the convent of San Paolo in particular, Abbess Maria Benedetti, a Sforza "creature" from the time of her election, must have found it necessary to revive ties to the ruling dynasty through the medium of art.

Framed within the fractured political reality of late Quattrocento Parma and, by extension, of Italy, the winged dragon and the carnation on several of the tile surfaces, both Sforza devices (the carnation, one of Alessandro's, and

46

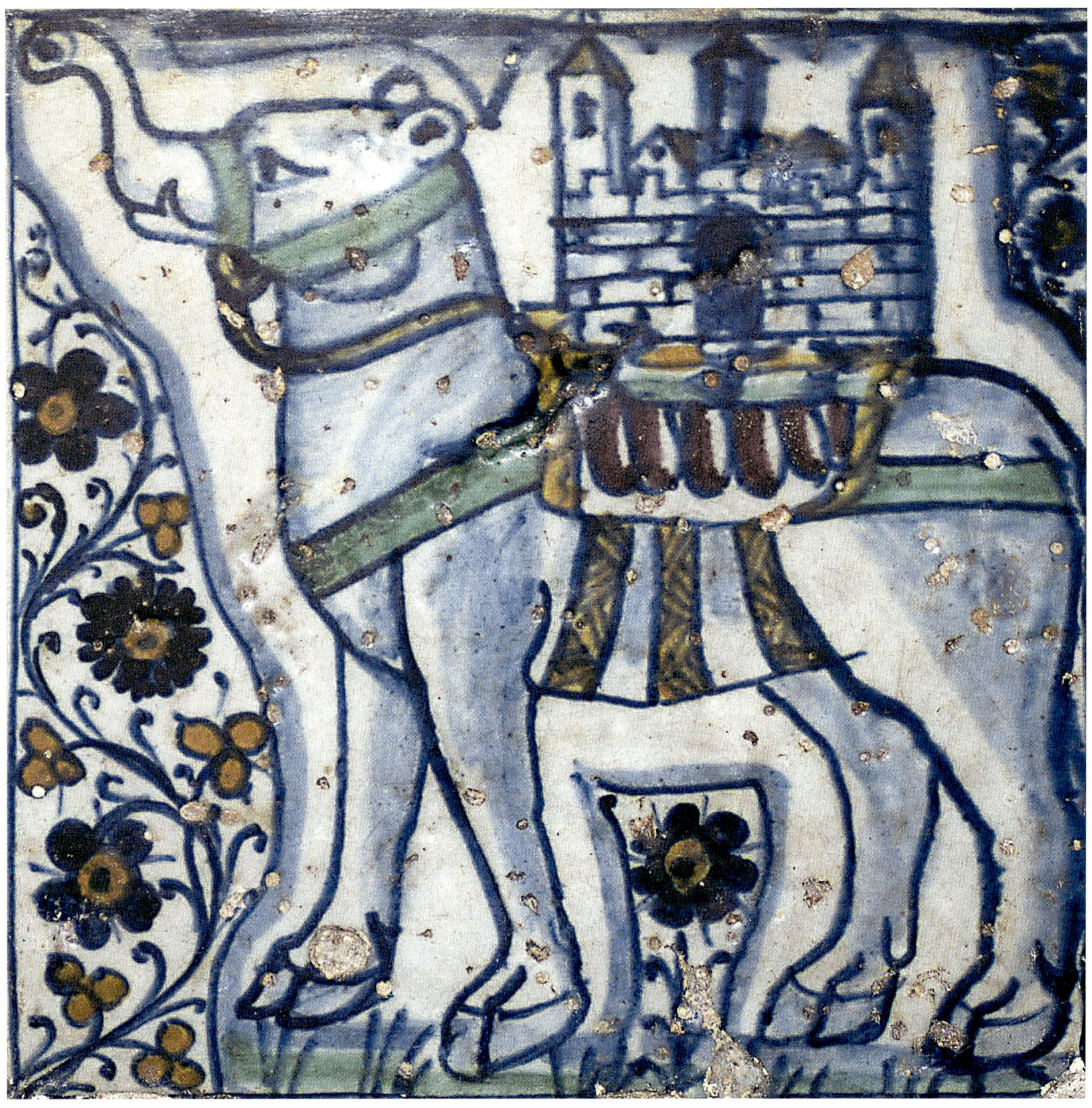

35 Elephant carrying a castle, 1470s, maiolica floor tile, 19.2 × 19.2 cm (7⅝ × 7⅝ in), Parma, Galleria Nazionale

dragon wings part of Costanzo's), could assume broader cultural meanings, intersecting the history of San Paolo with that of the Sforzas. As a marker of status and identity, for instance, the dragon wings appear in a finely illuminated manuscript celebrating Costanzo Sforza and Camilla of Aragon's wedding in Pesaro in 1475.[75] Walking and looking down at the charming tiled floor, the nuns engaged with the Sforzas' metaphors of power, their courtly festive atmosphere, and the discourses of love and courtliness reflected in the wedding manuscript. Taking pleasure in representations on the maiolica tiles that were designed to fuse reality and courtly myths, the nuns were simultaneously made participants in the Sforzas' cultural values and in their political agenda. The commission of the tin-glazed tile floor from Pesarese potters therefore constituted a calculated choice of a medium much in fashion at the Sforza courts. Abbess Benedetti's investment in that medium would have associated her with the Sforza rulers at a key moment in

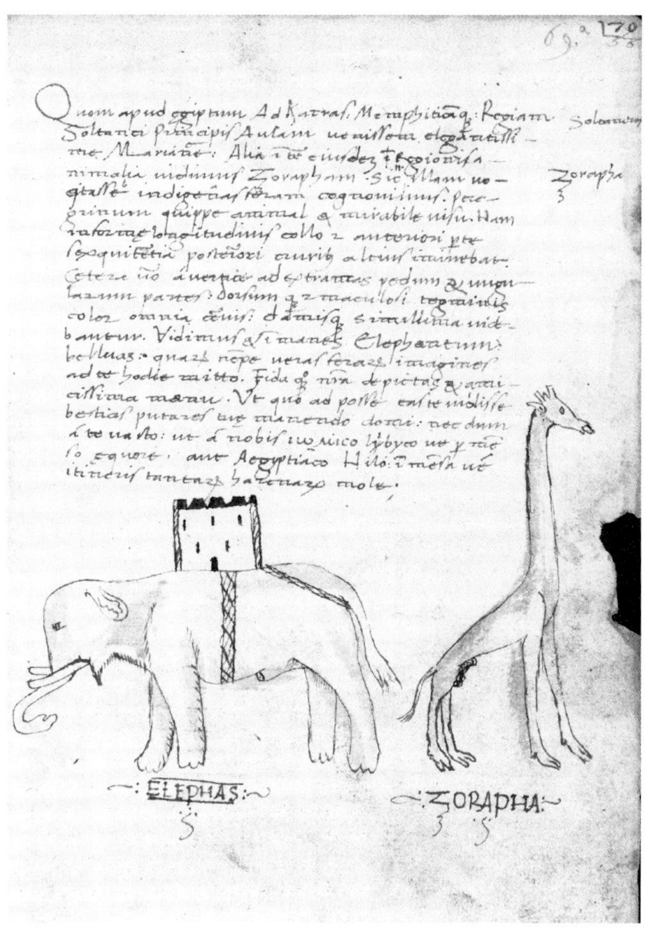

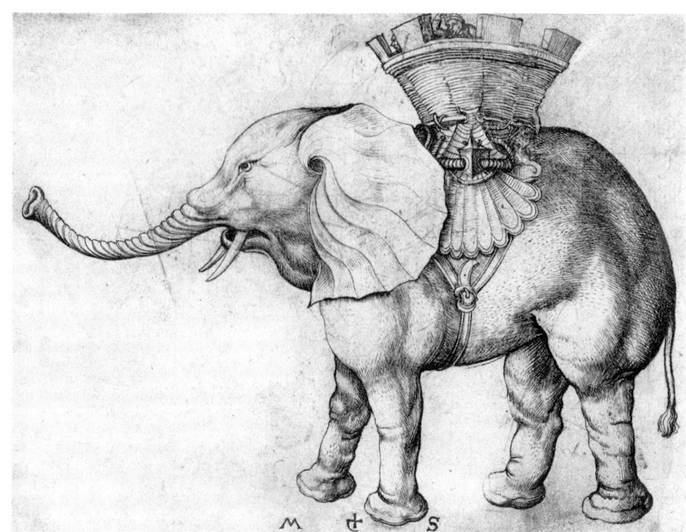

Left 36   After Cyriacus of Ancona, *Elephant and Giraffe*, ca. 1440, Oxford, Bodleian Library, Ms. Canon. Lat. Misc. 280, fol. 69r

Above 37   Martin Schongauer, *The Elephant*, after 1483, 10.7 × 14.6 cm (4⁷/₃₂ × 5³/₄ in), New York, Metropolitan Museum of Art

Facing page 38   Anonymous artist, "Regina Ebrea," from *Ordine delle nozze dello Illustrissimo Signore Meser Costantio Sfortia*, ca. 1475–80, 20.6 × 13.7 cm (8⁷/₆₄ × 5²⁵/₆₄ in), Vatican City, Biblioteca Apostolica Vaticana, Ms. Urb. Lat. 899, fol. 88r

the history of her convent when alliances needed to be reclaimed and reinforced. At the same time, a figurative and ornamental maiolica tiled floor represented the conscious choice of a patron to enhance the enjoyment of viewing for inhabitants and guests as they moved across its splendid horizontal surface, turning imported courtly subjects into sites of semiotic density and pleasure.

A remarkable and still overlooked figuration of this nexus of cultural, political, and artistic concerns is found on the tile depicting an elephant bearing a castle on its back (fig. 35). The cross-fertilization of images of this motif spreading across time and media includes Matthew Paris's colored drawing from the *Cronica majora* (1240–53);[76] an illumination in Fra' Niccolò da Poggibonsi's *Libro d'Oltremare* (1346–50);[77] a drawing after Cyriacus of Ancona dating to the 1440s (fig. 36);[78] an illumination, either by Mantegna or Giovanni Bellini and dating to around 1453, from Jacopo Marcello's *Passio Mauritii et sotiorum eius* manuscript; and a print by Martin Schongauer (fig. 37) and its sculpted version on the façade of Palazzo Fantuzzi in Bologna (1517).[79] A full-page miniature from the Sforza wedding manuscript

records an imaginative recreation of this very subject (fig. 38), featuring an elephant bearing on its back a golden baldachin under which stands a crowned lady holding a scepter. The inscription, "REGINA EBREA," identifies her as the Queen of Sheba.[80] This image encapsulates a performance by an elephant automaton staged in 1475 by the local Jewish community for the Sforza couple on the theme of the Queen of Sheba's offer of gifts to King Solomon, which the accompanying text vividly describes:

an elephant bigger than an ox, with its trunk and with its teeth so well counterfeited that it almost seemed real, and its bearers were invisible so that it seemed to move by itself . . . [a] marvelous artifice . . . and on the back of this elephant was a golden chair shaded by an umbrella made of gold. And a Jewish woman sat in this chair, crowned like a queen and dressed in gold, and behind her came two other similar elephants; on their backs they carried a turreted castle with pennants, full of the damsels of that queen, holding lilies and banners in their hands . . .[81]

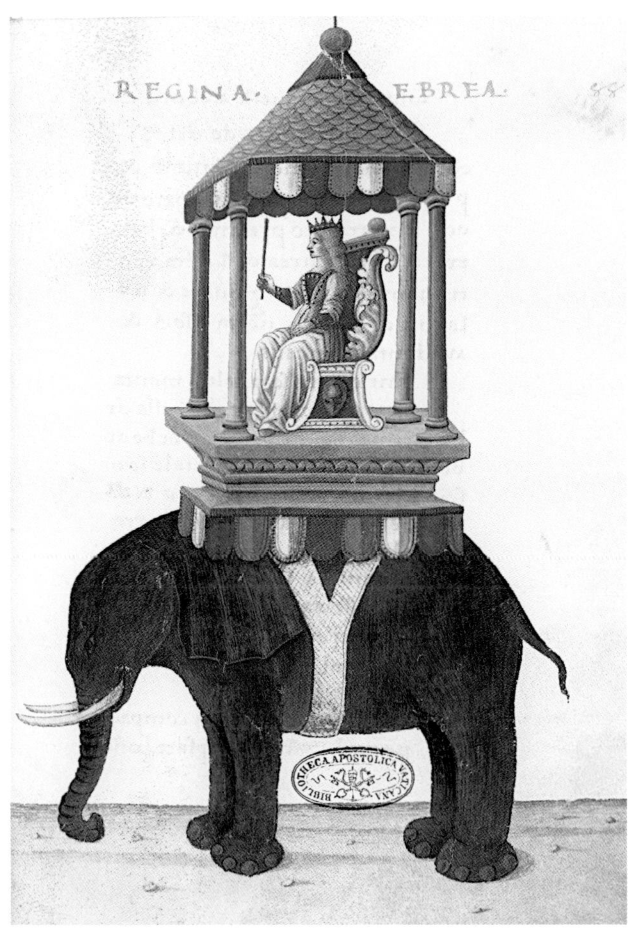

With five days of banquets, orations, and impressive performances, the 1475 Sforza wedding celebrations presented many wondrous sights for the married couple and their guests, which are recorded in the thirty-two colorful illuminations of the wedding manuscript. Here, the model of the loaded elephant is redesigned as an elephant bearing a lady, its author having adjusted and adapted a popular ancient motif to a festive purpose, encoding a chain of antiquarian, performative, and celebratory discourses within the image.[82] But, more importantly here, this tile representation inscribes the genesis of the San Paolo tiled floor within Pesaro's sophisticated courtly milieu, establishing 1475 as the *terminus post quem* for the possible production of the tiles by a local workshop. While this helps to establish a chronology, it also raises questions. Did the potters themselves assist in or witness the automata performance, or, given the prestige of the commission, perhaps have access to the Sforza antiquarian corpus? Or was the production of the maiolica floor tiles in tune with fifteenth-century working practices characterized by close contacts and shared motifs among painters, sculptors, goldsmiths, and potters? Whatever the case, the

extraordinary richness of the subjects displayed on the tiles and their makers' sensitive approach to the medium suggest that the maiolica corpus of San Paolo constituted an ambitious enterprise undertaken by a workshop of fine potters.[83]

Whoever the potters were, they were of Pesarese origin and produced an extraordinary tin-glazed tile floor that transformed the conventual spaces that it defined. Walking on the pavement with their eyes cast down, the nuns would have marveled at the representation of the elephant bearing a castle on its back. To some it would have appeared a charming subject with encoded subtexts, while to others it might have seemed almost a commentary on cloistered life, reinstating the model of enclosure as a secure way of living, but at the same time ridiculing it with the fortified architecture made portable and movable. The model of the confined life is both subverted and made playful on the tile surface. Women are protected within enclosed buildings, but their seclusion is tenuous indeed if entrusted to elephants – one of the most exotic and fashionable animals at fifteenth-century Italian courts.

THE TALE OF THE TILE PAVEMENT

Abbess Benedetti's investment in the maiolica tile pavement and the motivations behind it seem clear enough, but the questions raised by the varying dimensions of the tiles, and the uncertainty regarding their original location and function necessitate additional qualification. Dating to 1834 and the earliest surviving document, Paolo Toschi's report on the maiolica corpus transferred to the local Accademia states that the tiles were removed from a chapel overlooking the nunnery's garden. According to Scarabelli Zunti, however, Benedetti's tiles had been "laid down in some rooms of her convent."[84] Giuseppe Campori's book of 1879 on maiolica and porcelain in Ferrara records that 154 tiles from San Paolo were found in "a room in the proximity of the convent's gate."[85] Unfortunately, there is no way of determining with certainty whether Toschi, Scarabelli, and Campori were referring to the same set of tiles, so the discrepancy in their accounts could simply indicate inaccuracies and partial recording. Or perhaps the scholars were alluding to two sets of tiles laid down in separate, distinct spaces, that is, a corpus ornamenting a garden chapel, and another that paved a chamber or chambers adjacent to the gate of the convent. In her study, Fornari Schianchi neutralized the contradicting evidence by relying on Toschi's earliest report, suggesting that the tiles were laid in a prayer room whose walls are decorated with episodes from the life of St. Catherine of Alexandria.[86] Abutting the convent's high wall on the north, this so-called "cell of St. Catherine" (see Chapter Four) overlooked the garden. The issue seemed settled, but more recently it has been established that orchards occupied that northern zone of the nunnery during Maria Benedetti's tenure (1460–84). Aldo Spina and Giuseppina Longhi's excellent documentary research into the convent's history has proven that the maiolica floor tiles recovered by Toschi in 1834 were probably removed from what was then a chapel carved into the western wall and connected to Abbess Giovanna Piacenza's celebrated residence (on which more in Chapter Four).[87] Overlooking the abbess's garden, this now lost structure postdates 1507 when she began transforming the convent's western zone into an independent court for herself. I propose that after her election that year Abbess Piacenza adapted and, possibly, commissioned new tiles to pave an audience hall that was later remodeled into a chapel, which was in turn torn down in 1855.[88]

To recapitulate, what it is today known as the San Paolo tin-glazed pavement is a corpus of tiles of different dimensions that were perhaps laid down in distinct monastic spaces and produced in two campaigns. From a preliminary cross-checking of the formal features, subjects, and dimensions of the tiles, it appears that the majority of the smaller tiles, including that depicting the elephant and castle, was made after 1475, while the corpus in the larger format could have been manufactured after 1507. Additional technical research, however, is needed to substantiate this working hypothesis, which the rest of the chapter will attempt to corroborate in several other ways.[89] It seems clear, nonetheless, that Giovanna Piacenza recycled some of her predecessor Benedetti's floor tiles and also commissioned a number of new ones, including the unquestionably early sixteenth-century white-and-blue rectangular tiles (see fig. 30), a scenario that could account for some repeated iconographies, different dimensions, and the absence of Giovanna's own arms on the tiles.[90] There could have been many reasons for the transfer of some of Benedetti's tiles and the imitative gesture of investing in a tin-glazed pavement with profane content. In one way or another, it was meant symbolically to reinforce Giovanna Piacenza's own maternal lineage, inscribing its leading female members within the history of the convent of San Paolo. Overlooked records confirm that Piacenza was actually a niece of Giovanna Benedetti, her namesake, who in turn was the sister of Abbess Maria Benedetti.[91] In other words, Giovanna Piacenza was Maria's niece. This Giovanna's possible transfer of some of Benedetti's tiles would not be simply a case of recycling, which was common in monastic buildings, but an episode of reuse and reinstallation of an artistic corpus charged with personal, familial, and symbolic associations. The adaptation of the Benedetti tiles stresses the notion of the genealogical transmission of authority from one female member to another, but the new and old tiles were utilized each within their own specific ideological framework. Maiolica floor tiles were ultimately material manifestations of a monastic culture that, as will be seen later, emphasized the visual, the power of the gaze, and the kinaesthetic experience, recognizing that the very horizontality of splendid pavements and their perceptual mode were sources of delight, morality, and, simultaneously, claims of defiance and disobedience.[92]

A final question remains open: if Giovanna Piacenza had some tiles made to pave a meeting place, imitating her ancestor's gesture of redefining a space with a splendid tin-glazed revetment, where had the earlier corpus of tiles been laid? And what would the function of such a room have been in the 1470s, when the convent's core claustral block, including the cloister, the nuns' choir, and the chapter house, occupied the eastern zone? Given the standardization of claustral planning, it can be surmised that, in addition to these core buildings, the few other spaces included in the eastern block were the abbess's lodging and the parlor. Research by Sheila Bonde and Clark Maines on the spatial layout of French medieval abbeys has shown that abbots' dwellings tended to be placed within the claustral zone, either to the east or the west end, in the vicinity of the choir. Their discussion of elite spaces used as administrative offices and reception sites, and serving as connecting areas between the monastic and the secular worlds, has further demonstrated that some of these places had tiled floors consistent with a monastic tradition of fine pavements designed to signal the function of these loci.[93]

Reflecting back on the history of San Paolo with this information in mind, it follows that in 1469, on Antonia Torelli's death, her residence returned to the disposal of Abbess Maria Benedetti. I would argue that she transformed it into a place for herself by, among other things, paving one chamber with the maiolica tiles. A room devoted to business and recreational activities brightened and ornamented by the tiles made by Pesarese potters served as the abbess's representational site, a *camera abbatissa* and a parlor combined. Nuns accessed this chamber from the cloister, while visitors would have been escorted to it conveniently from the nearby eastern gate.[94] A maiolica tile floor of secularized content therefore represented the cultural aspirations of the abbess and her community, transforming an art form traditionally intended as a marker of elite administrative spaces into what could be seen as a new beginning. A floor usually serves purposes distinct from the display of art, but in the rarefied world of San Paolo it became the vector for the exhibition of colorful, tin-glazed *picturae*, the manifestation of these sophisticated religious women's search for alternatives to their prescribed roles. Connected with a medieval monastic tradition of decorated pavements that religious writers criticized as "curious artifacts," the San Paolo tin-glazed tile floor with a world of pleasure and beauty inscribed on its surface encompassed forms, memories, and meanings for an audience that was able to reimagine and experience them in multiple ways.[95] A viewer's sensorial experience in moving across the tiled floor with eyes downcast was the ultimate determining factor for the choice of this medium, redefining a conventual space intended for the cultivation of virtue through good administration, conversation, and the contemplation of art.

DOWNCAST EYES, MONASTIC RESTRICTIONS, AND DISOBEDIENCE

Laid down in the spaces of San Paolo, the horizontal tin-glazed tiles can be seen as episodes in defiance of austerity and poverty rules. The adornment of floors with sumptuous revetments had long been deplored by monastic writers and reformers. St. Bernard of Clairvaux's *Apologia* (ca. 1124–5) is a case in point. Lashing out against wasteful decorations of religious sites that distracted worshippers, St. Bernard coupled the horizontality of lavishly ornate floors to the vulgar behavior of ambulatory devotees spitting on floors and treading on their sacred representations, condemning the investment in such fine art forms as acts against true devotion:

> Why is it that we do not at least show respect for the images of the saints, which the very pavement which one tramples underfoot gushes forth? Frequently people spit on the countenance of an angel. Often the face of one of the saints is pounded by the heels of those passing by. And if one does not spare the sacred images, why does one not at any rate spare the beautiful colors? Why do you decorate what is soon to be disfigured? Why do you depict what is inevitably to be trod upon? What good

are these graceful forms there, where they are constantly marred by dirt? Finally, what are these things to poor men, to monks, to spiritual men? Unless perhaps at this point, the words of the poet may countered by the saying of the prophet, "Lord, I have loved the beauty of your house and the place where your glory dwells." I agree, let us put up with these things which are found in the church, since even if they are harmful to the shallow and avaricious, they are not to the simple and devout.[96]

The abbesses' awareness of St. Bernard's excoriating comments cannot be established, but their choice of fine maiolica floor decorations undoubtedly made a strong claim against his views and the string of monastic strictures on the governance of the body and the prohibition of enquiries beyond the simple causation of matters. In particular, lowered eyes and controlled bodily movements became the means to create a visual culture that promoted phenomenological perceptions, imaginative journeys, and ethical messages.

As Michel de Certeau observed, traversing a place transforms it into a space and the agent of this transformation is one's footsteps, bodily movement coupling with intensified sensory perceptions to make the experience of one's environment simultaneously both physical and visual.[97] In the peripatetic mode of seeing and touching the surface underfoot, not only do viewers' eyes absorb subjects as they move across the ground, but also their motion simultaneously exposes them to an intensification of the sensorium and the immersion into the painted fiction displayed under their feet. In other words, the perception of ornamented floors permitted a phenomenological experience of the visible world. Viewers' movements across ornate floors and their capacity to activate the full import of the representations underfoot stimulate acute perceptions, which begin with onlookers' physical traversal of the architectural space and their active engagement in order to reimagine and produce links among the representations. Splendid and varied floor decorations invite the viewer to step on them to enjoy motifs and subjects from multiple angles, directions, and itineraries, implicating the onlooker in a kinaesthetic experience of the fiction underfoot.[98] Certeau has further posited that the act of walking and traversing spaces enhances forms of anamnesis, the exploration of "deserted places of [the] memory" and the recovery of old memories and, ultimately, of the inner self.[99] Through walking, the observer engages in mental concentration, which in turn induces an alerted state of mind and a return to past experiences. The very horizontal flatness of floors affects the viewer's vision, perception, and movement on it; therefore, gazing down and simultaneously touching the floor propel an intensified cognitive experience of the represented subjects under one's feet. Studies have shown such contemplative engagement with reference to ancient and medieval artifacts, but can the same be claimed about the Renaissance tin-glazed floors in monastic settings?[100] Were they only about a tradition of forms and formulas made anew, or was there something more at work?

With its secularized content and alluring figurations the San Paolo maiolica pavement might have appeared to some onlookers as the appropriate décor of a convent space, the suitable adornment of a cultivated religious community. Others would have appreciated the abbess's investment in the new medium of maiolica that redefined the floors of chapels and domestic chambers at a relatively low cost. But cloistered women seem to have been aware that the tiled floor's appeal, its profane content, and the prescription of nuns' downcast eyes potentially inscribed subversive dimensions into its perception, reclaiming the power and centrality of the gaze that monastic regulations had long despised. The very motion that rules recommended, the prohibition of *otium* (leisure) and the enjoyment of secularized subjects made possible the unfolding of the stories collected in the decorations underfoot. Reflecting on monastic comportment literature, models of peripatetic vision, and the horizontality of the maiolica floor tiles therefore reveals that the kinaesthetic experience of the pavement could be turned into a calculated act of identity, resistance, and even catharsis for a community of sophisticated nuns. The charming tiled floor took over a surface that viewers traversed with their feet, transforming it into an artwork that commented on and threatened religious restrictions. Constantly advised to keep their eyes down, nuns refashioned this requirement into an experience leading to pleasure and insubordination, self-affirmation and presence. The phenomenological experience that the floor decorations promised, and their splendor, attracted movement across them, amounting to a disregard or even rejection of the rigid rules imposed on nuns. But the experience of mobile perception for nuns treading on profane subjects could also have implied purgation of their past selves and present misbehavior, turning the actions of walking and seeing into an exercise with morally beneficial implications. As Certeau put it, "walking makes possible procedures for forgetting."[101] Exposing and contemplating secular themes could ultimately be a way of neutralizing them through their recovery in the mind and transformation into cleansing agents.

Several regulations, including the Benedictine Rule, instruct individuals to keep their heads bowed, a posture recommended in the Scriptures. The practice of monks and nuns bowing their heads and lowering their eyes when walking, meditating, or praying was intended to signal their humility, as Chapter 7 of the Benedictine Rule posits:

> The twelfth step of humility is concerned with the external impression conveyed by those dedicated to monastic life. The humility of their hearts should be apparent by their bodily movements to all who see them. Whether they are at the work of God, at prayer in the oratory, walking about the monastery, in the garden, on a journey or in the fields, wherever they may be, whether sitting, walking or standing they should be free of any hint of arrogance or pride in their manner or the way they look about them. They should guard their eyes and look down. They should remember their sins and their guilt before the judgment of God, with the words of the publican in the gospel for ever on their lips as he stood with his eyes cast down saying: Lord, I am not worthy, sinner that I am, to lift my eyes to the heavens. Or the words of the psalmist might fit just as well: I am bowed down and utterly humbled.[102]

The idea that outer behavior revealed the inner workings of the soul had long been a staple in Christian thought. If physical and spiritual dispositions were intimately connected, the manipulation of one entailed the modification of the other. If monks were told to keep downcast eyes, nuns, considered humbler and of lower status than their male peers in the Roman Catholic Church, were expected and further pressured to control their bodies in order to discipline their souls. Novices were asked to avert their gazes in public and in front of superiors as a sign of obedience and self-restraint. The comportment rules for nuns and their gazing down at the tiles' poetic subjects therefore made the interplay among the secular, forbidden representations, the irony, and play built into the floor all the more fascinating to them and historically revealing to us. If the tiles with their set of female and male heads and profane stories were meant to amuse, refresh, teach, or redeem "bad" nuns who trod on them, their content spoke to the religious women of their identity as sophisticated cloistered ladies, their need for relaxation, and escape from tedious routine. Stepping on and looking down at the pavement's images might have invited some nuns to engage in imaginative journeys of delight and delectation. Others may have rationalized the profane subjects and secularized painted

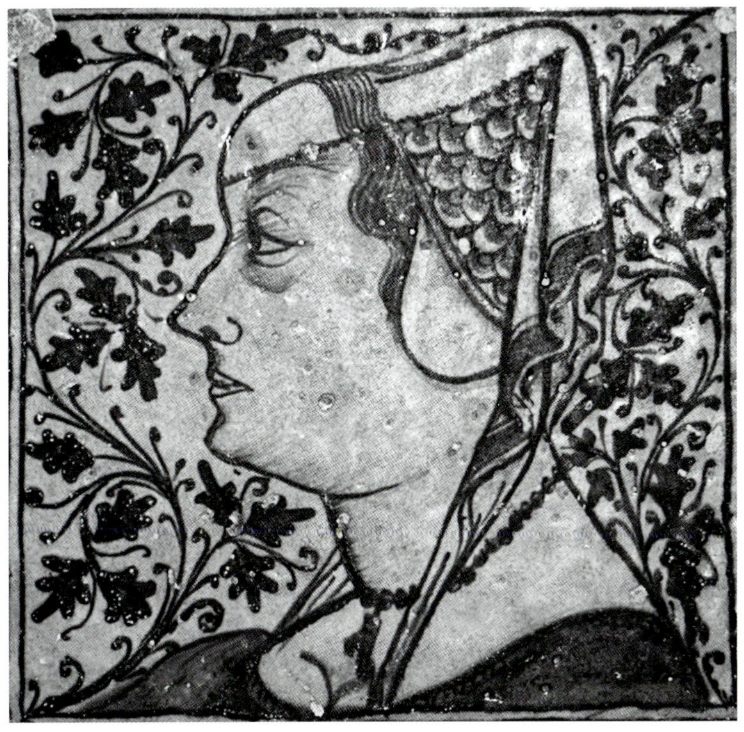

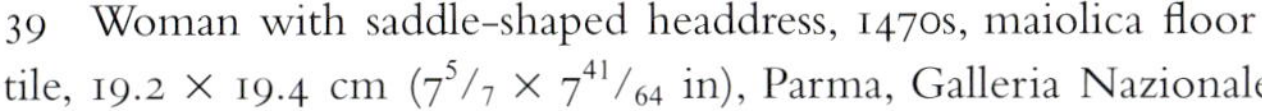

39 Woman with saddle-shaped headdress, 1470s, maiolica floor tile, 19.2 × 19.4 cm ($7^5/_7 \times 7^{41}/_{64}$ in), Parma, Galleria Nazionale

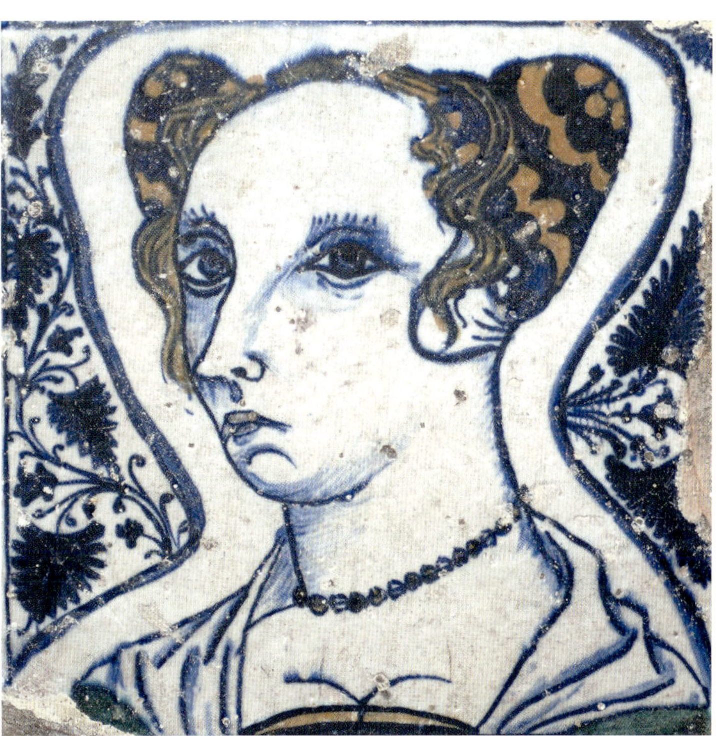

40 Young woman with small chignons, 1470s, maiolica floor tile, 19 × 19 cm ($7^{31}/_{64} \times 7^{31}/_{64}$ in), Parma, Galleria Nazionale

women underfoot as negative exemplars on which they trampled and passed beyond as they crossed the maiolica floor, purging their senses while gazing at superfluous decorations to recall St. Bernard's words, thus articulating processes of regeneration via the beauty of art. By proposing secular scenes and games on the floor decorations of the convent, the tiles engaged a community in multiple and unanticipated ways, treading with positive, negative, or mixed feelings on the tiles whose representations were easily able to intrude on the lived space of the room itself.

PICTURING BEAUTIFUL WOMEN ON MAIOLICA FLOORS

The original layout of the tiles cannot be reconstructed given the lack of documentation, which makes it impossible to comment on the pattern of the decorations as a unified whole. Rather, the way to proceed is to establish registers of semantic discourse among the tiles, regrouping them in similar categories of subjects and genres, including heads of female beauties, male heads, chivalric scenes, tarot motifs, and mythological narratives. To begin with, the richness of

the head-and-shoulder images of beautiful women in profile, elaborately coiffed, is truly impressive. Some *belle* wear saddle-shaped headdresses called *a sella* (fig. 39), fashionable until the 1470s, and have eyes demarcated by light shades. Others have shaved forehead hairstyles, with small chignons (the so-called *a corna* fashion creating a half-moon shape; fig. 40) or close-fitting caps concealing the ears. Some women have their hair tied with colorful ribbons and strings of pearls. There are pairs of female heads in profile, either with a turned-up nose or displaying contrasting characters (fig. 41): an older woman with an aquiline nose is coupled with a young girl with a more regular profile.[103] Several female representations are in profile but a few display three-quarter-length women whose gazes are directed out at the viewer, catching one's eye. Indeed, this act of gazing out connects and engages figures and viewers in multiple ways.

The wide range of female beauties pictured on the tiles, including those in décolleté or with a shawl and their hair covered, as well as fancifully garbed girls with flowers instead of words springing from their mouths and arrows piercing their hearts (fig. 42), attest to the potters' extraordinary inventiveness in their figurative models. In general,

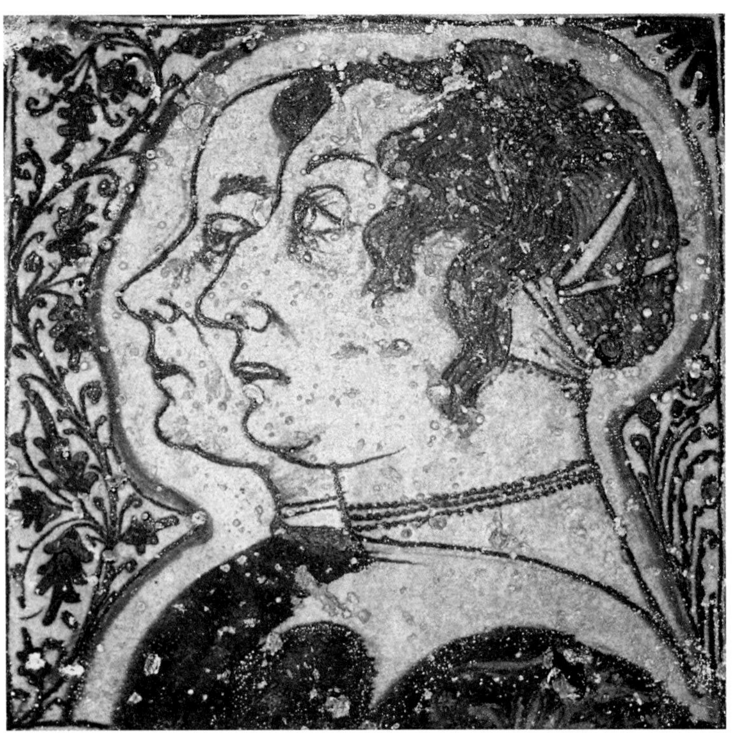

41   Female heads in profile, 1470s, maiolica floor tile,
19.2 × 19.2 cm (7⅝ × 7⅝ in), Parma, Galleria Nazionale

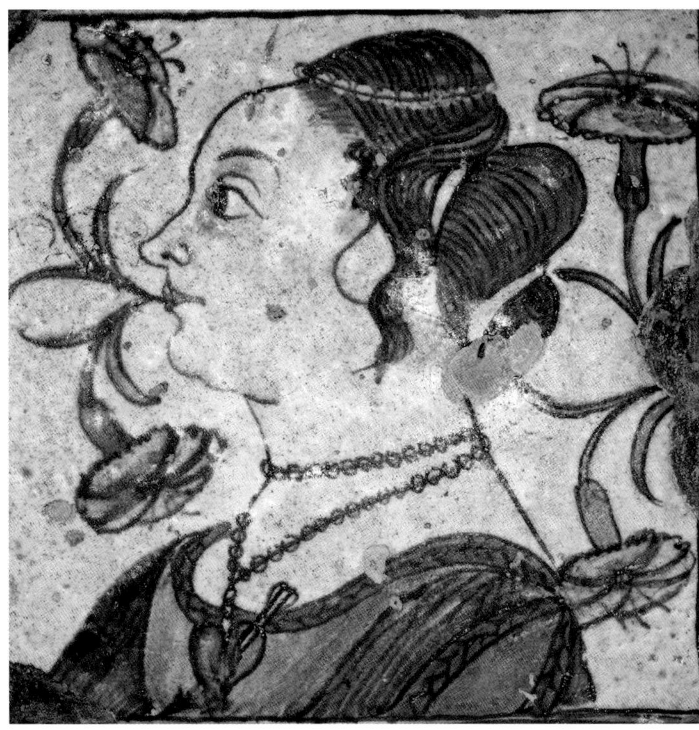

42   Head of a woman, 1470s, maiolica floor tile, 19.2 × 19.2 cm
(7⅝ × 7⅝ in), Parma, Galleria Nazionale

the female heads do not include inscriptions or mottoes. Either in Gothic or in classical lettering, women's first names (see fig. 33) along with the praise "bella" (Rosa Bella, Isadora Bella) appear on separate tiles. Names and *belle* heads could originally have been matched to form verbal and visual clusters on the floors, as may be seen in the maiolica pavement of the Vaselli chapel in Bologna's San Petronio. Dating to 1487, this tiled floor of Faentine production even includes a couple of female heads with a misogynistic inscription: "ugly face and lovely buttocks" (BRUTO.VIXO.E[T].B[EL].CUL[O].).[104]

This rendering of beautiful women on maiolica objects conformed to the Petrarchan tradition that canonized feminine beauty in a set of standardized features — blond hair, fair skin, red lips, and rosy cheeks, among others. The reception of *belle* images as exemplary models of female virtues relied on an ancient literary tradition revived by Petrarch, Boccaccio, and their followers.[105] Scholars have debated if female heads on pottery items can be considered "portraits" of historical individuals, given that heads on tiles, dishes, and jugs produced in a specific center tend to present identical formal features. By showing the same profile head on two jugs accompanied only by different names and serving to represent both an ancient heroine and a modern beauty, these representations, Luke Syson has concluded, are not true portraits, taking no account of "the individualized likeness of the named women."[106] Fine tin-glazed objects, especially plates, bearing beautiful heads were canonical love gifts offered by men to their betrotheds. Marta Ajmar and Dora Thornton have noticed, however, that when accompanied by historical names, stylized and stereotyped female heads bear intentionality, and they may be seen, under certain conditions, as portrayals of Renaissance individuals. One crucial example proposed by these scholars is a tile from San Paolo featuring a female head in profile that the full, historical name on the scroll above (fig. 43) turns into a portrait.[107] I am less interested in the debate about "true" or "idealized" portraits on the tiles than in the information that these representations give in relation to the mode of viewing the maiolica pavement.

On this somewhat damaged tile is shown the head of a young woman in profile, with blond hair pulled into a complicated chignon and a jeweled necklace at her throat. Within the scroll the full name *Lucrec[i]a Bregoza* (standing for Lucrezia Bergonzi) identifies the sitter as a real, historical individual. An unpublished document corroborates that Lucrezia

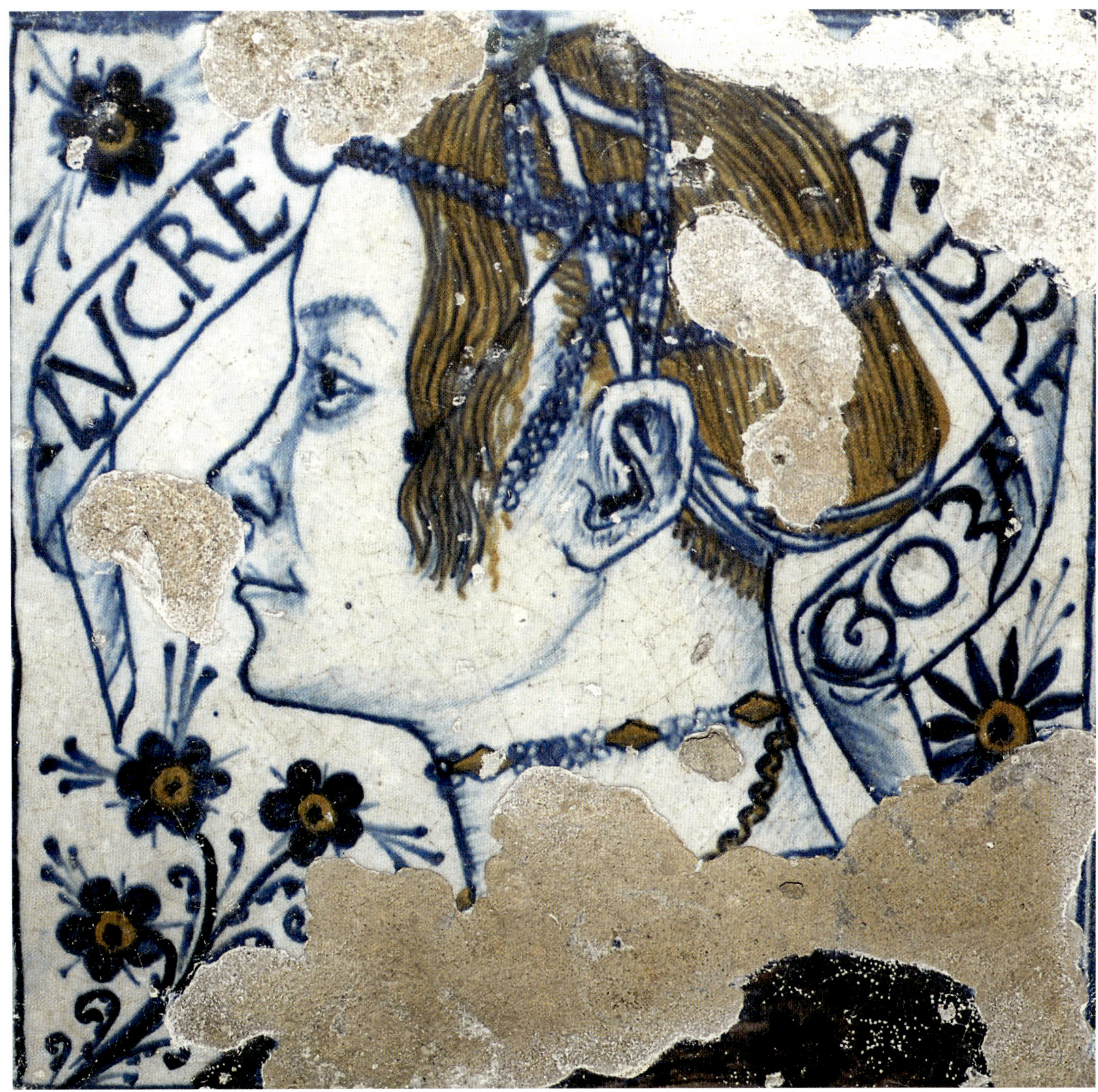

43   Lucrezia Bergonzi, after 1507, maiolica floor tile, 21 × 21 cm (8¼ × 8¼ in), Parma, Galleria Nazionale

Bergonzi was among the novices who professed vows before the newly elected Abbess Giovanna Piacenza on May 23, 1507.[108] The daughter of Paolo Bergonzi and one of Giovanna's maternal cousins, Lucrezia must have been in her full youth when she took her vows. Subsequently, a record of 1509 mentions her among the choir-nuns of San Paolo assisting the abbess. She did not live long, however, if the classicizing lettering found on another tile evoking the sudden death of a certain "Lucreccia" refers to her.[109] Be that as it may, Lucrezia's portrait confirms that some new tiles were probably ordered after Giovanna Piacenza's abbatial election in 1507, and that the professed nun Lucrezia was depicted on one. While Lucrezia's is perhaps not the only "individualized" face reproduced on the tiles, it would be a mistake to jump to the conclusion that all of the female heads on the tiles could refer to then living individuals. Yet the head of a young

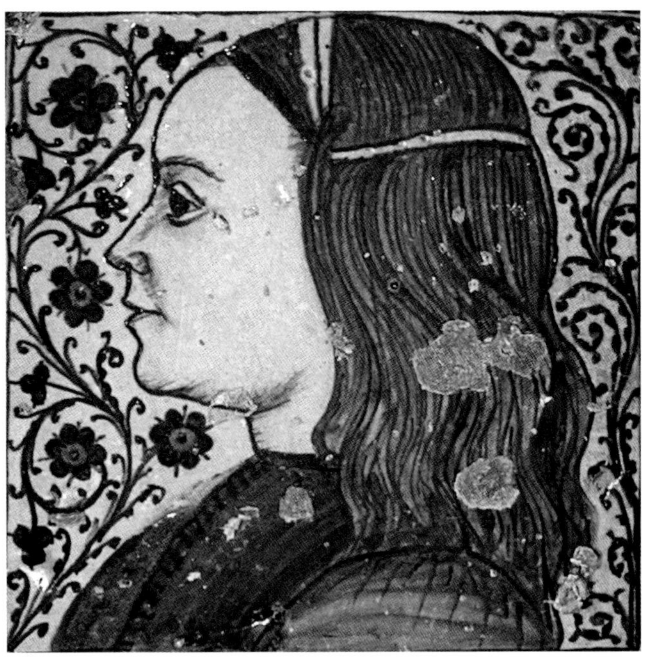

44   Head of young girl, 1470s, maiolica floor tile, 19 × 19.2 cm ($7^{31}/_{64}$ × $7^{5}/_{8}$ in), Parma, Galleria Nazionale

girl with blond hair falling to her shoulders, lively eyes, and an intense expression (fig. 44) far surpasses stereotyped models, and moreover bears physical similarities to the blond girl holding the crosier in Loschi's *Madonna of Mercy* (see fig. 20) and to the one carrying the basket in his *Last Meeting* (see fig. 22). Whether the sitter is Simona Benedetti or another family member is irrelevant. What matters most is the spectacle of female individuals being presented in Loschi's murals and in the maiolica pavement, documenting an intelligent meditation on nuns' viewing modes and engagements. It seems, therefore, intentional that the *belle* displayed on the tile floor are all in lay rather than religious clothing, since nuns would have walked on the pavement and thus trodden on female worldly selves, a possible form of purgation of nuns' worldliness, which ultimately could count as a defense for such a splendid maiolica floor. Instead, in Loschi's frescoes set on vertical walls and visible from across the room, the portrayed nuns wear their monastic habits.

Whether it was Lucrezia taking vows in the convent or her premature death that spurred her commemoration on the tile, what is astonishing is that she is rendered as a young girl, advertising her physical appeal as if she were not a nun deprived of that superficial allure through tonsure and the religious habit. Lucrezia's portrait is a startling, paradoxical image in many ways. Nuns were not supposed to be "real"

individuals in that way, or to be seen as attractive girls, because they were meant to exist only as perfected, spiritual beings. Could Lucrezia's portrait have been modeled on a lost drawing, or was there a model executed before she entered the convent? These hypotheses have been advanced, for example, in reference to Pisanello's portrait medal (dating to 1447) showing an unveiled and secularly dressed Cecilia Gonzaga, who was in reality already a professed nun by this time (see fig. 5). Or is the tile portrait of Lucrezia symptomatic of something else? What was the purpose of reimagining and remaking the nun Lucrezia as a beautiful, unveiled girl? Even the recognition of a relation between Lucrezia's image and the documented, forbidden dresses of the nuns (see Chapter One) cannot fully resolve the existence of the tile image. Lucrezia's idealized image challenges our conventional parameters of the female sacred self, simultaneously renegotiating discourses of youth, beauty, sensual desire, and devotion. The sitter's combination of desirability and unavailability, modesty and ostentation, made this portrait an ambiguous image of a nun, promoting the very femininity of which regulations deprived cloistered women, but which could have existed in the memory for the mind to recover and reimagine.

To some viewers crossing the pavement, Lucrezia's appealing face, like Petrarch's sonnets in praise of the portrait of Laura, might have evoked the innocence of her soul, making them pause to consider the ambiguous, liminal status of patrician cloistered ladies caught between secular and sacred worlds. To the nuns in motion with downcast eyes, engagement with Lucrezia's portrait could have prompted reflections on past and present realities, a life of renunciation with provocations and disobedience, or it could have been an incentive to abandon the old worldly self. Lucrezia's portrait stands between appearance and reality, masking and simulation. It hints as much at the playful reversal of a religious self tolerated in some elite convents where prohibited embellishments (clothing, make-up, dyed hair) and alterations of appearances are documented, as at the practices of reconfiguring reality to purge and/or delight the self that was encouraged by traversing the maiolica pavement.[110] Walking on the pavement's images that blurred the distance between fiction and reality, onlookers would have been struck by this embodiment of Lucrezia's beauty, as well as by the portrait's defiance of monastic strictures. It is as if the beauty that regulations attempted to fold away and suppress resurfaced in this tangible image, a charming representation of a nun as a beautiful girl, a metamorphosis and masquerade of a living individual who was not meant to exist in that way.

Exploring these concepts of self-reflection and transformation, representation and masquerade, Caroline Walker Bynum's comments on Narcissus's self-representation seem particularly fitting: "for even if we gaze at our own reflection . . . that gazing is a mark of who we are, and who we are is, in part, what we have been . . . the identity we carry with us."[111] Lucrezia's portrait makes claims for an appealing persona that religious rules wanted to erase, and simultaneously constructs a new self that existed in the imagination, as an image that spectators re-enacted through walking over and contemplating it. Her status was permanently altered when she professed her vows and became a cloistered individual, but at the same time the renewed, spiritual self remained connected with the graceful, youthful persona wanting to be seen and discovered as such. To expand on this tension further, let us turn to other unconventional portraits of cloistered individuals, which propose the recreation and reversal of the represented self. At a basic level, this discussion makes clear that art-historical narratives have largely discounted the phenomenon of convent "beauties."

PORTRAITS OF NUNS, THEN AND NOW: METAMORPHOSES OF THE FEMALE SELF

Another uncanonical representation of a nun that has long perplexed scholars is the exquisite, small *Portrait of a Nun from San Secondo* (see fig. 2) attributed to Jacometto Veneziano. Shown in half-length and facing to the left, this beautiful young woman does not appear at first glance to be a nun, wearing as she does a fashionable and suggestively cut outfit that exposes her left shoulder. The graciously arranged white headdress wrapped over her ears and across her throat covers her hair, but it is so elegantly crafted that it does not suggest a monastic veil.[112] Now separated, Jacometto's female portrait was once joined to a portrait of a male sitter, both with painted reverses (figs. 45 and 46). This ensemble was first described in 1543 by the Venetian connoisseur Marcantonio Michiel as in the collection of Michele Contarini: "a little portrait of Messer Alvise Contarini . . . who died some years ago. In the same small

45 and 46 Jacometto Veneziano, *Portrait of Alvise Contarini* (recto and verso), ca. 1485–95, oil on panel, 11.4 × 7.9 cm ($4^3/_6 \times 3^7/_6$ in), New York, Metropolitan Museum of Art

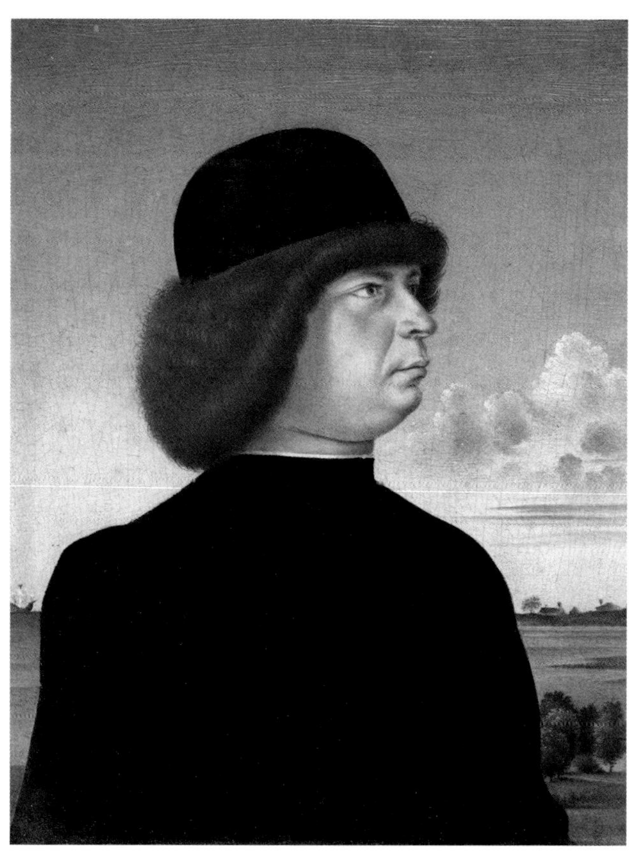
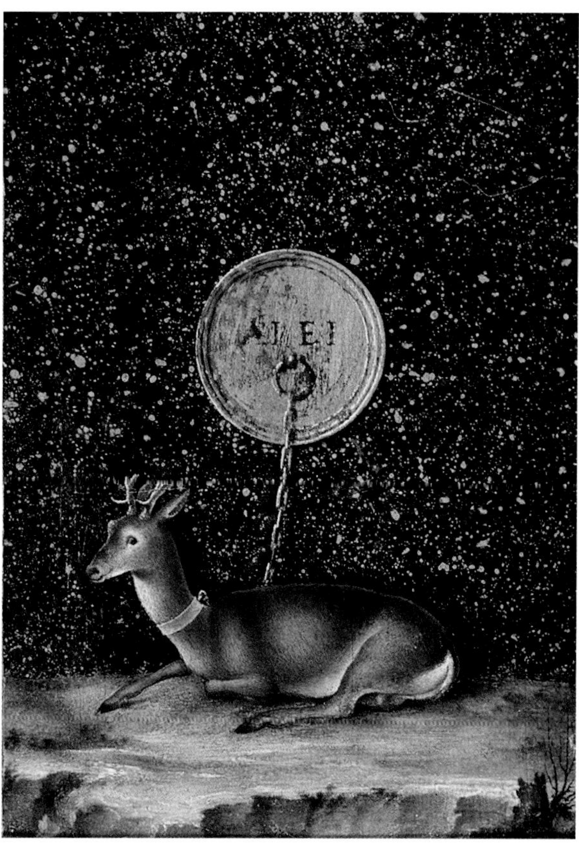

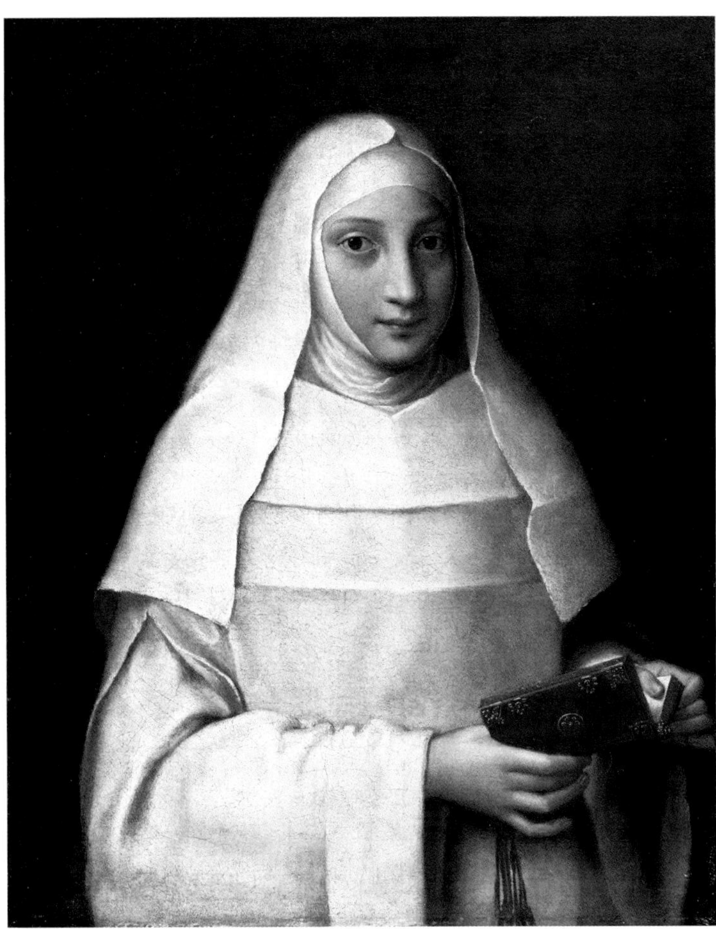

47 Sofonisba Anguissola, *Portrait of a Nun (perhaps the Artist's Sister)*, ca. 1551, oil on canvas, 75 × 59 cm (29$^{17}/_{32}$ × 23$^{15}/_{64}$ in), Southampton, City Gallery

picture, there is opposite, a portrait of a nun of San Secondo, and on the cover of these portraits is a small deer in a landscape . . . it is by the hand of Jacometto, a most perfect work."[113] Today there is some agreement that Michiel's description can be associated with the pair of miniature portraits by Jacometto in New York and that they can be dated around 1485–95.[114] Set against a background of both land and sea, Jacometto's male sitter is shown in a three-quarter view facing to the right. Following Michiel's description, he has been identified as Alvise Contarini, from a founding family of the Venetian Republic. On the reverse a deer rests on a rocky ledge, chained to a golden roundel bearing the inscription AIEI, the Greek for "always, forever," an allegorical representation standing for ideals of continence and fidelity. The reverse of the female portrait, in contrast, is in such ruinous condition as to be virtually illegible to the naked eye.[115]

What has most disturbed scholars is the secularized appearance of the female sitter and her manifest physical allure. One would have expected a nun to be veiled, with covered shoulders and no décolletage. David Alan Brown has written that "Michiel's identification of the sitter as a nun . . . seems odd" in view of her fashionable, secularly tailored costume.[116] It is easy to see that the sitter's dress totally disregards the features of the Benedictine habit and the orthodox representation of the religious self – the covered, devout, humble cloistered woman displayed, for example, in Sofonisba Anguissola's *Portrait of a Nun (perhaps the Artist's Sister)* (ca. 1551; fig. 47), Giovanni Battista Moroni's *Portrait of Abbess Lucrezia Agliardi Vertova* (1556–7), and Diego Velázquez's *Portrait of the Venerable Mother Jerónima de la Fuente* (1620). These works have contributed to shape our view of the early modern female religious self but this viewpoint is in need of critical refinement. It may be productive to counterpoise these images with documentation dating to the 1570s that reproaches nuns for their sumptuous dresses, lascivious hair styles, and veils, which all reflected secular taste. For instance, Bolognese Tridentine authorities commented that it seems that nuns masquerade and celebrate Carnival for months.[117] Isabella Campagnol's recent study has demonstrated that patrician lay and cloistered women in early modern Venice had similar clothing, make-up, and beauty treatments, making it impossible to trace any clear divide between the sacred and the profane.[118] In short, the secularized costume of elite nuns was perhaps more of a reality in Renaissance Italy than has been so far acknowledged.

Didactic writings addressed to nuns, including the illustrated *Prologo de l'ordine del vivere neli monasteri de monache* (1497), had always condemned superfluous embellishments for nuns. Chapter 28 of the *Prologo*, in particular, censures consecrated women who wear lavish attire and "outer ornaments" as weapons to arouse men's desire and concupiscence. It threatens nuns that, because of the ornamentation they deploy to seduce men, they will betray their heavenly spouse and thereby incur God's anger:

[These nuns] . . . place their glory in precious stones and rich garments. Their innate libidinous nature not being enough, they search for opportunities to provoke [men's] sexual arousal. No doubt they desire that men's gazes fall upon them and their gems, and once captured, with suggestive glances they can more easily set men on libidinous fire. Oh public prostitutes, why do you proudly find your glory in sumptuous costume and superficial adornments?[119]

Echoing contemporary attacks on women's excessively lavish garments, including Girolamo Savonarola's lament on Florentine girls' sumptuous attire and décolletage, the *Prologo* prescriptions build on a body of misogynist literature denigrating women's and nuns' nature and attitudes. A paradigmatic text of this tradition is Andreas Cappellanus's *De Amore* (ca. 1180), in which a young, naive interlocutor is admonished to avoid nuns' company:

> So be careful . . . not to visit isolated spots in the company of nuns, nor to seek an opportunity of addressing one of them, for if she realises that the place is suitable for wanton sport, she will not hesitate to grant what you desire, and to devise consolations that burn; you will hardly ever avoid the wicked acts of Venus and you will commit ill-omened crimes. Seeing that the charm of nuns forced me to waver, with all my clever brain and the advantage of infinite learning in love, how will your inexperienced youth be able to confront them? So you must avoid such love.[120]

The appeal of younger nuns, the manipulation of their habits, hair, and make-up to exalt their physical beauty and their resistance to strictures were not simply sinful attitudes remarked on in misogynistic literature and reproached by Tridentine authorities, but they were possibly experiences and/or memories whose ambivalent traces can also be found in paintings.

Exalting her beauty rather than her piety as a self-adornment, Jacometto's female sitter does not conform to our standardized view of conventual life, which is, however, partial and misconstructed. Nor are rules of enclosure and segregation reflected in the original relations between the male and female portrait sitters, whom Jacometto had face each other, fitting them into a small boxlike frame to form an unusual pendant of portraits that were otherwise hidden. In fact, it does not constitute a conventional diptych because the dimensions do not match.[121] The male portrait (11.4 × 7.9 centimeters) is larger in height and width than its female pendant (10.2 × 7 centimeters). According to a recent technical examination, the female portrait's "painted surface is complete and has not been trimmed . . . the panel has edges of ungessoed wood and from this we may surmise that the gesso ground was applied following the application of an engaged frame (now lost); conversely, that of the male portrait is gessoed to its edges."[122] It can therefore be assumed that originally the male sitter's image was on the top in the box-frame and was removable by sliding it over the female portrait, a construction that can also be seen in

another work, Albrecht Dürer's *Portrait of Hieronymus Holzschuher* (1526). When the upper panel was removed, the two pictures by Jacometto would appear side by side. When closed, the portraits instead formed a precious, small box similar to those exchanged by lovers as a sign of their mutual affection.[123]

The closeness of the sitters within the box-frame, almost a surrogate of their bonds in real life, the object's portability, secrecy, and preciousness, all seem to be at odds with the female sitter's religious status. Scholars have consequently rejected Michiel's identification of the sitter as a nun, proposing instead that she is a lay patrician lady. It has been suggested that the sitter is Daria Querini, the wife of Alvise Contarini. As a widow she would have entered a convent like San Secondo, but maintained a certain freedom and independence, as her secular costume reflects. Jacometto's ensemble therefore has been turned into a token of the couple's conjugal love and fidelity that resisted time and adversities.[124] But this reading immediately raises questions. Was Michiel, who had sisters housed in local institutions and was therefore a writer informed about Venetian convents as well as art collections, really in error? Or is our perception of Renaissance elite monastic culture biased and preconceived? Michiel's notation that the portrait depicts "a nun from San Secondo" is not a generic comment.[125] On the contrary, it is a specific reference pointing to a Benedictine convent in Venice that housed patrician women, as described in Flaminio Cornelio's eighteenth-century history of local religious institutions.[126] The convent was exempted from local episcopal control in 1177, then placed under papal jurisdiction. Located on the island of San Secondo, between Mestre and Cannaregio on the lagoon, which Rossella Lauber has recognized as the small island visible in the left background of the female sitter portrait, the convent was inhabited by nuns known for their relaxed behavior and fashionable clothing, and for admitting visitors.[127] Despite their tenacious opposition, the disordered San Secondo nuns were finally taken over by observant sisters in 1519 and a strict regime of enclosure was imposed on them.[128] The convent's inhabitants thus forever lost the power to live their lives as they wished.

Regulations forbade nuns to own profane or lascivious pictures, as well as portraits of those whom they had loved. Nor were representations of female seculars tolerated. Yet the customs of a noble life, and nuns' refined taste and imagination, can provide the context within which to inscribe Jacometto's portrait of an alluring nun. What is more, Jacometto's unconventional rendering of a female religious self is only one of a small group of representations of secularized nuns and nuns-to-be. This corpus includes Pisanello's portrait medal of Cecilia Gonzaga and Jacometto's so-called *Portrait of a Woman, possibly a Novice of San Secondo* (fig. 48). The latter figure wears an elegant white tunic with folds, and has a headdress somewhat similar to that shown in the image of the nun from San Secondo. This similarity does not seem merely stylistic or chronological, however. A sonnet of 1447 by the Paduan notary Ulisse Aleotti refers to a now lost portrait of a nun by Andrea Mantegna. It praises Mantegna's virtuosity in depicting "an angelic face behind a veil that distracts every soul for its splendor." Centered on the word-image *paragone* trope, the sonnet celebrates Mantegna's unsurpassed skills that made the nun's portrayal "alive and true."[129] The chronicle of the Venetian convent of Le Vergini also describes a portrait (*effigem*) of Abbess Isabeta Querini executed at the time of her consecration in 1366, which was "utterly graceful and beautiful."[130] Rather than resisting the figural dissonance that these portraits present – their very strangeness and ambivalence, to use Georges Didi-Huberman's words – one could see them as amounting to a tradition of (forbidden) portraits of elite religious women reimagining themselves as beautiful ladies, and transcending their historical personas.[131] The delicate *Portrait of a Nun* by Jacometto and the portrayal of Lucrezia Bergonzi on the tile surface are the material evidence of a courtly monastic tradition, marking significant moments of this overlooked genre of female portraiture that refashioned the religious self in unconventional ways, and even sustained forms of masquerade.

Jacometto's male and female portraits in New York suggest the bonds of love and affection that united their sitters, sentiments of earthly love and desire that could have distracted the nun from achieving a privileged relationship with her heavenly spouse. As much as spiritual love was preached and aspired to by nuns in the devotional exercises that punctuated their lives, wordly love, pleasure, and physical delight – whether as realities, fantasies, or memories – coexisted with their spirituality and religious practices. Nuns were ordered to forget their preclaustral experiences, and were recommended to abandon their earthly selves to acquire a cleansed memory in which only the voice of the scriptures could be heard. But works of art like this portrait by Jacometto make evident the extent to which such prescriptions were eluded or met with difficulty in elite communities. Nuns not only manipulated rigid monastic norms but also accepted reimagined versions of their beautiful selves painted on panels and tiles, as well as cast on medals, to impress the eyes and minds of those who loved them most.

Jacometto skillfully rendered his female religious sitter in miniature style, turning this image into a crucial, paradigmatic episode of the kind of courtly conventual art that ecclesiastical authorities tried to eradicate both before and immediately after the Tridentine legislation on convents. The *Portrait of a Nun from San Secondo*, the tile depicting Lucrezia Bergonzi, and Pisanello's portrait of Cecilia Gonzaga, are surviving examples of paramount significance for recovering this overlooked and largely effaced courtly monastic visual tradition. These portraits present religious individuals, their relations, thoughts, memories, and desires, transferring identities from the real world into the fictional reality of art and vice versa. The elite nuns of San Paolo must have enjoyed the games of self-recreation and self-representation played out on the tiled floor that was designed to interpret the space itself, while walking across it helped viewers to reconstruct the nuns' sophistication and struggles to become perfected selves. Likewise, Jacometto's female portrait transported its historical audience beyond its immediate environment and had the power to substitute, or at least compensate for, the earthly delights missing in the convent life. And as a whole, these portraits produce moments of provocation and moralizing content, shaped by the way patrician nuns saw and imagined themselves, thus providing modern spectators with an experience by which to situate themselves in relation to these representations.

LOVE, PASSIONS, AND THE ALTERNATIVE WORLD

Returning to the San Paolo maiolica floor, the tiles with *belle* heads have their counterpart in images of male heads, in either profile or full face, wearing fashionable outfits and head coverings. Idealized male heads as a painted genre depended on the classical literary tradition of famous men, which was revived in the Renaissance by Petrarch and Bartolomeo Facio, among others.[132] Although some male heads on the tile surfaces present individualized features such as one man's aquiline nose (fig. 49), there are several instances of a type (fig. 50) that is also found on contemporary Pesarese maiolica jugs (fig. 51) and vases.[133] This similarity implies that these representations are not portraits, although in some cases they may have been accompanied

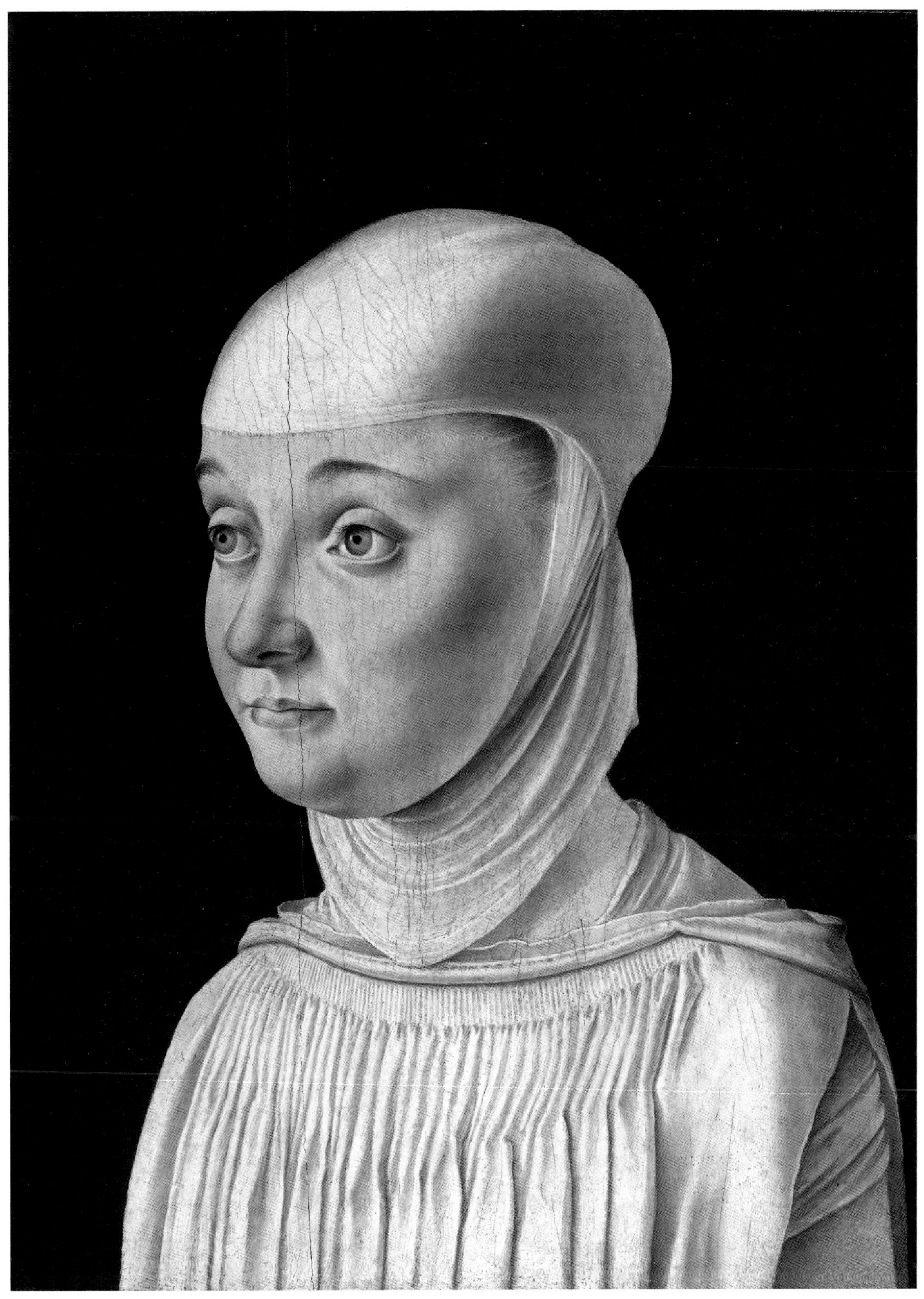

48 Jacometto Veneziano, *Portrait of a Woman, possibly a Novice of San Secondo,* ca. 1490, oil on wood, 24 × 17.5 cm ($9^{29}/_{64}$ × $6^{57}/_{64}$ in), Cleveland Museum of Art

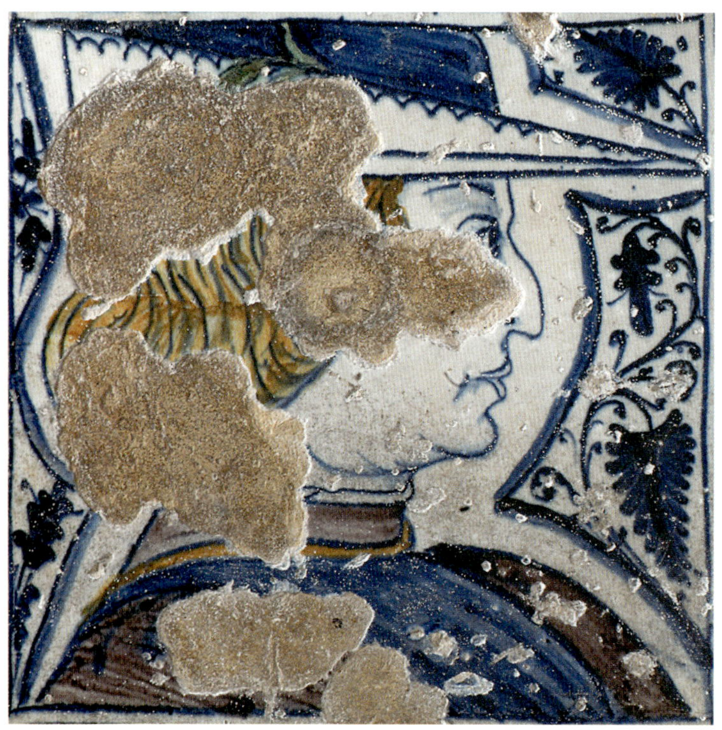

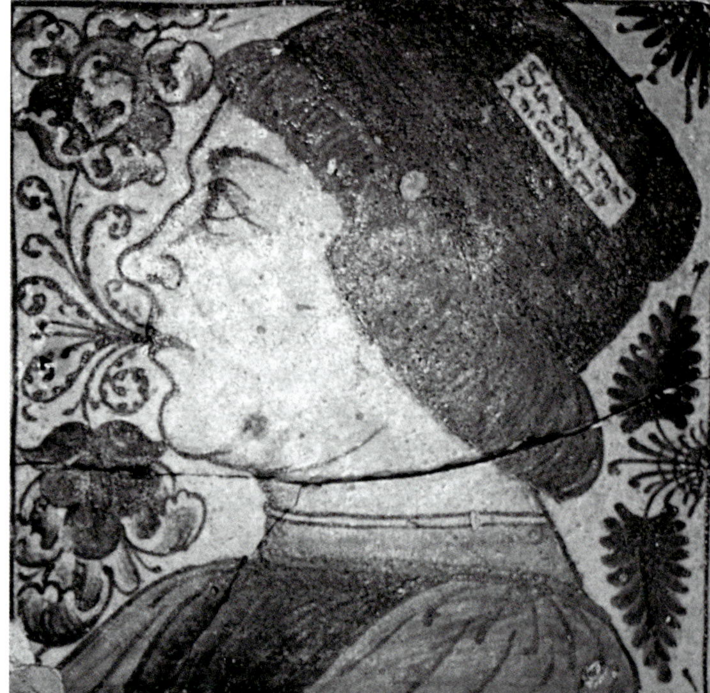

Above 49   Male head, after 1507, maiolica floor tile, 21 × 21 cm (8¼ × 8¼ in), Parma, Soprintendenza Belle Arti e Paesaggio per le Province di Parma e Piacenza

Right, top 50   Male head with inscription "to be delivered into Nicodemo's hands," 1470s, maiolica floor tile, 19 × 19.2 cm (7¾ × 7⅝ in), Parma, Galleria Nazionale

Right, bottom 51   Pharmacy jar with head of young boy, ca. 1470–80, Cambridge, Fitzwilliam Museum

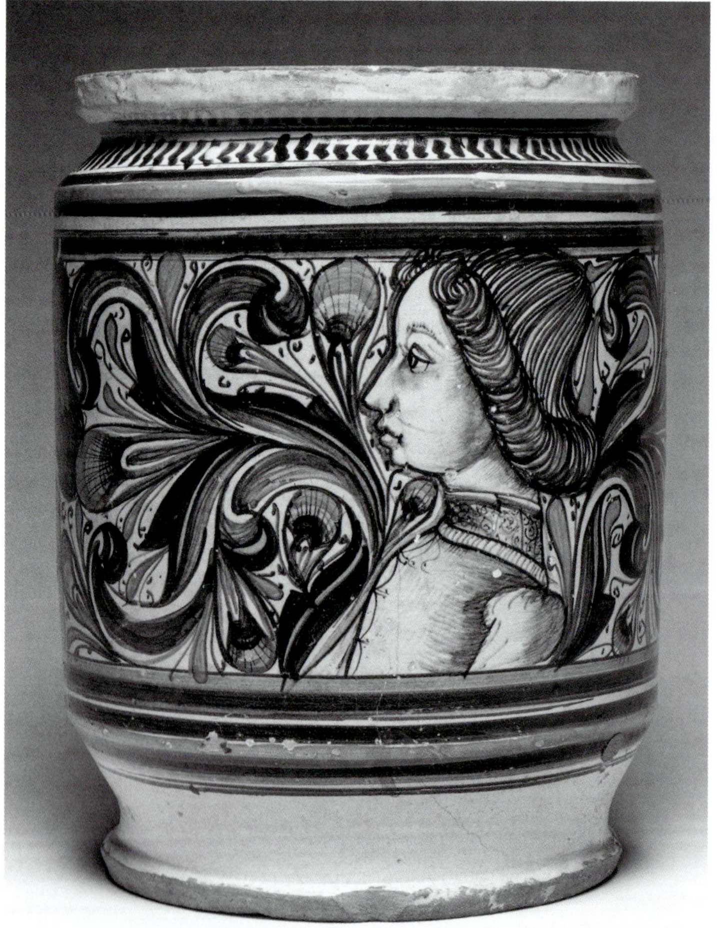

by proper names in Gothic letterings, such as those with "Bondi Pedro" (fig. 52) and "Bondi e Bonanno." Given the presence of a tile with Lucrezia Bergonzi's portrait, however, it would probably not be hazardous to assume that a few male images capture local gentlemen who are to be associated with the convent. As Bishop della Pergola's denunciation of 1457 confirms, a few lay male individuals had lodgings within San Paolo.

Another intriguing image is that of a youth in three-quarter view, whose agonized cry of love is synthesized in the "aime" lament (fig. 53) displayed on the banderole and echoed in his lovelorn expression. Hat-badge inscriptions on some male heads in profile record potential love messages like "to be delivered into Nicodemo's hands" (see fig. 50), "to be delivered into Zouano's hands" (*sia data in man a Nicodemo*; *sia data in mano a Zouano*), which are compre-

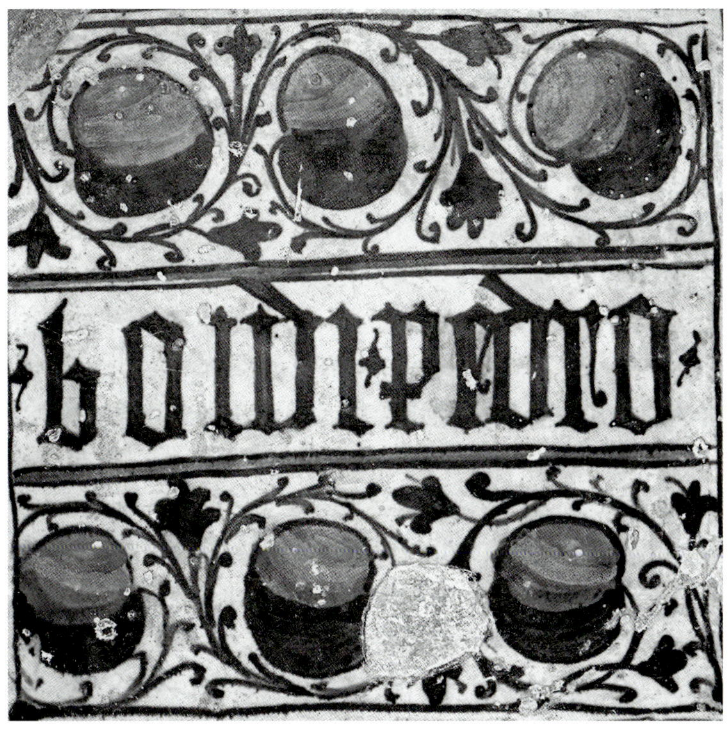

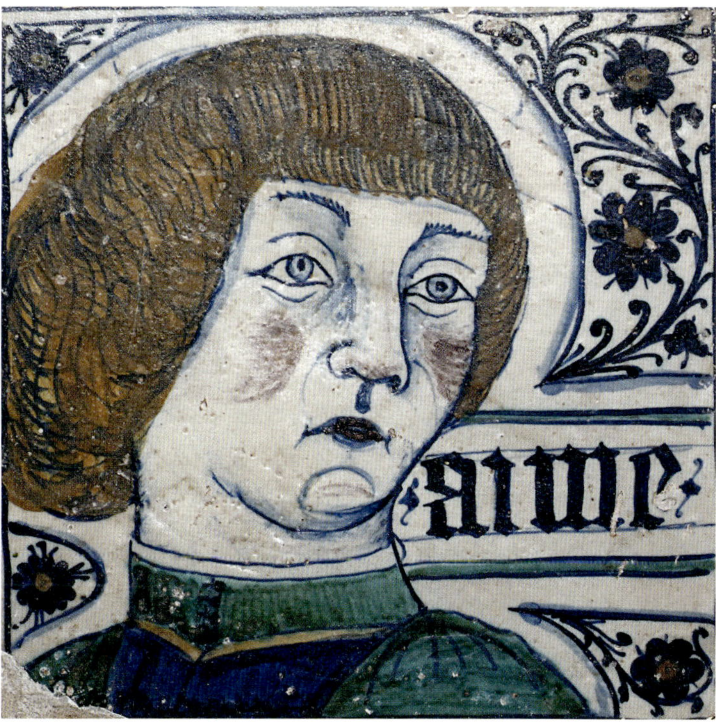

52   Gothic inscription "Bondi Pedro," 1470s, maiolica floor tile, 19 × 19.2 cm (7¾ × 7⅝ in), Parma, Galleria Nazionale

53   Lovelorn young man with Gothic inscription "aime," 1470s, maiolica floor tile, 19 × 19.3 cm (7¾ × 7⅓ in), Parma, Galleria Nazionale

hensible only within the games of courtesy and gift exchanges between lovers. What record would have been more playful and pleasurable to the nuns' downcast eyes than the semantics of love staged and fictionalized in the appealing heads on the floor tiles? The courtly poetic tradition of love from which these representations derive revolved not so much around intimacy or sexual relations, as idealization and imagination, transforming love into a liaison to be gained by individuals' special merits. As Niklas Luhmann remarked, symbolic communications should not "be confused with the circumstances in question . . . love as a medium is not itself a feeling, but rather a code of communication, according to the rules," through which these feelings are expressed and simulated.[134] Male and female heads on the tile surfaces fused together experiences of affection, beauty, and desire, as well as their reimagination and evocation, merging dialogues of fiction and reality for reflection by viewers. The repertoire of love metaphors on the tiles conspicuously includes ornamental cups filled with amorous motifs such as hearts pierced by arrows (fig. 54), cherries, grapes, and figs with their double messages of Christian and earthly love.

Courtly and chivalric culture informed the subjects of several other tiles featuring knights clad in elegant costumes or clothed in armor with helmets and lances shown astride their horses (fig. 55). Others feature imaginary warriors' heads (fig. 56), depending on the *teste divine* tradition (*all'antica* heads of warriors) of Verrocchio and Leonardo. The knights riding their horses on these surfaces are fashionable descendants of the heroes described in the courtly literature of love, adventures, and jousting of Arthurian tradition, which entered Italian vernacular literature with Matteo Maria Boiardo's *Orlando innamorato* (1482–3).[135] Occasioned by civic celebrations and festivities, tournaments were a notable feature of public life in fifteenth-century Italy and would have been familiar events to religious and lay spectators alike. Divided into brigades, youths were the protagonists of jousts and tournaments, displaying banners with insignia of love. Tournaments were as much manifestations of courtly love as theaters of power and masquerade.[136] In particular, engaging descriptions of tournaments are recounted in a popular romance entitled *Philogene Libro d'Arme e d'Amore* compiled by the local *litterato* Andrea Bajardi and published in Parma in 1507,

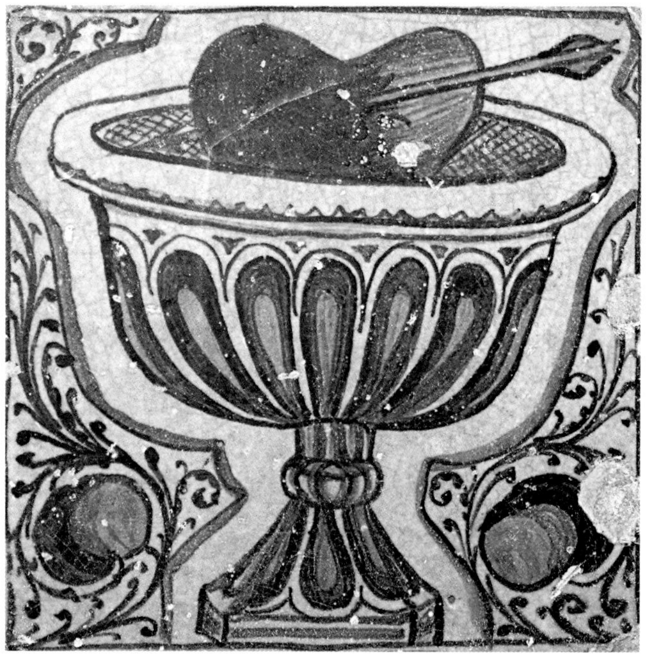

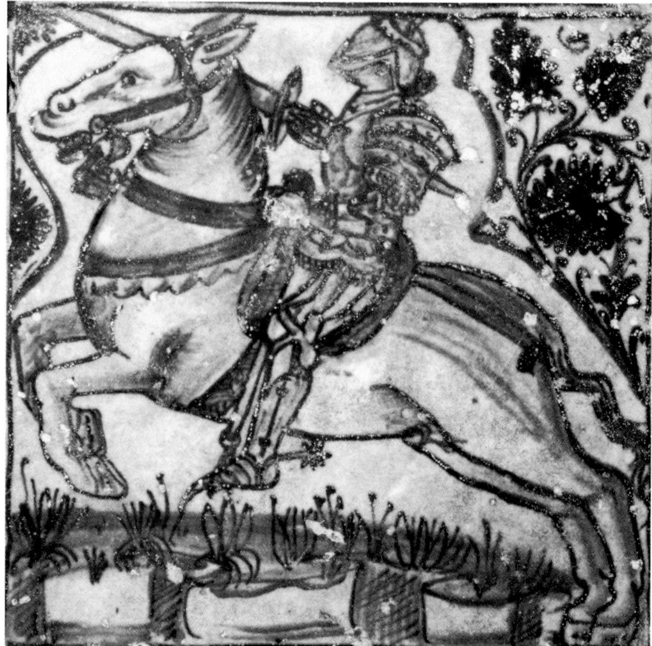

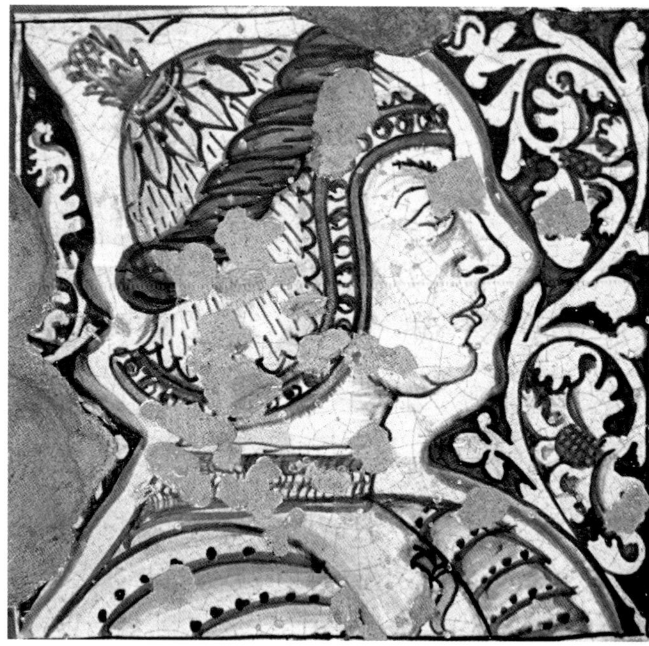

Above 54   Vase with heart pierced by arrow, 1470s, maiolica floor tile, 19 × 19.2 cm (7¾ × 7⅝ in), Parma, Galleria Nazionale

Right, top 55   Knight in armor, 1470s, maiolica floor tile, 19 × 19.2 cm (7¾ × 7⅝ in), Parma, Galleria Nazionale

Right 56   Head of a warrior, after 1507, maiolica floor tile, 21 × 21 cm (8¼ × 8¼ in), Parma, Galleria Nazionale

Facing page 57   Horse with Maria Benedetti's *stemma*, 1470s, maiolica floor tile, 19 × 19.2 cm (7¾ × 7⅝ in), Parma, Galleria Nazionale

narrating the mishaps of love between its protagonists, Adriano and Narcisa. Local readers would have been enthralled by Bajardi's account of a sumptuous train of knights in showy dress riding through the streets of Parma before a tournament.[137] The local chronicler, Leone Smagliati, records in similarly impressive detail the tournaments and other public festivities held from 1494 to 1518 in the city, including the *festa del balon* (ball game festival) that attracted crowds of citizens.[138]

Related to this courtly tradition, representations on other tiles include trotting horses, whose trappings feature Abbess Maria Benedetti's crest, a subject also repurposed in the variant of a page holding the reins of a groomed horse with the abbess's *stemma* (fig. 57). This display of Benedetti's arms as a kind of concealed portrait and as a marker of her patronage would have given viewers special pleasure. Such tiles speaking of the abbess's courtliness further associate the image with her right – like that of bishops and feudal

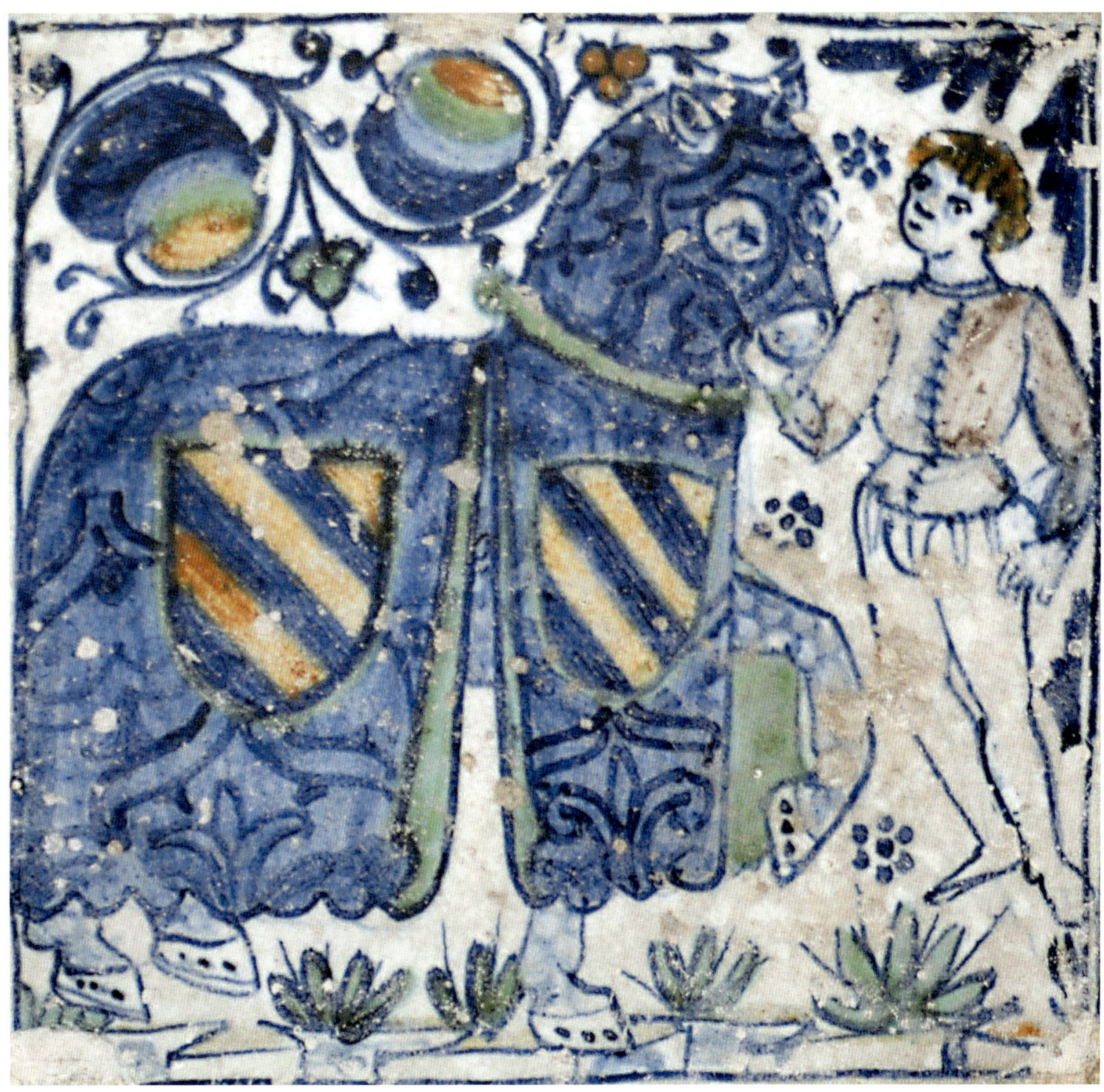

lords – to have well-equipped horses for visiting the convent's outlying properties. In addition, it could have been a reminder that wealthy monastic communities were meant to provide horsemen to cities for their defense. Perhaps only a select audience was aware that horses were among the gifts that Benedictine abbesses and bishops exchanged during symbolic marriage ceremonies, the culmination of bishops' solemn entry rites into cities. Standing for the Church, abbesses received the horse, an animal carrying noble, virile connotations of sexual prowess. Documentation from Florence, Pistoia, and Troyes relates these celebrations and their evolution through the late Middle Ages and Renaissance as bishops gradually curtailed abbesses' power and agency.[139] Markers of the abbess's self, and signifiers of the rights and rites in which she was a key player, the images on the tiles communicated messages and were symptoms of a courtly monastic visual culture, transforming conventual spaces into places of pleasure, ethical reflections, and disobedience.

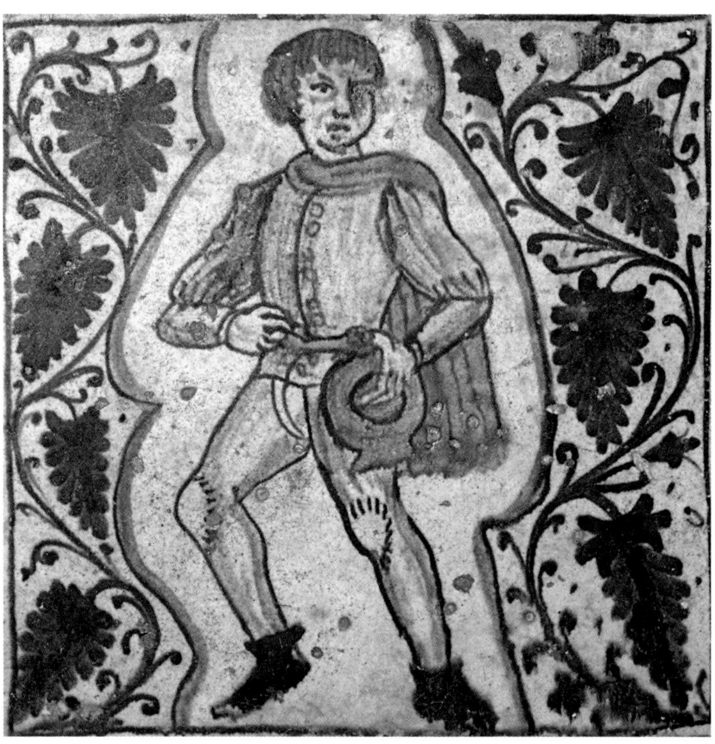

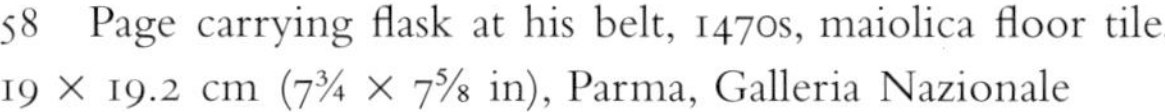

58 Page carrying flask at his belt, 1470s, maiolica floor tile, 19 × 19.2 cm (7¾ × 7⅝ in), Parma, Galleria Nazionale

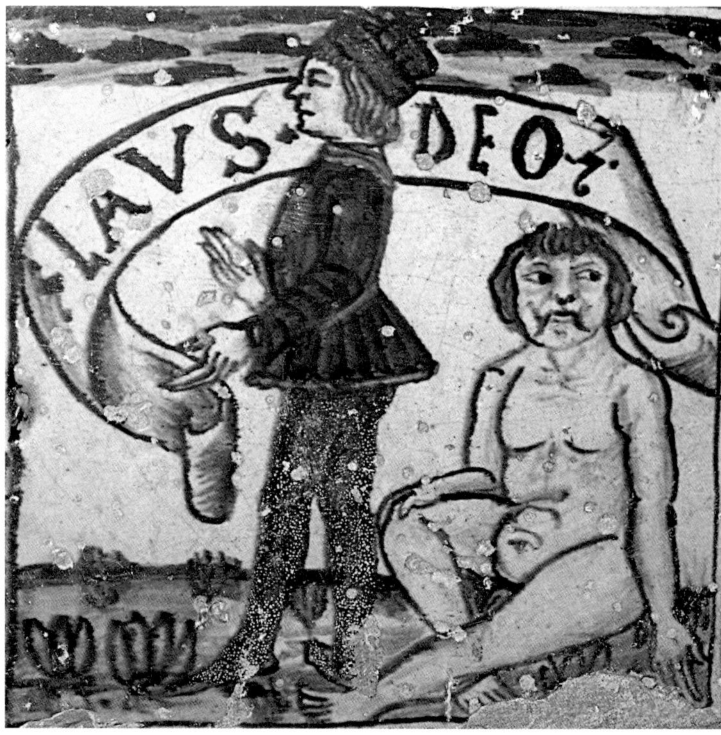

59 Two men and inscription "Laus Deo," 1470s, maiolica floor tile, 19 × 19.2 cm (7¾ × 7⅝ in), Parma, Galleria Nazionale

When crossing such an ornate pavement, one could not have but noticed tiles with male pages turning with sidelong glances and carrying flasks at their belts (fig. 58), holding swords, or accompanied by young men with whips. This body of images is known to have been derived from tarot cards, which were popular in the fifteenth century, and which comprised minor and major arcane cards, court cards, and trump cards with allegories. The earliest painted and printed tarot packs are associated with the courts of Milan, Pesaro, and Ferrara. Both Francesco and Alessandro Sforza owned lavishly decorated sets of tarot cards and their investments in them indicate that card playing was considered a courtly pastime to develop intellectual skills and self-control, and that it was deemed appropriate for rulers.[140] While playing cards were also a component of the training of elite women, this practice was seen as totally inappropriate for nuns. Cards, however, are often among the items confiscated by ecclesiastics from convents during the late Cinquecento.[141] The potters designing the San Paolo tiles must have been familiar either with the Sforza tarot set or with related sketches and prints in circulation since the mid-Quattrocento. Subjects from tarot cards were not uncommon for maiolica objects in general, but the numerous iconographic variations seen in

the San Paolo ensemble reinforce the impression of the pavement's rich semantic qualities and interpretative possibilities.

The pavement's festive flavor and the courtly world that it reflects and transmits would have engaged the nuns of San Paolo at multiple levels. It furthers the perception that they wanted to rule their secluded court as an alternative world to that which monastic strictures allowed – a world in which beauty, love, wisdom, and the contemplation of art were equally valued. Yet walking on the pavement would also have meant passing over representations of secular life. Indeed, while prayer and the perfection of their beings remained central to the lives of elite nuns, spirituality was practiced in parallel with imaginative journeys afforded by the absorption of art.[142] Few tiles capture the spirit of these multilayered experiences as does that depicting a finely dressed gentleman who stands while turning his back on a naked, seated figure (fig. 59). Their opposition could not be greater and alludes to the dichotomy between the refined world of urban civility and the arcadian world of primordial life, with the gentleman holding and pointing to the scroll that, by implication, praises God for lifting humankind out of its primitive savagery: *Laus Deo* (praise be to God).

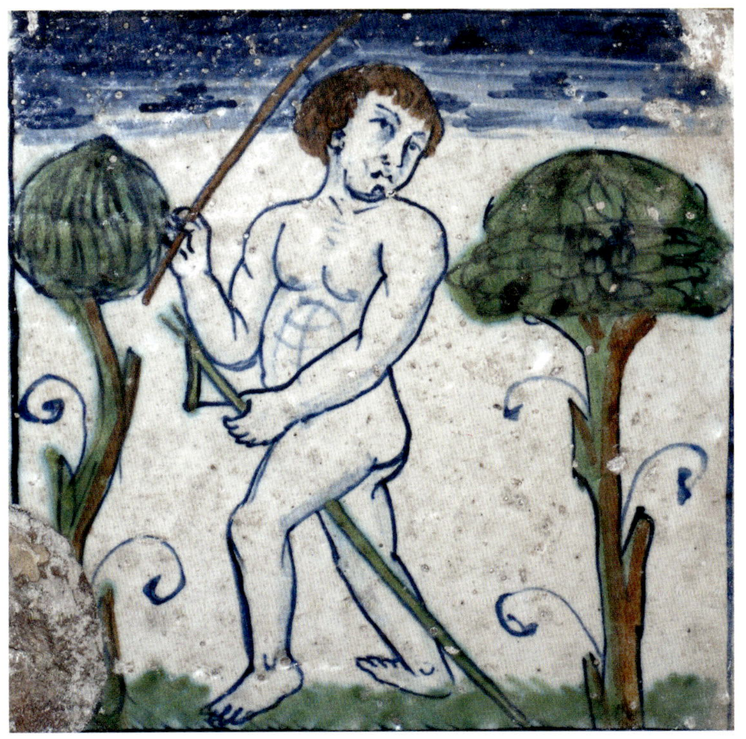

60 Putto on hobbyhorse, 1470s, maiolica floor tile, 19 × 19.2 cm (7¾ × 7⅝ in), Parma, Galleria Nazionale

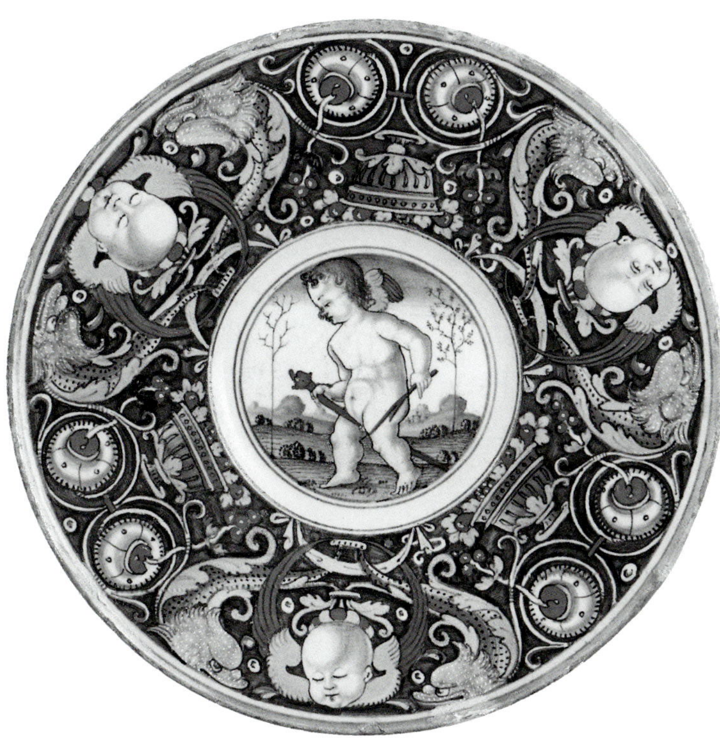

61 Plate with putto on hobbyhorse, ca. 1490, maiolica, Oxford, Ashmolean Museum

Playfulness, too, is recorded on tiles showing putti with games including one on a hobbyhorse staring at the beholder with a stick in his right hand (fig. 60). While the motif of putti at play is extremely common in Italian maiolica, less common is that of a putto glancing out at the viewer, seeking direct eye contact with those treading on the pavement. The putto's nudity and the hobbyhorse positioned almost as if he straddles it, carry sexual implications. Repeated on Pesarese maiolica plates dating from the 1490s to the 1510s (fig. 61), and on a tile originally from a floor in the Lando chapel (1510) in Venice's church of San Sebastiano, this motif embodies the earthly, sexual dimension of love played out in a landscape and almost seems to mock the tradition of knights' chivalric love.[143] A similarly ironic flavor characterizes the image with a castle in which women seem to be prisoners. From the castle's open portal a dog exits freely, while from the tower windows on either side appear two women with discontented expressions (fig. 62). Could this image be intended as a sardonic comment on the condition of women cloistered in buildings but with their chastity at risk, the doors open to potential intruders? The castle's door is left open to possible trespassers and is only guarded by a fierce-looking dog, challenging assur-

ances of confinement and strict separation among the sexes, and inviting viewers' perception and stimulation.

Along the same lines, several other tiles figure a young woman tying a man, naked except for a loincloth (see fig. 31), to a tree trunk. At the top, the Gothic letters read "non fare" (do not do this). Deriving from the Petrarchan tradition of love, this subject thematizes the tyranny of love, and the pain and vulnerability of lovers. This motif of the naked lover tied to a tree relates to the figure of Eros bound to a tree, thus incapacitated with respect to love. But the ambiguous tile scene also recalls an early Florentine engraving attributed to Baccio Baldini in which a woman has bound a lover to a tree and extracted his heart from his chest (fig. 63), an effective metaphor for the cruelty of love.[144] In the tile, if the woman is castigating her lover, the words contradict her act. Or is the male voice warning her not to proceed on such torture and humiliation?[145] However viewers may understand this representation, a woman freeing or imprisoning her lover, the point of view expressed by the command, whether in a male or female voice, remains elusive. In a basic way, the tile's message seems to be that lovers led by their passion are trapped by the bonds of love, its pleasure, and tyranny. Desiring and simultane-

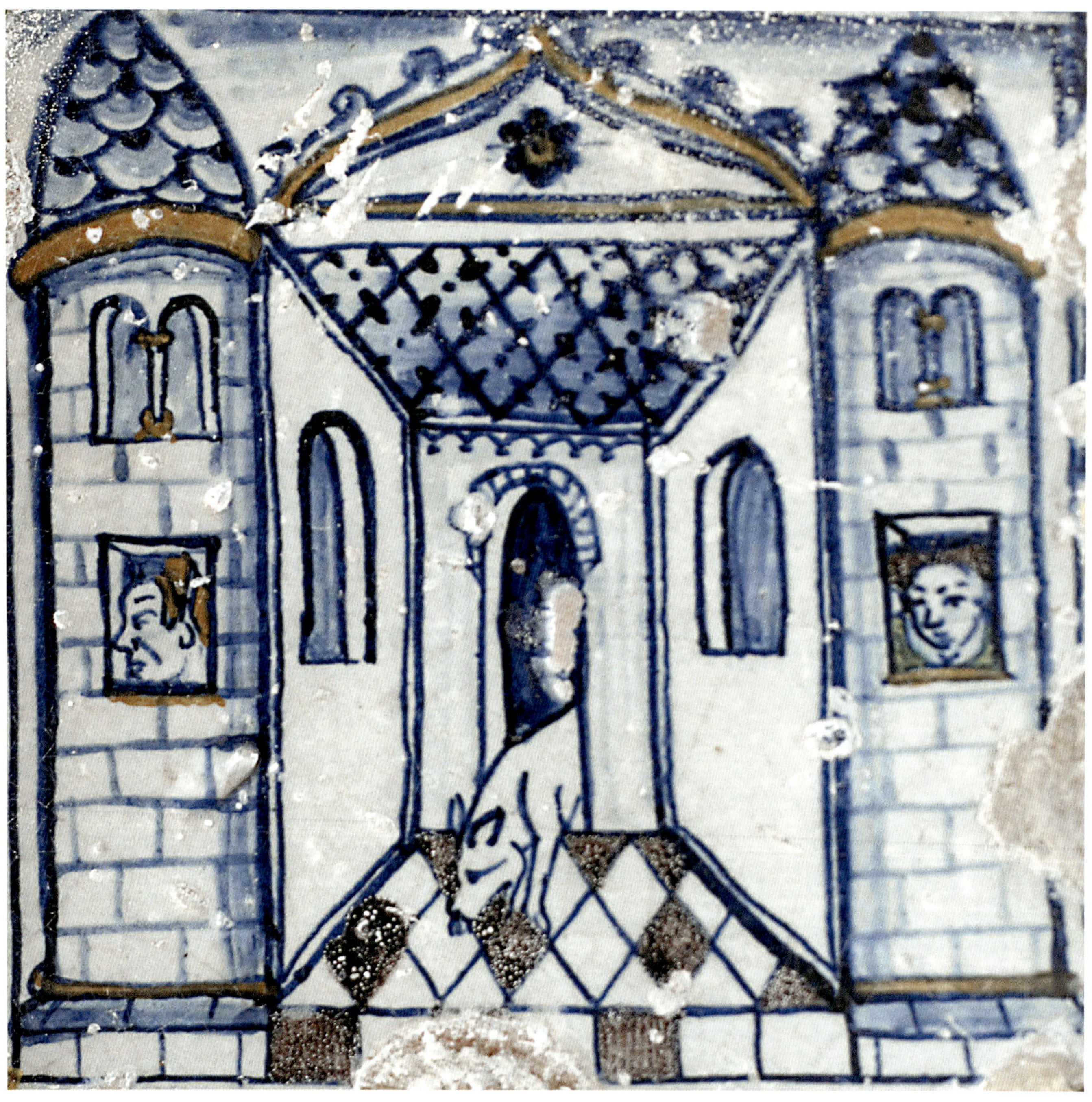

62   Women locked in a castle, 1470s, maiolica floor tile, 19.2 × 19.2 cm (7⅝ × 7⅝ in), Parma, Galleria Nazionale

ously fearing the emotions of love, this scene presents love as a burning passion and a cruelty, a sweet and a bitter story. Or it could be a suggestion to nuns to avoid the whole drama.

Laid horizontally on the floor, the colorful tiles drew viewers' eyes in multiple directions, with several twists and turns to engage actively with the richness of the pavement underfoot, its courtly fictions, and allegorical and moralizing messages. Spectators encountered tiles depicting young girls with a unicorn or a dog, images that stand for notions of virginity and fidelity, virtues to which in the Renaissance women were urged to aspire, and which must have had a particular appeal to an audience of nuns. In addition, representations of beautiful women gazing at

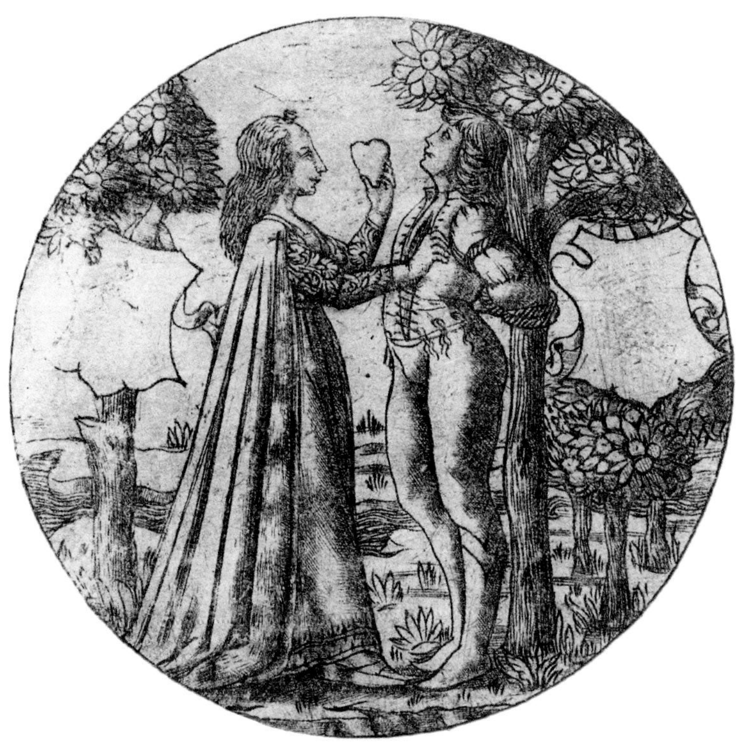

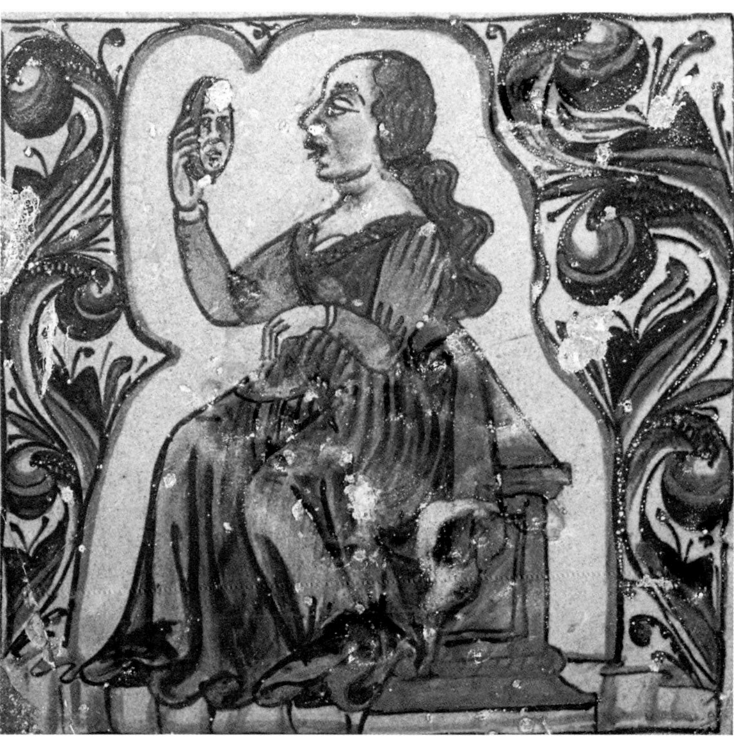

63 Baccio Baldini, attr., *Cruelty of Love*, ca. 1465–80, engraving, d. 10.1 cm (3³¹/₃₂ in), London, Trustees of the British Museum

64 Young woman gazing at herself in a mirror, 1470s, maiolica floor tile, 19 × 19.2 cm (7¾ × 7⅝ in), Parma, Galleria Nazionale

themselves in mirrors could either be seen as reflecting notions of lust, vanity, deception, and idleness, or could have evoked more positive ideals, such as trust and prudence. Mirrors in fact were interpreted in dramatically different ways depending on the context in which they appeared. They were intended, for example, as signs of love's faithfulness in the *Roman de la dame à la licorne* (the Lady and the Unicorn, ca. 1350), where women's self-gaze in the mirror signaled their perpetual love.[146] On the tile surface, the female figure mirroring herself and holding a compass in her left hand (fig. 64) instead points to the virtue of prudence, reflecting a paradigm of Christian wisdom recommended in monastic life. The iconographic richness of the floor tiles encompasses multiple registers that spoke to nuns about their virtues, imagined identities, and misdemeanors. To modern viewers, in contrast, they speak of a sophisticated courtly monastic culture, its ideals of spiritual nourishment and relaxation, and the kinaesthetic experience of this art form that, while freeing the mind from the challenges that a confined existence brought about, also commented on monastic obligations and reinterpreted the very architectural space that it defined. The power of vision, bodily movement, and intensified scrutiny

are the privileged vehicles of the enjoyment of the floor decorations, and simultaneously the affirmation of the courtly culture that they evoke and assert.

Looking down and walking across the pavement, beholders took in themes of love and beauty, including the mythological stories of Pyramus and Thisbe and the Judgment of Paris from Ovid's *Metamorphoses* and Virgil's *Aeneid*. Occupying the entire tile surface, these subjects could be enjoyed with particular effectiveness by onlookers familiar with their classical sources. Rules forbade nuns from reading either epics or romances, but these texts circulated in convents, as is confirmed by inventories of nuns' personal belongings.[147] The Ovidian story of Pyramus and Thisbe recounts the tragic love and death of a pair of ancient lovers. Pyramus commits suicide because he wrongly believes his beloved Thisbe has been killed by a lion.[148] When Thisbe finds the dead Pyramus, she impales herself on the same sword as her lover. The pottery painter who rendered the figures on the tile in a crude perspectival setting (fig. 65) made the protagonists look away from each other, as if to indicate that their contrasted love was an affair to be avoided. The Pyramus and Thisbe myth is about a disastrous love that ends in death, with onlookers con-

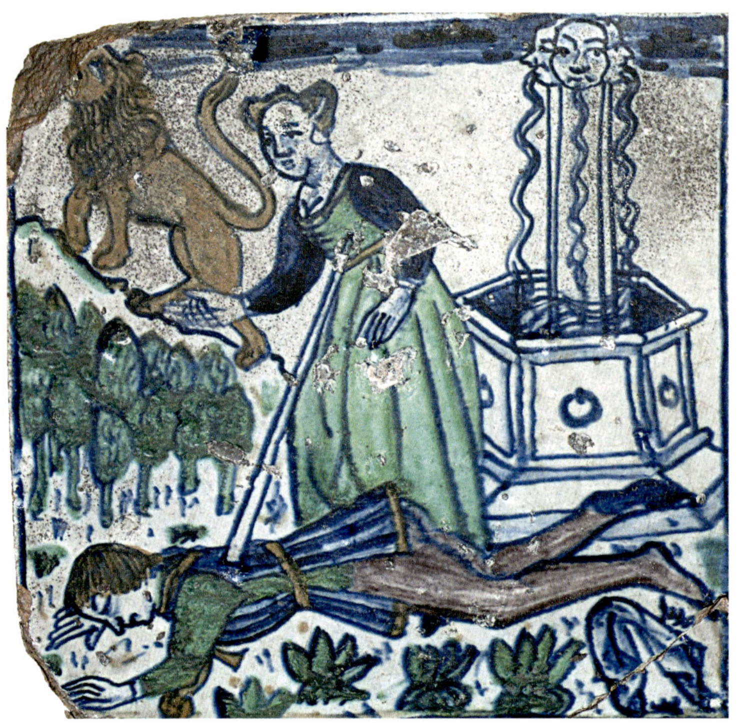

65 Pyramus and Thisbe, 1470s, maiolica floor tile, 19 × 19.4 cm (7¾ × 7⅓ in), Parma, Galleria Nazionale

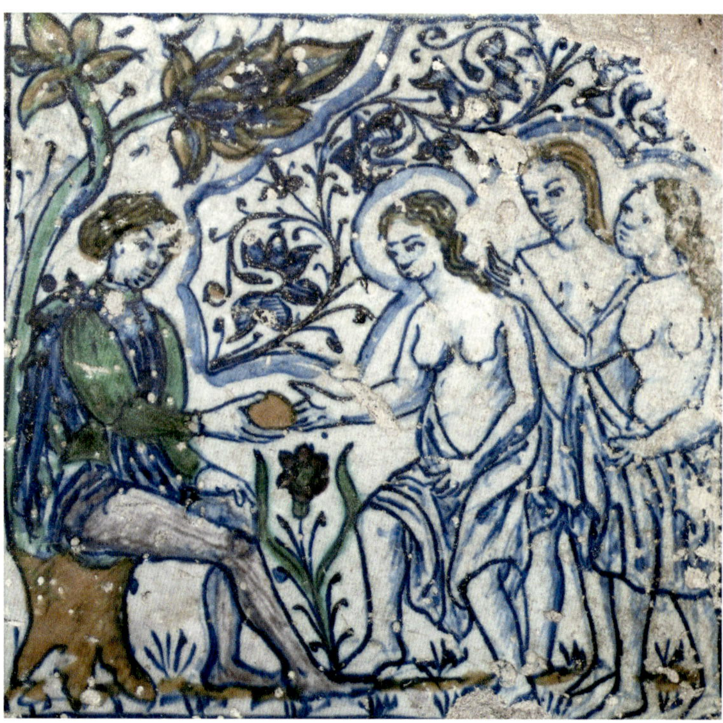

66 Judgment of Paris, 1470s, maiolica floor tile, 19 × 19.1 cm (7¾ × 7⁴⁄₆ in), Parma, Galleria Nazionale

fronting the reality that illegal or adverse love affairs often have negative outcomes. In Sabadino degli Arienti's *Gynevera de le clare donne* (ca. 1492) the tale of Pyramus and Thisbe's suicide is an occasion for a moral lesson on the tragic end of disobedient conduct.[149]

The *Judgment of Paris* (fig. 66) depicts the familiar story of the shepherd Paris who, when asked to select the loveliest from among three goddesses, Venus, Juno, and Minerva, chose the divine Venus, the personification of love.[150] The myth is the beginning of the history of Troy and its destruction, thus also a story linked to a tragic outcome. Seated on the left, the handsome Paris, dressed as an aristocratic knight, gazes at the three goddesses whose garments expose their breasts but not their pudenda. He has already chosen the foremost, Venus, to whom he hands the golden apple. The rest of the tile field is decorated with palmettes and flowers, standard motifs in Pesarese pottery of the late Quattrocento. These potters certainly used printed sources for rendering these mythological scenes, copying their models and adding the brilliant colors permitted by the maiolica medium.[151]

Exotic and fantastic animals such as lions, leopards, camels, and dragons, appear on the tiles, as well as the more domestic repertoire of rabbits, dogs, tortoises, birds (fig. 67), stags, fish, and swans. In general, each animal occupies the entire tile surface, though in some cases they are distributed in multiples. Animal representations could have been seen as carriers of specific meanings derived from the tradition of medieval bestiaries, or combined with other subjects to convey broader messages, as has been proposed for the Vaselli pavement in Bologna's San Petronio.[152] Conversely, the large number of tiles with peacocks and Gothic foliage patterns confirms that these elements either served as borders around the floorings, or were used as fillers to create pauses between tiles with different subjects. In addition, numerous tiles show inscriptions of adages and popular wisdom sayings including "Per ben far" (to do well), "Chi ben fa, ben ha" (he who does well, receives good [things]), "Aspetto il tempo" (I wait for the moment), which probably commented on particular figural themes or enhanced certain communications, thus inviting beholders to engage with and enjoy the floor.[153] On one tile, the saying "Sola Fides" (faith alone), figuratively illustrated by the clasped-hands motif (fig. 68), proposes a basic word–image nexus of trust and faith, a popular ensemble that reappears on Pesarese maiolica jars

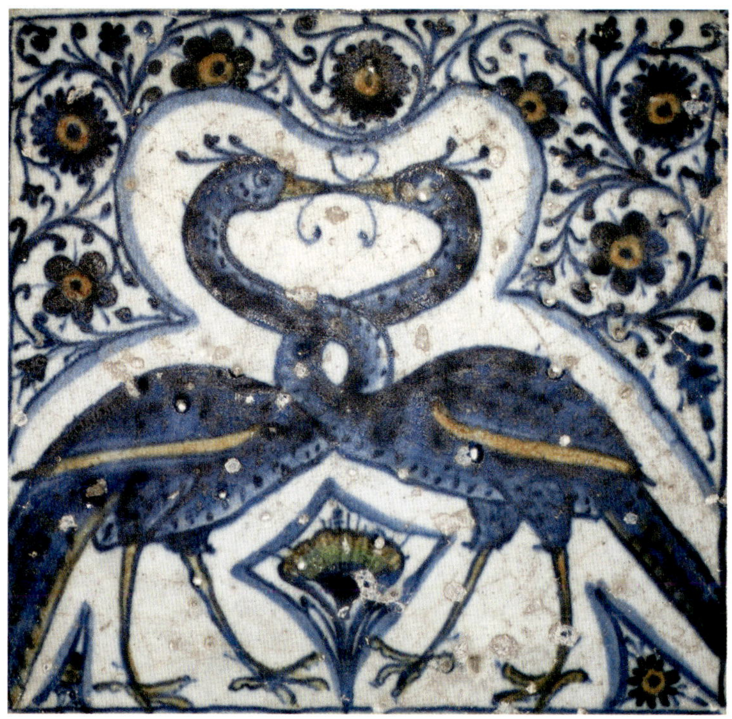

67   Birds, 1470s, maiolica floor tile, 19.2 × 19.4 cm
(7⁵/₈ × 7¹/₃ in), Parma, Galleria Nazionale

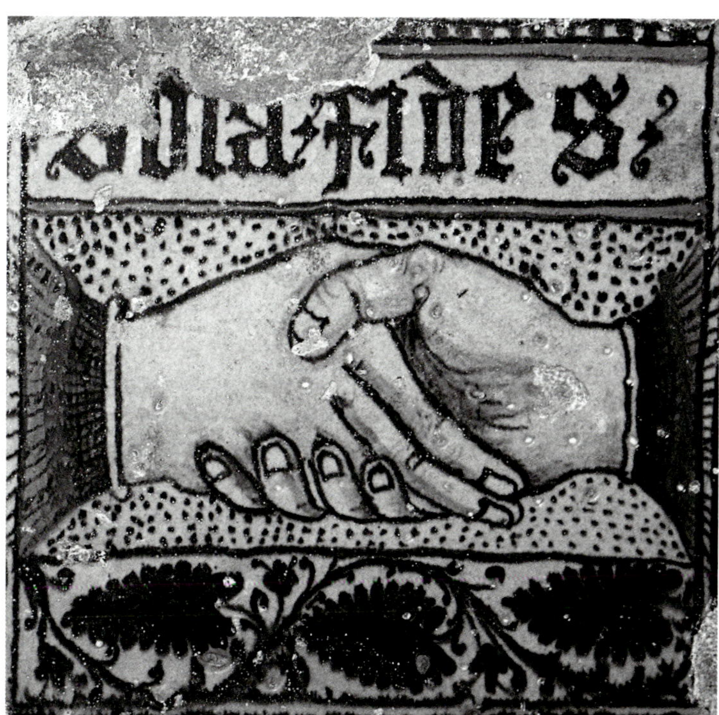

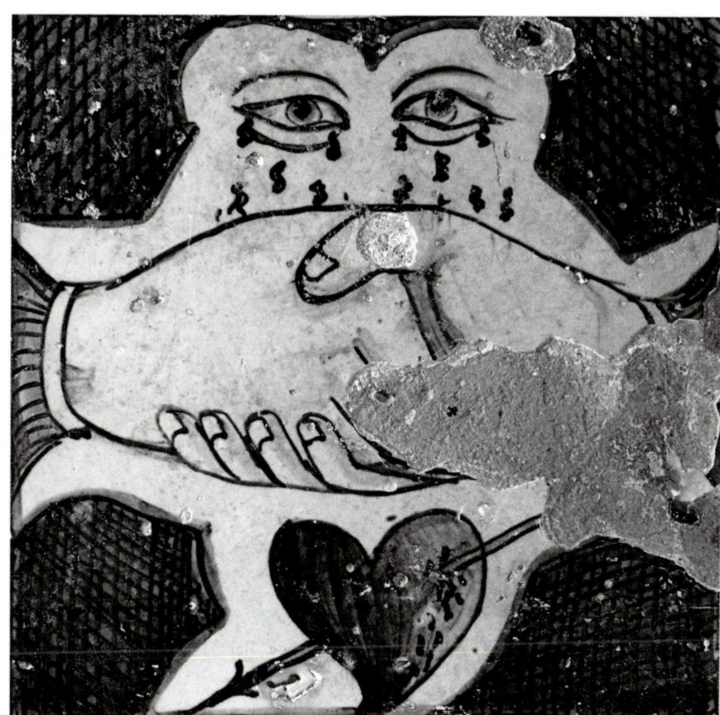

of the 1470s, the Lando chapel tiled floor, and elsewhere. A similar, slightly more complex verbal-visual conceit on sight, trust, and love is represented by the rebus on another tile displaying a vertical alignment of eyes, clasped hands, and a heart pierced by arrows (fig. 69), enticing beholders to pause and scrutinize the splendid floor as they moved across it.[154]

Ornate maiolica tiled floors formulated strong responses to monastic discourses of female passivity and humility, deprivation and obedience, reclaiming the phenomenology of gaze and touch as a means to access the world. The tile decorations recreated conventual spaces for experiences of delight, tactile pleasure, and ethical nourishment, transforming floors into artworks that spectators traversed and viewed back and forth in a circuit of endless beginnings and endings. Both the engaging maiolica tiles and the rather more sober imagery of the frescoes of Jacopo Loschi communicate meanings and memories of an elite secluded world, constituting crucial examples of the courtly conventual visual culture that developed in Renaissance Italy. By the late fifteenth century, elite convents had metamorphosed into courtly *cités des femmes* that proposed renewed intersections of their inhabitants' agency and the art objects surrounding them.

Top 68   Inscription "Sola Fides," 1470s–after 1507, maiolica floor tile, 21 × 21 cm (8¼ × 8¼ in), Parma, Galleria Nazionale

Above 69   Visual rebus, after 1507, 21 × 21 cm (8¼ × 8¼ in), Parma, Soprintendenza Belle Arti e Paesaggio per le Province di Parma e Piacenza

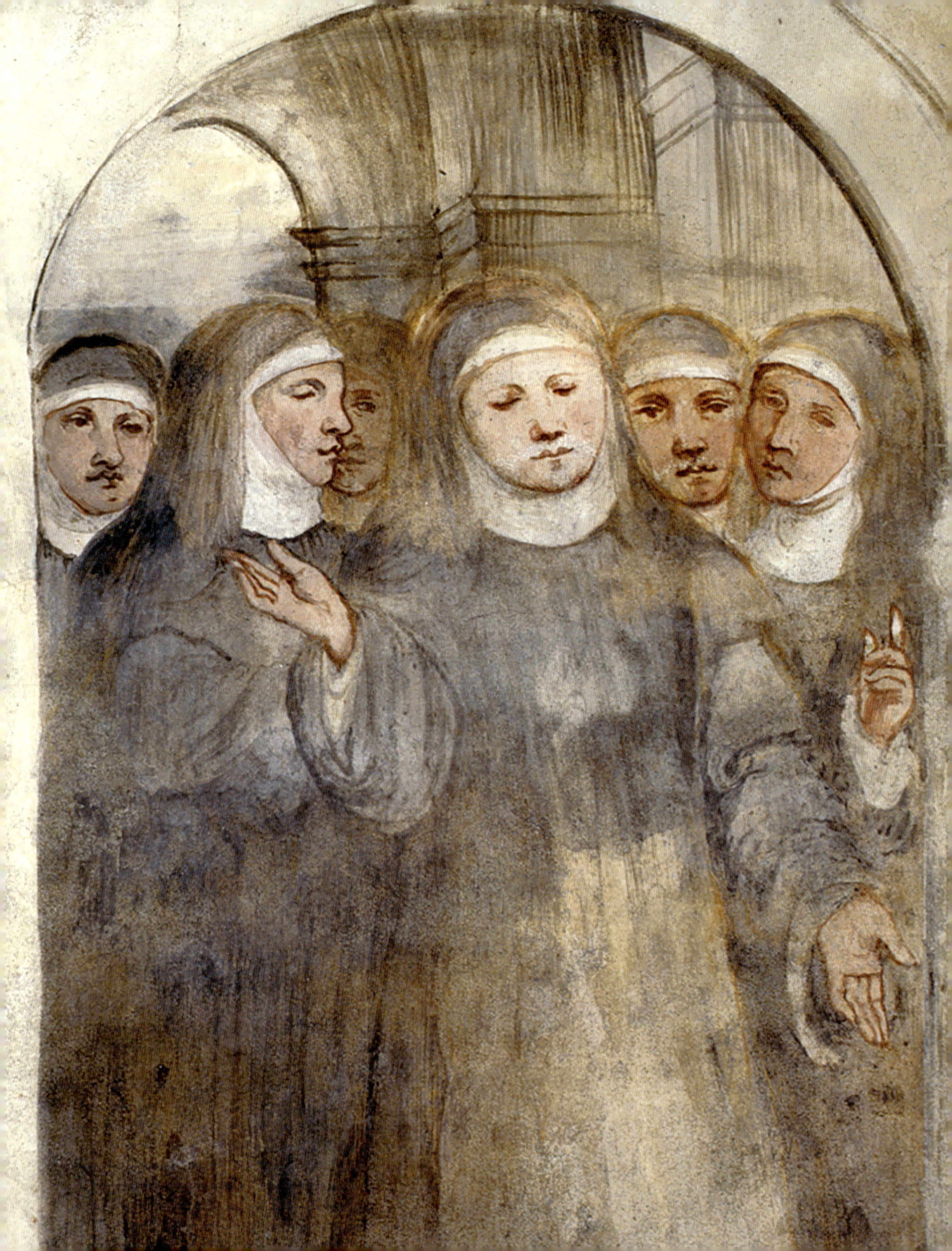

3
Art, Contemplation, and Splendor

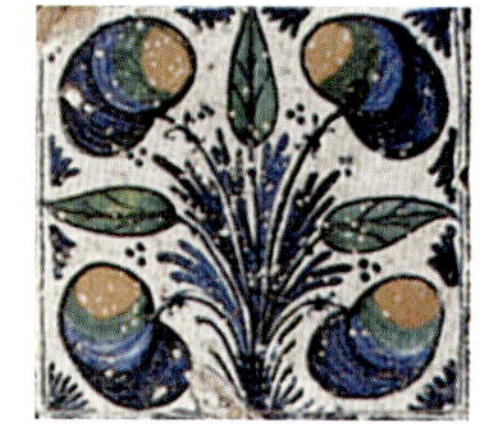

In a letter addressed to the prioress of San Domenico in Pisa, dating to 1493, the outspoken Dominican friar Girolamo Savonarola admonishes nuns to live in simple, unadorned cells "with no surplus," and to pursue a life of prayer and penitence in imitation of Christ.[1] Savonarola condemned the secularized lifestyle of his peers and their sumptuous possessions that distanced them from the contemplative, ascetic spiritual values typical of early monasticism. Erasmus echoes the same concern in one of his colloquies of the 1520s, where the protagonist wonders "what possible excuse there could be for those who spend so much money on building, decorating, and enriching churches that there is simply no limit to it."[2] Both Savonarola and Erasmus knew well that aristocratic nuns' cells and their churches were places whose fine embellishments and furnishings negotiated and encapsulated religious women's spirituality, their noble status, and liminal continuity to the outside society. Nuns' cells projected the wealth and intimate world of their inhabitants, while their decorated choirs indexed the role of sacred art as an agent of devotion and meditation.

In the early sixteenth century, the role of Christian art in stimulating religious practices faced renewed scrutiny as part of the contentions between Protestant reformers and Catholics. Although upper-class nuns did not participate in this debate directly, they could not remain totally untouched. Some became increasingly concerned with the beauty, illusionistic nature, and effects on the viewer of the sacred images they commissioned for their monastic settings, which were seen more as manifestations of artistic virtuosity and engines of the imagination than tools of spiritual communication. The Lombard artists Girolamo Romanino and Bernardino Luini, who worked for reformed Benedictine female communities, executed frescoes that engaged the viewer in forms of meditative experience, and simultaneously stimulated reflections on the mediating nature of painting itself. These works and the precious objects that nuns kept in their cells enhanced the process of "aristocratization" that transformed convents into sites of material and devotional splendor.[3] To understand the implications of this corpus, I first discuss the few surviving ornaments known to have adorned nuns' cells (fragments of fine maiolica objects and a frescoed frieze). Then I shall consider Romanino and Luini's murals in churches in Brescia and Milan, works that inscribe nuns within their subjects, turning the women's invisibility into a tangible presence to trigger beholders' empathetic reactions, and reflecting on the ontological status of the image that represents what is secluded and obscured. Finally, the finely crafted wood intarsia choirstalls produced in early sixteenth-century Parma will be addressed, suggesting how even furnishings could be a source of pride for their patrons and, at the same time, of rivalry among local religious communities. As a whole, each set of these works is seen to negotiate and transmit the views and agency of artists, nuns, and onlookers, and their concerns of devotion and artistry, spirituality and refinement, visibility and invisibility. But this corpus also constituted a phenomenology of media and materials that enriched conventual spaces, making what art represents all the more physically present to the viewer's gaze and touch.[4] These works ultimately dramatize sets of opposing values – spiritual and worldly discourses, ideals of contemplation and ambition – that speak of the complex functions that images and material artifacts played in elite conventual environments of the Italian Renaissance.

NUNS' CELLS: PRIVACY AND MATERIALS

In accordance with the Council of Trent's decree on consecrated individuals (1563), the bishop of Parma, Ferrante Farnese, visited local monastic institutions in 1579 and prohibited, among other things, any future installation of elaborate fireplaces or depictions of families' arms on the walls and doors of nuns' cells. Extant embellishments and devices were only tolerated, he writes, "out of compassion for nuns' inanity."[5] Cells were filled with all kinds of vain adornments, Bishop Farnese continued. What are the useless ornaments that the bishop refers to? What was it about this practice that he so deprecates? As a Tridentine ecclesiastic, Bishop Farnese well knew that patrician nuns' cells or apartments had been inhabited by generations of women from the same family, and had therefore long been marked by family arms.[6] Cells were repositories of both status and monetary wealth, and were manifestations of nuns' ownership. Purchased with family capital, such cells did not return to the convent at a nun's death but were managed as real estate property, at the owners' disposal to be passed down or sold.[7] Bishop Farnese's condemnation of the futile artifacts adorning cells as inappropriate to the spirit of devotion associated with such sites, speaks of the reality of cells as places of *otium* and leisure. Weaving together visual and documentary sources, the following discussion traces the contrasting perceptions of the decorated cell expressed by rigid pre- and post-Tridentine ecclesiastics like Bishop Farnese, on the one hand, and by the more open-minded Counter-Reformation art writer Giovanni Battista Armenini (ca. 1533–1609), on the other, articulating the fine line that existed between excess and the functional component of nuns' ornamented cells in the

eyes of their historical viewers. Adorned cells further are seen to have negotiated the entanglements between the enclosed life of nuns and of their portable objects whose precious textures enveloped nuns' existence from the very moment of their entry into convents.[8]

Warmed by fireplaces (which allowed for cooking), cells were the places for nuns to retire to pray, have private meals, sleep, and even to receive guests. The fine maiolica tableware and glass objects recently excavated in an area once occupied by the Benedictine convent of Sant'Antonio in Polesine in Ferrara are remarkably revealing examples of the material culture of Renaissance aristocratic religious communities. Built between 1258 and 1268 with funds supplied by the marquis Azzo Novello d'Este to house his daughter Beatrice, the convent of Sant'Antonio was inhabited for centuries by cultivated, noble nuns.[9] Albeit in fragments, the recovered early sixteenth-century Faientine maiolica plates featuring amatory subjects and female heads originally adorned nuns' *credenze* and tables.[10] Fragmented incised slipware (*ceramica graffita*) jugs and dishes with figural decoration of Ferrarese production have also resurfaced. This maiolica corpus confirms the domestic opulence of patrician nuns' tables, testifying that cloistered women shared with their lay sisters outside the *claustrum* the same material culture of refinement, spending, and consumption as imperative and desirable markers of status.

In addition to domestic items, cells were filled with fine devotional objects, books, and other precious possessions that nuns could bequeath to whomever they wished. Referring to German medieval institutions, Jeffrey Hamburger has perspicaciously observed that "private possessions . . . were at least as common as the sermons, treatises, and Rules that admonish against them."[11] Depicting the *Dream of St. Ursula* in 1495, Vittore Carpaccio shows the princess St. Ursula's bedroom as a spacious chamber with marble door frames, glass windows, a canopy bed, antique gilded bronze statuary, maiolica flower vases, and a corner study furnished with a writing desk, stool, and an open bookshelf (fig. 70). This interior, albeit not a monastic but a well-appointed Venetian-style lay woman's bedroom, offers a glimpse into the world of comfort, study, and refinement that patrician nuns could have afforded in their cells.[12] Its material richness is probably not dissimilar to that captured in the posthumous inventory of Abbess Lucrezia Matina (d. 1521) from the Benedictine convent of Santa Margherita in Polizzi (Palermo). Among the items owned by the mother superior were several Flemish carpets, a finely illuminated prayerbook, and a silver crucifix and saltcellar.[13]

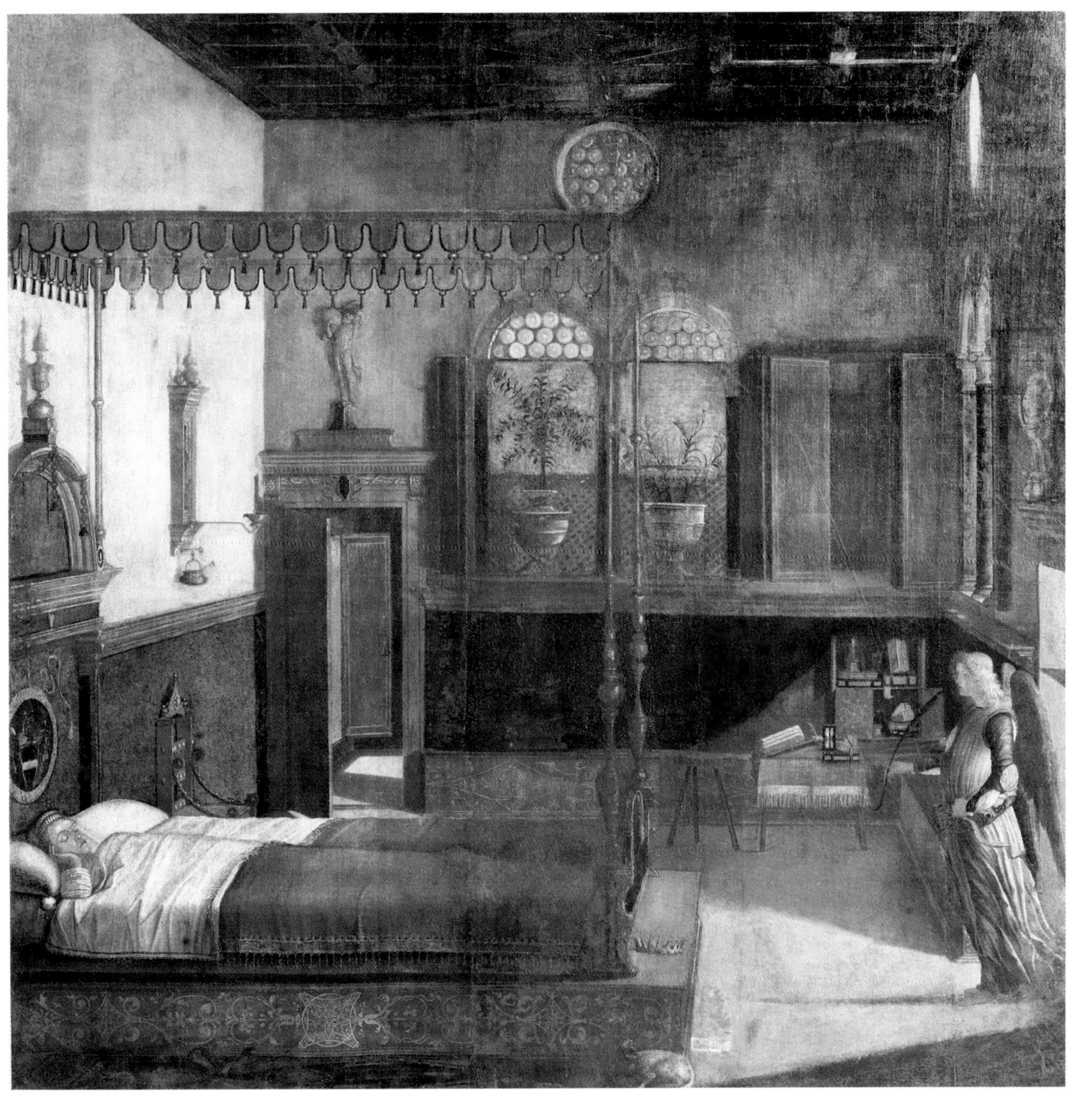

70   Carpaccio, *Dream of St. Ursula*, 1495, oil on canvas, 274 × 267 cm (107$^7/_8$ × 105$^1/_8$ in), Venice, Accademia

"Indecorous" objects – including books of romance and epic literature, painted nude figures, mirrors, cards, and dice – were discovered by Tridentine clerics in the cells of Bolognese nuns in 1576.[14] The most compelling record regarding such illicit possessions, however, concerns the nun Giulia Caracciolo from Sant'Arcangelo a Bajano in Naples. In her rooms, in 1577, the vicar found furnishings ornamented with ebony and ivory, pictures with mythological subjects (Cephalus, Diana, and Endymion), refined carvings, marble busts, crystal vases, a mirror that reflected objects twice life-size, a guitar, a Persian carpet, and still other fine items of exquisite work. The cleric reprimanded the nun for cherishing such forbidden artifacts, but Giulia did not remain silent and passive, instead responding that she was

of noble parentage and was segregated in the convent without rights and against her wishes. Why should she not enjoy a few "innocent objects" in her rooms? And she continued:

> "You, minister of Heaven, you come here to commit cruelties beyond my family's savagery, you who preach charity come here to take away from a wretched woman a last and frivolous illusion and to remind us of a cruel and harsh fact: that age in which [because] we had no capacity to know worldly things, they [our parents] tricked us into renouncing our life."[15]

No doubt, Giulia felt entitled to enjoy the "innocent" objects she owned, and that they were neither indecorous nor vain.[16] Rather, she saw them as appropriate manifestations of her social status and as compensation for her secluded life. The works denoted something more, however, than their physical presence. Gazing at works of art with profane subjects and finely wrought objects gave solace, as if the pictures, their aesthetic appeal, materials, and tactile qualities could almost substitute for the earthly delight of which Giulia was deprived. As artifacts of secular content and material preciosity they created multiple effects: that of the mimetic fiction that paintings represented, and those of the vibrant materials, effects that all served to activate the imagination and transport the mind.

The Neapolitan ecclesiastic regarded Giulia's possessions as dangerous and scandalous intrusions of the forbidden outside world into the seclusion of the convent, artifacts that had the power to raise emotions and propel the mind into endless journeys and distractions. In contrast, the nun referred to her objects as "innocent" items. Even after her cherished possessions were transferred to the convent they retained evocative qualities and agency, as if they brought with them their own secular implications.[17] They were repositories of stories and textures, animation and intentions, that could efface the crude reality of the unwanted life Giulia was forced to lead. Regardless of the styles and forms of the artworks, they were owned by the nun as property and enjoyed as objects with nobler values than their strictly economic ones. They established sentimental connections with the viewer through their subjects and materials. Their contemplation blurred distinctions between reality and fiction, intentionality and functionality, impressing their narratives and features in the nun's mind and invoking emotional responses. It is easy to imagine that a few of Giulia's (prohibited) possessions were part of her dowry or were given to her by relatives. The mobility of fine objects, their profane narratives, textures, and agency do not sit well with nuns' enclosure, or with monastic strictures. Refined artworks expanded the boundaries of nuns' cells and gave their inhabitants access to the outside world. Linking the separated realities of the spiritual and material spheres, they therefore complicate our understanding of their intersections and values.

Embellished cells were not merely characterized in negative terms, though, during the period. Even among the clergy there were those who expressed more support than the rigid Neapolitan vicar would have admitted. The painter-cleric Giovanni Battista Armenini wrote clearly about the didactic function of art in nuns' rooms in his *De' veri precetti della pittura* of 1587. In accordance with the Counter-Reformation's approach to sacred images, Armenini describes religious art as an aid for deepening devotees' faith and spirituality, and as an instrument of meditation and contemplation. Sacred art of charming beauty, in particular, is said to be appropriate to nuns' cells to incite their sincere expressions of faith. Armenini further states that frescoes are the proper media for enclosed women, whereas movable canvases transferable to different houses are more suitable to itinerant friars.[18] Media and materials therefore prove relevant to Armenini's reasoning, making the connection between the stationary nature of frescoes and nuns' enclosure apparent. Armenini goes on to suggest a list of subjects obviously suitable to nuns' quarters, that is, representations from the life of the Virgin, the Passion of Christ, and female saints. But, more importantly, he adds that images should be executed by talented masters and, most significantly, be pleasing to the eye. He recommends images of emotional appeal that would "dispose them [the nuns] to suffer all the more and would arouse in them a passionate sense of charity and divine love."[19] Armenini advocates charming art of simple, straightforward content, depicting female protagonists as the most appropriate means to arouse nuns' devotional sentiments, stressing his belief in the power of lovely art to create somatic effects in believers. According to Armenini, pleasing images are works not only to be beheld but also to be absorbed in order to liberate the viewer's emotional responses. Their efficacy ultimately depended on the artist's skill in making the devotional message tangible and real to the beholder. Armenini further reports that clumsy art by mediocre masters is detrimental to activating feelings of piety, thereby recognizing the importance of the aesthetic experience of art:

> It is certain that works by clumsy painters move nuns in their simplicity to laughter and to lascivity, whereas works of emotional appeal would touch the depth of their hearts. Then, in monastic spaces, either private or communal rooms, I should want the painted figures to be clothed very modestly and their inventions woven with purity and devotion, reserving the grandiose display of variety and styles for those places that are magnificent and grand.[20]

Despite the criticism expressed by Protestant reformers on the appeal of sacred art and the long-standing monastic tradition condemning the excess of pleasurable stimuli, Armenini saw no contradiction between charming images illustrating religious subjects and the tenets of secluded life, between nuns' ornate quarters and the genuine spirit of conventual life. Nuns' solitary prayers in cells, at the very least, disrupted the communitarian spiritual experience shared in nuns' choirs.[21] Armenini's comments may be related to the ideal of the hermitic life, an isolation that has long been understood as the privileged condition of contemplation and prayers. The painter-cleric Armenini maintains the value of the aesthetic experience, stating that pleasing, devout images are like *dispositifs* (mechanisms) for intensifying piety and adherence to Christian tenets. In making his recommendations for decorated nuns' cells, he probably had in mind the murals executed around 1440–45 by the Christian painter *par excellence*, Fra Angelico, in the friars' cells in San Marco in Florence.[22]

Armenini distinguishes between a devout style in painting and one which is more grandiose and not suitable to nunneries, a distinction that seems to echo the critique that Michelangelo had expressed decades earlier. Michelangelo referred to nuns and monks as unable to grasp the intellectual foundation of the modern Christian image: their apprehension could only lead to an empathetic relationship with art, but not to the comprehension of its deeper message.[23] Similarly, for nuns Armenini recommends devotional subjects charged with sentimental power and that do not entail dense theological doctrines, a view that, in turn, resonates with his era's misogynist perception of women as intellectually inferior. Or, might Armenini's remarks be an inadvertent acknowledgment that appealing images impressed themselves strongly on the minds of monastic individuals trained in memory techniques and were used to develop mental images of the information collected through the eyes? Be that as it may, Armenini never made a distinction between poor and aristocratic nuns, but his observations better suit patrician cloistered women whose decorated rooms proposed a realignment of Christian and aesthetic values, spirituality and material opulence. This is particularly apparent in communities sponsored by ruling families such as the Gonzaga, Malatesta, and Este, who founded and supported convents also to enable their female members to live like courtly ladies not in palaces but in monastic courts.

The Este in Ferrara were a case in point: Duke Alfonso I's wife, Lucrezia Borgia (1480–1519), entered the local convents of the Corpus Domini and San Bernardino on several occasions during her lifetime.[24] Founded in the early fifteenth century, the Corpus Domini, in particular, was endowed with land, income, and property by the Este and other local patricians, including Giovanni Romei (1402–83). At his death, Romei donated his own palace, located near the convent and subsequently incorporated within its pre-

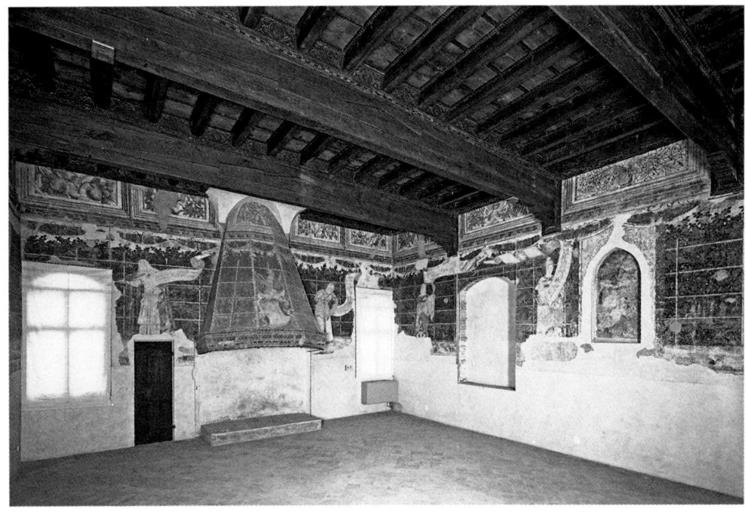

71   Anonymous artist, painted room with sibyls, ca. 1455, Ferrara, Casa Romei

cincts, to the community. In around 1455, Giovanni had two chambers of the now so-called Casa Romei painted with sibyls and prophets by an anonymous artist still using Gothic forms.[25] As Matilde Gagliardo has observed, the sibyls' scrolls bear inscriptions foretelling Christ's advent (fig. 71), but their placement within a verdant bower and their association with representations of chaste love, including those of the blind cupid and the lady with the unicorn, point to themes of female chastity and marital fidelity. Romei's painted chambers transmitted an atmosphere of visual elegance and spirituality that the Este women apparently felt pertinent to their retirement in the convent. When in 1502 Lucrezia Borgia entered the Corpus Domini to recover from childbirth, she stayed in the Casa Romei. Her daughter Eleonora (1515–75), who professed vows at the Corpus Domini, inhabited the Romei chambers on a permanent basis.[26] Although the commission for these murals cannot be ascribed to the nuns, the decorated rooms became their domain, a site governed by ideals of sophistication and devotion, comfortable lifestyle and spiritual achievements.

Domains of the personal self, cells were places whose adornment could be paid off with convent funds and which were controlled by ambitious abbesses. Dating to November 1519, a recently rediscovered document relates that Abbess Giovanna Piacenza from San Paolo in Parma paid the local painter Michele Mazzola (ca. 1469–after 1528), the uncle of the better-known Parmigianino, for decorations on the wood ceiling and upper walls of the nuns' dormitory.[27] As part of the convent's renovation campaign (discussed in Chapter Four), the abbess sponsored the construction of a

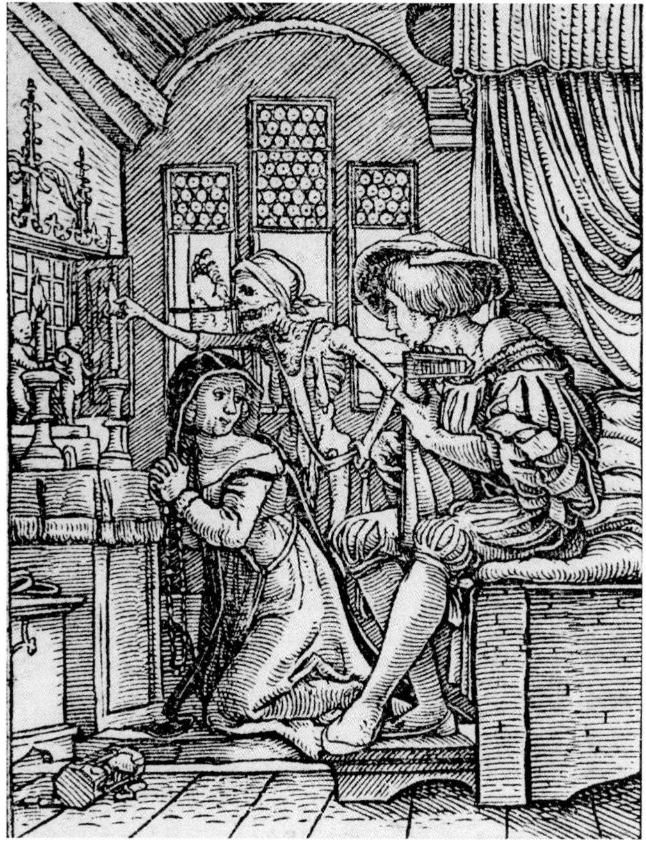

72 Designed by Hans Holbein the Younger, Printmaker, Hans Lützelburger, The Nun, from the *Dance of Death*, ca. 1526, published in 1538, 6.6 × 4.9 cm (2⅓ × 1⁵/₆ in), New York, Metropolitan Museum of Art

new nuns' dormitory that consisted of a long corridor located above her ground-floor apartment. Surviving pictorial fragments attributable to Mazzola include a damaged frescoed frieze of harpies and monsters.[28] Embellished nuns' cells in San Paolo were not, however, secluded, protected spaces. Dating to February 1579, a report by the Apostolic Visitor Giovanni Battista Castelli urged walls (*muraglie*) to be raised the better to isolate the convent from adjacent houses in order to make it more difficult for intruders to gain access to nuns' rooms.[29]

Male visitors to nuns' cells had been a constant preoccupation of early modern ecclesiastical authorities, who spent considerable energy on repressing such forbidden interaction. Sexual relations between nuns and men and same-sex relationships are both documented in convents.[30] In monastic writings, sexual intercourse with nuns was treated both as a sacrilege and a cause of contagious diseases.[31] Rules are not clear about the kind of sins that nuns

might commit, but allude in general to potentially unchaste behavior and admonish those with religious vows not to gratify the desires of the flesh. Conversely, literary writers are comparatively vocal on the topic. An unpublished version of Baldassar Castiglione's *Libro del Cortegiano* (1528) records the tale of a man found in bed with a nun, who wittily claimed not to have been caught in a compromising situation, but simply to being lazy, as he did not get out of bed early enough not to be caught![32]

Similarly, Pietro Aretino's first *Ragionamento della Nanna e dell'Antonia*, printed in 1543, published a roguish narrative on conventual life. A dialogue between two courtesans (one of whom, the mature Nanna, had experienced the three states of female life: nun, wife, and courtesan), the *Ragionamento* begins with a description of Nanna entering a convent as a young girl. Written with a strongly misogynist flavor, Aretino reports that the beautiful and innocent Nanna felt that she had entered "a tomb alive" when she joined the religious community. However, her life within the claustrum turned out to be full of delights and gratifying experiences, including delicious food and abundant sex. As Aretino recounts, Nanna was first taken on a tour of the convent buildings where she saw images of erotic subjects hanging on the walls of a large ground-floor chamber. After a lavish meal in male company, she retired to her cell, where she could spy on the sex performed in the abbess's adjacent room until a young friar joined her. As she engaged in the sexual encounter, she gave thanks for having taken her vows, considering the life of nuns "to be a true paradise."[33] Indeed, Aretino's fiction of a sexually driven convent life ultimately took to task nuns' frail nature, their inability to control their physical impulses, and their disregard of religious prescriptions.

Aside from Aretino's ribald and picturesque account, patrician nuns are known to have allowed male outsiders to play music and sing in their spaces. Ecclesiastical authorities viewed music as either a form of interior renewal for women, or as an art potentially connected to sinful behavior. Music could become synonymous with sin, given that nun-musicians interacted with male teachers, and that their angelic singing moreover provided moments of relaxation and opportunities for socialization. As trained musicians the Ferrarese aristocratic nuns of Sant'Antonio in Polesine had male musicians accessing their institution, but the entry of such guests caused disruption in the community. In 1524, the alarmed abbess sent a plea to Alfonso I d'Este to restrain his niece's musical passion in order to avoid incidents in the convent.[34] Perhaps the print *The Nun* (ca. 1526–38; fig. 72) designed by Hans Holbein the Younger captures some of the concerns of the Ferrarese abbess. In the print, a beautiful young nun kneels before a portable altar in her well-furnished cell or bedroom. Instead of looking at the altar, she turns her head toward a lute-playing gentleman seated on the bed, as if lured by his music. The youth tenderly returns her gaze as a prelude to their physical conjunction. The personification of death (in this context, sin) steps in from behind to extinguish the candles on the altar, and an hourglass is thrown on the ground.[35] Holbein's print represents the moment before the couple's resistance is overcome and the senses take control of the mind, casting the cell as a site of passionate intimacy and, consequently, as a place of symbolic death. Permeable and porous spaces, nuns' quarters were thresholds where the profane and the sacred met, the private and the public spheres mingled. Cells were the manifestations of their occupants' agency refracted in material objects, which encapsulated the spirituality, necessity for relaxation, and the need of compensation of elite nuns.

NUNS' CHOIRS: DEVOTIONAL SPLENDOR AND TANGIBLE PRESENCE

As places reserved for professed nuns only, nuns' choirs were liturgically crucial spaces, reflecting the choral, communitarian aspect of monastic life. In the churches of all orders, the religious community was set aside from the laity, but in convent churches this separation often resulted in permanent architectural divisions. Usually a wall divided a church in two, together forming the conventional double monastic church type.[36] There was, however, no fixed position for the nuns' choir: it was sometimes located behind the high altar of outer churches (the retrochoir type) or to the side, but choirs could also be raised (see Chapter One). Indeed, each solution had specific visual and acoustic implications for nuns. Separating but at the same time connecting religious and lay communities participating in the rite of the Mass within a shared space, choirs and their ornament and furnishings had long been the focus of nuns' attention.

Medieval nuns' meditation on devotional images in their choirs, their corporeal identification with the painted or sculpted subjects surrounding them, even exhibiting on their bodies actual signs of Christ's suffering, are known forms of female piety. Scholars have characterized their devotions as visionary and ecstatic, involving an imaginative perception of art whose primary emphasis was not on its aesthetic quali-

ties. Devotional art was primarily intended to inculcate spiritual messages in nuns, and was perceived as a tool to reach a perfected state modeled on the lives of Christ, the Virgin, and the saints.[37] From the end of the fifteenth century onward, nuns' perception of art became more articulate and nuanced. The rise of a new conception of Christian art seen as the manifestation of an artist's invention and recognizable for its distinct style – an art stimulating its audience through its classicizing features, strategies of representation, and reinvented subjects – gradually shifted onlookers' expectations and their approach to the work's material presence. The emergence of this modern religious art coincided with a major spiritual and political crisis that fractured Europe from the 1510s onward, bringing to the surface a debate over the function of Christian images as instruments of devotional instruction, a means of communication between artists and viewers, and between believers and God. The Roman Catholic Church's defense of the role of sacred images against the criticism of Protestant reformers sustained the didactic function of Christian art and the cult of venerated icons, miraculous images (or the sphere of "popular" visual culture), and, at the same time, promoted religious art imbued with aesthetic appeal and intentionality. Contemporary artists experimented with pictorial motifs, reinvented iconographies to amalgamate votive images with aesthetically driven art, and reworked genres of traditional Christian subjects, showing a renewed understanding of the efficacy of their works in transmitting religious meaning to the believer.[38]

Amid spiritual and cultural pressures and artists' varied responses to devotional ends, Renaissance aristocratic nuns did not remain a passive audience. Different from their medieval predecessors who encountered simplified, even "ugly" art, early sixteenth-century upper-class religious women wanted their images to represent Christian truth in pleasing and naturalistic, mimetically convincing compositions that would effectively capture onlookers' minds. An overlooked record attesting to this shift concerns the Parmese nuns of San Paolo who commissioned the local painter Alessandro Araldi to decorate the walls of their now-lost choir in 1505. The provisions of the commission reveal the nuns' concern about the efficacy of the painter's works, reflecting a change in attitude toward the Christian image, which had come to be seen as an instrument of aesthetic effects and devotional splendor rather than a strict vector of Christian doctrine. As mentioned in Chapter Two, the nineteenth-century renovation of the church of San Paolo caused the loss of the Christological murals painted by Araldi between 1505 and 1507. The surviving documentation, however, remains of extreme interest in disclosing the abbess's awareness of Araldi's limited pictorial skills and the adjustments she felt were necessary to nourish his imagination.[39] Dating to May 1505 and outlining the obligations between Araldi and a nameless abbess (either Cecilia or Orsina Bergonzi), the agreement, as was usual, first lists the scenes to be painted and their sequence on the choir walls placed behind the high altar of the outer church. The payment is then stated, promising Araldi a premium if three external *cognosenti* (experts) approved five of his pictures.[40] It is, however, the next provision of the agreement that is of relevance here, because it raises questions about the performative aspects of the artist's murals. An entire paragraph is dedicated to a possible trip to Milan, stating that if the abbess wishes Araldi to study Leonardo's *Last Supper* or any other work, the better to execute his paintings in San Paolo, he should be compensated for the costs accrued, and also be given travel equipment (probably a horse).[41] It would be a mistake to consider this provision as standard, since it does not commonly appear in contracts. Often, contracts require a work to resemble an existing one, creating visual connections from one monastic house to the next, but the case projected in the Araldi agreement is quite different.[42]

The abbess, evidently knowledgable about the most innovative examples of Renaissance art, seems to consider Leonardo's *Last Supper* (1494–8) in the refectory of the Dominican friary of Santa Maria delle Grazie in Milan as a kind of academy, from which Araldi could have updated his style and compositions.[43] Much praised by contemporaries for its rendering of the apostles' varied psychological reactions to Christ's announcement of his betrayal, Leonardo's *Last Supper* is acknowledged in the document as a paramount example of modern monastic art. Like cultivated lay viewers, the abbess of San Paolo seems to have wanted inventive sacred images, and to see aesthetic value and spirituality mingled in efficacious artistic forms. As will be discussed in the following chapters, Araldi served the nuns of San Paolo on many occasions, but he was probably chosen out of convenience and availability rather than a convinced appreciation of his art. A local painter, Araldi studied the most advanced examples of modern art in northern Italy before Leonardo – works by Mantegna and Giovanni Bellini, respectively in Mantua and Venice – and then traveled to Milan to copy Leonardo's work.[44] Outside of these travels, he spent his entire career in Parma and lived in the San Paolo district, which certainly helped him maintain strong relationships with the nuns.[45] Despite his pictorial shortcomings, Araldi remained one of most credited

painters in the city before the ascent of Correggio and Parmigianino, whose artistic style, however, did not totally satisfy such sensitive beholders as the nuns of San Paolo.

Preoccupation with the appearance of sacred images, their beauty, and how their religious message was conjugated with artistry, was certainly not confined to the San Paolo community. Other patrician consecrated women on the peninsula attested a similar awareness of the aesthetic appeal of Christian art and its authorship. For example, the Clarissan nuns of Santa Maria di Monteluce in Perugia commissioned Raphael for an altarpiece representing the *Coronation of the Virgin* in 1505 (Rome, Pinacoteca Vaticana). Despite numerous enquiries and frustrations over the unfinished state of their work "begun by master Raphael," only after his death in 1520 did the abbess accept the completion of the altarpiece by the master's pupils, Giulio Romano and Gianfrancesco Penni.[46] In 1524 the German abbess Sabina Pirckheimer, the sister of the humanist Willibald, requested none other than Albrecht Dürer to instruct her own convent's painter-nun, evidently sharing similar concerns to those of her Italian peers for updating the devotional effectiveness of Christian art. By then, as Jeffrey Hamburger has put it, Christian images for a conventual audience "had to be not only true but beautiful as well. In a word, it had to be 'Art.'"[47] Monastic art had shifted from the realm of the merely instructive image to that of the beautiful, attracting the viewer through the force of its visual qualities to activate the imagination and elicit psychological effects. Educated, aristocratic nuns had become more and more aware of the aesthetic impact, power, and appeal of the image.

Generations of monastic writers had condemned the beauty of art as a source of distraction and waste. But the perception of charming images and the pleasure they afforded had gradually come to be identified as within the scope of conventual art itself in some Renaissance elite institutions. But, one wonders, what was the status of the Christian art made for these communities? And what may be said about the agency of images that depict cloistered women pointing their beholders to something beyond the fictive surfaces? To begin to answer these questions, I shall examine what are perhaps the most impressive Renaissance murals *in situ* in conventual churches in northern Italy, namely, the works of Girolamo Romanino and Bernardino Luini. In their murals, both artists depicted living individuals, turning frescoes into engines of communication and, simultaneously, reflections on the mediating nature of the art of painting. In Brescia, Romanino portrayed the enclosed, reformed nuns of Santa Giulia in an image placed on the intrados of a window in

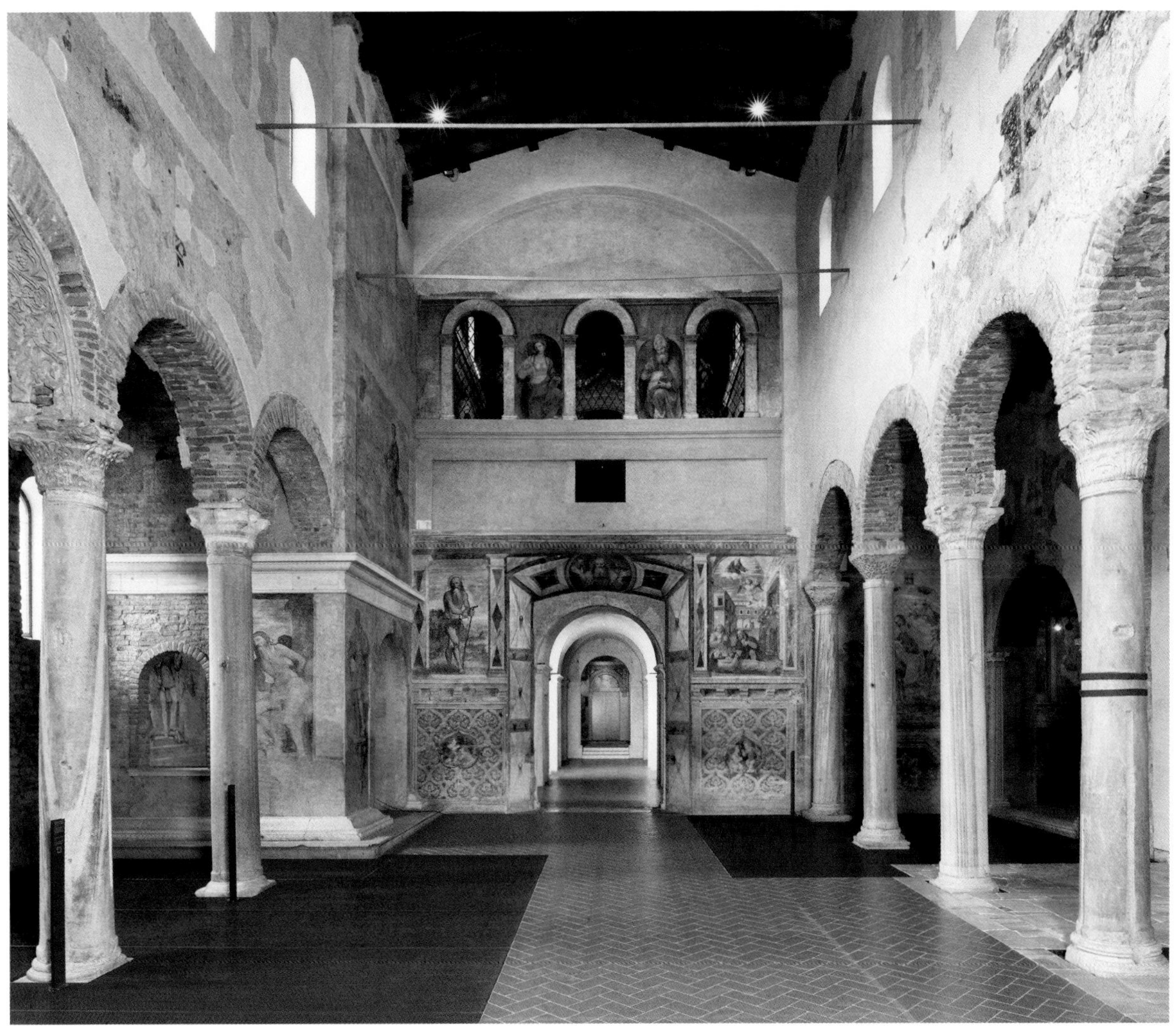

73   Brescia, Santa Giulia, view of the nuns' choir, with barred windows

the outer church, making their very act of looking out a dense perceptual experience for the viewer. Likewise, in his Milanese frescoes in both San Maurizio's nuns' choir and its outer church, Luini renders living, consecrated individuals, ultimately enhancing the religious community's spiritual self-perception and reception.

Santa Giulia, founded between 753 and 759 by the Longobard King Desiderius and Queen Ansa, was an esteemed Benedictine house in northern Italy. It enjoyed imperial protection and independence from local bishops, and its inhabitants belonged to the most prominent Brescian families.[48] In the general prologue of his *Vite* (1568), Giorgio Vasari refers to Santa Giulia as a complex built "at the greatest cost but in a disorderly manner," occupying an entire district in the city and including three churches. Its

elite inhabitants renovated their earliest church in the 1460s, which by then was being used as a treasury wherein to guard the convent's precious liturgical objects.[49] Thereafter, the community ordered the construction of a new choir, a two-story building abutting the façade of the extant church of San Salvatore (fig. 73). Regardless of the problem of its chronology (oscillating from the 1460s to the early sixteenth century in the literature), this choir in the tripartite organization of the nave, with classicizing arcades based on ancient models, has been described as "one of the earliest episodes in adapting the modern architectural language in Brescia."[50] The nuns' choir occupied the upper floor, while the space below was turned into a majestic entrance hall to the outer church for the laity. Thus the female cloistered community had a prime position above the lay congregation. Three

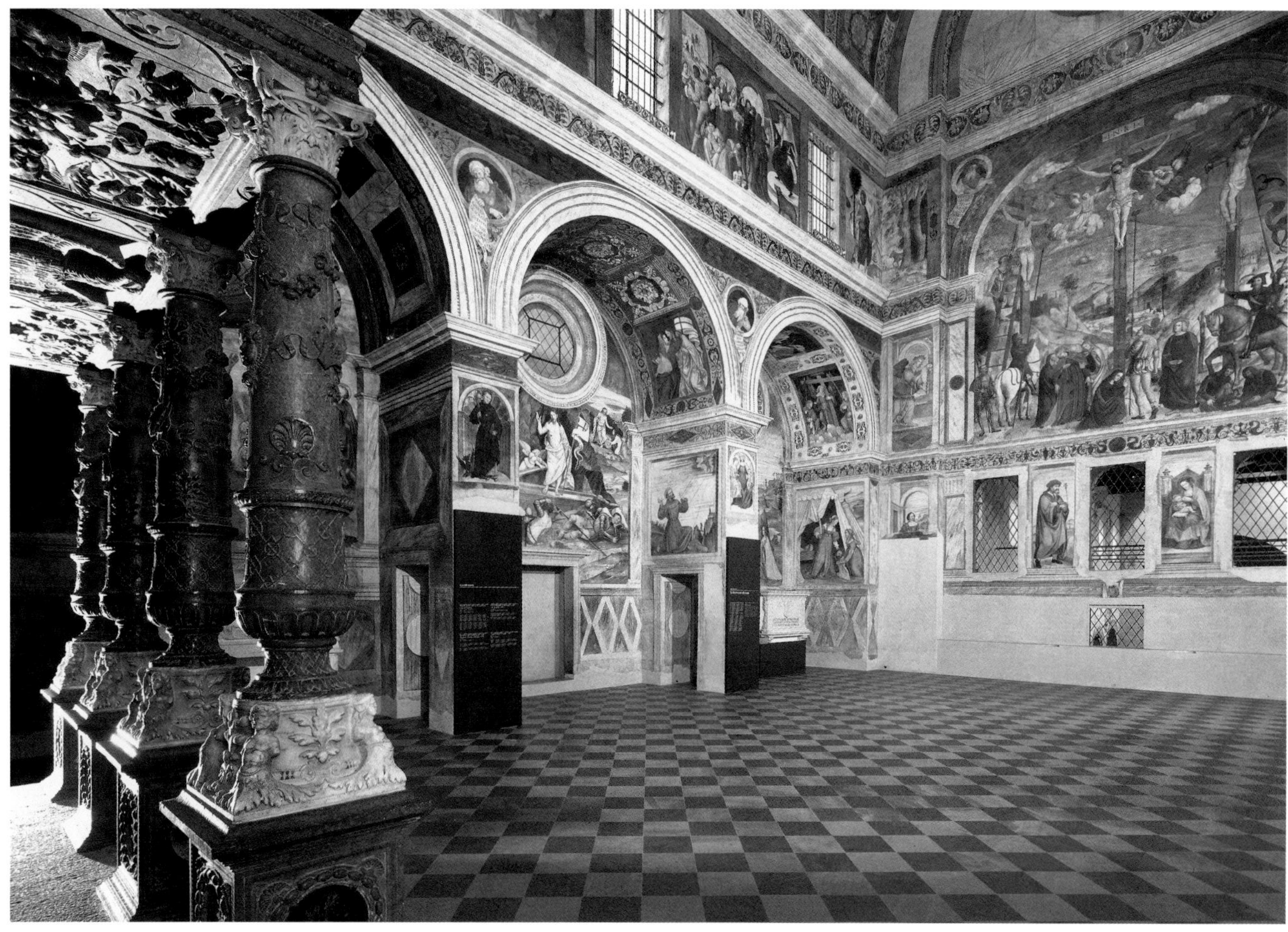

74 Floriano Ferramola, *Christ Crucified between the Two Thieves*, before 1528, fresco, Brescia, Santa Giulia

grated windows assured the nuns a view of the Host when attending Mass. The construction of the nuns' choir coincided with a turbulent phase in the convent's history, culminating in the community's affiliation with the Benedictine Cassinese Congregation in 1481, an affiliation reaffirmed in 1497.[51] Placed under the spiritual care of Cassinese monks, the nuns promised to obey the rules of the Congregation that had reformed the Italian Benedictine order. In consequence, a strict seclusion was enforced on the religious women, and the abbatial office became a one-year appointment. It seems, however, that the nuns maintained a certain independence. The Cassinese *Ordinationes* (regulations) of 1492 make clear that monks should not "involve themselves in the temporal affairs of . . . the nuns, unless only to give advice." Further, an obvious monastic tenet is reiterated, that only authorized monks had access to female communities and only when it was deemed necessary. The regulations

indicate, for instance, that a specific valid reason for appointed Cassinese monks to enter convents was to examine the state of repair of buildings.[52]

Amid a prolonged crisis and the horrors of a war that resulted in the sack of Brescia in 1512, the newly built nuns' choir of Santa Giulia remained unadorned until the mid-1520s. This lack of images could be seen as a deliberate choice, following the prescriptions listed in the Benedictine Rule, which the Cassinese reprinted in 1520, requiring choirs to be simple, imageless places of prayer.[53] In his recommendations to his reformed monks, the founder of the Cassinese Congregation, Ludovico Barbo (d. 1443), states that books, not images, should assist monks in their meditative exercises. His ideal of imageless devotion was rooted in the long-standing assumption that images deceive, projecting the divine truth in forms wanting to appear real beyond mere verisimilitude to the heavenly reality they

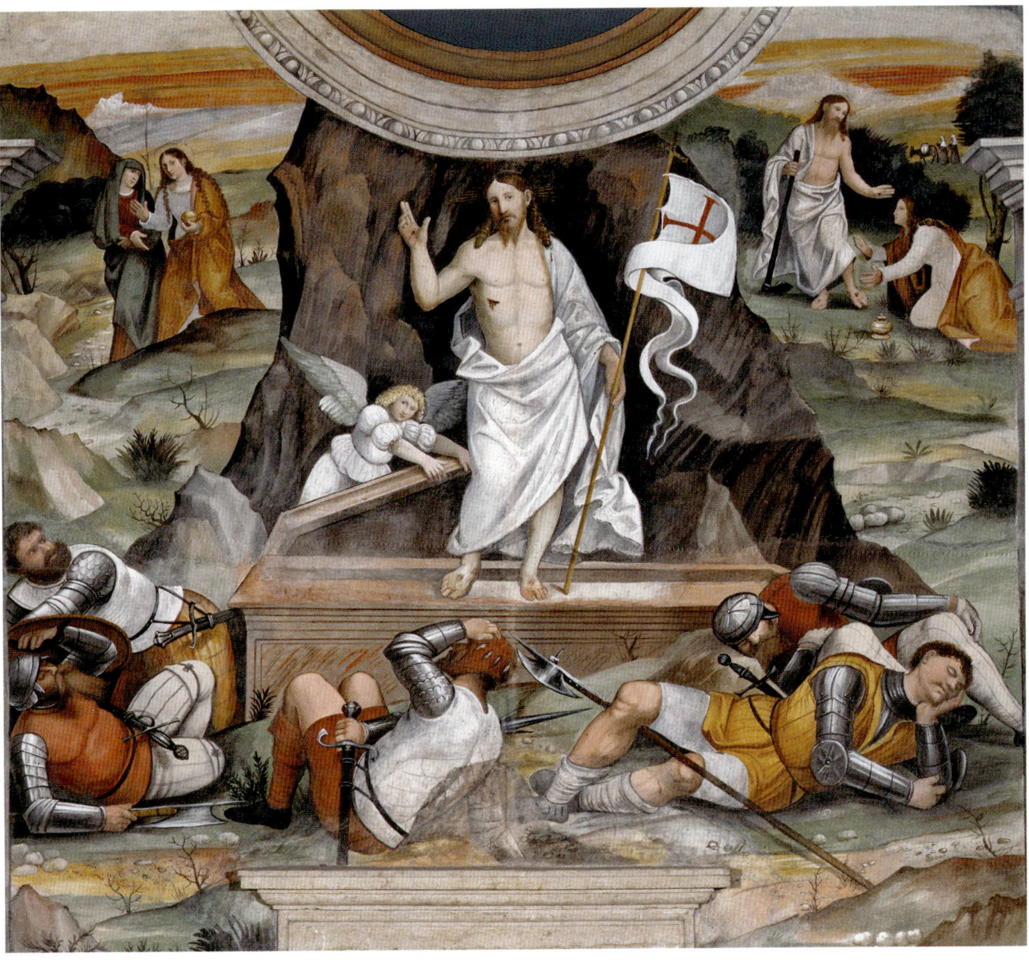

75   Paolo Caylina the Younger, *Resurrection of Christ* and *Noli me Tangere*, before 1532, fresco, Brescia, Santa Giulia

depict, and only functioning as a means of reference to the divine truth, which is invisible.[54]

In the 1520s the nuns of Santa Giulia decided to challenge these Cassinese views on images. First the local painter Floriano Ferramola and then, after his death in 1528, Paolo Caylina the Younger executed scenes from the Passion of Christ in their choir. Ferramola's and Caylina's murals are conventional in terms of their iconographies and compositions, but the overall result is impressive: their frescoes (see fig. 74) cover every centimeter of the choir walls and incorporate motifs to capture the religious women's eyes. The images invited them to meditate on the message of spiritual love that the nuns' mystical groom has for his virginal brides, and to enjoy the sweetness of their encounters with God through fervent prayers. Ferramola's monumental scene, *Christ Crucified between the Two Thieves* occupies the entire space above the three grated windows through

which the nuns could assist at the Mass, offering nuns direct and immediate access to Christ as suffering Savior and guarantor of salvation. In Caylina's multi-episodic *Resurrection* and *Noli me Tangere* (before 1532; fig. 75) on the wall of the left side chapel, Benedictine nuns are incorporated into the painted narrative. Behind the *Noli me Tangere*, in the right background, two miniaturized nuns walk with a donkey in a luminous and verdant countryside.[55] While such a detail reminds modern viewers of nuns' physical labor, the cloistered individuals instead saw their tangible selves inscribed within the history of Christian salvation. Caylina's image not only structures the itinerary of nuns in their meditative exercises, but also gives them physical presence within these spiritual paths, ultimately stressing their intercessory role for the wellbeing of fellow citizens.

Around the same time, the ground floor of the bell tower abutting the nuns' choir was transformed into a chapel. The

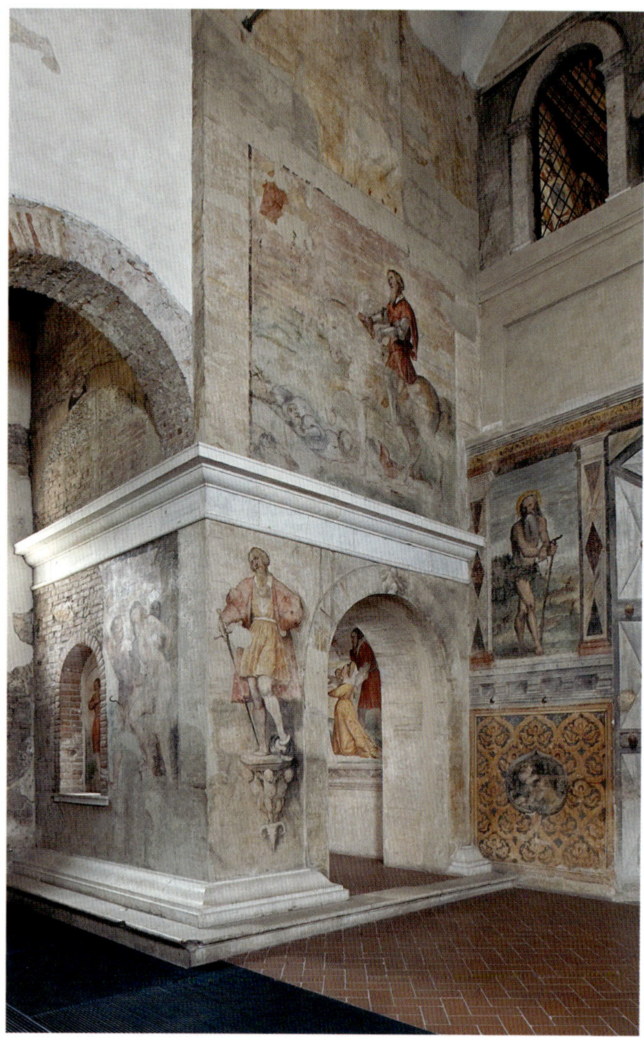

Above 76   Brescia, Santa Giulia, view of the chapel of St. Obizio, ca. 1526–7

Right 77   Girolamo Romanino, *Nuns*, ca. 1526–7, fresco, Brescia, Santa Giulia

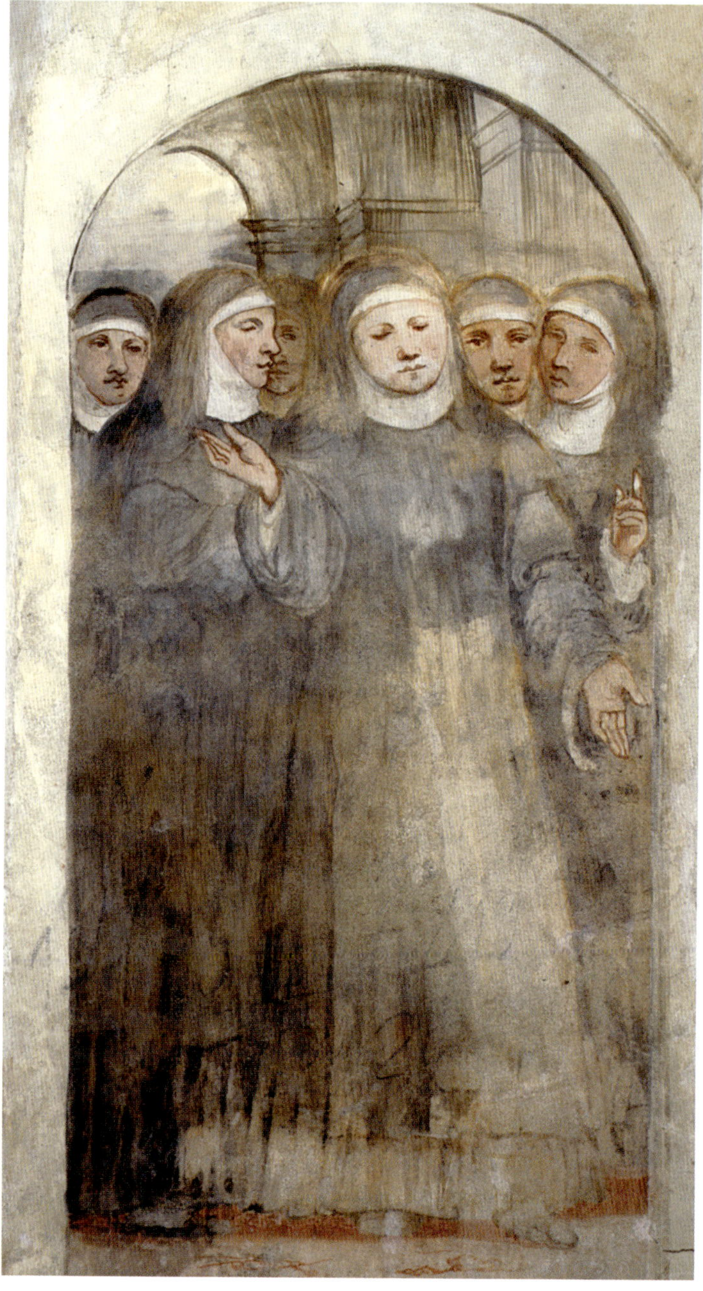

most experimental local painter, Girolamo Romanino, decorated the tower's interior and exterior walls with stories from the life of St. Obizio (fig. 76). A twelfth-century Lombard soldier who left the army having miraculously escaped death, Obizio subsequently became an oblate in Santa Giulia, where he was also buried.[56] Little is known about the circumstances of this commission to Romanino dating to around 1526–7. Here, it is relevant to consider a hitherto neglected image on the left intrados of the chapel's arched window, depicting a Benedictine community (fig. 77). Although the surface of the lower zone shows some

paint loss, six standing nuns can be seen gazing at St. Obizio, who appears on the opposite, right window intrados.[57] The very location of the image on the intrados, that is, at the threshold between the St. Obizio chapel and the outer church nave, projects this picture outward. The group of nuns is led by a central figure who may represent Abbess Adeodata Martinengo – who was elected to the office numerous times, including the years 1526–7 – given that her family's armorial device (the eagle) is painted on the chapel vault. Foreshortened from a high viewpoint, the standing nuns appear before what seems an open arched doorway revealing other walls and arches, which augments the effect of their proximity to our space. Fundamentally, Romanino's image has commemorative and celebratory purposes. It honors an elite secluded community, its abbess, and then a saint, Obizio (set in the opposite intrados), said to have been an ancestor of the Martinengo family and whose cult was centered in Santa Giulia. But there are still other ways to make sense of Romanino's fresco.

With artistic acumen, Romanino makes a few of the nuns look directly out at the spectator, while others have their eyes downcast as if to mimic both their appropriate comportment code and their real placement in the elevated choir where they gazed downward to take part in the Mass. But, in contrast to the obstructed gazes of the living nuns obliged to assist Mass through grilled windows, Romanino gives the painted nuns' eyes free access across the space, with no screen or grates to block their vision. Usually separated and constrained within their choir, the nuns of Santa Giulia are made visible, and their gazes address and confront us. It is as if Romanino's image opens the site where the nuns are confined, and stretches its boundaries out to meet our space. The painter has depicted those who are enclosed behind the choir and made his subject palpably present and tangible, directing our eyes to follow theirs. Alternatively put, in Romanino's fresco nuns enclosed in their raised choir behind grates and invisible to others in real life are given back their faces and an unobstructed view and are the protagonists in its painted fiction, which occupies the liminal zone of the window intrados in the chapel of St. Obizio.

On the exterior wall of the chapel, a standing St. Obizio rendered with an eloquent gesture and gaze directed at the raised nuns' choir serves as a connector, making the link between the real and the painted nuns on the intrados apparent and effective. Through its dialectic of convincing imitation and fiction, reality and illusion, Romanino's fresco makes the absent present, and the secluded real, an achievement said in Alberti's *De Pictura* (1436) to be the aim of painting itself.[58] If, according to Alberti, the modern image was like a window through which the viewer gazed to gain a view of the immanent world, Romanino returned his fresco to this role as a means of interpreting and commenting on monastic enclosure. Romanino's image is a visual fiction that points beyond itself to the real nuns, and which states its artistic ambitions, proposing a reflection on the mediating role of painting itself and its empathetic values. Klaus Krüger has discussed the mediating nature of the Christian image, the ambiguity between its pictorial devo-

tional discourse and its divine referent, and its staged representation of beholding, asking the viewer to confront its truth, which ultimately exists only as an aesthetic experience.[59] Developing from Krüger's mode of thinking about the pre-Reformation Christian image, one may see Romanino's fresco as a self-reflexive image intended not only to shape viewers' spiritual expectations and to incite their responses, but also to rethink the very subject of communication. Romanino's self-consciousness heightens the beholders' involvement. He aims to make real what his painting represented, producing the illusion of what is not visible in reality (the nuns) to our eyes, and ultimately proposing viewing as a source of knowledge.

Romanino's work captures the onlookers' gaze through the force of the artist's style, an unorthodox synthesis of Venetian and Lombard pictorial models and a manner that has been associated with contemporary linguistic debates, in particular, with the anticlassical literary idiom ("the maccheronic," a mixture of Latin and vernacular languages) coined by the Cassinese monk Teofilo Folengo.[60] The task of executing the St. Obizio cycle went to a local painter who was well established within the Cassinese Congregation.[61] Romanino's image extending the Santa Giulia religious ladies to the outside proves to have been a conscious effort on his part to reflect on the question of nuns' enclosure and invisibility in an image whose activation through vision gives the nuns a physical existence through the act of looking itself. It therefore provides us with insights on the performativity of the modern image that elite reformed nuns may have wanted as a subtle commentary on their secluded condition.

A different but no less compelling extension of religious women to the outside world may still be seen in Milan. The church of San Maurizio, often discussed as a crucial example of the renewal of monastic architecture in Lombardy, comprises two distinct zones separated by a dividing wall.[62] It was built according to a plan supplied by a major – albeit still unascertained – local architect, with possible candidates ranging from Gian Giacomo Dolcebuono to Cesare Cesariano.[63] Begun in 1503, the church was only consecrated sixteen years later. In a variation from the standard double-church type, the nuns' choir (fig. 78) placed behind the high altar is larger than the space reserved for the laity in the outer church, a clue that it was always the real center of gravity of such religious structures.[64] Communication between the two areas of the church was achieved by a grilled opening in the dividing wall directly above the altar. This solution, in fact, strictly secluded the

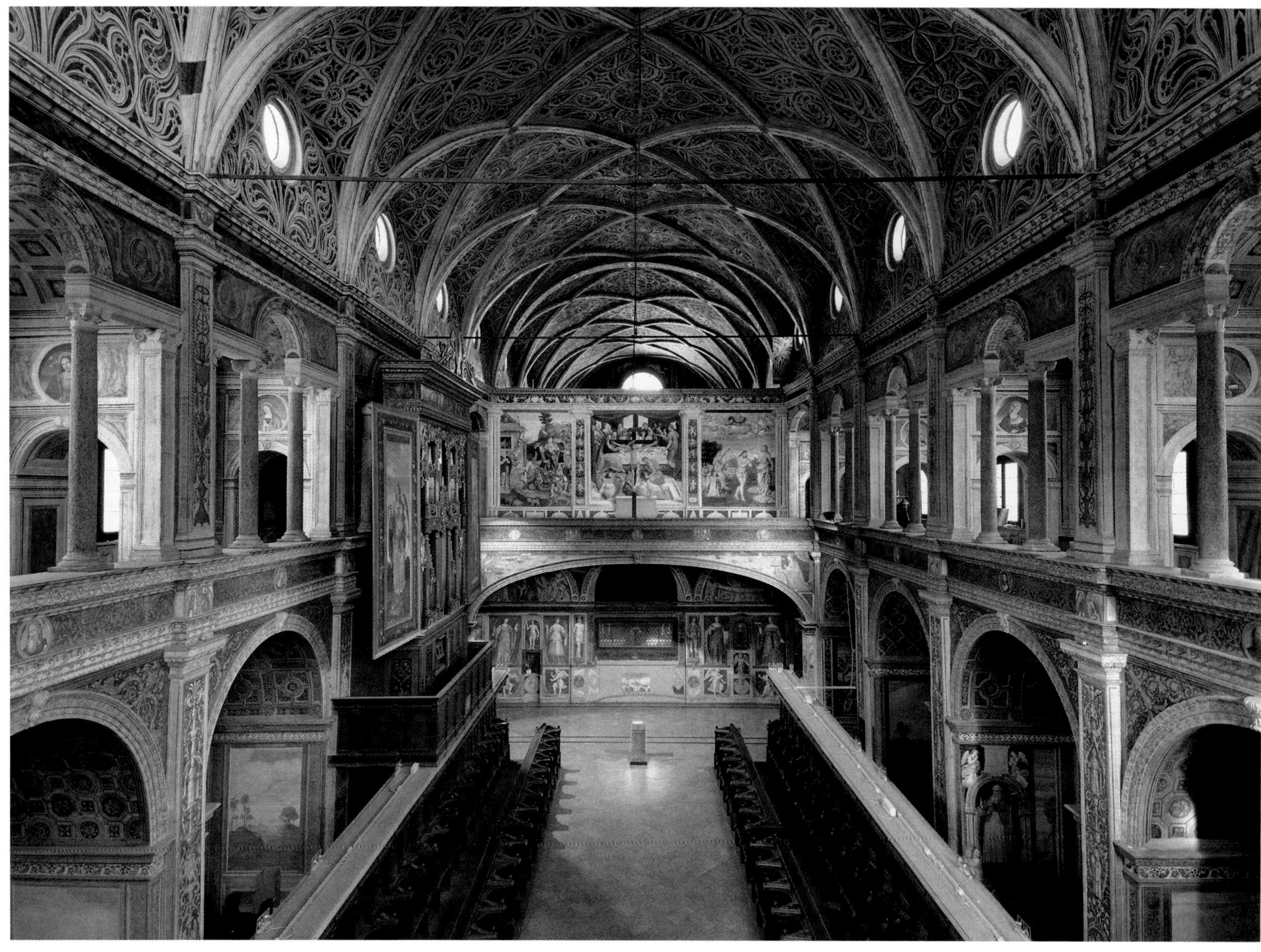

nuns in compliance with the regulations of the Benedictine Cassinese Congregation to which the community of San Maurizio provisionally adhered in 1480.[65]

The Lombard painter Bernardino Luini and his workshop, including his sons, worked both in the inner and the outer church, on either sides of the dividing wall, and in several of the chapels from the 1510s onward in different phases. In the nuns' choir (fig. 79) Luini's frescoes with episodes from the Passion of Christ occupy the dividing wall and the adjacent areas. Luini's murals have been variously dated from the late 1510s to the mid-1520s, and a recent proposal has even suggested around 1530–45 (that is, after Luini's death in 1532). Such a late chronology implies that their authorship largely fell on Luini's sons.[66] For the Christological scenes on the dividing wall in the nuns'

choir, the conventional date of the mid-1520s seems the most appropriate chronology, due to their formal, compositional, and structural similarities to Luini's murals on the other side of the wall (dated to those years or immediately before) and to contemporary works displaying identical compositional features. The frescoes' tripartite structure, in particular, comes close to that of late Quattrocento polyptychs (fig. 80), though its visual complexity clearly refers to High Renaissance models. Set against airy landscapes, the Christian episodes fill the top lunettes, as in the case of the *Way to Calvary*, while immediately below there are inscriptions in gold, staging Christ's drama verbally. Below the *Way to Calvary* stand a pair of female saints (Apollonia and Lucy) flanking a tabernacle surmounted by the figure of the bleeding Christ. The saints are placed above illusionistic

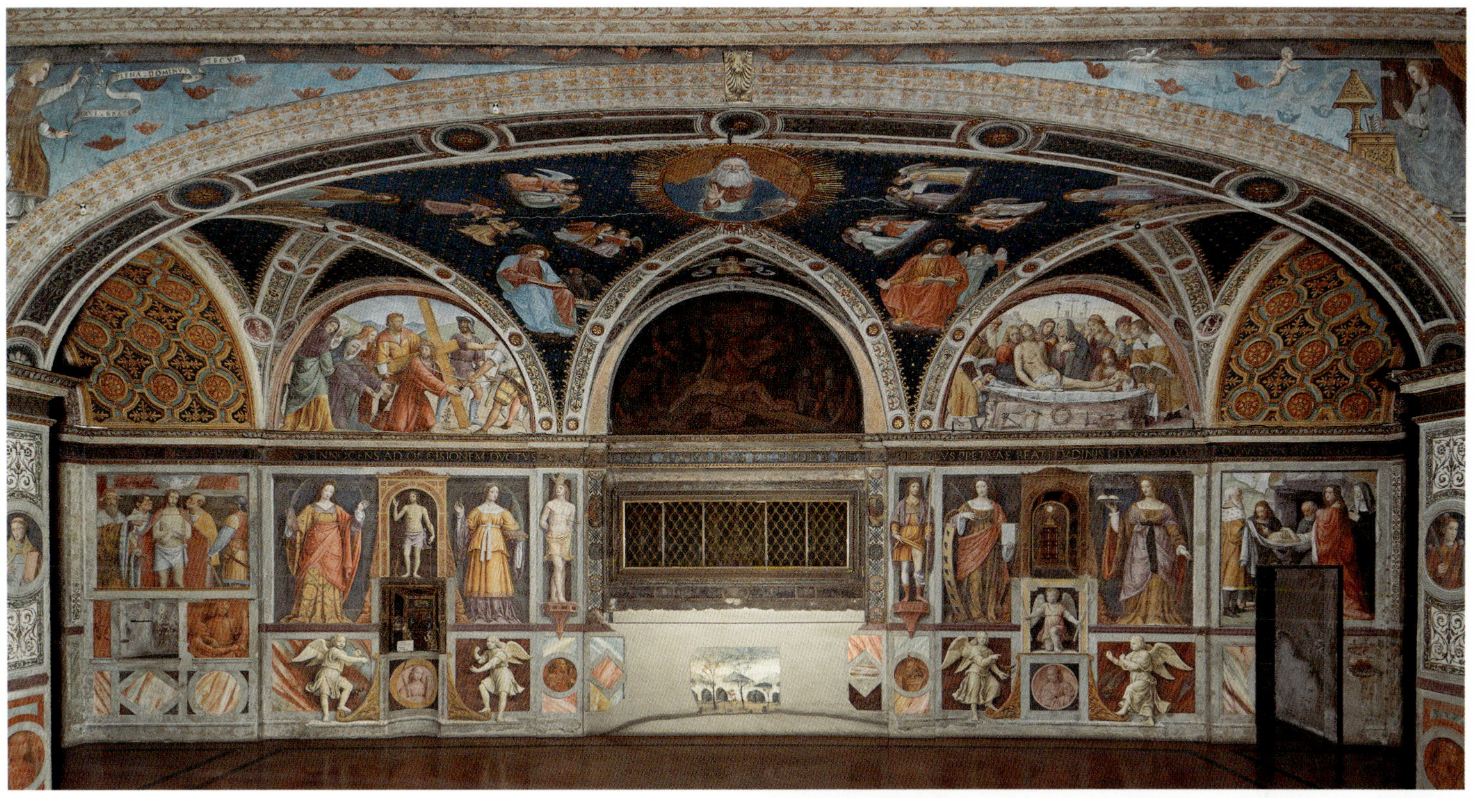

Facing page 78   Milan, San Maurizio al Monastero Maggiore, inner church or nuns' choir

Above 79   Milan, San Maurizio al Monastero Maggiore, frescoes by Bernardino Luini on the dividing wall between inner and outer church

Right 80   Bernardino Luini, *Way to Calvary* and female saints, ca. 1522–4, fresco, Milan, San Maurizio al Monastero Maggiore

marble dados, completed by monochrome angels and at the center a tondo with a bust of St. Barbara, architectural features and figures carried out by Luini's assistants. It has been recognized that they also executed the two male saints on the lateral pilasters of the central grilled opening. As a whole, this ensemble creates contrasting interplays of projection, flatness and depth, rich chromaticism and grisaille effects, *all'antica* decorative elements and fictive architecture. Luini's vivacious pictorial syntax declares his fusion of Leonardesque qualities – human, emotional, charming – with the vibrant, bright coloring of the Lombard and Venetian traditions, further nurtured by a probable encounter with Raphael's art and Roman antiquarianism in the papal city, which he may have visited before 1521. Luini was an inventive painter with an acute sense for familiar gestures,

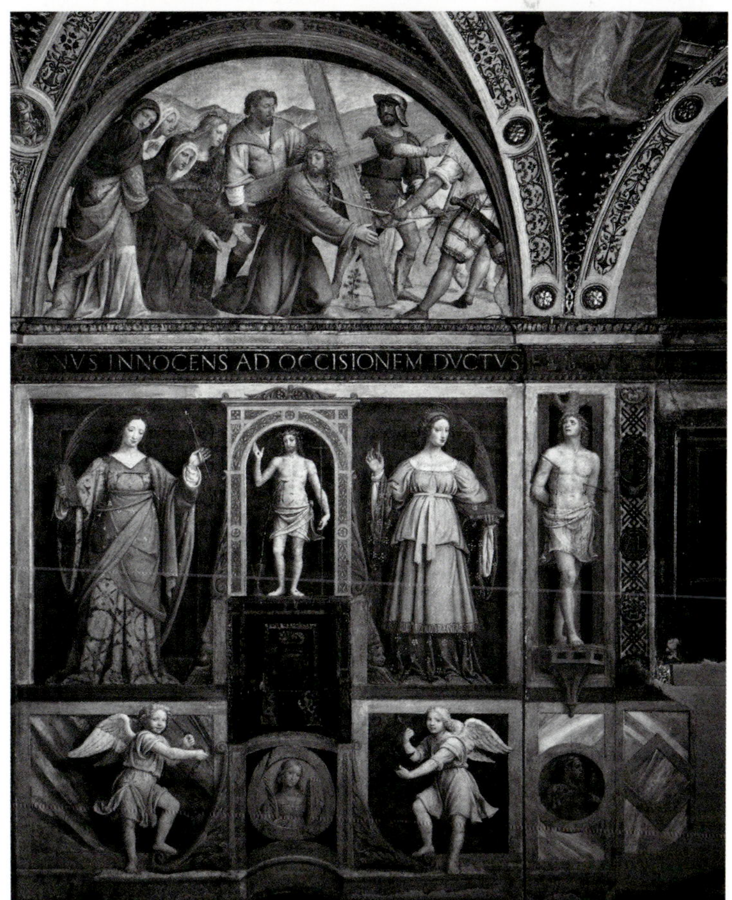

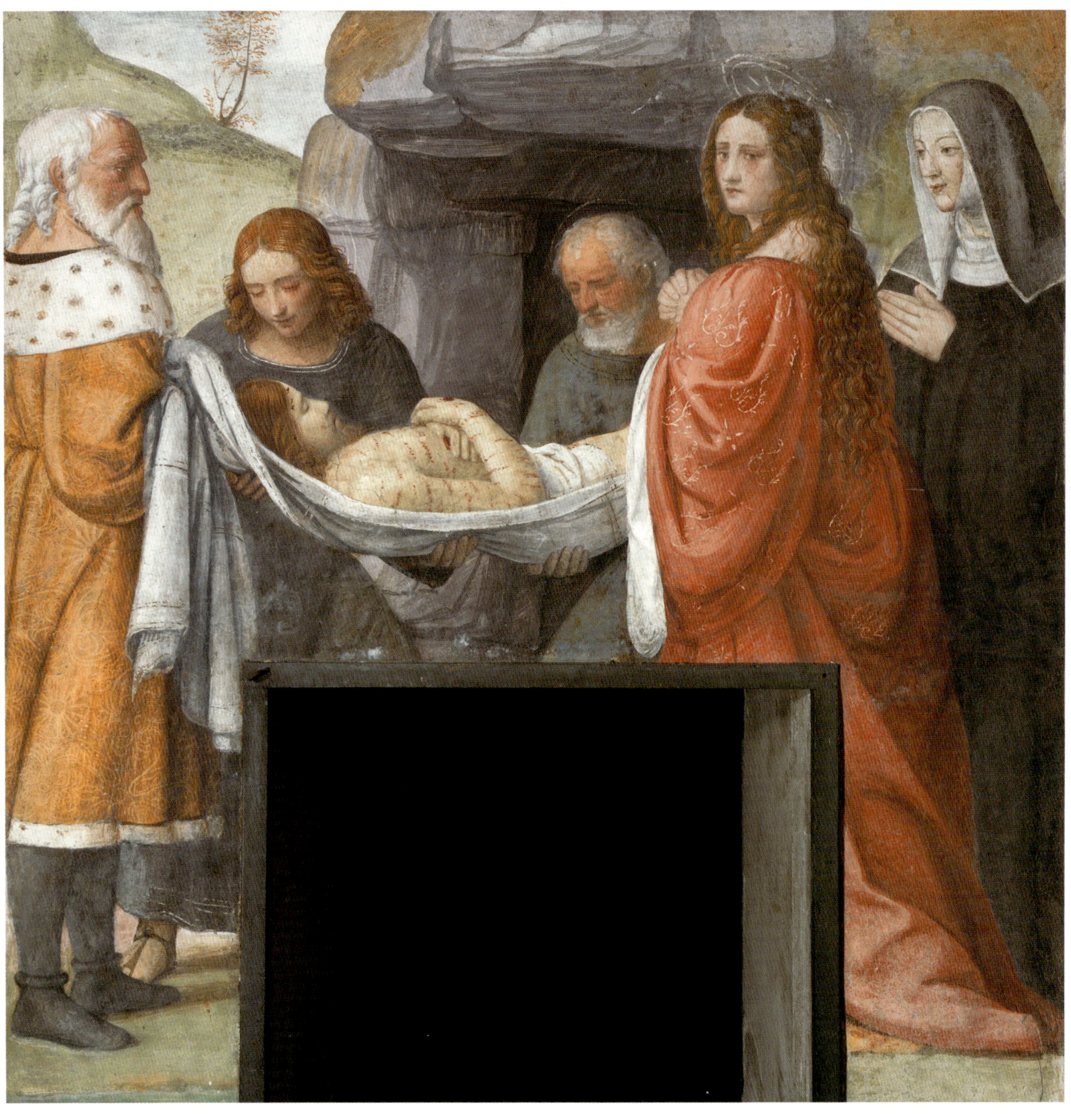

81   Bernardino Luini, *Entombment*, ca. 1522–4, fresco, Milan, San Maurizio al Monastero Maggiore

tender faces, and the rhythmic placement of figures, convey-ing the impression of sacred events vividly underway before our eyes.

A mural on the right end of the dividing wall depicting the *Entombment* (fig. 81) is another case in point. Although partly destroyed by a doorway opened in 1864 to facilitate communication between the two churches, it conveys the Christian drama through the restrained pain of the protago-nists, and their intimate gathering around Christ's dead body. These features differ markedly from the dramatic pathos and sculptural effects of Raphael's most famous *Entombment* (the Pala Baglioni, 1507) and, measured against that model, can almost be taken as a declaration of Luini's own artistic self. Luini's *Entombment* is notable for both the absence of the Virgin and the insertion of a praying nun who visually recalls the St. Scholastica (see fig. 85) depicted in a lunette on the opposite side of the dividing wall, facing the laity, putting the nun on almost the same footing as the celebrated female saint of the Benedictine order. If, as sug-gested, both portray Abbess Alessandra Bentivoglio (whose

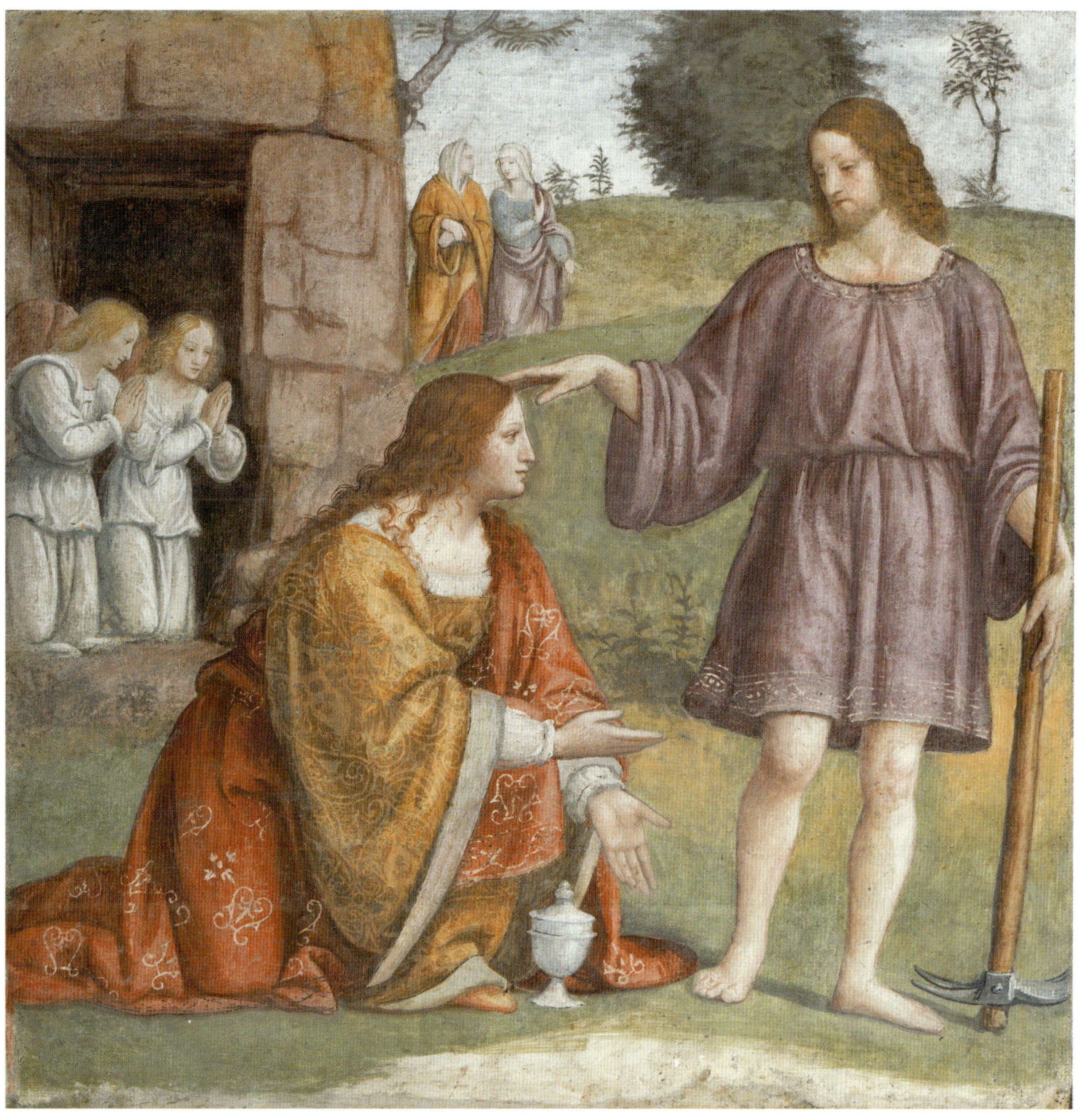

82   Bernardino Luini, *Noli me Tangere*, ca. 1522–4, fresco, Milan, San Maurizio al Monastero Maggiore

given name was Bianca), who took her vows in San Maurizio and was many times elected abbess, her very representation serves as the connector between both zones of the church and the religious and lay community. Furthermore, the abbess's presence in Luini's *Entombment* would surely have enabled nuns' sympathetic identification with this subject.[67] Pictorial effects such as presence and tangibility, familiarity and closeness are Luini's compositional strategies to orient and attract the spectator's gaze so that the act of beholding became a form of prayer in itself. Luini's fusion

of figures and landscape in the adjacent *Noli me Tangere* (fig. 82), characterized by the unusual gesture of Christ touching Mary Magdalene's head, also resulted in a greater degree of narrative clarity and monumentality, which in turn gave focus to the nuns' prayer and, as the Benedictine Rule recommends, to the "tears of devotion that come from the heart."[68] The pairs of angels and women participants, specifically, would have served to exalt the nuns' spiritual links to the subject. Overall, in San Maurizio, Luini has taken the devotional aspects of biblical narratives and translated them

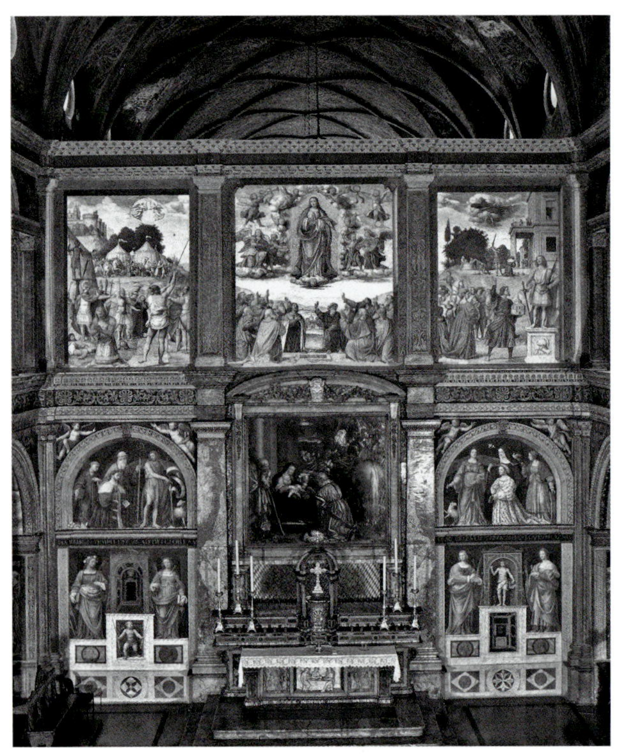

into modern creations, offering double beauty in his frescoes: first, in the form of pleasing representations of religious episodes that, as meditative moments, were intended to lift the eyes and minds of nuns; and second, in the insertion of Christian stories to verdant settings that transformed the spatial and temporal limitations of the nuns' choir, opening its solid walls onto expansive views of God's creation.[69] Merging sacred scenes and the beauty of nature within its own frame, Luini ultimately evokes the power of Christian art to elevate and ennoble the soul, which has its roots in the writings of Petrarch and contemporary

Left 83   Milan, San Maurizio al Monastero Maggiore, overview of the outer church

Below 84   Bernardino Luini, *Alessandro Bentivoglio and Saints*, 1523–4, fresco, Milan, San Maurizio al Monastero Maggiore

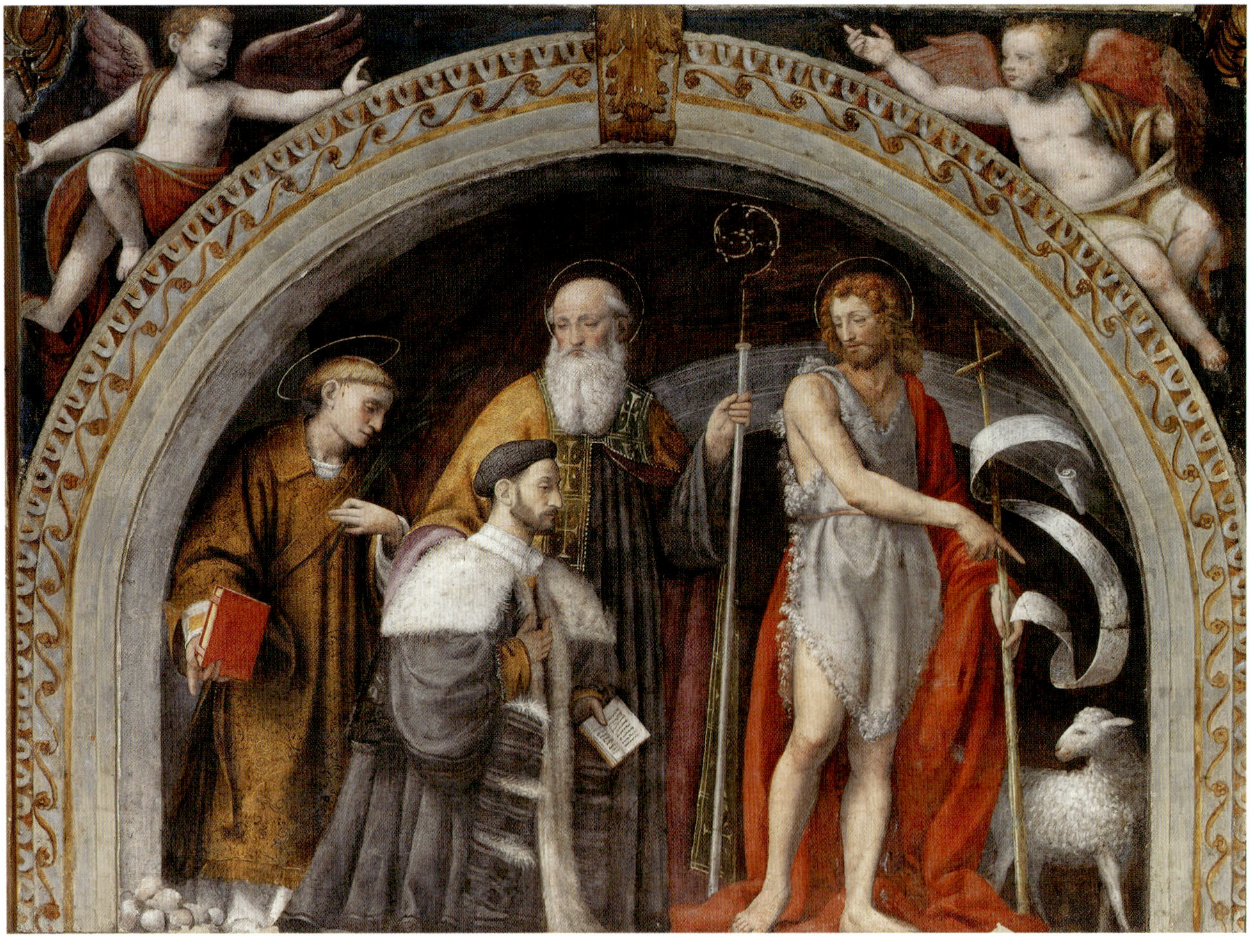

Facing page 85   Bernardino Luini, *Ippolita Sforza Bentivoglio and Saints*, 1523–4, fresco, Milan, San Maurizio al Monastero Maggiore

humanists (Erasmus included) who regarded the *vita contemplativa* as essential for spiritual transcendence.[70]

On the wall facing the lay congregation (fig. 83), Luini's lunette frescoes (widely dated to ca. 1523–4) present saints and two kneeling donors who have been identified as Alessandro Bentivoglio (fig. 84) and his wife Ippolita Sforza (fig. 85) or, alternatively, Ginevra Bentivoglio (Alessandro and Ippolita's daughter) and her husband Giovanni del Carretto.[71] Regardless of their identity, the question is why the Bentivoglio family members feature so prominently in the outer church of San Maurizio. Rulers of Bologna, the family fled the city when it was seized by Pope Julius II's army in 1506, and found refuge in Milan. In 1517 Alessandro and his wife acquired a palace near the convent of San Maurizio, a residence that evolved into an unofficial court of poets, artists, and musicians described in several novels by Matteo Bandello (1554).[72] Meanwhile, the newly built church of San Maurizio became the family's spiritual center, and three of the Bentivoglio daughters – Bianca, Ippolita, and Isabella – took vows in the convent. Luini's

model of dynastic portraits inserted into religious scenes, making claims for political leadership and searching for divine protection, evokes a genre of imagery that the Bentivoglio had favored in their native Bologna. This is exemplified in Lorenzo Costa's altarpiece (1488; fig. 86) in which the Bentivoglio clan flanks a central, enthroned Madonna and Child.[73] Some 35 years separated the images by Costa and Luini, but Costa's prototype continued to encapsulate the values of the Bentivoglio courtly world. In San Maurizio, the kneeling figures accompanied by saints appear less as dynastic leaders than devotees, putting themselves under religious protection. Excommunicated in 1506, Alessandro and Ippolita Bentivoglio were affiliated with the Cassinese Congregation twelve years later, in 1518, enjoying spiritual benefices normally reserved for consecrated individuals. If, however, it is Ginevra Bentivoglio and her husband who are represented in Luini's murals, they stand for the heirs of the Bentivoglio family. The prominence of these Bentivoglio figures in the frescoes, ultimately, signals their status as good Christians

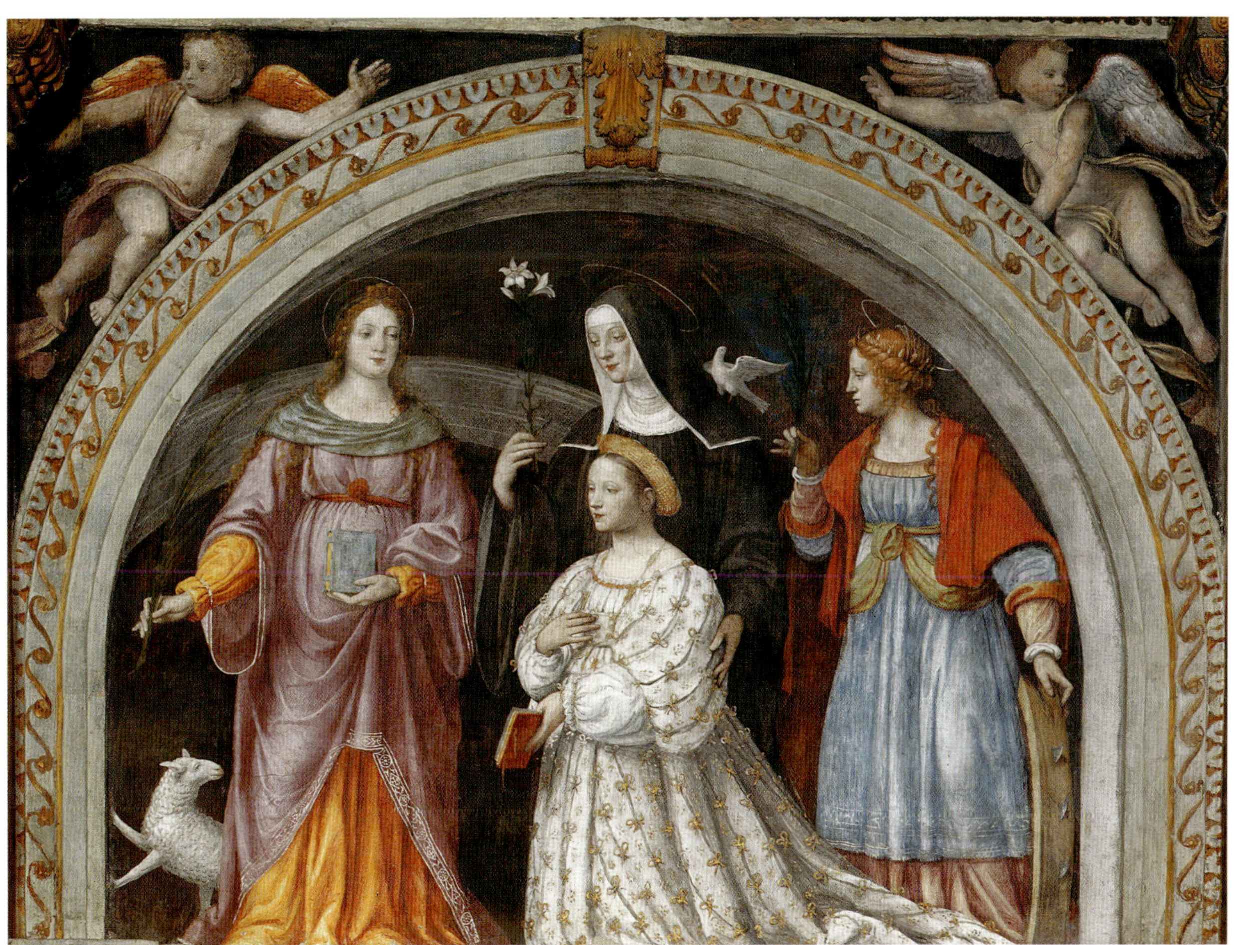

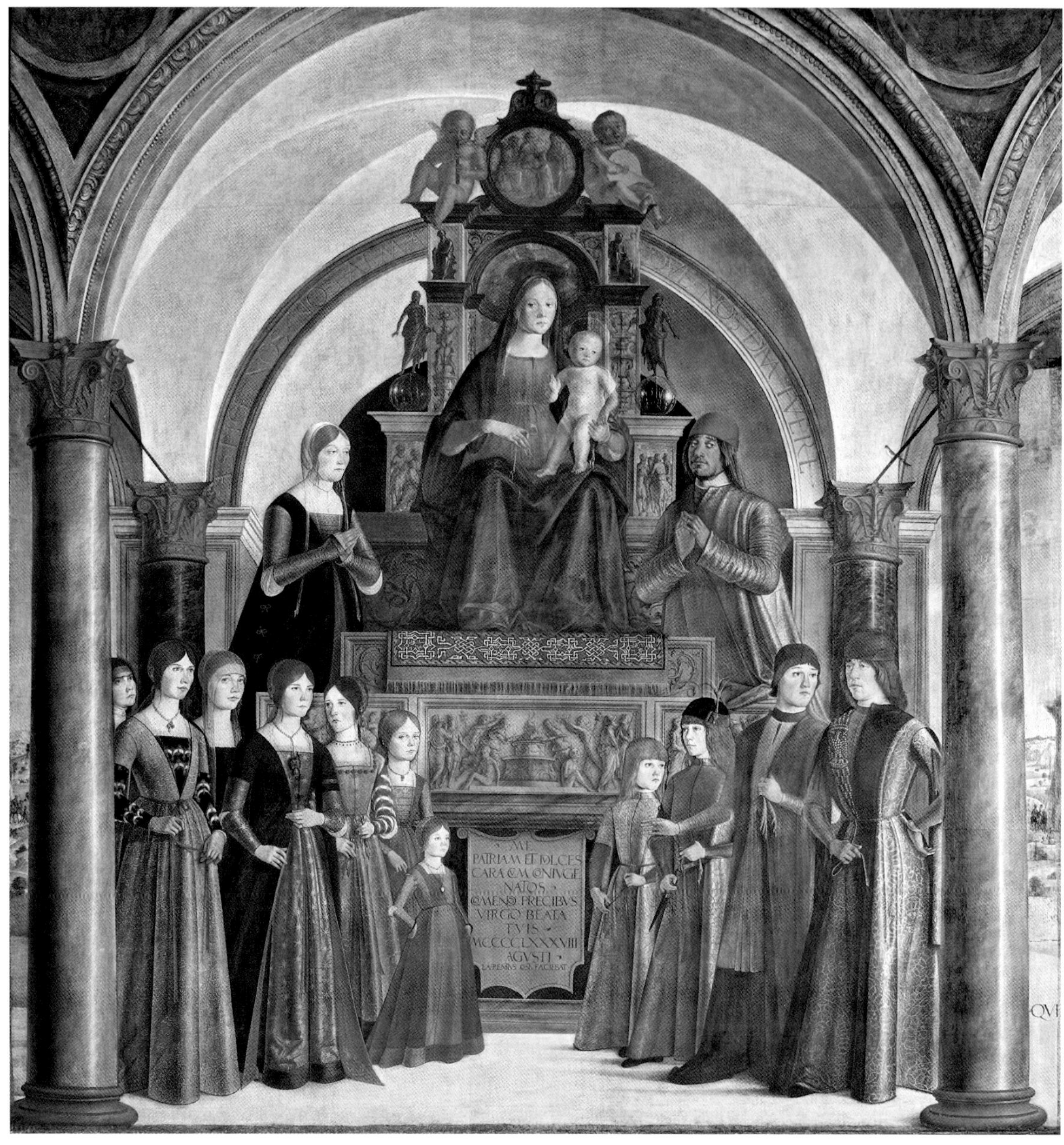

86   Lorenzo Costa, Bentivoglio Altarpiece, 1488, tempera on canvas, 368 × 332 cm (144$^7/_8$ × 130$^{45}/_{64}$ in), Bologna, San Giacomo Maggiore

rather than their political or social rank. The heroine-saint of the Benedictine order, St. Scholastica, accompanies the female figure. As mentioned earlier, the saint may have been given the likeness of Alessandra Bentivoglio, Alessandro and Ippolita's daughter, who was the abbess of San Maurizio in 1522, that is, at the very time when this pictorial monument to the family's history and piety took shape in the outer church of the convent.

Elected six times despite the Cassinese rule of one-year tenure, Abbess Bentivoglio and her community had ambi-

tions to make their decorated choir the model it later became. Although the documentation for this enterprise is lacking, the pictorial transformation of the church of San Maurizio and the inclusion of the abbess's image in the murals suggest that the female cloistered community was not excluded from the aristocratization process that redefined their church with these persuasive, pleasing forms. While Luini acknowledged the nuns' eminent sponsors in the outer church, his other set of images, which fuse Christian spirituality, living nuns' presence, and landscape views,

92

ornament the nuns' choir. These works transformed the site into a unique place of devotional magnificence produced and embodied by the aesthetic effects of art itself.

WOOD INTARSIA STALLS: REFINEMENT AND COMPETITION

Murals were not the only art forms that appointed nuns' choirs. Works in other media, including panels, canvases, miniatures, and inlaid wooden stalls also furnished these female liturgical spaces, and were among the artifacts that elite nuns increasingly scrutinized to bring them into line with their modern artistic values. Stalls, in particular, were indispensable fixtures of monastic choirs and their adornments had long been monitored. For example, in 1490 the General Chapter of the Cassinese Congregation ruled that inlay decoration (probably wood intarsia or floors) could be used in the monks' choir only but not in the outer church, where it would cause too much distraction and "admiration and murmuring" among the laity.[74]

Richly ornamented with fine intarsia, Luchino Bianchino's stalls for the choir of San Paolo in Parma (fig. 87) are recorded by the city's chronicler. Leone Smagliati, annotating every event concerning this convent in recognition of the nuns' status, reports the completion of the choir in January 1510. It is described as a monument to civic pride on which two local masters, the painter Alessandro Araldi and the woodcarver Luchino Bianchino, had worked under the supervision of Abbesses Orsina Bergonzi and Giovanna Piacenza.[75] Smagliati's words are hardly exaggerations. The project for the intarsiated choirstalls was initiated earlier, however, than has so far been recognized. Dating to April 4, 1503, a recently rediscovered document testifies that the energetic Abbess Cecilia Bergonzi first promoted the commission.[76]

Featuring liturgical items (books, candlesticks, and crosses), polyhedrons, writing implements, and perspectival city views, Bianchino's large intarsia panels in the stalls are refined works that display his virtuoso skill in the rendering of buildings and artifacts as geometric solids. Ideal cities receding in one-point perspective and an array of objects visible within cabinets through half-open shutters proclaim Bianchino's perspectival knowledge and chromaticism.[77] Within Bianchino's geometric elaboration of his subjects, the arms of Abbesses Bergonzi and Piacenza appear in four panels.[78] Surmounting an ideal city view in one panel, the

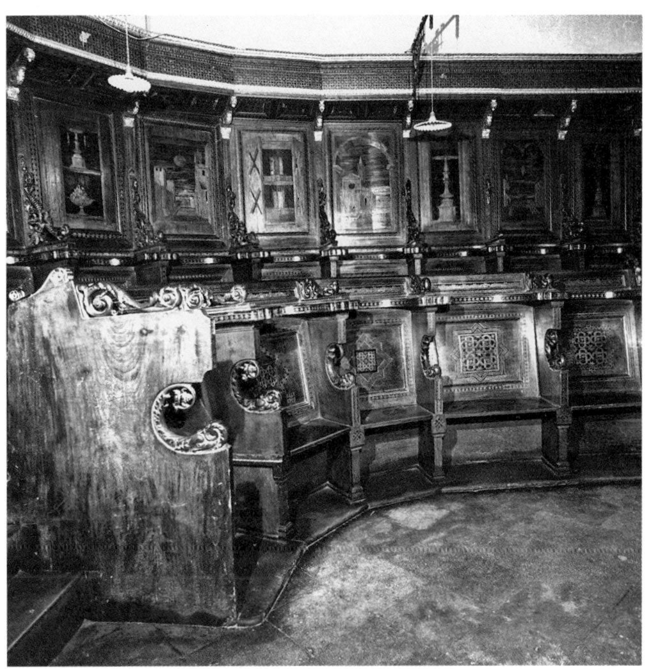

87   Luchino Bianchino, choirstalls, 1510, Parma, SS. Trinità dei Rossi, now Santa Teresa del Bambin Gesù

dark-toned Bergonzi shield (three crescents horizontally disposed and separated by a band) is suspended on a half-rotating polyhedron, while in the other panel the device marks the archway of a city gate (fig. 88). Conversely, the lighter-toned Piacenza arms (three diagonally disposed crescents) hang from the central corbel of a double arch framing an urban perspective (fig. 89), with foreshortened buildings that lead the eye in depth toward a distant landscape. In the other Piacenza panel, the abbess's device is shown on an archway through which the eyes again travel back into a distant view. Double symbolic representations of abbesses' arms were not infrequent in conventual artworks, usually alluding to conflicts and clashes inside the communities. Arms are potent reminders that even furnishings and inlaid works were entangled with notions of status and power, and that they, too, could become tokens of rivalry and competition. To address these questions in the San Paolo context, it is first necessary to take a step back and revisit the choir project at its inception during the tenures of Abbesses Cecilia and Orsina Bergonzi, their exploitation of the courtly dynastic model, and investments in the arts.

To begin with, the election of Cecilia Bergonzi as abbess in 1484 was contested. She was elected by a minority of nuns, while the majority of votes were cast for another nun, Caterina Bravi. The Milanese political authorities inter-

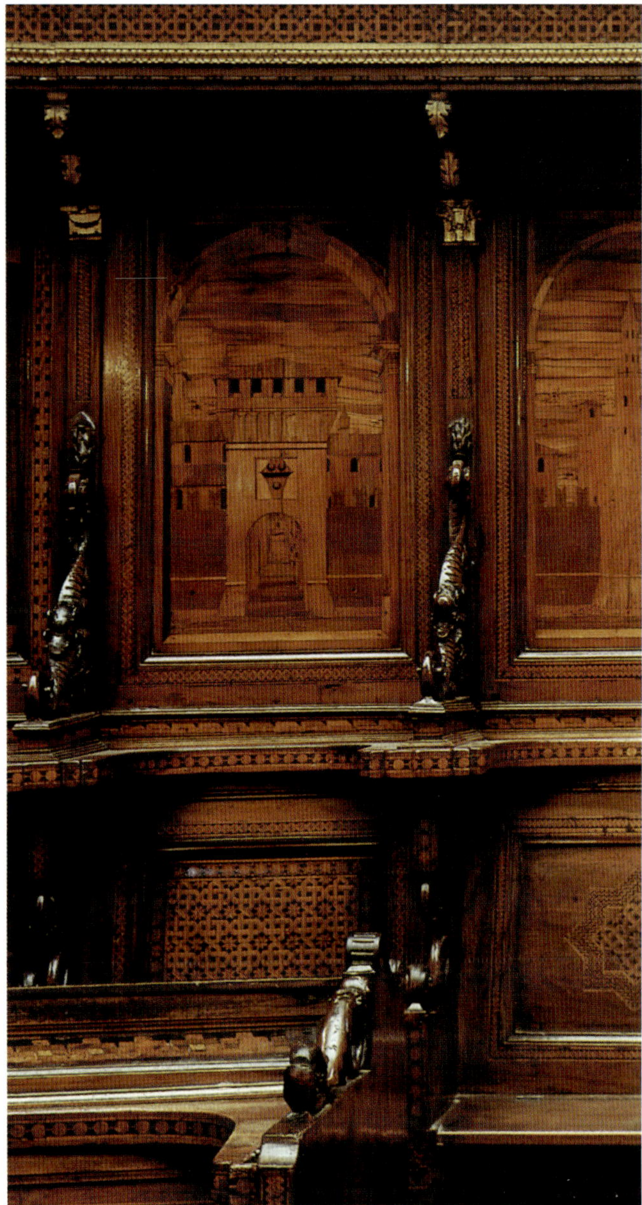

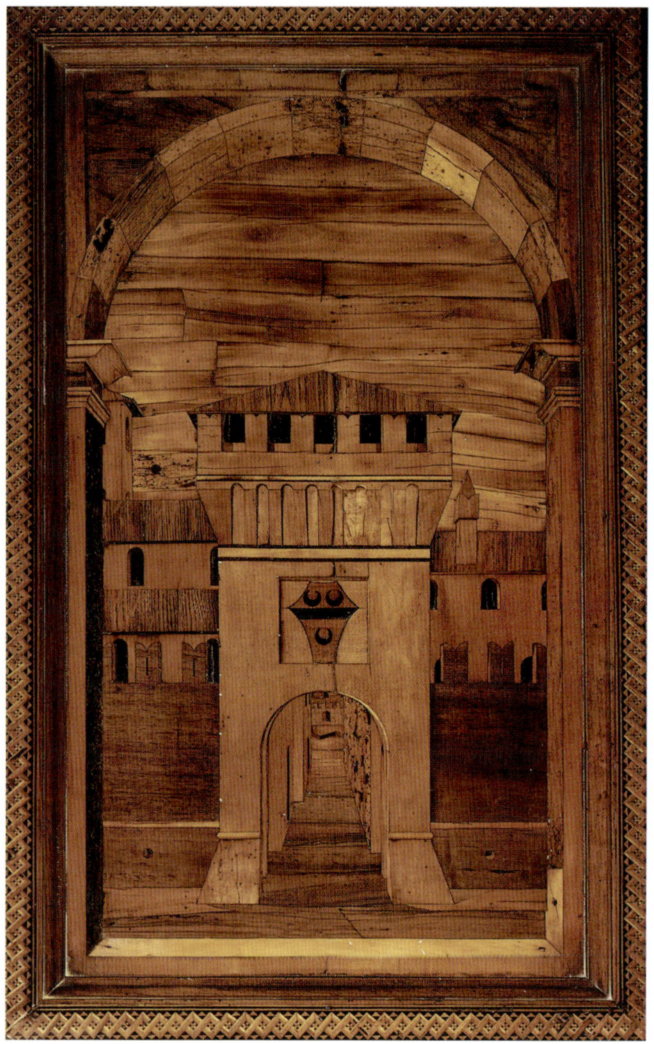

Left and above 88   Luchino Bianchino, panel with Bergonzi arms, 1510, wood intarsia, 40.5 × 24.5 cm ($15^{15}/_{16}$ × $9^{41}/_{64}$ in), 95 × 35 × 17 cm ($37^{13}/_{32}$ × $13^{25}/_{32}$ × $6^{11}/_{16}$ in), Parma, SS. Trinità dei Rossi, now Santa Teresa del Bambin Gesù

vened in the process, rejecting Bravi's candidacy, and their representatives helped Cecilia Bergonzi obtain papal confirmation.[79] Despite the confirmation bull issued on September 23, 1484, Bravi along with a few defiant nuns refused obedience to Abbess Bergonzi. At least one document was drawn up recording Bravi as the abbess of San Paolo.[80] Given the strong ties between the nuns and their natal families, this monastic dispute evolved not only into a legal suit, but also erupted into street violence among armed supporters of both religious women.[81] It took Cecilia Bergonzi two years and a half to gain obedience from all her nuns. In February 1487, the penultimate step was to grant Caterina Bravi a perpetual allowance (*vitalizio*) and to

refund the nun's relatives the legal fees they had accumulated in her defense.[82]

In the following decade, Cecilia manifested a strong sense of self in several remarkable commissions. She promoted the renovation of the nuns' choir, the construction of the eastern arm of a new cloister (see fig. 97), and the erection of higher walls, proudly presenting her achievements in inscriptions that are now lost, but are known thanks to eighteenth-century transcriptions.[83] Prominently placed on the convent wall and visible to passersby, one inscription stated: "Abbess Cecilia, the great glory of the Bergonzi family, second to none in virtue, built [this wall]."[84] Partaking in the long-standing custom of investing in architecture to confer glory

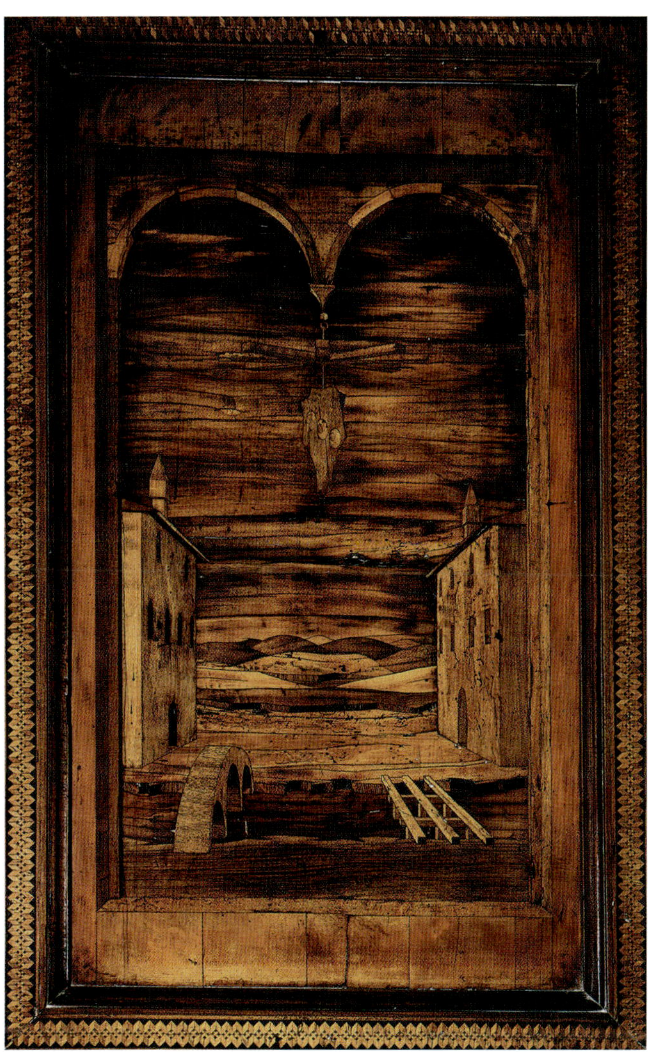

89   Luchino Bianchino, panel with Piacenza arms, 1510, wood intarsia, 40.5 × 24.5 cm ($15^{15}/_{16}$ × $9^{41}/_{64}$ in), Parma, SS. Trinità dei Rossi, now Santa Teresa del Bambin Gesù

speaks, in particular, of the abbess's closeness to such local humanists as Taddeo Ugoleto. A professor of Greek and humanities, Ugoleto served from 1475 at the court of Buda as the librarian and the tutor of Matthias Corvinus's illegitimate son. After Ugoleto returned to Parma in 1490, he became a crucial figure in the rise of a humanist culture there. Along with his brother, he established a printing press in the city, but as a result became impoverished, as is declared in his biography by Pierio Valeriano, *Ill Fortune of Learned Men* (ca. 1529).[85] Ugoleto is known to have treasured small-scale antiquities in his Parmese residence, as attested by an unpublished drawing featuring an ancient stele in his possession, in the antiquarian sylloge assembled by the epigrapher Michele Fabrizio Ferrarini (d. before 1493).[86] While the vogue for inserting inscriptions on palace façades, courtyards, and garden loggias is well documented in Italian cities from the early 1490s, only a few humanists in Parma, including Ugoleto, took part in it. Ugoleto could therefore have been instrumental in Abbess Cecilia's exploitation of inscriptions for her own celebratory purposes.

After some twenty years in office, Cecilia wanted to ensure her family perpetual power over San Paolo and so maneuvered to pass the abbatial office to her niece, the young nun Orsina, turning the Bergonzi female progeny into a convent dynasty.[87] By asking Pope Julius II to appoint Orsina as a *de facto* abbess sometime in 1505, Cecilia disregarded a foundational monastic norm that gave nuns the right to vote for their abbess. As Kate Lowe has acutely observed, "abbesses' elections provided the only known opportunity for women to vote on the Italian peninsula at the time."[88] Dating to 15 April, 1505, Pope Julius II's bull granted Cecilia her request, praising her virtues and accomplishments.[89] The daughter of Cecilia's brother Francesco, Orsina had assisted her aunt Cecilia for some time by 1505. Competent at administration, Orsina is described in the bull as having sufficient education (*literatura*) for the abbatial office, although she was not yet 28 years old, as required to become eligible. Both Orsina's minority and the suppression of the community's voting rights were evidently concerns that did not much matter to Abbess Cecilia, nor to Julius II. The papal bull further specifies that Cecilia could keep various entitlements, such as the right to reclaim her title should Orsina step down or die, and to keep her office's allowance of 1,000 gold florins. Further, Cecilia was to exercise equal supervision to that of the administrators (*presidentes*) of the Cassinese Congregation.[90] The *de facto* abbess Orsina was to secure the completion of several artistic commissions, among which the ornamentation of the choir was paramount. In short, in 1505 the hegemony

on patrons, Cecilia linked her own virtue to the construction of the convent walls, displaying her sense of pride and virtuosity. The persona in the inscription connects her fame to her family, however, not to her religious community. Abbess Cecilia did not present herself adorned with the virtue of humility. On the contrary, she manifested an ambitious and, arguably, egocentric personality.

The choosing of encomiastic inscriptions in praise of oneself aligned Cecilia with contemporary palace owners who asserted their virtues and glorious genealogies in antiquarian inscriptions. Modeled on classical examples of praise for illustrious individuals, Renaissance inscriptions repurposed them as propaganda. A celebratory inscription

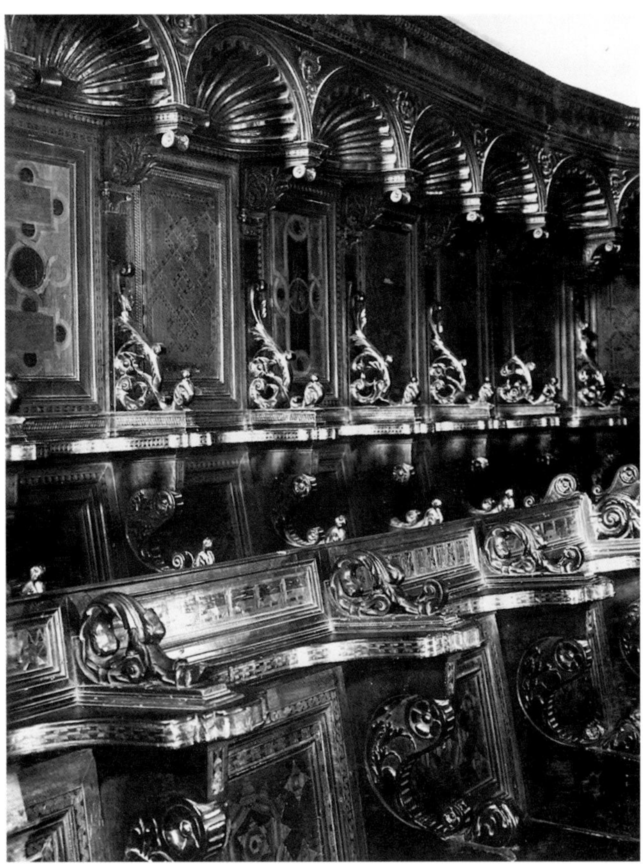

90   Giovanni Giacomo Baruffi, choirstalls, 1505–7, Parma, Sant'Ulderico

of Abbesses Cecilia and Orsina Bergonzi in San Paolo had the makings of a female dynasty.

Reckonings occur, nevertheless, and dynasties perish. Orsina's abbatial office lasted only two years. She was unexpectedly found dead on April 25, 1507, as the scrupulous Parmese chronicler reports. That very day the Bergonzi dynastic control over San Paolo ended abruptly. The nuns immediately congregated and unanimously elected Giovanna Piacenza as their abbess.[91] With Giovanna's election, the nuns at least reasserted the right to elect their abbess. This detailed account of the convent's history illustrates two matters: the extent to which the choir's refurbishing had become a source of pride for the community and its female leaders, and how the competing financial investments of Abbesses Bergonzi and Piacenza affected the production of the wood intarsia stalls. Although opposed on several other grounds, both abbesses held the belief that a noble self should be manifested through the display of sumptuous adornments, contrary though this was to monastic tenets.[92]

Bianchino's two rows of choirstalls are arranged in a U shape. In the 1860s they were transferred from the badly deteriorated choir of San Paolo to the then oratory of SS. Trinità dei Rossi, now known as the church of Santa Teresa del Bambin Gesù, which is still their home. They were adjusted to fit the small retrochoir behind the main altar of the church and now abut the walls (see fig. 87), with thick curtains hiding them from the public.[93] Two large stalls were adapted to become doors, six were lost, and in general the distance between the large and the small row of stalls was reduced. The unusual double stall now found at the center of the stalls resulted from joining together two stalls.[94] In short, the surviving choirstalls consist of twenty large intarsiated stalls, ten smaller stalls, and a lectern.[95] Originally, however, Bianchino's stalls may not have been placed along the walls. As was typical in pre-Tridentine monastic churches, stalls occupied the central portions of choirs, forming independent zones for nuns' worship and musical performances.[96] Trained by the famed painter-carvers Cristoforo and Lorenzo Canozi da Lendinara, Luchino worked both as a woodcarver and an architect-engineer in early sixteenth-century Parma. Although some subjects appearing in the San Paolo stalls repeat motifs from Bianchino's previous sets, they are a tour de force of geometry and painterly effects, but not, as Massimo Ferretti has recognized, of plasticity.[97]

A manifestation of civic and conventual pride, San Paolo's splendid intarsia stalls spurred the other local Benedictine communities, in particular the nuns of Sant'Ulderico and San Quintino, to compete in the refurbishing of their own choirs, the sort of competition that was another salient component of the patronage of elite monastic institutions. In Parma, noble abbesses had occasion to observe one another's artistic investments. For example, the abbess of Sant'Ulderico, Cabrina Carissimi, is documented among the guests invited to the banquet celebrating Giovanna Piacenza's election in 1507. She stayed late for the party and, as an unpublished record relates, was lodged in the convent guesthouse (*in camera deputata pro alogiamento*).[98] To understand this context of conventual rivalry I turn to consider the making of the choirstalls for Sant'Ulderico and San Quintino, and explore the working conditions of woodcarvers involved in the commissions.

Placed behind the altar, the choirstalls still in situ in Sant'Ulderico comprise 24 large stalls (fig. 90) and 14 smaller ones, also arranged in a U shape.[99] Different from the San Paolo enterprise, the provisions of this commission are specified in a surviving contract dated April 4, 1505.[100] Drawn up between Abbess Cabrina Carissimi, assisted by six nuns, and the local woodcarver Giovanni Giacomo Baruffi, the document regulates the materials, costs, and features of the stalls. It specifies that their visual imagery be modeled on the (now-lost) stalls of San Francesco in Parma, except for those with "prospective" (city views). In place of city views, Baruffi is requested to represent "varied and multiple ensemble of intarsiated motifs [*grupi de tarsie varii et diversi*] of good and perfect design to fill the surface . . . Learned individuals are to find them beautiful and praiseworthy; and the work should display virtuosity and proportion."[101] Could the contract's specification for *grupi* be seen as a reference to the knot-patterns (or *groppi*), that is, the cords looping around themselves to make geometrical, repeated forms? They appear in drawings and engravings after Leonardo and were used to advertise his academy in Milan.[102] Several existing large stall panels in Sant'Ulderico show curvilinear cords interlaced in various ways against a darker background to confer a sense of plasticity and painterly effects to the carved patterns. Whatever the case, the knot motif stood for protection, security, secret matters, and eternity in ancient cultures. A well-known apotropaic device, the knot was a symbol of enchantment and protection against demonic spirits.[103] But for modern viewers, once again, what is significant is the nuns' deep awareness of the forms expressed in the works to be made for them.

The contract further indicates that Abbess Carissimi prepaid Baruffi the cost of the material (walnut) and wanted her stall panel alone adorned with "a large, good, and beautiful architectural view."[104] She promises to supply Baruffi with a furnished residence (a two-story house with a courtyard).[105] The exact location of this house, which the carver kept until the completion of the commission in 1507, remains unclear: was it within or outside the convent precinct? It was there that Baruffi may have had his workshop. Chapter 66 of the Benedictine Rule allows "all the facilities [which are needed . . . including] workshops for various crafts" within monastic confines.[106] Indeed, this prescription worked best in male communities, and at least one painter, Correggio, is known to have resided within the Cassinese monastery of San Giovanni Evangelista in Parma from 1520 to 1523 while engaged on works for the monks, a still undervalued aspect of the interrelationships between art and monasticism and the shifting role of sacred art in the age of religious reform.[107]

In the case of San Quintino, the choirstalls were carved by Marco Antonio Zucchi, who began working on the commission in 1512.[108] Part of the furnishings still in situ in the church's choir, which also included an altarpiece by Francesco Marmitta of ca. 1500–05 (Paris, Louvre), the 16 large stalls and 6 smaller ones are arranged in two U-shaped rows.[109] Located behind the main altar, the large stall panels present geometrical motifs, while only the stall for Abbess Giovanna Sanvitale, which was carved as the commission test piece, displays an ideal perspective view. As in San Paolo, each stall has ornamented rests and classicizing finials. Despite their differences, the stalls of San Quintino, Sant'Ulderico, and San Paolo therefore all had features of devotional magnificence set into their very materiality. Due in part to the imagery demonstrating the science of perspective, intarsiated ornamentation like that found on these stalls appealed to the minds of cultivated observers. In his *De Partibus Aedium* (1494 and 1516) the Parmese humanist Francesco Mario Grapaldo speaks of intarsiated images as *emblemata*.[110] In Roman mosaic floors, *emblemata* were the historiated tessellated panels separated from each other by multiple borders. During the Renaissance, they were extended to embrace the figural insertions in marble floors, walls, or as studs with devices that were worn on clothing.[111] Despite the fact that Vasari characterized woodcarvers as men endowed with diligence rather than imagination in design, sophisticated viewers perceived intarsia as a craft that allowed its makers to display their own inventions.[112] Echoing Leonardo's *groppi*, the varied "knots" (*grupi*) requested by Abbess Carissimi can be seen as kinds of *emblemata*, and their various interwoven patterns the result of reimagining them in multiple ways without losing the force of the ornamental design. As a form of interlace decoration, knots were an ornament elevated to an end in itself.

Embellished choirs, ornate choirstalls, and outfitted cells enlivened the corporate and private living spaces of elite nuns, and were works that celebrated and glorified their historical viewers. The religious images by Romanino and Luini in particular make claims as to the efficacy of Christian art and its aesthetic values, promoting the emergence of a courtly monastic art that did not simply echo Renaissance artistic trends but aimed to reflect on their very subjects and messages. As will be seen, further evidence of this courtly visual culture is found in the spaces inhabited by abbesses and the ornaments within their rooms.

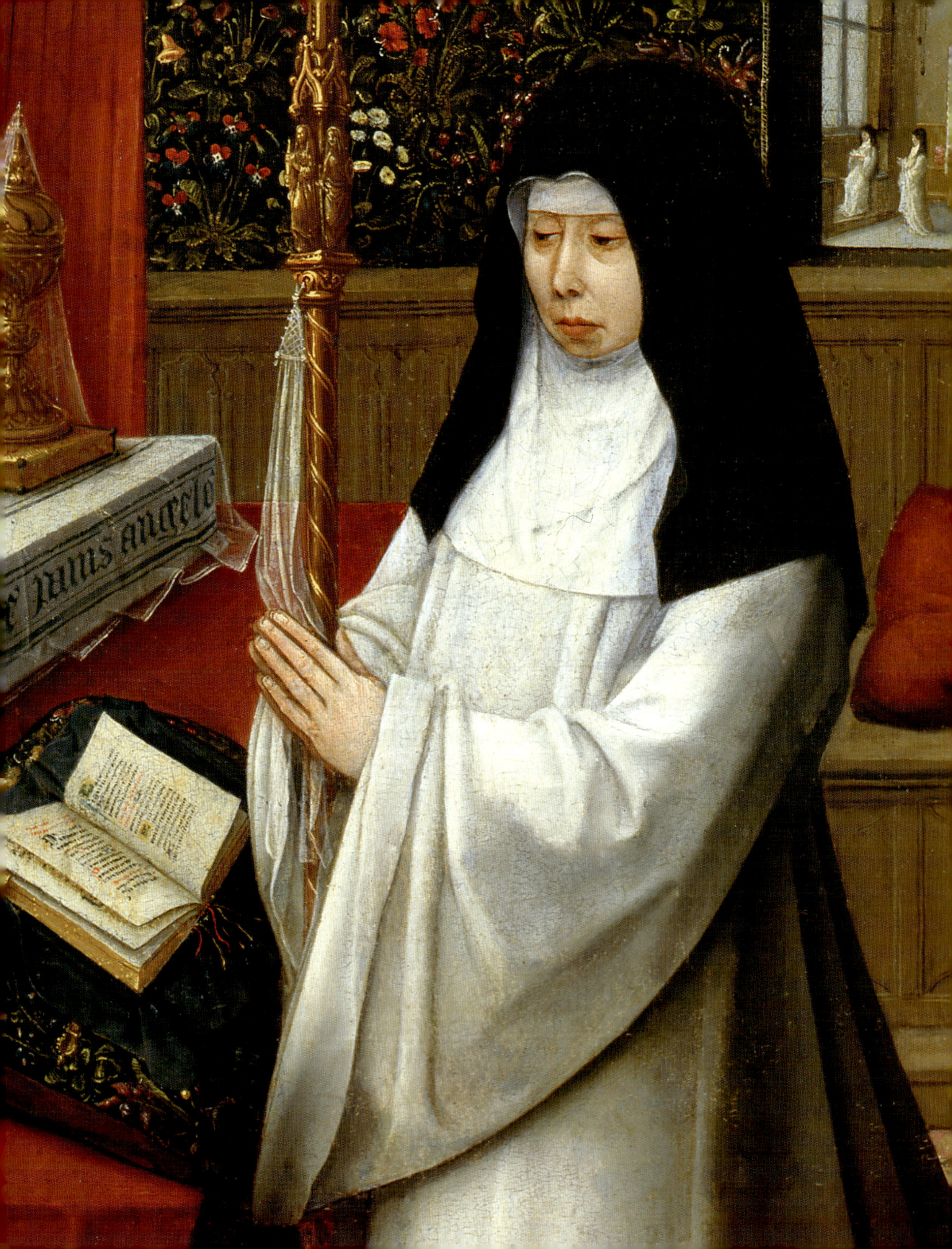
panis angelo

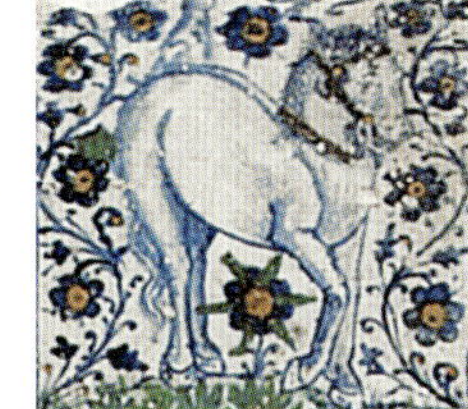

4

Giovanna Piacenza's Abbatial Apartment

SPACE, GENDER, AND SELF-IDENTITY

Monastic rules do not prescribe that abbots should live in rooms separated from the rest of the community. From the Middle Ages onwards, however, aristocratic abbots had independent lodgings from which to carry on their administrative and pastoral duties. Abbots' dwellings in large, affluent monasteries progressed from small chambers to discrete residences, later transformed into luxurious palaces. At Cluny in the twelfth century, abbots occupied a few rooms on the upper floor of the narthex of an abandoned church. Conversely, the abbot of the Benedictine monastery of Santa Giustina in Padua inhabited a so-called palace, an ensemble of independent chambers that also served to lodge dignitaries and guests. The reformer of the Benedictine order (then Cassinese), Ludovico Barbo (1381–1443), suppressed this abbatial palace, which he described as a den of "vice and fornication." Regardless of Barbo's views, the tradition of elite monastic residences continued to flourish. Sixteenth-century records relate that at the Cassinese monastery of San Benedetto Po (Mantua) the abbot's palace adjoined the guesthouse and infirmary, forming a separate court to welcome visitors. Seventeenth- and eighteenth-century noble abbots are documented as having inhabited magnificent castles with gardens, fountains, lakes, and pools such as at St. Florian Abbey near Linz (Austria).[1]

Bishops, too, lived in elegantly furnished residences located in the main city of their dioceses. The halls and chapels of ecclesiastical apartments were often finely decorated.[2] For example, the bishop of Albenga, Napoleone Fieschi, had sibyls, prophets, and stories of the infancy of Christ painted in his apartment chapel by the so-called Maestro di Luceram between 1459 and 1466. During the tenure of Filos Roverella as the bishop of Ascoli Piceno, the Vicentine artist Marcello Fogolino depicted scenes from the story of Moses (ca. 1547) in a room of the bishop's palace.[3]

In contrast to the fairly well-studied residences of monastic and male ecclesiastical authorities, much less is known about the dwellings of their female counterparts, upper-class abbesses whose administrative responsibilities and rights placed them on equal footing with their male peers, although as women they were considered inferior and ranked lower in the Church's hierarchy. Patrician abbesses inhabited independent quarters in their convents that functioned as the centers of their networks.[4] But the furnishings and ornaments of many of these residences were often stripped away in the decades preceding and/or subsequent to the Tridentine decree on religious individuals (1563). What little visual evidence has survived of this female monastic tradition is therefore precious. The early eighteenth-century portrait of Abbess Elisabeth Ernestine Antonie von Sachsen-Meiningen by Johann Peter Harburg (fig. 91) constitutes an astonishing late manifestation of this tradition. It presents a German canoness of a *Frauenstift* (convent whose members were not bound by vows) in Bad Gandersheim (Lower Saxony), not garbed as a religious but in rich attire and shown playing with her lapdog in a refined domestic setting. Sitting at a table displaying finely illustrated books and a collection of *naturalia*, she is seen against a backdrop revealing other books and statuettes, proudly exhibiting a private space devoted to the cultivation of her persona.[5]

Jean Bellegambe's *Abbess Jeanne de Boubais* (fig. 92), painted between 1507 and 1533, transmits a more sober but no less fascinating style of life in an abbatial interior. Holding the crosier and with her family arms suspended above, Abbess Boubais is captured in prayer in her private chapel, a site delimited by a wooden bench and a mille-

91   Johann Peter Harburg, *Abbess Elisabeth Ernestine Antonie von Sachsen-Meiningen*, 1734, 162 × 244 cm (63$^{25}/_{32}$ × 96$^{1}/_{16}$ in), Lower Saxony, Bad Gandersheim, Gandersheim Abbey

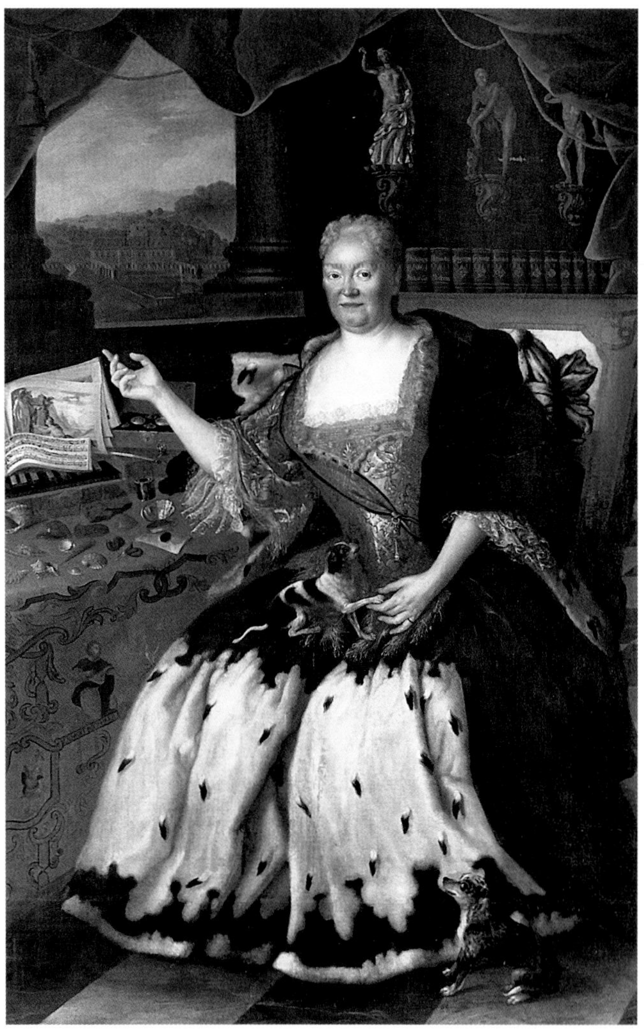

fleurs tapestry mounted on a wall panel. Through an opening to the right of the tapestry, the spectator's eyes are transported into a room furnished with a bed, cabinet, two window seats, and a clock. A religious woman (or the abbess herself) oversees another sister, who is seated at the window reading from a book. The bed and cabinet seem to suggest that this chamber served as Jeanne Boubais' own bedroom.[6] Bellegambe's image offers a rare glimpse into a sixteenth-century convent residence, picturing cloistered women at their devotions and studies.

Abbatial apartments had been adorned both north and south of the Alps since the Middle Ages, as seems to be confirmed by an early fourteenth-century tapestry panel from the Dominican house of St. Katherine in Freiburg. The panel features eleven medallions (fig. 93), the first and last of which incorporate the Freiburg Malterer family arms with the names ANNA on the left and JOHANNES on the right. In between, the nine scenes represent episodes of men humiliated by women, including Phyllis riding a bridled Aristotle and Iwen surrendering to the enthroned wife of his enemy Ascalon, both stressing the topos of the power of women.[7] At the same time, they underscore elite cloistered women's level of sophistication in the later Middle Ages. Taken as a whole, this small body of work speaks of a female conventual visual culture that, despite ecclesiastical authorities' cyclical campaigns of suppression and repression, continued to thrive and resurface in different forms, media, and times in aristocratic convents until the secularization of religious orders in the nineteenth century. But there is something more fundamental at stake in this corpus.

The paucity of surviving works documenting this tradition has largely contributed to its historiographic neglect. Even its most impressive manifestation, Abbess Giovanna Piacenza's ornate residence in San Paolo in Parma, has been totally obscured as regards its position within the history of female monasticism, nor has it ever been considered within that framework. Since Erwin Panofsky and Ernst Gombrich's contributions, Correggio's enchanting painted chamber (see Chapter Six) has been seen as the expression of Abbess Piacenza's patronage and the painter's artistry, disregarding the issue of Correggio's intervention within a sophisticated monastic culture that he remade anew and that interacted with spheres of gender, power, and learning in wholly unanticipated ways. The cultivated abbess of an urban convent, Giovanna Piacenza was subject to a regime of appropriate comportment and to rules of enclosure, modesty, and austerity, which she challenged by creating an elaborately decorated noble residence for herself. Her apartment not only

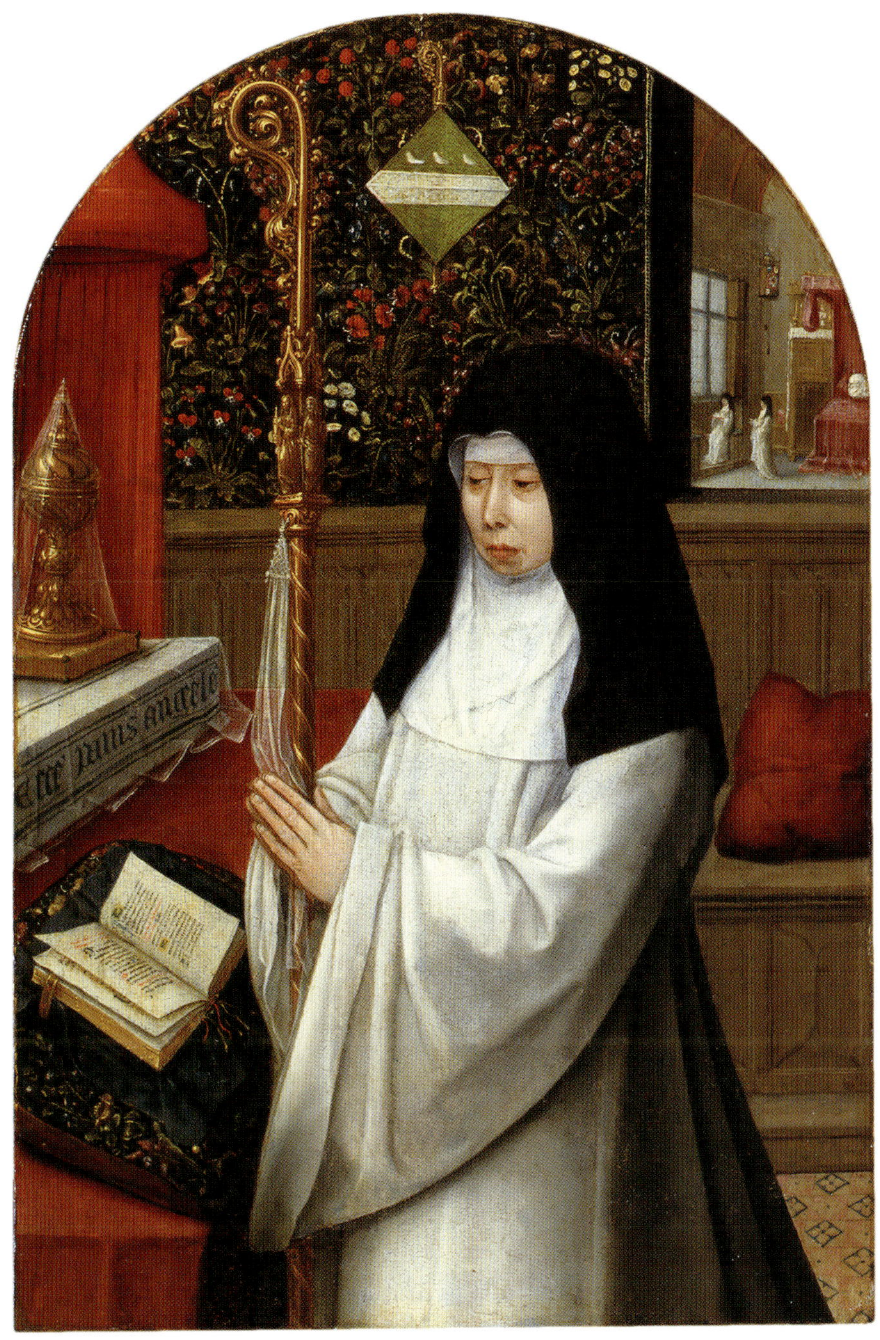

92   Jean Bellegambe, *Abbess Jeanne de Boubais* (verso), ca. 1507–33, 40.4 × 25.1 cm ($15^{29}/_{32} × 9^{7}/_{8}$ in), Pittsburgh, Frick Art and Historical Center

represented a world that amalgamated monastic, courtly, and social values and transgressed boundaries of conventual decorum, but also itself made that world.

A notarial document of 1524 (to be examined shortly) states that the abbatial dwelling occupied the ground floor of a new building (fig. 94). It further refers to open-air structures overlooking a garden. In essence, the record shows that Giovanna did not resort to having a single chamber for herself carved out from extant conventual spaces. Instead, she sponsored the construction of a building whose finely decorated interior and exterior spaces would afford its owner and visitors opportunities for pleasure and contemplation, delight and meditation. As a reassessment of Abbess Giovanna Piacenza's ornate residence, this chapter argues that the apart-

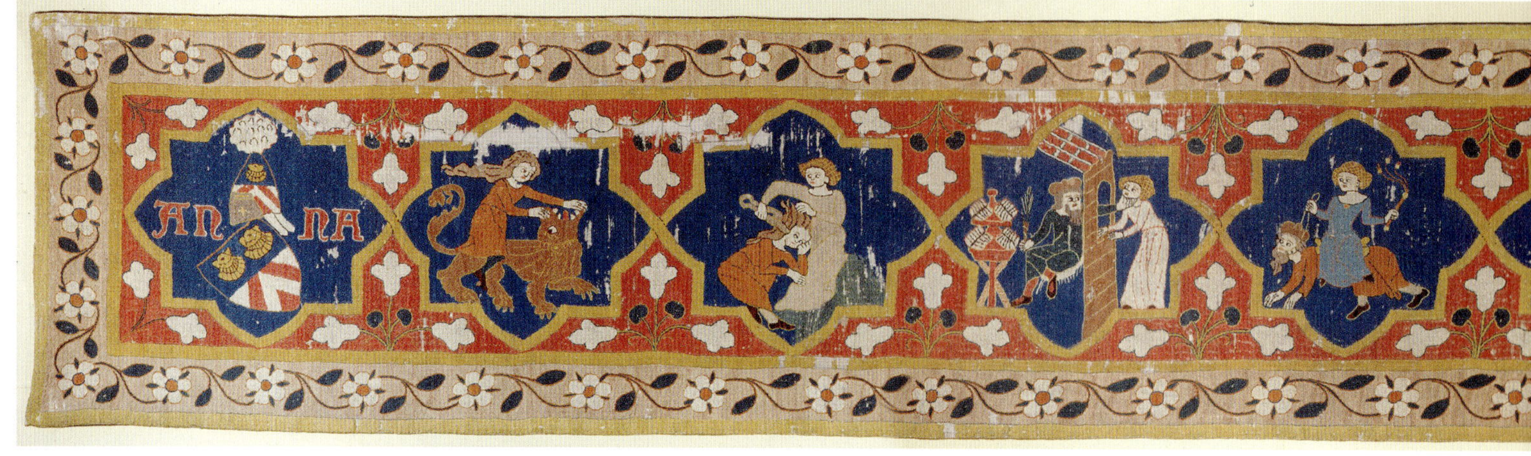

ment adapted the typology of the male ecclesiastical *palatium*, shifting the gender and power relationships to an unprecedented degree. Giovanna's own quarters exposed features of "other" spaces in distinct ways. Building on the notion of "other" spaces, that is, heterotopic spaces that do not fit into the standard dichotomy of sacred/profane, enclosed/open, I argue that the abbatial rooms and their exterior surroundings constituted an "other" space, a convent court that recognized status and roles for cloistered women unavailable outside,

Above 93   Tapestry presenting courtly subjects, 1320–30, wool, 67.5 × 491 cm (26½ × 193⁵/₁₆ in), Freiburg, Augustiner Museum, detail

Below 94   Parma, San Paolo area, aerial view

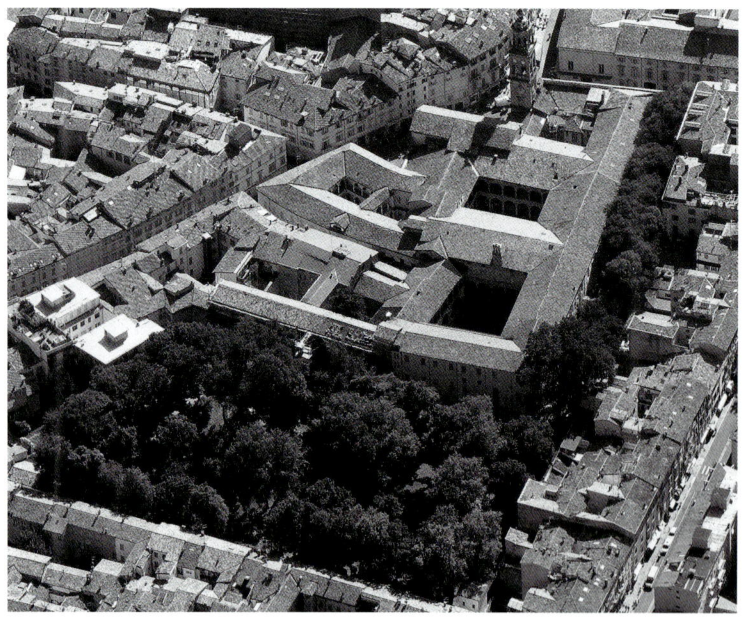

staging a myth of female power and leadership tinged with wit.[8] Relevant to this critical rethinking of the abbatial apartment is the little-studied intarsiated wood and incised stone corpus, a set of multilingual inscriptions and ingeniously conceived devices that furnish the viewer with precepts of stoic discipline and humorous, *double entendre* messages. This body of words and signs was not displayed alongside Correggio and Araldi's frescoes, but marked door thresholds, asking visitors to pause and meditate as they accessed the rooms. And Mary Carruthers has long reminded readers that letters were considered "to be as visual as what we call 'images' today" in the monastic tradition.[9] Before addressing what this corpus at San Paolo encoded, one must first consider the early sixteenth-century campaign for the construction of the abbatial residence as an independent court opposite the convent's north gate. It will be seen that it was Alessandro Araldi who probably decorated the walls adjacent to this entrance with murals exalting female learnedness. And finally I shall turn to the earliest justification of Giovanna Piacenza's artistic investments, written by the nuns' confessor Lorenzo Cornigli as early as 1522 in defense of the "venustas" (beauty) of the abbatial chambers.

HOLDING THE *CURIA* AND THE CONVENT COURT

Giovanna Piacenza's abbatial office (1507–24) coincided with a period of wars and calamities that plagued the Italian peninsula. The collapse of the Milanese Sforza regime in 1499 and the protracted fights for political domination caused instability in the city of Parma, which had been annexed to the Sforza duchy some 40 years earlier. Conflicts and sudden

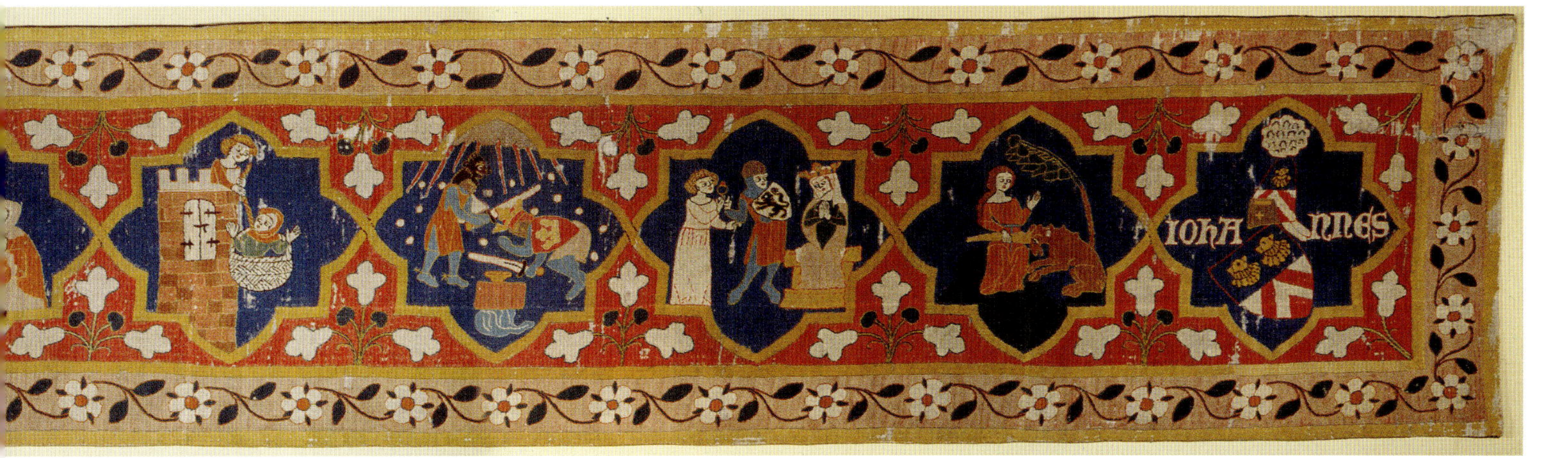

shifts of power brought the papacy and the French alternately into control of Parma in less than two decades. Violence and street fighting afflicted the citizenry and deepened their sense of insecurity, spurring radical forms of devotion such as the "bonfire of the vanities" in 1510. Cards, dice, wigs, cosmetics, and mirrors, among other objects deemed to be occasions of sin, were burned in a public bonfire in Parma's main square. Local youth carrying banderoles with the insignia of Christ celebrated this act of purification, which culminated in the severe beating of prostitutes across the square.[10] Prostitutes were recurrent victims of society's anxiety in the Renaissance. But during the French occupation of Parma (intermittently between 1499 and 1521), not even its patrician female citizens were safe from abuse. As Smagliati records, the French army commanders organized "reprehensible" parties that well-bred local girls were constrained to attend, involving masquerades and plays.[11] In the midst of street violence, scandals, and various other forms of disorder and maltreatment, life was hardly peaceful even for cloistered women.

Supported by her family and sponsors, Abbess Giovanna Piacenza resisted attempts by the ecclesiastical authorities to enforce strict seclusion on her community on three occasions, in 1512, 1514, and 1523, each time with less determination and strength and the gradual acceptance of some restrictions. Attempts to reform the nuns were ultimately successful well before the Tridentine decree. Local ecclesiastical and political authorities joined forces to implement rigid cloister regulations over the unruly community of San Paolo following Giovanna's death in 1524. The major changes entailed reducing the abbess's lifelong tenure to one year and shifting control of the convent's vast estate from the abbess's family members to civic authorities.[12] As a result, the community's artistic investments shrank dramatically. But, to step back in time, first I consider the relations that bound Abbess Giovanna to a group of politically ascending Parmese citizens who sponsored her monastic career and assured the manifestation of her agency in the investments she promoted in San Paolo.

Giovanna Piacenza was born into a rising patrician family that exercised control over one of the factions that dominated Parma's government in the early sixteenth century. Her ancestors had long lived in the district of Santo Stefano, and their continued residence in that neighborhood reflected their sense of urban identity. Giovanna's father, Marco Piacenza (or Boroni), came from a merchant family, while her mother Agnese was the daughter of Giovanna Benedetti and Sebastiano Bergonzi.[13] Beside Giovanna, the couple had at least two other children, Cesare and Caterina. As part of the family's strategy of accruing social influence and maintaining its patrimony undivided, Giovanna entered San Paolo, while her sister Caterina married Scipione Montini Rosa, the nephew of Bartolomeo Montini (ante 1460–1524), an influential canon of Parma's cathedral and the Apostolic Protonotary. The marriage consolidated the families' alliance and, through other unions, the Bergonzi, Piacenza, and Montini were tied to the Colla and Prati, forming a close-knit urban group that used the same strategies as old feudal clans on its path of political ascendance. Among these strategies was that of permitting women to invest in the arts in exchange for their role in enhancing the clan's agendas.[14]

The nuns of San Paolo unanimously nominated Giovanna Piacenza as their abbess in April of 1507 but the validation of her election was not a smooth process. The relatives of the previous Bergonzi abbesses questioned Giovanna's age and worthiness in an attempt to undermine her

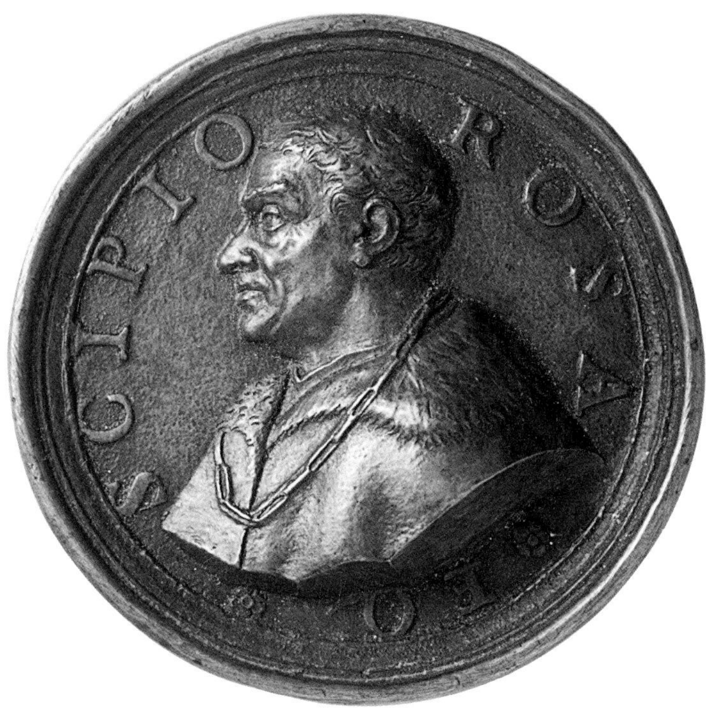

Above 95   Giovan Francesco Bonzagni, *Scipione Montini Rosa*, 1515, bronze portrait medal, d. 7.55 cm ($2^2/_3$ in), Parma, Museo Archeologico

Below 96   Plan of Giovanna Piacenza's ground-floor apartment and upper floor, convent of San Paolo, 1800–04, Parma, Archivio di Stato, Fondo Sanseverini, fol. 20d

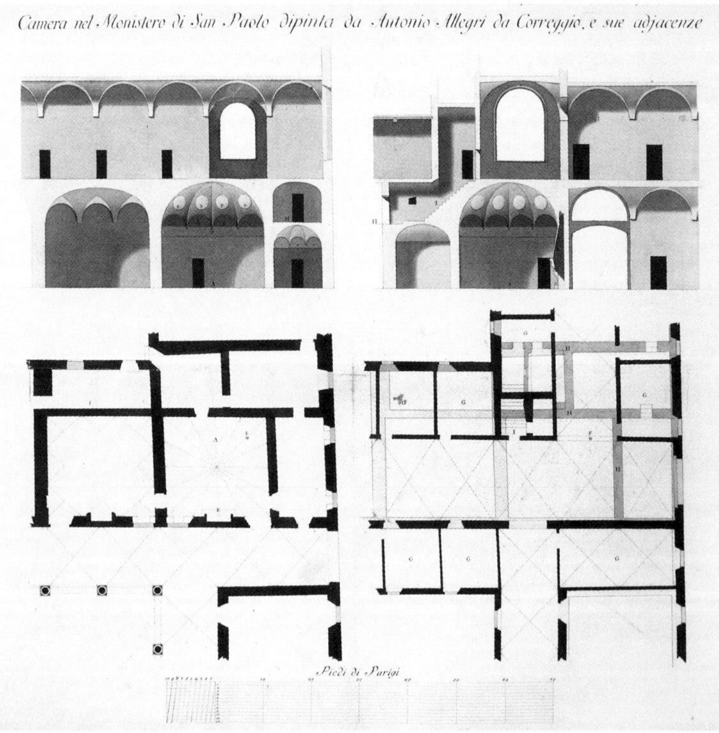

election.[15] Julius II appointed Canons Bartolomeo Montini and Lattanzio Lalatta to settle the issue. The prioress of San Paolo and Giovanna's mother were interrogated regarding Giovanna's age and fitness for an office that carried an annual income of 1,300 florins. Lalatta and Montini then approved Giovanna's election, but the papal confirmation was issued only eight months later, Montini was, however, eager to turn Giovanna's election into a public event to celebrate the abbess and simultaneously display his clan's standing. A two-day celebration was scheduled in early May of 1507.[16] Civic officials, ecclesiastical dignitaries, and families attended the religious rites officiated by Niccolò Bracciano, the bishop of Lydda (Israel) and not by Parma's bishop, Giovanni Antonio Sangiorgio. Firstly, five novices, including Lucrezia Bergonzi (encountered in Chapter Two), took their vows before the bishop. Then, during the solemn Mass celebrated at the high altar of the convent's church, the bishop blessed Giovanna Piacenza as the abbess of San Paolo. While the bishop chanted the Vespers, the new abbess along with twelve nuns accepted Drusiana Bergonzi, one of Giovanna's young cousins, as a novice. Recorded in notarial documents, these ceremonies sealed an agreement among the Bergonzi-Montini-Piacenza families, and its ramifications extended to Giovanna Piacenza and her convent.

A leading figure of this group was Canon Montini. He was instrumental in the abbess's election and in settling disputes that had long engulfed San Paolo. A self made man, Montini bequeathed his estate to his nephew, Scipione Montini Rosa. Represented in profile in a bronze medal probably struck by Giovan Francesco Bonzagni in 1515 (fig. 95), Scipione was Giovanna Piacenza's brother-in-law.[17] Scipione's appointment as the convent's revenue collector caused much strife with the previous collector, Giovan Francesco Garimberti, culminating in the latter's assassination in 1510.[18] Scipione and his cohorts, including the abbess's brother Cesare, were found responsible for the homicide. Garimberti's mother took the case to trial in order to ban the already fleeing Scipione from Parma. On this occasion, even the holy precincts of San Paolo were violated in the search for the fugitives.[19] So close was the relationship between the abbess and her clan that her ornate residence could almost be seen as the manifesto of this urban group. But the abbatial apartment is more than a declaration of the social and political status of a local clan. It is principally about a monastic tradition reinvented in a liminal conventual setting.

Giovanna Piacenza's lodging (fig. 96) occupied the ground floor of the edifice built in the years immediately after her election. Conceived as part of the convent expansion, this

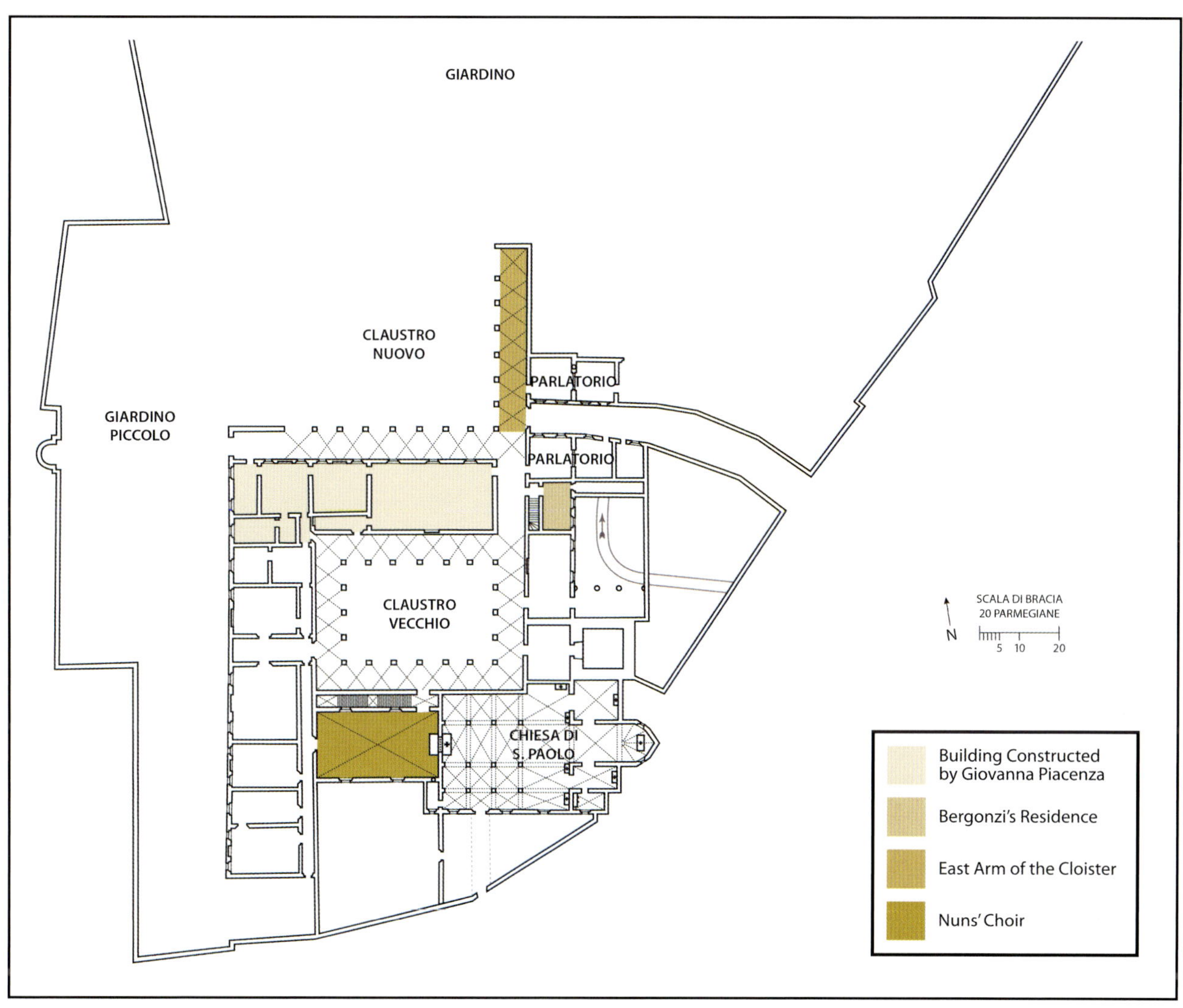

97   Convent of San Paolo, Parma, redrawn from Paolo Gozzi's late eighteenth-century plan

simple building followed a design supplied by the Parmese architect Giorgio da Erba.[20] Its upper floor was devoted to the nuns' dormitory, and corner staircases secured communication between the floors. The building (fig. 97) closed off the old cloister on one side, and overlooked the in-progress new cloister on the other. Paralleling the nuns' choir, this two-story edifice featured a ground-floor loggia, an architectural element typical of contemporary Parmese palaces, pointing to the sharing of motifs between monastic and noble domestic architecture.[21] This conventual building made claims to ideals of honor and leadership not through architectural differences, however, but through the charm of its interiors.

The new building marked a decisive shift in the conventual topography of power or, better, it constituted a conscious act in the restructuring of power. It marginalized the residence of the previous Bergonzi abbesses located in the eastern zone (fig. 97). One of its surviving ground-floor chambers displays a ceiling decoration attributed to Alessandro Araldi, which consists of simplified lozenges marking four vaults each containing a tondo (ca. 1500–07; fig. 98).[22] The Bergonzi arms fill two tondos, while the others feature busts of St. Paul and St. Catherine of Alexandria, respectively the convent's dedicatee and the ideal of learning for the female inhabitants.[23] According to Francesco Barocelli, the much damaged lunette paintings on the upper walls represent episodes from the life of Sant'Homobonus (?–1197), a prosperous merchant from Cremona who donated his wealth to the poor.[24] While the murals thematize the ideal of charity that the Benedictine Rule describes

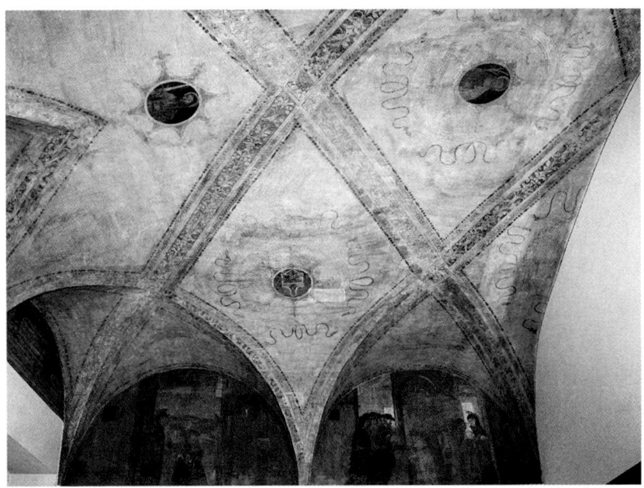

98   Alessandro Araldi, painted ceiling, ca. 1500–07, Parma, Pinacoteca Stuard

as the crucial virtue from which all others derive, the images are too poorly preserved to reach any definitive iconographic conclusions. The most important point here, however, is that the Bergonzi dwelling was disregarded in the early sixteenth-century renovation of the convent, an act that amounted to a conscious turn against the previous abbatial agenda. The new edifice not only reorganized the convent spaces but also expanded the nunnery toward the north, a move signaling Giovanna Piacenza's concern for the growth of her community and her interest in creating a separate court for herself. And this achievement was proudly proclaimed in an inscription.

Elaborating on the Renaissance tradition that inscriptions honored and commemorated the owners of palaces, the now lost inscription, known thanks to Ireneo Affò's transcription, reads: "Joanna Placentia, appointed abbess to the best of communities, not neglecting its older parts for the richer perpetuation of its splendor, constructed a convent, bringing the greatest things under its new roofs."[25] Carved on a marble slab and displayed on the western façade, it established the equation between the building (literally, the "new roofs," which can stand for a structure and, by metonymy, a palace) and the magnificence of the convent, portraying the abbess as its instigator. Rather than acknowledging the code of monastic simplicity and austerity, the inscription emphasized the abbess's adherence to discourses of splendor and honor that made investment in architecture and outlays of fine adornments imperative and desirable. Magnificence was the quintessential manifestation of an individual's position in society and, as Giovanni Pontano's

De Nobilitate (1501) claims, constructing splendid buildings was an advertisement necessary for the declaration of a ruler's power, status, and distinction. Nobility of living and magnificence had to be coupled with decorum, however, implying both a rational approach to planning residences appropriate to their occupants' standing and the relationship of one part to another, as discussed in the contemporary architectural treatises of Alberti, Grapaldo, and Cesare Cesariano, among others.[26]

This inscription also presented the abbess as equally concerned with the preservation of "old things," which could have alluded to both ancient artifacts and old structures. Although there exists no other information about her attitude toward antiquity, the inscription seems to confirm her respect for the surviving fragments of the past. At a time when ancient walls, materials, and objects were often dismantled or melted down, their reuse in buildings can be considered as partial preservation from total destruction.[27] The adaptation of ancient structures had a long history in monasticism. Many religious institutions were built on old foundations and materials were often recycled in new constructions. Grapaldo's treatise, *De Partibus Aedium* (1494; 1516), in particular, makes clear the connection between Roman villas and monastic complexes. It could have been inspired by Flavio Biondo's *Roma Triumphans* (1472), which records that old monasteries had been built on the remains of Roman sites.[28] Attentive readers were certainly fascinated by this association between monasteries and classical foundations, present and past histories, ancient and modern civilizations, which could be further reworked and personalized in a conventual site inhabited by a cultivated abbess.

The new edifice built by Abbess Giovanna Piacenza accommodated her ground-floor residence, an ensemble of chambers first described in the notary's record appended to the convent enclosure paperwork drawn up on August 28, 1524. On her deathbed, Giovanna succumbed to the reform of her nunnery, and left her residence along with its exterior structures at her successor's disposal:

Below are described the dwellings and the spaces newly built at the order of the Lady Abbess herself in the said convent: a hall, or large room, at ground level above a storehouse, with two chambers adjoining that same hall, an oratory and a portico at ground level leading into the said hall, chambers, and oratory, and with a little room adjoining the said chambers; likewise, another space above that and a storeroom, and a kitchen with the equipment of the said kitchen and a storeroom [for the abbess] found

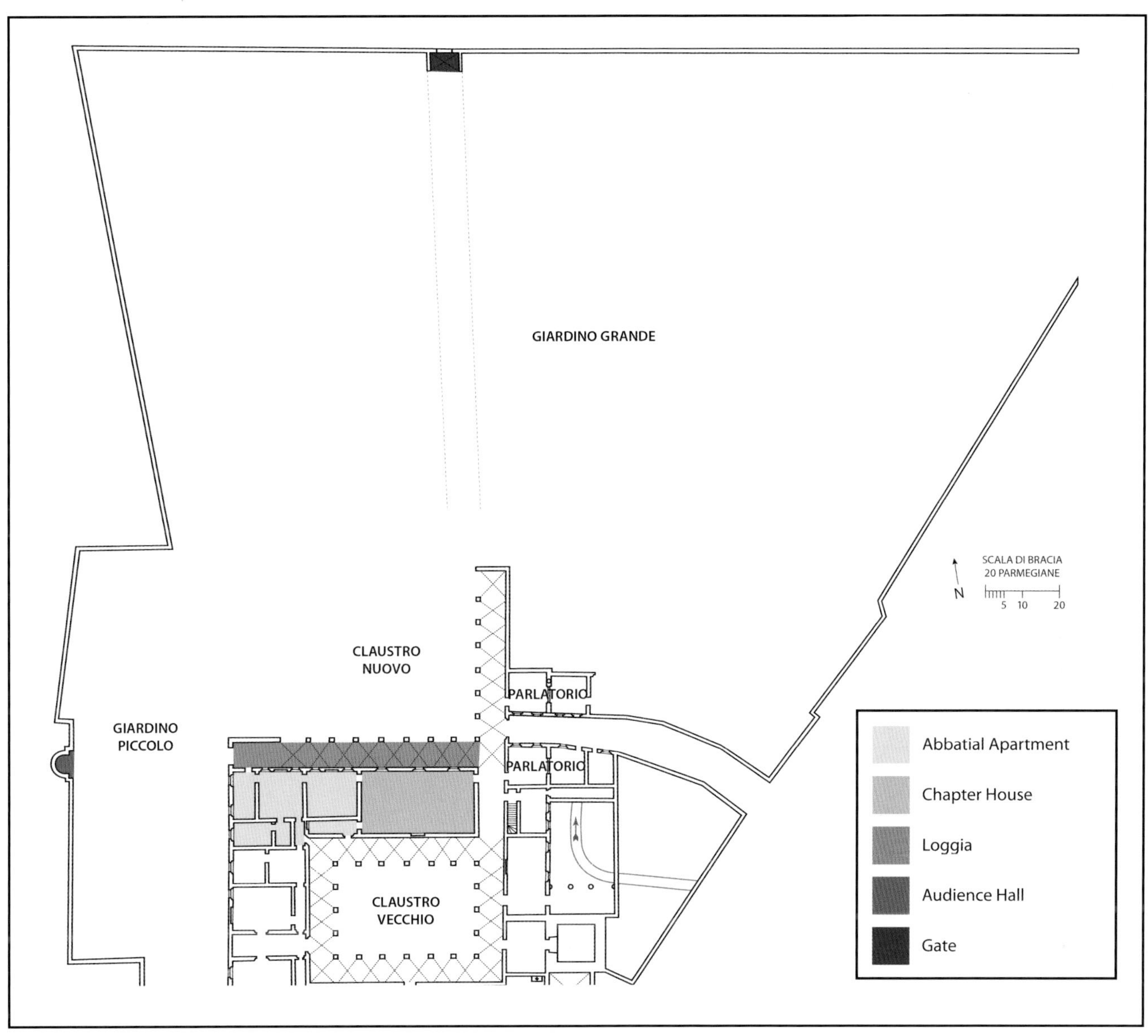

99   Convent of San Paolo, Parma, redrawn from Paolo Gozzi's late eighteenth-century plan, detail

below the said chambers and oratory, while another larger storeroom is set back below the said hall, said to be for the nuns; likewise a smaller garden with a loggia adjoining the said garden that faced out onto the public street, and the house of those from Ferraria, and a small audience space; likewise, the tools and ornaments of the said spaces, reserved for the Lady Abbess herself, that is, those things which seem to be for the Lady Abbess herself for her use and of other persons deserving of it.[29]

It is our good fortune that Giovanna Piacenza's dwelling, albeit with alterations, still exists today.[30] Both the layout of the rooms and the exterior structures visualized in Paolo Gozzi's late eighteenth-century copy of the convent plan deserve probing. The large hall first mentioned in the record was not, strictly speaking, part of the abbess's private domain: it served as the chapter house (fig. 99). It gave access through a single door to two almost identical square rooms with fireplaces (which made them habitable in the cooler seasons), and then to an oratory. The back part of the residence included a *camerino* (small room), and three cell-like spaces along the side. Below were a kitchen and storehouses. The presence of the equipped kitchen meant that the abbess could have independent meals and serve guests in her quarters, which probably also functioned as the convent guest-house. Overlooking a garden, the residence is described as surrounded by external, open-air structures, that is, a loggia defined as a *curia* in the record, culminating in a small audience hall (*locus audientiae parvae*).

Typical of conventual settings, Giovanna Piacenza's apartment is characterized by cell-like interiors rather than by the large reception chambers of the Medici palaces in Florence or the Ca' Loredan in Venice.[31] Giovanna's cell-like rooms may be aligned with those in Isabella d'Este's apartment in the Gonzaga palace in Mantua that, as Stephen Campbell has observed, "brought with it a specific physical comportment" connected to reading and meditation.[32] The use of abbatial ground-floor interiors for living and hospitality may also seem at odds with the upper-level apartments in many patrician palaces. Renaissance architectural treatises comment on the hierarchy of stories, recommending upper-floor rooms for reception and private activities. Grapaldo's *De Partibus Aedium* devotes separate books to the lower- and upper-story chambers. But activities typical of upper-level rooms could be carried out in ground-floor interiors during summer to avoid the heat. Paolo Cortesi's *De Cardinalatu* (1510) describes the arrangement of rooms in the cardinal's palace, taking into account meteorological factors and the multi-functionality of spaces on different levels.[33] As noticed by Brenda Preyer, despite the advice offered in the architectural literature, it has proven difficult to sustain the primacy of upper-floor rooms over those on the ground floor of the Renaissance palace:

> There were important rooms on the ground floor as well . . . [In] the Medici Palace [in Florence there] were a rectangular sala . . . followed by a square camera, an anticamera and a scrittoio . . . The suite on the ground floor of the Medici palace might have been used for summer living by members of the family, but the quantity of rich trappings stored in chests in the camera also suggest that it accommodated guests. On the other side of the courtyard was Lorenzo's camera *terrena* . . . where the celebrated paintings by Paolo Uccello depicting the *Battle of San Romano* were placed.[34]

If in palaces the distribution and use of rooms was fluid, no single, fixed model existed for monastic dwellings either. Sheila Bonde and Clark Maines's scholarship has made clear that the arrangement of the abbots' residence varied according to each community's history and customs. Each institution seems to have proceeded differently, with options ranging from two-story independent houses, ground-floor dwellings, and upper-floor chambers located at the end of dormitories.[35] In general, upper-floor chambers were reserved for sleeping and private meetings, while administrative business was conducted in ground-floor parlors and adjacent rooms, but no strict hierarchy of floors existed in convents. A ground-floor dwelling could therefore depend on numerous conditions, including a monastic tradition modified in the light of ideals of civility and refinement.

Giovanna Piacenza's ground-floor residence reflected her status as a sophisticated religious lady open to the alteration of the surveillance system imposed on religious individuals (see Chapter One). As St. Gregory describes, the founder of the Benedictine order, the fourth-century St. Benedict, while praying in his cell on the top floor was able to check on his disciples asleep in the dormitory below. It is tempting for scholars to associate this model of the watchful eye with Michel Foucault's discussion of Jeremy Bentham's famous Panopticon building.[36] Despite the temporal and conceptual differences between the two systems, both monks and inmates were watched without being able to tell if they were being monitored or not, either by St. Benedict in his high-up cell or by a watchman in a prison's central tower. Conversely, the ground-floor residence of Abbess Piacenza welcomed visitors rather than functioning to control nuns' comportment; it manifested a status and visibility rather than insisting on a fortified architecture of seclusion. Simultaneously it was the site of communication of messages of leisure and sophistication, a place where the gaze of nuns was not limited or controlled. As will be seen in the following chapters, the act of seeing beautiful art was interwoven with practices of the renewal of the spirit.

Approaching the abbatial residence from the convent's northern gate and being escorted to her independent court, visitors were exposed to the now lost exterior structures to the west of the abbess's apartment. What is known of these? What was their purpose? The 1524 notary's record describes a loggia (*curia*) adjoining a small garden and an audience hall. The convent plan indicates that this audience site was an apsidal-shaped space (fig. 99) carved out of the high western wall of the monastic complex. At a basic level, it can be inferred that this sequence of spaces created a continuum between inside and outside, providing the nuns and their guests outdoor areas for recreation. But, as is often the case with conventual buildings dramatically altered across the centuries, what remains to enable us to imagine these open-air structures are mainly clues found in the documentation. Drawn up in September 1507, an unpublished record states that the local stone carver Antonio d'Agrate was requested to provide nine pairs of columns for the north loggia surrounding the abbatial apartment. It further specifies that the columns should match those already installed in the cloister (that is, the eastern arm; see fig. 97) for a harmonious juncture.[37] According to Giuseppina Longhi and Aldo Spina, the columns formed a loggia of nine classicizing rounded arcades, which were later reduced to five, as we see them today (fig. 100).[38] Longhi and Spina could not, however, provide further specifications about the loggia and the audience hall. I propose that this audience space was originally paved with colorful maiolica tiles. As a whole, the west zone held a special significance for the abbess, as is confirmed by the commission of new tiles, and the probable recycling of the Benedetti tin-glazed tiles to adorn it (see Chapter Two). Contemporary treatises, including Alberti's *De Architectura* (1485), recommend paving porticoes and loggias with mosaic, terrazzo (a hard, compacted flooring), or bricks. A place for walking and conversation, contemplation and spiritual refreshment, the loggia and the adjacent audience hall enhanced the onlooker's enjoyment of the secular subjects depicted on the maiolica tiles underfoot.[39]

It is also interesting that the notary's description refers to the loggia as a *curia*. But what exactly did this term mean in the Renaissance? In the Roman world, the term *curia* was used to indicate the hall set aside for Senate or clerical meetings. By and large, it referred to any kind of meeting loggia.[40] In the Middle Ages, it came to stand for the administrative entourage of rulers and bishops, and by extension the gatherings of elites in courts. In general, Renaissance architectural treatises and contemporary documentation deploy the term interchangeably with reference to porticoes, loggias, courtyards, and other places where meetings could be held.[41] Grapaldo's *De Partibus Aedium* does not discuss the *curia* as a distinct place, stating instead that galleries overlooking gardens and filled with statues or paintings encourage walking, thus proposing an identification between the ambulatory contemplation of nature and that of art.[42] Likewise, the convent garden loggia and the audience hall promoted immersion in the beauty of nature and the reading activities associated with a solitary life of contemplation outdoors, proclaiming the power of the natural environment to confer repose, as exalted in Petrarch's *De Vita Solitaria* (1346–56) and his *De Otio Religioso* (1347–57). Since Petrarch's reinvigoration of the Stoic paradigm of virtuous *otium* associated with nature, and of the praise of the quiet life of study in retreat from hectic urban life, countryside villas and

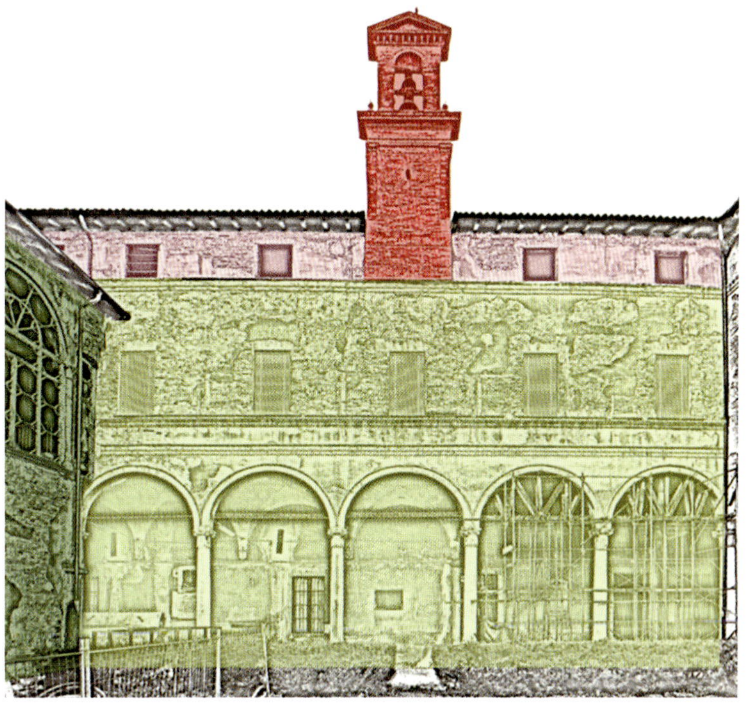

100   Parma, San Paolo, loggia and façade of the abbatial building (in light green); top floor built later (in pink); and bell tower (in red)

garden loggias were transformed into spaces for such studious gatherings.[43] Among the activities facilitated by loggias were conversations but also dining and theatrical performances. It is thus no surprise to read in Cortesi's *De Cardinalatu* that the household of a cardinal requires a dining room that "overlooks a covered walk (xystus) and a garden (toparium) so that their cheerful aspect will make dining (accubatio) the more pleasant."[44] The garden loggias of private villas were often decorated with images of memorable deeds of illustrious men and mythological scenes. In Mantua, the painter and architect Giulio Romano designed Palazzo Te for Federico II Gonzaga (1500–1540), which features a secret garden loggia adorned with moralizing subjects. In Rome, Agostino Chigi's Villa Farnesina has an open-air loggia painted by Raphael and his workshop (ca. 1518–19) with episodes from the fable of Cupid and Psyche.[45]

Whatever the sources for the conception of the *curia* and the garden audience hall in San Paolo were, the *Hypnerotomachia Poliphili*, the 1499 illustrated romance narrating the experiences of the lovesick Poliphilo, may have been relevant. Declaring its novelty through woodcut illustrations of hybrid architecture and antiquarian fantasies accompanying the text, the *Hypnerotomachia* was widely consulted in Parma.[46] Several passages describe porticoes and garden pergolas, even imaginatively paved with perfumed floors whose scents inebriated the senses.[47] Several woodcuts reproduce porticoes and pergolas, reflecting its maker's acquaintance with the topiaries that filled Renaissance gardens and that are described (but not illustrated) in one of the early imitations of the *Hypnerotomachia*, that is, *Il Peregrino*, a romance published in Parma by the local cleric Jacopo Caviceo in 1508.[48] Caviceo narrates the tormented love affair of its protagonist, Peregrino, picturing garden pergolas as spaces for the delectation of the senses.

Connecting the exterior to Giovanna Piacenza's interiors, the loggia is therefore described as a *curia* in the 1524 document for good reasons, I believe. Retaining its semantic richness both as a meeting place and as the courtly entourage of rulers, the *curia* can be understood to designate the garden loggia and the audience hall as ideally almost a unified zone; simultaneously, it may be extended to include the lay and monastic community around the abbess, her conventual court. The term, on the one hand, indicates a physical meeting space and, on the other hand, points to a community sharing beliefs and cultural values, reappropriating for a woman the male ecclesiastical model of holding a *curia*. But the concept is even richer in its implications than one might expect. In monastic literature, the notion of *curia* had initially a negative connotation linked to improper comportment. The monk Pier Damiani (1007–1072) vehemently criticized clerics who left the church to serve at courts, constituting rulers' *curia*, and launched bitter invectives against their frivolous conduct in the secular world. By the twelfth century, however, their worldly pomp came to be seen as a form of elegant manners and was deemed appropriate to clerics' duties in the world.[49] The term *curia* therefore tied together the monastic and the secular spheres and its cognate, *curialitas* (courtliness), referred to the combination of refinement, elegance, and restraint required in courtly settings. Often seen as the distinct traits of court life, courtliness and the control of emotions have been discussed by Dilwyn Knox as a comportment code that was derived from "Christian morality and its implementation in lay society during the Middle Ages and Renaissance."[50] It is known that the tradition of courtliness developed into Baldassar Castiglione's *Libro del Cortegiano* (published in 1528 but in the making for fifteen years), which, with its stress on social grace and appearance, cultivation and irony, vividly sketches a picture of the Renaissance court. Castiglione records conversations on various topics purportedly taking place at the court of Urbino in 1507 among a restricted group of elite personages sharing a code of social and ethical behavior, learning, and virtue.[51]

As a place to congregate controlled by a woman, a convent court could be seen to anticipate an assertion made by Erasmus in his colloquy *The Council of Women* (1529). Inspired by the supposed existence of an ancient senate of women during the reign of the Roman Emperor Heliogabalus (218–22 CE), Erasmus has one female interlocutor exclaim: "Bishops have their synods, congregations of monks their chapters, soldiers their assigned stations, thieves their rendezvous . . . Of all living creatures, only we women never have intercourse."[52] The convent court at San Paolo seems to have fulfilled this Erasmian claim in advance, providing women with the opportunity to congregate and entertain, and further endowing them with status and power unavailable on the outside. It was a place that had no direct identification with the typical courts of Renaissance Italy. Their dynastic structure of political and military power did not pertain to convents, although one could argue that unreformed, aristocratic abbesses held rights that approximated those of political rulers, including the imposition of dynasties over nunneries, and therefore that elite convents approximated Renaissance courts. But the notion of the convent court that I am evoking here is that of a "third" or an "other" space that belonged to times and dimensions different from those outside, a space that was real and yet "elsewhere" than the Renaissance court that existed in the imagination of a community with shared values. It was a place that was simultaneously real and mythical, and imbued with a variety of relations, concerns, and negotiations. The convent court signaled elite nuns' adherence to norms of civility, a code of classical and Christian virtues appropriated by male rulers and patricians alike, and to the belief in the power of art to nourish, delight, and unite that community. But a convent court was also riddled with paradoxes and incongruities, and took the "form of a contradictory site." While it was tied to discourses of social status, female leadership, and cultural attainments, it may also be said that it constituted a "space of illusions . . . a heterotopia of compensation."[53] It encompassed a Renaissance court of a different sort and, by its very hybrid status, its pictorial and carved decorations staged a myth of female leadership and virtue, but also sustained games of *double entendre* and irony.

At a time of social and political turmoil, the convent court may ultimately have been a site in which elite nuns (particularly Abbess Giovanna Piacenza who late in her life seems to have suffered from an illness and was often in bed from 1519 onward), local *litterati*, and ecclesiastics could congregate for the pleasure of cultivated company, the enjoyment of art, and reading, fending off the devastations of wars and violence that plagued Parma's citizens during the first decades of the sixteenth century. Crucial traits of these court environs were urbane wit and banter, discourses which affected the activation of meanings in the abbatial decorated rooms. The ideal of wit (*facetia*) coupled with sophistication competed with that of courtliness to produce the code of comportment, refinement, and levity appropriate to courtly settings.[54] These ideals and their fiction found productive intersections in texts published in early sixteenth-century Parma by humanists likely to have frequented the convent court.

Proponents of a pedagogy of levity as a cure for the spirit include the Parmese humanists Taddeo Ugoleto, Francesco Mario Grapaldo, and Giorgio Anselmi. This triumvirate of scholars coauthored an emended edition of Plautus's comedies in 1510, in which they claim to have purged the text of the numerous mistakes made in the previous edition published by Giovanni Francesco Boccardo Pilade in 1506, and to have based their emendations on a newly discovered Plautine manuscript rather than on mere conjectures. The Parmese edition was foremost a defense of a philological approach to ancient texts, as incarnated in previous Plautine editions commented on, among others, by the Bolognese humanists Filippo Beroaldo and Giovanni Battista Pio.[55] Bologna had long been a center that favored Plautus over Terence. Indeed, despite the ongoing debate about the effects of comedy that, as Francesco Patrizi's *De Institutione Reipublicae* (1520) put it, "corrupts the mores of men and makes them effeminate, and drives them towards lust and dissipation," comedy was a highly popular literary genre, especially in sixteenth-century Bologna. As Loredana Chines has observed, local humanists recognized in Plautus a kind of humor that suited their conception of the *vir facetus* (clever man), turning witticism into a recommended virtue for accomplished individuals to face life's adversities.[56] As Beroaldo states, he found in Plautus's comedies both a handbook of conduct and a representation of veiled truth that entertained via *ludus* (humor, play), jesting, and *lepor* (wit). Seconding Beroaldo's view, the Parmese triumvirate argued that Plautus's comedies offer a picture of an everchanging reality captured in its mutable, protean contexts and that humor and doubling effects are its engines. The world's multilayered reality is shaped and simultaneously covered up through puns and wordplay, which present truth in other than straightforward or direct ways.[57]

As is known, irony and gaiety are also described in monastic writings, in reference to the detachment, light-heartedness, and joy that religious individuals experienced when communicating with the divinity. Monastic authors refer to various kinds of humor: the joyous irony that originated "in the enthusiasm aroused by wisdom, differing from vain laughter that engendered nothing but foolishness."[58] Gaiety was ultimately seen as the assurance that one was disciplined, diligent, and controlled. In conclusion, the now lost garden loggia (*curia*) and the audience hall, along with the embellished abbatial apartment, constituted *loci amoeni* (pleasances) devoted to activities that renewed the spirit; they promoted gatherings of nuns and their guests enhanced by the beauty of art and nature that captured the senses. These interconnected places did not merely replicate an outside Renaissance court but created the convent court. They cannot, therefore, have been intended as manifestations of a casual project of the abbess's. In these spaces, conversation, study, and the contemplation of painted subjects with eyes raised up and not cast down, were practices for enlivening the spirits, marking the convent court as an "other" space, one in which female power and learning could blossom, despite confined, conflictual, and paradoxical circumstances. Shared by the convent community, these values were communicated to and reinforced for passersby in a set of overlooked frescoes at the very entrance to the convent, the north gate.

THE CONVENT GATE: STUDIOUSNESS AND FEMALE VIRTUES

As thresholds to the outside world, convent gates were zones that were policed and regulated to preserve their inhabitants' seclusion. Barriers to intruders, the entrances to convents perhaps accrued richer signification than palace portals, marking the liminal zone between the sacred and the secular worlds, the zone where the holy space of nunneries terminated and the open realm of the lay public began. As discussed in Chapter One, gates acquired a specific role in the rite of girls' physical entry into convents. The early sixteenth-century reshaping of the claustral space of San Paolo could not leave this crucial liminal area untouched. Facing the abbatial residence, the northern gate transmitted to visitors and passersby specific messages about the virgins who lived inside.

Abutting the convent high wall on the north, the so-called "cell of St. Catherine" (see Chapter Two) was walled up only in 1850 in order to preserve its heavily damaged

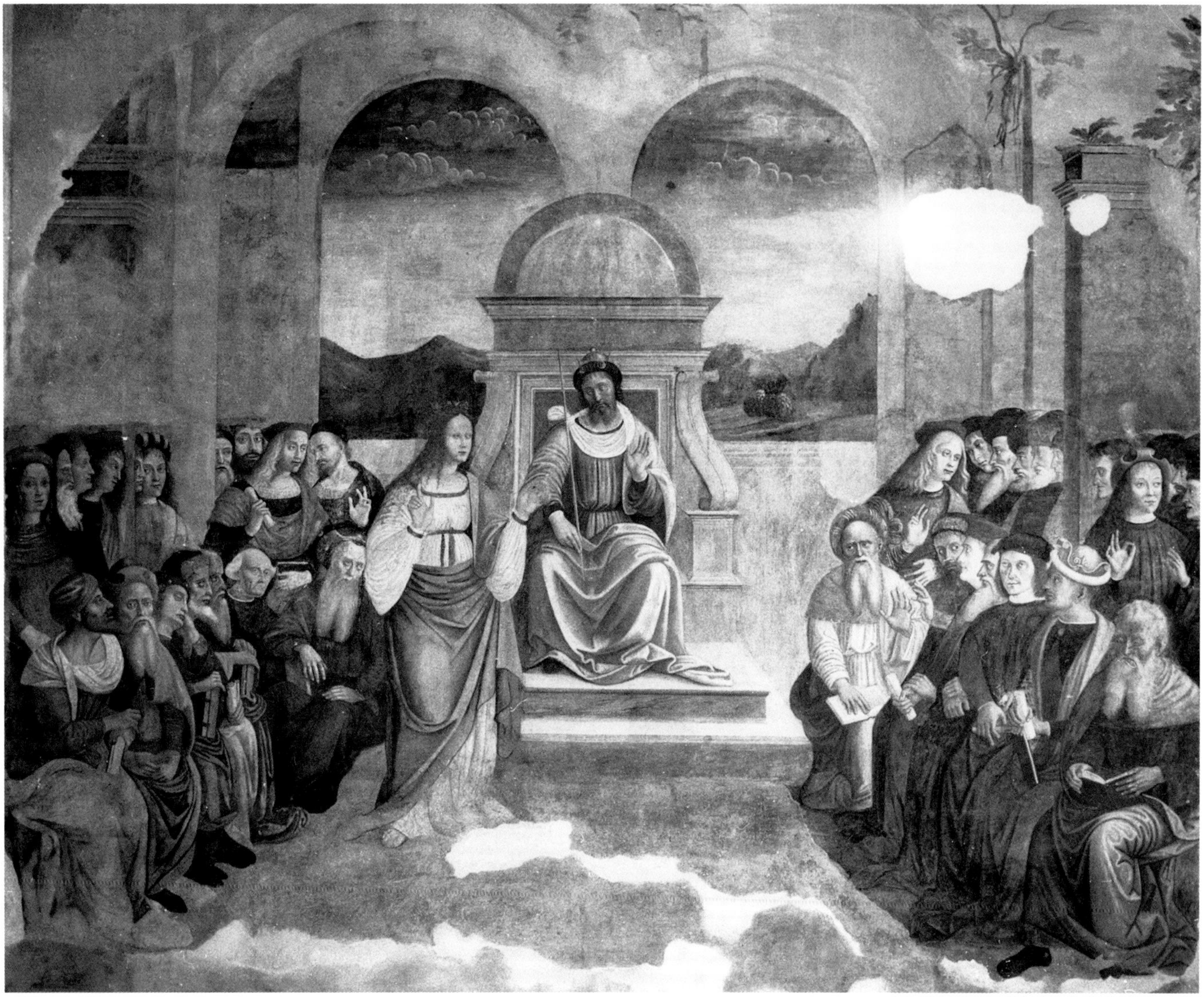

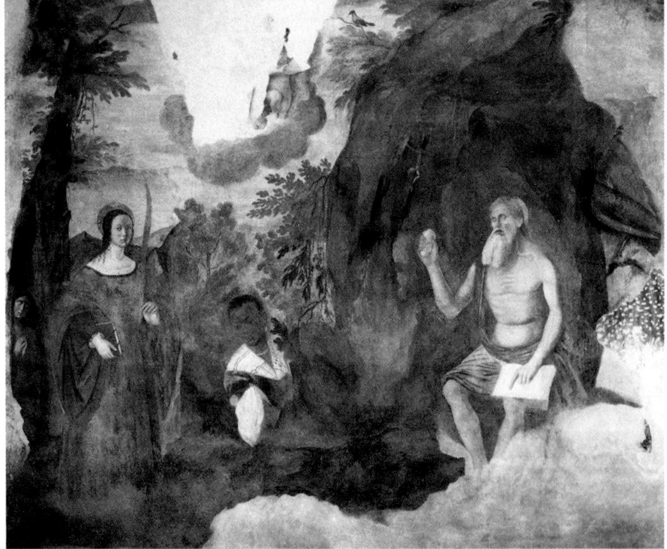

Above 101   Alessandro Araldi, attr., *St. Catherine of Alexandria Disputing with the Philosophers*, after 1507, fresco, 426 × 360 cm (167 × 141 in.), Parma, San Paolo

Left 102   Alessandro Araldi, attr., *St. Catherine of Alexandria with St. Jerome*, after 1507, fresco, 471 × 360 cm (164 × 141 in.), Parma, San Paolo

early sixteenth-century murals. Attributed to Araldi, they represent *St. Catherine of Alexandria Disputing with the Philosophers* and *St. Catherine of Alexandria with St. Jerome* (figs. 101 and 102). These frescoes were not originally displayed on the walls of a prayer room, as has often been suggested.[59] Araldi's frescoes are on opposite walls of a space that originally communicated directly with the public street. This space was therefore located at the interface between the convent and the outside world, addressing both (see fig. 99). It was common to find gatehouses by the convent gates, with gatekeepers in control of contact between the religious and the outer community. This office was inevitably governed by an older nun, assumed to be capable of resisting secular temptations.[60] Whether or not the murals were originally connected with the gatehouse cannot be ascertained, but they were on the entrance to the convent itself and were probably executed by Araldi after he had worked in the nuns' choir (after 1507). There seems to be little doubt that the abbess, possibly Giovanna Piacenza herself, suggested a subject like St. Catherine disputing with the sages, thus demonstrating her learning, to stand for a sophisticated religious community at the then main gate of its convent. Just as the vestibules of palaces were ornamented to celebrate and honor the owners, so the decoration of convent gates bore the imprint of their inhabitants.

Araldi's *Disputation* shows St. Catherine standing to the right of the enthroned Emperor Maxentius within a large hall that opens through two windows onto a landscape stretching into the distance. Clothed in a tunic and robe, she raises her hands in oratorical fashion as she delivers her speech to confound the beliefs of the pagan philosophers gathered around her. Separated into two groups, the old sages, seated or standing to either side, react differently to her defense of the Christian doctrine. Some seem disoriented, others talk among themselves, using gestures that mimic Catherine's, while still others offer pensive attention. One avidly consults his book to find arguments to refute the saint. Another seems to have just read a pertinent passage to challenge St. Catherine, pointing his finger at a page. Another philosopher is absorbed in listening, his eyes closed and his head resting on his hand. Despite the sages' various reactions to the saint's speech, Araldi's figures do not make a choral, unified ensemble. Each sage remains somewhat separate from his neighbor and, typically for Araldi, their gestures seem formulaic rather than credible manifestations of emotional involvement. Several philosophers have individualized faces, and might even be portraits of local individuals, but Araldi leaves viewers hanging in possible empathetic relationships with them, an effect now dramatically exacerbated by the degraded surface of the mural.[61] St. Catherine addresses the philosophers seated opposite her at some distance and has her back turned to others, a slightly uncomfortable compositional solution that both Masolino da Panicale and Pinturicchio, for example, avoided in their own *Disputation of St. Catherine* images. Both of those present the female saint among the sages, using her fingers to enumerate her points in the manner of a philosopher-teacher and not as if delivering a lecture, as in Araldi's mural.

The other image by Araldi, which exhibits more serious lacunae, depicts St. Catherine holding a book and the palm of martyrdom, symbols of her learning and virginity. Behind her and now only partially visible is a kneeling female (a nun?), while opposite is the penitent St. Jerome, his left forefinger indicating a book possibly meant as that containing his letters to Marcella, Paula, and Eustochium, three women who retired to convents.[62] Between the saints is a kneeling, black-skinned figure, which in compositional terms is incongruous: a recent restoration has revealed it to be a seventeenth-century repainting or replacement. Due to its extensive damage and lacunae, this mural leaves us with more questions than answers. However, it seems reasonable to say that its content exalts the standard belief that conventual life was the best condition for women, advertising as it were the conviction of those who lived inside. St. Jerome's praise of the religious life describes it as a marker of status for women that raises them above their sex.[63]

Secluded within their sacred precincts, the nuns of San Paolo wanted to rise above their sex by promoting an image that would reflect their cultivated selves and perhaps willingness to debate through the exemplum of St. Catherine. In the early modern literature, St. Catherine of Alexandria stood as a *figura* of learning and as the protector of universities.[64] For nuns, to read about her life could have been bound up with the self-affirmation of a cultivated status, or viewed in connection with sites of female studiousness like convents. The fifteenth-century *Catalogus Sanctorum* by Petrus de Natalibus portrays St. Catherine as the cultured female counterpart to the *miles Christi* (soldier of Christ).[65] Knowledgable in Greek and Latin, Catherine won over the old sages with her eloquence and ability to debate. As a model for both consecrated and lay women, the saint's erudition was not seen as incompatible with her female gender. Her biography figures prominently in the Renaissance literature in defense of women. For example, in Jacopo Filippo Foresti's catalogue of outstanding women (1497), the story of St. Catherine revolves around her expertise in the liberal arts and sacred scripture, giving great emphasis to the episode of her disputation with the philosophers.[66] A correspondent of Isabella d'Este, Abbot Agostino Strozzi, in his *Defensione de le donne* (Defense of Women; ca. 1501) further exalts St. Catherine's admirable "erudition in all the disciplines."[67] And, he continues, she is among those women who excelled at preserving their virginity, preferring martyrdom to its loss: they are better than men in their beliefs and spiritual practices. In his *De Istitutione della Femina Christiana* (first Latin edition 1524), Juan Luis Vives portrays St. Catherine as a laudable figure, but he remains ambivalent about the role of learned women in society. As Vives puts it, women could be learned, but eloquence is not really necessary for "good and wise" women.[68] Silence is considered women's supreme virtue: therefore he adhered to the long-standing misogynist view that women were by nature inferior, talkative creatures.[69] In one of his pungent critiques of these views, Erasmus has an abbot prone to vices proclaim to his sophisticated female interlocutor: "It is not feminine to be brainy." And, he added, "books ruin women's wit."[70]

Women's learning matched with political power posed major challenges and threats to the male-oriented society of the Renaissance, especially when women like Eleonora d'Aragona ruled while their husbands were away – in her case, Ercole d'Este, who was absent from Ferrara in 1486–7. Eleonora's model of erudition and leadership is exalted in Bartolomeo Goggio's *De Laudibus Mulierum* (ca. 1487) and Antonio Cornazzano's *Del modo di reggere e di regnare* (ca. 1478–80).[71] In general, however, female education remained a troubling terrain even for humanists. Contemporary cultivated women like Isotta Nogarola, Cassandra Fedele, and Laura Cereta were cast as threats to the natural order. Eloquence was considered a masculine sphere, and women who succeeded in that art were perceived as male souls mistakenly born in female bodies. As Margaret King observed, cultivated women were even criticized by their female peers for having risen above them via their cleverness.[72] Based on these ambivalent discourses about female learnedness in the Renaissance, Marta Ajmar has concluded that contemporary images of St. Catherine's *Disputation* usually had "a doctrinal function as opposed to [being seen for] their specifically female exemplary values."[73]

Araldi's *Disputation*, painted in proximity to or at the convent gate, seems instead to constitute an ideological statement from and about the cloistered women inside. Addressing both secular and monastic viewers, Araldi's image proposes the ideal of a sacred femininity nurtured through study and contemplation and even through debating, challenging the model of the passive religious self upheld in the monastic literature: an abbess had the power to rule and some male prerogatives, such as running a community. Sensitive to the image of themselves that they displayed to public viewers of the mural, the religious women of San Paolo represented by St. Catherine appear as privileged interlocutors of the divine and as upholders of Christ's teaching through their literacy. The power of teaching and

consecration was withheld from women in the Church. Nuns were prohibited from preaching publicly and were excluded from performing the Mass and sacramental rites. They were permitted to instruct other nuns only in appropriate comportment, not in questions of faith. Araldi's *Disputation* was not intended to address or alter this established order of things. Rather, what it figures is a learned female acting with eloquence rather than silence, casting the convent of San Paolo for future nuns as a place of learning and debate, and simultaneously reassuring families that their daughters' virginity was secured through their very education. At the convent threshold, Araldi's image ultimately conveyed the message that nuns cultivated themselves through reading, and that their learning was put to good use to defend their virtuous, noble lifestyle against attempts to enforce strict regulations on them.

WORDPLAY, GAMES, AND ETHICS

Confronting Araldi's image of the Christian learned female at the gate prepared guests to encounter Giovanna Piacenza's separate court. While it is fair to say that her residence could be seen as a kind of confirmation, reinforcement, and refinement of that view of the female religious sex proclaimed at the gate, it would be mistaken to stop at just that claim. Although the original furnishings and some of the carved ornaments of the residence are lost, the abbess's decorated chambers still convey a vivid picture of the owner's understanding of the power of art to transmit messages about what it meant to be a learned cloistered lady in Renaissance Italy. Today, visitors access the abbatial space via a mid-nineteenth-century entrance and are forced into an established itinerary within the rooms that have been turned into museum galleries. As my research has uncovered, originally there were multiple points of access to the chambers, and the movements of guests were regulated according to their status, rank, profession, and relations to the convent's inhabitants. Some individuals were only admitted to certain areas, while others were permitted further inside.

After going through the northern gate, ecclesiastical authorities, literati, business professionals, and relatives would all probably have had different experiences of the conventual space. Documentation confirms that business professionals were directed to the large hall (the chapter house; see fig. 99), the first room mentioned in the 1524 notarial record, following an east–west route into the interiors. In contrast, religious dignitaries and literati participating in the

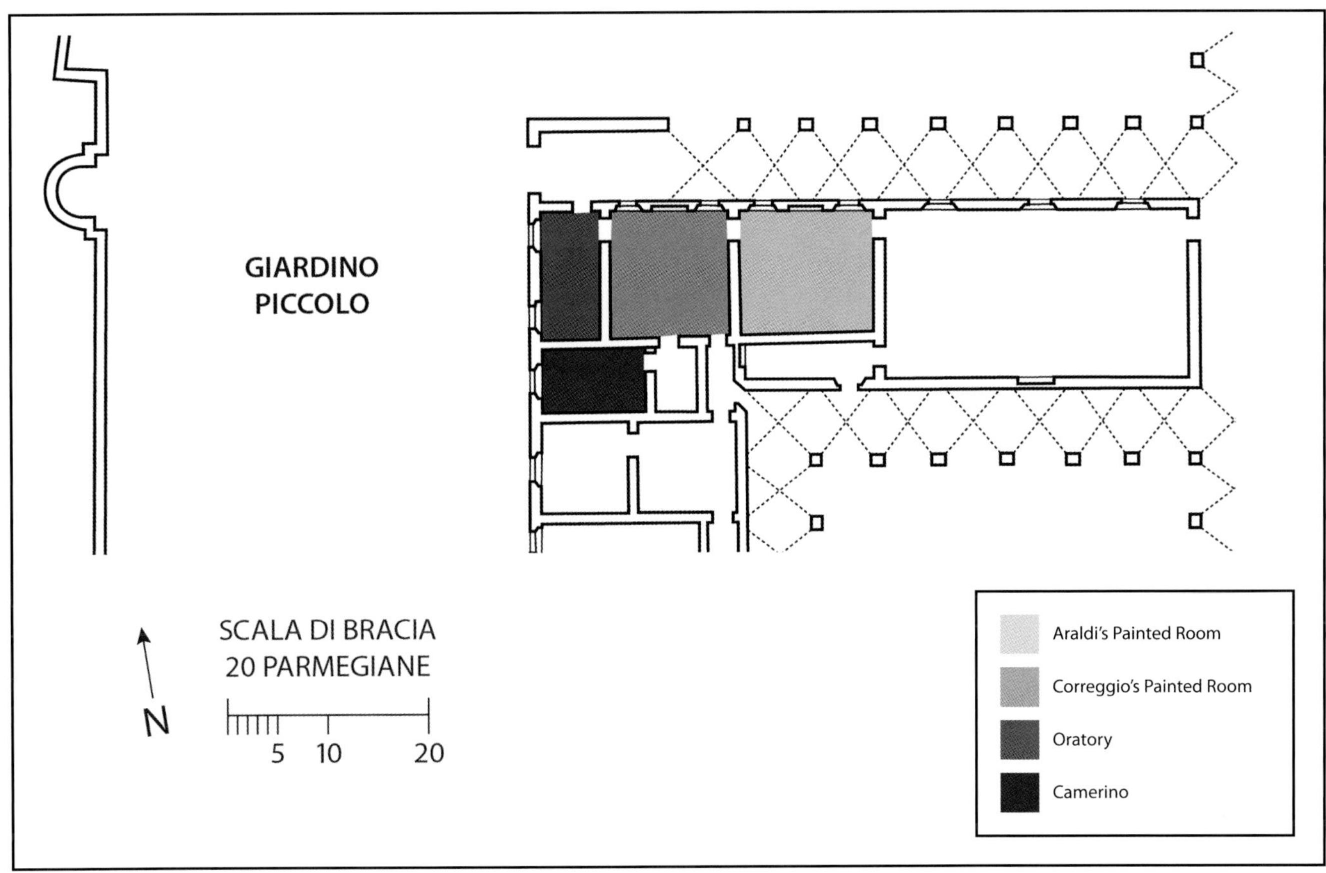

103   The abbatial apartment redrawn from Paolo Gozzi's late eighteenth-century plan, detail

convent court were probably escorted through the loggia to the abbess's apartment, proceeding along a west–east axis to reach the chambers. Nuns' relatives had access to the parlors in the eastern zone and, if necessary, could get to the abbess's lodging through the cloister. From their upper-story rooms, nuns could descend to the abbess's domain, entering a sort of antechamber that communicated with Correggio's painted chamber. It is my contention that, without forcing any group or individual into a fixed itinerary or a predefined tour of the convent, outsiders were made participants in the circuit of knowledge proposed in the convent spaces from multiple points of access. This circuit of knowledge was sustained through an ensemble of pictorial images and incised and intarsiated inscriptions that speak of predilections for forms that veil and play with meanings.[74] The network of carved and intarsiated inscriptions is not well known in the scholarship, but is extremely revealing and deserves closer attention. As an ornamental apparatus, it provides clues about both the original function of the chambers and the dense intersections between signs and image forms, language and ornament that afforded viewers insights into a refined monastic tradition and its values.

It is instructive to put the 1524 notarial description that assumes an east–west axis of access into the abbatial apartment next to Gozzi's plan of the convent, and to use both visual and textual evidence as a guide in entering Giovanna Piacenza's quarters (fig. 103). Accessing the residence from the eastern end meant first entering the large hall that served as the chapter house where the community congregated to make decisions. Through a doorway, visitors passed from this communal room to the heart of the abbess's quarters. The adjoining quadrangular chambers, frescoed by Araldi and Correggio (see Chapters Five and Six), served as a reception/dining room and a bedroom respectively. Next to the Correggio chamber was the abbess's private chapel.

Recorded as an oratory in the 1524 documentation, the function of this room has been debated in the literature, but it seems confirmed by previously neglected sources. The local engineer Smeraldo Smeraldi's unpublished report of his visit to the convent in 1598 mentions first Correggio's frescoes and then a back room through which he reached the outside garden, where the community wished a fountain to be built.[75] According to Affò's description of the residence after its rediscovery (1794), this back room served as a sacred space connecting Giovanna's interiors to the outside *curia* and the apsidal-shaped audience hall (a "niche" in Smeraldi's word).[76] In his *De Partibus Aedium*, Grapaldo discusses private chapels placed in communication with owners' most intimate chambers as places embellished to enhance solitary forms of prayer.[77] Cortesi in his treatise adds that "it should be understood that the more erudite are the paintings in a cardinal's chapel, the more easily the soul can be excited," by guiding the eyes to "the imitation [*imitatio*] of acts, by looking at [painted representations of] them."[78] Located in contaminating proximity to the chamber that Correggio adorned with profane subjects, the abbess's oratory may have served to sanctify her own persona and office.

That oratory is, however, forever lost to us. It was reduced in size and transformed into the present-day entrance hall (fig. 104) to the apartment in 1856.[79] An impressive wood intarsia frieze, recently attributed to the woodcarver Marco Antonio Zucchi, now runs along the upper walls of this hall. Affò reports that this frieze originally lined the adjacent *camerino*, a room embellished with a fine paneled ceiling and facing onto the garden beyond.[80] It has been posited that the *camerino* was assigned to the abbess's assistant, but it is implausible that a helper slept in so ornate a room (perhaps she slept in the small, square room facing onto Correggio's room). In the Renaissance, intarsia paneling was often used to embellish studies, rooms where individuals took pleasure in reading books and contemplating precious objects to free their minds from agitation and anxiety. What is more, the intarsia frieze features ingeniously conceived versions of the abbess's arms along with four pairs of Latin and Greek sentences each set in discrete ovals, constituting an appropriate decorative ensemble for a study; they strongly suggest that the back *camerino* could originally have served as Giovanna Piacenza's study.[81] Grapaldo speaks of the appropriate location of a study being near the chapel and the bedroom, further advising his readers on the categories of books, manuscripts, and seals to be collected, and how to display them.[82] Nothing is known of the abbess's own library, nor has information resurfaced about her fine possessions. They might have not been dissimilar to the ancient coins and modern statuettes displayed in the almost contemporary *Portrait of a Collector (Marco Garbazza?)* painted by Parmigianino (fig. 105), which captures the precious artifacts preserved in the domestic setting of a prominent local citizen.[83]

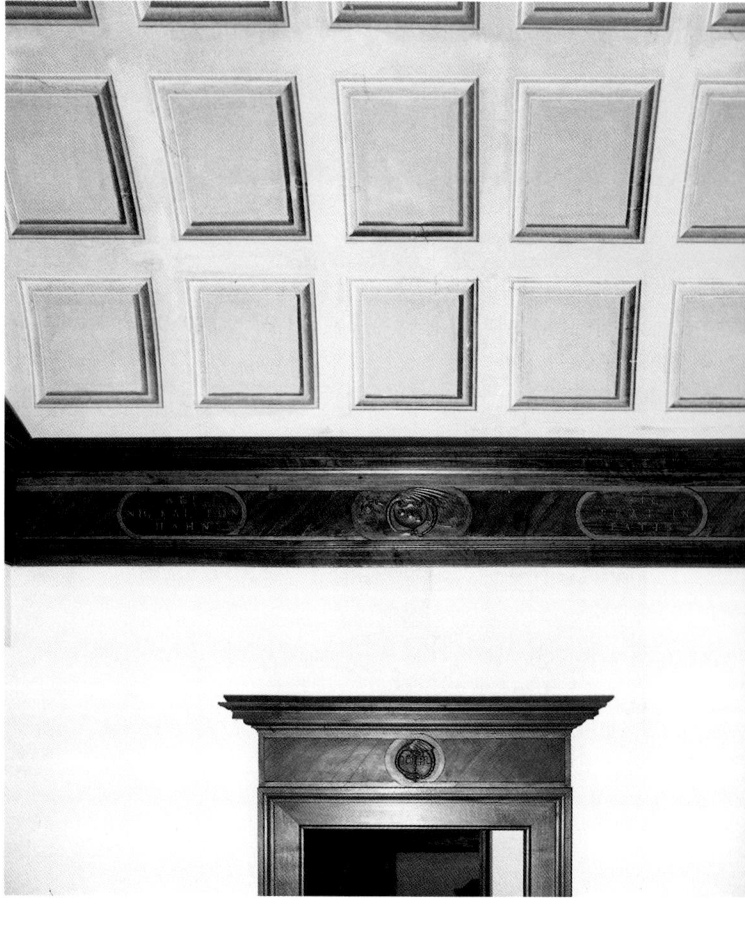

Offering viewers Latin verses culled from classical authors paired with abstruse Greek sentences and interposed with playfully inventive versions of Giovanna Piacenza's arms, the intarsia frieze presents a visual–verbal ensemble whose meaning is not immediately apparent. The Greek words constitute anagrams of the abbess's name, while the Latin are passages of ethical import. Together they form sets of dual-language sentences exploring the fine line between learning and ornament.[84] According to Angelo Pezzana's nineteenth-century description of their original placement, a pair of Greek and Latin intarsia sentences was displayed on each wall but their exact arrangement is hard to reconstruct.[85] Over the entrance door of the *camerino* appeared the Greek inscription ΗΝ ΕΝΙ ΠΤΙΛΩ ΚΑΝ ΗΑ (Behold, I have wings and I ascended; fig. 106), and adjacent on the left was the Latin IOVIS OMNIA PLENA (All is full of Jupiter; fig. 107); on another wall the Greek ΗΝΙ ΠΑΝΤΑ Η ΕΝΙΚΛΩ (All things are at hand whereby I thwart) and the Latin ERIPE TE MORAE (Tear yourself from delay) were visible;[86] on the wall opposite the entrance door the Greek ΙΩΗΝΤΕ ΚΑΙ ΠΛΑΝΗΝ (Both clamor and roaming; fig. 108) accompanied

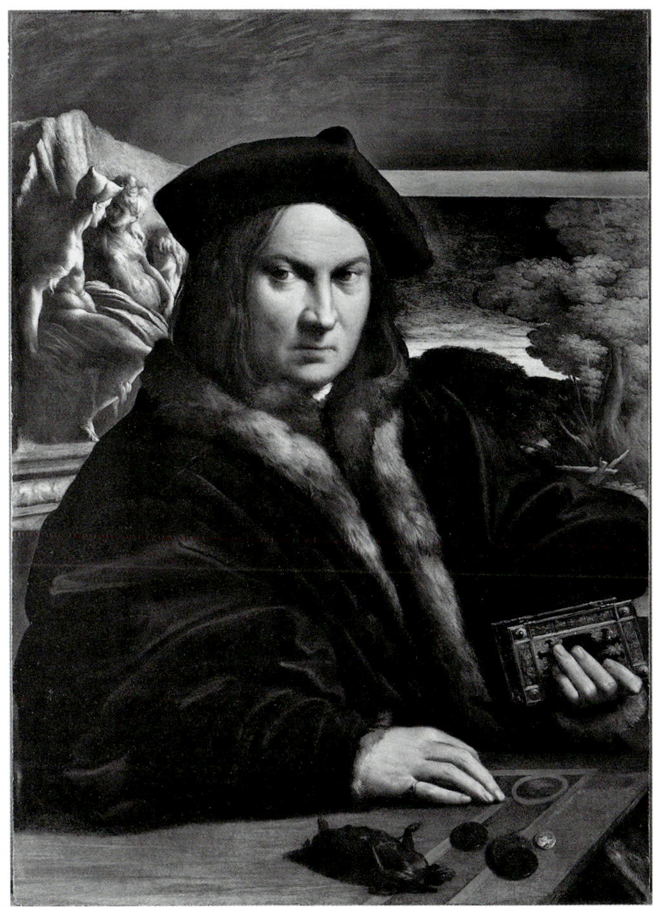

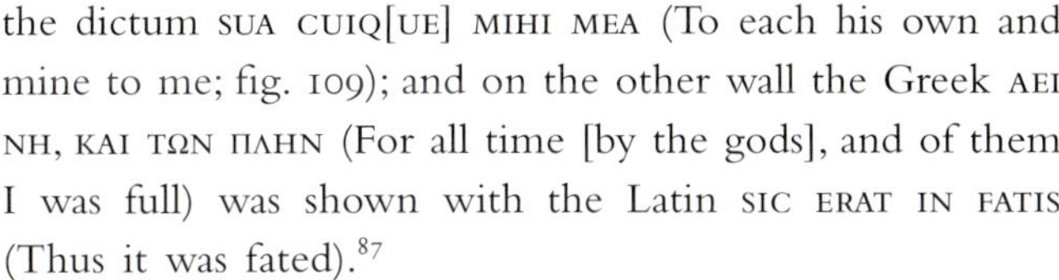

the dictum SUA CUIQ[UE] MIHI MEA (To each his own and mine to me; fig. 109); and on the other wall the Greek ΑΕΙ ΝΗ, ΚΑΙ ΤΩΝ ΠΛΗΝ (For all time [by the gods], and of them I was full) was shown with the Latin SIC ERAT IN FATIS (Thus it was fated).[87]

Recent efforts to make sense of these sets of inscriptions as unified, bilingual sentences have had limited success; therefore, in what follows, there will be no attempt to read them as semantic units. The Greek phrases border on the nonsensical, disguising the abbess's name in word- and sound-play rendered in the unfamiliar Greek alphabet to make cryptic and witty puzzles. They are not clear sentences, nor are they grammatically correct because the urge was to form anagrams of the letters of the abbess's name. In his writing, Giulio Camillo (ca. 1480–1544) speaks of this practice of reordering proper names' letters having its roots in the kabbalistic tradition to which the local elite was exposed.[88] It is probable that either Ugoleto or Anselmi, fine scholars of Greek, composed the anagrams of the abbess's name. In 1506, Anselmi vied with Erasmus in the translation of Euripides's *Hecuba*, one of the Greek drama-

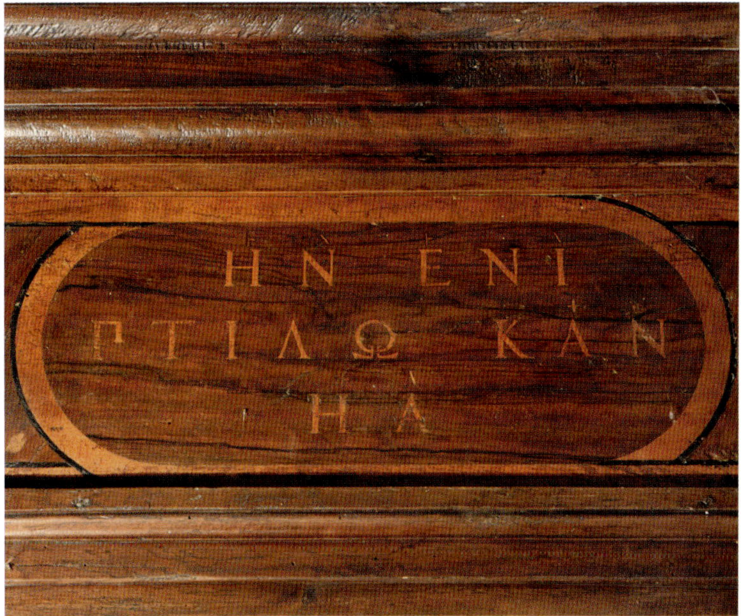

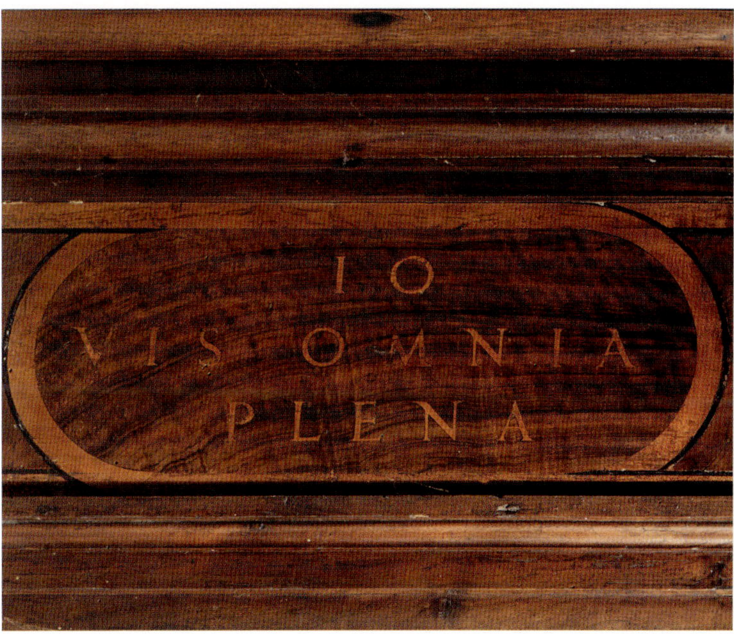

Facing page 104   Marco Antonio Zucchi, 1510s, wood intarsia frieze, 363 × 421 cm (142 × 165 in.), Parma, San Paolo

Top, left 105   Parmigianino, *Portrait of a Collector (Marco Garbazza?)*, 1523–4, oil on panel, 86 × 94 cm (33^{55}/$_{64}$ × 37^{1}/$_{64}$ in), London, National Gallery

Top 106,   Marco Antonio Zucchi, Greek inscription, 1510s, wood intarsia, Parma, San Paolo

Above 107,   Marco Antonio Zucchi, Latin inscription, 1510s, wood intarsia, Parma, San Paolo

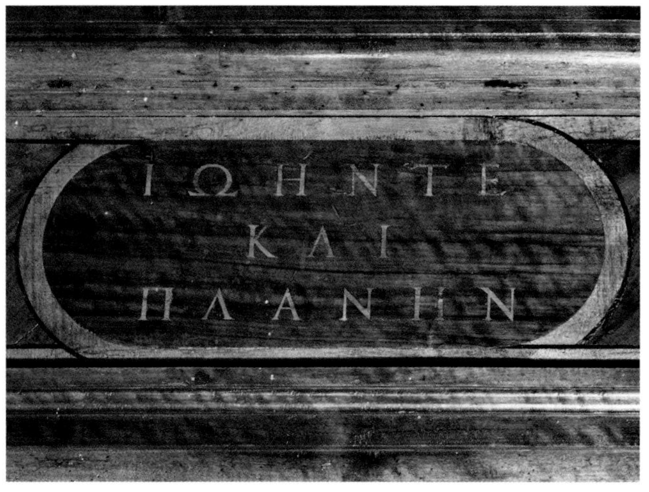

108   Marco Antonio Zucchi, Greek inscription, 1510s, wood intarsia, Parma, San Paolo

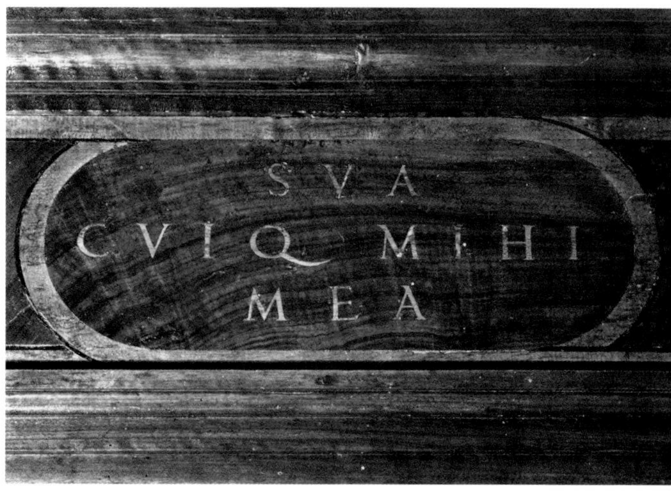

109   Marco Antonio Zucchi, Latin inscription, 1510s, wood intarsia, Parma, San Paolo

tist's tragedies known in the Renaissance.[89] Ugoleto was responsible for the notes and some entries of the *Lexicon Graeco-Latinum*, edited by Johannes Crastonus in 1483.[90] Trained in the *ars memorativa*, Abbess Giovanna Piacenza enjoyed anagrams of proper names: as a mental rubric, a name constituted a mnemonic.

Anagrams and word puzzles were considered linguistic gems worthy of admiration, appreciated for their capacity to remain in one's mind, enhancing forms of meditation and mental engagement. Their decipherment was not what mattered most, though. Rather, it was the endless possibility they offered of generating associations, encouraging individuals to bring to bear their own learning to expand and inflate the contents. These mnemonic exercises were meant to instruct an audience, to help it store information and create mental images, thus returning a distracted, bored, or preoccupied mind to the paths of ordered thought. Memory was perceived as the engine of ideas in the early modern monastic world. Anagrams and puzzles, in particular, suited meditation on what St. Augustine defined as a "productive and healthy difficulty," that is, they provided food for thought, to generate knowledge and delight, keep the mind active, but also potentially to tease it.[91]

Puzzles, anagrams, and wordplay that altered meanings were much enjoyed in courtly gatherings, as Castiglione in his *Libro del Cortegiano* declares: "it is amusing to quote a verse or so, putting it to a use other than that intended by the author, or some other well-known sayings used in the same way or with a word in it changed."[92] To make his point, Castiglione refers to the story of a group of friends winning a bishop's clemency for a priest who, while exercising his mission as a confessor, had impregnated five nuns:

> as they [the friends] kept on pleading and recommending the culprit, urging in his excuse the temptations of his position, the frailty of human nature and many other things, the bishop said: "I will do nothing for him, because I have to give account to God." And when they repeated their pleas, the bishop said: "What answer shall I give to God on the Judgment Day . . ." Then Messer Marcantonio at once answered: "My lord, say what the Evangelist says, 'Lord, thou deliveredst unto me five talents: behold I have gained beside them five talents more.'" Whereupon the bishop could not refrain from laughing, and greatly mitigated his anger and the punishment that was in store for the offender.[93]

Wordplay and anagrams of proper names highlight the tension between appearance and reality, shadow and substance, making communications about oneself less obvious than they might first appear. Walls filled with puns and anagrams are evidence of one's character, predilections for games of reversal and transformation, and secrecy, marking one's refusal to put oneself on the same level as other viewers.[94] As François Rigolot has commented, the puns and anagrams of the proper name allude "to the person's self-celebration with all the wit of the double hermeneutical register."[95] The Greek words promote such commemoration, curiosity, and irony, which concealed and reimagined reality, and, at the same time, amazed and mystified the beholder by their abstruse characters and signification – a light-heart-edness proclaimed throughout the apartment not in opposi-tion to the images but in dense dialogues and intersections with them. They present the abbess as a *domina faceta* (clever lady), recasting the model of ancient rulers as cultivated and well-mannered *viri faceti* for a religious woman.[96]

Sophistication, playfulness, and concealment are also manifested in Giovanna's reinvented personal device, the three diagonally disposed crescents crossed by a crosier and encircled by a winged snake devouring its tail (fig. 110). As an abstraction of the abbess's persona, this reimagined device is of particular interest not merely as a *stemma* but as a pliable sign of the self. To begin with, the motif of the snake tied into a knot is known in Greek as an *ouroboros*, and was believed from pre-Christian civilization onward to have magical and apotropaic powers. The *ouroboros* sign can thus be interpreted as a symbol for warding off negativity, to protect the abbess and her nuns.[97] When guests were admit-ted to religious houses, prayers were requested to protect the community from potential demonic incursions. This sign's apotropaic value was therefore the fending off of any evil introduced by lay individuals (enemies, detractors, and others) into a holy place dedicated to the pursuit of Chris-tian virtues. Given the likelihood that the community of San Paolo was exposed to debates on magic (see Chapter Five), the quasi-magic implications of the *ouroboros* sign should not be underestimated. But there are other ways in which this symbol of the tail-eating snake was read, which alluded to notions of eternity and cyclicality; it was also known as an Egyptian hieroglyph standing for the idea of the universe.[98]

Charles Dempsey offered an engaging reading of the riddle encompassed in a slightly different permutation of Giovanna's arms (fig. 111), which features the *ouroboros* encir-cling her initials, IO.PL. Dempsey interpreted this as proclaim-ing the abbess's universal presence (IO[ANNAE OMNIA] PL[ENA = All is full of Giovanna), echoing the Virgilian dictum IOVIS OMNIA PLENA (*Eclogues*, 3.60; All is full of Jupiter) that appears in the intarsia frieze.[99] Visitors who, like Castiglione, enjoyed deciphering puzzles and wordplay could not but have been intrigued and amused by the playful reinventions of Gio-vanna's arms that designated her apartment as a place which was all about herself, and, simultaneously, disclosed her pro-pensity for games of *double entendre* and wit.

In his writing defending Giovanna Piacenza, the priest Cornigli instead describes the abbess's device in terms of its sensory quality, speaking of it as a fragrance that pervades the space with its "soft and pleasant scent" (*odorem suavitatis*

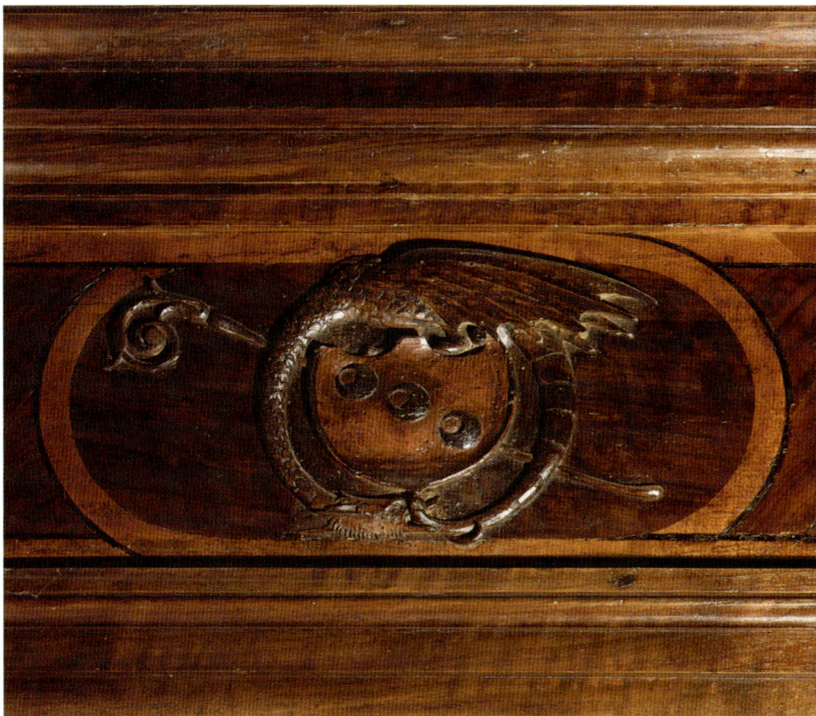

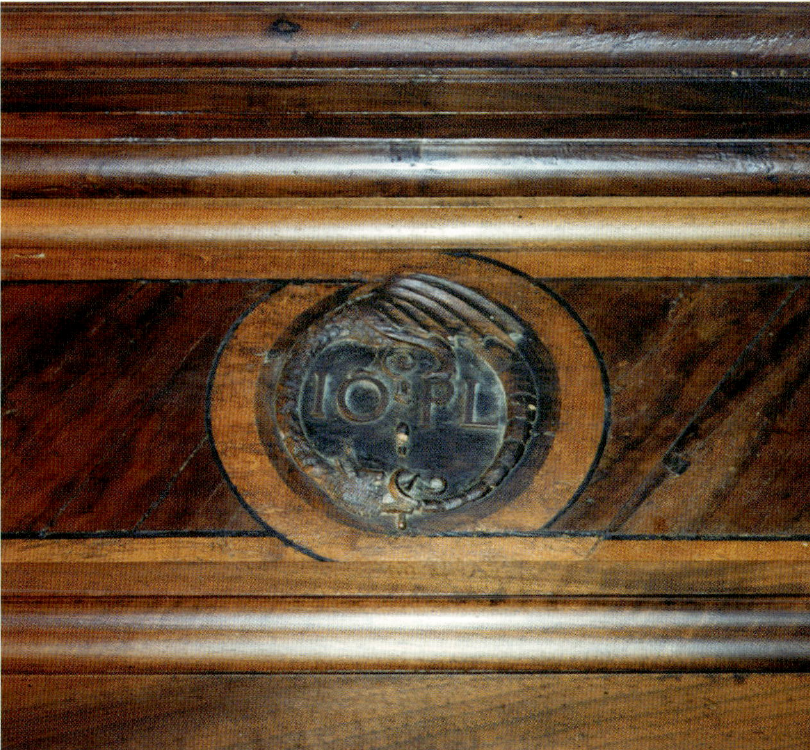

Top 110 Marco Antonio Zucchi, arms of Giovanna Piacenza, 1510s, wood intarsia, Parma, San Paolo

Above 111 Marco Antonio Zucchi, arms of Giovanna Piacenza with IO.PL. initials, 1510s, wood intarsia, Parma, San Paolo

et gratiae). Reworking the opening verses of the Song of Songs, a unique text in the Hebrew Bible that celebrates carnal love, that sensually evokes the bride's kiss as "better than wine fragrant with the best ointments," and that refers to her name as "perfume poured out," Cornigli transforms a marker of self-identity into a sensory metaphor. In other words, he turns the abbess's insignia into a fragrance that fills the air, keeping spectators engaged through more than their eyes.[100] The perfume asserts the abbess's presence as it penetrates the lungs. Unlike sight, which is about distance, smell is a sense that speaks of immediacy, intimacy, and closeness, a sensory evocation of the invisible made penetratingly tangible. Fragrances captivate, inebriate, and beguile us in different but no less fascinating ways than do the eyes. And one wonders if Cornigli's reference to a vaporous aroma scenting the atmosphere drew on Michael Psellos's eleventh-century *Cosmographia*, a summa of Byzantine sources on magic. Discussing perfumes and their theurgical associations, Psellos writes: "perfumes [*aromata*] give off a vapor which drives away evil spirits and which at the same time restores to the materials affected by it the presence of more benign spirits."[101] In a Renaissance world in which demonic spirits were believed to cause diseases and misfortune, fragrances functioned as protectors against them. Be that as it may, Cornigli postulates a sensorial experience related to the abbess's *stemma*, which is linked to the rich Renaissance semantics on devices intended as metaphorical portraits of historical beings, markers of social status, signs of apotropaic power, and perfumed vapors that animate the space and make the mind tingle.

As for the Latin *dicta* in the ovals surrounding the abbess's arms, they insist on Stoic precepts of self-confidence, and admonitions against wasteful leisure, inviting viewers to reflect and meditate. Latin sentences propose a plural message whose understanding depends on the reader's ability to uncover their linguistic play. The saying ERIPE TE MORAE (Tear yourself from delay; Horace, *Odes*, 3.29.5; fig. 112), from Horace's famous ode to Maecenas asking him to leave Rome and politics to relax in the countryside, recommends the avoidance of laziness, idleness, and all fruitless activities. Classical authors had defined their virtuous leisure as *otium negotiosum* (productive leisure), but the risks of *otium* as a temptation for sloth, and its associations with the sluggish loss of the will to act or time-wasting idleness were equally underlined. In the writings of the Church Fathers, the pagan ideal of *otium* was associated with idleness, and therefore seen as contrary to Christ's teaching. Chapter 48 of the Benedictine Rule proclaims:

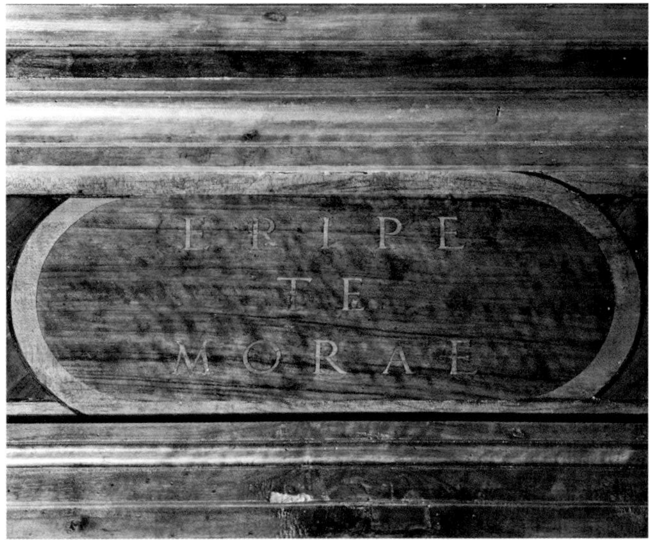

Top 112   Marco Antonio Zucchi, Latin inscription, 1510s, wood intarsia, Parma, San Paolo

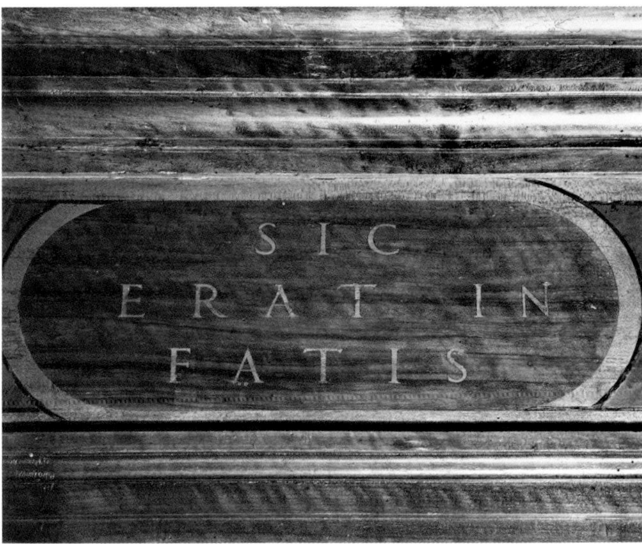

Above 113   Marco Antonio Zucchi, Latin inscription, 1510s, wood intarsia, Parma, San Paolo

"idleness is the enemy of the soul."[102] Monks were instructed to occupy themselves with manual and contemplative activities to safeguard them from sloth, because languishing in tranquility was dangerous to their spiritual progress. Yet, at the same time, Christian writers held that the monastic life was the true embodiment of *otium negotiosum*. Since Petrarch's *De Otio Religioso*, the ideal of *otium* was connected to the withdrawn, solitary life of contemplation and study as a means for reaching a perfected being. Perhaps, however, such an ideal needed to be reinstated and proclaimed in the study of an abbess dedicated to the pursuit of the same mission. The Horatian verses are an invitation to virtuous activities of leisure and contemplation that marked an appropriate use of time. The *Eripe te morae* inscription ultimately seems to emphasize the idea that the study was Abbess Piacenza's kingdom, a place she had conquered and now controlled, with everything at hand to enjoy *otium negotiosum*.

The other quotation in the intarsia frieze – SUA CUIQ[UE] MIHI MEA (To each his own and mine to me; Cicero, *Tusculanae Disputationes*, 5.22.63; Erasmus, *Adagiorum Chiliades* [1508], 1.ii.15; see fig. 109) – centers on the notion of ownership, evoking the propensity of individuals to prefer what is their own (for example, family, country, or lover). It proclaims a sense of pride in one's own things, which, however, had to be dissociated from immoderate applause for them, which Erasmus sums up in his commentary on *philautia* (self-love), a universal failing: "you will find no one so modest, so thoughtful, or so clear-sighted that he will not be blind . . . when it comes to putting a value on something of his own." And, he continues, self-love is a healthy attitude, as long as it goes only "so far as to make each of us tend a little to favor . . . our own arts, business, or discoveries," but one must avoid blind *philautia*, and constantly examine and strive to know oneself.[103] For Erasmus, the process of self-knowledge is not to be deprecated as long as it involves a realistic assessment of one's talents and shortcomings. The abbess's status, and the perpetual power connected to the office, brought Giovanna Piacenza the opportunity to become a prominent abbess-lady, to transform herself from someone insignificant into a figure of public importance.[104] But in the case of a cloistered woman who had promised to deny herself in service to God, such an image ran the risk of being perceived as the manifestation of pride, and it therefore needed to be tempered. The readjustments must have been particularly urgent in the case of an abbess positing an image that challenged prescriptions of female passivity and subordination, which may be summed up in the ambiguous message of the accompanying Greek words: ΙΩΗΝΤΕ ΚΑΙ ΠΛΑΑΝΗΝ (Both clamor and roaming; see fig. 108).

The Ovidian quotation SIC ERAT IN FATIS (Thus it was fated; Ovid, *Fasti*, 1.481; fig. 113) in the next oval is a crucial passage from the consolatory speech delivered by the Arcadian Carmentis, the ancient goddess of prophecy and mother of Evander, one of the early inhabitants of Rome. Carmentis's narrative begins with a description of Evander's birth and exile from Arcadia to Rome, then proceeds to the prediction of the city's greatness. In an attempt to cheer the exiled Evander, Carmentis states that there was no wrongdoing on his part, or crime of his own making to explain his misfortune, and therefore his guiltless conscience should spur hope and confidence.[105] By evoking the notion of fate, Carmentis's passage frees individuals from direct responsibility for their hardship, separating the anger of the divine from the innocence of mortals. Intended to offer consolation to forlorn beings, it proclaims belief in the power of fate over human actions, universal over individual history. It encourages viewers to put present difficulties in perspective, with the promise of a better time to come. For Christian believers, adversity was not only considered an occasion for affirming one's personality as greater than that of one's enemies, but also as an opportunity to endure obstacles in order to demonstrate one's strength and faith in God's mercy.

REGENDERING THE MALE ECCLESIASTICAL PALACE

The same combination of ethical and playful registers is shown in the inscriptions, or *tituli*, the one-line captions carved into the *pietra serena* lintels of the doors in the apartment. This work may have been carried out by the local stonecutter Giovan Francesco d'Agrate, who seems to have served as the supervisor, consultant, and agent for the provision of stone materials and whatever carved stonework items were needed, including fireplaces, benches, window frames, fonts, and lavabos.[106] Carved in the early 1510s, the *tituli* created spatial relationships between and among the rooms of Giovanna's quarters, demanding the beholder's interaction and signaling that the chambers were intended for the pursuit of virtue. There were originally four Latin *tituli*, but only one, the saying O[MN]IA VIRT[UTI] PERVIA (All is accessible to virtue; fig. 114), has survived. However, the content and placement (on which more later) of the other three are known from Affò's description.[107] Escutcheons carrying the abbess's arms were carved at the center of each caption, an assemblage suggesting that the message of the *tituli* circled back and forth around her persona, making her presence central despite her physical absence. It is a corpus rarely discussed in the literature, and it fulfilled its purpose by its material display of information in carved form. Comprising quotations from classical authors as well as commonplaces, the *tituli* proclaimed

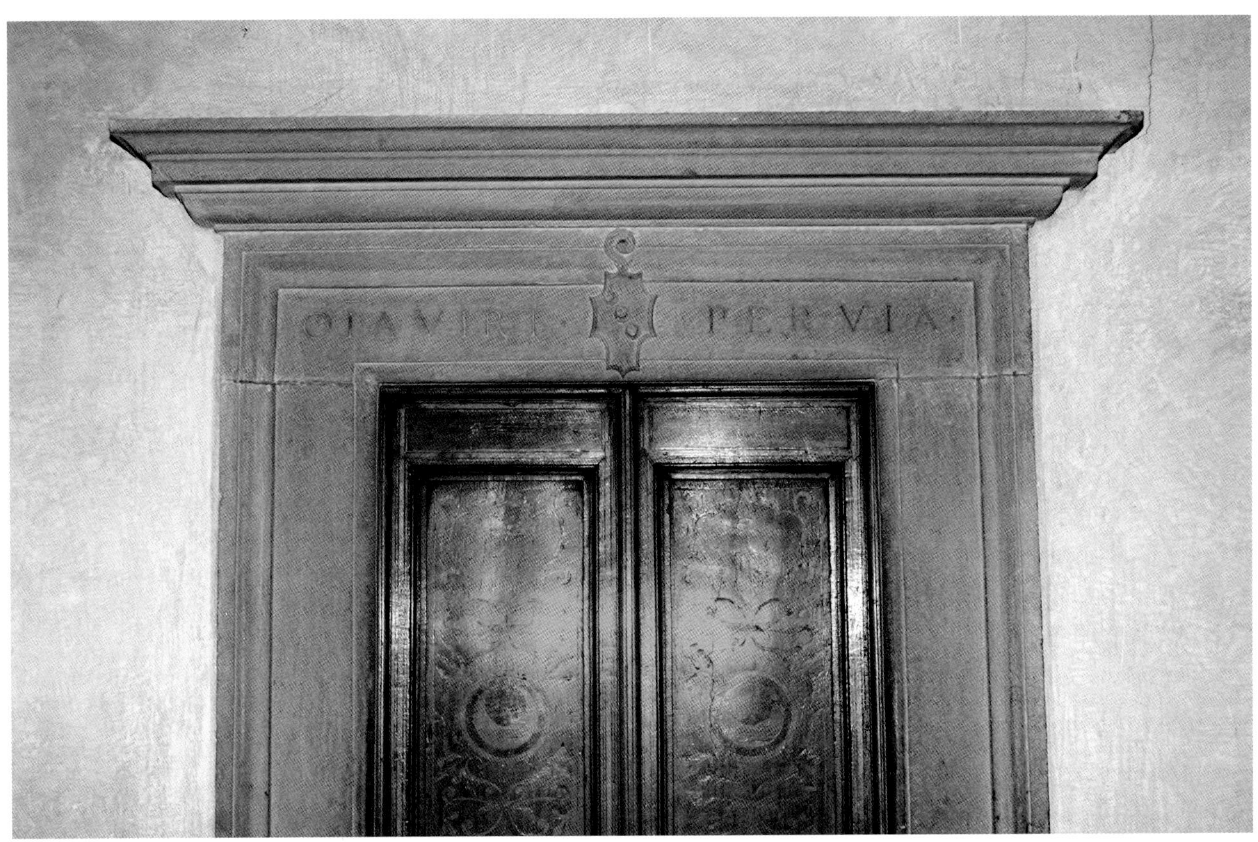

114 Giovanni Francesco d'Agrate, *titulus*, early 1510s, *pietra serena*, Parma, San Paolo

ideals of self-love, fame, and virtue. Their originality resided in their selection from a variety of sources and their novel placement on door lintels, claiming for the monastic community and their guests the knowledge they spelt out. But the *tituli* simultaneously pointed to places and times beyond what they asserted, serving to bridge past and present, universal and personal experiences. As a whole, the *tituli* can be seen as a kind of abbreviated *florilegium*, that is, a compilation of excerpts from classical and religious writings that monks were instructed to assemble as part of their memory training. Given their brevity, the *tituli* are there to be memorized, expanded into chains of associations, and then mentally recomposed. At a basic level it can plausibly be posited that the *tituli* of the abbess's domain made up her own *florilegium*, engaging the beholder with *sententiae* that served as an antidote to agitation and distress. As Petrarch suggests in his *Remedies for Fortune Fair and Foul* (ca. 1354), succinct sentences that the mind retrieves and meditates on are apt exercises to protect oneself against sudden changes of emotion, helping to restore a state of inner calm and equilibrium.[108]

Inscriptions were more, however, than just markers of a self or tools in mental relaxation. Because they stand at thresholds, *tituli* symbolically framed the abbess's interiors. Their very liminal location must have alerted observers, that is, the ecclesiastics, professionals, humanists, and the nuns admitted to the interiors, that their message was not necessarily univocal and stable, but shaped between rooms of different function, size, and nature. A local audience might have noticed, for example, that the humanistically driven content of the *tituli* in the abbatial rooms substantially diverged from the doctrinal bent of those in the bishop's palace in Parma. Bishop Giovanni Antonio Sangiorgio (1499–1509) had Christian moralizing sayings painted on the walls of the ground-floor loggia of the episcopal palace.[109] Although Renaissance bishops were rarely in residence in their dioceses and their administrative power was delegated to vicars, while substitutes (*suffraganei*) exercised their pastoral mission, the episcopal palace incarnated the authority of the bishop's office.[110] The chronicler Smagliati reflects the sense of amazement that the newly restored bishop's palace aroused in local citizens assembled in the

Cathedral for the 1507 Christmas Eve Mass. Facing the Cathedral, the imposing bishop's palace with its *tituli* and portal bolstered civic pride, as Smagliati remarks. The palace stood in for the bishop, celebrating his office and persona as a religious and political mediator.[111]

These *tituli* could also be read as signs of patronage, as has been argued for those in the countryside villa in Alatri of the humanist Giovanni Tortelli (ca. 1460), and in the Farnese palace in Rome.[112] *Tituli* also took the form of rebuses sometimes used as a kind of artistic signature. In the *vita* of the architect and painter Bramante (1444–1514), Giorgio Vasari reports that Pope Julius II poked fun at Bramante for having copied lintel puns "from a door in Viterbo. There one Maestro Francesco, an architect, had placed his name, carved in the architrave, and represented by a St. Francis (*Francesco*), an arch (*arco*), a roof (*tetto*), and a tower (*torre*), which interpreted in his own way, read 'Maestro Francesco Architettore.'"[113] *Tituli* over doors could be more than assertions of authorship, however. In a woodcut illustration from the *Hypnerotomachia*, Poliphilo, Logistica (interpreted as Reason or Speech), and Thelemia (Desire and/or Will) stand at a gate before three doors carved out of the living rock and inscribed with *tituli* in Latin, Greek, Hebrew, and Arabic (fig. 115). The *tituli* ("Gloria Dei, Mater Amoris, Gloria Mundi") refer to the realm of Queen Teleosia, which lies beyond the gate.[114] Poliphilo has to make a choice based either on will or reason on which path to follow.[115] The women instruct him but fail to persuade him to take either the path to the *vita contemplativa* (the life of contemplation) or the *vita activa* (human action and business). Poliphilo instead goes through the central doorway, opting to explore the realm of *Mater Amoris* ("the nurse of love") in which he ultimately finds his beloved Polia.[116] In sum, *tituli* over lintels were polysemic signs that guided and invited Renaissance viewers to engage with their messages in multiple ways.

In the monastic tradition, inscriptions on lintels were common as mnemonic tags that, much as the Benedictine sayings *Ora et Labora* (pray and work) and *Silentium* (silence) declare the mission of religious life, or were associated with spaces used for specific rituals. The fourth-century Bishop Paulinus, for example, describes "four little rooms with the colonnades inserted in the longitudinal sides" of his basilica at Nola (south of Naples) reserved for devotees to pray. Each room was marked over the door by a *titulus* to indicate its specific function.[117] Appropriated in patrician and ecclesiastical palaces as doorframe ornaments, *tituli* signaled more than the purpose of a chamber in an abbess's apartment.

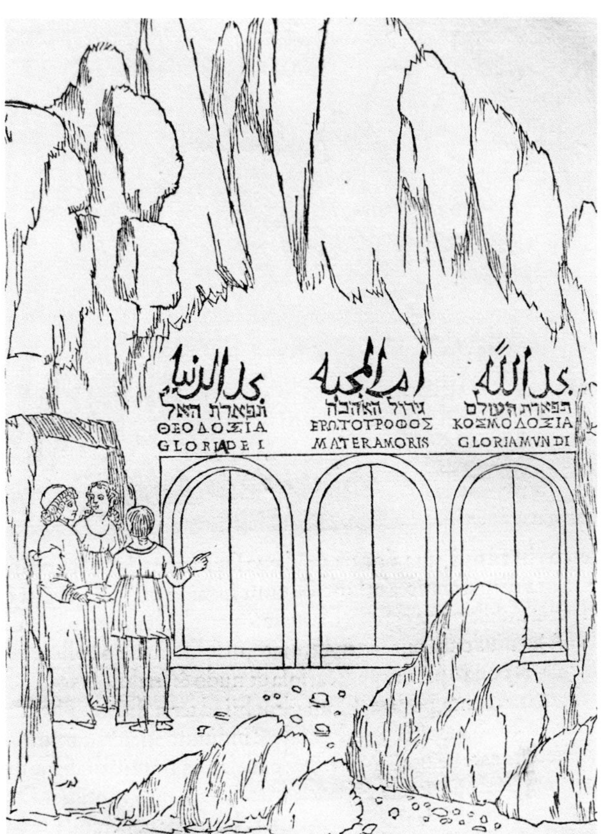

115 Inscriptions on lintels, from the *Hypnerotomachia Poliphili*, woodcut, h8r, 12.8 × 17 cm ($5^3/_{64}$ × $6^{11}/_{16}$ in), (Venice 1499)

They were invitations to reflect on ethical and spiritual matters, accompanying the ambulatory viewer into the rooms. Above the doorway to the chapter house, guests encountered the saying NEC TE QUAESIVERIS EXTRA (Seek not outside your own self) from the first satire of the Roman poet Persius.[118] This satire is a bitter critique of Persius's own time, a pungent reflection on its decadent mores and morals. In adherence to a Stoic precept, Persius's verses scornfully declare his disregard of public opinion and assert reliance on his own judgment alone. Erasmus's commentary on Persius in his adage *Extra quaerere sese* (To seek outside oneself) reminds readers of Persius's self-reliance, which Erasmus condenses in this sentence: "Measure yourself by your own capacity and not by public opinion."[119] Placed at the threshold of the chapter house, where the community congregated to make decisions, Persius's words imparted the Stoic ideal of self-sufficiency and autonomy (*autarcheia*) in making fair decisions, beyond the susceptibility of emotions or factual contingencies. It encouraged residents to be self-assured and, at the same time, presented the abbess as a self-reliant individual who looked to her own conscience instead of others as her guide. If the words do not necessarily ask the viewer to share this Stoic precept they nonetheless pose its importance.

Early Cinquecento humanists read and extensively commented on Persius's satires. But there were also those who wanted to deprive students of Persius's writings, like the playwright Ugolino Pisani of Parma (ca. 1410–1450), who banished Juvenal and Persius along with love poets from public lectures in the university.[120] Conversely, the Parmese Taddeo Ugoleto played a crucial role in reassessing Persius's centrality. Matthias Corvinus sent Ugoleto, then his librarian, to Italy in 1487–8 to hunt for codices, and to organize and supervise the team of scholars, scribes, and artists involved in the production of manuscripts for the Corviniana Library in Buda. In Florence, Ugoleto met Politian and Bartolomeo Fonzio, whose treatise *Tadeus vel de locis Persianis* (Thadeus, or Passages from Persius; ca. 1488) investigates some dense passages in Persius's *Satires* and refers to their conversations on the topic.[121] During Ugoleto's years at the Corvinus court in Buda, many texts of ancient and modern authors were copied and illuminated for the library, including Philostratus's *Imagines*, Alberti's *De Re Aedificatoria*, and Filarete's *Trattato di Architettura*. The last was translated into Latin by Antonio Bonfini, who seems to have had Ugoleto's help in producing the richly illustrated version of Filarete's text now in the Biblioteca Marciana in Venice.[122] Once he had returned to Parma (in 1490), Ugoleto brought with him his collection of manuscripts and texts, including copies of Plautus's comedies, Pliny's *Naturalis Historia*, and Boccaccio's *Genealogiae Deorum Gentilium*.[123] Ugoleto's documented relationship with Bartolomeo Montini, the canon who was closely linked to the community of San Paolo and who served as the godfather of Ugoleto's youngest son Elpidio in 1513, shows that until his death (before 1515) Taddeo was an active participant in the convent court.

The threshold between the chapter house and the painted room by Araldi was marked by another carved inscription, GLORIA CUIQUE SUA EST (To everyone his glory). Taken from Tibullus's elegy to Priapus (1.4.77), the saying is proverbial.[124] Elegy 1.4 is one of Tibullus's most playful poems, in which Priapus assumes the role of a teacher-adviser on love for distraught lovers. Priapus's "to everyone his glory" was a proud boast of himself as a master of love, but his cocky stance was short-lived. He himself was maltreated by a mischievous lover, whose victims were forced to seek remedies to cure their woes. Tibullus's verses are replete with humor and *double entendre*, amusing his readers with the very conceit of Priapus's *gloria*, his oversized penis and, at the same time, his pedagogy of love. They further seem to echo the Stoic dictum *suum cuique* (Let each have his own) and reinforce the perception that the chamber's owner wanted to play a role of her own choosing, and was deserving of her own glory. The *titulus* therefore recombined the Stoic doctrine of trust in the self with a hint of irony, playing with the notion of self-glory and fame.

Moving through Piacenza's apartment, the viewer encountered another inscription over the doorway to Correggio's painted room. Here was carved DII BENE VORTANT (May the gods turn things for the best), invoking a general ideal of the common good and strength for facing life's adversities. It was not a prayer in the Christian sense but, rather, an optimistic invocation of one's inner forces for better things to come. The phrase is found in many plays by both Terence and Plautus, including the latter's *Aulularia* (257, 272). Given that an edition of Plautus's comedies was reprinted in Parma in 1510 under the care of Ugoleto, Grapaldo, and Anselmi, it is fair to assume that Plautus was the source.[125] Reinforcing the beliefs expressed in the intarsia frieze inscriptions, this consolatory message could have sustained viewers, including the abbess, in resisting hardship and attacks on their reputation

Within Correggio's chamber, the southern door carries the only still extant *titulus*, which reads O[MN]IA VIRT[UTI] PERVIA (All is accessible to virtue; see fig. 114). It was carved in classicizing capital letters according to the model of probably the earliest printed pattern-book of letters that ever appeared in Italy, Damiano da Moille's alphabet, published in Parma around 1483.[126] A slightly reworked version (*omni virtute praevia*) occurs in an address to the Virgin in a popular Franciscan hymn.[127] Its associations with Correggio's images will be addressed in Chapter Six, but here it is the placement of the inscription that needs emphasizing, which, at almost the same height, stands opposite the inscription over the fireplace (see Chapter Six). This gives the inscription a strategic location for its intersection with the themes embodied in Correggio's secular subjects.

This corpus of *tituli*, inventive devices, and Greek and Latin sentences, along with the paintings, aligned the abbatial apartment with contemporary ornate male ecclesiastical residences, making it a female-gendered response to the typical magnificent male ecclesiastical interiors, which functioned as centers and transmitters of authority, identity, and sophistication. In particular, abbesses and bishops shared the same symbols – the pastoral and the throne – the insignias of the power of their offices that were permanently present in their apartments. As the *Prologo de l'ordine*

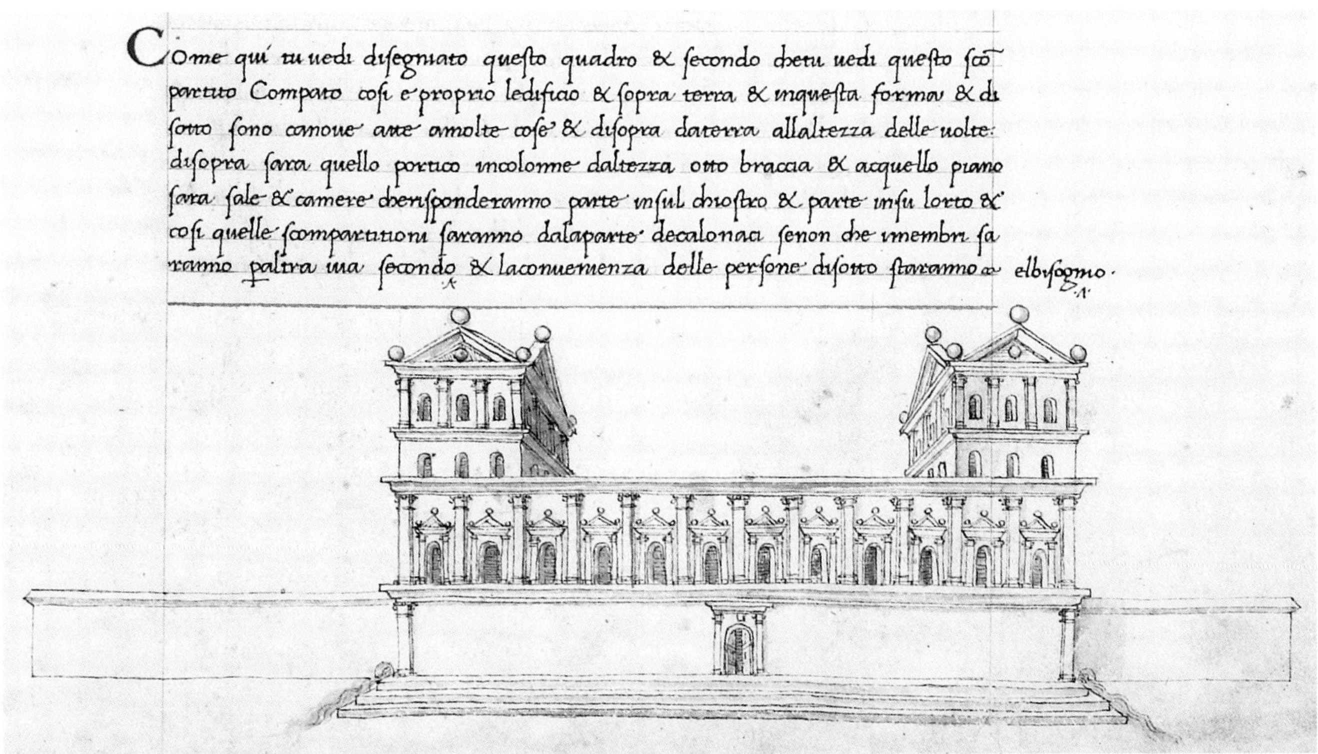

116   Bishop's palace, from Filarete, *Trattato di Architettura*, ca. 1460–64, book IX, 66r, Florence, Biblioteca Nazionale Centrale

del vivere neli monasteri de monache (1497) illustrates, female communities were under the jurisdiction of bishops, and several of its woodcuts picture nuns kneeling and praying before the bishop, a manifestation of religious women's submission to male ecclesiastical leadership.[128] As discussed in Chapter Two, the convent of San Paolo was exempt from local episcopal supervision and subject solely to papal jurisdiction, and its independence had long fractured relationships with local bishops. Early modern bishops were often members of the elite, living away from their assigned dioceses, accumulating benefits, and conducting what amounted to secular lives. Bishops exercised a pastoral mission and held temporal powers; they engaged in political business and entertained high-profile guests, playing roles that religious reformers questioned in the early sixteenth century as contrary to the spirit of a genuine religious life as practiced in the primitive Church. The Council of Trent (1545–63) attempted to remedy these abuses, asserting that bishops had to reside in their dioceses, that the temporal powers of their office were to be reduced, and that periodically they had to undertake visits to the churches and religious institutions in their dioceses.[129] This model of episcopal supervision was pioneered, among others, by the zealous bishop of Bologna, Gabriele Paleotti (1522–1597), better known to art historians for his treatise on religious images than his episcopal mission.

As a symbol of ecclesiastical authority, the bishop's palace, along with the usually nearby cathedral – the site of the bishop's *cathedra* (seat) – brought together the Christian community, constituting the spiritual focus of Italian Renaissance cities. In planning the ideal city of Sforzinda (ca. 1460–64), the architect Filarete anticipated some of the criticism to come, turning the episcopal palace into a building that embodied the bishop's pastoral mission more than his political role. In Filarete's *Trattato di Architettura* the bishop's palace is described as a two-story building with towering wings; his accompanying drawing presents the palace as a massive edifice (fig. 116) with a simplified façade perforated by an enfilade of windows because, as Filarete puts it, the palace is the seat of a resident bishop sharing his space with canons and priests. The bishop's representative rooms are distributed on the upper floors and, rather than being decorated with painted images, Filarete proposes they be ornamented with semiprecious stones, which could be seen either as a precious sign of *iconophobia* or as a reflection of architects' long-standing disdain for illusionist murals that were perceived as

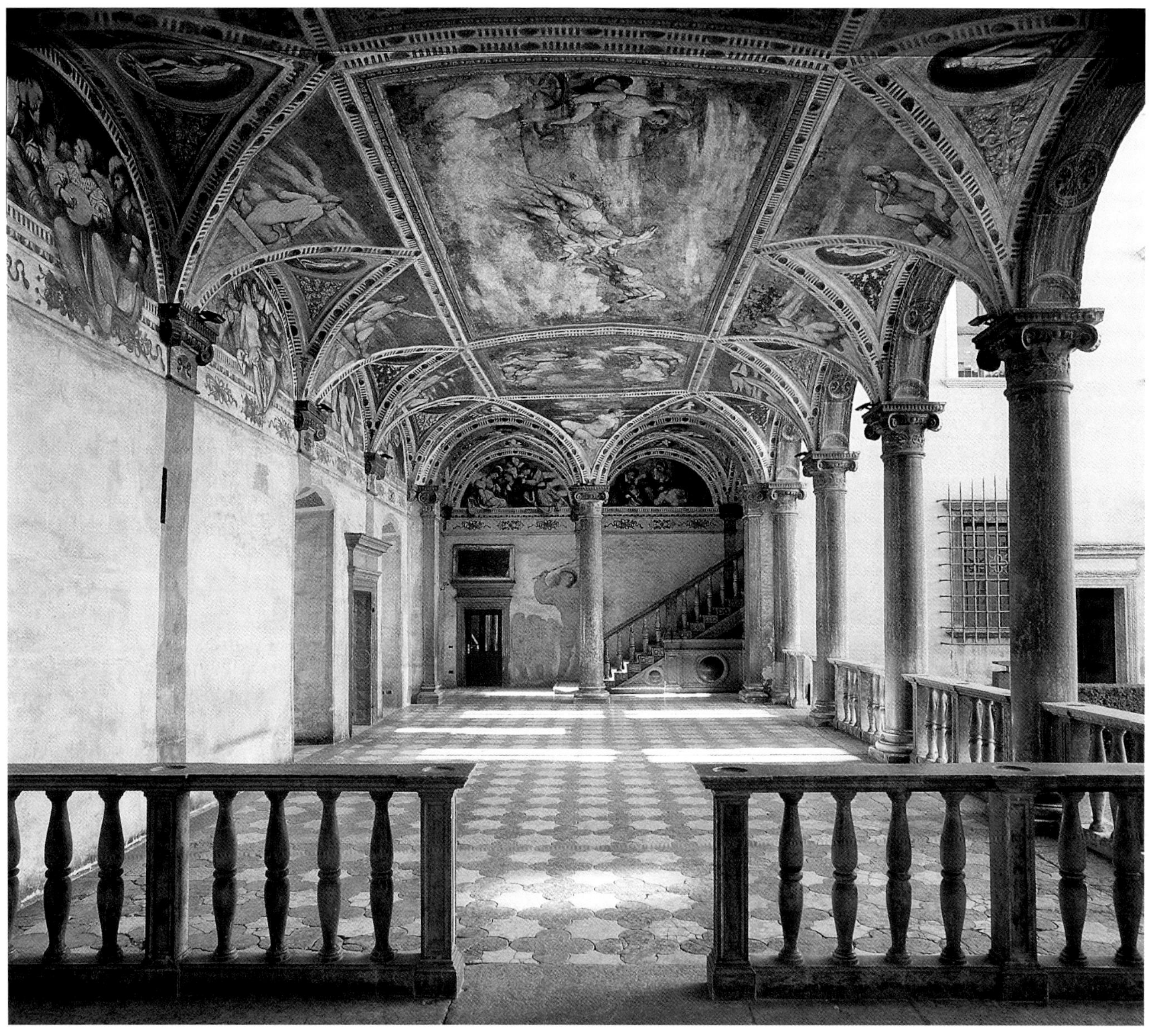

117   Loggia of the Magno Palazzo, Castello del Buonconsiglio, Trent

altering the beauty of pure architectural form.[130] Likewise, for the palace façade, Filarete prescribed marble ornaments, suggesting a building devoid of images as the counterpart of the bishop's renewed pastoral role in his diocese. But Filarete felt that he almost had to apologize for his thoughts because

> that [building] will not seem very suitable to many . . . [But] I have done this solely for the following reason. It seems to me that when the shepherd is near his sheep they are more wary. They do not go beyond the limits of good behavior, especially at night, for when the shep-

herd has shut up his sheep, he no longer has any concern for the wolf. Thus, when the good shepherd is near his sheep both day and night, they are kept safer.[131]

Extant bishops' palaces that could be seen as comparable to Giovanna Piacenza's interiors include the Castello del Buonconsiglio in Trent, to which the episcopal seat was transferred in the late fourteenth century. The castle was renovated and ornamented by Bernardo Cles (1485–1539), the prince bishop of Trent elected cardinal in 1530. One of his predecessors, Prince Bishop George of Liechtenstein,

126

had acquired the castle in 1390 and commissioned a tower room to be decorated with the Labors of the Month. Cles enlarged and remodeled the building, transforming it into a splendid palace (also called the Magno Palazzo), which features a large reception room, a library, and a courtyard with an open-air loggia (fig. 117), among other spaces. Despite prolonged absences from Trent, Cles managed to have several chambers decorated by a team of acclaimed artists, including Girolamo Romanino, Dosso Dossi, and Marcello Fogolino.[132] The bishop's court physician, Pietro Andrea Mattioli, composed a long poem describing the decorations' mixture of Christian, mythological, and anti-quarian themes, a text that was published a few years after the completion of the project in 1536. The correspondence of the absent bishop with his local supervisors and the painters proves that Cles was concerned with matters of decorum, but that he considered secular subjects appropri-ate for his residence. In one of the bishop's rooms, Dosso Dossi and his brother Battista painted scenes from Aesop's *Fables* that stand out for their refinement, charm, and the-matic unity. On the vault of the loggia, Romanino's frescoes (ca. 1531–2) present a less thematically coherent but none-theless exceptionally alluring ensemble, juxtaposing pagan themes (the Three Graces) and historical subjects (the Death of Cleopatra) with nude figures (fig. 118). In particular, Romanino's *ignudi* (nude bodies) and Dosso's depictions of pagan gods raised contemporary eyebrows. Critics saw the depicted gods as evocations of persistent pagan cults, and the nude bodies as trespassing the rules of decorum. Mat-tioli defended Dosso and Romanino's images from charges of indecency, positing that the *ignudi* were proofs of Romanino's great artistry.[133]

Returning to Giovanna Piacenza's decorated apartment with this understanding of a contemporary Renaissance bishop's ornate episcopal residence, I suggest that in the former, the model of the ecclesiastical *palatium* was adapted to assert ideals of power, self-identity, leadership, and refine-ment, regendering that male model to manifest a female courtly monastic culture that culminated in one of the most fascinating creations in the history of Italian Renaissance art: Correggio's painted room (see Chapter Six). Both these residences were spaces expressing their religious owners' cultivated personae; they were sites of power relations, they encouraged aesthetic and intellectual divagations, which in the case of the abbess's interiors required sustaining and defending. Reversing the code of monastic austerity into discourses of aesthetic delight, splendor, and levity, the abbess's appropriation of the male ecclesiastical palace model

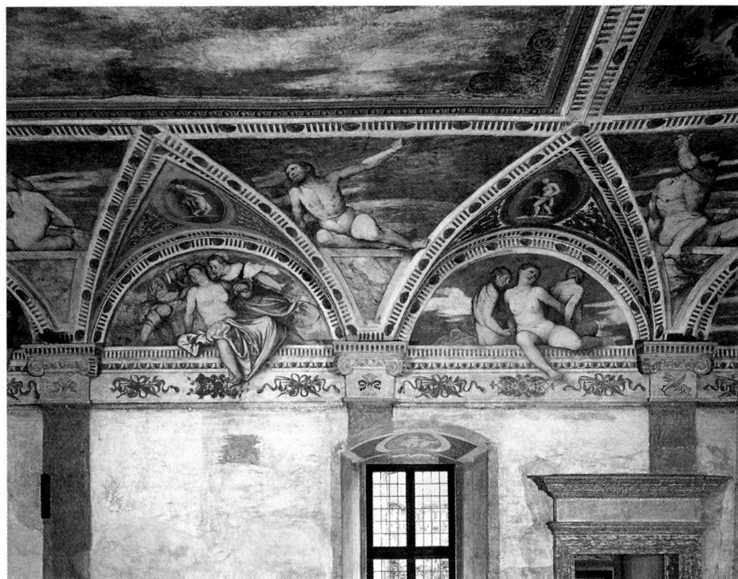

118   Girolamo Romanino, nude figure, and *Death of Cleopatra* and *The Three Graces*, 1531–2, fresco, Loggia, Castello del Buonconsiglio, Trent

was found by critics to be highly inappropriate for a clois-tered woman. Well beyond the criticism leveled at Cles, Giovanna Piacenza's ornate rooms became the target of attacks that can be surmised from Cornigli's defense of her space. It is easy to imagine how the rooms' charm and lavishness were linked to notions of curiosity, waste, disrup-tive sensory emotions, and disobedience: and what is worse, they had been commissioned by a religious woman.

QUESTIONING BEAUTY

Composed in 1522 as a preface to a lost gradual ordered by Giovanna Piacenza from Lorenzo Cornigli, the Latin pro-logue text written by this local calligrapher and priest is now known thanks to Angelo Pezzana's nineteenth-century tran-scription.[134] It is, above all, a defense of the abbess's invest-ments in art and architecture that transformed the convent's spaces into splendid Renaissance interiors. Composed in the epideictic rhetoric of praise, Cornigli's too-often overlooked text is conceived as a eulogy of the abbess portrayed as a paragon of the virtues of conventual life and as a model to be imitated by those whose lives were devoted to serving God. Surely, Cornigli had personal interests in fashioning such an image of female excellence and spiritual leadership, since he served as the confessor of the nuns of San Paolo.

Giovanna's lifestyle and ornate apartment, which declared a preference for material comfort and magnificence, drew criticism. At least one document dating to 1515 reveals that the relatives of the previous Bergonzi abbesses had attempted to discredit Giovanna and to tarnish her reputation.[135] As a cloistered woman, she was expected to obey monastic regulations and show modesty rather than audacity of comportment, but in the self-image she projected through her artistic investments, she appeared learned and endowed with authority, manners, and a sense of humor. On the one hand, Cornigli's writing addresses these views, presenting the abbess as an exemplary observer of monastic rules, while on the other, he emphasizes that her apartment was marked as a site of moral values. From a cloistered woman of strong mind and sophistication battling ecclesiastical attempts to reform her institution, Giovanna Piacenza was metamorphosed into a champion of religious conduct and a praiseworthy embodiment of her office's duties. Consider the list that Cornigli offers: praise for the abbess's imposition of strict cloister rules over her community; for the correction of nuns' abuses and wrongdoing by both punishment and good example; for the regulation of profligacy in food and undue attention to fashion in clothing; and finally for the construction of high walls to protect the nuns from male intruders. All of these measures portray Giovanna Piacenza as a commendable abbess, concerned for her flock and responsible for implementing concord and discipline among her nuns, in adherence to rules that forged equality among them. In short, the nuns of San Paolo lived in an environment that was ideal for the fulfillment of their mission to serve God.

After this laudatory introduction, Cornigli proceeds to his justification of the abbess's expenditure, describing her investments as pious acts. Evoking the theology of magnificence that preachers had developed in the fifteenth century, Cornigli posits that investments in beautiful art were made for the honor of God.[136] Art, he continues, is made tastefully for that purpose, after which he praises the ornate residence erected by the abbess for its charm (*venustas*) and usefulness (*utilitas*).[137] Beauty and utility had been associated with architecture since antiquity. In his *De Architectura*, Vitruvius speaks of "strength, utility, and beauty" as the principles on which all of the other architectural tenets must be based. Palaces were thus to be built in consideration of beauty and functionality, and of the enjoyment that they can bestow on their owners. According to Alberti's *De Re Aedificatoria*, a well-designed building had a positive effect on citizens and civic affairs because its presence and appearance could calm passions and con-

vince the unruly to return to order. Additionally, several commentaries of Cicero's *De Officiis* published in the Renaissance link the concept of a charming and useful house to notions of virtue and *commoditas* (comfort): the latter is defined as "use with delight" in opposition to mere utilitarian use.[138]

In his justification of the splendor of Giovanna's abbatial residence, Cornigli, who may have been writing with these texts in mind, connects what is alluring, appealing to the viewer's eyes to its utility. The sensory pleasure afforded by the experience of viewing the decorated residence becomes charged with a moral value. Echoing Alberti, who had written that appropriate and skillfully made paintings improve the ethics and morale of viewers, Cornigli recognizes that the contemplation of appealing interiors could inspire the audience's admiration, providing intellectual at the same time as visual delight. Investments in splendid adornments were therefore justified by making them profitable for the mind, and thus the charge of ostentation could be avoided by their owners.[139] In other words, Cornigli defends the material splendor of the abbess's residence because of the knowledge and inspirational pleasure that magnificent quarters generated, distancing the ideal of lavish display from the dangerous discourses of wasteful luxury. The distinction was subtle but critical for responding efficaciously to potential attacks leveled at the abbess's chambers as a repository of female vanity.

Luxury, cultivation of pagan learning, and excessive beauty had long been preoccupations for religious reformers aiming to banish them from monastic spaces for all they stood for (including immorality and potential idolatry). St. Gregory the Great, St. Bernard, Pier Damiani, and Girolamo Savonarola, among others, associated art's precious materials and high costs with vanity. All such forms of refinement were viewed as distracting monks from prayer and from the cultivation of a privileged relation with God.[140] The twelfth-century Abbot Suger's response to similar criticism was to claim that material preciosity served as a spiritual aid, and that aesthetic beauty drew beholders beyond refined materiality toward the immaterial and divine.[141] Despite Suger and subsequent defenders of splendid ornament in religious settings, religious reformers continued to raise the alarm against the deceptive power of images, exposing the vulnerability of art to censorship and being banned.

The excessive beauty of images, and especially religious images, could corrupt viewers' minds and behavior, and their improper use could engender sloth (*otium*) and neglectful conduct. Petrarch in his *Remedies for Fortune Fair and Foul* made conciliatory remarks about viewers' excessive emotional involvement with images and the attendant risk of idolatry. As he puts it, "great minds . . . are captivated by these things [the beauty of art]" and, rather than take brief enjoyment, they "continue to venerate with sighs of admiration," entangling the eyes and the mind to the point of precluding the contemplation of higher things. The beauty of art thus risks presenting itself as an obstacle to the divine truth that images are meant to convey. Petrarch proposes moderation as the antidote.[142] Insistence on moderation was the countermeasure that humanists and art theorists, from Petrarch to the late sixteenth-century Gregorio Comanini, suggested in attempting to draw a line between enjoyment and distraction, reflections and rapture provoked by appealing art. But such a line remained ambiguous, residing very much in the eyes and mind of the beholder. As Cornigli was aware, that fine line may have been crossed in the abbess's interiors, where the powerful allure of the art was apt to intoxicate, seduce, and confound the spectator. And local critics perceived such feelings in the chambers painted by Araldi and Correggio, the subjects of the following chapters.

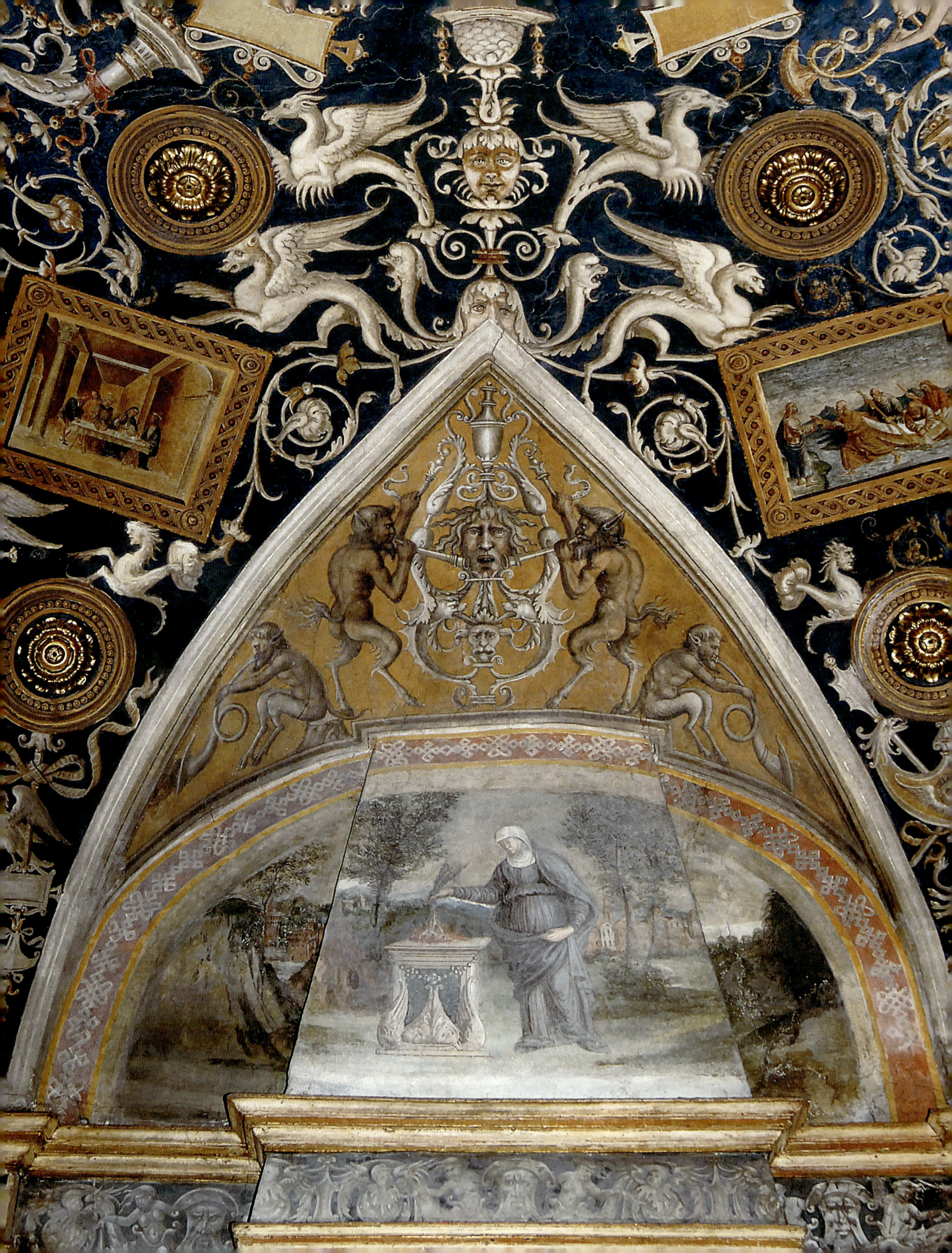

5

Monstrosities, Female Exemplarity, and the Ideal of Regeneration

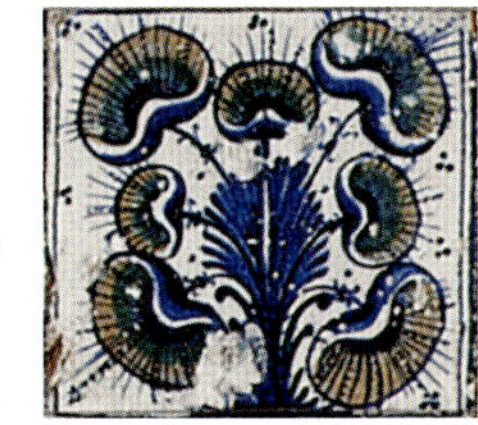

Alessandro Araldi's decoration of a room within Giovanna Piacenza's quarters in San Paolo transformed a simple architectural space into an impressive setting, a display of antiquarian, biblical, and monastic culture (see figs. 103 and 119). Perforated by two windows flanking the fireplace on the northern wall, this small, almost square room (measuring 6.5 × 7.10 meters; ca. 21 × 23 feet) was ornamented for the pleasure, comfort, and entertainment of the abbess, and of the monastic and lay community forming the convent court. Araldi transmuted the octagonal vault into an *all'antica* surface (fig. 120), creating a highly structured jungle of demons, dragons, trophies, and floral sprays typical of grotesque decoration, as rediscovered in the Domus Aurea in Rome, and since the early 1480s widely deployed in Renaissance art.[1] Set against a dark blue ground, mythical and fantastic creatures, masks, fictive relief carvings, and cornucopiae are stacked to form eight column-like "candelabra," each occupying the center of a vault spandrel of equal width, and revolving around an illusionistic oculus at the top. The four candelabra sprouting diagonally across the ceiling consist of quasi-grisaille grotesques and drolleries interwoven with colorful Christian scenes in roundels. These circular images are framed by putti – or *spiritelli* (sprites), as the airborne creatures were called in the Renaissance – further serving as connectors to the adjacent and equally colorful rectangular pictures (fig. 121 and see fig.

123). In elaborate *trompe l'oeil* frames, these eight religious narratives are demarcated above and below by actual stucco-gilt rosettes, which together enhance the circular rhythm of the pictorial surface. Above the rosettes are eight putti on antique tablets and linked by a rich foliage festoon, who in turn, like mini-atlas figures, hold up the marble balustrade of the oculus on their fingers (fig. 122). A kind of symbolic eye, the central oculus is an illusionistic hole opening to an azure blue sky, which accommodates seven music-making *spiritelli* (not eight, thus breaking the symmetry of the number eight around which the entire vault is organized) in unlikely postures, set against a clumsily foreshortened railing. Blowing horns and trumpets, they look down into the chamber in a bid for contact with the viewer. Across the vault space, sphinxes, harpies, griffins, ribbons, vine tendrils, and Abbess Giovanna Piacenza's colorful device (three black diagonally disposed crescents set against a red field) are further squeezed into an arrangement that strikes modern visitors with its polyphonic array of forms.

At the base of each central quarter of the octagonal vault is a lunette image, and the semicircular pendentives at the four corners accommodate two each, giving a total of twelve lunettes. Ten feature either pagan heroines or virtuous acts personified by women (fig. 123); the eleventh hosts a Roman triumph, and the twelfth an Egyptian-derived hieroglyph (the two feet walking on water). Several of the

Facing page   detail of fig. 123

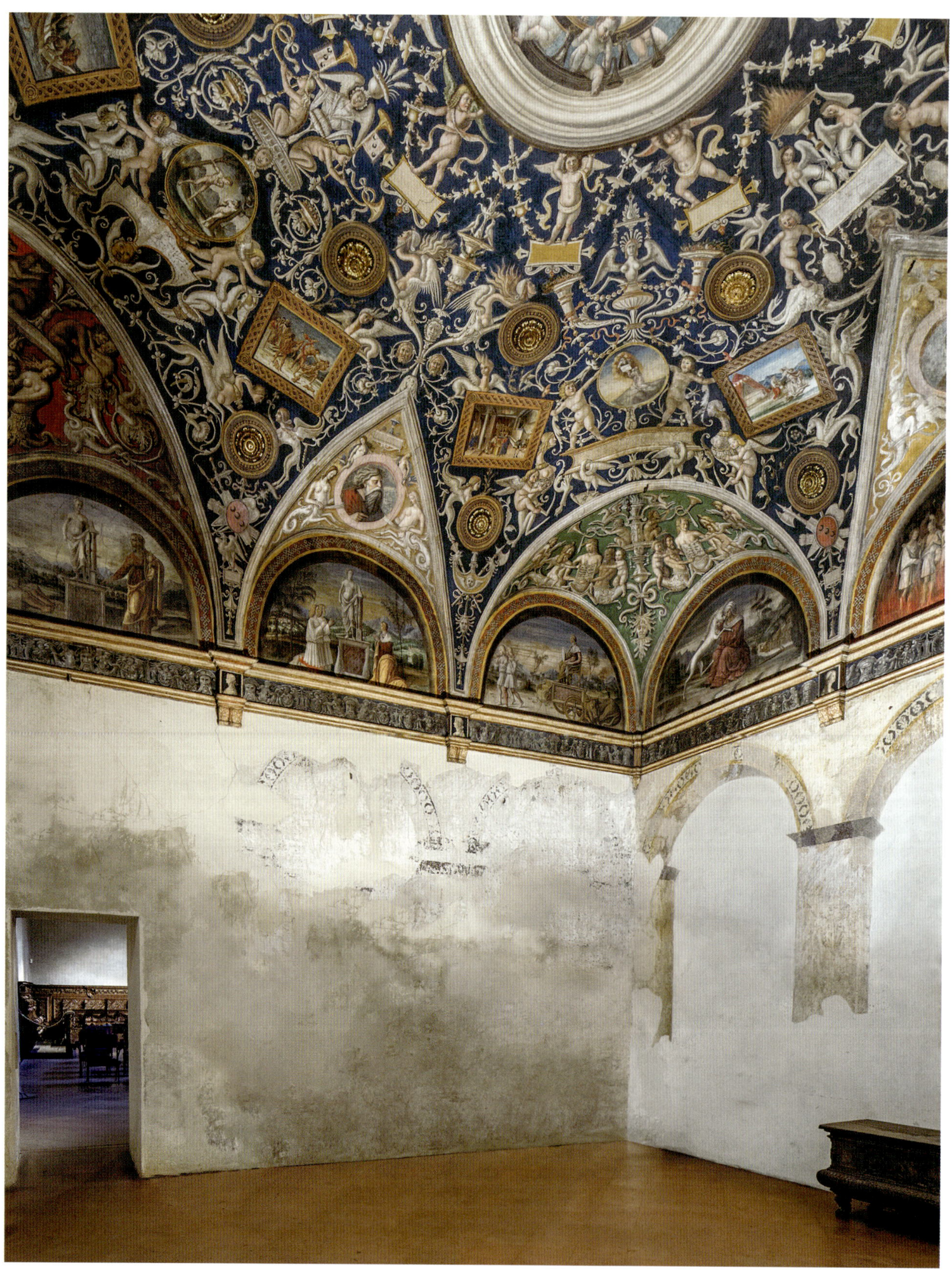

119 Alessandro Araldi, frescoed room, ca. 1514–15, Parma, San Paolo

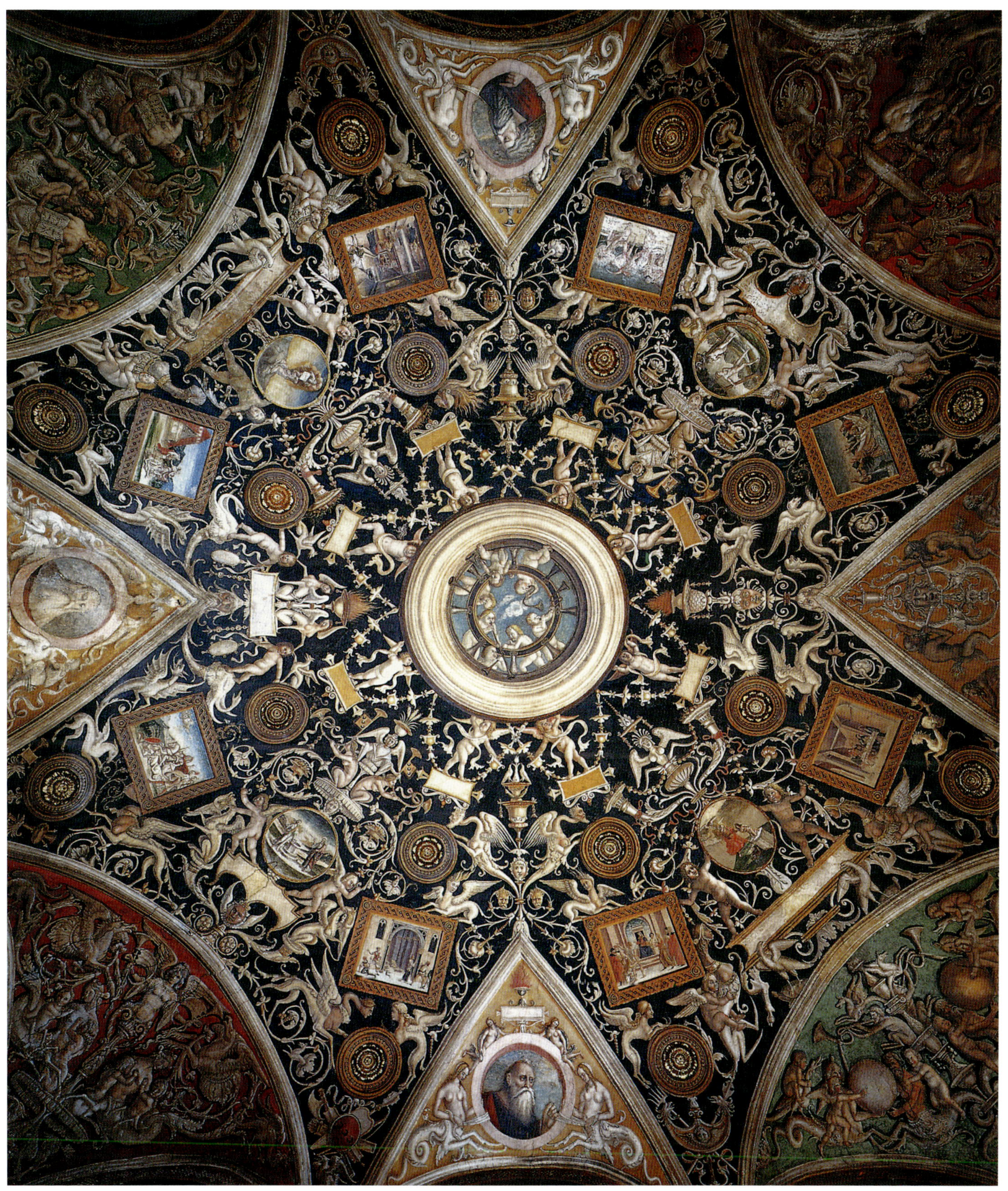

120   Alessandro Araldi, frescoed vault, ca. 1514–15, 7.10 × 6.5 m (ca. 21 × 23 feet), Parma, San Paolo

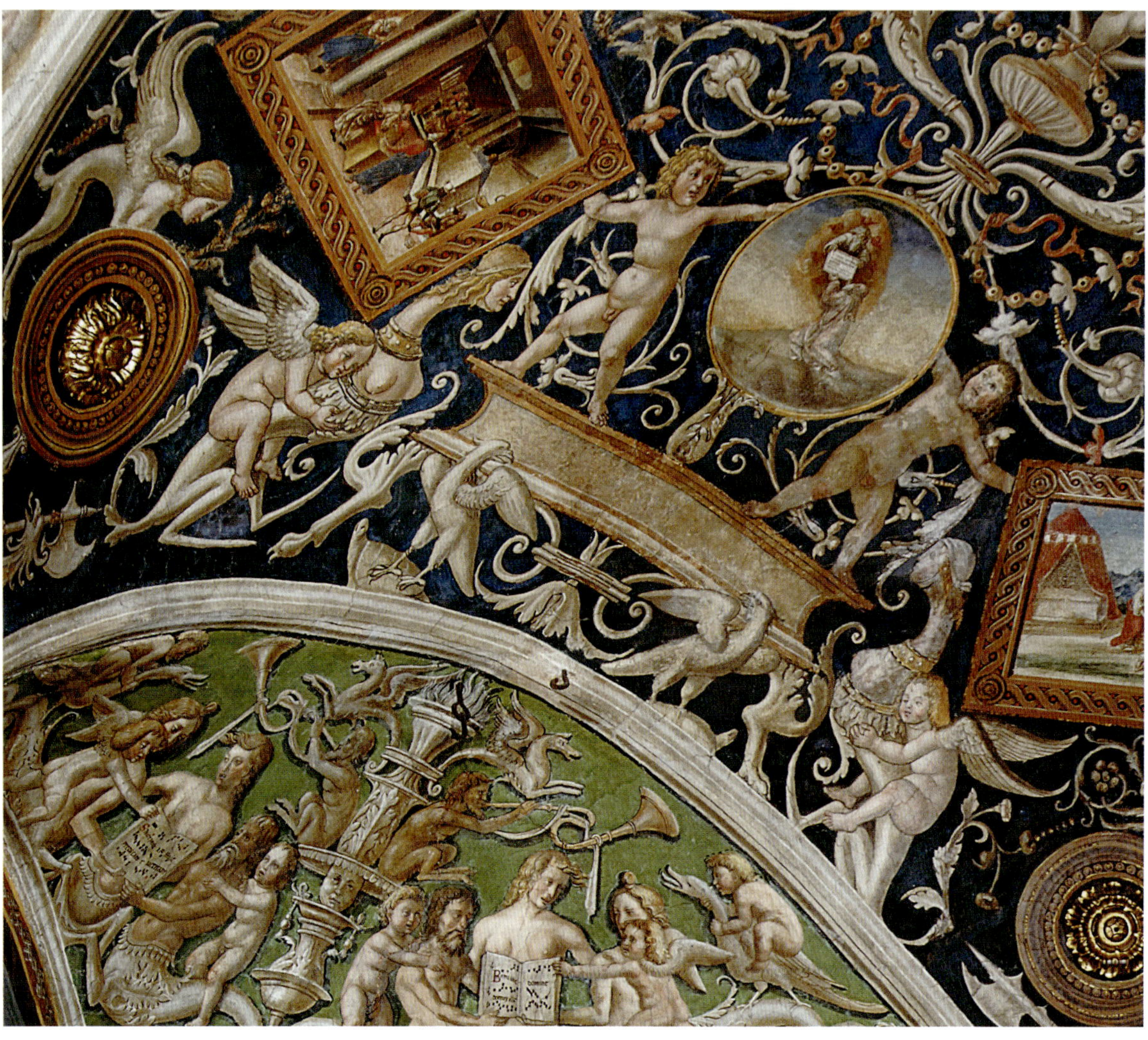

121 Alessandro Araldi, candelabrum, *spiritelli*, stucco rosettes, ca. 1514–15, fresco, Parma, San Paolo

lunette images are characterized by a composed, single human or allegorical figure standing in marked contrast with the chaos of hybrid creatures flaunting acrobatic postures in the upper vault. Aquatic monsters, satyrs, and centaurs fill the colorful semicircular corner pendentives, while pairs of sirens naughtily arouse old men leaning out of roundels in three of the four triangular pendentives of the vault (see fig. 119). A cornice displaying a parade of monochromatic marine monsters irrupted by profile heads delimits Araldi's decoration.[2] Traces of painted arcades survive on the south and west walls, but their chronology remains problematic. On the northern wall, the *pietra serena* mantelpiece (fig. 124) bears a celebratory Latin inscription from Psalm 66.12: *Transivimus per ignem et aquam et eduxisti nos in refrigerium MDXIIII* (We went

through fire and through water, but you have brought us out to a place of refreshment 1514).

Apart from the fireplace, nothing is known about the original furnishings of the chamber, but given its size it is fair to assume that it was reserved for small groups of guests. The abbess's private kitchen located below, together with the fireplace seem to suggest that it functioned as a dining room, or a *basilica*, according to Grapaldo's curious definition of dining reception spaces in his *De Partibus Aedium* (1494; 1516). Reminiscent of Vitruvius and Alberti's discussions on the topic fused with his own philological erudition, Grapaldo calls a *basilica* a reception room in which rulers could enjoy elaborate displays and performances during private meals. According to Grapaldo, the *basilica* denotes its owner's status and dedication to learning and conviviality

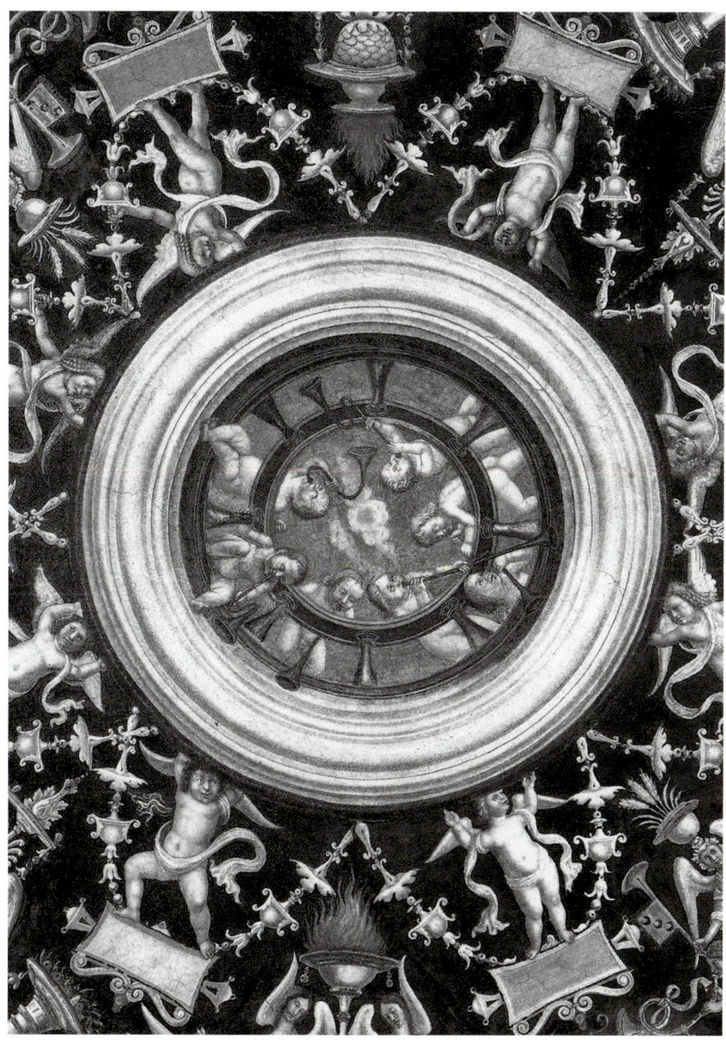

122   Alessandro Araldi, oculus and supporting *spiritelli*, ca. 1514–15, fresco, Parma, San Paolo

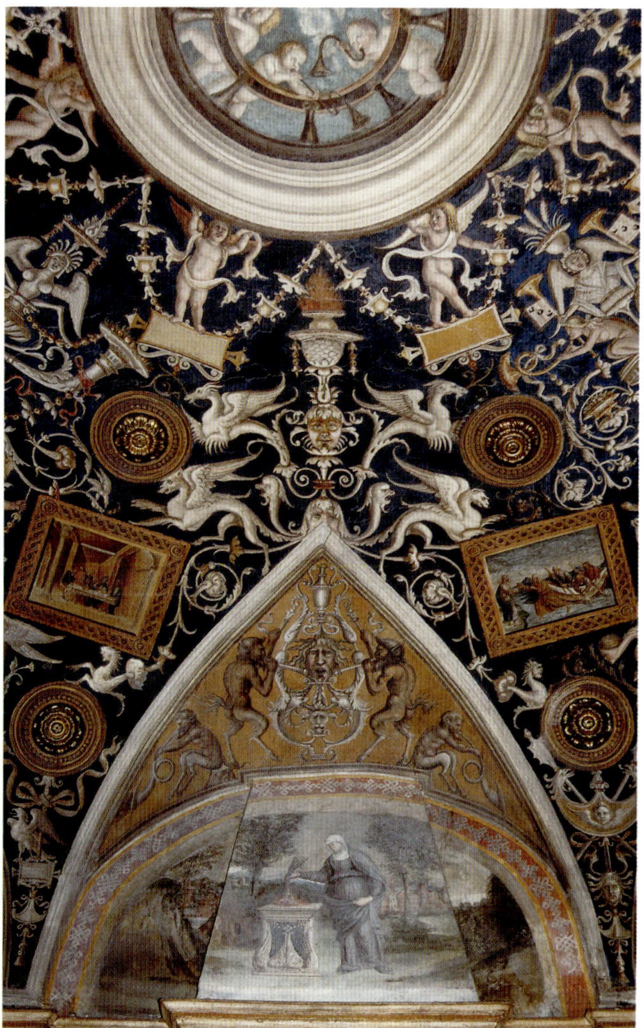

123   Alessandro Araldi, lunette with virtuous act personified by a woman, ca. 1514–15, fresco, Parma, San Paolo

promoted through conversation and the enjoyment of food, as described by ancient authors (Plutarch, Macrobius, and Aulus Gellius) and revitalized in Erasmus's colloquies.[3]

No documentation has surfaced about this painted chamber. Since the rediscovery of the abbatial apartment in the 1770s, Araldi has been mentioned as its author on connoisseurial grounds and due to his long-standing service to the nuns.[4] The chronology of the commission has been inferred from the date carved on the mantelpiece (1514). Incised in classicizing capitals probably by the local *scalpellino* Giovan Francesco d'Agrate, the passage from the Psalms and the date flanked by Giovanna Piacenza's arms form an unusual ensemble, suggesting more than the chronology of a room that lay at the heart of the abbatial residence and which had already been inhabited for some

time by 1514. The mantelpiece date is not merely a chronological marker. It is a clue richer in symbolism than has been previously understood. Three crucial events took place in 1514 with consequences for the convent for years to come. In June, the long-standing litigation between the Benedictine nuns of San Paolo and the Cassinese monks of San Giovanni Evangelista over mills and water rights was concluded, thanks to canon Bartolomeo Montini's mediation.[5] Almost simultaneously, after four years of exile, Giovanna Piacenza's brother-in-law and Montini's nephew, Scipione Montini Rosa, the convent's accountant who had been accused of murder, returned to Parma. Additionally, that year the nuns were successful in fending off a second ecclesiastical attempt to seclude them (see Chapter Four). These events would have brought to the religious com-

135

124   Giovanfrancesco d'Agrate, mantelpiece with inscription from Psalm 66, before 1514, *pietra serena*, Parma, San Paolo

munity a sense of social and economic security after years of accusations, suspicions, and struggle to remain independent.[6] The mantelpiece date is therefore an invocation of a real moment in time and the watershed marker for the season of serenity that the nuns could enjoy after years of uneasiness and conflict. Anchoring the psalm's message to a real time, it also inscribed the history of the community of San Paolo into the universal history of Christianity. The incised date, ultimately, establishes more than a simple chronological relationship to Araldi's images (probably executed around 1514–15) by connecting their subjects to the historical reception of their audience and greatly enriching our perception of this painted chamber as a site of *refrigerium* (regeneration, nourishment, repose).

Entering the chamber, the beholder is almost overwhelmed by the parade of dragons, satyrs, and other fantastic creatures overhead in the vault, experiencing a confusion that the hieratic patterning and dynamic postures of the grotesques only partially offset. At first glance, it may seem an awkward stacking of hybrid creatures lacking pictorial allure, but a second look reveals that relationships of similarity and dissimilarity bind the figures together, and that horizontal, circular, and orthogonal patterns govern their reiteration and contraposition. Repetitions, correspondences, and oppositions of figures infuse unity across the surface and, at the same time, set up multiple modes of viewing, which makes vision spatial and simultaneously focused on a specific set of images. The candelabra, assemblages of antiquarian motifs, masks, and monstrosities, invite viewing across orthogonal and diagonal axes. In contrast, the putti in their circular concatenation that magnifies the central eye-oculus can be said to ring the vault space. Personifications of vital spirits, the putti look down at the viewer, seeking direct eye contact as the latter moves across the room.[7] The lunettes, finally, with their moralizing themes of female virtuosity framed by strapwork ornament, set a horizontal mode for the gaze. Taken as a whole, Araldi's images therefore invite the spectator to look up and globally scan the surface to discover its formal and semantic associations from a variety of perspectives, without any real position of command over them.

By gazing attentively at Araldi's painted drolleries, one realizes that the majority are unbridled, frenzied female monsters compressed into the vault but almost reaching into the viewer's space. Each figure is connected to the next through gestures and movements that glance off each

125   Alessandro Araldi, harpies, ca. 1514–15, fresco, Parma, San Paolo

other, but simultaneously affect the onlooker through their sinister faces, plays, and aural themes. Among the female demons, those who resemble the mythical harpies in particular strike the modern beholder with their animated contortions and lively facial expressions. Believed to be wind spirits, the harpies (fig. 125) are caught in mirroring postures, and some sport electrified hair, wings, possessed faces, and tails that merge into the candelabrum structure. Others are grasped by *spiritelli* (see figs. 1 and 131) who seem to have twisted the harpies' heads right round. Still others play trumpets so forcefully that the loud blasts curl festoons around the instruments. These figures' outlandish qualities are not just a matter of the transformations typical of grotesques, including tails of dolphins becoming volutes or acanthus leaves. The bodily distortions and demonic expressions given to these hybrid creatures seem intentional, as does their almost magnetically charged appearance. Araldi stages a parade of frenzied, spirited entities, which it would be restrictive to regard as mere manifestations of an up-to-date *all'antica* decoration. This corpus of pagan and supernatural figures coexists with religious narratives, some of which emphasize themes of female virtuosity. The message of the sacred stories is, in turn, strengthened

by the content of the lunettes below, proposing an ensemble that resonates well with the room's sophisticated owner, Abbess Giovanna Piacenza.

The sharing of the same patron has often led to a comparison of Araldi's images with the dazzling frescoes by Correggio in the adjacent room, resulting in the stigmatization of the former for the limited visual force of his style. The explanation has been that Araldi responded unimaginatively to iconographic instructions given him by the abbess and/or her consultants, either canon Bartolomeo Montini or the humanists participating in the convent court. Araldi's commission for San Paolo has even been linked to the work he executed in Parma Cathedral, for which a contract survives, enumerating the subjects that the Cathedral's *fabbriceri* (administrators) wished Araldi to translate into pictorial form.[8] Even if Araldi was a passive receptor of instructions and his local patrons required images based on pre-established programs, his painted chamber in Giovanna Piacenza's residence was an enterprise of a completely different order from his frescoes in Parma Cathedral.

In general, the decoration of private chambers depended on consultations among patrons, artists, and often learned advisers, but any subject could be translated by painters with different degrees of imagination in rooms that, as Henri Lefebvre remarked, are both real and fictional sites: "the ideal and the real space, the complex pictorial fiction and its physical site cannot be set apart because each involves, underpins, and presupposes the other."[9] The architectural structure of the abbatial vault with its combination of pendentives and spandrels informed Araldi's pictorial decisions. But decorated chambers, including Andrea Mantegna's famous Camera Picta (ca. 1465–74) in Mantua with its interplay of antiquarian pseudo-reliefs, medallion portraits, *spiritelli*, and group portraits of the Gonzaga family, have also long been seen as pictorial extensions of their patrons' status and power, places through which owners celebrated and negotiated political and social messages. More recent scholarship has complicated these accounts of patronage, arguing for both the permeability of painting that holds the "positions of beholder and beheld" and artists' agency in reinventing the pictorial subject itself.[10] Whoever suggested the subjects visualized by Araldi in the abbatial room, they composed themes that encompassed the world, the outlook, and the poetics of secrecy and irony of an elite conventual community. The artist may have required supervision and expert counsel in creating works in a genre outside his conventional religious oeuvre. For, while Araldi devised pictorial forms of a certain *fantasia*, transforming the vaulted space into a site of moderate (certainly not breathtaking) aesthetic delight, he managed to engage with discourses of magic and cryptic communication to generate images that unfold into chains of plural readings. As such, his ceiling served as a still much underestimated precedent for Correggio's adjacent painted room: both chambers deal with what lies beneath the surface, and is being made visible in images capable of opening up multiple paths of reflection and association.

Connections between the conceptualizations of these two painted rooms in San Paolo have gone unrecognized and unexplored in the literature. Araldi's images, for instance, have been interpreted as stations on a spiritual journey through which the abbess would reach the condition of *refrigerium* promised in the lines from the psalm.[11] Inspired by Erwin Panofsky's study of Correggio's frescoes, this reading has enriched modern comprehension of the iconography of the lunettes, but at the same time, a set of religious and moral significations was superimposed, and Araldi's corpus of fantastic creatures was treated as a second-hand ornament of the ethical discourses embedded in the images below. While it is not incorrect to assume that the room's messages revolve around the dialectic, tension,

and antithesis declared in the fire-*refrigerium* inscription, the systematic way in which the images have been interpreted as reflecting this spiritual trajectory is forced. It precludes an understanding of the meanings sustained by Araldi's energized monsters and of the biblical stories that stand, in turn, in dynamic relationships, with the exempla of female virtue depicted in the lunettes. The subject of this painted chamber, I would argue, is any occupant of the room, Giovanna Piacenza included, gazing up at images that comment on the fluid boundaries between legitimate and illegitimate knowledge, the mind and the imagination. Though instructed to govern their bodies rigidly, to keep their eyes cast down, to search for learning only to serve God better and not to look for or to attain knowledge for themselves, Giovanna Piacenza and her elite nuns challenged these monastic strictures. Araldi's painted vault invites its beholders to raise their eyes upward to activate the images overhead that engage with discourses of magic, Christian morality, and irony. As the fifteenth-century German churchman Nicholas of Cusa states in his writings, which were known to the Parmese audience, seeing has a transformative force, and in impressing themselves on a viewer's eye and mind, images could enhance understanding, contemplation, and produce admiration, turning the spirit from affliction to *refrigerium*. Cusa also asserted the hermeneutical value of paradox as the "coincidence of opposites," that is, the manifestation and performance of opposing values. Viewed through these lenses, the notion of *refrigerium* carved over the mantelpiece presupposes the insights brought by the images, proclaiming painting as an engine for attaining a state of equilibrium and repose and (not least) keeping adverse forces at bay in a contradictory world. In this chapter my itinerary is first to address the psalm inscription and its implications, and explore how it is tied to some pictorial clues (such as the fire motif). I then link Araldi's spirited creatures to discussions on magic and hermetic knowledge secretively carried out in Parma's elite circles, to see how these beliefs complicate and inflate the messages that the images communicate, and how they are opposed and in tension with the exercise of female virtues (sacrifice, chastity, and *pietas*, among others) depicted in the lunettes.

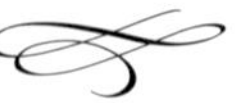

By now, readers are familiar with the fact that the chamber painted by Araldi could be reached both via the eastern and the western axes of access. Regardless of which entrance the viewer uses to enter the room, the northern fireplace, a trapezoidal hood supported by *pietra serena* scroll brackets, with its carved passage from the Psalms, immediately draws the eye by virtue of its material presence (see fig. 124). The lines, "We went through fire and through water, but you have brought us out to a place of refreshment," declare that those who put their trust in the Lord will reach the promised *refrigerium*. In his fourth-century commentary on the Psalms, St. Jerome associates this verse with the inner workings of faith, which strengthens and ultimately redeems human beings. Citing the writings of both the Prophet Isaiah and the Jewish scribe Sirach, Jerome emphasizes that the believer may overcome every possible difficulty by trusting in God, and may thus attain uplifted spirituality and contentment.[12] St. Augustine instead discusses this passage and its fire–water opposition in terms of inner purification aided by religious rites that help to prepare individuals to receive the sacraments, including Baptism.[13]

Meditation on the Psalms had long been a significant aspect of monastic life. Psalms were recited and chanted during Divine office, and used for prayers and memory exercises. Penitential psalms were recommended for recitation while imagining oneself in the difficult condition evoked in the verses themselves.[14] With their request for protection against unknown forces and dangers, they emphasize individuals' internal troubles, facilitating introspection, catharsis, and the healing of the soul. Joyful psalms, in contrast, were intended as prayers for salvation. Repetition of the Psalms is equally crucial in order to enhance their spiritual effects. Chapter 18 of the Benedictine Rule specifies the order of the Psalms' recitation, ensuring that the entire Psalter is rehearsed each week. Certain psalms are to be recited on a daily basis, at particular hours, or on specific liturgical feasts.[15] A crucial assertion of the therapeutic role of the Psalms is expressed in Erasmus's commentaries on the Psalms (1515–45). Erasmus states that the recitation of psalms requires the apprehension of their inner truths, and that the litany of repeating "a great string of psalms every day but with the tongue only, not with the spirit" is of no benefit.[16] He further recognizes that nuns' constancy in their prayers and their recitation of the Psalms

are often the result of their secluded condition rather than of authentic piety. The appropriate recitation of psalms, Erasmus continues, is to unfurl a map of salvation and to recognize the working of faith through them. In his previous writing, the *Enchiridion Militis Christiani* (*The Handbook of the Christian Soldier*; 1512), Erasmus advised readers to break psalms into short sentences and to meditate on their core message to acquire nourishment: "Meditation on a single verse will have more savor and nourishment if you break through the husk and extract the kernel, than the whole Psalter chanted monotonously with regard only for the letter . . . [It is an] aberration . . . [to think that] the culmination of piety [is] to recite the greatest number of psalms possible each day."[17] The prominence of the verse from Psalm 66 carved on the fireplace in Giovanna Piacenza's chamber ultimately suggests the role that such meditative exercises played for the abbess. The fire–*refrigerium* opposition declared by the psalm in its metaphorical language is both a reassurance that false promises, sinister fortune, and the effects of destructive events could be withstood by the exercise of virtue, and simultaneously an affirmation of the belief that God's benevolence and love ease humankind's suffering.

The spiritual core of the psalm verse encapsulates only one aspect of this dense verbal construct, however. The fire–*refrigerium* antithesis or, to put it differently, sufferance–regeneration, was a pivotal metaphor in both love poetry and Stoic philosophy. Human beings constantly have to heal the pain and distress provoked by the burning emotions of love, fear, sorrow, anger, and grief, and so forth. In Petrarchan vernacular love poetry, in particular, the fire–*refrigerium* motif had long expressed the unbalanced passion of lovers. The lover, enflamed by the gaze of his cruel or absent beloved, burns with ardent feelings and desire for that which he cannot attain. In the first book of Pietro Bembo's *Asolani*, a dialogue on love published in 1505, Perottino speaks of the uncomfortable conditions of those afflicted by love: "one lives in fire like a salamander, another freezes like ice."[18] Tormented by longing for their beloved, these individuals were much in need of healing. As Letizia Panizza argued, the cures recommended for a soul afflicted by excessive love were readings by classical and modern authors, including Cicero's *Tusculan Disputations* (book 3) and Petrarch's *Remedies for Fortune Fair and Foul* (book 2).[19] Dedicated to Azzo da Correggio, lord of Parma, Petrarch's *Remedies* (ca. 1354), in particular, discusses how best to navigate calamities and shifts of fortune and love, proposing, among other therapies, the memorization and pondering of short

passages (*sententiae*) culled from spiritual or literary writings
(see Chapter Four). First proposed by Stoic philosophers
and later reinvigorated in Petrarch's writings, this practice
of repeating and meditating on short passages of ancient
lore in order to attain a refreshed and renewed state of mind
may confirm that the tension evoked in the fireplace
inscription was meant to stimulate a viewer's productive
thinking, contributing to the healing of his or her afflicted
soul and the regaining of a balanced self.

In the San Paolo room, the psalm passage also performs
a witty play with the fireplace beneath. The Latin *ignem*
(fire) constructs a word game, imbuing the carved fire–
refrigerium antithesis with a lighter connotation, which is
echoed above in the burning vase motif that tops the
north–south painted candelabra (fig. 126). This burning vase
stands in metonymic relationship to the fireplace and its
inscription. As a visual cue, it brings pictorial lightness to
the ensemble, but the burning vase was also a motif known
to the Renaissance. It has not been previously noticed that
Araldi's burning vase resembles the right-hand hieroglyph
filling the strip above the base of the pyramidal-shaped
candelabrum in a woodcut illustration from the *Hypnerotomachia Poliphili* (fig. 127). In the accompanying text the
image is explained as alluding to a concept of shared love.[20]
The burning vase motif therefore functions as a decoration,
a pictorial pun, and a hieroglyph. In addition, flames are
prominent in the lunettes featuring female sacrifices (see
fig. 123), a visual reiteration that is rich in signification. In
general, visual cues serve to direct the viewer to the themes
embedded in an image, but the quasi-magical capacity of
fire to draw and hold the eye should be stressed. Considered
the base and foundation of all four elements, fire is the most
dynamic and vital. Fire can further be linked to rites evoking
spirits, and thereby to doctrines on magic that were secretly
debated in contemporary Parma. Thus, it is conceivable that
the fire motif and the hybrid creatures displayed across the
vault were charged with particular meaning for a local audience. While the taste for grotesque work had become
almost commonplace by 1500, in Parma the overlooked
confluence of the interests in magic, the occult, and the
language of Egyptian hieroglyphs (to be examined in the
next section) sets a specific context for assessing both the
theory and practice of art and, in particular, such products
of artists' *fantasia* as grotesques.

Renaissance *grotteschi* were perceived as simultaneously
new and ancient. Long considered as without significance
except for the delight they generate by their transformative
force, grotesques should be recognized, Philippe Morel has

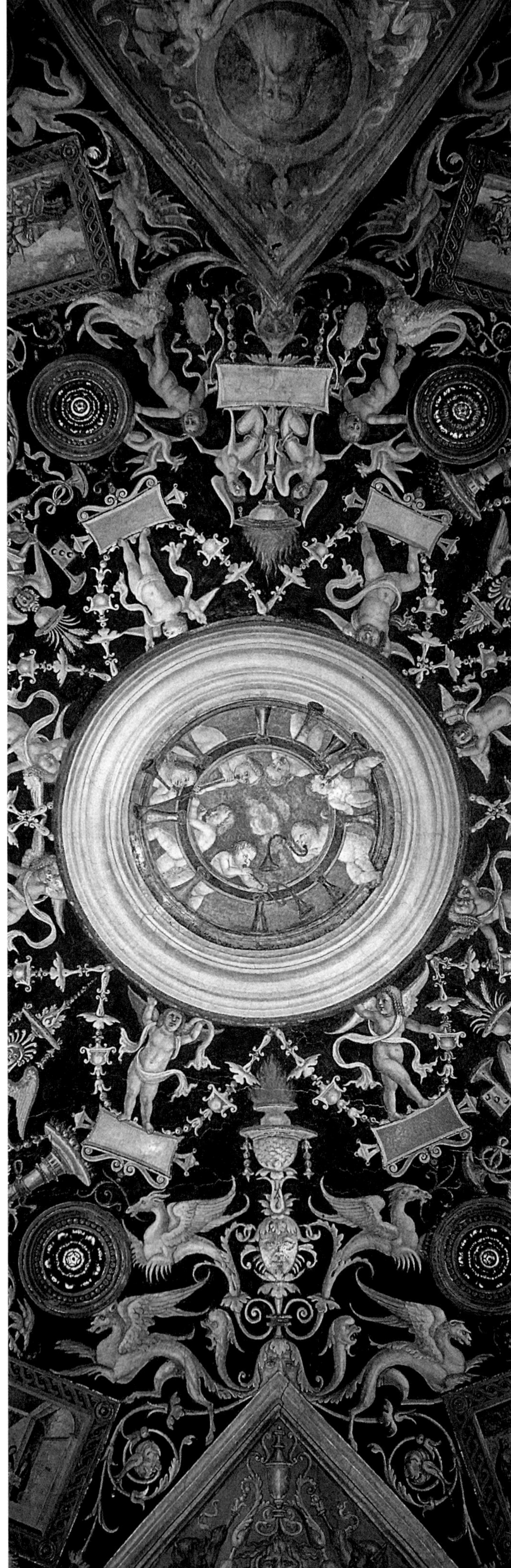

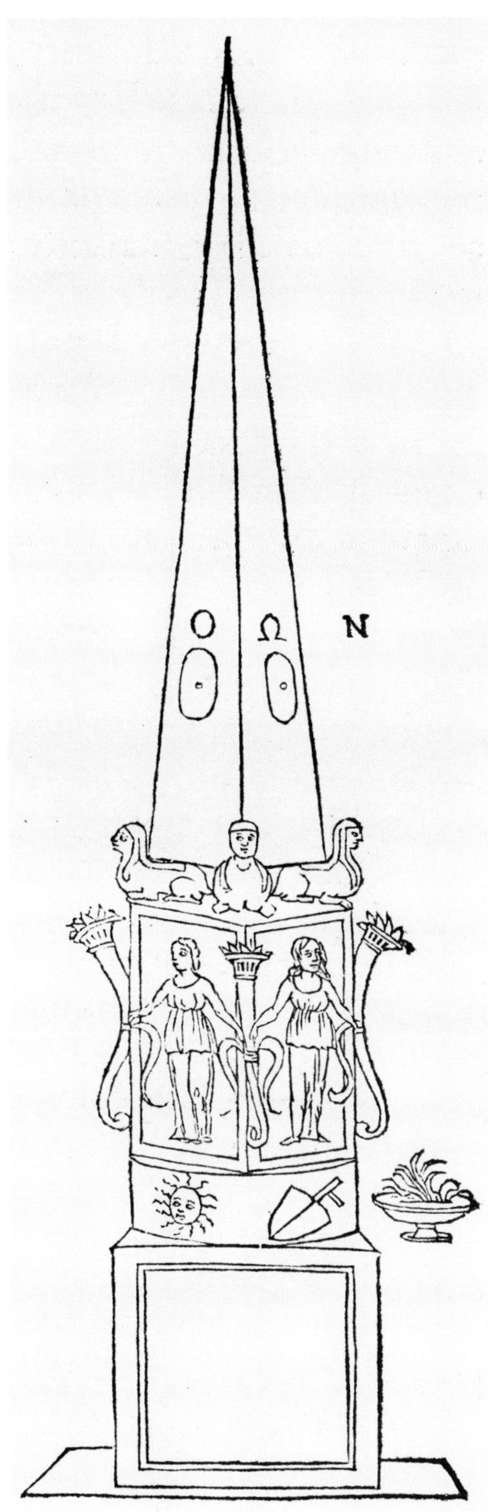

Facing page 126 Alessandro Araldi, candelabra with burning vases and masks, ca. 1514–15, fresco, Parma, San Paolo

Above 127 Candelabrum with a burning vase motif, from the *Hypnerotomachia Poliphili*, woodcut, h5r, 18 × 6 cm (17³/₃₂ × 22³/₆₄ in), (Venice 1499)

strongly argued, as having their own syntax, themes, and vocabulary. Morel posits that grotesques disrupt the very status of the image by calling into question both its content and function, bewildering beholders' perception of the ground from which they emerge and into which they are woven and metamorphosed.[21] Other studies have proposed that grotesques functioned as "middling things" between categories, "following principles of analogy, sympathy, and antipathy."[22] Grotesques were employed to create fluid and ambiguous relationships between spheres of knowledge, but they have also been perceived as forms of social criticism, sensory stimulation, and wonders of apotropaic power.[23]

Since antiquity, grotesques have sparked controversy. They have long stood for the creative power of the imagination and for an unregulated fantasy capable of generating highly charged, sensual, and dangerous images. The skeptical remarks of the first-century architect Vitruvius on decorative assemblages of curious forms nonexistent in nature and which he defined as "dreams of painters," register his disdain, and the dangers of the rule of *fantasia*. To avoid errors and not to put meaning at risk, nature must be imitated, thundered Vitruvius.[24] Similarly, Horace opens his *Ars Poetica* (19 BCE) with a critique of nonverisimilitude, which he compares to dreams produced by illness, criticizing poets who assumed the same license as painters.[25] In his *Craftsman's Handbook*, the fourteenth-century painter Cennino Cennini instead sees irrational representations as resting at the intersection of poetic and artistic discourses, justifying them as products of an artistic license that exalted *fantasia* rather than the copying of visible things. The process of creating these imaginative forms in turn pushed Renaissance artists to compete with nature in its generative power.[26]

Artists devised their own repertories of *grotteschi* that the sixteenth-century sculptor and theorist Benvenuto Cellini saw as appropriate for decorating "chambers, baths, studies, halls, and other places of like nature."[27] Conversely, contemporary religious writers censored grotesques as forms that went beyond the proper, didactic function of images. In his treatise (1582), the Counter-Reformation archbishop of Bologna, Gabriele Paleotti, dedicated three chapters to *grotteschi*, condemning them as vain chimeras, children's playthings, thereby dangerously loosening the imagination. He even brought moral charges against grotesques, describing them as figments of degenerate or lunatic minds.[28] Paleotti's view relied on a long tradition of religious writings in which representations of hybrid creatures are criticized as forms of curiosity and excess, and associated with the waste and deception of pagan cults. St. Bernard of

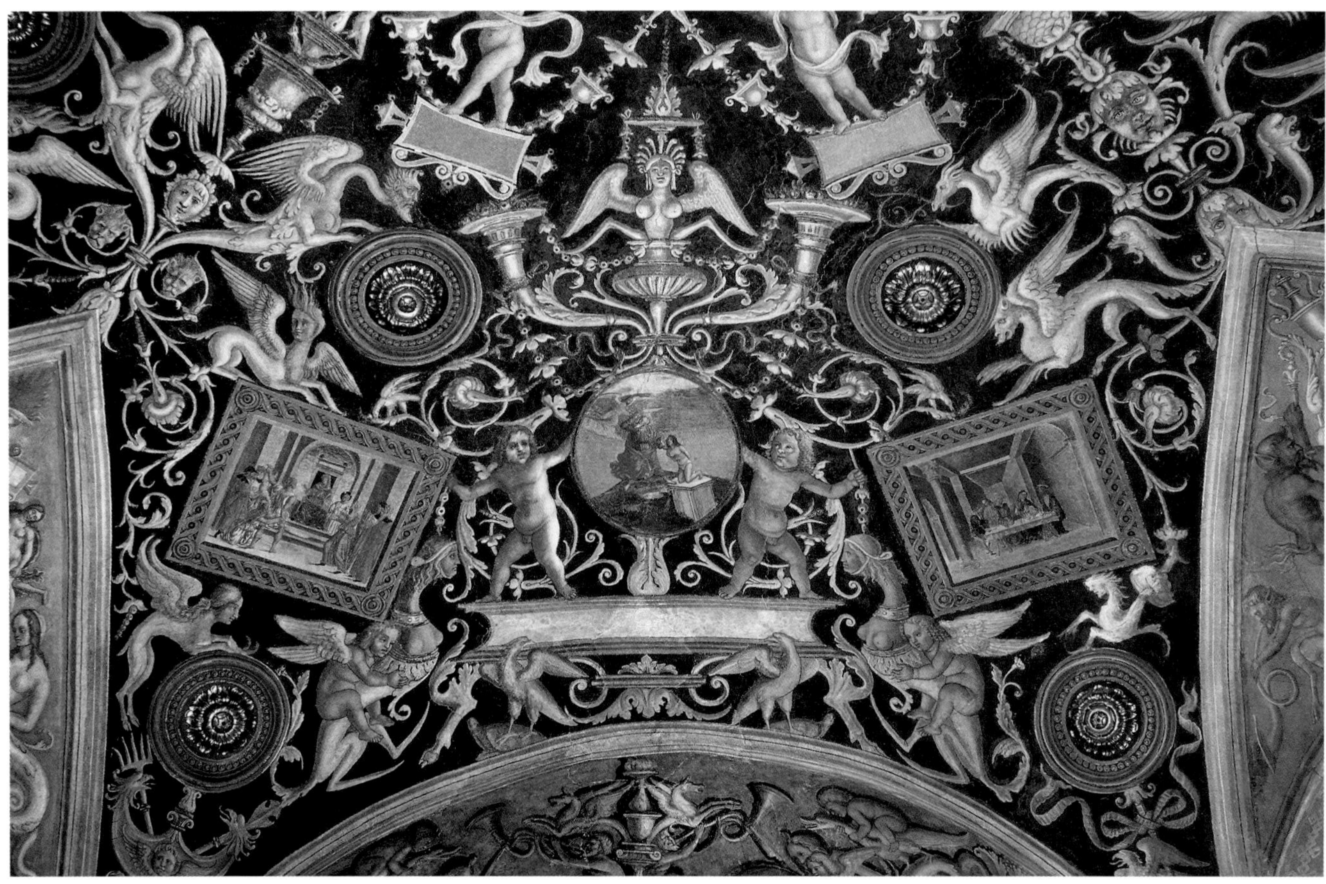

128   Alessandro Araldi, hybrid creatures, ca. 1514–15, fresco, Parma, San Paolo

Clairvaux's *Apologia* (1125) and St. John of Salisbury's *Policraticus* (1159) speak of fantastic creatures sculpted on medieval cloister capitals as products of dreams and impaired vision with the power to divert monks from their prayers and duties.[29] This attention to monstrous representations that stimulated free inquiry was equated to forms of carnal appetite. But, as Thomas Dale has argued, the contemplation of monstrous forms may have also had its benefits. By gazing at sculpted monstrosities, medieval monks saw materialized versions of infernal spirits that were believed to enter the body by diabolical means and alter one's behavior. As a result, monks could meditate on these malevolent spirits and be reminded of the inner struggles they had to undergo in order to achieve a perfected being.[30]

Possible reminders of emotional turmoil and prescribed monastic comportment, Araldi's hybrid creatures and harpies are curious representations juxtaposed in pairs and multiples, and mirroring one another. Some have exposed breasts emphasized by low-cut corsets and stucco golden necklaces, and carry winged putti on their backs (fig. 128). Their overt

sexuality is palpable and notable, too, are their ominous facial expressions. The major issue today with this corpus is that *grotteschi* are products of *fantasia* and they have little to do with copying. Yet Araldi's painted demons and drolleries are not products of his own imagination, nor are they reinventions of antiquarian motifs from the Domus Aurea. They are citations from other artists. Araldi does not seem to have undertaken first-hand investigations in Rome.[31] By the early sixteenth century, the language of *grotteschi* had spread throughout the Italian peninsula by means of paintings, illuminations, and above all, prints, any number of which may have served as sources. For example, Peregrino da Cesena and Nicoletto da Modena published decorative prints showing hybrid figures playfully touching, punching, and biting one another. Illustrating the "flourishing of the arts made possible by the advent of peace," an ornamental panel by Nicoletto that is part of a series of four he engraved after his trip to Rome in 1507, in particular, presents aural themes, including Apollo and Marsyas's contest at the top and pipe-playing satyrs seated on opposite sides

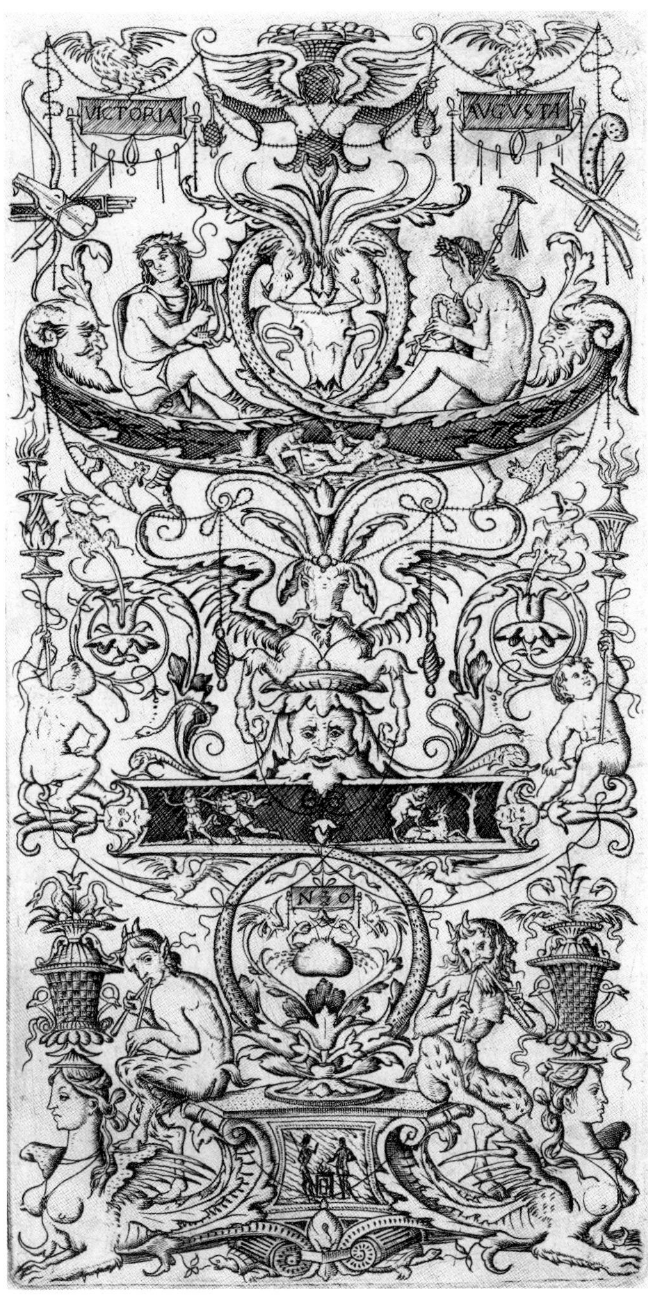

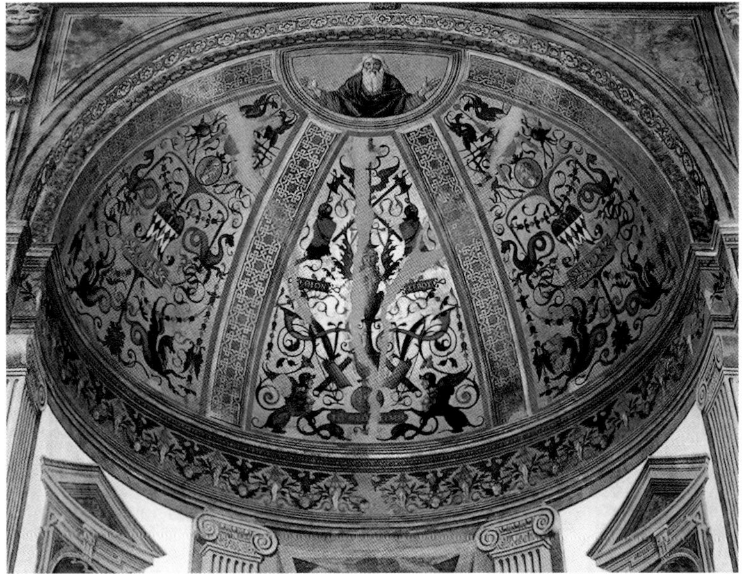

Left 129   Nicoletto da Modena, ornamental panel with grotesque figures, after 1507, engraving, 26.4 × 13.2 cm ($13^2/_6$ × $5^1/_6$ in), London, Trustees of the British Museum

Above 130   Cristoforo Caselli, grotesques, 1506–7, fresco, Parma, Cathedral

at the bottom (fig. 129). Fantastic animals, floral sprouts, and putti fill the rest of the panel.[32] Similarly, several woodcuts from the *Hypnerotomachia Poliphili* illustrate hybrid animals with foliage tails, mermaids, and aquatic monsters reinvented from extant ancient and contemporary monuments.[33] In Parma itself there were works that may have engaged Araldi, as well. The local painter Cristoforo Caselli filled the vault of Canon Bartolomeo Montini's chapel in the cathedral with grotesque candelabra set against a fictive mosaic (ca. 1506–7; fig. 130) and surrounding the central oculus with God the Father.[34] In addition, either Caselli or Gio-

vanni Antonio da Parma painted a monochrome frieze with grotesques and scenes of sacrifice (ca. 1514) in the left transept of the Cassinese church of San Giovanni Evangelista. Likewise, Araldi could not have been ignorant of Cesare Cesariano's frescoes. An artist and architectural theorist, Cesariano painted his own variant of grotesques along with faux-marble discs (the *rotae*) within imitated coffers in the ceiling of the sacristy of San Giovanni Evangelista (1508). In his vernacular translation of Vitruvius's *De Architectura* (1521), Cesariano did not comment on Vitruvius's criticism of fantastic creatures, but as a painter he created grotesques, probably justifying them as the expression of the "pleasing license of fine ingenium" (*legiadra bizaria del vago ingegno*), as his translation of Vitruvius put it.[35]

Whatever Araldi's exact visual sources were, the repetitiveness of his monstrosities gathers the chaos of the pagan and supernatural world into clusters of signification. If not manifestations of artistic *ingenium*, Araldi's magnetically charged creatures signal at least his concern to animate mythical and hybrid creatures, mingling and juxtaposing human bodies with artificial things and the linking of Christian and pre-Christian knowledge. The four diagonal candelabra (see fig. 120) pile up quasi-grisaille harpies, eagles, masks, cornucopiae, and fictive marble tablets, along

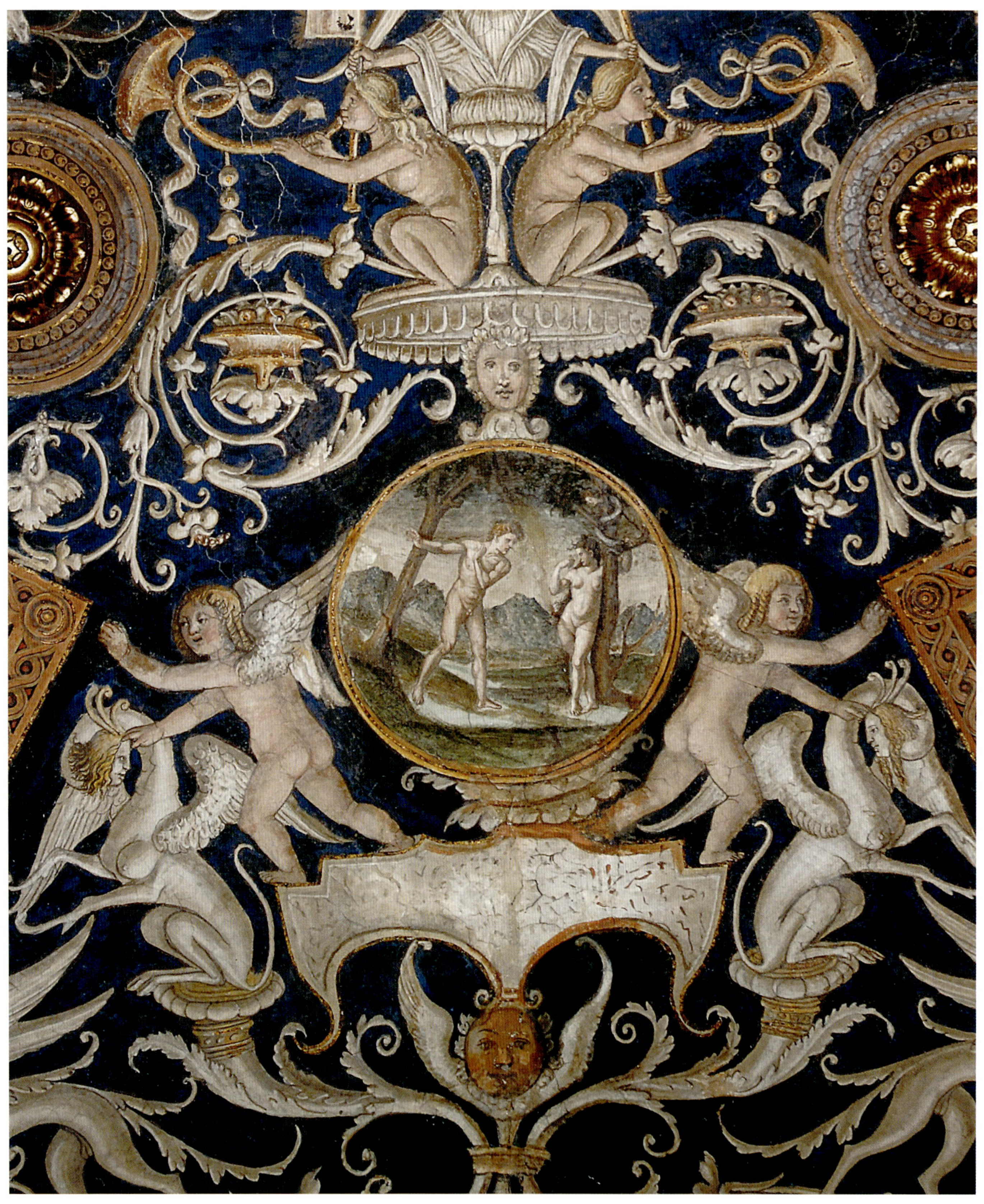

131   Alessandro Araldi, *Fall of Adam and Eve*, ca. 1514–15, fresco, Parma, San Paolo

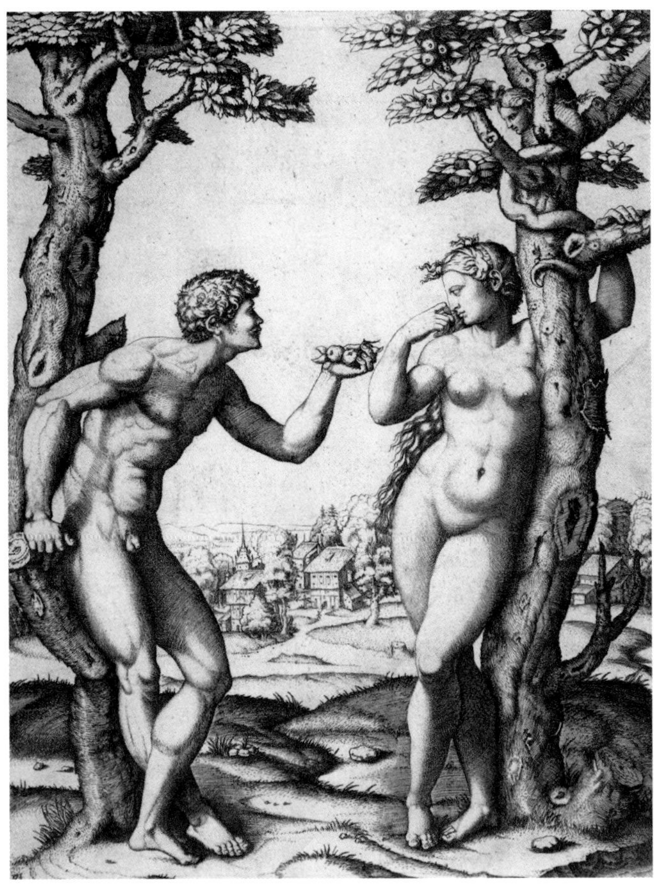

132 Marcantonio Raimondi, *Fall of the Progenitors*, ca. 1511–12, engraving, 24.2 × 17.6 cm (9¹/₇ × 6⁵/₆ in), New York, Metropolitan Museum of Art

with colorful biblical scenes in roundels, making a composite of contrapositions and associations. Set within golden frames, the sacred episodes are thus separated from the ground of the grotesques; their brightness and vivid palette stand out against the flat, dark space and grisaille tonalities of the grotesques and marble tablets, as if one dimension intersected the other, becoming almost its route of access. These composite candelabra further evoke a *paragone* of materials (gold, marble, and modern painting) to enhance a tactile perception of the ensemble. Proceeding from the northern side, the biblical roundels feature the *Fall of Adam and Eve* (fig. 131), *Punishment of Isaac, Christ and the Woman of Samaria*, and *Moses with the Tablets of the Law*. At a closer look, the derivations of these compositions may easily be recognized. They can be described, albeit anachronistically, as "bricolage" images combining motifs from various sources. In his *Adam and Eve* representation Araldi adapted the figures from Marcantonio Raimondi's print (ca. 1511–12;

fig. 132), which, in turn, had amalgamated the gestures and poses of the *Fall of Adam and Eve* from Michelangelo's and Raphael's models.[36] Raimondi's engravings provided contemporary artists with a readymade vocabulary of inventions, enabling the circulation of motifs and faster spread of ideas.[37] Araldi portrays Adam in the pose of Michelangelo's Sistine ceiling Adam expelled from the Garden, without offering fruits to a distressed Eve (as in Raimondi's print), who leans against the tree around which the serpent is wound. Adam and Eve are shown with conventional gestures and postures because they are dependent on contemporary models, but some informed viewers might have known that Eve's culpable role had been reframed in positive terms by two fifteenth-century female writers.

Church Fathers had long presented Eve's part in the Fall in a strongly pejorative light, but female Renaissance voices, like those of Isotta Nogarola and Laura Cereta, had been raised in defense of the first woman. In her dialogue *De pari aut impari Evae atque Adae peccato* of 1451, Nogarola argues for Adam and Eve's equal share of responsibility for the original sin, stating that they sinned differently but with equal pride.[38] Throughout the dialogue, Nogarola defends Eve's action, undermining the logic of patristic exegesis and rebutting her interlocutor Ludovico Foscarini, Adam's defender, by positing that if a woman is inferior by nature, as was traditionally held, then she should not bear more of the blame than men for the original sin. The contemporary female writer, Laura Cereta (1469–1499), insists that Adam and Eve's shared sin is the result of their common origin.[39] In his *De Originali Peccato* (composed in 1509 but only published twenty years later), the German humanist Heinrich Cornelius Agrippa went so far as to shift the blame for the Fall away from Eve, turning her into a sinless figure.[40] He writes that Eve was not responsible for the Fall because the order to obey was given to Adam before Eve's creation.

Connected with Araldi's religious tondi are the eight rectangular sacred stories (see figs. 120, 128 and 133) rendered to look like modern paintings hanging on the surface of the vault. They appear as small easel works in finely wrought wooden frames suspended against the pictorial surface, that is, *quadri riportati* (literally, transported paintings, as if designed for hanging on vertical walls) on the opposite scale from the colossal *quadri riportati* that Michelangelo painted on the Sistine ceiling (1508–12). Apart from their status as illusionistic images with their own internal perspectival organization, their regular spacing around the vault confers a symmetry and order to the ensemble. Griffins with open

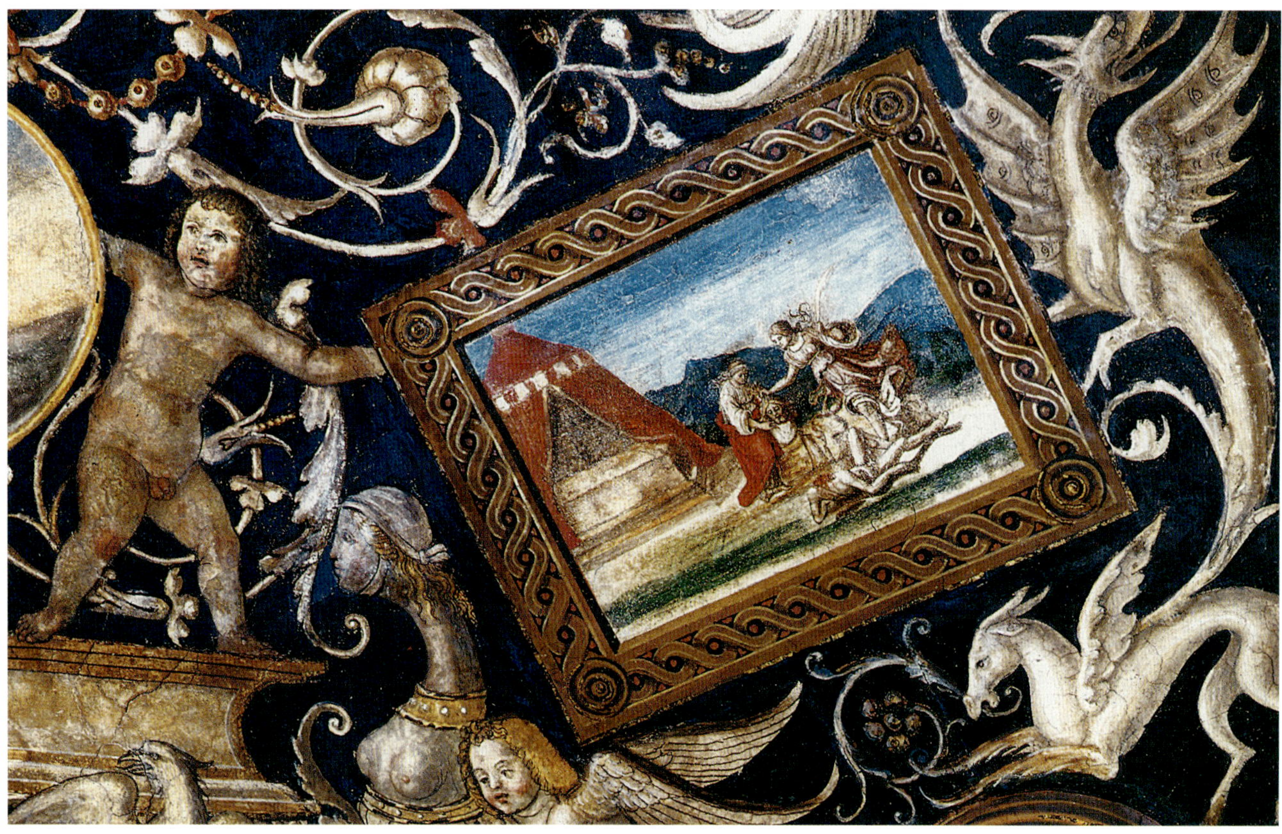

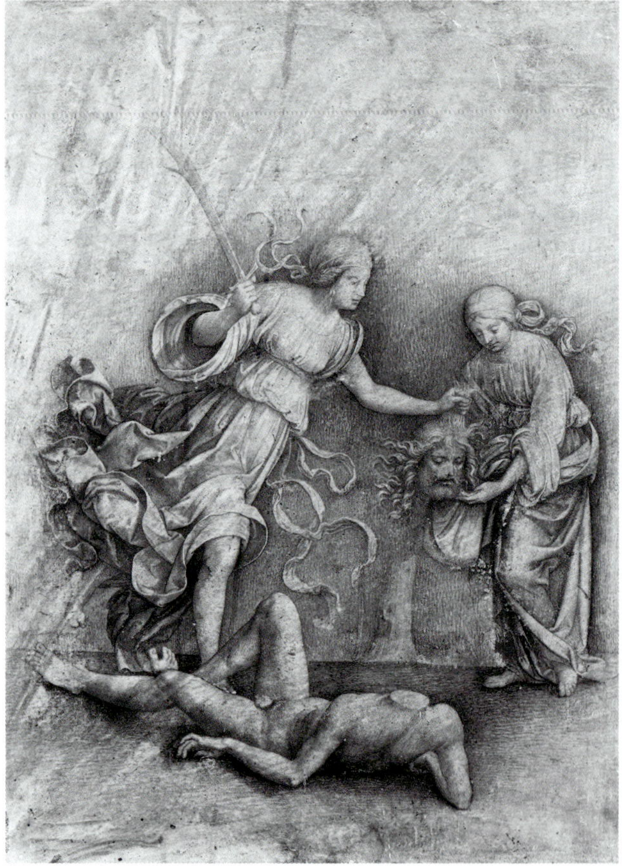

jaws or, alternatively, sphinxes balance on the frames of these biblical stories, an eye-catching juxtaposition of the mythical and the sacred. Symbols evoking enigma and mysteries, the sphinxes gaze back over their shoulders with spirited expressions beneath punkish hair (see fig. 125). The sacred scenes, while not representing dense theological subjects, stand out in several instances for their thematics of female courage and piety, as in the *Judith and her Maidservant with the Head of Holofernes* and the *Massacre of the Innocents*. In addressing their audience of nuns, these episodes could at least have been seen as questioning the traditional gender discourse of the Renaissance. They underscore the essential role of women in the trajectory of Christian salvation, challenging the long-standing view that women were weak and fragile creatures. Araldi's *Judith and her Maidservant* (fig. 133), in particular, celebrates the Hebrew heroine who used beauty and intel-

146

ligence in the service of God and her people, leading her
to triumph over male weaknesses. Zanichelli has argued that
Araldi took his compositional structure from a fine drawing
of the same subject by the Bolognese painter Francesco
Francia (ca. 1505; fig. 134), but Araldi's miniaturized protagonists dwarfed by the gigantic tent diminish the efficacy of
the scene.[41] With its rapacious soldiers wrestling infants from
their mothers' arms, Araldi's *Massacre of the Innocents* (fig. 135)
derives instead from Raimondi's well-known print (ca. 1511–
12; fig. 136) from Raphael's celebrated composition which
renders the drama enfolded in this cruel story with a particular charm and loveliness.[42] Adding a throne with the
onlooking Herod and his turbaned advisers, scaling down
the protagonists to near figurines, and reducing their number
to a minimum, Araldi does not achieve the pathos and
beauty of the Raphael/Raimondi prototype.

Araldi's mechanical imitation and recycling of his visual
sources speaks of his conception of painting as a bricolage
of references rather than as a true product of *fantasia*.
Alberti's and Leonardo's treatises refer to painting as an art
of the imagination having the power to affect the beholder,
but Araldi's citational images freeze the viewer's emotional
engagement. He seems to be more an *à la page* assembler
than a creator of motifs of his own. Employed with ambition, citations are capable of being ironic comments on a
pictorial canon, as shown in Gerolamo Romanino's *Resurrection* (ca. 1525, Capriolo, Brescia) in which Titian's resur-
rected Christ from his celebrated Averoldi altarpiece in
Brescia is quoted with inventiveness. Similarly, Defendente
Ferrari turned Raphael's alluring Roman Madonnas into
peasant-faced, anticlassical variants made for a peripheral,
Piedmontese public. Visual citations, references, and adaptations of motifs caught the attention of Renaissance spectators, especially when the models were reworked with witty
connotations or translated into other scales and media, but
such sophistication does not seem to have been within the
reach of Araldi, whose images manifest an almost mechanical imitation or recombination of models, with limited
creative effort on his part.[43] More indebted to prints than
to first-hand study of paintings or sculptures, Araldi's works
speak of his derivative approach to the art of painting and
of a mediated relationship to the newness of the art of
Raphael and Michelangelo in Rome. Nonetheless, his
works represent the most advanced attempt before Correggio to establish a vision of modern art in early sixteenth-
century Parma. It is, however, equally true that with
Correggio's ascent Araldi's citational style immediately
became old-fashioned.

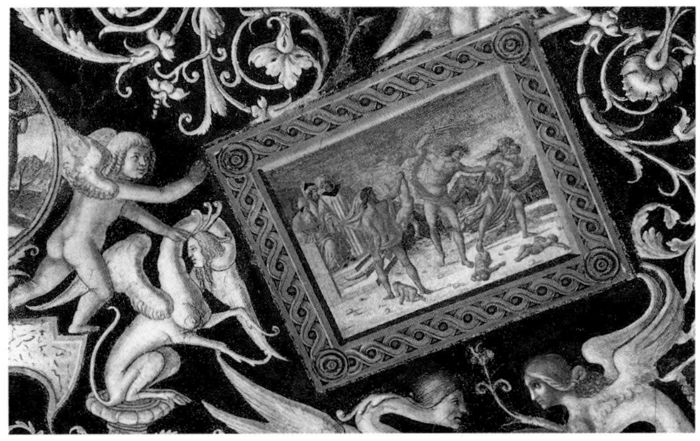

Above 135   Alessandro Araldi, *Massacre of the Innocents*, sphinxes
and harpies, ca. 1514–15, fresco, Parma, San Paolo

Below 136   Marcantonio Raimondi after Raphael, *Massacre of the
Innocents*, ca. 1511–12, engraving, 28 × 42.6 cm (11^{1}/$_{3}$ × 9^{41}/$_{64}$ in),
London, Victoria and Albert Museum

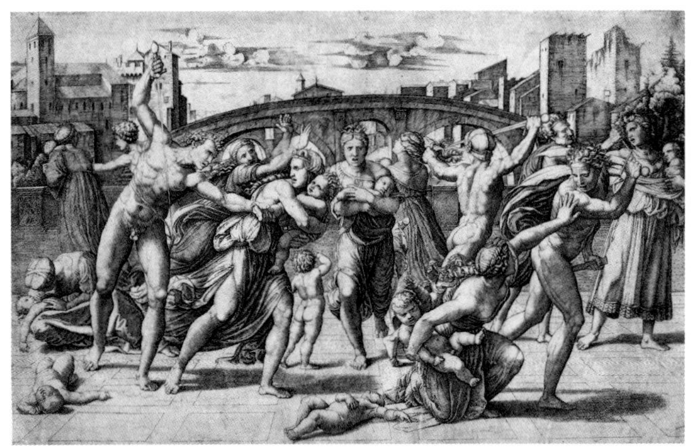

ON MAGIC AND VISION

Despite their somewhat limited aesthetic appeal and lack
of pictorial inventiveness, which have long constituted an
obstacle for understanding their chains of communication,
Araldi's hybrid figures form a corpus of possessed creatures
in liminal continuity with Christian narratives, which
comment on the boundaries between sacred mysteries
and Christian revelation, imagination, and vision. Araldi
employed the visual to stimulate reflection on what lies
beneath the surface, and on the mysteries of nature, religion, and art. In particular, as markers of the fluctuation
between pre-Christian and Christian mysteries and the
long-standing symbol for paganism in Christian art represented by an idol on a column, the four diagonal candelabra are topped by curious creatures positioned as if they

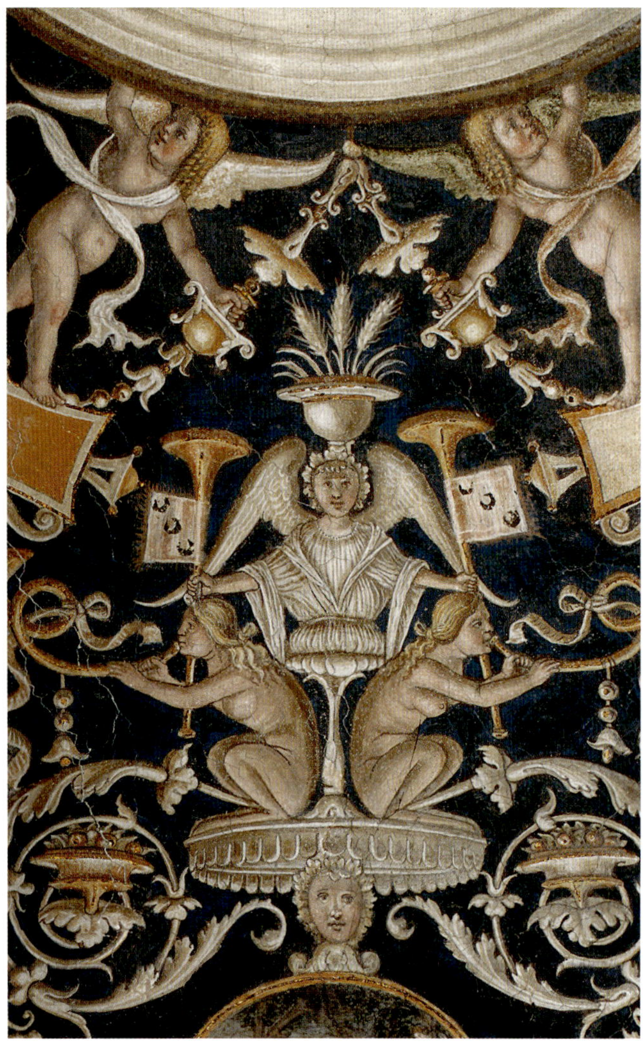

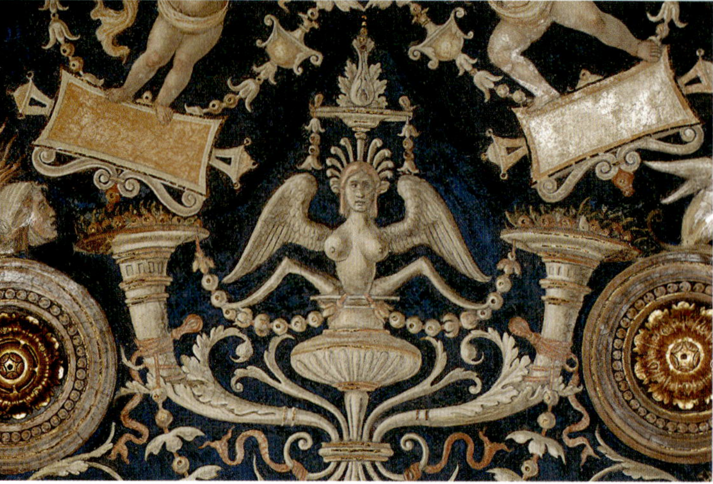

were idols (see figs. 120 and 137).[44] Two candelabra are surmounted by a winged and draped bust-length, female figure carrying on her head a vase and holding banners bearing Giovanna Piacenza's arms, recalling a now lost figure once painted on the great cloister of the Cassinese monastery of Santa Giustina in Padua (fig. 138). It is known that these lost frescoes exhibited historical and religious narratives, mythological fables, hieroglyphs, and grotesque composites deriving from the *Hypnerotomachia* illustrations.[45] Araldi topped the other candelabra with a winged, naked figure with exposed breasts and a bizarre headdress of rays that comes close to that of the Egyptian goddess Isis.[46] It is not the newness of Araldi's figures that needs stressing here, given that similar ones also occur in Peregrino da Cesena's niello prints from the early 1500s. What matters is their status as curious, enigmatic images and the linking of subjects from pre-Christian and Christian lore, which is further attested in another monastic commission in Parma.

The library of San Giovanni Evangelista, decorated between 1573 and 1575 by the artists Giovanni Antonio Paganino and Ercole Pio, features grotesques, hieroglyphs, emblems, episodes from Jewish and Christian histories, and words in Greek, Hebrew, and Latin.[47] This unusual combination of verbal and enigmatic visual representations has been interpreted as a *theatrum Sapientiae* (theater of wisdom), an encyclopedia of moral and pedagogical knowledge intended to provide viewers with truths of spiritual and ethical import. Grotesques, hieroglyphs, and emblems were not perceived as paradoxical or inappropriate forms of communication in at least a few cultivated Benedictine Cassinese communities. They were, rather, assertive of the marked preference for images that hide truths and that stretch the interpretation of their subjects over time. Combining depictions that are not immediately decipherable and that unfold into plural interpretations and, possibly, indeterminacy, opens images to multiple and even contradictory associations with both legitimate and illegitimate knowledge.

Investigations into the sacred mysteries, the occult, and magic had long preoccupied patristic scholars and ecclesiastical authorities, and images representing irrational, hybrid creatures were coupled by analogy with portents seen in nature. Nuns, who were not meant to raise their heads or to use their eyes to expand their understanding beyond the Christian revelation, had long been detached from knowledge of the world's most secret traditions. The search for hidden learning, for magic, and beliefs in the efficacy of materials signal dissatisfaction with the Christian interpretation of the universe. Despite ecclesiastical condemnation of those who wanted to know what was not appropriate for them to know, and the censorship to which studies in the occult had long been subject, these investigations were vig-

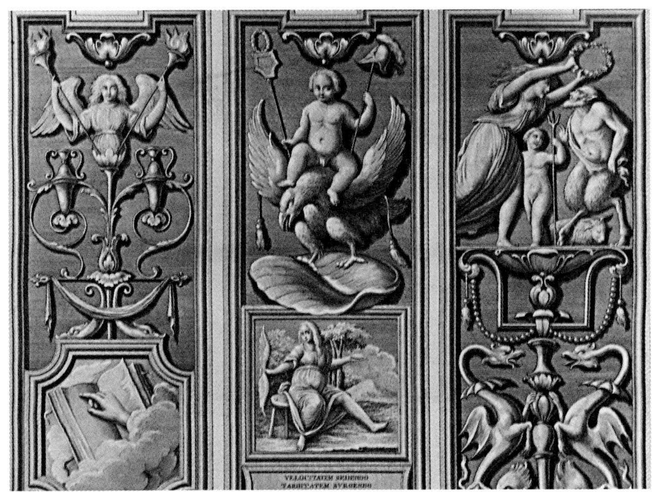

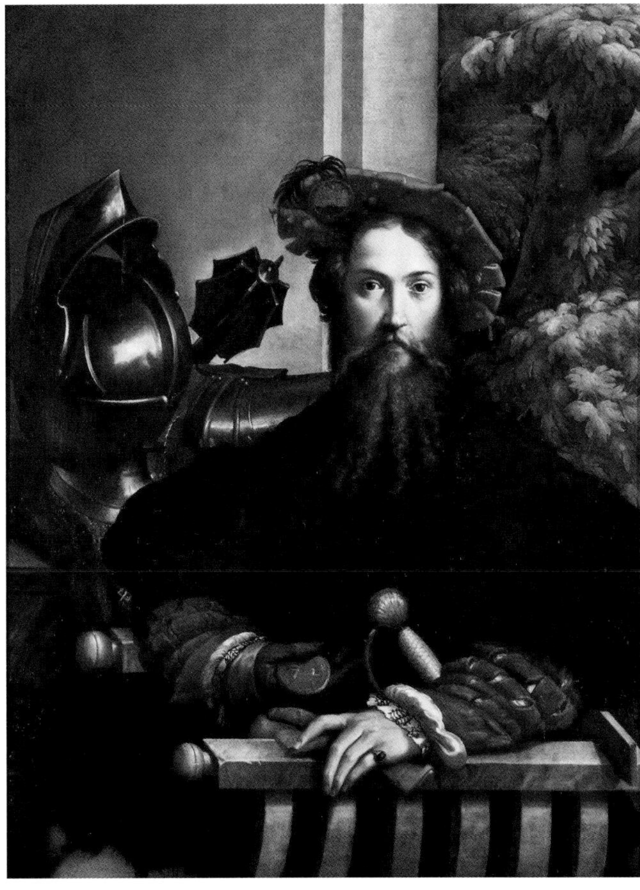

Facing page 137   Alessandro Araldi, female hybrid creatures, ca. 1514–15, fresco, Parma, San Paolo

Above 138   Francesco Mengardi, detail of engraving of lost fresco decoration in the great cloister of Santa Giustina, Padua, 95.5 × 41.5 cm ($37^{19}/_{32}$ × $16^{11}/_{36}$ in), from *Arabeschi del Chiostro Maggiore del Monastero di S. Giustina in Padova*, 1794, Piacenza, Biblioteca Passerini-Landi

Right 139   Parmigianino, *Portrait of Galeazzo Sanvitale*, ca. 1523–4, oil on canvas, 109 × 81 cm (43 × 32 in), Naples, Capodimonte

orously pursued in Renaissance Italy, Parma included. Abbess Giovanna Piacenza was an educated woman almost certainly aware of the criticism of the appetite for illegitimate knowledge, what St. Augustine had defined as "the joy of knowing [illegitimate] things."[48] In his repertoire of female spirited demons and binding motifs, including the quasi-magic rings of *spiritelli*, the fire that catches the eyes, and the virtual sound of instruments filling the air, Araldi's images make claims to the pursuit of illegitimate learning or at least to discussions on magic turned into a visual poetic. I propose to link Araldi's imagery to beliefs about magic and discourses of secret communication, and to see how his animated figures may also be symptoms of local debates on demonic powers believed to give rise to mental perturbation, fear, misleading perception, and general adversity.[49]

By the sixteenth century, the relationship between demonic and artistic practices was a common enough topic that it could serve as the screen against which Parmese artists created images that bound viewers through their quasi-magical powers. Captivation is indeed itself a form of artistic agency. While it is not my intention to turn Araldi or the convent court into credulous types who believed in magical

forces, they cannot, nevertheless, have been wholly immune to recondite allusions and mysteries found in books and art.[50] My aim is, rather, to uncover how Araldi confronted these discourses visually to fold into his painted ceiling meanings that intersect multiple traditions. In this context, it is productive to make a digression to some overlooked texts on magic and other writings by Nicholas of Cusa to assess the local debate on nature and its secret components, vision and imagination, and their reverberation in the theory and practice of art in Parma. Debates on the prophetic – not divine – nature of Christ, doctrines on magic combined with esoteric teaching and beliefs in the occult properties of substances have been associated with at least one other image produced in the city, that is, Parmigianino's *Portrait of Galeazzo Sanvitale* (ca. 1523–4; fig. 139). The lord of a fiefdom twenty kilometers from Parma and much involved in local politics, Sanvitale is depicted holding a medal tilted to show the cryptic numbers 7 and 2, which have been interpreted as signs for the name of God according to the so-called Christian Kabbalah. But there is far more to be said about these topics in early sixteenth-century Parma, which were favored among select circles and communities.[51]

One wonders if the local elite was aware of the curious, self-taught prophet, Giovanni Mercurio da Correggio (supposedly a member of the family who ruled a fiefdom on Parma's eastern outskirts and had influenced the city's government for centuries), who appeared in Rome on Palm Sunday of 1484 and preached in St. Peter's as if he was the mythical Hermes Trismegistus, presumed Egyptian priest and prophet contemporary with Moses. As Brian Curran has observed, Mercurio was viewed by many as a charlatan, a bizarre product of the Renaissance fascination for Egyptian culture, but he was taken seriously by at least one humanist, Ludovico Lazzarelli. The latter's preface to the translation of the hermetic *Definitiones* (ca. 1494) is dedicated to Mercurio.[52] Lazzarelli's text discusses the wisdom of the Egyptians and of Hermes Trismegistus, considered the founder of an ancient theology that included prefigurations of Christian and alchemical doctrines. Such religious and magical topics the Florentine scholar Marsilio Ficino was almost simultaneously addressing in his writings, reconciling hermeticism with the philosophy of Plato, and proclaiming Hermes Trismegistus as the founder of pagan theology and inventor of Egyptian writing. Ficino's commentary on Plotinus's *Enneads* (1492), in particular, inscribes the study of Egyptian hieroglyphs within the context of Neoplatonism, speaking of it as a language of symbols that encapsulated an entire discourse in one fixed image without the need for discursive reasoning.[53] Ficino's discussion of hermetic writings ventured onto more slippery ground in his *De vita coelitus comparanda* (1489), exploring matters inherent to astrology and sympathetic magic, addressing the making of statues and the practice of the Egyptians who "insert into them . . . the souls of demons . . . to help people or even to harm them."[54]

Condemned by the Church Fathers because they were implicated with idolatry, these practices on theurgy and magic had crucial coverage in Parma in one previously unexplored text, now in the Biblioteca Laurenziana in Florence. Better known for his astrological and musical writings, Giorgio Anselmi the Elder (ante 1386–1449?) is the author of the *Divinum Opus de Magia Disciplina*, which summarizes the medieval Arabic treatise *Picatrix*, a synthesis of the previous literature on astronomy and magic, prescribing rituals for petitioning the planets, prayers for summoning demons, and recipes for making potent drugs.[55] Composed in five books, Anselmi's *Divinum Opus* is principally a defense of magic. Anselmi declares that a philosopher can be a magus if he employs his knowledge for good ends. Following a brief introduction, the first book discusses the categories of magic (natural, celestial, and ceremonial), while the second offers an extensive treatment of demons. Anselmi focuses on how to evoke them with a series of addresses, saying that demons materialize in smoke, and their gaseous forces can be released and controlled through the burning of incense. In the subsequent books Anselmi explains, among other topics, that the virtues of all things in the natural world are transmitted into their constitutive materials, and that crystals and semiprecious stones are vessels of occult powers instilled in them by astral rays, which could be catalyzed by proper invocations. The power of magnetic stones is also discussed at length. Another topic covered by Anselmi is scapulimancy, a rare form of divination in which the right shoulder blade of a sheep or ram was utilized.[56]

Anselmi junior (already encountered in Chapter Four and with ties to the convent court) attempted to publish his ancestor's *Divinum Opus* in the early sixteenth century. As Paola Zambelli has written, Anselmi seems to have been a member of a secret circle of international scholars involved in the study of the occult, which included Ficino and Cornelius Agrippa.[57] In a letter of 1510 addressed to the German Benedictine Abbot Johannes Trithemius, accompanying a draft of his *Occulta Philosophia* (published in 1533), Agrippa refers to Anselmi the Elder's *Divinum Opus* as a source he had consulted with profit. One of the most influential scholars on magic, Agrippa is a controversial yet nodal figure in the transmission of the magic tradition. In his text, Agrippa posits that all objects emanate spirits and that they entangle human beings with invisible threads, transferring their qualities onto men. As an extension of the sense of touch, the eyes are described as permeable, vulnerable, and porous: spirits leave the body through the eyes, and external spirits penetrate through the windows of the eyes in fluid exchanges. As Michael Cole has proven, Agrippa believed that air is particularly conductive for carrying "species into the body."[58] Agrippa further discusses the art of binding, arguing for the magus's power to bind "men into love, or hatred, sickness, or health," and suggesting a repertory of binding tools (including rings, amulets, and charms), but he also indicates that binding can happen through "strong imaginings, passions, and images." In sum, images are players in the world of enchantment.[59]

Agrippa's Parmese interlocutor, Anselmi, a medical doctor and the author of a lost text on human physiology, is portrayed in a drawing (fig. 140) executed by Parmigianino after Anselmi's death on September 21, 1530, as annotated on the sheet. At first glance it seems that the

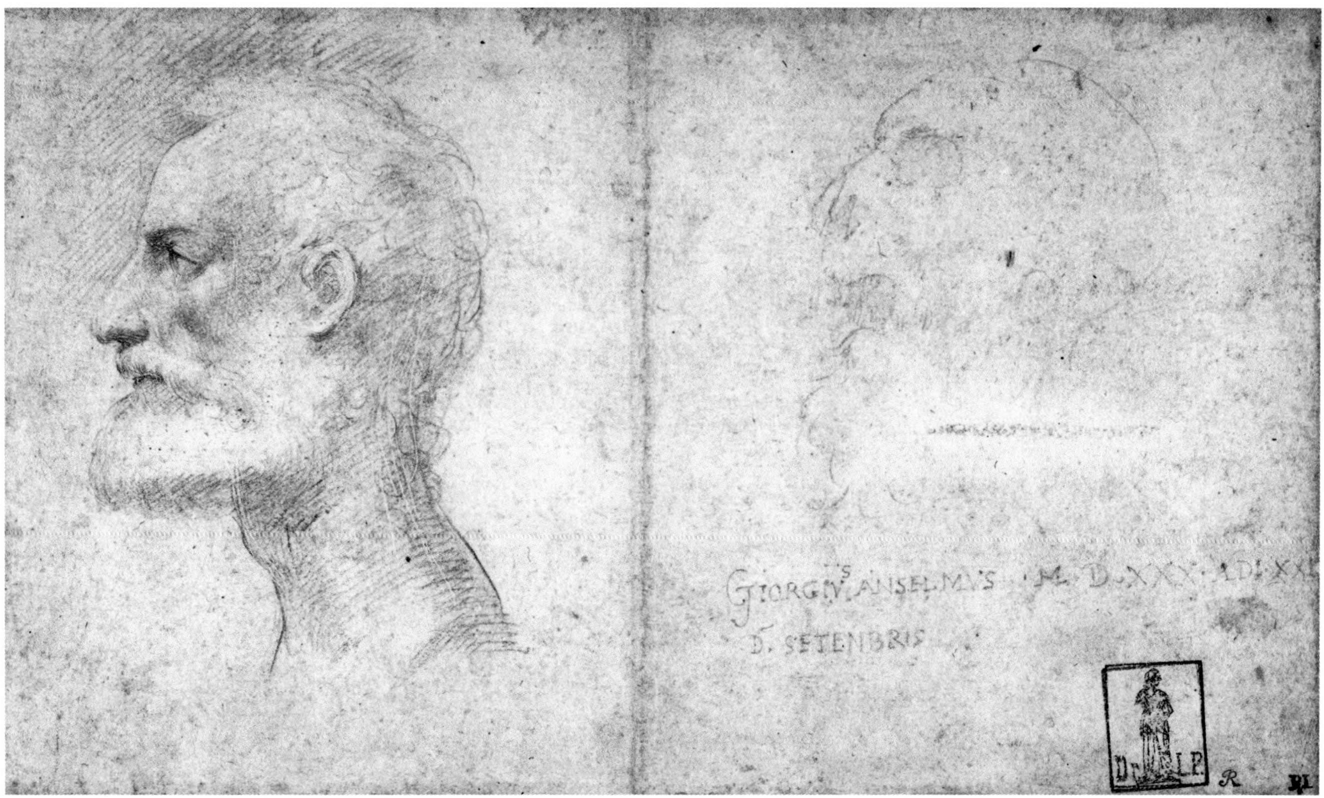

140 Parmigianino, *Head of Giorgio Anselmi*, with study of a skull-like head, ca. 1530, red chalk, 13.9 × 23 cm (5¹/₃ × 9¹/₁₆ in), New York, Metropolitan Museum of Art

faintly visible skull on the right could have been intended as a generic study for a *memento mori*. But in the light of Anselmi's exposure to texts on magic it is more productive to see it as a symptom of these interests.[60] Anselmi's regal profile head is sketched on the left, facing away from the skull, a juxtaposition of the living and the dead. If so, the skull is linked not only to Anselmi's profile head but also to his invisible yet implied body, reflecting the decay of that body in its head. This skull may be ultimately intended as a memorial of Anselmi's own self whose bodily matter is consumed and deprived of its vital spirits after death.[61] Discourses on magic were coupled in Anselmi with interests in Egyptian hieroglyphs. Anselmi's own romance, *In Cupidinem Captivum* (On Captive Cupid, 1506), which bears a dedication to his friend the epigrapher Michele Fabrizio Ferrarini, describes an imaginary library in Cupid's temple with texts in Greek and Latin, and "many with hieroglyphs." Ferrarini (who died before 1493), in turn, assembled antiquarian sylloges that document the earliest known Renaissance copies of real Egyptian hieroglyphs taken from monuments in Rome.[62]

The Parmese audience read other pivotal texts – which have largely been ignored in the modern scholarship on the arts in Parma – in particular, Nicholas of Cusa's *Tractatus et Libri*, printed in 1502 under the aegis of Rolando II Pallavicino (d. 1509).[63] Pallavicino, the ruler of a fiefdom on Parma's western outskirts, and his relatives had tremendous cultural ambitions despite their limited political power.[64] The 1502 edition of Cusa's collected writings is a reprint of his Strasbourg publication (1488), and comprises the key texts on philosophy, theology, astronomy, and religion of one of the most prolific thinkers of fifteenth-century Europe. Proposing his mathematics-based doctrine for the comprehension of sacred mysteries, Cusa supplied Parmese readers with sensitive views on the most salient topics debated in the Renaissance Western world. Against the traditional Aristotelian and patristic polarity describing the male as the ideal sex, in Cusa's *On [Intellectual] Eyeglasses* the local audience would have read his paradigm of the coincidence of opposites, inferring that women are not passive beings and that they could bring new perspectives to the equation. Typical of the method by which he approaches current topics, Cusa selected a curiosity, in this case a beryl (a transparent gemstone), that becomes the focus of his reflections on controversial matters including the role of women in male-dominated Renaissance society.[65]

In his *On Learned Ignorance*, Cusa begins to speculate on the problem that God is beyond the reach of human beings. He posited that God is unknown because he escapes all comparative relations but, through sight and perception, individuals can learn to recognize God's infinitude through his likeness. Cusa says that God fashioned the world using the rules of geometry, and that monstrous, alien creatures inhabit the planets, too. He then hints at the discourse of vision, suggesting that the mind assimilates the objects it sees. Studies on vision had intensified in the later Middle Ages, spurred by new translations of Arabic texts on optics. It was believed that vision involved optical rays travelling between objects and the eyes. Some writers posited that the rays emanate from objects and pass into the eyes and mind (intromission theory). Conversely, others held that the eyes sent out rays (extramission theory).[66] In his *The Layman on Mind*, Cusa adheres to the intromission theory, stating that the eyes absorb the exterior object (its likeness), while the intellect assimilates the object by abstracting – from the sensory image – a concept.[67] Vision ultimately relies on the mind. As he puts it, "the mind . . . makes various fine or coarse configurations [of the objects] in accordance with the varying pliability of the arterial spirits present in the sense organ." And he continues: "Since mind makes . . . assimilations in order to have concepts of perceptible objects . . . mind acts as a soul, enlivening the body."[68]

Cusa's *On the Vision of God* expands this model of vision, referring to a modern icon of the face of Christ (probably painted by the Flemish artist Rogier van der Weyden) that he sent to the Benedictine monks of Tegernsee (Germany) to accompany his text. Despite the image's immobility on the wall, it is said that the eyes of God look out and see each viewer in the room, even those in motion, thus positing no escape from God's all-seeing eyes. God's all-seeing power had long been a powerful metaphor in monastic writing (see Chapter One), but Cusa makes a different argument. By viewing the icon of Christ on the wall, monks could grasp a deeper understanding of the nature of God. Cusa speaks of rays radiating from the image (God's eyes) looking at each viewer and simultaneously filling the whole space.[69] Using an illusionistic technique, the painting itself looks and its rays pervade the monastic space: it has been noticed that the painting creates a coexistence of all the eyes, each of which is seen and directed by the one

gaze of God. While Cusa's argument adheres to the intromission theory, he simultaneously refers to an image whose power of captivation saturates the enclosed monastic space, creates the community of devotees around it, and impresses itself forcefully on the viewer's eyes.[70] As Michel de Certeau put it, it produces admiration and astonishment because the unimaginable is being made visible, and astonishment became "the gesture, at once ethical and poetic, of responding to an excess by turning toward the imperceptible. The domain of surprise will be the birthplace of discourse."[71] Amazement overcomes believers as if they were before a magical phenomenon. This digression regarding texts on magic and Cusa's writings is not to trace iconographic links between Araldi's images and these spiritual sources, nor just to assess the cultural background against which local informed audiences could have projected the messages of his works. Rather, these discourses on demonic entities, physiological theories of vision, and the power of forms to catch onlookers' attention constitute compelling evidence for rethinking the status of art in Renaissance Parma and mobile spectators' perceptual experiences of artworks. In his painted vault Araldi employed the visual through its most enigmatic and ambivalent genres (grotesques and hieroglyphs) to experiment with its quasi-magical capacity to fasten the eyes to it. Notwithstanding his own artistic limitations, his dynamic hybrid figures convey to the beholder an intriguing sense of veiled truths and simultaneously of enchantment, both of which affect the viewer's contemplation of and emotional relationship to the work.

Araldi's spirited, female-gendered creatures (see fig. 125) capture the invisible forces believed to lie beneath the surface of the earth, which menaced the world of chastity, sacrifice, and courage that the lunettes encompass. These are the fears and forces that Anselmi senior and Agrippa would have related to demonic powers and that could have materialized in conflicts or in ecclesiastical authorities' and detractors' attacks. As proposed earlier, in their associations or contrasts with the biblical stories in the framed panels, they can be seen to negotiate the fluid boundaries between Christian and pre-Christian mysteries, the world of nature and the history of Christianity. But there is more at stake in Araldi's painted room. The female figures, candelabra composites, and fire-hieroglyph motifs gravitate toward the fictive sky-blue oculus inhabited by musician *spiritelli* whose quasi-angelic appearance opposes the surrounding dark world of monsters. Rendered in delicate tones, the putti are in clear sunlight (see figs. 120 and 122) and in striking contrast to the shadowed ground

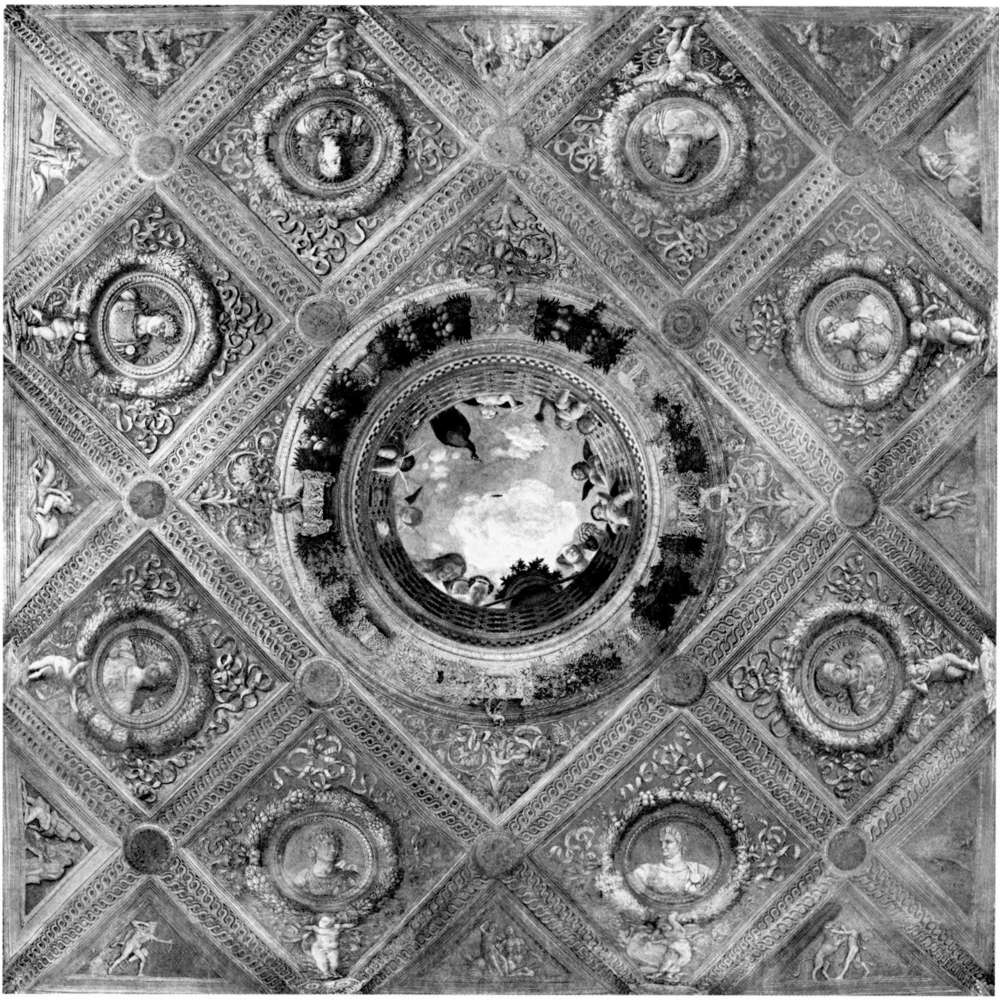

141 Mantegna, Camera Picta ceiling with fictive oculus, ca. 1465–74, fresco, Mantua, Palazzo Ducale [Gonzaga palace]

of the demonic figures. Looking down at the beholder in the chamber below, the *spiritelli* draw attention to themselves by their recklessly unstable positions, and the almost heard blasts of their trumpets and horns. Their quasi-angelic features, blondish hair, nudity, and joyful demeanor make them seem celestial beings, bringers of life and nourishment, seeming to fill the air with the sound of their instruments to stir the viewer's soul. The music-making *spiritelli* have their mocking counterparts in the bagpipe-playing satyrs who occupy the top green corner pendentives (see fig. 121) and in the harpies in the candelabra blowing trumpets (see fig. 125), turning the chamber into a hall of virtual music saturated with loud wind and brass sounds. But as Agrippa remarks, sound was a potent binding element, which Araldi seems to have deployed as a form of visual fascination.

Depicted as outside the oculus but leaning over or under its balustrade to teeter precariously on the edge, the putti make every effort to enter the spectators' space and to engage with them, as the sounds they make with their horns pervade the air. Putti occupying the summit of a room are not a motif that Araldi needed to invent. Decades earlier, Mantegna had animated the illusionistic oculus of his Camera Picta (fig. 141) with charming putti and five women and a bird, luring beholders below with their ambiguous smiles, perilous postures, and inviting gestures.[72] Araldi's *spiritelli* are somewhat less appealing creatures, but not less compelling: the blast of their trumpets makes the air pulsate with quasi-angelic forces to counteract the surrounding space filled by demonic creatures. The putti's twists and turns humor and cheer beholders, but, as noted earlier, there are only seven instead of the expected eight in the oculus. Eight (or its dividends two and four) is a semi-magic number around which the vault space is structured (indeed, eight putti support the outer edge of the oculus), pointing to late medieval doctrines on the power of numbers that could aid contemplation of the secrets of nature.[73] The seven horn-playing putti cannot, therefore, stand only for a quasi-angelic message because their number evokes other discourses and may even turn into the artist's own pictorial signature. If versed in music and cosmology, observant viewers might have connected the seven putti to the ancient cosmological system of the seven planets and the related Pythagorean theories of the music of the spheres, all of which had been discussed in the treatises of Giorgio Anselmi senior and another eminent fifteenth-century local scholar, Franchino Gaffurio.[74] Both treatises describe the cosmos as structured in harmonic proportions and explain that through mathematical knowledge one may ascend to the understanding of divine things. But as horn-players, the *spiritelli* further recall the idea of trumpeting heralds, playing on the name of the artist himself, Araldi (Heralds). The trumpeting *spiritelli* may, thus, stand as a form of signature, establishing Araldi's authorship of the painted ceiling at its summit, the oculus, the eye that gazes back at us. One may even find it ironic that Araldi's ambitious but awkwardly foreshortened *spiritelli* stand for the artist's signature, given that they lack the qualities of perspective and *ingegno* that the oculus and its occupants command.

Araldi was not the first or the last to adapt Mantegna's composition for decorating a private chamber. As observed by Giovanni Agosti, from the late fifteenth century onward, each generation of Northern Italian artists confronted Mantegna's audacious foreshortening, illusionism, and daring pictorial inventions, but each master was impressed by a different Mantegna.[75] The decorative scheme of the Camera Picta was adopted by Alessandro Pampurino with minimal variations featuring the Muses (ca. 1500) in a room in Cremona, which probably served as a monastic *studiolo*.[76] Garofalo in turn turned the balustrade motif into a balcony on which fashionably dressed spectators disport themselves in the chambers of Palazzo Costabili (ca. 1513) and Sacrati (now Palazzo Vescovile, ca. 1519–20) in Ferrara. These painted rooms made viewers aware of the pictorial performances being staged for them, transforming acts of looking into awareness.[77] Similarly, Araldi's images stage the spectacle of the forces of disorder latent beneath the serene surface of virtuous deeds, the illusions caused by demonic powers, which exemplary women control and counteract. Looking at Araldi's representations, the beholder realizes that not

even a sophisticated religious community was totally innured against finding supernatural explanations for its difficulties. A painted room became the place to comment on these forces, to display the means of enchantment as converted into visual poetry, and to reflect on the ontological question of looking upward by a female community in an "other space." Simultaneously, it was also the site to promote a serene, composed female exemplarity as the way to hold the invisible forces of chaos at bay, or, at least, to stage the tension of these forces, enabling one's own regeneration as proclaimed in the mantelpiece inscription: "We went through fire and through water, but you have brought us out to a place of refreshment."

EXCELLENCE OF THE FEMALE SELF AND THE EXERCISE OF VIRTUE

Moving across the room and looking at Araldi's sequence of lunettes, one becomes immediately aware that several of them concern female figures involved in sacrifice, defeating male monsters, or fulfilling familial duties, which magnify women's dedication to virtue. Disciplined female figures dominate the lunettes as if the rigid control of the body required in the convent was almost transferred to the discourse of painting itself (see fig. 123). The lunette images confront beholders with themes exalting women who display such virtues as chastity, and caring for others, portraying them as charismatic heroines and personifications of spiritual and moral leadership, in striking contrast to their actual lack of authority in the Church. Despite the fact that women have always been faithful followers of Christ, educators and pillars of the Church, they were deprived of equality with men in the Church hierarchy. Women's exclusion from the priesthood, derived from a prohibition traditionally ascribed to St. Paul, was a limitation that Agrippa addressed in his *Declamation on the Nobility and Preeminence of the Female Sex* (1509–29), going as far as to say that women could serve as priests.[78] Nor were consecrated women permitted to preach in public, though their exemplary lives and deeds had long been deployed as models to inspire religious and lay audiences. Araldi's lunettes propose views of women, *exempla*, standing for virtuous comportment and ethical values, amounting to a proclamation of the excellence of the female sex. In this sense, the lunette images can be seen as the visual counterparts of arguments raised in such Renaissance writings as Baldassar Castiglione's *Libro del Cortegiano* (1528) and Agrippa's *Declamation*. The latter is especially ambiguous in its fusion of material from hermetic and cabalistic lore, but it may well have been circulated in Parma given Agrippa's connection to Anselmi. As Barbara Newman put it, "sliding between straightforward eulogy of women and bold inversion of misogynist *topoi*, the treatise escapes the usual confines of the '*querelle des femmes*'" (the debate on women).[79] Attempting to reverse the long-standing cultural belittlement of women, Castiglione and Agrippa's texts, and a few others, address the status and education of the female sex, simultaneously supplying to readers *exempla* of virtuous women.

Such *exempla* had long been adopted to illustrate religious or moral precepts with the aim of persuading the audience. The best-known classical collection is Valerius Maximus's *Memorable Deeds and Sayings*.[80] From the Middle Ages on, preaching *exempla* were compiled into written collections, such as the biographies of ancient heroines (1374) by Giovanni Boccaccio. By the Renaissance, readers began to draw *exempla* from other sources, including the Bible, and either to discover new *exempla* or to re-evaluate the traditional ones. As a result, the interpretation of *exempla* was conditioned by readers' subjective engagement with texts, giving *exempla* less stable meanings.[81] In his *De Copia* (1512) Erasmus speaks of *exempla* as *paradeigmata*, or striking images, the purpose of which was not only to "make [one] case look convincing, but also to dress it up and brighten, expand, and enrich it."[82] As tools of rhetorical persuasion, what mattered was not their illustration of exemplary models but their expansion of semantic possibilities. John Lyons aptly wrote that "an example is not a moral concept but a discursive one."[83] Quoting Erasmus, Lyons continued:

> the death of Socrates can be used to show that death holds no fear for a good man, since he drank the hemlock so cheerfully; but also to show that virtue is prey to ill will and far from amidst a swarm of evils; or again that the study of philosophy is useless or even harmful unless you conform to general patterns of behavior. This same incident can be turned to Socrates' praise or blame.[84]

It was therefore up to the audience to extrapolate from the multiple messages of *exempla*. All in all, *exempla* document the Renaissance appreciation of ambivalence and the plurality of signification.

This brings us back to the central problem of Araldi's lunette images and their chain of associations: what are the implications of images displaying subjects of female exemplarity? How were these images invented? It has long been

recognized that several of the lunettes reproduce the reverse imagery of Roman coins. Less well-known is that ancient coin reverses were defined as *symbola* in the Renaissance, personifications or allegorical representations, making the meanings of the lunettes unstable and oblique.[85] In a letter to Pellegrino Morato dating to 1544, the Ferrarese humanist Celio Calcagnini uses the term *symbolum* to describe the image on coin reverses, referring to the old practice of inventing symbols and words for coins with recondite social, religious, and cultural values.[86] The most explicit reference to these *symbola* comes from the mid-sixteenth-century Paduan humanist Alessandro Maggi, who refers to coin reverses as symbols or hieroglyphs (*symbola seu hieroglyphica*).[87] The Parmese audience further read in Cusa's *The Bowling-Game* (De Ludo Globi) that coinage represented a community, declaring not simply the use of symbolic signs on coins, but also the shared understanding of the signs. Coins preserved the faces, names, and deeds of great men of the past, and their images condensed the political and intellectual life of communities, with *symbola* rich in multilayered communications.[88]

As noted by Francis Haskell, the study and collecting of ancient coins put Renaissance scholars in "close and exhilarating contact with aspects of the past that were not accessible in other ways."[89] Little wonder that such Parmese humanists as Anselmi junior and Ugoleto possessed collections of *medaglie*, a term that, as Luke Syson has noted, was used interchangeably for both ancient coins and modern medals in the early modern era.[90] Dating to 1518, Ugoleto's posthumous inventory records that he had a "medal box with 183 medals in copper; 63 in silver, 10 medals of "archimia"; 10 carnelians; 8 limonites and 8 chalcedony stones."[91] The uncommon reference to medals of "archimia" could be associated with either alloy medals or medals used in alchemical rites: the belief in the occult power of the materials of coins, despite detractors including Petrarch, persisted well into the sixteenth century.[92] Petrarch was an avid coin collector, and wanted to inspire his contemporaries to emulate the virtues of the illustrious men portrayed on coins. The pleasure that collectors took in contemplating these small ancient objects that compress knowledge in their "intelligible dimensions," and their interplay between text and image, raised suspicions among late Cinquecento clerics: Paleotti, for example, commented negatively on the contemporary fascination with coins.[93] The portability of the medium further turned coins into one of the preferred media for transmitting antiquarian knowledge: artists copied, replicated, and reinvented the tiny images on coins

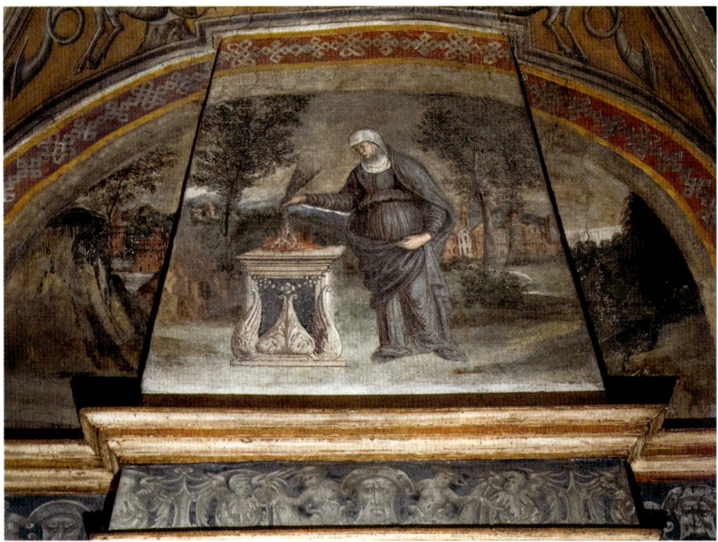

Above 142   Alessandro Araldi, scene of female sacrifice over the chimney hood, ca. 1514–15, fresco, Parma, San Paolo

Right 143   Scene of sacrifice, from *Hypnerotomachia Poliphili*, woodcut, m4v, 12.7 × 12.5 cm (5 × 4$^{59}/_{64}$ in) (Venice 1499)

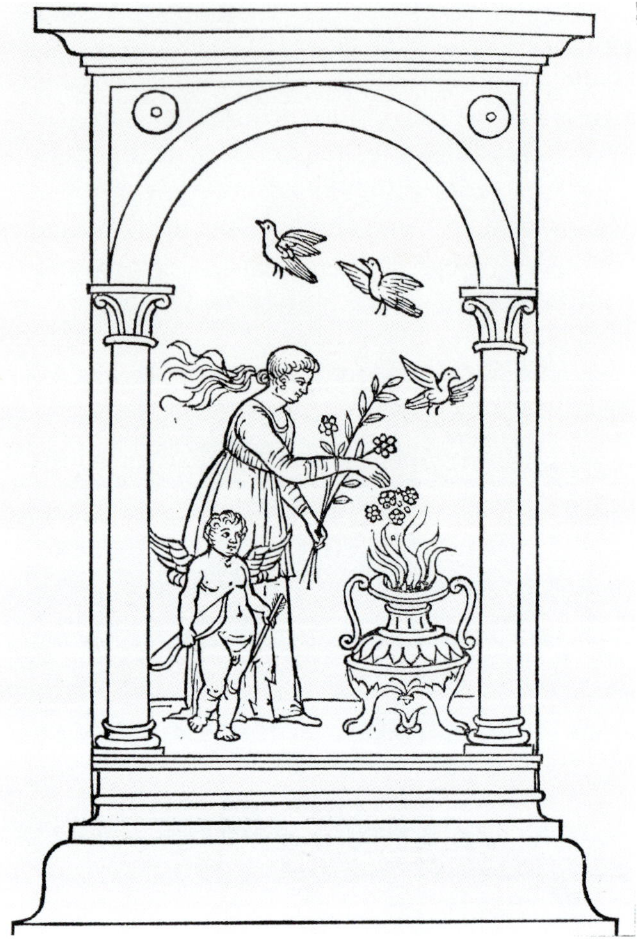

in a wide variety of media. Reproducing the relief subjects of ancient gems, coins, and plaquettes in marble works was a practice adopted with ambition by the Lombard artist Giovanni Antonio Amadeo (1447–1522).[94] A less talented artist, Araldi used ancient coins as sources for his lunettes, creating *symbola*, that is, images that are open to multiple readings and playful implications for enjoyment by the convent court.

Araldi creates separate framed pictorial fields for each hemispherical lunette, but also groups several of them iconographically, as in the case of the three scenes narrating the myth of the Argive brothers Cleobis and Biton on the eastern wall (see fig. 154). My discussion takes the images above the fireplace on the northern wall, centered on subjects of female sacrifice, as its point of departure, assuming that the fireplace and its surrounds would have had an immediate impact on anyone entering the room. These northern lunettes, however, do not mark any "real" point of origin because vision is spatial in the room and one's eyes move across the painted surface endlessly. In the remainder of this chapter, I consider the most telling lunette representations, which revolve around themes of Christian morality, specifically *pietas*, fortune, chastity, and a blissful end, stressing the active practice of Christian and ethical virtues and the assertion of one's agency. Taken together, the lunettes amount to a manifestation of the strengths of wise and courageous women, proposing an agenda of female virtue that can withstand the forces (invisible and material) that threaten it, and which can lead to *refrigerium*.

Distinctively pagan in flavor and painted over the raised trapezoid chimney hood, the central lunette depicts a woman in dark robes making an offering of wheat on a burning altar (fig. 142). Like Mantegna in his Camera Picta, Araldi treats the fireplace zone as a pictorial space, but he was less capable than his celebrated colleague in making effective use of it: Araldi's sacrifice rests on an uneven surface, and is compositionally somewhat unresolved. Images of pagan sacrifice sometimes include a crowd around the priest pouring libations onto the altar or performing the sacrifice, as seen, for example, in Raphael's tapestry cartoon of the *Sacrifice at Lystra* (1516), while Araldi's choice of a solitary figure intent on her sacrificial duty and immersed in a landscape distances the viewer's emotional engagement.[95] Although the gestures and poses of this female figure may be somewhat conventional, the image recalls (albeit in reverse) a woodcut illustration from the *Hypnerotomachia* showing a young woman

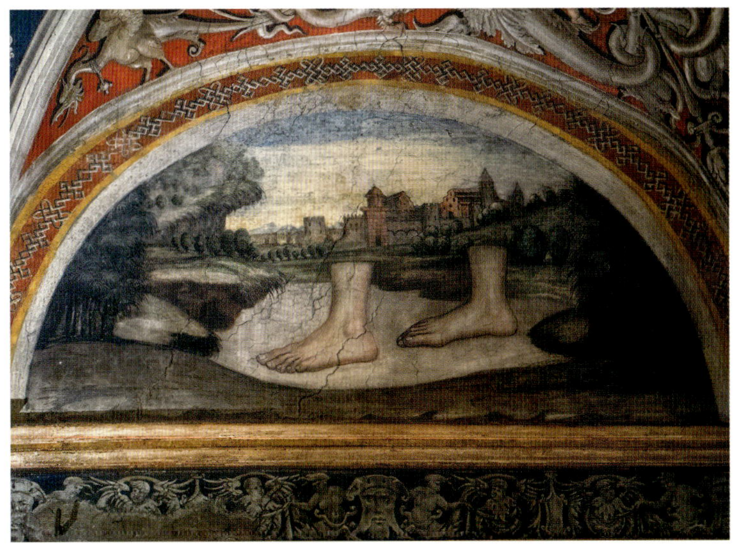

144 Alessandro Araldi, hieroglyph of the impossible, ca. 1514–15, fresco, Parma, San Paolo

accompanied by a putto, making a sacrifice before a burning vase (fig. 143).[96] Araldi's sacrificial, pagan subject has been seen as thematizing *pietas* intended as devotion to God, the convent, and the family, a virtue essential to consecrated women. It is a subject that insists on sacrificial rites as constantly renewing virtue in action, particularly fitting in a monastic context. Novices, indeed, promised to become living sacrifices to God.[97]

Yet it is almost impossible not to notice the touch of wit in this female figure wearing quasi-monastic clothes, before a burning altar. Along the vertical central axis, the element of fire is repeated several times: from the image it travels down to the real flames of the fireplace, and its verbal manifestation incised on the mantelpiece, while over the lunette it reaches up to the burning vase motif topping the north–south, perpendicular candelabra (see figs. 123 and 126). Across the room, too, the opposite, southern lunette (see fig. 146) features Aemilius Paulus's triumph surrounded by flames (a subject to be examined in due course). Flames are sparks of light and heat and affect sight, but here they may further comment on difficulties in the course of life. In contrast, at the center of the triangular pendentive over the lunette, two satyrs torment a desperate-looking mask with their loud music, below which is a small, mocking version of the same mask, aligned with more masks above the lunette. Known as *larve* in the Renaissance, masks have been explained as alluding to uncontrolled fears and mental perturbations.[98] Although Araldi's desperate mask face seems a motif derived from ornamental panels by Nicoletto da Modena or Pere-

grino da Cesena, the painter employed it to reflect playfully on the fire–*refrigerium* inscription, making an ironic notation to the suffering stated in the verse from the psalm.

Turning to the far northeastern lunette, the viewer finds an unusual depiction of a landscape with two feet walking on water in the foreground (fig. 144), an awkwardly rendered hieroglyph.[99] Described in Horapollo's *Hieroglyphica*, an ancient text of Egyptian sign letters discovered in 1419, the hieroglyph with two feet walking was known to signify impossibility.[100] Araldi must have learned of this Egyptian sign from the printed or abridged manuscript copies of the *Hieroglyphica* that were circulated in the early sixteenth century. It seems that the antiquarian Cyriacus of Ancona (1391–1453/55) prepared an abridged version of 36 signs of the *Hieroglyphica* probably copied into the epigraphic sylloge assembled by the antiquarian Ferrarini.[101] Like Anselmi, Ferrarini was fascinated by the abstruseness of Egyptian signs, which were described in Alberti's *De Re Aedificatoria* (published in 1485) where the theorist champions hieroglyphics as a substitute for language.[102] This Albertian precept is visualized with impressive clarity in the funerary monument of a contemporary influential Parmese canon, Vincenzo Carissimi. Dating to around 1520, a recently discovered sketch shows Carissimi's wall sarcophagus (fig. 145), which incorporates three Egyptian hieroglyphs: a helmet with a dog's head, a bucranium with branches tied to its horns, and a bird-headed lamp.[103] Copied from the *Hypnerotomachia*, the three hieroglyphs are decoded in a discursive sentence: "Patientia est ornamentum custodia et protectio vitae" (Endurance is the ornament, care, and protection of life). In Carissimi's tomb design, instead of a conventional inscription carved in *all'antica* lettering, three hieroglyphs comment on the deceased canon's virtues. Indeed, these Egyptian signs were decipherable only in sophisticated circles with an awareness of the *Hypnerotomachia*, the convent court of San Paolo included.

Araldi's surreal walking feet on a pond limit somewhat the beholder's appreciation of this Egyptian sign and reveal his confused confrontation with enigmatic images, especially if it is compared with the same hieroglyph rendered by Albrecht Dürer in the topmost panel of his woodcut of the triumphal arch for Emperor Maximilian (ca. 1518).[104] In Dürer's print the hieroglyph convincingly bears the idea of the emperor's military accomplishments that "all men had thought impossible." Araldi's hieroglyph, instead, points to the militant virtue of women that attains impossible things. By implying that women are capable of achieving impossible things and of confronting adversity with virtue (espe-

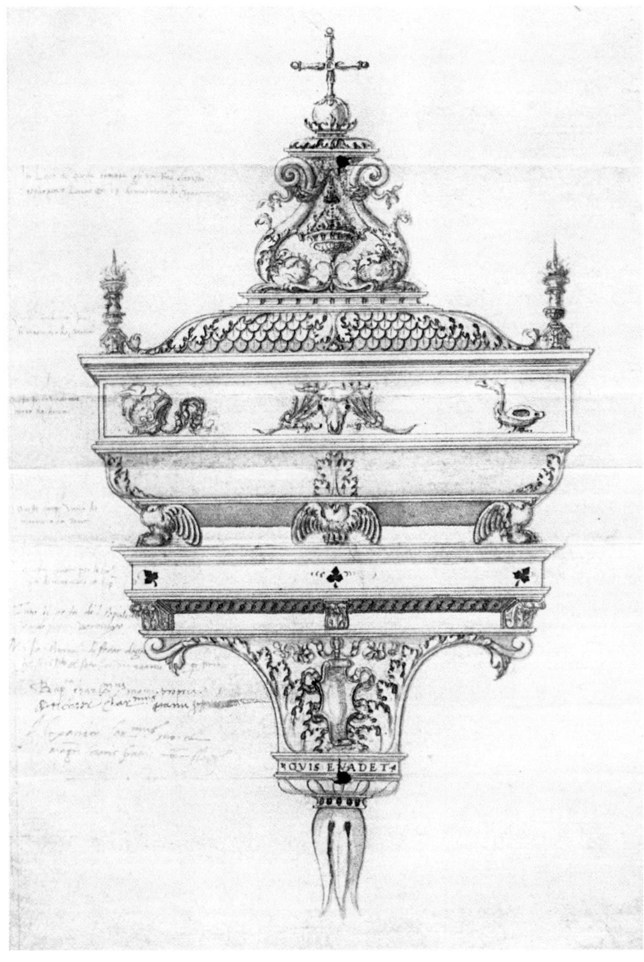

145 Giovanfrancesco d'Agrate, *Project for Carissimi Tomb,* ca. 1520, Parma, Archivio Distrettuale Notarile

cially if they follow the example of their divine spouse, Jesus Christ, who walked on water), Araldi's depiction could have been intended to parry the abbess's detractors, who attacked her leadership and status.

In the lunette opposite the fireplace, the viewer sees an image of a Roman triumph (fig. 146), displaying a table piled with spoils and trophies at its center, while the victorious general and his captives are arranged on either side. Differing from Mantegna's canvases of the triumph of Julius Caesar – with their remarkable parade of foreshortened soldiers, musicians, and captives with their booty, all designated with a wealth of detail and which were immediately copied in prints[105] – Araldi's fresco of the triumph of Aemilius Paulus, the Roman general who defeated King Perseus of Macedon at Pydna in 168 BCE, portrays the figures in semi-grisaille silhouette flanking the trophies, while a crowd of Roman citizens is relegated to the background.[106] From the

left, Aemilius and his older sons confront the defeated Perseus and his attendants on the opposite side in a flattened composition that derives from a coin image celebrating the triumph. Araldi's primary alteration of this model was to surround the scene with flames. Described by Plutarch, Aemilius's triumph was commented on by several Renaissance authors, including Leonardo Bruni and Francesco Albertini.[107] Plutarch narrates that before and after Aemilius's celebration, which lasted three days, the general's younger sons died and "no Roman . . . [failed to] share the father's grief . . . all shuddered at the cruelty of Fortune, seeing that she had not scrupled to bring such great sorrow into a house that was full of congratulations, joy, and sacrifices, or to mingle lamentations and tears with paeans of victory and triumphs."[108] Consuming all things, the flames remind beholders that even military triumphs, the highest celebratory moment of a career dedicated to civic service, could turn from occasions of glorification into moments of grief, alerting the audience to beware the illusions that good or bad fortune creates and the necessity to steel oneself against its sudden turns. As Plutarch puts it, "[Aemilius] said . . . that he had never dreaded any human agency, but among agencies that were divine he had ever feared Fortune, believing her to be a most untrustworthy and variable thing."[109] Araldi's representation effectively captures Aemilius's self-control and noble determination, despite the sudden turn of events. Among the paraded prisoners, Perseus's young children were led along as slaves, generating pity among the Romans. This sentiment is encapsulated in the woman in the left background, carrying one child while pulling another close to her.[110] Set opposite the fireplace, this triumph imagery reinstates the dichotomy of the psalm inscription, the incessant flux of emotions (fear and relief, grief and rejoicing), but also reminds viewers that fortune can at any time disrupt the lives of human beings, who should equip themselves through virtue to endure its unexpected effects. It further reinforces the north–south visual axis within the room centered on the element of fire, its messages, and quasi-magic power to catch the eyes.

The adjacent image proposes instead a curious variant on the allegory of the maiden and the unicorn, which traditionally refers to the virtue of chastity. Here the unicorn is jumping into the lap of a woman to embrace and kiss her (fig. 147). This differs from most earlier depictions of the subject, including an exquisite portrait attributed to Raphael (ca. 1505–6; Rome, Borghese Gallery) in which a demurely attired, sober-faced blond maiden holds a miniature domesticated unicorn in her lap.[111] Araldi seems to allude to the

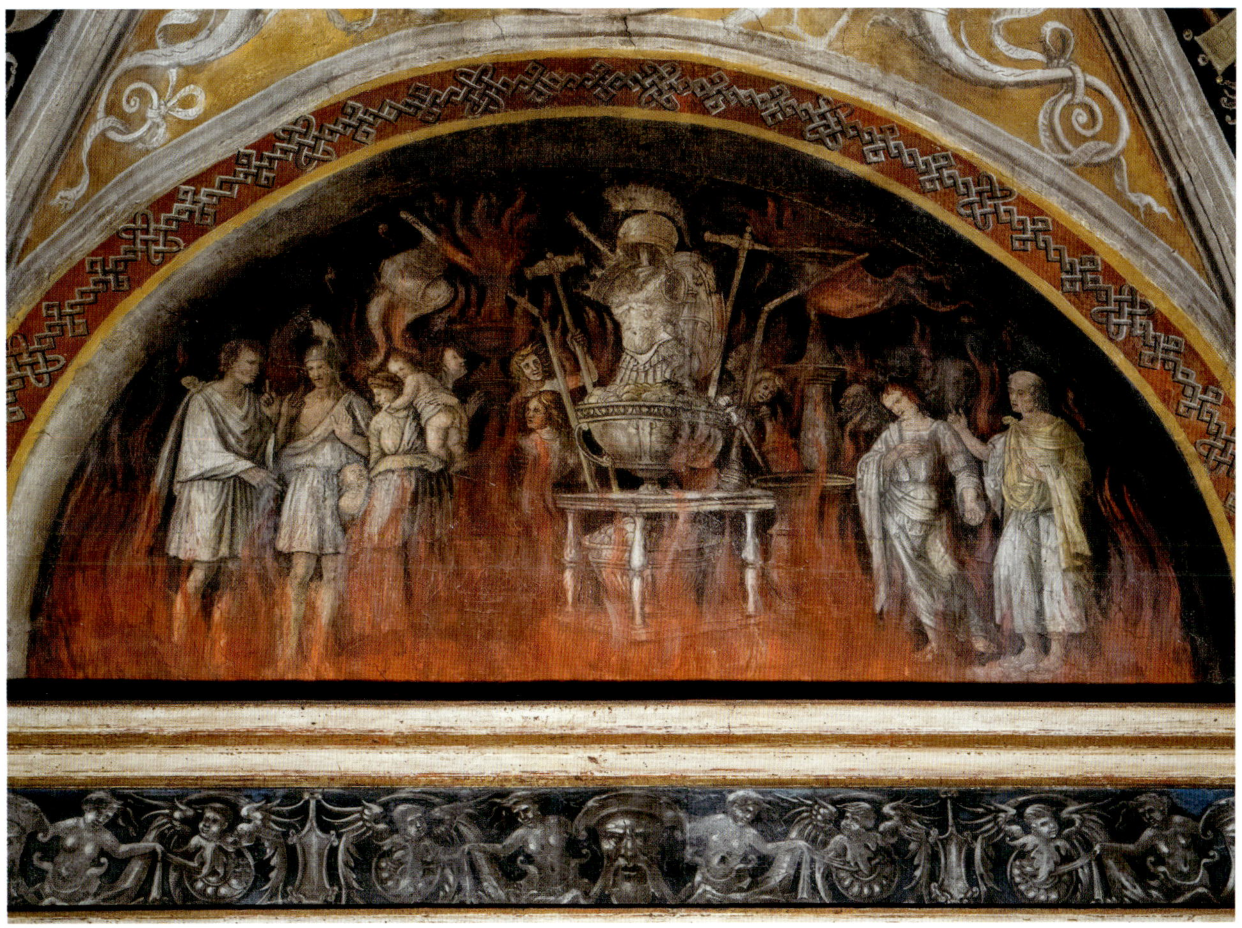

146   Alessandro Araldi, *Triumph of Aemilius Paulus*, ca. 1514–15, fresco, Parma, San Paolo

erotic side of the encounter. His unicorn is large, aggressive, and voracious, while chastity is not suggested by a youthful female, as in Raphael's and numerous other paintings of this popular subject. The female protagonist is instead a robust, mature woman with a lined face in a red gown (as was the convention), which Zanichelli has interpreted as a monastic uniform.[112] A white veil covers her head, leaving her neck and shoulder exposed. If the lunette depicts a consecrated woman, the red dress would be unusual, though the exposure of her shoulder would match one of the most contested features of Jacometto Veneziano's *Portrait of a Nun from San Secondo* (see fig. 2), discussed in Chapter Two. It is more likely that Araldi's image stresses a notion of eroticized chastity, reverberating with Correggio's sensual Diana imagery (a standard personification of chastity) in the adjacent room (see Chapter Six). Or would the theme of this lunette have something to do with Horace's castigation of artists' *fantasia* ("savage [shall never] mate with tame"), expressing the painter's challenge to embody poetic license itself?[113]

Be that as it may, it is impossible not to notice the eroticism of the woman's embrace of the unicorn, her hands caressing its neck in a gesture of passionate love, and their mouths aligned to kiss.[114] Araldi makes the unicorn's physical desire complement the woman's receptive behavior: the unicorn places a hindleg on the woman's right knee to gain leverage, while its forelegs apparently embrace her torso, bringing its head and mouth close to hers, gestures of passion which the woman does not spurn. This image seems to invoke the sensual tone conveyed by an engraving attributed to Baccio Baldini (ca. 1465–80) presenting a young girl, known as Marietta, holding and caressing a unicorn in her lap that gazes at her with adoring eyes (fig. 148). Leonardo studied this composition in several drawings, and in one (ca. 1478–80; Oxford, Ashmolean Museum) he portrayed the maiden as pointing at the unicorn, whom she holds by a leash. A figure that on its own conventionally stood for the ideal of chastity, the unicorn was conversely also associated with opposite values such as pleasure and lust. In the popular

159

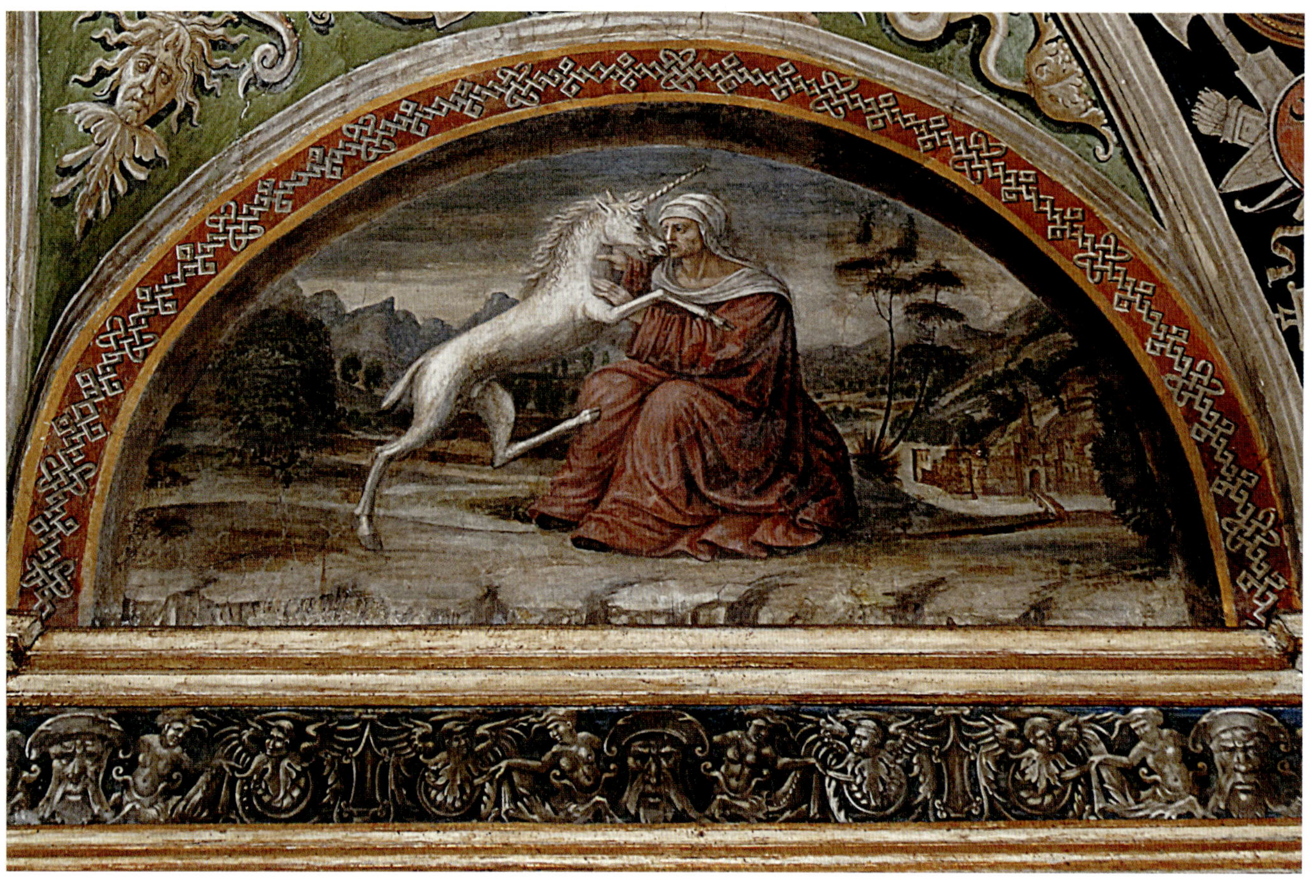

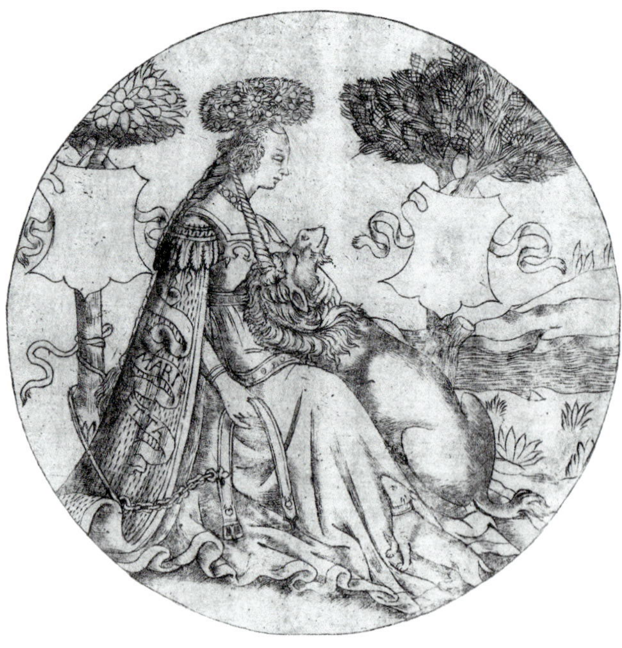

Above 147   Alessandro Araldi, lunette with virgin and unicorn, ca. 1514–15, fresco, Parma, San Paolo

Below 148   Baccio Baldini, *Emblem of Chastity*, ca. 1465–80, engraving, d. 15.3 cm (6^1/$_{32}$ in), London, Trustees of the British Museum

Fiori di Virtù – a medieval anthology of virtues in which morals are related to animal behaviors, and a text that Leonardo had in his library – the unicorn is described in terms of licentiousness and intemperance in a passage that Leonardo recorded in his notes on the tales of animals.[115] Leonardo describes the unicorn as a "puzzling creature [that] because of its intemperance not knowing how to control itself before the delight it feels toward fair maidens, forgets its ferocity and wildness, and casting aside all fear it will go up to the seated maiden and sleep in her lap and thus the hunters take it."[116] Confronting Araldi's image in which the embodiment of female virtue is aligned with its feminine, eroticized side, the viewer might have been reminded of nuns' probable struggles to maintain physical purity and the menaces to female chastity that, whether actual or anticipated, were a major concern in female religious communities. All in all, this image of unbridled passion shows a debauched model not to be followed by nuns but, at the same time, addresses its possible implications in the conventual world. If the female is meant as a monastic, the crude, moralizing message would be that nuns who give in to lust are no better than those who engage in sexual relations with animals.

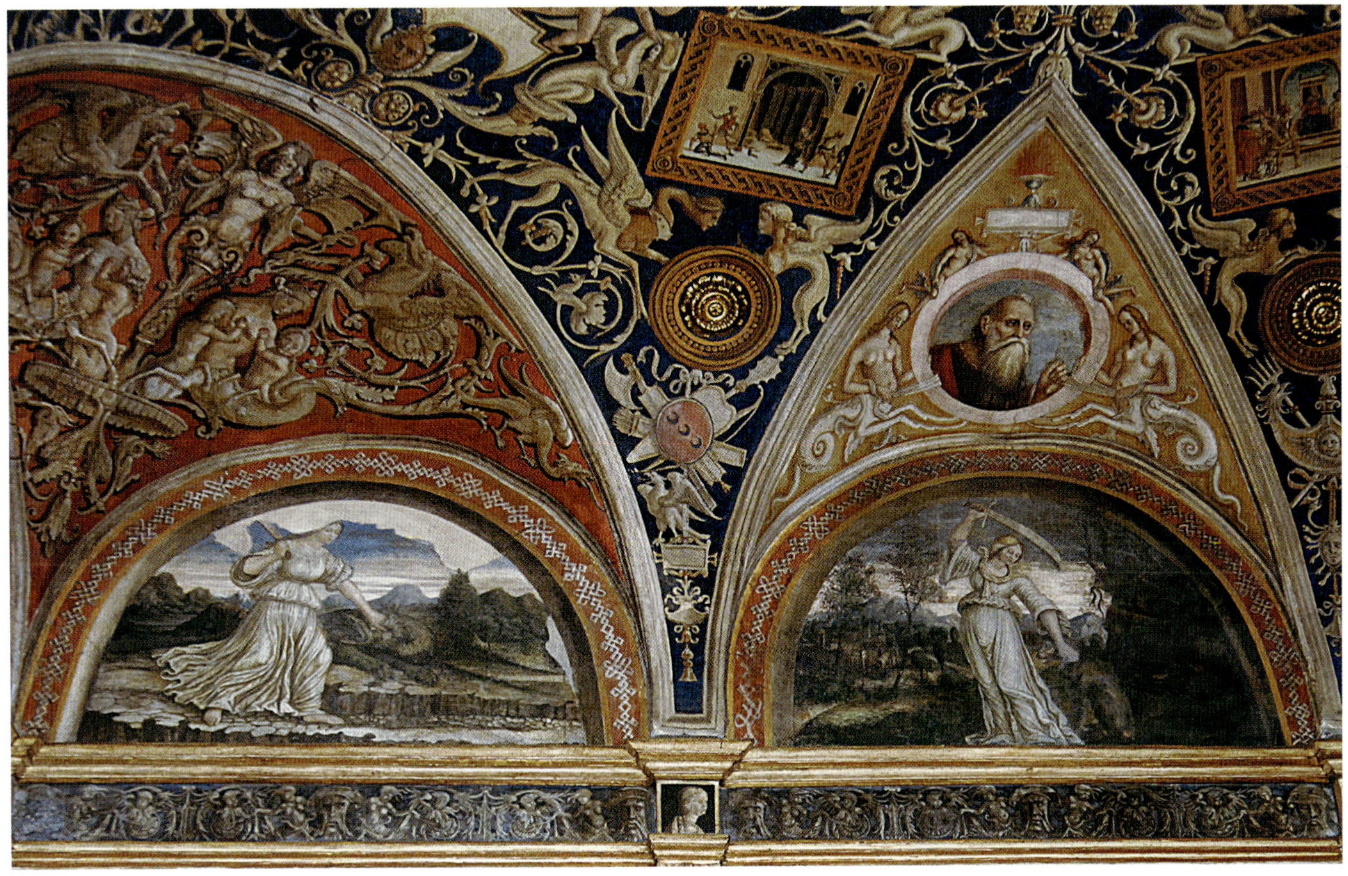

Above 149   Alessandro Araldi, female figures killing beasts,
ca. 1514–15, fresco, Parma, San Paolo

Right 150   Giovanni Antonio da Brescia after Mantegna, *Judith
with the Head of Holofernes*, 1497–1507, engraving, 31.5 × 22.6 cm
(12^{13}/$_{32}$ × 8^{57}/$_{64}$ in), London, Trustees of the British Museum

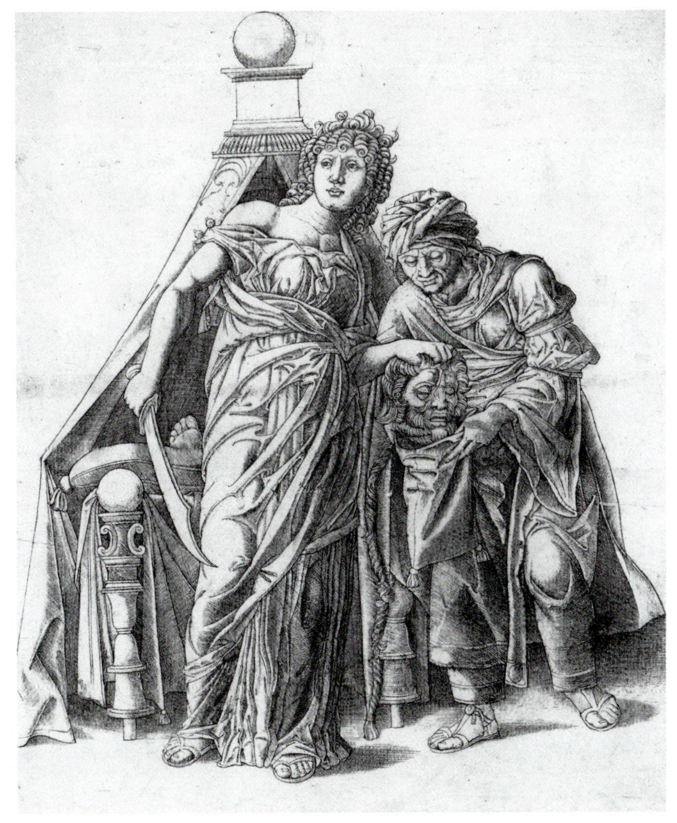

The spectator in Araldi's room might notice that this
subject is balanced by representations of the active, even
aggressive, exercise of virtue in two images on the western
wall with female protagonists overcoming beasts (fig. 149).
In the right-hand lunette, a young woman brandishes a
falchion with which she will slay a squatting ape-like figure
in her grasp. Araldi captures the moment preceding the
violent end of the beast, emphasizing the girl's strength and
readiness to perform the deed. In the other image, the
woman, also facing right with sword in hand, is about to
kill a dragon. Both Araldi's protagonists generically recall
Mantegna's figure of Judith with the head of Holofernes,
which was circulated thanks to drawings and prints, including those by Giovanni Antonio da Brescia (1497–1507;
fig. 150).[117] Araldi's figures are less evocative than their Man-
tegnesque model, but he used that prototype to reverse the

long-standing argument presenting women as vicious and debased individuals. The shift of gender is crucial: here, aggressive female protagonists triumph over vices embodied by monstrous, male creatures. As Horst Woldemar Janson observed, apes were often associated with vices and with the devil instigating inappropriate behavior in humans; they had been treated as a sort of debased man in monastic literature, similar in physical appearance but lacking men's ability to reason. In addition, the ape was likened to the art of painting as an inferior imitation of nature and its creative powers.[118] Araldi gives his ape a human posture, making it appear a cowed male who has succumbed to the strength and moral stature of the female wielding the sword, and possibly pointing to the vainglory of men who sought immortality through their deeds. Themes of vanity and vainglory identified with the male amplify, by contrast, women's courageous actions, spiritual perfection, and excellence. These two images amount to a proclamation of wise, powerful, and warlike women engaged in the defense of the world, rather than reacting with timidity or passivity to the turn of Fortune or adversity.

Looking at the southern wall, the display of the active exercise of virtue is confirmed by another lunette that declares itself to be about a quintessential female virtue: it portrays a young girl breastfeeding an elderly man, the personification of the so-called Caritas Romana. A story of parental care and familial bonds, the Caritas Romana is exemplified by the dutiful Pero, who saved her father Mycon (or Cimon in other accounts) from starvation by breastfeeding him in prison (fig. 151). The story of Pero is narrated as an exemplum of *pietas* in Valerius Maximus's *Memorable Deeds and Sayings*.[119] The viewer's perception of Pero's caring responsibility is, however, slightly compromised due to Araldi's clumsiness in rendering her breast, the focal point of the image. It seems that the organ is detached from her bust and raised, as she presses it to Mycon's mouth. Aside from Mycon's chained feet, Araldi omits any allusion to his prison, and the sloping, bucolic setting and low horizon confer nobility on the figures who loom large at the center. The story of Pero and Mycon was a fairly popular subject in the Renaissance and was translated into many media.[120] As a theme of filial devotion, Pero feeding her father came second only to the story of Aeneas saving his aged father from burning Troy. In his biographies of ancient heroines, Boccaccio adapted Pero's story into that of an unnamed Roman girl breastfeeding her mother, a change of gender that the French writer Christine de Pizan maintains in her *Book of the City*

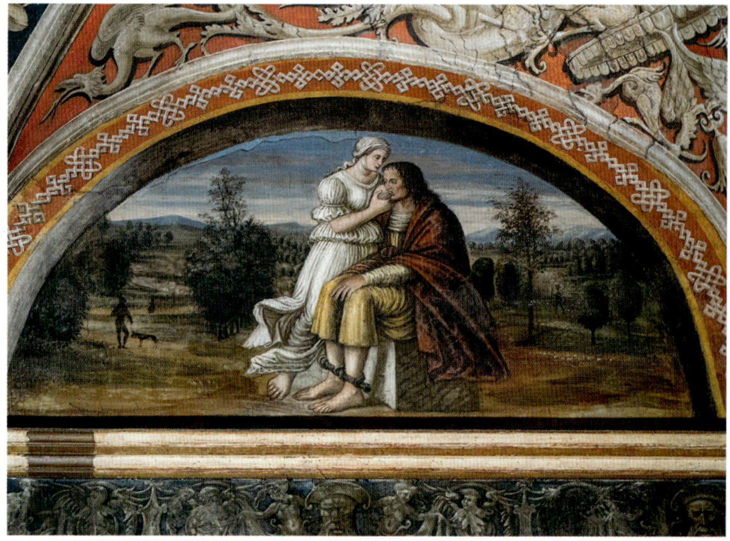

151 Alessandro Araldi, *Caritas Romana*, ca. 1514–15, fresco, Parma, San Paolo

of Ladies (1405), emphasizing the daughters' care for their old parents in contrast to their brothers'. In his *Gynevera de le clare donne* (ca. 1489–92) the Bolognese *literato* Sabadino degli Arienti praises women for caring for elderly fathers, allocating it as the distinct province of women.[121] Araldi returns to the ancient version of the Caritas Romana, stressing daughters' compassion for their fathers. He portrays an intimacy between relatives that was seemingly not problematic or disturbing to contemporary viewers, concentrating on the theme of *pietas* rather than any incestuous relationship.

In the semicircular pendentive above the Caritas Romana (see fig. 152), the theme is parodied in the aquatic monsters nursing their offspring like human mothers, set against a red ground. It was probably inspired by Lucian's description of an image by Zeuxis, which, in turn, Jacopo Sannazaro narrates in his *Arcadia* romance (1504) as painted by Mantegna on a maplewood bowl.[122] Lucian states that Zeuxis

avoided painting popular and hackneyed themes . . . he was always aiming at novelty . . . Among the bold innovations of this Zeuxis was his painting of a female Hippocentaur feeding twin Hippocentaur children, no more than babies . . . She holds one of her offspring aloft in her arm, giving it the breast in human fashion; the other she suckles from her mare's teat like an animal.[123]

Araldi substituted aquatic creatures for terrestrial monsters, but the textual reference seems clear enough. In reworking

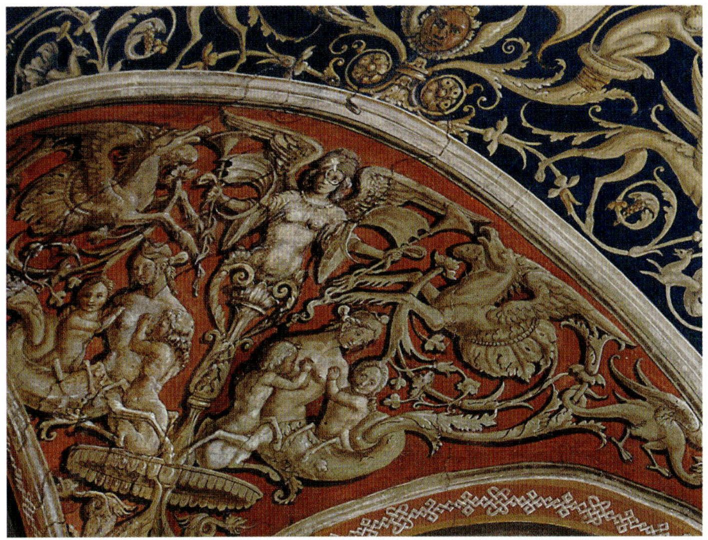

152   Alessandro Araldi, corner pendentive with hybrid figures feeding offspring, ca. 1514–15, fresco, Parma, San Paolo

this subject Araldi may have drawn inspiration from a contemporary niello print by Peregrino da Cesena (after 1507; fig. 153) showing grotesque work and a satyress nursing babies at the top.[124]

As noted earlier, the three lunette images on the eastern wall differ in iconographical structure from all of the others that act as independent, discrete units. They form a narrative centered on the ancient myth of Cleobis and Biton, twin sons of Cydippe, priestess of Hera in Argos (fig. 154). Recounted by Herodotus, Plutarch, and Valerius Maximus as a story of virtuous life and death, maternal love and pride, the myth of the Argive brothers is associated with the plague in Servius's commentary on Virgil's *Georgics*. The youths' unfailing obedience to their mother is rewarded by a gentle death:

> it was the custom for the Argive priestess to go to the temple of Juno [Hera] drawn by cattle, and on the sacred day no cattle could be found; for a plague that was (as we say) passing through Attica, had consumed them all; the two sons of the priestess, Cleobis and Biton, yoked themselves up and carried their mother to the temple. Then, Juno, approving their piety, offered to the mother that, whatever she wanted, she might ask for her sons; and in pious response she said, that whatever the goddess knew to be useful to mortals, she should give them. And so the next day the sons of the priestess were found dead.[125]

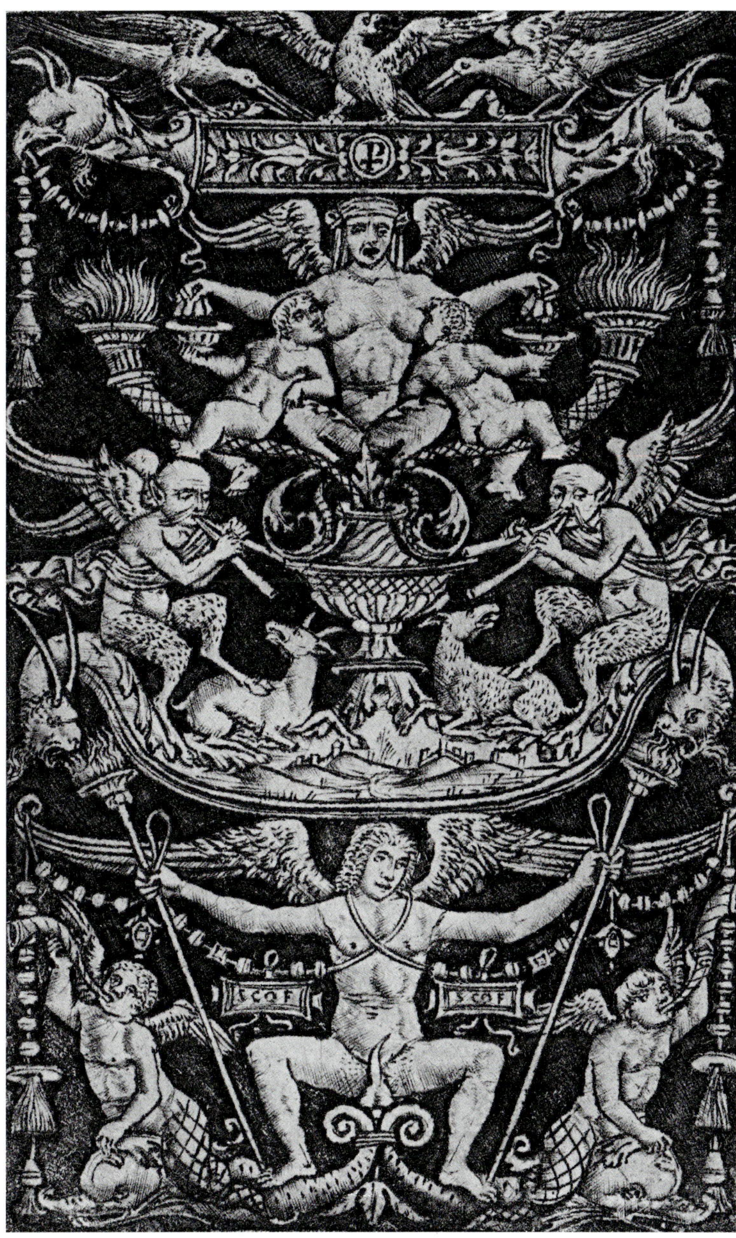

153   Peregrino da Cesena, *Panel of Ornament with Satyress Feeding Babies*, after 1507, niello print, 7.1 × 4.4 cm (2⁵/₆ × 1⁴/₆ in), Washington, D.C., National Gallery of Art

Herodotus describes the boys as athletes and prizewinners, insisting on their physical strength. In Rosso Fiorentino's depiction of the myth for Francis I's Gallery of Fontainebleau (ca. 1536–7; fig. 155), for example, the twins are depicted with muscular bodies dragging their mother's chariot, looking exhausted and strained.[126] In Araldi's conception, the twins are presented as blond ephebes who gently, almost effortlessly, tug their mother's chariot. It was precisely the youths' survival of the plague that made it

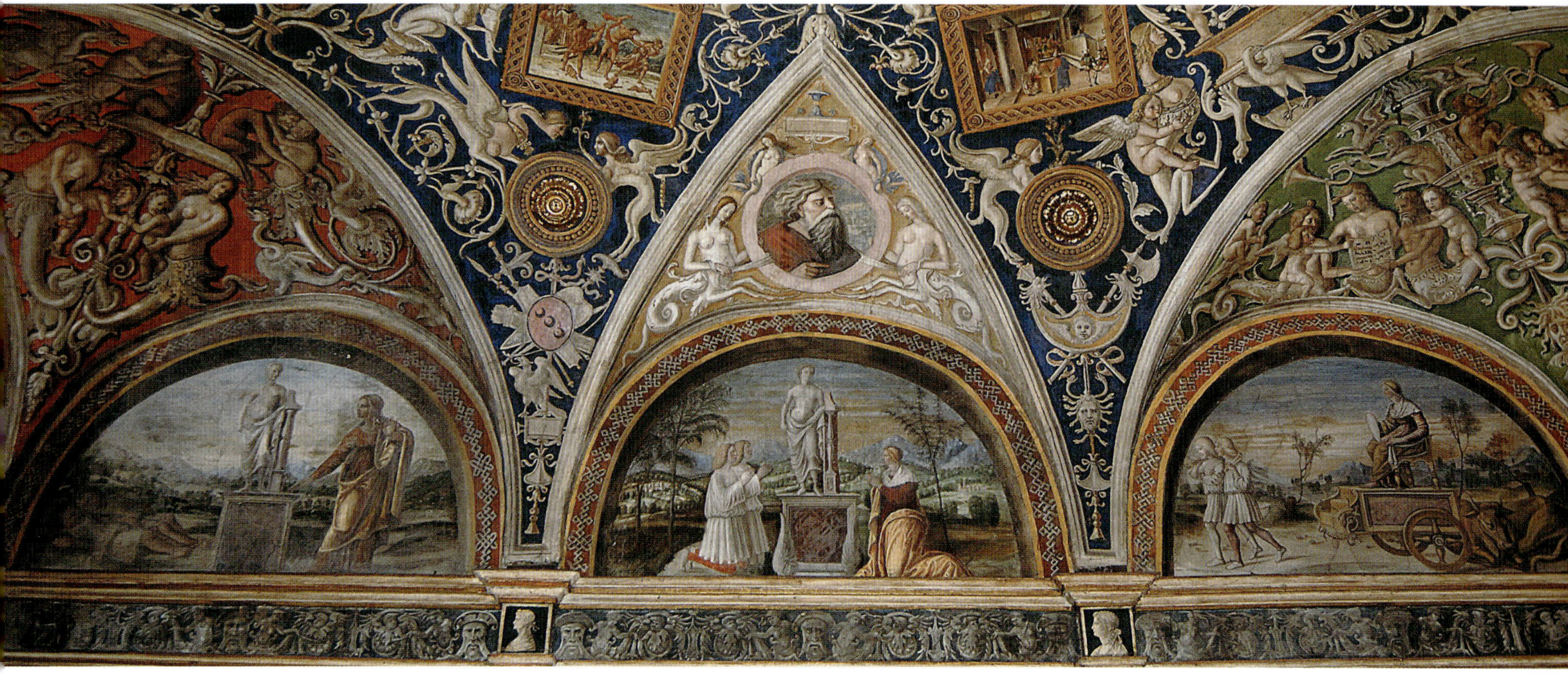

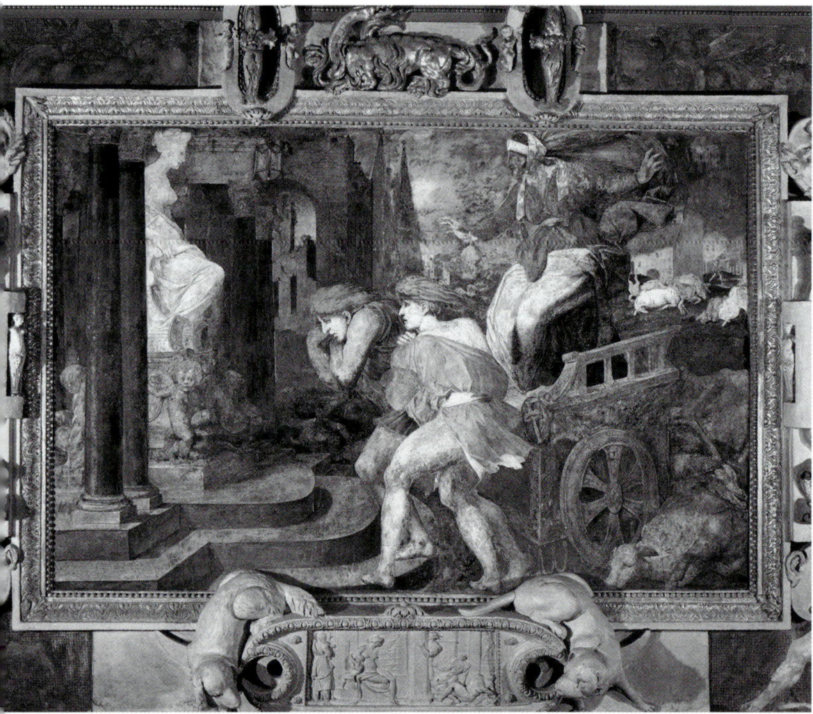

Top 154   Alessandro Araldi, lunettes with Cleobis and Biton, ca. 1514–15, fresco, Parma, San Paolo

Above 155   Rosso Fiorentino, *Cleobis and Biton,* ca. 1536–7, fresco, Fontainebleau, Château de Fontainebleau

possible for Cydippe to perform her duty to the goddess Hera. Rosso's fresco signals this by a desolate landscape of ruins and dead animals, giving the scene a sense of finality. In Araldi's composition, which ultimately derives from a third-century coin, it is difficult to detect devastating plague and famine: in the tranquil landscape, the cattle behind Cydippe's chariot seem to be merely resting rather than dead.

Next, Araldi has the Argive brothers and their mother kneel before a statue of Apollo (not Hera, as Servius had specified and as Rosso later depicted). Here Cydippe is requesting the god to grant the twins the greatest reward that a human being can receive, that of dying sweetly in one's sleep. This outcome is depicted in the third image, where the brothers, portrayed as sleeping children, and their mother flank the Apollo statue.[127] As the ancient sources recount, the Argive brothers died without the stain of sin, and their self-sacrifice and premature death were both the source of their perennial fame and bliss.[128] To informed conventual audiences, the Argive brothers' obedience and care for their mother might have appeared an apt subject when contemplating a pious and dutiful life. Such an audience would have known that in Plutarch's *Life of Solon,* the brothers' virtuous conduct is contrasted with that of the wealthy, inglorious Croesus in order to magnify the Argives as an exemplum of the fortunate life. The late Cinquecento artist and theorist Pirro Ligorio corroborates this view,

164

referring to the myth as a paradigm of the blissful life.[129] The brothers' loving familial bonds seem echoed or commented on in the pendentives above, where aquatic monsters demonstrate various forms of affection. A monstrous couple holds babies who reach out for each other, while satyrs embrace their female counterparts in passionately charged gestures. *Exempla* and their visual parodies or glosses ultimately serve to reinforce the antitheses of fire–*refrigerium* and suffering–regeneration embedded in the decorative scheme of Araldi's frescoed room.

Araldi's painted chamber for Giovanna Piacenza mounts an argument about the role of painting as the motor of regeneration, and of activating the beholder's emotions, but also about the illegitimate knowledge that wise women should possess to withstand life's conflicts, pursuing virtue with lightness. The wise choose various paths including the visual and its therapeutic power to achieve regeneration. It is probable that the abbess and the convent court retired to take meals in Araldi's painted chamber, conversing and perhaps touching on the occult, magic, and the hermetic Egyptian language embodied in the images overhead, reproducing and producing *refrigerium*. Albeit a performance of limited aesthetic virtuosity, Araldi's *all'antica* decorative display must have satisfied its original audience, and would serve Correggio well in the creation of his stunning frescoes in the adjacent room.

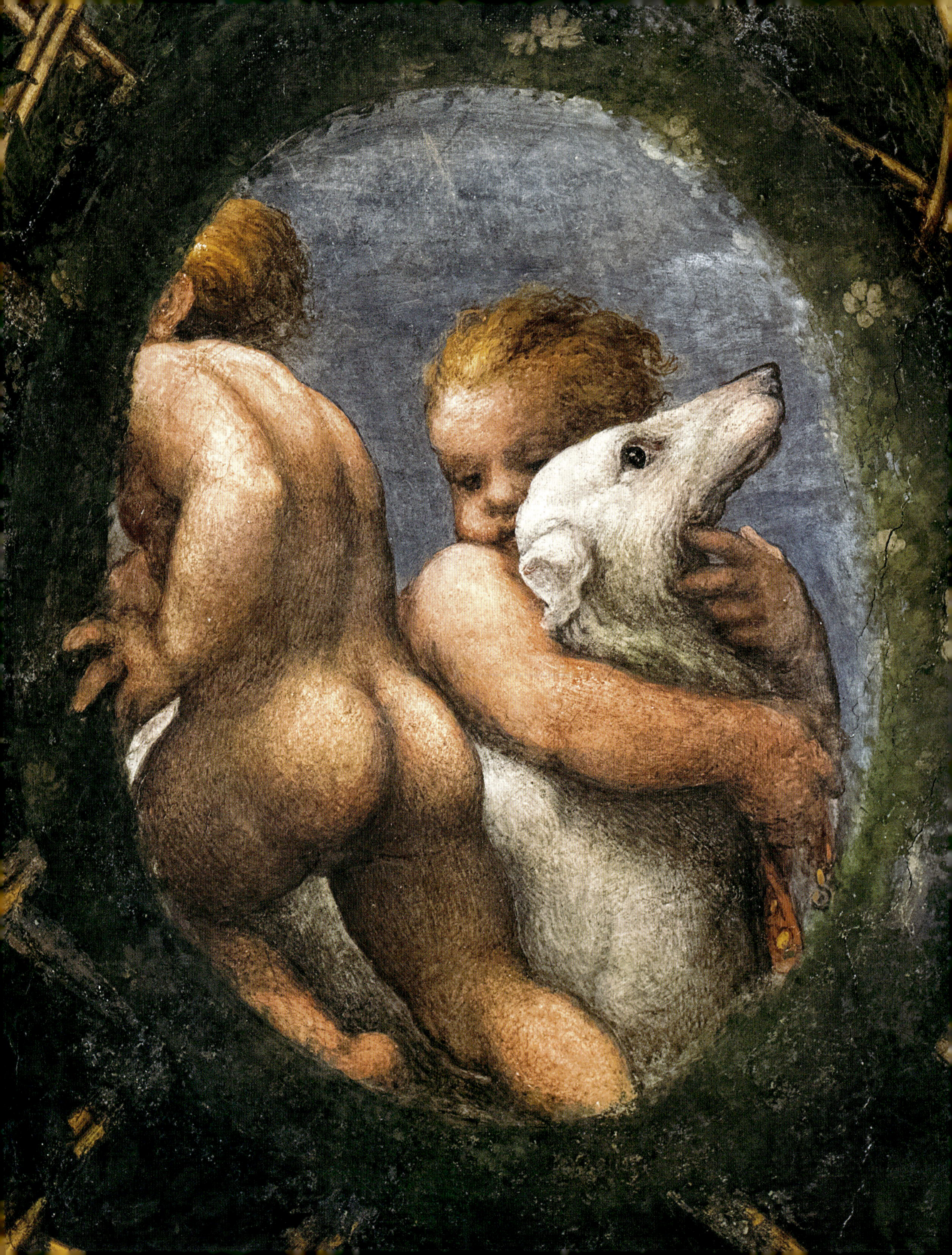

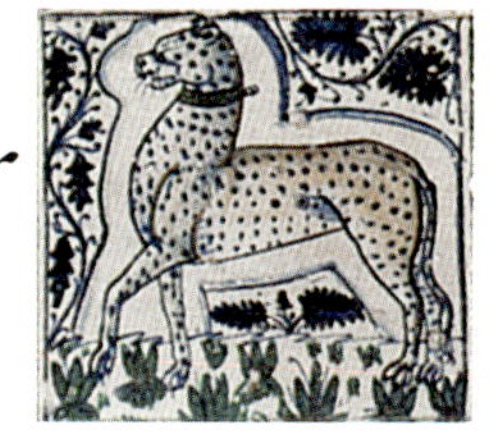

6
Correggio's Wit, Irony, and the Enigmatic Image

Correggio's decoration in Abbess Giovanna Piacenza's private chamber at the core of her apartment is nothing short of revolutionary. His frescoes are a synthesis of illusionism, artifice, and allure, an unconventional amalgam of pagan subjects charged with palpable appeal in a monastic setting. The artist transforms the chamber's real masonry umbrella vault, consisting of sixteen concave spandrels, into a garden bower with reed ribs, wicker trellis webbing, and garlands of fruit and vegetation knotted around the abbess's gilded stemma at the zenith (fig. 156; see figs. 1 and 103). Imagining the vault as a verdant bower expanding down and outwards from the central arms, Correggio devised a solution that evokes Leonardo's famous Sala delle Asse (1498–9; fig. 157) in the Sforza castle in Milan. But Correggio's structure is far more complex than that of the Sala delle Asse, enhancing the conception of the garden bower opened by oculi proposed by Mantegna in his *Madonna of the Victory* altarpiece (1495–6; fig. 158).[1] To rethink Mantegna's fiction of the verdant semidome perforated by circular openings in this altarpiece, which Correggio must have studied during his stay in Mantua in the early 1510s, he pierced each spandrel of his pergola with an open-sky oculus, revealing a colorful parade of naked putti or *eroti* engaged in joyous play (fig. 159).[2] The verdant bower rests on a fictive architectonic and sculptural structure articulated by a cornice on which sits a series of semicircular lunettes, four on each wall for a total of sixteen. The stonelike, gri-

saille figures (with only occasional touches of gold) in the lunettes feature pagan gods, mythological subjects, and allegories, and the illusionistic marble cornice that sustains them is interrupted only by the windows on the north wall (fig. 160). With the exception of these two bays, each lunette and the bottom of each rib is demarcated by a pair of rams' heads resting on a vase-like element. Each head pins a segment of the continuous length of fabric that stretches along the entablature under the lunettes, and supports colorful sacrificial implements such as libation vessels and platters. This placement of the rams' heads (see fig. 159) reinforces the sense that each lunette is a separate unit, a slightly concave sculptural surface receding into the masonry supported by the fictive architectural frame.

The contrast between the monochrome, classicizing, self-contained lunettes and the colorful upper band of putti directly over them could not be more striking. These frolicking, jocose *spiritelli* capture the viewer's eyes with the sheer loveliness of their games, interacting with each other as though a continuous train of lively creatures were animating the pergola from outside, sometimes staring in while engaging in their pastimes. The puttis' jollity is enhanced by their palpable physicality and soft modeling in warm flesh tones, as much as the cool, *all'antica* style of the lunette faux-marbles correlates with their content and intended obscurity. It is as if Correggio's different pictorial modes are

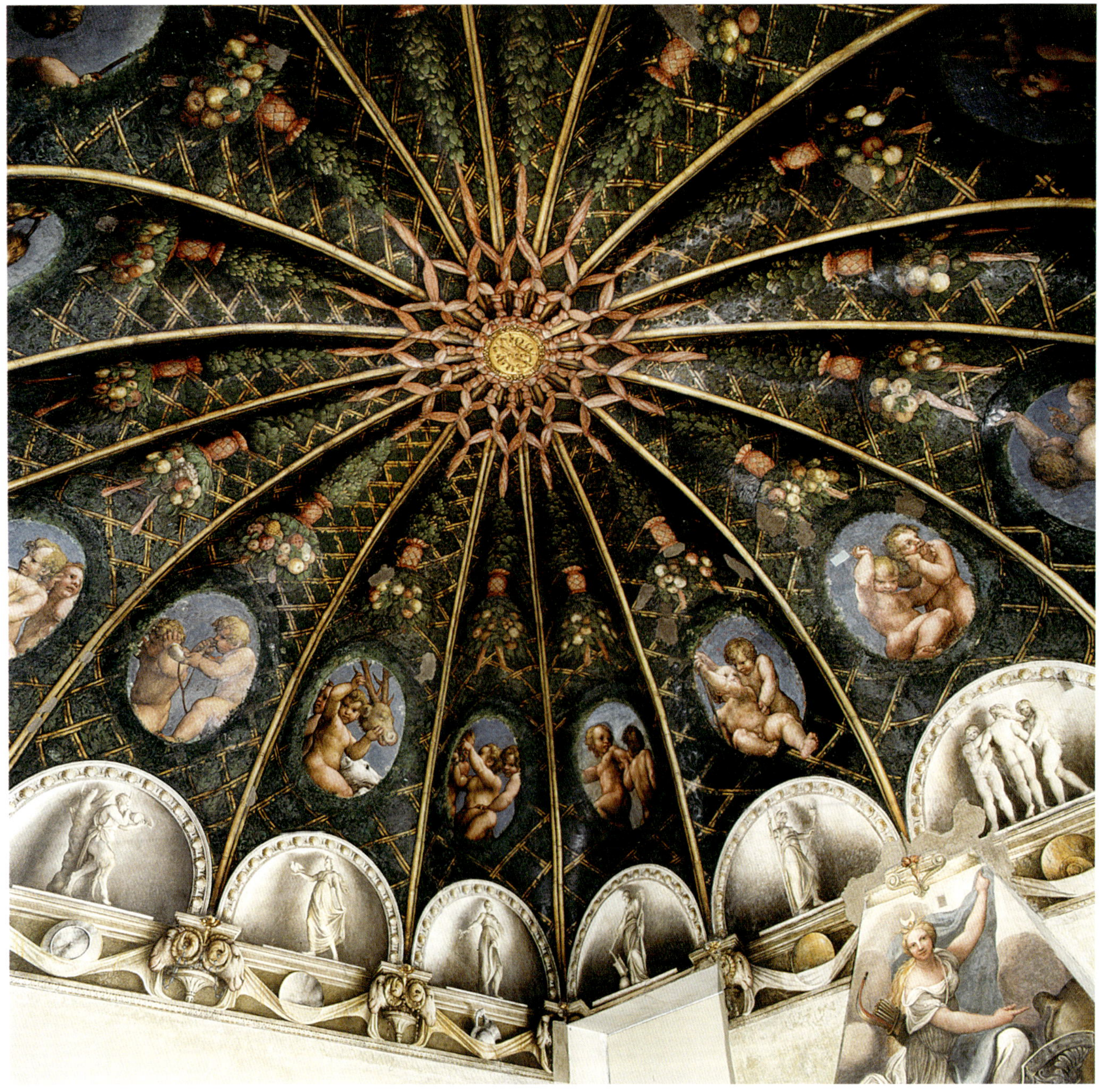

156   Correggio, frescoed vault, ca. 1518–19, 6.75 × 6.45 m (ca. 22 × 21 feet), Parma, San Paolo

meditated reflections on the effects of the represented subjects on the spectator. In the same spirit, on the trapezoid hood of the northern fireplace, Diana, the classical goddess of the hunt and a personification of chastity, is rendered as an unmistakably sensuous figure (fig. 161). This voluptuous Diana is shown ascending to heaven in her chariot and spreading a variegated dark blue mantle behind her. As in the adjacent room painted by Araldi, the mantelpiece bears an inscription in elegant Roman capital letters: IGNEM GLADIO NE FODIAS (Stir not the fire with a sword). An aphorism of the ancient Greek philosopher Pythagoras, this arcane utterance was commented on in Erasmus's *Adagiorum Chiliades* of 1508 with reference to the virtue of prudence.[3] Opposite the fireplace, the *pietra serena* lintel of a door carries the words O[MN]IA VIRT[UTI] PERVIA (All is accessible to virtue; as discussed in Chapter Four, see fig. 114), stressing

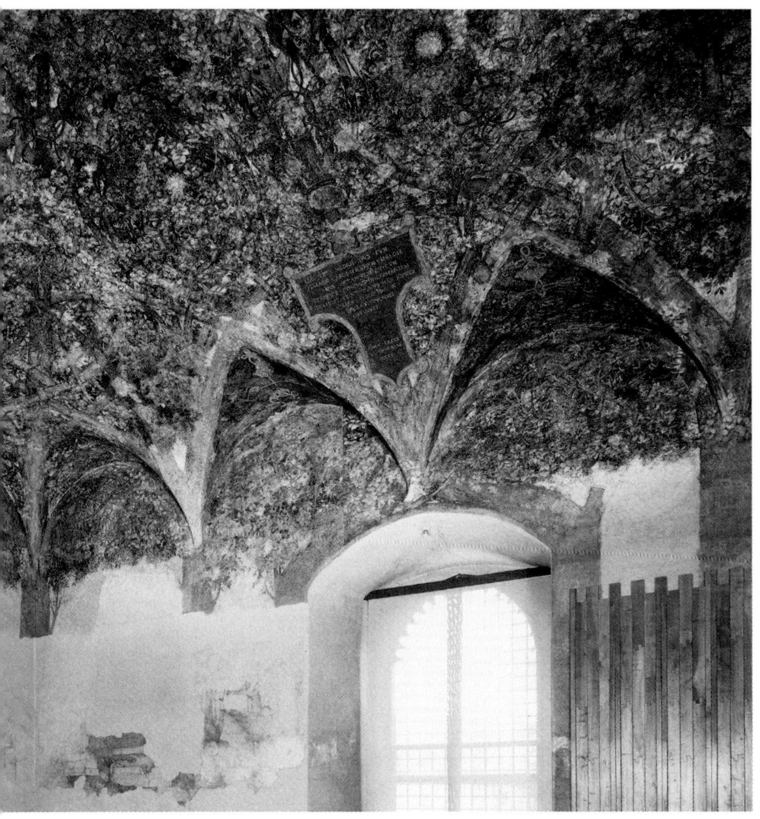

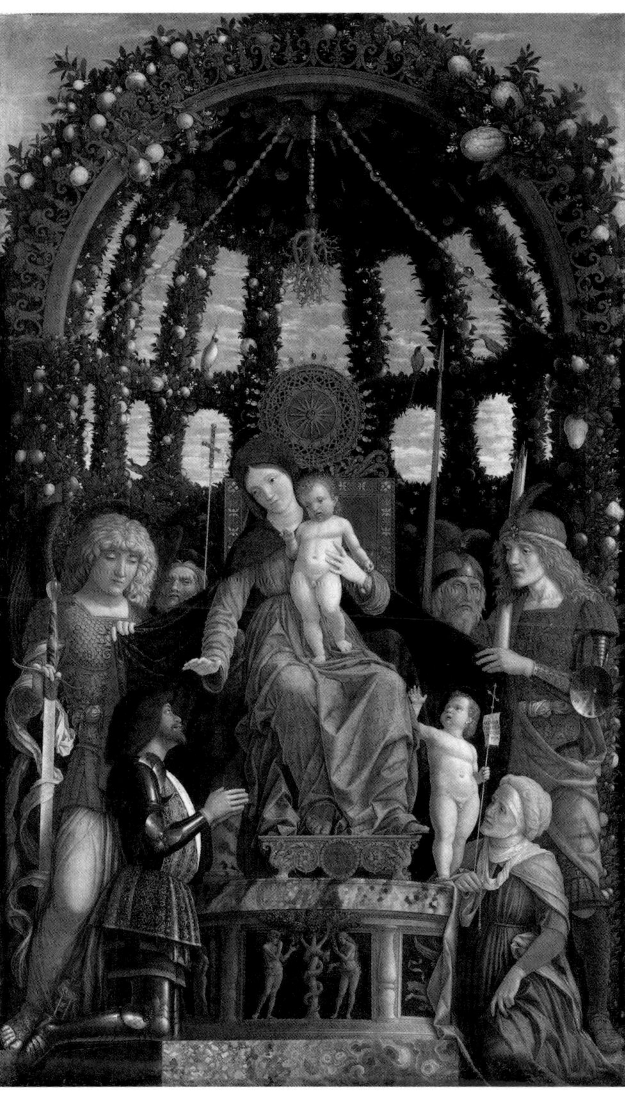

Above 157   Leonardo, Sala delle Asse, 1498–9, fresco, Milan, Sforza Castle

Right 158   Mantegna, *Madonna of the Victory*, 1495–6, tempera on canvas, 285 × 168 cm (112 × 66 in), Paris, Musée du Louvre

the dedication to virtue of the room's owner, Giovanna Piacenza, and the pursuit of precepts of timeless wisdom.

Almost totally unviewable until their rediscovery in 1774, exactly 250 years after Giovanna Piacenza's death (1524) and the enforcement of strict seclusion on the convent of San Paolo, Correggio's frescoes have never since lacked critical attention. Studies have been polarized under the rubric of the artist and his female patron, however, largely discounting the conventual tradition in which this paradigmatic painted chamber is rooted. Correggio's images are not peripheral representations of a secular culture staged in a convent space, nor did they occupy its margins. Rather, they reflect the ambiguous liminal identities of noble cloistered women, their learning, and paradoxical world, proposing a sensory experience that enchants and haunts the viewer. Twentieth-century scholarship has been concerned generally with decoding Correggio's images at the expense of interrogating

how they operate within the painted chamber and its wider monastic context. In his influential study on Correggio's murals, Erwin Panofsky demonstrated that they are tied to a sophisticated literary tradition, arguing passionately for the humanist foundation of their subjects. Panofsky's study was primarily a testing ground for his iconographic approach to the interpretation of Renaissance allegorical images.[4] Since Panofsky's contribution, other readings of Correggio's frescoes, informed by different methodological positions have been put forward, calling into question Panofsky's interpretation itself and, in general, the relation of Renaissance art to humanist culture. Ernst Gombrich advanced an explanation that centers on Giovanna Piacenza's blazon (the three crescents) and the figure of Diana on the fireplace with its heraldic correlation to the abbess.[5] Conversely, Maureen Pelta, Maurizio Calvesi, and Barry Collett have found religious content in Correggio's profane subjects.[6] Informed by

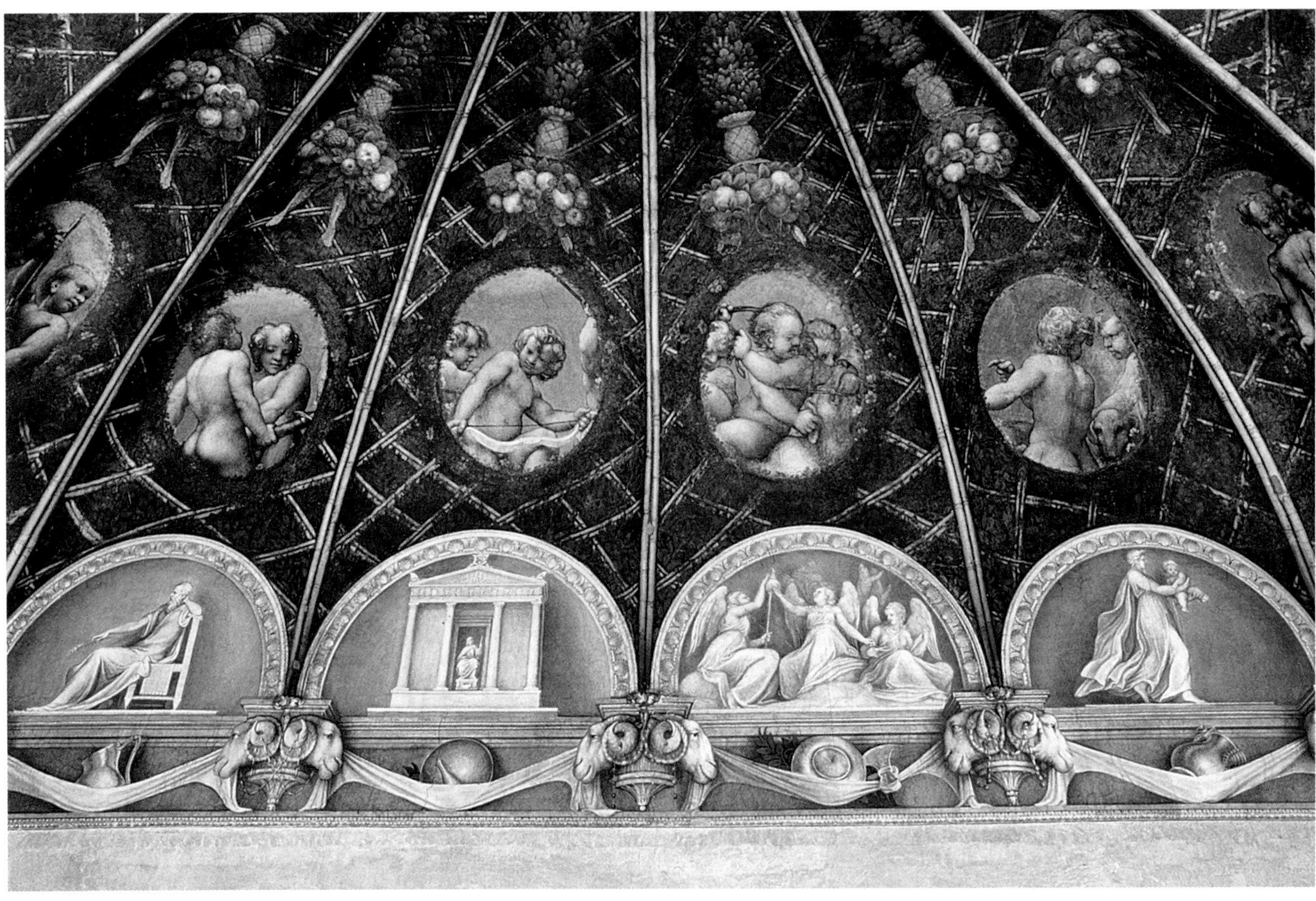

159   Correggio, south wall, ca. 1518–19, fresco, Parma, San Paolo

gender studies and reception theory, Regina Stefaniak and Alessandro Nova have related the frescoes to discourses of gaze and vision. Both scholars have re-evaluated the role of the beholder, whose emotional responses Correggio elicits through the appeal of his art. Stefaniak has argued for the intersection of the aggressive, piercing, and biting eyes represented in the room, associating the configuration of the gaze with the myth of Diana and Actaeon. She ultimately sees the ceiling as a "dense icon of remedies against the evil eye," stressing more the abbess's than the artist's viewpoint embedded in the decoration.[7] Nova has instead underlined the polysemic content of Correggio's images, recognizing that the opacity of the lunettes was intended almost to bemuse and impress the onlooker, reclaiming their centrality to the conception of this painted room.[8] Yet, the question of how Correggio's jocose and abstruse subjects work to make this painted chamber a meaningful whole, and the nature of the dialectical tension among its different visual components and their relations to discourses of virtue, irony, and enjoyment, still remain problematic.

There are structural differences between the higher and lower zones of Correggio's decoration and among its vertical, diagonal, and horizontal registers. The colored putti and the monochrome lunettes articulate a range of relationships and oppositions, juxtaposing and commenting on one another. The putti's luminous and beguiling appearance, as well as their sheer physicality in relation to the entirety of the room decoration, call to the viewer, demanding that he or she take a closer look. By contrast, the milky, intaglio-like *all'antica* lunettes and their enigmatic content perplex and disorientate, while the amused rams' heads below tease and tantalize any spectator who is intrigued and eager to understand the images overhead, expanding from Giovanna Piacenza's gilded stucco arms at the zenith of the room.[9] Notwithstanding the separate pictorial components, the spectator perceives the space as a unified ensemble. Scholars have wondered whether this unifying structure depends on the seductive forms that Correggio gave his subjects, or on the fact that the decoration is a projection of the persona of Abbess Giovanna Piacenza, or again, whether it should

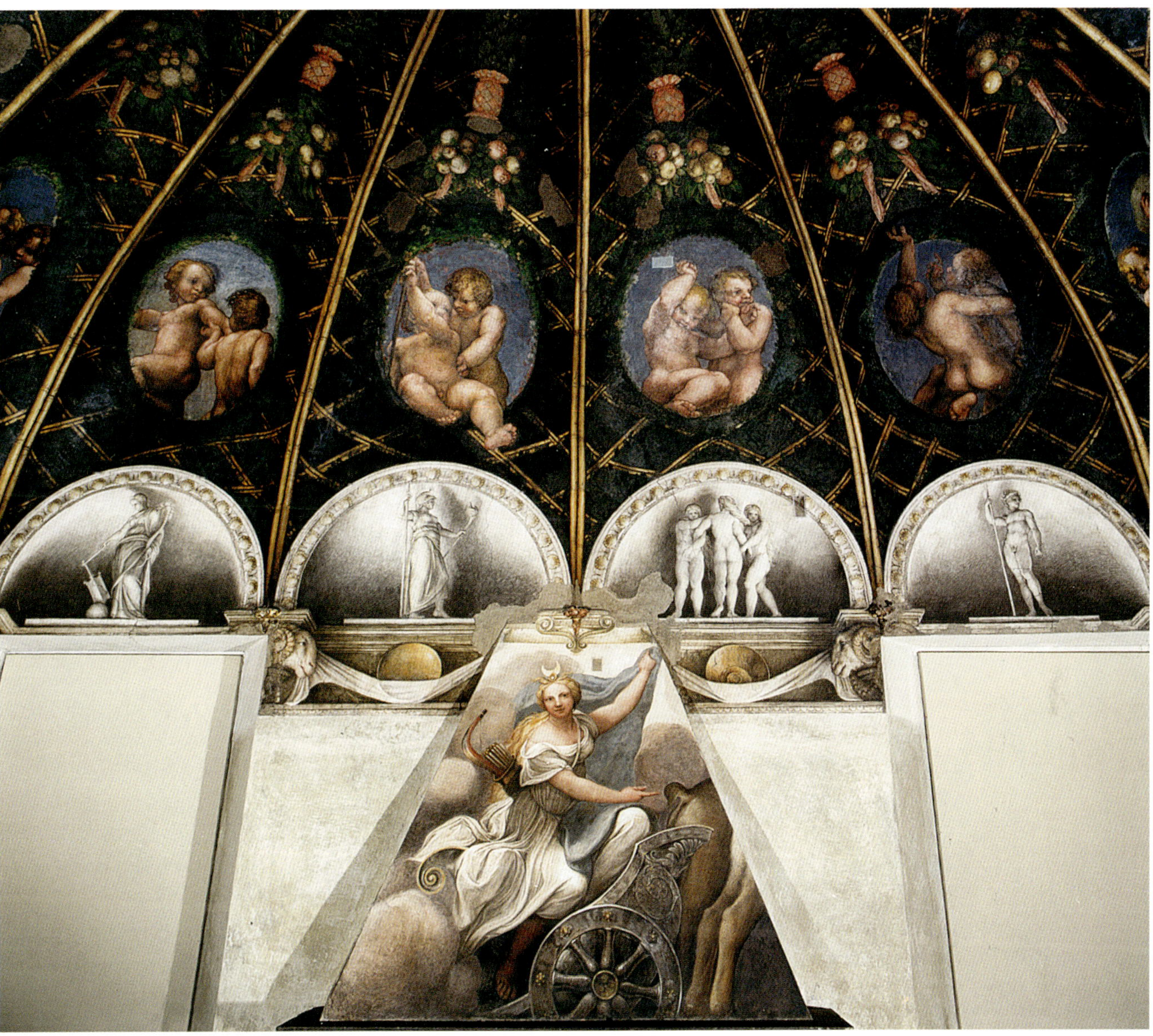

160   Correggio, north wall, ca. 1518–19, fresco, Parma, San Paolo

be seen as an extension of an adviser's intellectual output. Such queries can have no single answer, however, because what is at issue is a question of method itself. The adoption of an iconographic and (its partner) iconological method by Panofsky has advanced appreciation of the humanist foundation of Correggio's images. Yet, in this painted chamber that impinges lastingly on the audience's senses, a one-to-one assignment of a text to an image is insufficient to explain how its multiple visual components operate, demanding the mobile beholder's affective enactment and constantly evoking the presence of the abbess. The San Paolo painted chamber is as much a space uniquely created by Correggio's reinvention of his sources, as it is the materialization of the beliefs of the abbess and her conventual community. Ultimately, its value as a unified pictorial surface greatly exceeds the sum of its parts.

Beyond iconographic reinventions, Correggio also exercised an interpretative role through the forms he chose to use in order to capture the viewers' emotions, creating an appealing style of painting that has engaged historical and modern visitors. The images' sensual loveliness unifies the decoration but at the same time challenges the beholder to recover their open-ended communications. A tension lingers in this model of prolonged viewing enticed by the beauty

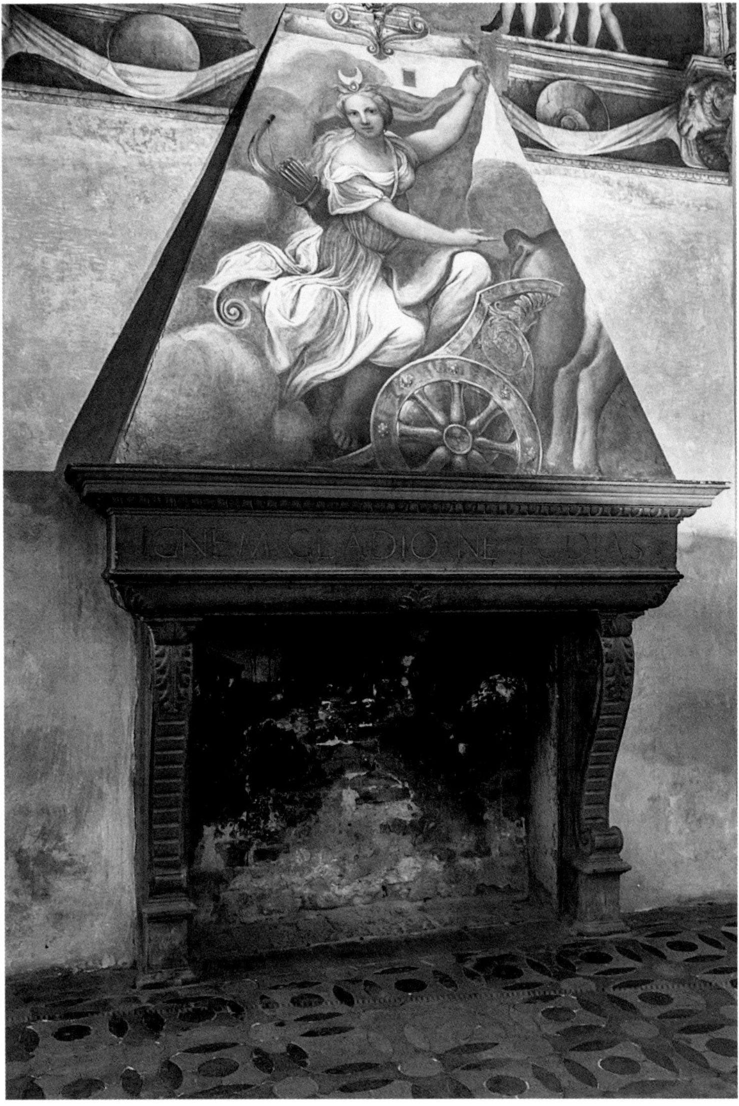

161   Correggio, *Diana*, ca. 1518–19, fresco, Parma, San Paolo

Gravitating around this majestic Diana is the cortege of sporting putti, who evoke the myth of the hunt through their various trophies and games. Both Diana and the putti embody the theme of the hunt that in the Renaissance stood as an ideal of poetic, intellectual, and spiritual pursuit for the attainment of virtue.[10] Two contemporaneous texts printed in Parma, Jacopo Caviceo's romance *Il Peregrino* (1508) and Nicholas of Cusa's philosophical writing *The Hunt for Wisdom* (*De Venatione Sapientiae* reprinted in 1502), revolve around the hunt. Caviceo turned the chase into a conceit for the pursuit of love by his protagonist, Peregrino. After numerous misadventures, including exposure to a conventual community in Ravenna where his beloved Genevera had found refuge, Peregrino enjoyed only momentary solace in his amorous hunt, because of Genevera's premature death. In contrast, in his *Hunt for Wisdom* Cusa takes the trope of the hunt to engage readers in a search for wisdom and the divine. Hunting in the form of observation and collection supplies the knowledge that transforms one superficial form of seeing into another, that is, a path for recognizing the invisible through the visible.[11] The hunting metaphor provides some keys to Correggio's representation of Diana and the putti, but these figures are mainly valued for their performance qualities, to rivet and enchant the viewer, ultimately making one's search for meaning revolve around discourses of levity and irony. Correggio's images propose an oscillation between paradigms of seriousness and lightness, sensory delight and intellectual engagement, letting the eyes be drawn away into the alluring world they depict. All in all, though, the hunt alone is insufficient to recover the full import of images that stage a spectacle for ambulatory viewers, whose gazes and movements complete the decoration and make it a living presence.

The eroticized Diana, the mocking putti, and the abstruse lunettes juxtapose pictorial modes that unfold into plural readings and ironic associations, introducing a sense of indeterminacy and concealment. This chapter is constructed around these tensions, positing that Correggio's decoration is about the power of the visual to teach, tease, and disorientate the onlooker, who is bound to it in affective and empathetic relationships. It confronts the images' iconographic instability and modalities of conveying messages, especially with reference to the historical audience's expectations. Beginning with the lightly clad huntress Diana, rendered with sensual flair and paired with the Pythagorean saying, it considers some of the responses that this goddess and the mischievous *spiritelli* in the garden bower unleash, drawing dynamic intersections between the images and

of art and its enigmatic, abstruse contents: our senses are captivated by the artist's tactile forms, but the sensations that ripen in our body can by distraction almost inhibit us from accessing what lies beneath, the latent meaning. On the one hand, the beholder is exposed to an aesthetic experience that demands sustained viewing and enactment. On the other hand, Correggio's exceptional, obscure, *all'antica* passages in the lunettes require and challenge informed beholders to bring out meaning by decoding subjects that are not univocally or transparently aligned to their signifiers. The sensual figure of Diana on the fireplace, the goddess of the hunt, is another case in point of this tension folded into the images.

beholders' concerns and in-motion viewing experiences. In a further step, the very opacity of the lunettes is inscribed within the Renaissance debate on *aenigmata* (enigmas) to see how it engages with ethical precepts (prudence and foresight, among others) enfolded with levity.

Correggio makes his subjects simultaneously abstruse and ironic, poetic and dense, opening up paths to contemplation and reflection, and turning them into pictorial *ludi* (games) with the power to affect and transport spectators beyond what is depicted in an "other space." His images can be seen as the visual counterparts of the poetic of the *serio-ludere*, which had a long history and modern incarnations in such writings as Cusa's *The Bowling Game* (*Ludo Globi*; 1502), Erasmus's *Adagia* (1508), *Praise of Folly* (1511), and *Colloquies* (1519 and 1533). These texts comment on key ethical topics of the Renaissance period using games and humorous stories and the paradoxical theme of the wise fool as teacher. Erasmus's texts in particular ridicule both those who take the things of this world too seriously and those who do not take them seriously enough, conveying sharp criticism of contemporary habits, mores, and institutions. These writings invite productive thinking, and pose a tension between apparent reality and its serious and ludic dimensions.[12] Whoever devised the themes of Correggio's images was a fine scholar well versed in classical literature and with a fondness for parodies, who composed subjects for a room devoted to the cultivation of virtue destined for reception by sophisticated nuns and their guests. Although no documentation has emerged to confirm it, the humanist Giorgio Anselmi with his many ties to the San Paolo convent court (Chapters Four and Five), is the most promising candidate as the ideator of the subjects.[13] In Correggio's interpretation, the room's thematics are treated in an obscure and playful way, ultimately giving back to the nuns the visual and tactile sensory pleasure paired with knowledge of mythological stories that monastic regulations deprived them of enjoying. The images also taught nuns ethical values through the pagan literature, proposing a renewed role of the profane in the sacred. Through these lenses, Giovanna's room can ultimately be viewed as a place of learning coupled with fun (*ludus litterarum*), proclaiming the exercise of pagan and Christian virtues with feminine levity.[14] As Elissa Weaver has discussed, early modern nuns staged theatrical performances within their *claustra*, shaping their own version of monastic fun.[15] Correggio's painted room reinvented that tradition of monastic performances to create the convent court of San Paolo, and simultaneously to turn it into a peak in the history of Italian Renaissance painting.

Whether or not he was aware of the modern styles of Raphael and Michelangelo in Rome, Correggio established his own vision of modern art in San Paolo, rivalling antiquity through an innovative and unique rethinking of artistic, courtly, and monastic traditions.

STUPOR, INTOXICATION, AND CHASTITY

Regardless of how Correggio's room is entered (that is, from the chapel to the northwest or the chamber frescoed by Araldi, or from the space connected with the cloister and the upstairs nuns' cells; see fig. 96), visitors are dumbfounded before his murals, which transform the act of looking into an experience of emotional perception and sensation. Leonard Barkan's comments on the elation produced by Correggio's painting in terms of his discovery "of a new Ovidianism that proceeds from an aesthetic investigation of the styles of his own art" points in a promising direction, but I would posit that the poetic origin of Correggio's artistic thinking lies elsewhere.[16] The artist's imagery is delightful to the point of enrapturing the spectator, evoking marvel, perplexity, and astonishment. In a long poem entitled *Stupori* whose poetic implications are closer to Correggio's pictorial achievements than has been thus far understood, Giorgio Anselmi personified these sensations in the figure of Stupor. Composed in imitation of Catullus's poem devoted to Attis, the Greek deity of vegetation, and narrating his madness, self-castration, and final surrender to the goddess Cybele, Anselmi's poem substitutes Stupor for Cybele, presented as the child of Night with a fawn-like appearance, whose worship brings numbness and astonishment to his followers. Stupor is described first as the motor of civilization, and its benefits in overcoming violence and war are extolled so that it is seen as a principle of the order of nature itself. In time, however, Stupor transforms into a god who provokes delirium and an intoxication of the senses. Developing ideas from Lucretius's *De Rerum Natura* and Politian's *Nutricia*, Anselmi portrays primitive life as coming to an end with the appearance of Stupor, whose seductive effects elicited from human beings a frenzied dance. Anselmi's poem attests its author's erudition in the narration of Stupor's multiple incarnations (a survey of classical mythology), but at the same time it also ends by bringing too many ideas into the mix, turning Stupor into Eros, Genius, and Chaos, and even into the maker of the Homeric Trojan Horse that bore the army into Troy. Despite the zigzags of Anselmi's poem, Stupor emerges as an engine of world civilization, but also as the cause of its apathy, and then of its descent into chaos. So it is no wonder that Anselmi ends his poem with a plea for Stupor to leave the poet in peace.[17] Although stylistically dry and lacking narrative clarity, Anselmi's poem and the personification of Stupor invited Parmese readers to reflect on the sensations of amazement and fascination, turning ecstatic transports into experiences with ambiguous outcomes. Anselmi and his German interlocutor Agrippa von Nettesheim knew well that fascination was associated with magic powers and that it could be used to generate positive or negative effects. There was risk involved in seeing a beautiful object, since fascination with certain materials and works was believed to permit malignant spirits to penetrate the body.[18] But here it is equally important to underline that the feeling of amazement and the power of seduction poetically embodied by Anselmi parallel Correggio's visual poetic in San Paolo and, although no simple correlation should be asserted, his frescoes in this monastic setting similarly propose stimulation and performance as crucial ingredients of the spectacle of painting. With its intermingled pictorial registers and figures and forms of impressive beauty, Correggio's painted room was designed to orchestrate sensation and impulses, locking the beholder into a mutual relationship.

If this doctrine of sensory seduction as education had a bearing on the conception of the decoration, there is no real beginning or end to the viewer's reception of the spectacle staged in the chamber. Panofsky insisted that the frescoes on the western wall constitute a starting point for decoding the murals, but his suggestion is not convincing in that the onlooker is captivated by Correggio's images along multiple directional axes all at once, and simultaneously asked to interact with them.[19] Whichever access route taken and images first encountered, the figure of the huntress Diana over the fireplace, both for its large scale and prominent location, dominates the space. Often interpreted as an allegorical figure of the abbess herself, as the crescents (a primary attribute of Diana) constituted the abbess's arms, Diana replaces the heraldic devices that traditionally adorned Renaissance fireplaces. Differently from Mantegna, in whose Camera Picta the fireplace wall is merged into his narrative, Correggio treats the chimney hood as a distinct site, most probably adhering to advice by the architect Filarete. Translated into Latin for Matthias Corvinus in around 1488–9 with the possible assistance of Taddeo Ugoleto, Filarete's *Trattato di Architettura* recommends decorating chimney-pieces with their own separate ornament, such as the nar-

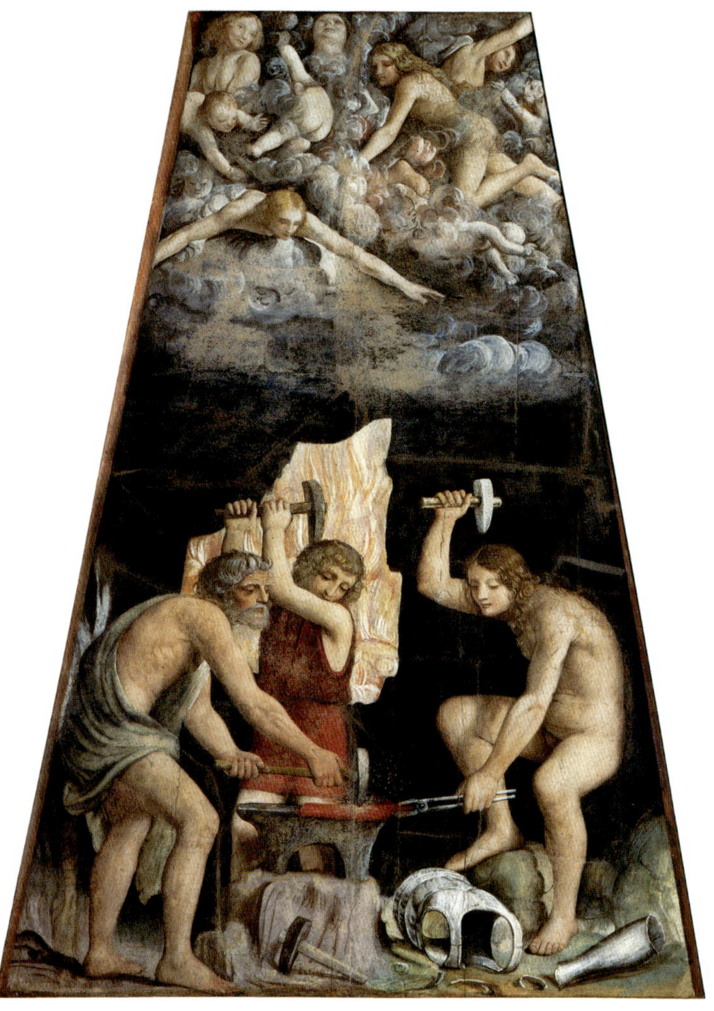

162   Bernardino Luini, *Venus at the Forge of Vulcan*, ca. 1513–14 or ca. 1520–21, fresco transferred on panel, 240 × 163 cm (94$^{31}/_{64}$ × 64$^{11}/_{64}$ in), Milan, Pinacoteca di Brera

rative of Tubal-Cain and Vulcan, an apt subject for the location.[20] Filarete's advice resonated well with the Lombard artist Bernardino Luini, who portrayed *Venus at the Forge of Vulcan* (variously dated ca. 1513–14 to ca. 1520–21; fig. 162) over the fireplace of a room in Girolamo Rabia's Villa Pelucca outside Milan.[21]

The trapezoidal hood in Giovanna Piacenza's chamber features a full-scale eroticized Diana paired with the inscribed Pythagorean aphorism. If the abbess wanted to be seen as a virile, nubile woman exercising power, Diana, a goddess whose authority lies in her athletic chastity, is the fitting representation (fig. 163). Diana seems to have power over the frolicking putti above her, as if they are the substitutes for her usual cortège of nymphs. But Correggio rendered Diana as a sensual figure, exalting her feminine

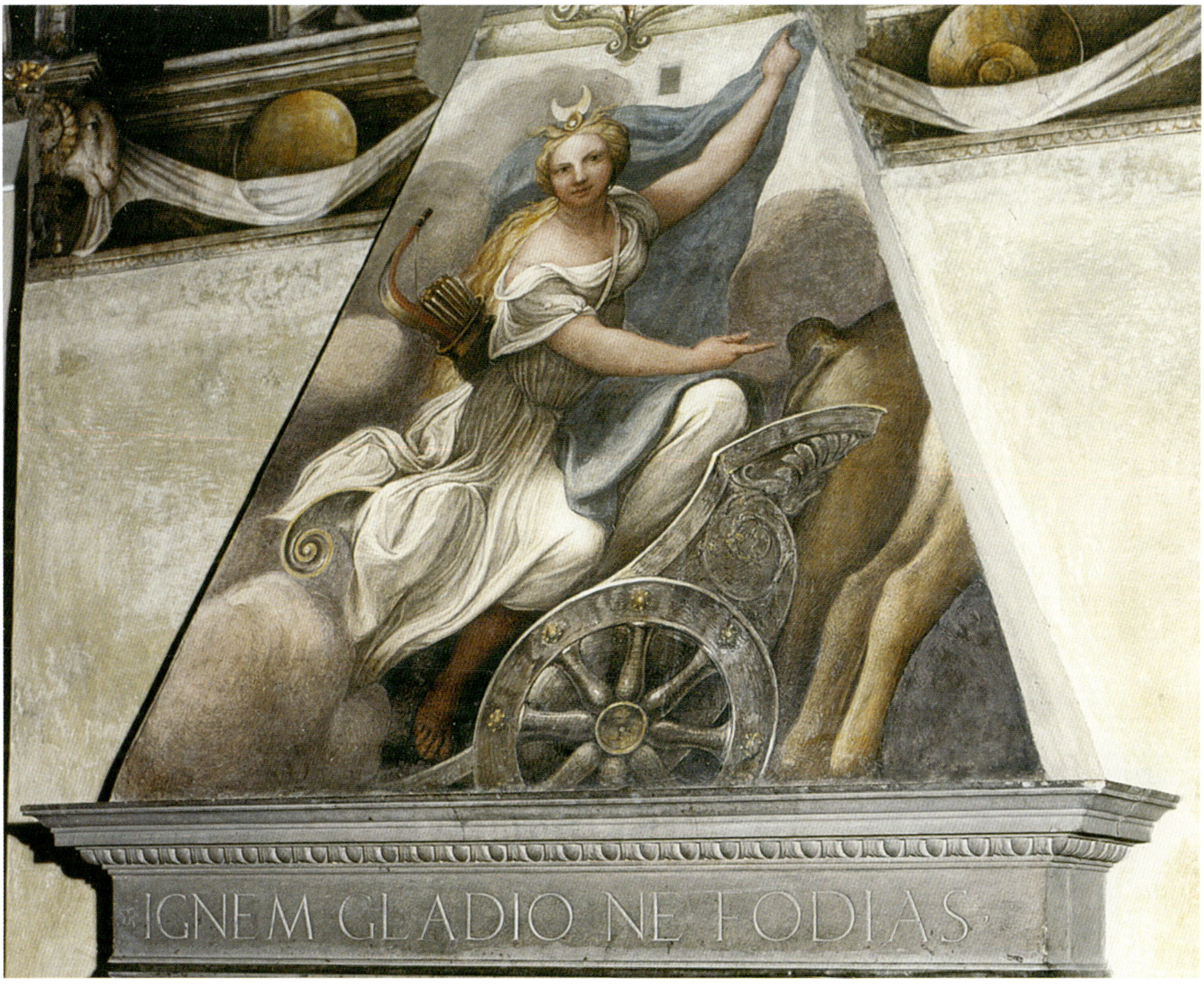

163   Correggio, *Diana* and the inscription on the mantelpiece below, ca. 1518–19, fresco, Parma, San Paolo

appeal and charm by means of her warm skin tones and a generous décolletage that even exposes an undergarment's lace. This may seem perplexing for a figure that has a heraldic relationship with and temperamental parallel to the abbess herself. But interpretations of this sexualized Diana may have diverged depending on the gender of its historical viewers. As Caroline Walker Bynum observed, late medieval male authors defined women as virile when they renounced the world, made religious progress, or exercised power, while female writers of the same period referred to themselves or their peers in similar circumstances either as androgynous or female.[22] Men writing about women assumed that their spiritual conversion and perfected state were accompanied by a sort of gender reversal, making them virile. Instead, women saw their peers' experiences

differently: no renunciation of femininity was implicit in the exercise of virtue. In sum, Correggio's eroticized Diana could stand for the embodiment of virtue and authority from a female perspective, and was indeed, created for a community of nuns.[23]

A full-bodied, voluptuous figure on a double-wheeled chariot with long blond hair bound only at the nape of her neck, Diana is presented in a short white gown that bares her right shoulder, further exposing most of her arms, a lower leg, and an unshod foot. These features adhere to the description of the goddess in Claudian's *De Raptu Proserpinae* (The Abduction of Proserpina), a poem included in Claudian's corpus reprinted in Parma under Ugoleto's aegis in 1493.[24] The bow and quiver, Diana's customary attributes, are slung over her back, while the crescent moon at the

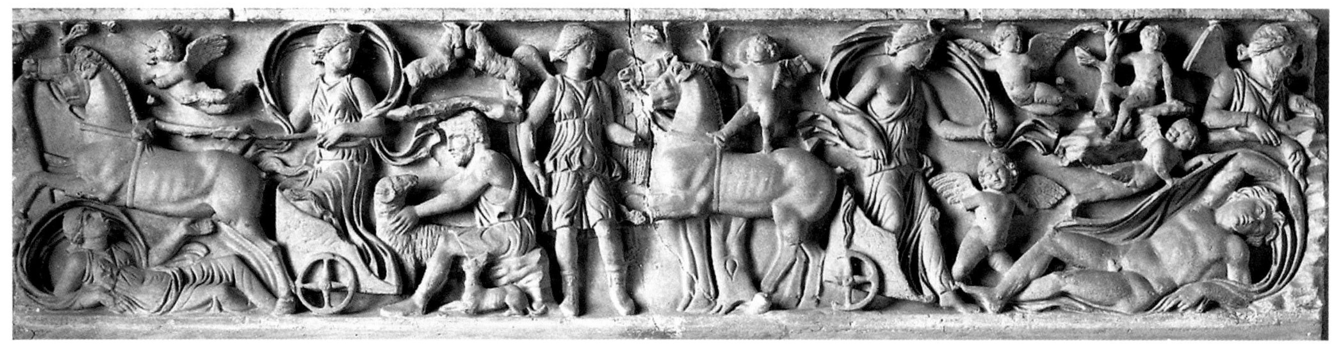

164   Roman sarcophagus, Diana on a chariot, 3rd century, Mantua, Palazzo San Sebastiano

crown of her head rises from an open shell embellished by a shining pearl. Seated *contrapposto* with her legs bent and her body turned three-quarters to our right, Diana looks over her right shoulder to gaze directly out at the spectator while raising her knee as if to dismount from or perhaps to remount her chariot. With her raised left hand she spreads out a windblown blue veil behind her, amid soft, vaporous clouds, while with her right index finger she points toward or past the hind legs of the horse pulling her vehicle. That gesture could be taken almost literally as an invitation to leave the room, since her finger points toward the door to Araldi's painted chamber. In his reinvention of Diana, the artist either adhered to the textual tradition (Claudian's description) or, as suggested by Corrado Ricci, drew inspiration from ancient sarcophagi reliefs featuring the sleeping Endymion and the enamored Diana on her chariot, with winged putti, and shepherds (fig. 164).[25] Roman sarcophagi reliefs, revetment plaques, and other fragments of the past were routinely copied by Renaissance artists, and it is probable, though virtually impossible to determine with certainty, that both the textual and the visual traditions contributed to Correggio's formulation.

One conspicuous detail in this alluring Diana image, namely, her gesture of pulling across the blue veil, is particularly telling, as it denotes the fusion of Diana with Luna, the moon goddess, a conflation with a long poetic history summarized in Lilio Gregorio Giraldi's *De Deis Gentium Varia et Multipla Historia* (1548).[26] As virgins, Diana and Luna, one active during the day and the other at night, have features in common, and their conventional appearance is indebted to Claudian's text. Catullus's ode to Diana (*Carmen Dianae*, included in the edition published in Parma under Francesco Puteolano's aegis in 1473), describes one goddess turning into the other.[27] Anselmi's own *Hymn of Diana* merges Catullus's and Claudian's descriptions, and it

enumerates the goddess's spheres of influence and her manifestations as Ilithyia (the Roman Lucina), Hecate (Trivia, the goddess of sorcery), and Luna.[28] In the final invocation, Anselmi calls on Diana to calm the turmoil of his own time, subsuming the coming of Luna in his request. Correggio's visual conflation of Diana-Luna can ultimately be seen to herald the coming of night, the time of meditation, silence, and speechless wonder, into the abbess's room. Nightfall, in turn, offers a clue about the function of the chamber as a bedroom.

In the Renaissance, bedrooms were retreats from the noise of public life, spaces for leisure, recreation, and the restoration of the inner self. They served, it is known, as multifunctional spaces reserved not only for sleep, but also for meetings, business, and cultural activities.[29] Mary Carruthers's discussion of what she calls the "mystery of the bedroom" further provides a context for the memory work enhanced in such intimate spaces, arguing that monastic bedrooms were

> associated with the bridal chamber of the Song of Songs. And while all the sexual associations of fertility and fruitfulness resonated in this bedroom mystery, its goal [was] cognitive creation, and its matrix [was] the secret places of one's mind, the matters secreted away in the inventory of memory, stored and recalled, collated and gathered up, by the "mystery" or craft of mnemotechnical invention.[30]

Dominating the decoration, Correggio's Diana-Luna solicits viewers' productive and imaginative thinking and, simultaneously, engagement with the other subjects in the lunettes that evoke themes of chastity, prudence, and female power (on which more later), recombining and shuffling their messages into chains of associations and paths of intensified perception and feeling.

Correggio's sensual Diana, it is fair to posit, invites subjective confrontation and mystical transport that would not be dissimilar from those mentioned in a letter from the Ferrarese humanist Gaspare Sardi in 1548 when describing his feelings of joy at gazing on the precious, fine objects that his friend Agostino Righini kept in his well-furnished chamber. Sardi's two dense Latin lines read: "contemplari suavissimaque cum admiratione oculis collustrare; animo inbibere; pectori infingere; cordique adserere" (to contemplate [the works] with the most gentle admiration is to illuminate the eyes; to imbibe [them] in your soul; to fix them in your heart and to sow them in your spirit).[31] The sequence of verbs used by Sardi – *contemplari* (to contemplate), *collustrare* (to illuminate), *imbibere* (to imbibe), *infingere* (to impress), and *adserere* (to sow) – mirrors the chain of emotions provoked in the body by the objects. First the eyes are caught and illuminated by the works, after which feelings flood the body, and are transferred to the mind and the heart in a circuit of perception and stimulation, sight and insights, turning the contemplation of art into a therapy for the soul. Sardi's comments provide a positive assessment of the experience of viewing beautiful art, pointing to its gentle admiration and prolonged seeing in intimate spaces as tools of a synaesthetic experience that, as will be considered next, nonetheless required caveats given the vulnerability of the body in looking. Specifically instructed not to search for learning and pleasure through their eyes, nuns were particularly at risk for what they might see around and above themselves.

The real danger of art as an enhancement of pleasure and as a source of empathetic feelings is stressed in the pairing of the Diana representation with the Pythagorean aphorism *Ignem gladio ne fodias* (Stir not the fire with a sword) carved on the mantelpiece. This ensemble forms a visual–verbal construct that was theorized as an emblem in the following decade, anticipating a genre of text–image interactions that Andrea Alciato treated in his *Emblematum Liber* (1531). As far as Pythagorean utterances are concerned, during the fifteenth century they were thought to be gnomic precepts (also known as *symbola*) intelligible only to the initiated. Over the sixteenth century, Filippo Beroaldo's *Symbola Pythagorae Moraliter Explicata* (1500) and Erasmus's *Adagia* – two texts that arrange *symbola* under commonplace headings and explicate them – were widely used as textbooks, and thus Pythagoras's sayings became familiar to a wider audience. While Politian made fun of Pythagoras's maxims, Beroaldo and Erasmus took them seriously as precepts for conducting an ethical life.[32]

Traversing the history of the Pythagorean precept, Erasmus in his 1508 edition connects the aphorism *Ignem gladio ne fodias* with the virtue of prudence, treating it as a warning against provoking the wrath of powerful or angry men, "for the more the fire is stirred the stronger it grows."[33] Erasmus adds that the saying could be intended to caution against futile actions. A wise person is invited not to choose a tool inappropriate to the task at hand, or else risk unexpected, even unpleasant, consequences, and to observe suitable behavior and a careful choice of words, which might mean communicating in a veiled fashion or through arcane sayings. One of the cardinal virtues, prudence was indeed necessary for guiding the abbess's words and actions when religious authorities attempted to enforce enclosure on her convent, and to put an end to her lifetime office. To define Giovanna Piacenza's aggressive defense of the independence of her institution in terms of prudence might appear paradoxical to us today. But the exercise of prudence could imply firm and decisive actions against one's opponents, as described in Castiglione's *Book of the Courtier* (which was circulated in manuscript form long before its publication in 1528).[34] As John Martin has aptly observed, prudence could also prompt the cultivation of a certain discretion with regard to one's own convictions, an ambiguity that might lead to dissimulation. As a foil to the control of emotions, dissimulation became a means to disassociate outer behaviors from inner feelings, promoting the governance of the body and the mind.[35]

The Diana imagery and the Pythagorean saying can appear to us as an admonition to refrain (prudently) from intruding in the convent's business: after all, the virgin huntress Diana was a combative, punitive goddess. But further, the visual–verbal ensemble over the fireplace stresses the meditative approach that the night brings to contingent concerns, while asserting the abbess's own example of prudence. Likewise in Araldi's adjacent room, the Pythagorean precept encapsulates a lighter dimension with its wordplay of the Latin *ignem* (fire) with its placement above the actual fire. Or in the play between the Latin *gladio* (sword) and the sword represented behind the shield with Giovanna Piacenza's gilded arms at the top of the ceiling (fig. 165). A symbol of the abbess's legitimate, juridical power over her convent, the sword functions as a visual cue, reinforcing the meaning of the inscription below and the abbess's potential investment in its truth: it is a proclamation of authority interwoven with the pursuit of virtue and associated with discourses of play. These parameters of doubling, reversal, and irony around and about the eroticized, prudent, chaste,

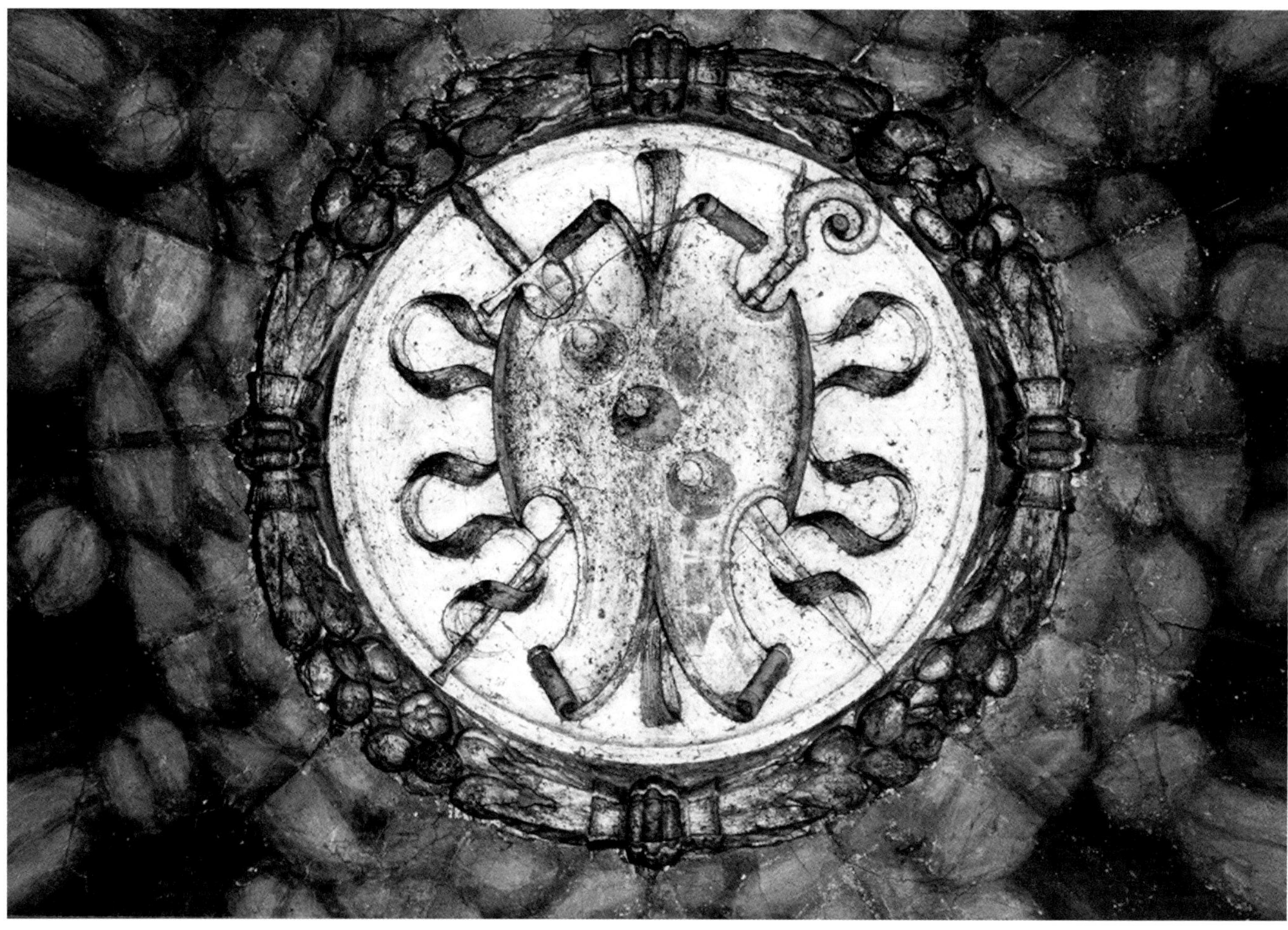

165   Correggio, Giovanna Piacenza's *stemma*, ca. 1518–19, gilt stucco, Parma, San Paolo

and punitive Diana over the fireplace must be emphasized. They create intriguing dynamics between being and imagining, reality and its appearance, making the identity of the painted room's owner, Abbess Giovanna Piacenza, more fluid and ambiguous than it may at first appear. No doubt the verbal–visual construct over the fireplace struck and intrigued onlookers, who would have been likewise captivated by the sensuous putti above in the vault, intruding into our space with their games, some of whom stare down at the visitors and thus demand a return of their gaze.

PARODY AND THE PICTORIAL LUDUS

Sixteen portholes opening to the sky puncture the lush foliage and fruit over the reed trellis of the vault bower, exposing life-size infants illuminated as if by brilliant sun-light, and bound together in a sequence by their interrelated actions. They exist in a natural environment on the exterior of the fictive bower, which they vivify with their joyous wrestling and frolicking, mimicking ancient rituals, playing musical instruments, embracing dogs, and carrying weapons of the hunt. Given their life-size scale and "real life" activities, these *spiritelli* apparently inhabit the same spatial and temporal dimension as do we, the viewers. Correggio studied their postures, attitudes, and games in preparatory drawings, only a single sheet of which survives, the sole evidence of the thinking that went into the invention of the putti. Dating to 1518–19 and squared for transfer, the drawing depicts three infants in an oval (fig. 166): a putto at the center holds a shield embossed with a Medusa's head toward which the other two infants gaze. The sheet has long been considered a final preparatory drawing connected to the figures in one of the eastern ovals, though in the fresco (see fig. 167), Correggio modified the arrangement of the

178

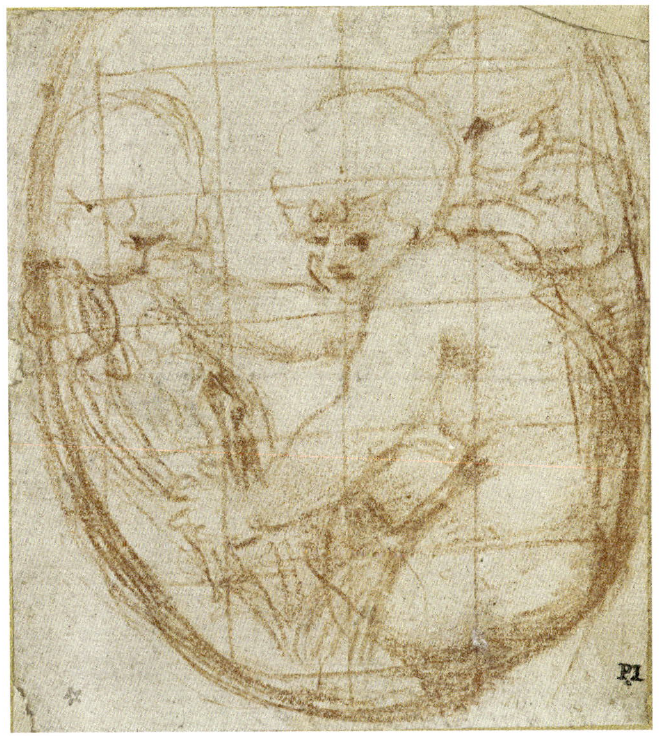

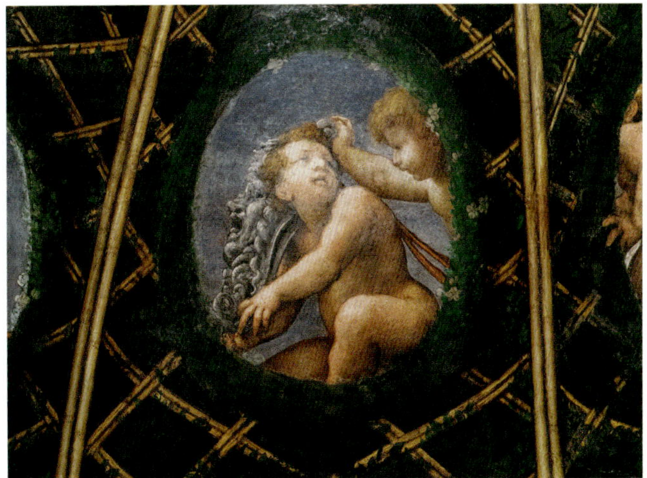

Left 166   Correggio, three putti in an oval, 1518–19, red chalk, 10.8 × 9.4 cm (4$^{1}/_{4}$ × 3$^{4}/_{6}$ in), London, Trustees of the British Museum

Above 167   Correggio, oval with putti, ca. 1518–19, fresco, Parma, San Paolo

central putto and reversed the shield.[36] However, rather than a final drawing, as Hugo Chapman has correctly posited, Correggio's sheet is probably an intermediate study that the artist made and squared up to develop his composition, ultimately refining his figures to achieve the pleasing circularity of the children on the vault.[37]

Although they are the result of meditated reflections, Correggio's children are immediate, fresh, and palpable figures. Modeled in pink tonalities, they are remarkable for their fleshy and vigorous physicality, cunning gazes, windswept hair, and endearing poses, many of which include exposing their buttocks to the viewer below. Set in pairs or trios in each oval, the putti interact with one another by means of gesture and action, staging a carefree parade of unending games of which the spectator gets only a tantalizing glimpse. In an oval on the east wall (fig. 168 and see fig. 172), a *spiritello* with its back turned walks away, only to reappear in the adjacent opening with a teasing gaze and caressing gesture toward his companion carrying the Medusa shield. Another putto in *profil perdu* on the north wall (see fig. 160) leans dangerously backward to pick fruit from a high bough, his partner guiding him from behind to indicate the best fruit; meanwhile, the naughty neighboring infant is about to throw something at the onlooker below, while his indifferent pair gazes with perplexity in the opposite direction. Another sits on the oval frame, shamelessly

exposing his genitals (fig. 169), while his companion's touching gesture attracts curious onlookers below to the infantile male sexual organ. Correggio's putti do not fail to beguile and amuse at every turn. In a densely populated oval, one of the *spiritelli* sits backward astride a mastiff that he heroically muzzles to keep it from attacking a terrified dog in the next oval (fig. 170; see fig. 159). Another porthole sports a pair of putti (fig. 171) the foremost of whom triumphantly raises a stag's head as a trophy of the hunt (and perhaps a reminder of the unfortunate Actaeon). In total, nine putti carry hunting weapons, while others hold or blow horns. Among the remaining *spiritelli*, several poke fun at ancient rites, showing symbols of love such as a wreath of flowers, while three have no specific attributes.

On the east wall, one putto wears a yellow mantle (the only one with a piece of clothing) and a gold crown, which his companion adjusts (fig. 172). Atop the crown is a massive rock identified by Panofsky as the *lapis manalis*, a meteoritic stone that the Romans used during the *aquaelicium*, the ritual invoking rain in times of drought.[38] From its repository in Rome near the Temple of Mars, the concave stone was dragged to the altar of Jupiter Elicius and drenched with water as a rite of sympathetic magic to make the heavens open. The double irony here is that instead of the highest Roman priest, an infant masquerading as a god performs this ceremony, and the *spiritello* in

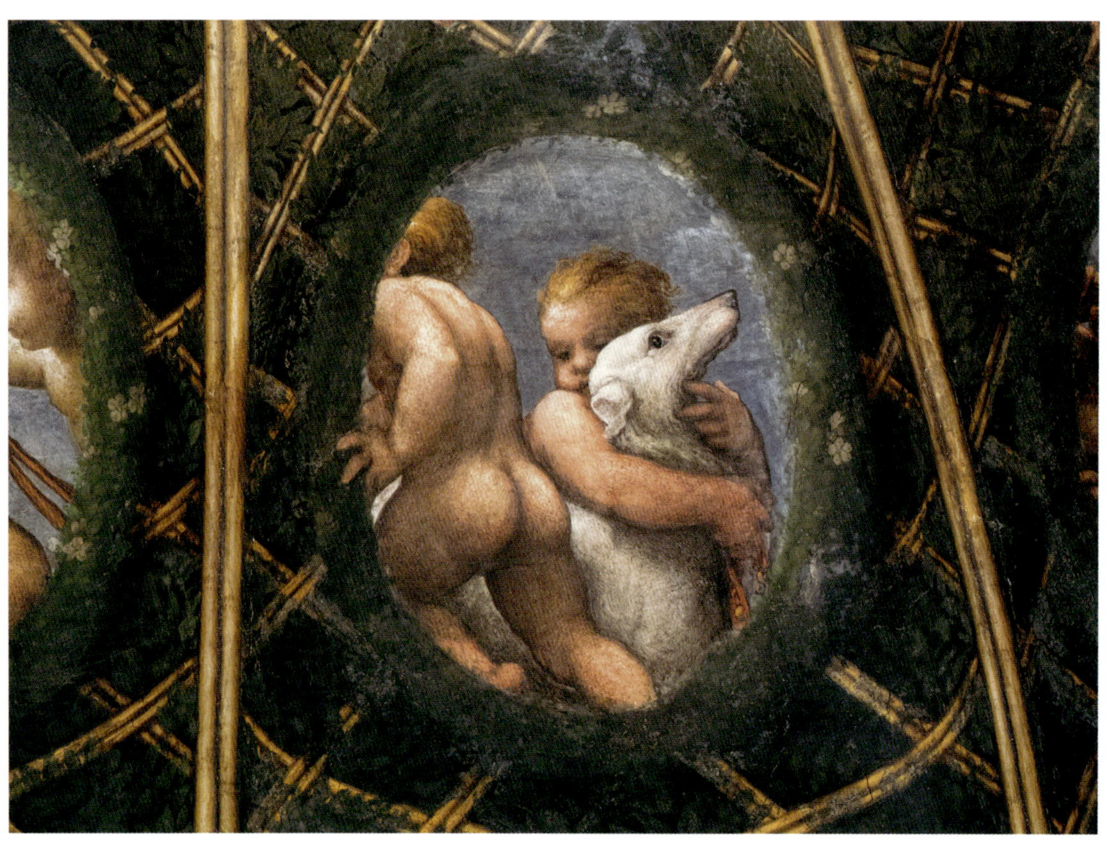

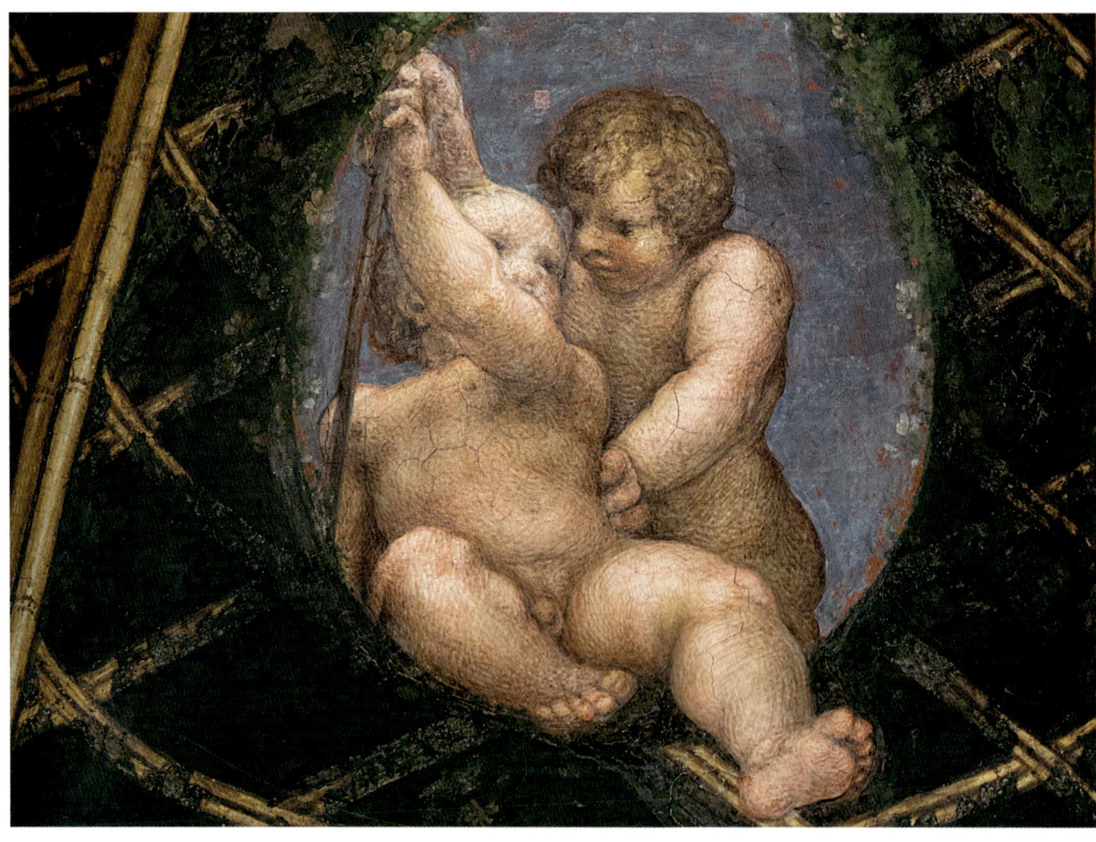

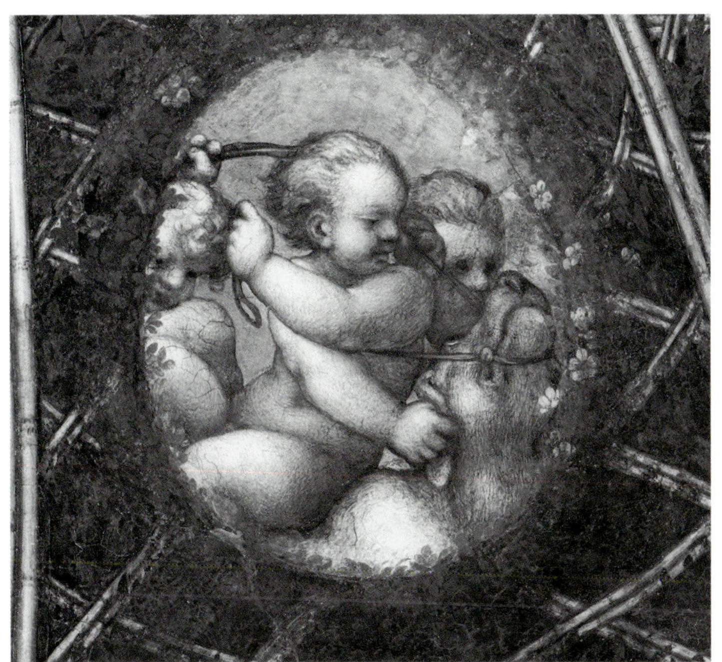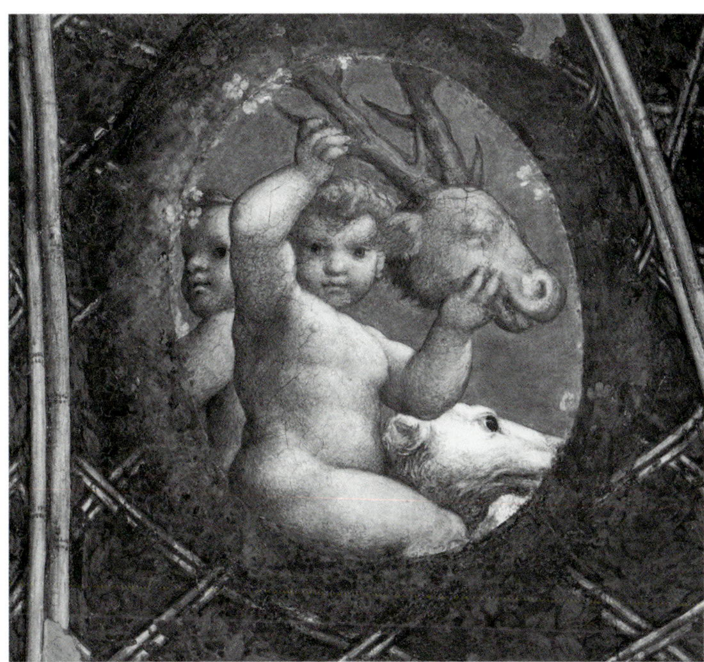

Facing page 168, 169   Correggio, ovals with putti, ca. 1518–19, fresco, Parma, San Paolo

This page 170, 171, 172   Correggio, ovals with putti, ca. 1518–19, fresco, Parma, San Paolo

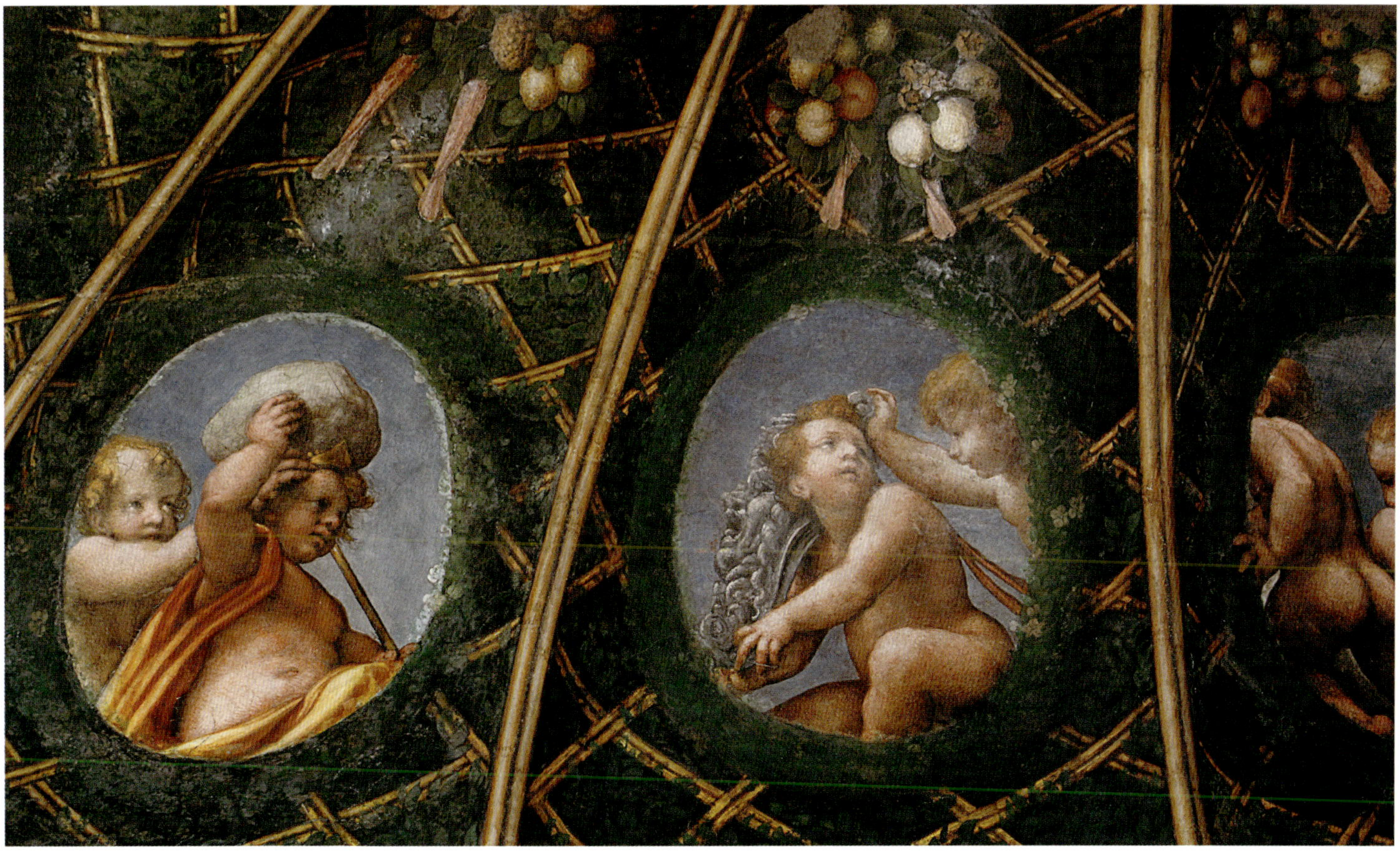

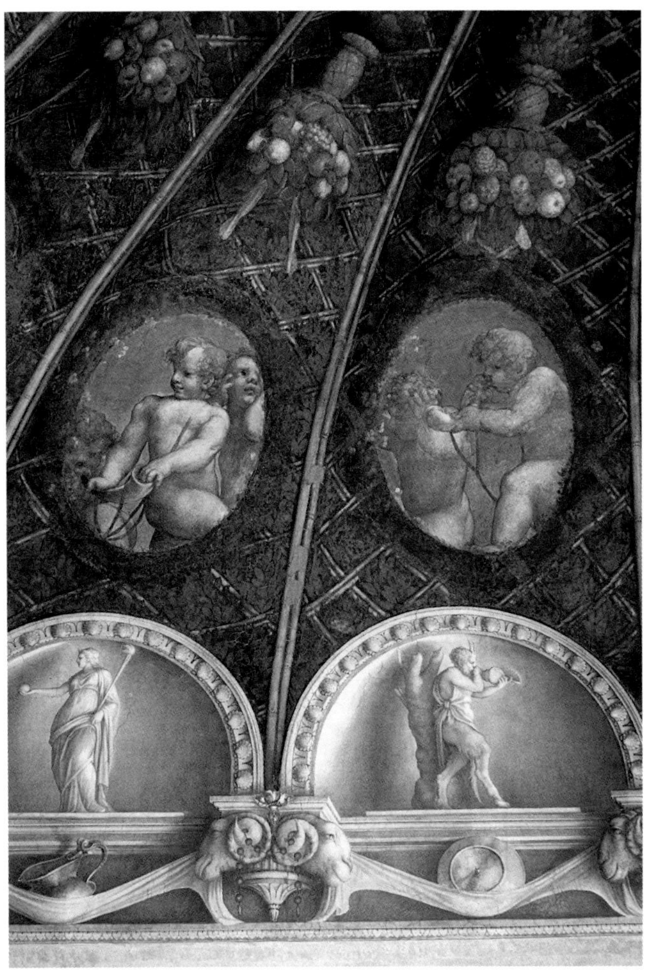

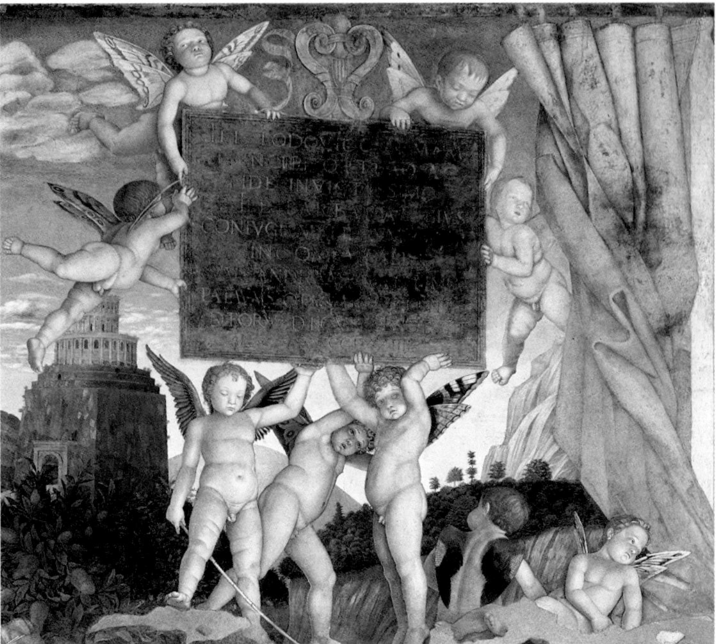

Left 173   Correggio, lunettes and putti on the west wall, ca. 1518–19, fresco, Parma, San Paolo

Above 174   Mantegna, putti carrying a dedicatory plaque, ca. 1465–74, fresco, Mantua, Palazzo Ducale

the adjacent oval proceeds toward him with the Medusa shield. It is as if Medusa's power to turn onlookers into stone may also nonsensically petrify the magic stone, annulling or ridiculing the rainmaking rite. With similar irony, some of the putti mimic – thereby burlesquing – the actions staged in the lunettes below (fig. 173), as in the case of the *spiritello* blowing a horn so forcefully that his companions, even those in the next oval, cover their ears, a witty notation on Pan blowing the conch in the lunette below (on which more later) and almost a burlesque on Araldi's horn-blowing putti in the adjacent room. The same humorous commenting characterizes the infant ready to shoot an arrow (see fig. 159; in Italian, *saetta*, which also means a "bolt of lightning," as Panofsky recognized), which is found above the lunette featuring Jupiter seated before his Capitoline Temple.[39]

Long before Correggio, putti had been recognized as carriers of meaning and vehicles for ironic commentary. Miniaturized *eroti* playing instruments, fighting with each other, and mocking warriors' actions appear on twelfth-

century Byzantine ivory caskets.[40] Closer to Correggio's time, Mantegna's winged putti fill the oculus of his Camera Picta and hold up the plaque declaring his artistic greatness (fig. 174). Descendants of Mantegna's infants, like those painted by Araldi, Correggio's *spiritelli* are, however, his own creations, exuding an erotic appeal and joyous optimism absent in those of Mantegna, and which radiate into the room below. The young Parmigianino saw and studied these remarkable *eroti* in around 1519 when his uncle was paid for work in San Paolo (see Chapter Three), translating them into the mischievous winged infants who inhabit the Sanvitale painted chamber (fig. 175). Correggio's erotic putti have their legacy in his own *ephebi* in the dome of Parma Cathedral (1530–34) and they also seem to resonate in the infants painted by Lorenzo Lotto on the beams supporting the ceiling of the Suardi oratory (ca. 1524; fig. 176) in Trescore (Bergamo). Lotto's putti offer grapes and urinate on the viewer, while populating the vine pergola that emanates from Christ's hands on the lateral wall. Symbols of regenerative life, these *spiritelli*, interspersed by scrolls

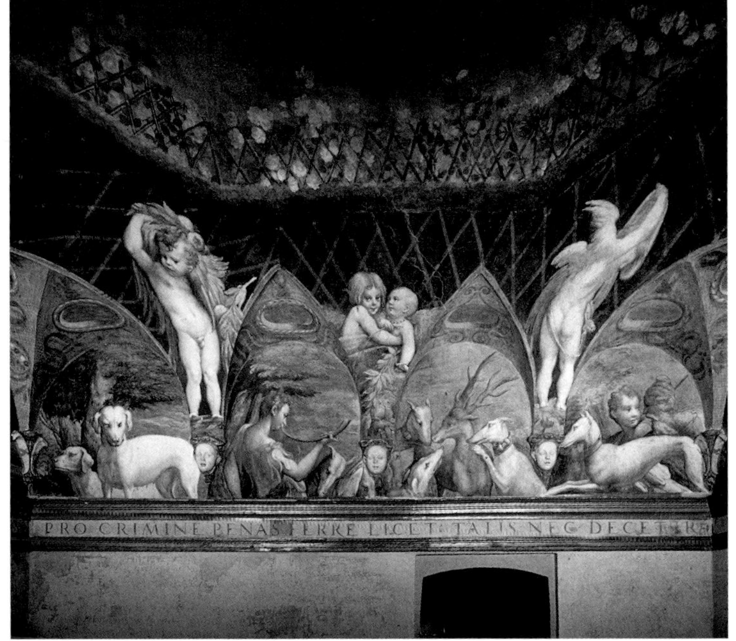

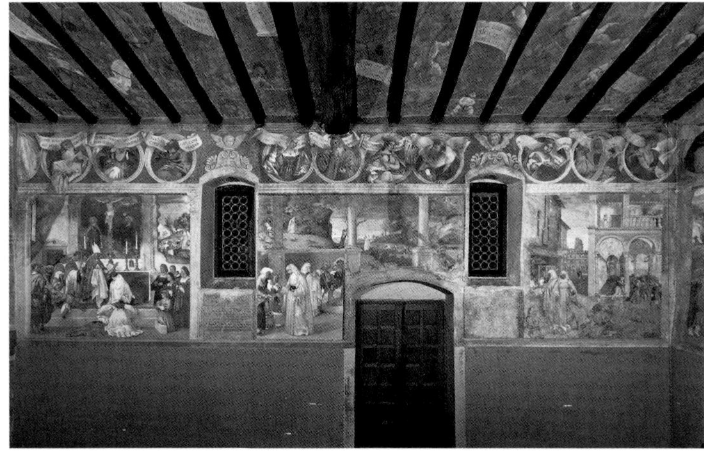

Left 175   Parmigianino, story of Diana and Actaeon, detail, ca. 1523–4, fresco, Fontanellato, Rocca Sanvitale

Above 176   Lorenzo Lotto, putti in the Suardi oratory, ca. 1524, fresco, Trescore (Bergamo)

with biblical inscriptions, have been interpreted as invitations to meditate on the Eucharistic theme of the decoration.[41] Similarly, Correggio's jocular creatures draw viewers' eyes upward and sustain their gaze through the force of their loveliness, vigorous carnality, and childish excitement. It is easy to imagine that these rambunctious babies compelled their historical female religious audience to transgress the monastic precept of lowered eyes to absorb such aesthetic delight, and, after sating their senses, also encouraged them to reflect on the more demanding portions of the room's ornament.

Yet more can be said about Correggio's putti. As Charles Dempsey has argued, putti were believed during the Renaissance to be sprites with the power to move the mind, carrying and transmitting feelings (love, awe, fear, and joy, among others).[42] They came to personify "any of those many different impulses that affect the body without conscious bidding, unwilled by the intellect. These impulses and sensations are caused by volatile, airy spirits that enter the body through such sensory organs as the eyes . . . or ears" and which are then transferred to the intellect.[43] Correggio's putti affect our feelings through their carnality and insistent eye contact, eliciting merriment and giddiness as if through sympathetic magic, so that we assimilate what is painted in our own feelings. As the Bolognese artist Annibale Carracci recognized around 1580 on viewing Correggio's *ephebi* in the dome of Parma Cathedral, they "breathe, live, and laugh with such grace and truth" that they induce us "to laugh and to feel happy along with them."[44] It has recently been argued that this sensory stimulation binding the viewer to what is represented overhead was excluded from Alberti's theorization of perspective as the paradigm for Renaissance painting.[45] The creation of painted chambers requiring the projection of three-dimensional illusionistic imagery onto curved surfaces with multiple viewpoints in order to accommodate mobile spectators looking up from different angles and in a process of evolving understanding, brought sensitive artists like Correggio to reflect on the broad implications of vision, subjective perception, and the medial nature of painting.[46] As the master of illusionism that he became through his spectacular dome paintings, Correggio first faced the question of peripatetic looking up and the potential psychological effects of painting on a spectator in the small, intimate chamber of San Paolo: he proposes a spatial and a synaesthetic experience engaging sight, hearing, and touch, turning life-size carnal and playful *spiritelli* into crucial components of his decoration. Figures of ironic possibilities foreshortened to make them seem real, they draw us to return to them continuously: their soft forms playing across the curved surface trigger a sense of closeness to them, appealing directly to our eyes and ears while simultaneously frustrating our sense of touch. They bring to life within the chamber the world of earthly physicality and of the senses, co-opting the viewer as an audience for their droll performances. Prohibited from seeking pleasure except in God, elite nuns made their eyes vehicles for accessing

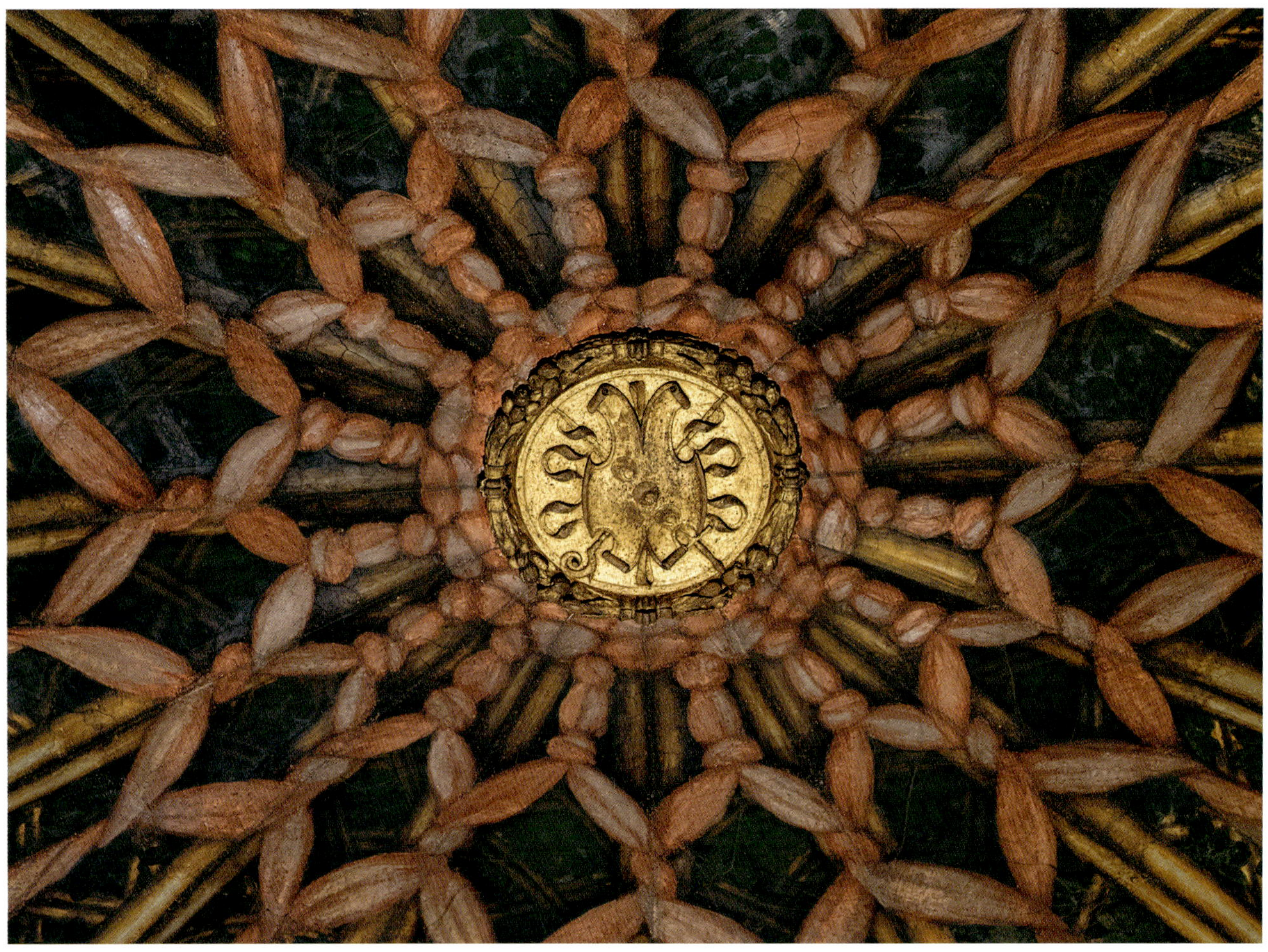

177 Correggio, Giovanna Piacenza's *stemma* and surrounding decoration, ca. 1518–19, gilt stucco and fresco, Parma, San Paolo

earthly delight. It is as if the putti staring at the beholder mirror and refract the historical nuns' illicit gesture of looking up.[47] These joyous, infantile creatures ultimately stand for nuns' forbidden pleasure in seeing for themselves, their perception of the physical world set apart from them, and for the animation of the prescribed silence of their conventual setting.

Correggio's verdant bower and its *spiritelli* depend from the abbess's arms at the apex of the room (fig. 177; see fig. 156). Radiating from the gilt shield that substitutes for the oculus such as those by Mantegna and Araldi, the abbess's presence fills the space. She is perceived as the motor of the decoration that she also completes, even in absentia, thus reinforcing in a humorous conceit her ubiquity, a quality usually reserved to God.[48] But there is more at stake here. Correggio inscribes the abbess's arms at the center of a sixteen-point double rosette of knotted and twisted ribbons. The points in turn support a ring of multicolored festoons

of fruits and vegetation interlaced with knotted tassels. Regina Stefaniak linked the motif of knotted ribbons with Agrippa's notion of binding, remarking that tools of enchantment like charms and rings were either bound or woven.[49] Giovanna's arms may have been recognized as having the quasi-magic power to bind the entire decoration together, while simultaneously, like a perfumed vapor filling the space, as Lorenzo Cornigli noted (see Chapter Four), it could be seen to have apotropaic power against evil influences. As discussed in Chapter Five, it is likely that the community of San Paolo was exposed to discussions on magic and was probably not immune to the temptation of finding supernatural explanations for its troubles. Consecrated women using their eyes to seek what was not meant to concern them – the nourishing spirit-putti of life, ancient mythological lore, and pleasure from richly sensual art – needed quasi-magic protection since fascination was believed to draw negative spirits into the body.

184

The *spiritelli* engaging in amusing, though futile, pastimes in Correggio's vault could also amount to a reinforcement of the Pythagorean saying that admonishes spectators to abandon vain activities. After all, nuns were advised to be constantly active or at prayer. Playful cupids in the context of a bedroom (and its implicit sexual associations) could, moreover, be reminders of the offspring of whom consecrated women with lives devoted to God were deprived. Even in a male-oriented society like that of early sixteenth-century Europe, which forced women into either claustration or marriage, the question of allowing women to make choices regarding their own lives was raised in at least a few of Erasmus's writings. In his *Girl with No Interest in Marriage* and *Repentant Girl* from around 1523–4, Erasmus points to the risks of forcing girls into lives that they do not want, and discusses the choices reserved to women. He questions the wisdom of committing oneself to a course of life without sufficient reflection: monastic life aims at a perpetually pure physical and mental state, requiring sexual abstinence and excluding procreation. Erasmus realistically sees the vow of chastity, virginity, as extremely difficult to honor.[50] From the broken vows of the nun Lucrezia Buti and the friar-painter Filippo Lippi (their son, the artist Filippino Lippi was born in 1457) to Alessandro Manzoni's narrative of the travails of the nun of Monza (1827), it is clear that in convents sexual intercourse was not as infrequent as authorities would have wanted. Erasmus insists that monastic life in general, and in this case that of women, be based on a true vocation, describing nuns as "ornaments" of the Church.

In playing desecrating games and mocking time-honored activities like hunting and performing pagan rituals, Correggio's putti display an exquisite combination of jollity and irony that binds the viewer. The more one becomes absorbed in their magnetic childish physicality and game-playing, however, the more one may recognize that they can be linked to Renaissance love lyrics and parodies, translating these literary genres into a pictorial poetic. Composed in imitation of Virgil's eclogues, Navagero's *Lusus* collection of amatory and arcadian sonnets (published only in 1530 but widely circulated before that date) has as a title and marker of its content the very name of a children's game (*paignon* in Greek, Latin *lusus*).[51] Representations of nature in its abundance of fruit and living creatures, Correggio's *spiritelli* as pictorial *ludi* replicate the vibrancy and comic spirit of Navagero's amatory poetic play in the modern art of painting. In their mocking features Correggio's putti also retain elements of Catullian parodies, which the Parmese audience particularly enjoyed.

Anselmi's fondness for Catullus, for instance, culminated in his parody of the *Phaselus* (The Ship). As Julia Gaisser has argued, this Catullian poem appealed to its audience because it was inspired by the only surviving parody thought to be by Virgil in the Renaissance.[52] Catullus's *Phaselus*, "the fastest of ships," is a speaking ship musing on its travels to the most prestigious locations of the Mediterranean world, reaching as far east as Asia Minor and then retiring to a quiet lake, probably the Garda, where it dedicates itself to Castor and Pollux, patrons of seafaring. The *Phaselus* is a lampoon of Roman epic poetry imbued with all the *double entendre* and unusual contexts of the boat's tales. Conversely, the storytelling object in Anselmi's poem is a book that recounts its adventures with subdued enthusiasm, almost as though they were secondhand tales, resulting in a total lack of excitement compared to that in Catullus's parody.[53] Published first in 1526 though composed over preceding decades, Anselmi narrates the various stages of Aeneas's journey from Troy to Rome, and then follows Trojan genealogy from Roman civilization up to Parma in the early sixteenth century. His narrative surely intrigued readers for the local associations it proposed and the connections to their age in its final plea for peace and concord. As was also true of Anselmi's poem dedicated to Stupor, his parody is ineffective in most of its attempted irony, but the author's erudition cannot but impress the reader. However, it is not iconographic links between Navagero's or Anselmi's texts and Correggio's putti that is in discussion here, but Correggio's reworking of the same poetic ground in pictorial terms. In other words, the jollity of the putti, their parodic and comic actions, match the spirit of Navagero's and Anselmi's poems. Dashing behind arboreal portholes in unsteady fashion to stage visual parodies of the hunt and ancient rites, Correggio's *spiritelli* greatly enhance the fascination of his painted room.

OBSCURITY AND AMBIGUITY VISUALIZED

Dating to 1598, Smeraldo Smeraldi's unpublished description of his visit to the convent of San Paolo culminates in his account of Correggio's painted room. Smeraldi's remarks constitute the earliest textual response to the images, composed by a local polymath (goldsmith, engineer, and cartographer) of acknowledged stature. Having gained the bishop's permission to enter the convent, by then fully *in clausura*, Smeraldi surveyed several of the monastic spaces

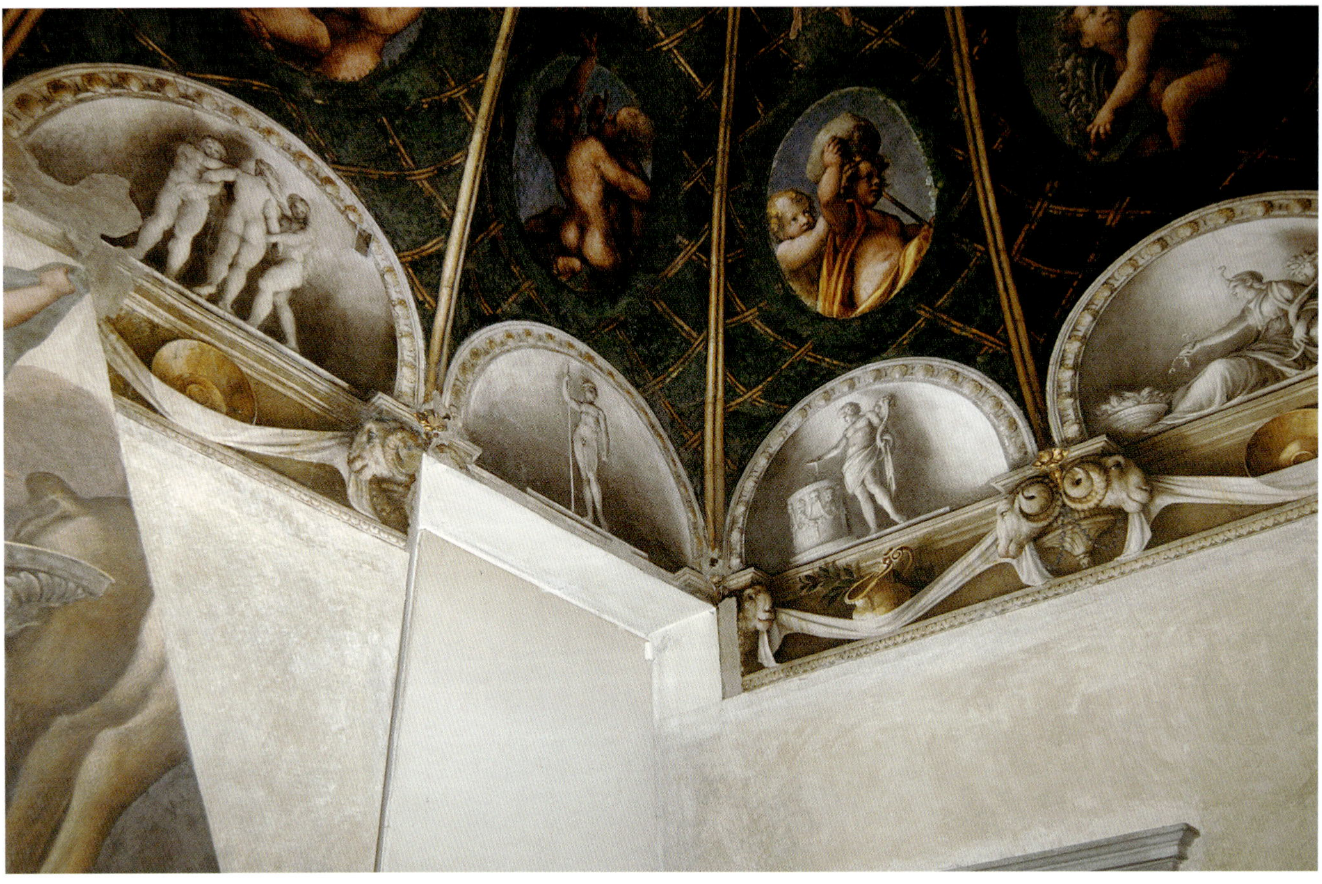

178   Correggio, fictive marble cornice and window, ca. 1518–19, fresco, Parma, San Paolo

that needed repair and improvements. Then he was accompanied to see Correggio's frescoes, which he praises for the artist's magisterial imitation of different materials and surfaces, evoking the beauty of nature, the *colorito* of modern painting, the *all'antica* grisaille style, and the luster of metals. Despite not addressing the imposing image of Diana over the fireplace, Smeraldi's description stresses Correggio's spectacular art and skill:

> an umbrella vault with lunettes at its base, transformed into a fictive pergola with trellises covered with vines and fruits, interspersed with ovals containing several lovely putti in varied and different attitudes and movements; the lunettes show small monochromatic representations. Below there is a cornice along which runs a festoon with vases, bowls, ewers, and other vessels imitating silver, beautifully rendered.[54]

Smeraldi's reaction to Correggio's achievements can be framed as much within the Renaissance *paragone* between painting and sculpture as within the discourse of painting's capacity to imitate different materials, eliding distinctions between surfaces and structures, appearance and reality. Less costly than marble revetments, the simulated sculptural lunettes, reeds and wicker garden bower, and the painted cornice literally reinvented the solid architecture, soliciting the spectator to detect the relations between the real and fictive surfaces, as manifested in the remarkable passage of the rich illusionistic cornice and the windows visible on the north wall (fig. 178). But Correggio utilized this intrusion of the real into the painted space to make the pictorial illusionism even more effective, modeling his figures according to the real light coming from the windows: different nuances are given to the lunettes on each wall, while those on the north (see fig. 160) are modulated with especially deep chiaroscuro, perhaps to imitate the contrasting light that the fire would have had on real sculpture.[55]

A similar tale of true and false claims, reality and illusion, was told to the local audience in a largely forgotten text by the fourth-century poet Ausonius, which was reprinted in Parma in 1499. A poem in almost 500 lines about the eponymous northern European river, the *Mosella* mentions the buildings and cities along its course. Ausonius employs tropes of the transient visual effects of water, asking the reader to take pleasure in his description of sights that are ambiguously true and false simultaneously. The poet evokes transparency, reflections, and refractions, asserting that the duality and dance between appearance and reality, mirroring and presence, distance and nearness, is the source of delight in his poem.[56] He requests that his readers recall the sights he describes, as much as the Parmese audience expected modern painting to simulate materials and surface textures, juxtapose the real and fictive, and be rendered according to principles of decorum and beauty (*vaghezza*), making its falsity persuasively true, and the mimetic the stimulating source of feeling. The document signed by Correggio in 1522 with the officials of Parma Cathedral is clear on this matter, stipulating that his painting should imitate "the living, the medal, and the marble, according to their placements and the requirement of the building, as well as the appropriateness and the beauty of painting itself."[57] Correggio's *Assumption of the Virgin* (fig. 179) in the dome of the Cathedral is a work of impressive pathos, a choral jubilee of divine entities, saints, angels, and clouds foreshortened from below, offering devotees a variety of spiritual messages as they approach the dome from different viewpoints. Certainly, the cathedral's officials, who included Scipione Montini Rosa (Giovanna Piacenza's brother-in-law, as noted), were well acquainted with Correggio's images in San Paolo, whose virtuoso illusionism also imitates reality and juxtaposes various textures, shaping games of education as delight.

Unlike Parmigianino's representations of the myth of Diana and Actaeon in the Sanvitale chamber (see fig. 175), or Luini's Ovidian frescoes narrating the fable of Cephalus and Procris in a room for Girolamo Rabia in his Villa Pelucca, the secular subjects of Correggio's monochrome lunettes do not derive from Ovid's text, nor do they propose myths of transformation or of the hunt. Rather, his pagan personifications are self-contained figures for which, as Pliny commented apropos those by the Greek painter Timanthes, "more is always implied than is depicted."[58] But how did Correggio achieve this magisterial result of pictorial brevity? And what is the genre of these succinct, abstruse images? In the earliest study on Correggio's frescoes (1794), Ireneo Affò recognized that his lunettes derive from ancient coins, and Corrado Ricci later identified half of the sixteen coins being imitated.[59] As discussed in Chapter Five, images on ancient coin reverses were considered *symbola* in the

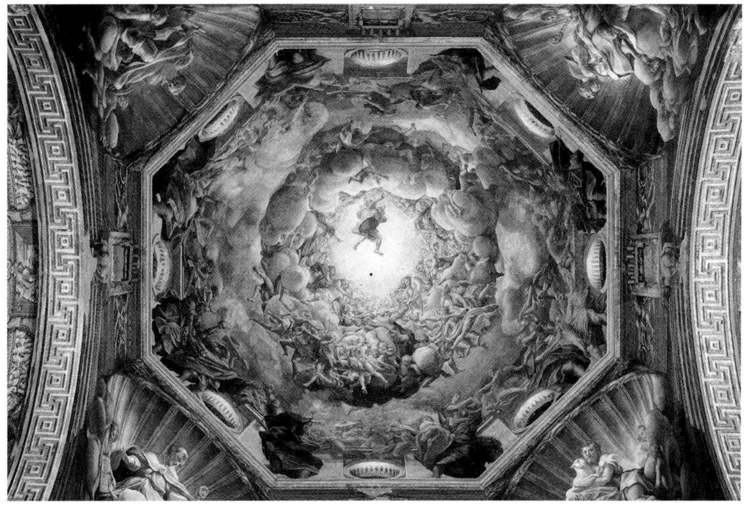

179   Correggio, *Assumption of the Virgin*, ca. 1530–34, fresco, Parma, Cathedral

Renaissance, a type of hieroglyphics, and therefore coins constituted the most appropriate source for enigmatic pictures. As Pietro Bembo stated in 1532, ancient coins demonstrated the skill of past artists and were objects of emulation for modern masters.[60] Contemporary artists' imitation of the reliefs on Roman coins was even parodied by the Bolognese poet Giovanni Filoteo Achillini, who poked fun at a certain painter Ombrone and his "cisterns full of precious coins" whose "various reverses [are] rendered with such craftsmanship as to make nature ashamed [at such artistry]." And Ombrone is said to have consumed "ten ducats' worth of candles to light up the coins to better contemplate them and, in so doing, to illuminate his mind."[61] Despite his mocking tone, Achillini was aware that the subtle interplay of texts and images on coins, their synthesized forms, and fine, low reliefs were manifestations of the power of art to outperform nature's creations. In his *Viridario* of 1507, Achillini elaborates on the enigmatic qualities of coin reverses and how they stimulate curiosity, which he associates with the fanciful antiquarian style of his fellow citizen, the painter Amico Aspertini.[62]

Modern scholars are not the first to notice that in the sixteenth century, coin reverses, adages, Pythagorean *symbola*, and riddles were all grouped under the genre of *aenigmata* (enigmas). Composed between 1502 and 1507, though not published until 1551, Lilio Gregorio Giraldi's text on *aenigmata* is one of the earliest works to treat the topic.[63] As pointed out by Maia Wellington Gahtan, Giraldi's intention was not to interpret enigmas "to unlock religious or philosophical knowledge long forgotten . . . Unlike most contemporary books on Pythagorean symbols or hieroglyphs, Giraldi's text does not discuss enigmas and *symbola* as mysteries."[64] Rather, Giraldi wrote that deciphering enigmas sharpens readers' minds, drawing on their knowledge to discover and expand latent meaning. In other words, decoding enigmas was a discursive exercise for Giraldi. *Aenigmata* bore knowledge compressed into succint forms (*forma brevis*) that made their obscure meaning the subject of conversation.[65] Renaissance scholars debated the value of obscurity both as a virtue and a pitfall. Philipp Melanchthon and Juan Luis Vivès, for example, condemned the inaccessible, meandering logic of medieval scholastic theologians who were accused of having led students into bewildering labyrinths and verbal chaos. Scholastic disputations were often incomprehensible and their arcane implications and inconclusive results were believed to be a major defect.[66] A more positive approach to poetic obscurity comes from texts published in early sixteenth-century Parma.

In their commentaries on Plautus's comedies, the Parmese triumvirate of Grapaldo, Ugoleto, and Anselmi concurs with Bolognese peers that in their unusual plots and bizarre language the Plautinian *fabulae* cover protean reality, and that the reader (defined as a "divinissimus chamaeleon") should be able to extract the core of ethical truths, recognizing comic tales and games as veiling complex reality.[67] The Parmese scholars' defense also echoes Petrarch's and Boccaccio's doctrine on recondite subjects. In his *Invective contra Medicum* (1353), Petrarch states that difficulty makes reading more stimulating because obscure passages could be invested with multiple, equally possible, interpretations. In the fourteenth book of his *Genealogiae Deorum Gentilium* (1360–74), Boccaccio writes that obscure subjects are artfully embellished to veil truth "in a fair and fitting garment of fiction."[68] Poetic obscurity also includes secrecy, which only the educated elite can grasp. The Cinquecento humanist Paolo Cortesi transferred this doctrine of obscurity to the decoration of a cardinal's palace, recommending that enigmatic pictures be displayed in summer rooms, including "riddles and fables [*aenigmatum apologorumque*]. Their interpretation sharpens the intelligence and [inspection of] their learned representation fosters the cultivation of the mind."[69] Cortesi's and Giraldi's enthusiasm for enigmas balances the disdain that Vivès and others expressed for poetic concealment, but this debate supplies the context for approaching Correggio's obscure lunettes, which spread the search for meaning across time.

The artist's faux-sculptural lunettes amount to the visual counterparts of this debate, in the sense that he conceived them as pictorial *aenigmata*, both because their iconographies derive from ancient coins (thought to be *hieroglyphica* in the Renaissance) and because Correggio made indeterminacy their focus.[70] Assimilating brevity and obscurity from the genre of literary enigmas, and employing imitation and reinvention of the sources, Correggio's lunettes are ambivalent, indeterminate visual tokens that enhance interpretations and meditation over time. The artist purposely devised subjects that resist linear identification and stability, as Dario Gamboni has shown with reference to contemporary images.[71] Enigmatic images oscillate between different possible readings, introducing a certain play with their representations and ambiguity about the objects for which they are signs, and whose subjects viewers pierce to recover their dynamic discontinuity through history.[72] They were conceived at a moment in which images as bearers of meaning underwent major rethinking in their structures and genres, by merging forms and figures in previously untested ways. In San Paolo, they addressed a female religious audience who wanted meaning to remain in *potentia*, opaque rather than transparent, and to be conveyed by playfulness.

Correggio was a young painter when he gave visual form to this poetic of obscurity around 1518–19. One wonders how an artist still inexperienced in grand projects could qualify for such an undertaking, and through what networks he was brought to the abbess's attention from his small hometown of Correggio (the capital of a fiefdom 25 miles east of Parma). Born Antonio Allegri probably in 1489, he spent some time in Mantua where in 1512 he is recorded as being a creditor of Mantegna's son Francesco.[73] By 1518 he had executed a few known paintings within a limited radius of his native town. A document transcribed by the nineteenth-century scholar Luigi Pungileoni testifies that Giovanna Piacenza traveled to Correggio in 1511 to serve as godmother to a newborn baby in the Fontanelli family.[74] While it is not surprising that an elite consecrated woman was able to travel outside her convent's precincts, this information makes it feasible that by 1518 she could have returned there and admired Correggio's imposing *Madonna of St. Francis* altarpiece (1514–15) and his *Portrait of a Lady* (ca. 1517–19). If the abbess did see these paintings, the earliest manifestations of Correggio's affective modern visual language, it could be that she was won over, and invited the artist to Parma to work on the decoration of her chamber. Alternatively, either Canon Bartolomeo Montini or his nephew Scipione Montini Rosa, both of whom had direct connections with the da Correggio ruling family and some interest in art, could have put the artist to work in San Paolo.[75]

The unprecedented aesthetic of delight coupled with abstruseness or, better, the *serio-ludere* poetics that Correggio created in the abbatial chamber shows his intelligent assimilation of Mantegna's and Leonardo's achievements interwoven with features of *lietezza* (merriment) of his own, which became the salient features of his style. Elsewhere I have argued that these qualities of his art should be seen in connection with his surname Allegri (*allegrezza* means joy), producing his distinct version of the modern manner as an extension of his own self.[76] The late Cinquecento painter Annibale Carracci first recognized Correggio's forays into modernity as the creation of a self-referential style of his own invention:

> Correggio's works were his own thoughts, his own conceptions, which one sees he drew out of his own head, and invented on his own, testing these only against the original. The others all lean on something that is not their own, either on the model, or on statues, or on drawings and prints. All the works of these others represent things as they could be, but Correggio's as they truly are.[77]

Discounting Annibale's perspicacious view, modern scholarship has often associated Correggio's style to an undocumented visit to Rome that is said to have occurred either before or immediately after the San Paolo commission.[78] That visit is believed to have provided the artist an opportunity to study Raphael's and Michelangelo's works and to derive from their classicizing, grandiose, energetic figures the basis for his own pictorial modernity. Without entering into this controversy (for which his understanding of and confrontation with ancient coins and modern works by Mantegna and Leonardo, to my mind, suffice), Corrado Ricci's early twentieth-century remarks remain helpful. They call for a less binary comprehension of Correggio, an artist too long considered a provincial and regional master:

> Yet even the criticism most wholeheartedly in favor of Correggio's Roman pilgrimage finds itself at a certain point forced to say and say again that Vatican influences were soon overcome by the painter's genius, that his memories of Rome grew distant and suffered shipwreck in the personal character of the artist, whose colors very soon showed a marked difference from those ground with the waters of the Tiber.[79]

Correggio's *Portrait of a Lady* and the almost contemporary San Paolo images proclaim a convincing and affective modern aesthetic of *lietezza*, capturing viewers through their pictorial elusiveness and drawing them into empathetic relationships with the emotions his art exudes.

Correggio's lunettes with pagan subjects and allegories speak of a classical culture but one working alongside Christian wisdom. While their content and tenor are secular and it is not appropriate to attribute religious implications to them, their messages embrace the humanist, irenic culture of the Renaissance that explored the relationships and the tensions between the pagan and the Christian world. The overlaps between ancient and Christian morality had one of their finest interpreters in Erasmus. Through the negotiation of pagan and Christian precepts, profane and sacred learning, Erasmus's writings aim to convey knowledge, spirituality, and also pleasure to his readers. As mentioned at the outset of this chapter, few of Erasmus's writings informed by the *serio-ludere* poetic (the *Adagia* and the *Praise of Folly* included) deal with serious topics, but he fills them with humor because, as he put it, learning itself needs its own relaxation (*maxime si nugae seria ducant*).[80] Similarly, as one of the discussants in his *Convivium Fabulosum* (The Fabulous Feast, 1524) oxymoronically remarks: "nothing is more fun than to treat jokes seriously."[81]

With this understanding of the lunettes' discourses of obscurity and irony in mind, a discussion of their iconographic indeterminacy has become possible. In the remainder of this chapter a selection of the themes of pagan and Christian morality embedded in the lunettes are considered, and it is proposed that art provided the nuns with learning and levity that they could have not obtained by other means. Correggio's allegorical representations allude to the virtues of chastity, prudence, and foresight, among others, juxtaposed to themes of punishment, sacrifice, and fortune, offering reflections on the choices available to women, and presenting different manifestations of the female religious self. These subjects bounce back and forth across the lunettes, reverberating against and with one another, echoing and expanding the messages of the Diana-Luna image dominating the room in dialectical circularity. The lunettes' poetic indeterminacy opens up a space for the mobile beholders' re-enactment of subjects, or what has been recently defined as the movement of the mind.[82] Correggio's images play with meanings and make their audience aware that their plurality of contents remains part of an unending game, that their seriousness and lightness are bound together inextricably. And, as enigmatic images, they are representative of a pictorial genre with only a few other Renaissance incarnations, including a lost painting in an underground grotto beneath the Sforza castle described by

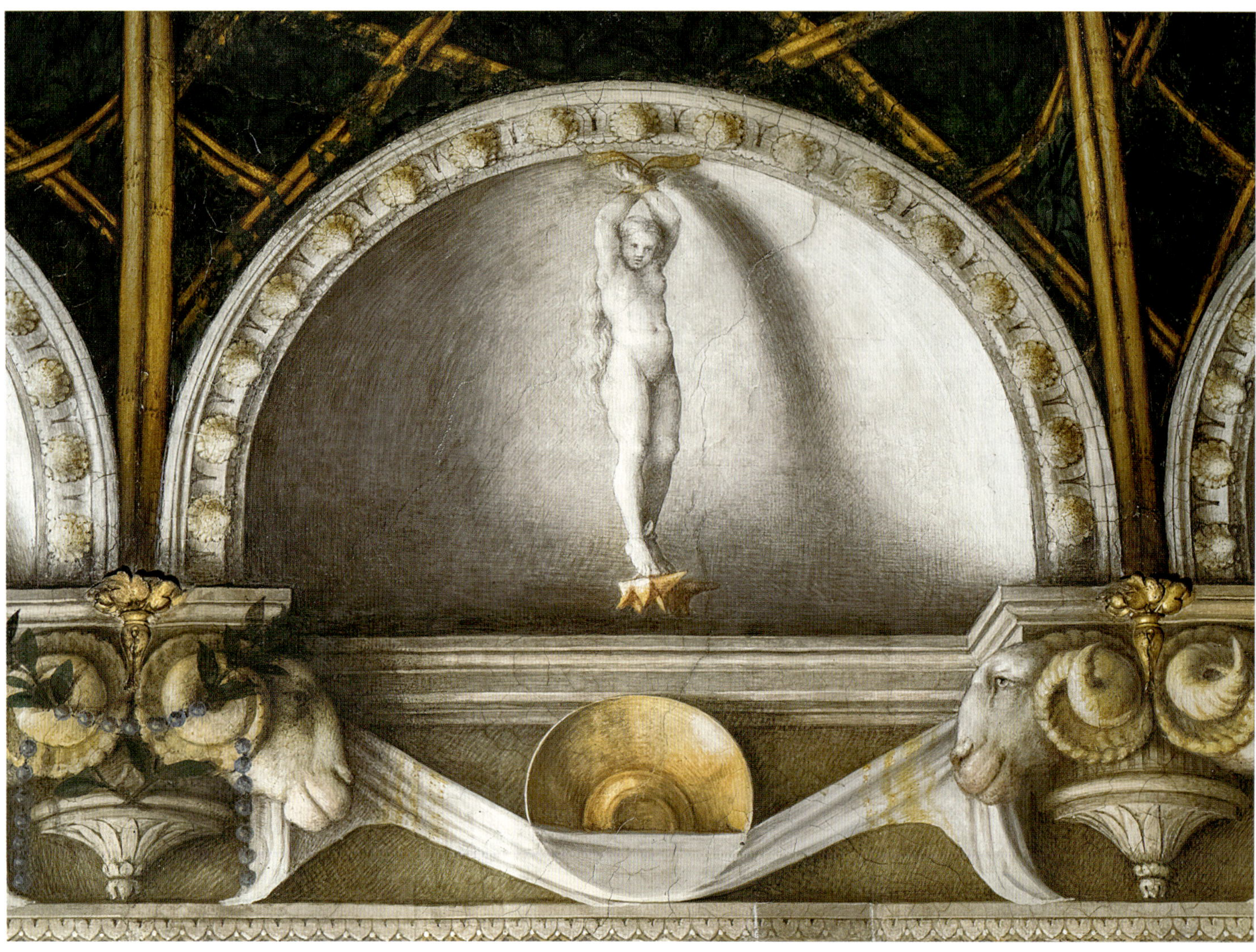

180   Correggio, *Punishment of Hera* and frame of seashells, detail, ca. 1518–19, fresco, Parma, San Paolo

Cesare Cesariano as a hieroglyph, Giorgione's works including his *Tempest*, Raphael's so-called *Dream of Scipio*, and the graphic oeuvres of Giulio and Domenico Campagnola, among others.[83] Later, Gabriele Paleotti vehemently censored abstruse pictures for their lack of transparency between pictorial signs and the objects represented, lamenting that their confusing effects enhanced only the wondering of the beholder's mind, but did not fulfill the didactic purpose of art.[84]

There is perhaps no better way to begin discussion on Correggio's lunettes than to acknowledge an often overlooked detail, their fictive ornamental frames of scallop shells (fig. 180). As Paula Findlen pointed out, shells were considered "jokes of nature" in the Renaissance, exhibiting "the 'irregular regularity' with which nature confounded

her observers."[85] Shells are therefore the most appropriate adornments of obscure, curious, and playful subjects, associating the jokes of nature with those of art. Similarly, the fictive marble cornice below the lunettes displays pairs of rams' heads linked by fabric festoons. These rams' heads with animated, intelligent eyes (fig. 181), teasing expressions, and strings of beads and even apparently of small fruit (blueberries) dangling from their horns, are set atop conic marble elements at the base of each rib, and suggest the inverted volutes of Ionic capitals. This composite could have been intended by Correggio as an architectural jest (a *scherzo*) to evoke the origins of the Ionic capital, an order that the Roman architect Vitruvius associated with temples dedicated to female goddesses including Diana, and was in discussion at the time among architects, painters, and schol-

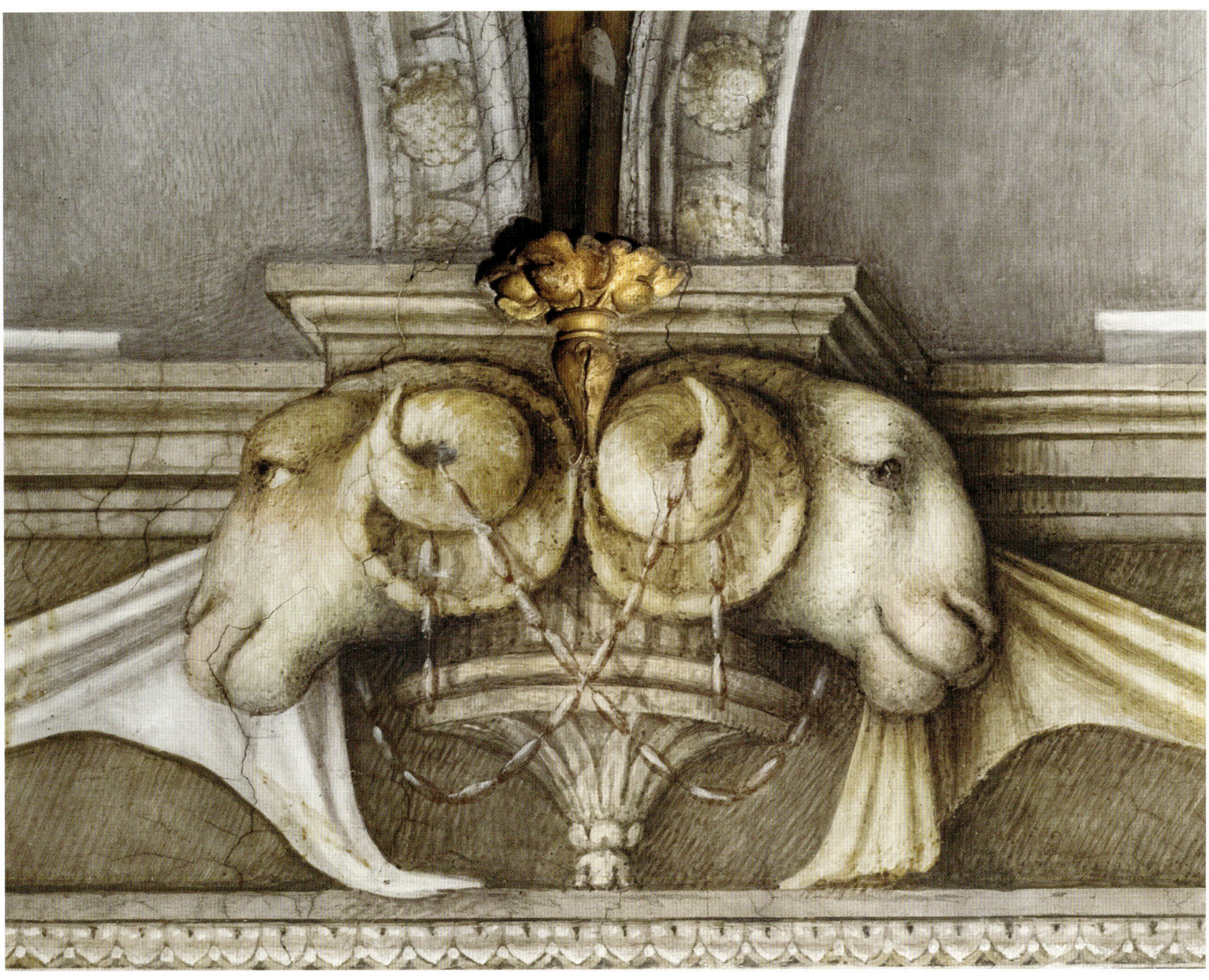

181 Correggio, rams' heads, detail, ca. 1518–19, fresco, Parma, San Paolo

ars, including Fabio Calvo in his 1514–15 vernacular translation of Vitruvius's treatise.[86] These festively bejeweled rams with horns rolled like fashionable ladies' braided hair, pinning the festoons to support sacrificial objects, seem to bespeak a female order, in contrast to the dry ox skulls (*bucrania*) that appear in metopes of the Doric order to celebrate male divinities (Jupiter or Mars). As signifiers of victories and heroic acts, ox skulls were set ornamentally into Roman temple façades and wall paintings, and were familiar elements to Renaissance antiquarian culture, as Giuliano da Sangallo's fine drawing of the ruins of the Basilica Aemilia in Rome attests.[87] Fictive stone oxen are set above the spandrels of Michelangelo's Sistine ceiling. In 1546 the sculptor Vincenzo de Grandi, better known as Vicentino, explains the subject of a bronze inkstand representing *bucrania* and festoons used by architects for "Doric works," reporting that *bucrania* signify "the hardship on which glory depends," while garlands stand for "no less than the triumph of virtue and the honor of glory."[88] Such *bucrania* cannot, however, have been anything other than a starting-point for Correggio's unusual, incarnate rams' heads. Depicted in natural colors, they have open mouths, seeing eyes, amused smiles, and mocking expressions, and, in brief, are emphatically animated despite their bodilessness. They also interact across the space as they share the task of pinning the drapery to hold the liturgical instruments, playfully gazing at each other, or more rarely out toward the viewer (see figs. 180 and 183). The humor of their big, homely faces downplays the abstruseness of the lunettes above and almost ridicules viewers intent on getting a closer

191

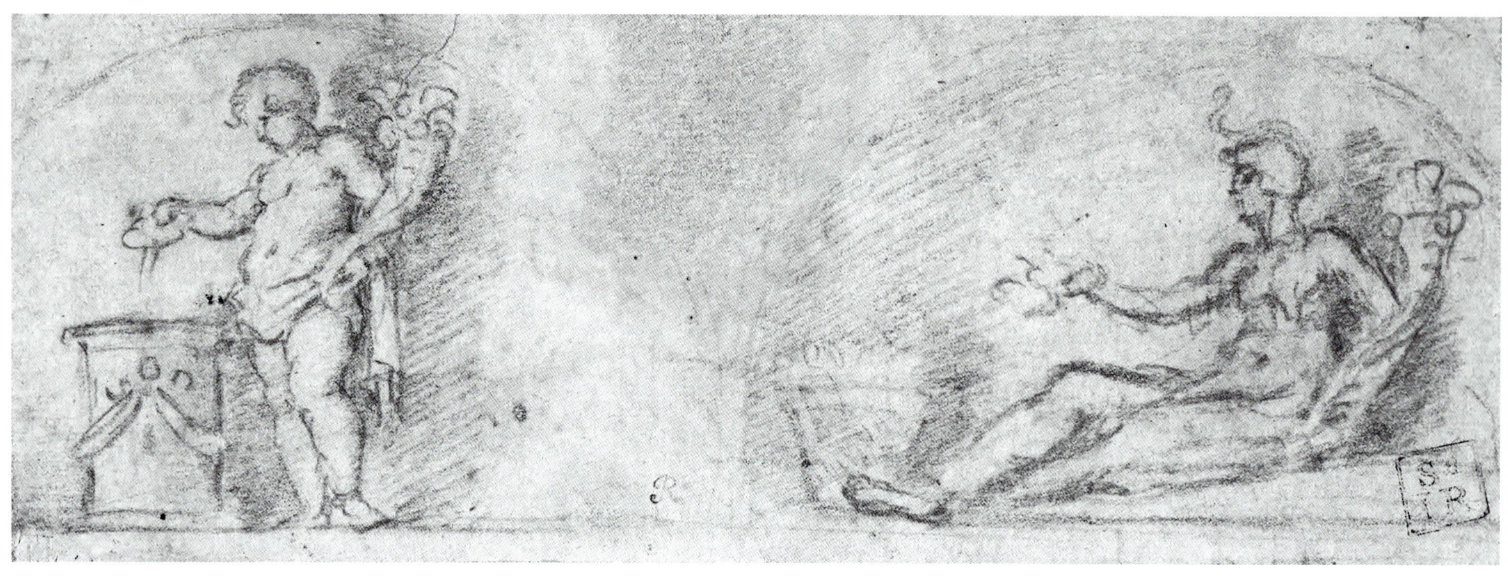

182   Correggio, *Genius and Africa*, ca. 1518–19, red chalk, 5.9 × 15.7 cm (2²/₆ × 6³/₁₆ in), London, Trustees of the British Museum

183   Correggio, *Genius and Africa*, east wall, ca. 1518–19, fresco, Parma, San Paolo

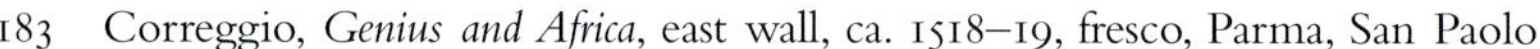

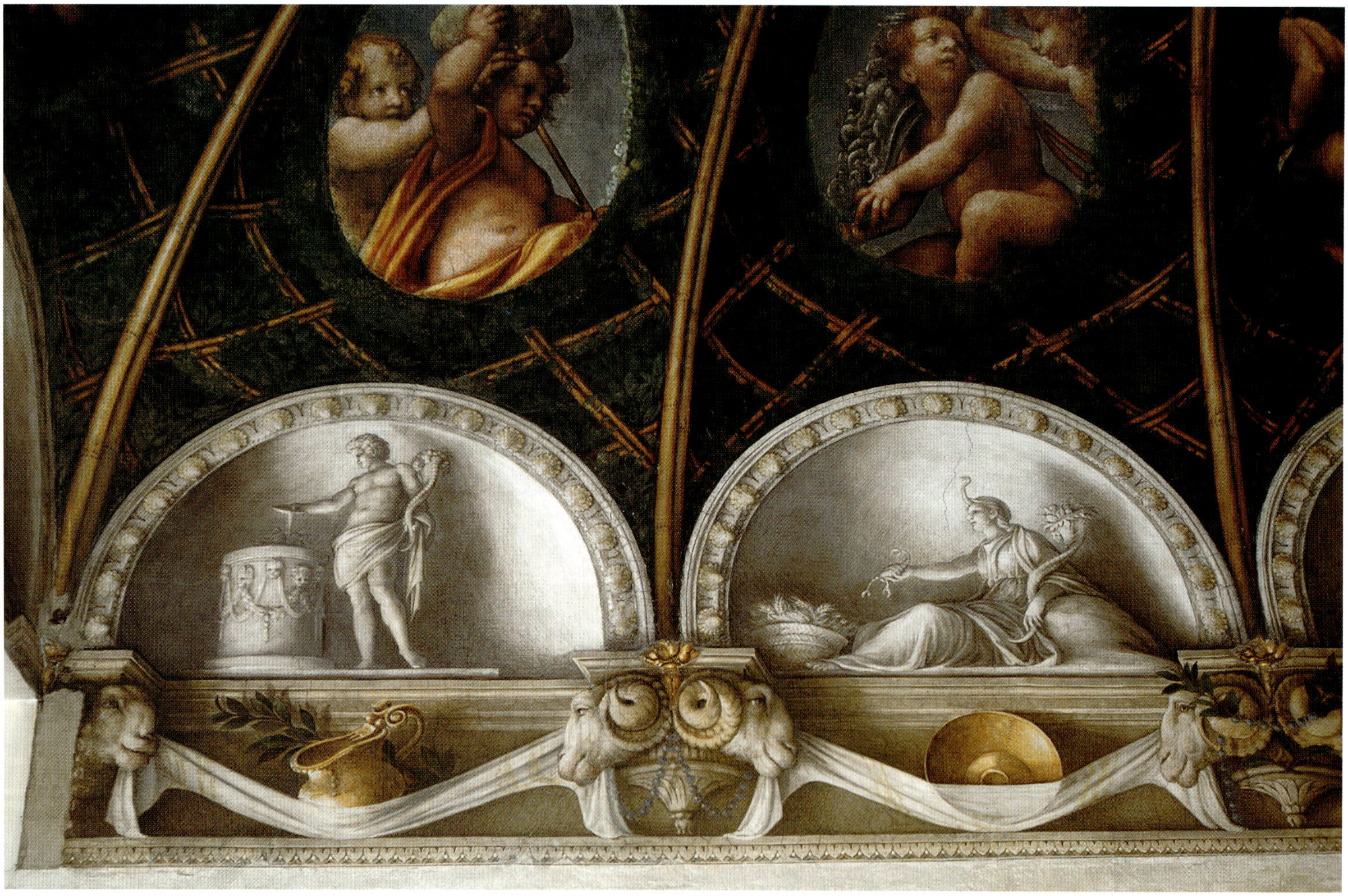

look to grasp recondite insights. They seem to enjoy being garnished with the colorful necklaces, and several even wear sprays of laurel, a touch of elegance and wit. Likewise, the fabric festoons hold items like patera, jugs, sacrificial knives, and laurel branches, that make colorful and delightful notations on the lunettes, and, insofar as the latter suggest temple rituals, could also further a reading of the structure that Correggio created as a sort of fantastic, rustic Ionic temple of the goddess Diana-Luna.

Only one preliminary drawing for the lunettes survives. On the sheet (fig. 182), Correggio translates the linear rigidity of metal coins into his soft graphic forms using red chalk. Although typical of his sketching technique with rapid strokes, the two lunette studies on the sheet also create pictorial effects through the chiaroscuro modeling. Copied from a sestertius of Emperor Nero bearing the inscription "Genio Augusti" and representing a standing, seminude youth holding a cornucopia and patera to make a libation, Correggio renders the figure of Genius as a putto on the left side of the sheet. On the east lunette fresco, however, the painter brought his figure closer to the coin model. With his muscular torso turned and foreshortened and a loincloth wrapped around his waist falling down to one side, Correggio's Genius (fig. 183) is a handsome youthful figure with a full head of hair, intent on pouring a libation over a cylindrical flaming altar.[89] In antiquity, a *genius* was a tutelary spirit protective of communities, cities, countries, and individuals, standing for nature and, by extension, for the procreative power of human beings. Each person was said to possess from birth a *genius*, a spirit of well-being that could, however, be compromised by unregulated appetites and a lack of moderation. In his *Aulularia* (Concealed Treasure) reprinted in Parma in 1510, Plautus ridicules both individuals indulging in comfort and those who denied their good *genii*. Plautus states the dilemma of the *genii* role without siding with either view.[90] Polydor Vergil's and Erasmus's early sixteenth-century texts further refer to two species of *genii*, a good and a demonic kind, the former seeking to aid individuals while the latter plotted their destruction through distraction, in a constant struggle for the control of the senses.[91] Correggio's exquisitely rendered Genius emblematizes the good spirit, the positive purveyor of protection for the community. By extension, it could be seen in relation to the socially emerging urban clan of the Montini, Piacenza, and Bergonzi (see Chapter Four) to which the abbess belonged, whose *genii* were being invoked to help them gain the political power that guaranteed the independence of the religious community of San Paolo.

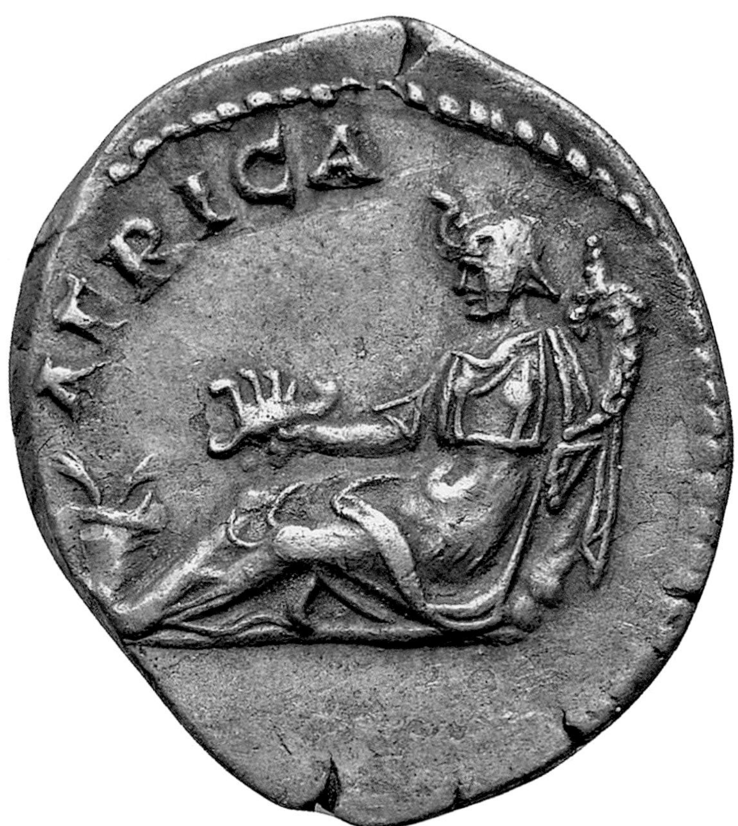

184 Africa (verso), denarius of Hadrian, 134–8 CE, London, Trustees of the British Museum

On the right side of the drawing, Correggio portrays a reclining nude female figure with a curious headdress, holding a cornucopia in her left hand and a scorpion in her right, while a basket of wheat lies at her feet, an adaptation of the allegorical representation of Africa derived from a Hadrianic denarius (134–38 CE). The coin (fig. 184) features the typical female Greco-Roman personification of Africa, who either appears kneeling or sacrificing before the emperor.[92] Africa is consistently described as a fertile if dangerous land filled with scorpions, snakes, and other venomous animals in ancient and early modern texts, including Pliny's *Natural History* and Claudian's *De Bello Gildonico*, which were both republished in Parma with annotations respectively by Filippo Beroaldo (1476) and Taddeo Ugoleto (1493).[93] In Correggio's preparatory drawing, Africa's headdress is unfinished (among other details), but the artist gives a languorous and sensual quality to the figure. The posture is retained for the fully draped image depicted on the east wall (see fig. 183), where a serpent substitutes for the elephant-scalp headdress of the coin imagery, and a globular-shaped knoll for the rock behind. The corn basket and cornucopia, both symbols of prosperity, can be associated with the wealth and abundance of the convent under Giovanna's tenure, by which expenditure on artistic commissions was permissible.

In discussing Correggio's drawing, David Ekserdjian and Hugo Chapman have concurred that the coins which Correggio studied and copied must have been worn to the point that he could not discern iconographic details, but was the accurate citation of models his objective? Perhaps a freer and more imaginative approach was required in the creation of enigmatic subjects. In addition to the representations of Genius and Africa, Correggio's lunettes with Fortuna and Vesta (see figs. 187 and 188), for example, derive from classical coins. But he also reinvented and adumbrated his references in other lunette subjects whose comprehension has eluded generations of interpreters.[94] So the question here is about the very nature of Correggio's conception of painting: imitation, or the intelligent amalgamation and reinvention of sources within the poetic of *enigmata*? Let us take a close look at the mysterious representation of what is widely recognized as Jupiter majestically enthroned within a Doric temple (fig. 185) and holding a scepter (or thunderbolt?) in his left hand. It has not been previously noted that for this image Correggio's source may have been a silver denarius of Petillius Capitolinus (43 BCE) showing an eagle symbolizing Jupiter on the obverse, and the hexastyle Capitoline temple on the reverse (fig. 186). Before 1515 Ugoleto gave his friend Anselmi this precious Roman coin.[95] Correggio synthesized and transformed the visual *symbola* of the coin into an evocative *all'antica* image of his own devising. He reworked the Jupiterian eagle into the enthroned Jupiter seated within the doorway of his temple, producing an original and ingenious rethinking and development of the iconography. Indeed, one can argue that Correggio could have inflated his imagination with other numismatic representations, too, of the popular Capitoline temple, including the sestertius struck by Vespasian in 76 CE, whose obverse shows the temple with its three cellae and statues of Juno, Jupiter, and Minerva.[96] Be that as it may, this process of invention is described by the Ferrarese scholar Giambattista Giraldi as Leonardo's working practice, that is, the collecting together of "sufficient material for the figure which [Leonardo] wished to paint, [to then] . . . proceed to give it shape and [do] it marvellously."[97] Correggio's possible adoption of the Petillius Capitolinus denarius as the basis for his lunette image would attest the extent to which his working method disguised its iconographic models, making them less recognizable and stable as part of the synthesizing process of imitation and invention

demanded by the genre of *aenigmata* itself.[98] The image of the temple on the south wall of the chamber follows its source with philological precision. As noted by Fabrizio Tonelli, the artist rendered the Jupiter Capitolinus building as a tetrastyle Doric temple set on a high podium, with metopes and triglyphs adorned by *bucrania* and pateras, and the tympanum with its acroteria, as described in the passage on this order in Calvo's translation of Vitruvius's *De Architectura*. Well before the Vitruvian text became foundational to the language of built architecture in Parma, Correggio had adopted its classicizing norms as a guide for his painted *all'antica* buildings.[99]

In his Capitoline temple Jupiter was honored as the Optimus Maximus, alluding to his supremacy over all the other gods and to the sacredness of the place itself. It was there that Roman military leaders made vows or rode in triumphal processions, and where rituals of purification and thanksgiving were performed to glorify and supplicate Jupiter.[100] Anselmi composed a poem in honor of the god: "O Jupiter Optimus Maximus, and you, all the gods and goddesses to whom I ritually vow and dedicate a shrine from the proceeds of my modest country estate along with solemn sacrifices and altars, to you I hereby and rightfully vow and dedicate the aforementioned monument, solemn sacrifices and altars."[101] Inscribing his Christian beliefs within the wisdom of pagan lore and not against it, Anselmi's poem matches in spirit Correggio's subject, further echoing the Virgilian *Iovis Omnia Plena* (All is full of Jupiter) inscription carved on the *camerino*'s intarsia frieze. These Virgilian verses associated with the abbess's initials within the *ouroboros* hieroglyphic sign bring out ironic contrasts between Jupiter's universal authority and the abbess's limited power, but by weaving one into the other, Correggio's Jupiter image reinforces the sense of levity that the convent court of San Paolo wished to see. The three objects that appear in the cornice festoon below – a gold paten, wine jug, and laurel branch – are related to ritual and seem to comment on the appropriateness of sacrifices reserved to Jupiter Optimus Maximus.

An inventive approach to visual references was also adopted by Correggio to devise the subjects of other lunettes, including that displaying the warlike Bellona (see fig. 190). Conversely, in the case of other representations, such as the Punishment of Hera, Pan *terrificus*, and the Fates, specific visual models have not been found, which suggests that the artist engaged in the creative rethinking of ekphrastic textual descriptions. In the Three Graces imagery (see fig. 194), he conflated ancient and modern visual sources,

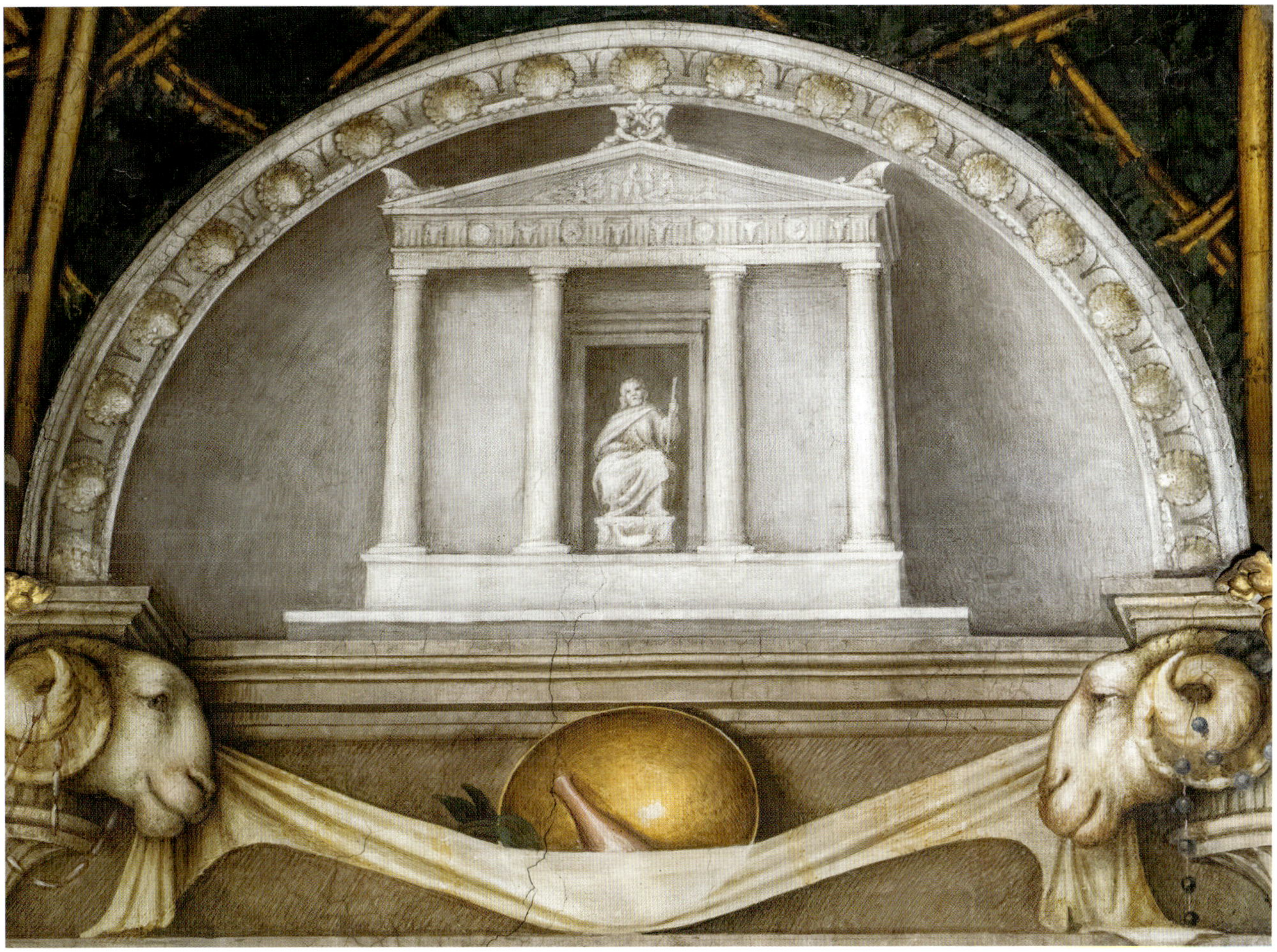

185   Correggio, *Jupiter Enthroned*, ca. 1518–19, fresco, Parma, San Paolo

186   Eagle on thunderbolt (recto) and Capitoline temple (verso), denarius of Petillius Capitolinus, 43 BCE, London, Trustees of the British Museum

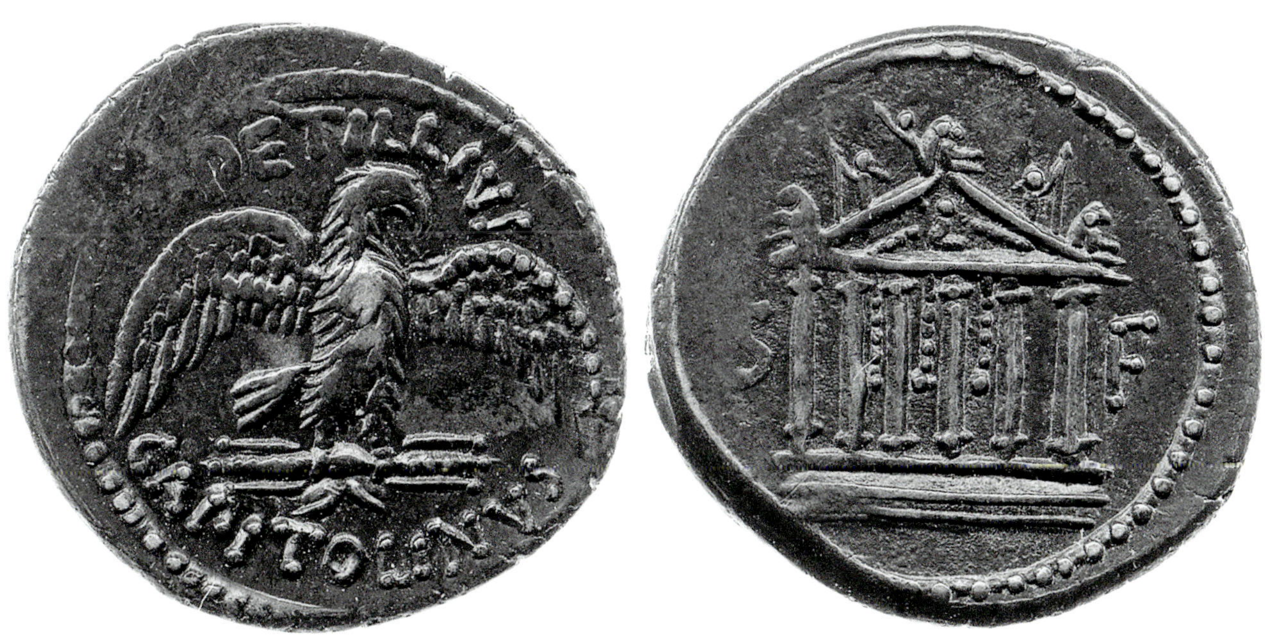

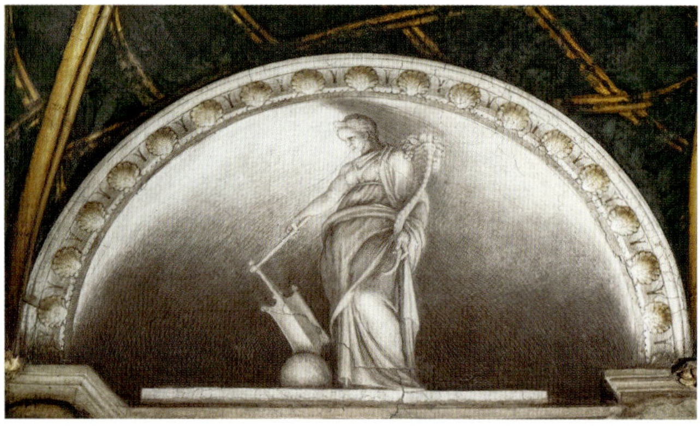

187 Correggio, *Fortuna*, ca. 1518–19, fresco, Parma, San Paolo

making its alluded-to antiquity an invention of the artist Correggio, rather than a mere facsimile of references, in a process that Claudio Franzoni has characterized as the fanciful rendering of the models, making them as appealing and modern as possible.[102]

A VIEW ON THE LUNETTES

On the far left north wall, an impressive image of Fortune stands out (fig. 187). Holding a cornucopia in her left hand and a rudder resting on a globe in the other, Correggio presents the personification of whimsical Fortune. He adapted the popular Fortuna Redux type impressed on a number of ancient coins, the cornucopia alluding to ideals of prosperity, while the rudder refers to the need to adjust to change.[103] Fortune and its accidental effects were among the topics most debated by Renaissance scholars concerned with how to counter her wiles with wisdom, while taking advantage of her unpredictable and sudden gifts and favors. Petrarch's *Remedies for Fortune Fair and Foul* (ca. 1354) offers advice on how to hold out against Fortune's whims and endure its caprices. In his *De Fortuna* (1512), Giovanni Gioviano Pontano, a friend of Anselmi, aligns Fortune and virtue, recognizing that *homines fortunati* (lucky men), in addition to their ethical strengths, possess the ability to work around the irrationality of Fortune. Summarizing classical and contemporary sources, in one of his adages Erasmus states that to merit Fortuna's favors, individuals must be daring. Erasmus advises his readers to "make a strong bid for Fortune; for it is for people who do this that things go well."[104] Likewise, in another adage, he recommends men to be active in pursuing their goals because Fortune does not listen "to the prayers of indolent and lazy men." And,

he adds, one should not be too confident to neglect its help either, nor "so dependent on that help that we let our duty go by default."[105] Within a room dedicated to the pursuit of virtue, this representation, like Araldi's triumph of Aemilius Paulus surrounded by fire, is meant as a reminder that Fortune's whims could impinge on individuals in opposing ways, and further, that what can empower human beings to circumvent her blows is the exercise of virtue. While Fortune impacts the history of humankind and the belief in her inevitable reverses liberates the individual from direct responsibility for difficulties, faith in the exercise of virtue works to mitigate Fortune's ups and downs.

Spectators can easily connect Fortune's downs with the image of the punishment of the Greek goddess Hera (see fig. 180) depicted on the east wall. The suspended nude figure, whose hands are tied and whose feet are weighed down by anvils, features Hera castigated for her insubordination by Jupiter. This story is a little remembered episode narrated in the fifteenth book of Homer's *Iliad* and rarely treated in Renaissance literature, with the exception of Valerius Probus's commentary on Virgil's *Eclogues* (1507) and Beroaldus's on Apuleius's *Golden Ass* (1510). Homer's corpus itself was not well known and was only printed in Florence in 1488–9 after several failed attempts.[106] Despite stumbles in publishing Homer, by the end of the fifteenth century, scholars of the caliber of Politian and the Bolognese Codro Urceo were celebrating the Greek poet as the sagest of the sages, a source of knowledge for the order of nature, for his ability to communicate truth in myths, and his mastery of practical arts, including welfare, medicine, and divination. Anselmi proclaims in the opening verses of his ode in praise of Homer's poems: "Why, reader, do you ponder so long over this work, astounded by the wonders of its content?"[107]

As Panofsky observed, the unusual story of the punishment of Hera lacked an iconographic tradition in the Renaissance. Correggio's image constituted a *unicum* before Giulio Bonasone's print of the subject in the 1560s, which rendered the goddess unjustly strung up by a cord, together with verses explaining her husband Zeus's bitter revenge against transgressors of his rule.[108] To the cultivated beholder familiar with the rare body of literature folded in the image, recognition of Correggio's subject was possible, but less informed spectators must have been startled before this young, nude figure with long, wavy hair who bears her suffering gracefully despite her evident physical torment. Touches of gold paint highlight the anvils dragging down her feet and the bands tied around her wrists, emphasizing details ekphrastically described in textual sources, and thus testifying to Correggio's literary accuracy in depicting his subject. If the textual sources were rare, the search for his visual models has frustrated scholars as well. But could Correggio have reworked another classical myth of punishment, that of the satyr Marsyas? If so, the painter regendered the figure and transformed the punished Marsyas (who was flayed by Apollo), often shown propped up against a tree and an arm suspended by his wrist tied over his head, into the castigated Hera. A few ancient statues of the flayed Marsyas were known in the Medici circle in Florence, and a drawing dating to around 1500 exists.[109]

Be that as it may, Correggio's representation explores the theme of female castigation that it displays. On a basic level, if the intention was to comment on a woman's married life as one of subjugation and punishment, this disquieting representation of the nude, shamed and punished Hera seems apt. But Correggio imagined Hera with an expression of resigned serenity, meeting her "punishment" lightly, as if suggesting that the physical discomfort is not as awful as the perpetrators intended. Either way, the fact remained that cloistered or married life brought women punishment in some form. Yet entry into an elite convent gave women the opportunity for education and the chance to pursue a "career," enabling their elevation from a relatively unremarkable life by historical standards to one, as in the case of Abbess Piacenza, imbued with power, status, and virtue. And one may further recognize that the Diana and Hera images comment on two aspects of Giovanna's role as the abbess of San Paolo. On the one hand, the imposing and powerful goddess Diana amplifies the abbess's authority over the convent's inhabitants, while, on the other, the Hera punishment image provides a reminder of the limits of that power, stressing a dialectic with the theme of male absolute authority portrayed in the Jupiter Capitolinus lunette. Seen through the nuns' eyes, instead, the Hera representation could amount to a warning that transgressions to rules would be punished. But this subject also raises more general reflections on the condition of Renaissance women subjected to male authority, inside and outside convents, where attitudes of defiance, disobedience of rules, and intellectual curiosity were viewed as aberrations or absolutely forbidden.

This notion of female punishment sets up a dialogue with that of the Roman vestal represented as a dutiful, consecrated woman, with her head covered and standing before a lighted altar, on the east wall (fig. 188). A personification alluding to consecrated women, this veiled figure

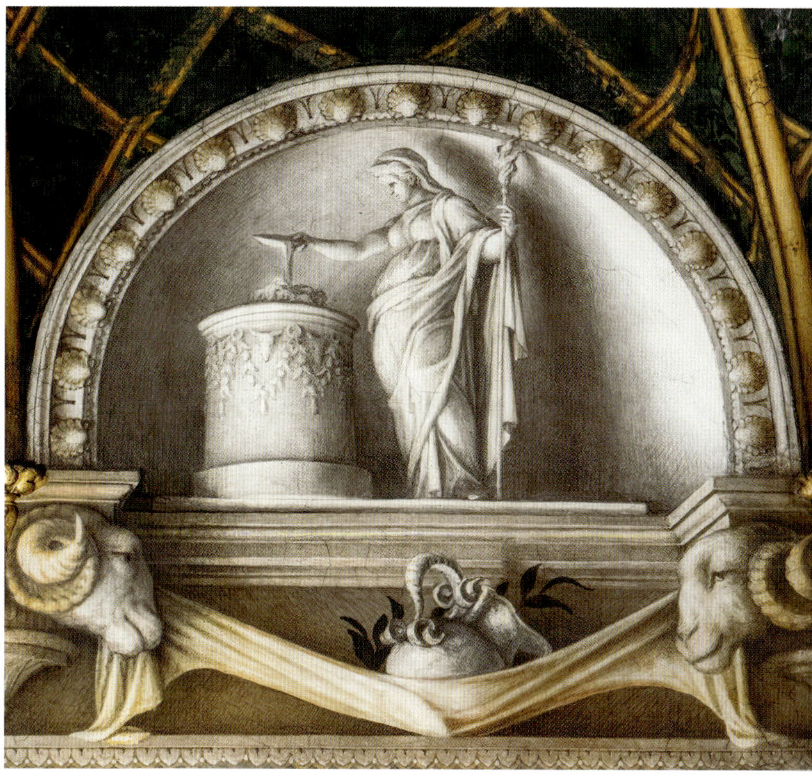

188   Correggio, *Vesta*, ca. 1518–19, fresco, Parma, San Paolo

faces left, holding a burning torch with her left hand while pouring a libation with her right. Vesta, the hearth, signified stability and permanence in the Roman world, and her temple was attended by vestals who perpetually maintained its sacred fire. Performing such a crucial duty, the vestals, virgins chosen by the Pontifex Maximus, agreed to remain chaste and that any negligence on their part would meet with terrible punishment (they were interred alive). Men were denied access to the enclosure of the temple of Vesta, and any form of male presence in the sacred precinct was believed an act of profanation. Given her virginity and the enclosure of her sacred zone, Vesta was not only intended as a manifestation of the sacred but also as "the root of sacredness itself: the inviolable."[110] Correggio's virginal, libating woman underscores her role as the guardian of the vestal's virtue, which is assured by keeping alight the sacred fire. The association between vestals and nuns is obvious, and was already long established by the sixteenth century as reported in Giraldi's *De Deis Gentium* (1548).[111] Correggio's image proclaims the role of nuns, their condition of chaste and secluded individuals whose prayers assured the wellbeing of fellow citizens, presenting them as vestal virgins maintaining the perpetual "fire" of convents.[112] A conventual

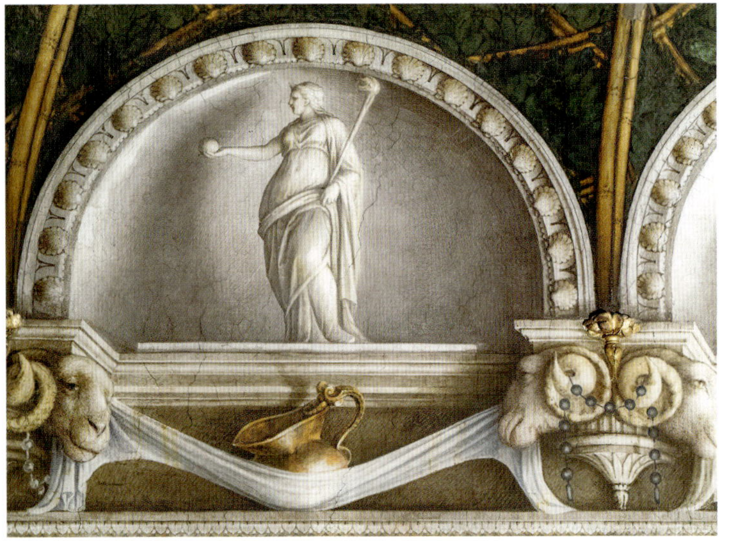

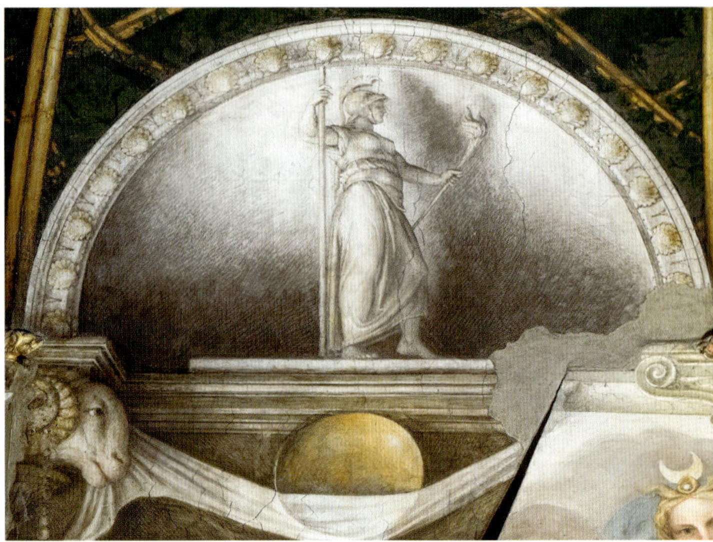

189 Correggio, *Providentia*, ca. 1518–19, fresco, Parma, San Paolo   190 Correggio, *Bellona*, ca. 1518–19, fresco, Parma, San Paolo

audience could have further been reminded of contemporary considerations on nuns' chastity not as a superior condition for women, but a way to enhance the perfection of their being. In his *Proci et Puellae* (Courtship), Erasmus speaks of purity as a condition first of the mind and then of the body. It resides, he says, not so much in the immaculate intact body as in the heart, from which impure thoughts and carnal desires must be banished. The vow of chastity was intended to prevent virgins' physical and moral pollution, and therefore to exalt their inner selves.[113]

Correggio's representations would have further invited associations with another image showing a female figure: she faces left, gazing at the globe she proffers with her right hand while holding a burning torch with the other (fig. 189).[114] It seems that here a popular ancient coin inscribed "Prov.[identia] Deor[um]" and depicting a figure bearing a globe in her right hand and a scepter or a cornucopia in the left, served as the model. Echoing the Aristotelian notion of *pronoia* (prudence), Providentia (foresight) was perceived as a necessary virtue for rulers to ensure the wellbeing of citizens and provide a stable succession to states. Foresight was desirable for the abbess because of the planning required to secure order and stability for the religious community, as Lorenzo Cornigli proclaims in his writing (see Chapter Four). The iconographic resemblance between Correggio's torch-bearing goddess and descriptions of Diana Lucifera (bringer of light, or Luna), a deity carrying a torch and itself another incarnation of the Diana-Luna on the fireplace, could have prompted recognition of

the links between this lunette and the Diana representation, all personifications of a Diana/abbess exuding authority, prudence, and foresight.

The exercise of prudence and foresight can, however, entail aggressive action to withstand difficulties, as suggested by a female figure in profile wearing armor and equipped with a spear, torch, and helmet (fig. 190). This north lunette depicts a bellicose goddess that stands in sharp contrast to conventional representations of virtuous females. Correggio's figure seems to derive from standard Minerva imagery from Roman coins, holding aloft a lighted torch instead of Minerva's shield, and with features characterizing this goddess as Bellona. The latter was described in Statius's *Thebaid* and Silius Italicus's *Punica* as a bellicose goddess. Brandishing the lighted torch, Bellona, whose very name suggests war, stirs up battle and has a hoarse cry "fraught with death."[115] Correggio gives no indication of Bellona's bloodthirsty aspects, instead investing her with a regal appearance, firm stance, and dignified strength that convey a sense of *prontezza* for battle. This may signal the abbess and her clan's willingness to defend their interests to the utmost: here one thinks of the assassination of the convent's revenue collector in 1510 (see Chapter Four). The warlike Bellona and the Diana-Luna representation set on a vertical axis on the north wall parallel one another, positing a determined female religious self defending the prerogatives of her community against ecclasiastics and detractors with *prontezza* for combat instead of passivity. It further reverberates with Araldi's representations of female figures killing

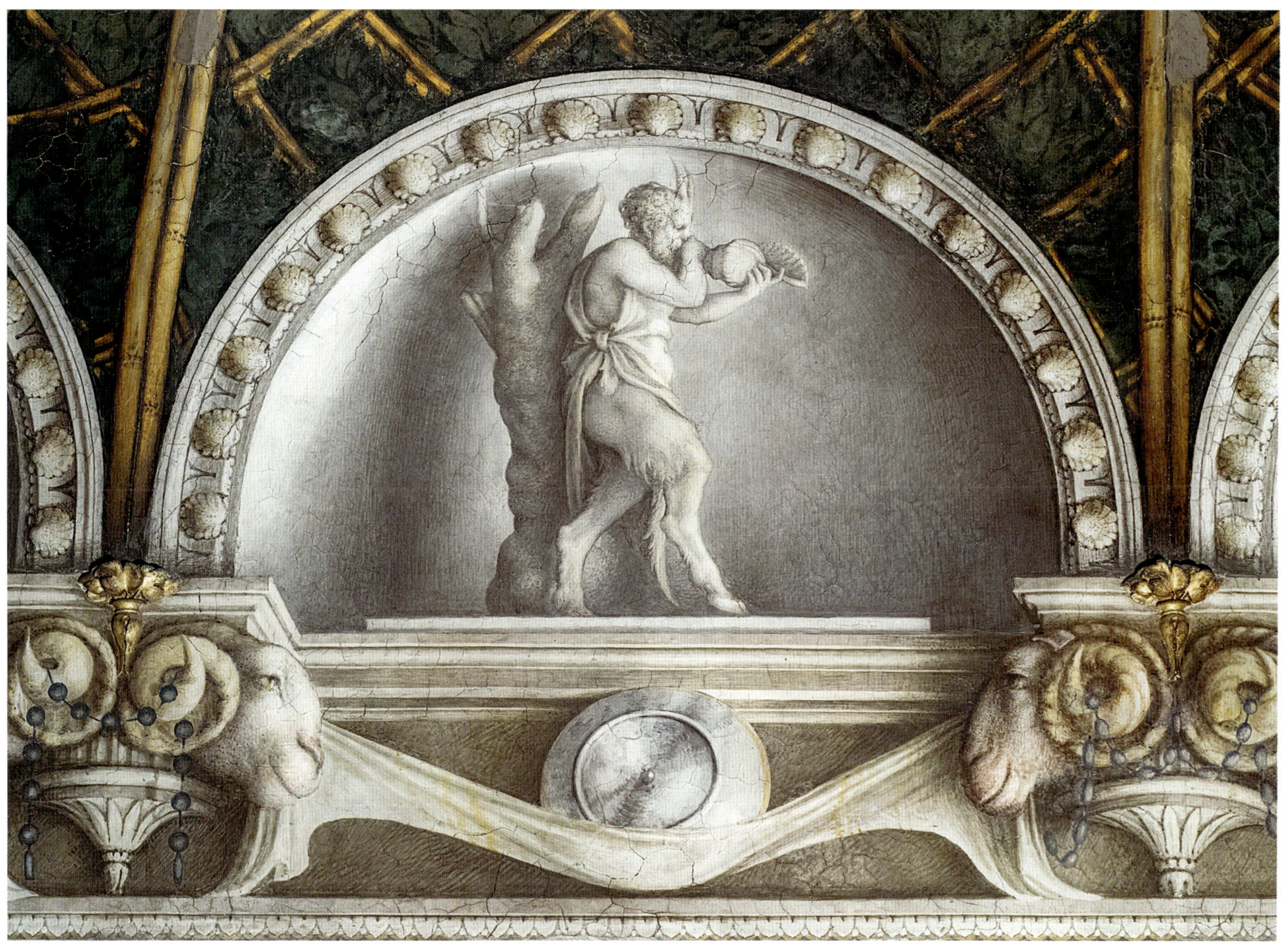

191   Correggio, *Pan*, ca. 1518–19, fresco, Parma, San Paolo

beasts, a linking of the themes around the painted rooms' lunettes that reinforces the message of wise women acting with firm resolve, not with timidity.

Yet, even the militant exercise of virtue does not prevent perturbations or inner turmoil, as embedded in an unorthodox image of Pan on the west wall. Leaning against a tree trunk and blowing a gigantic conch shell (fig. 191), Pan was described with these unusual iconographic features only by rare Greek scholiasts to Aratus's *Phaenomena*, reporting how Pan frightened the Titans with the sound of his conch when he was waging war against them. The story of this terrifying Pan first became known to Renaissance scholars through Politian, whose essay *Pan terrificus* (1489) associates the conch-blowing Pan with sudden feelings of panic.[116]

Erasmus's adage summarizes the ancient and modern references to the *Pan terrificus*, which inspired irrational terror, fear, and alarm. As Charles Dempsey has written, the ancients believed that sudden feelings of panic are "empty and without apparent cause, and hence irrevocable"; they are fears that seize the mind, especially before or during sleep. Renaissance medical writers speak of these perturbations as illnesses, while scholars of magic and superstition regarded them as influenced by supernatural forces.[117] In one way or another, whether through Politian, Manutius, Erasmus, or other sources on magic, information about this frightening Pan became available to scholars participating in the convent court and was passed to Correggio, who gave it a remarkable visual form. This Pan is a manifestation

199

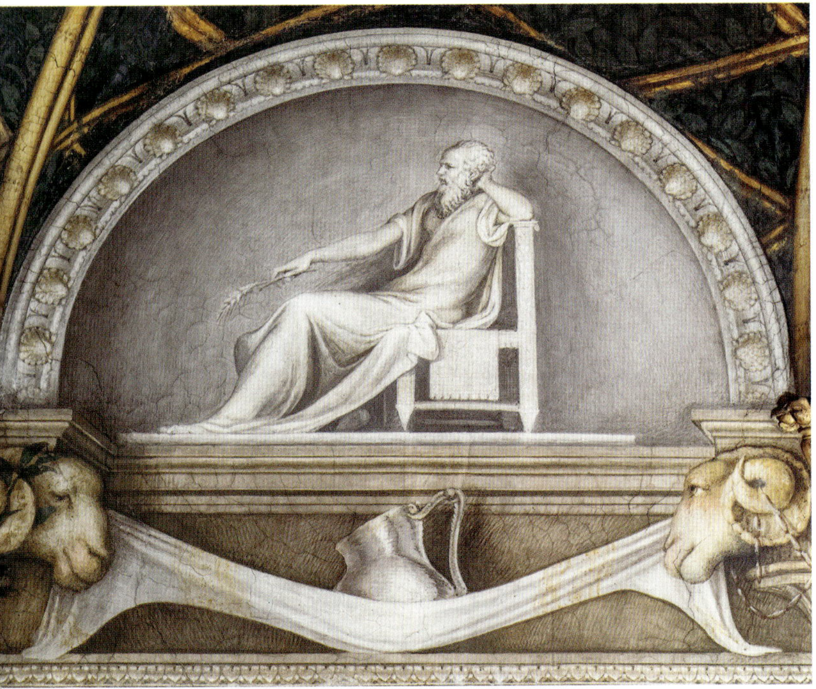

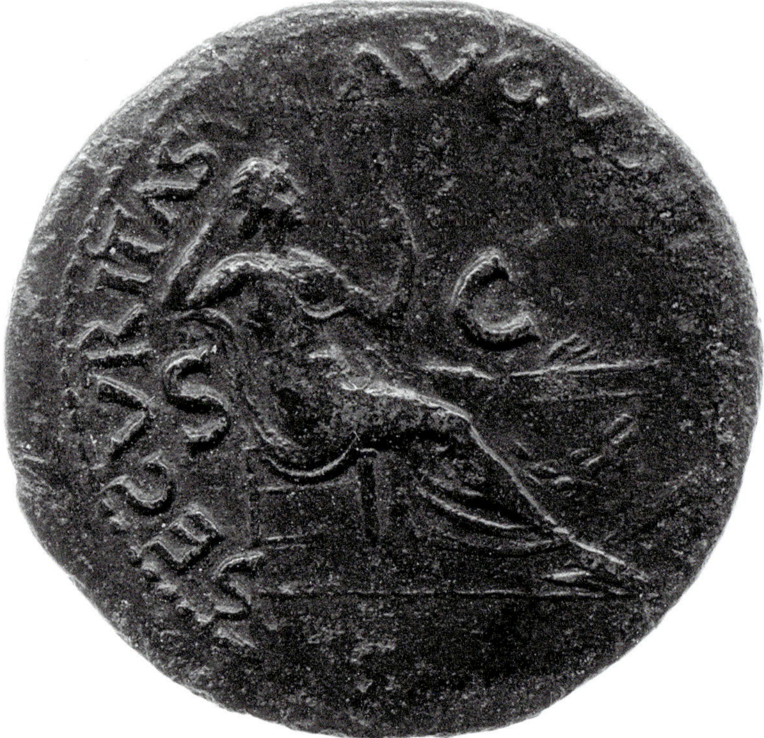

Top 192   Correggio, bearded old man, ca. 1518–19, fresco, Parma, San Paolo

Above 193   "Securitas Augusti" (verso), dupondius of Nero, 67CE, London, Trustees of the British Museum

of terror, either real or imagined.[118] Evoking nightmares and terrors striking mortals during sleep, this figure further supports the identification of the chamber as the abbess's bedroom.[119] As with the lunettes featuring the *Punishment of Hera* and the *Fates*, Correggio reinvented the figure on the basis of recondite references, and disguised his visual sources so that decoding the image hinges on the viewer's knowledge of rare texts. But, simultaneously, the beholder is fascinated by the appeal of the pictorial surface itself as the medium that elicits overhead viewing.

Correggio's *Pan terrificus* depiction could also be juxtaposed with an image facing the fireplace, a representation of a bearded old man (fig. 192) reclining on a chair and leaning his head on his left hand in introspection while holding out a tassel of corn with his right. Correggio's composition bears a generic resemblance to an image on the reverse of a dupondius of Emperor Nero (54–68 CE) featuring a seated male figure before a tripod, and the inscription "Securitas Augusti" (fig. 193).[120] He changed the direction the model faces, accentuated its relaxed, contemplative mood, suppressed the tripod, and substituted a grain tassel for the scepter, creating an idealized mature male who stretches his right hand over his left leg in a *tour de force* of *contrapposto*. Scholars have associated this pose with Giulio Campagnola's engraving of Saturn (ca. 1507), where the figure of the god, adapted from an ancient gem and holding either a reed or a corn stalk in his left hand, is set against a modern landscape derived from Dürer's prints.[121] It is unclear from a visual comparison if Correggio knew Campagnola's engraving, because even though both images portray similarly introspective and melancholy characters, Correggio presents his figure in a compressed mode, set in a timeless past, without the narration of any action. If viewers (mis)understood the connection with Saturn, they might have read into it notions of fertility, introspection, and melancholy temperament. Those more attuned to numismatic references could have related Correggio's figure to ideals of *securitas* (safety, confidence) in one's self and rights, a conceit that paralleled Persius's words "Nec te quaesiveris extra" (Do not seek outside yourself) carved over the lintel door of the chapter house. This is yet another instance of the links among the various ornaments in the abbatial rooms, which amplify and inflate one another in an expansive circularity. Carved and painted decorations echo and reflect one another in each of the rooms and then across the apartment, engaging the beholder in multiple ways with their verbal and visual communication.

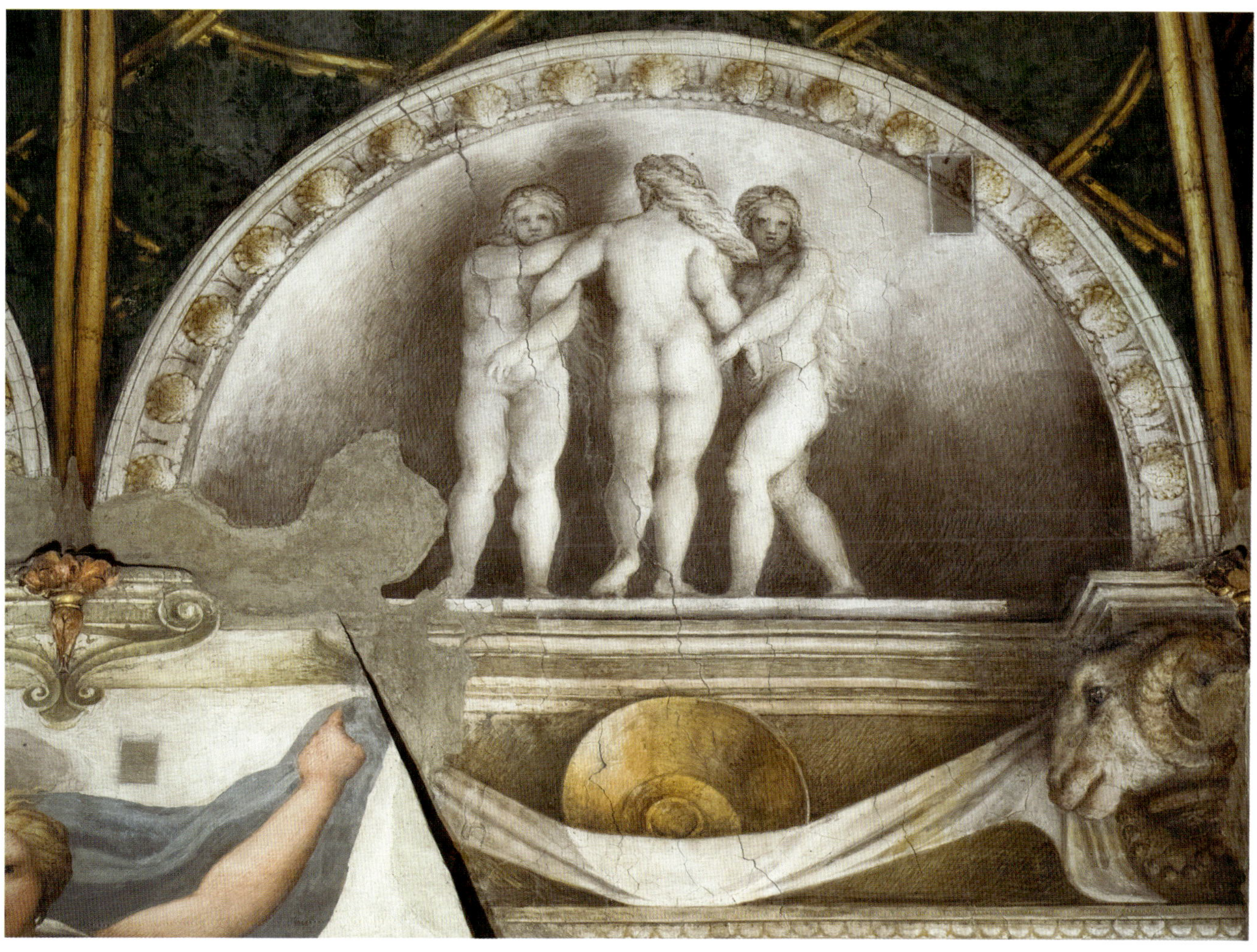

194   Correggio, *The Three Graces*, ca. 1518–19, fresco, Parma, San Paolo

Along with self-confidence come the benefits emblematized by the Three Graces (fig. 194) painted as voluptuous nude girls with free-flowing long hair, intertwined in a dancelike movement, the central Grace seen from the back and the others in frontal view. Correggio's arrangement assimilates poetic descriptions and modern models, including Niccolò Fiorentino's medal of Giovanna Tornabuoni (1486) and Raphael's *The Three Graces* (1502–5).[122] Their arms joined, Correggio's Graces exude elegant delicacy and finesse, evoking the ideal of giving and receiving. The central Grace steps to the right, both her sisters yielding as she passes the benefit to them. The right-hand Grace, as she receives this act of liberality, shifts toward the third partner of the dance, taking her hand so as to extend the benefit. She in turn embraces the central Grace and stretches her right arm to reach her other companion. Erasmus's "Naked are the Graces" adage states that the Graces preside over "human and generous actions," and refers to Horace's *Carmina* (1.30) and Seneca's *De Beneficiis*.[123] Another adage by Erasmus associates this concept of open liberality, the sharing of properties and fortunes, with the rules practiced in monastic communities, turning it into a principle of the ethical life.[124] Renaissance readers were aware that Horace describes the Graces as naked, while Seneca clothed them in transparent gowns. Niccolò Fiorentino, Raphael, and Correggio alike imagined their Graces as naked figures of voluptuous beauty. Correggio's Graces, denoting the cycle of giving, receiving, and returning benefits, translate the ideals of generosity and sharing among individuals, a way of life that bound consecrated religious women and their guests gathering in the convent court to contemplate art.

Related to contemplation and sharing as principles of conduct for one's life is another image on the south wall,

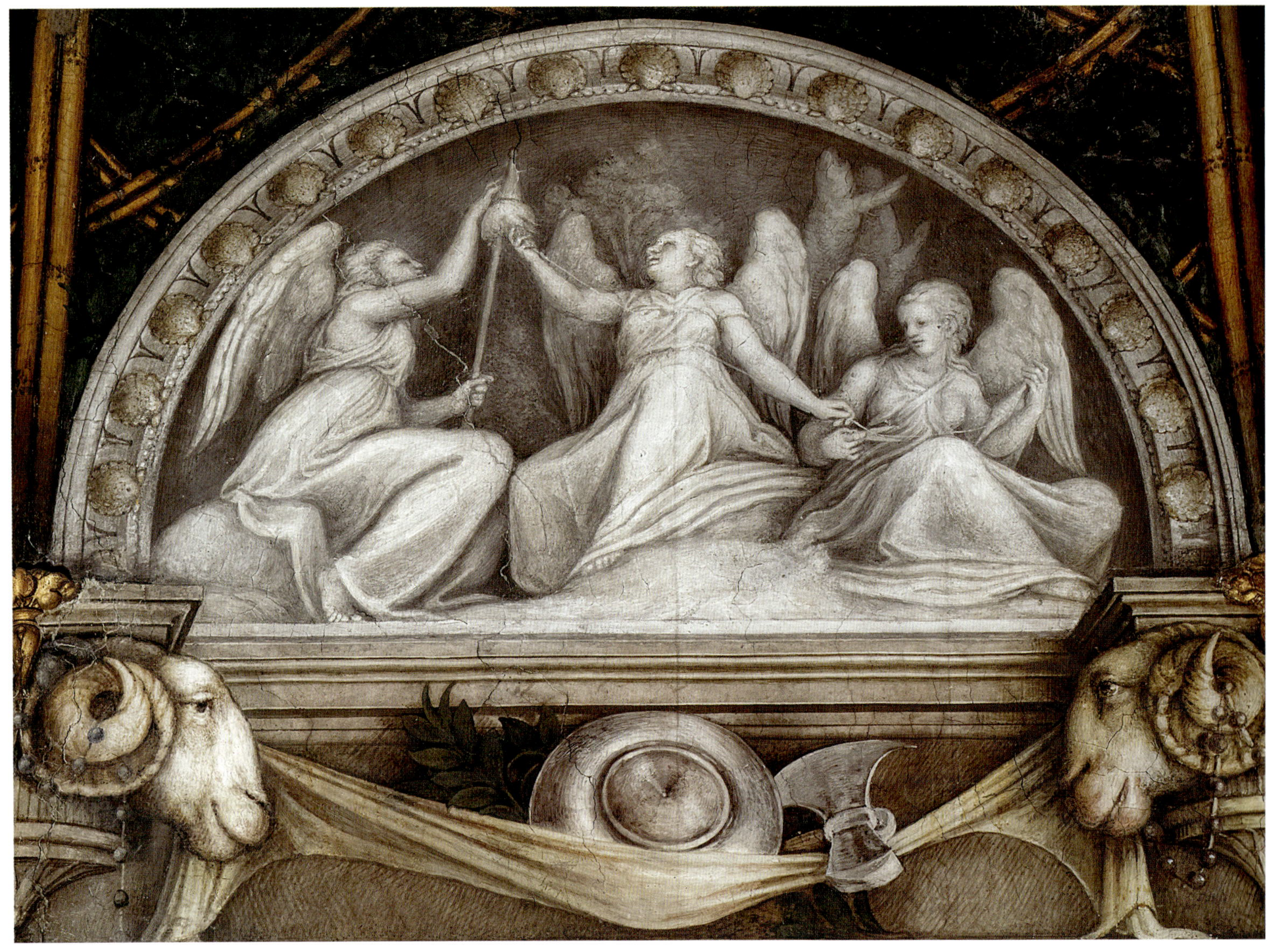

195   Correggio, *The Fates*, ca. 1518–19, fresco, Parma, San Paolo

featuring three attractive maidens seated side by side in a landscape (fig. 195). Depicted in the bloom of youth and wearing luxurious clothes, the three can be identified as the Fates who ordain human destiny. Clotho holds the distaff from which the thread of life is spun, Lachesis draws out the thread and measures it, and Atropos is about to cut it with a pair of scissors. In the cornice below, a sacrificial axe is shown along with a golden patera that, with the amused rams, make for a humorous comment on the weighty subject. More dramatic than the scissors, the axe confers a touch of levity to the gravitas of the lunette. Dressed in Renaissance-style garments that fully cover their bodies, the three girls are coordinated in gracious *contrapposto* move-

ments that reflect their roles. Panofsky recognized that Correggio's Fates break with the previous iconography in one remarkable way: they are winged. This characteristic has been associated with a Homeric *Hymn to Hermes* that describes the Fates as three "virgin sisters having wings, their heads besprinkled with white flour."[125] That hymn, like much of the Homeric oeuvre, was a fairly rare text at the time Correggio devised his composition, and the artist's literary accuracy must have greatly impressed the few informed spectators capable of linking this detail with the obscure text. The fact that the thread of life has not yet been cut indicates the notion of destiny, assuring us that there is a length of time assigned to each individual life decreed by eternal forces, thereby reiterating and reinforcing the aphoristic message of the "Sic erat in fatis" (Thus it was fated) carved on the intarsia frieze (see Chapter Four). Ultimately, this image proclaims the idea of a predetermined span of life but, given the message of several of the other lunettes, one may also infer that while the Fates and Fortune condition the lifespan and the events of a life, it is the choices and actions of the individual that in the final analysis are the markers of success or failure.

In conclusion, Correggio's lunettes juxtapose iconographies of virtues and moral precepts (chastity, prudence, and foresight) with themes of fortune, destiny, and perturbation of the mind. Designed to embellish activities of learning and reflection in the chamber they adorn, Correggio's frescoes are invitations to imagine and reimagine an "other space," stirring up sensations, and co-opting the mobile viewer and the painted space one into the other.[126] It is the *muta poesis* of painting that speaks loudly about the conventual culture that it created and defined. Paolo Valesio argued for a paradigm of silence that complements words with pauses, interruptions, and breaks, a mute poetic that magnifies speech through silence, distilling that which words cannot convey with sound and thereby making its truth more powerfully audible.[127] This poetic paradigm of silence that amplifies, expands, and recreates, seems folded into Correggio's painted chamber whose chain of concealment–irony–abstruseness prolongs the pleasure of the beholder across time. As a precept in convents and a figure for the intactness of nuns' bodies, silence is an apt metaphor for religious women, for whom silence was the recommended state of being. Correggio's murals have ultimately resisted all attempts to silence and erase elite nuns' sophisticated monastic culture. Viewed through these lenses, the pictorial poetics of silence subsumed in Correggio's frescoes is the appropriate cipher for Abbess Giovanna Piacenza's bedroom, the provoking manifestation of a conventual visual courtly culture that continues to seduce through the force of its appealing and abstruse painted fiction.

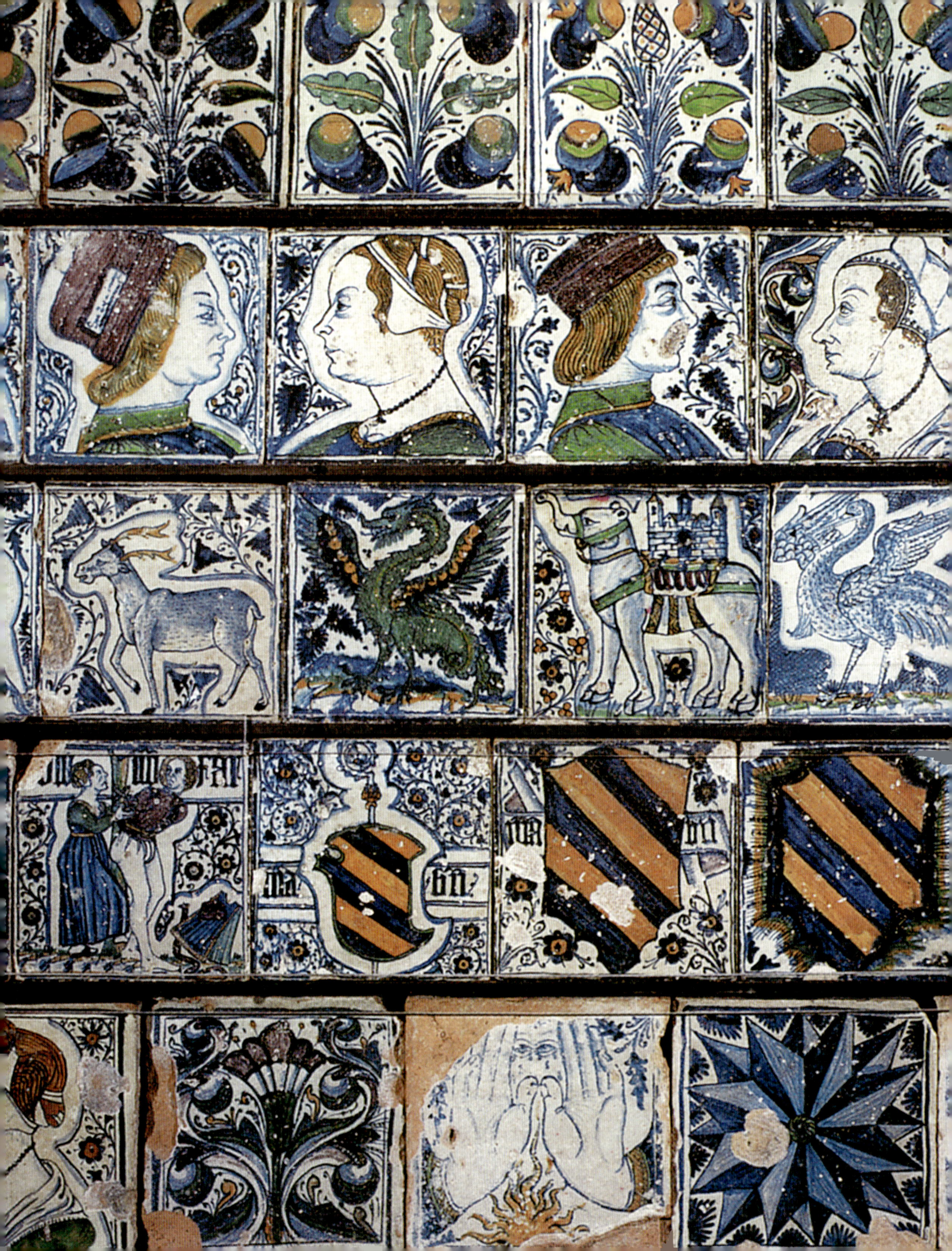

Conclusion

This book has traced the rise of what I have defined as a courtly conventual art in Renaissance Italy. It has explored a series of works with mythological and devotional subjects embedded with remarkable signs of cloistered women's authority and daring religious thoughts, works that startle modern viewers accustomed to the discourse of rigid separation between the monastic and the worldly, the sacred and the profane in the early modern period. My purpose has been to assess the role, value, and meanings of this unconventional artistic corpus produced between the 1460s and 1530s, that is, before the Council of Trent's rigid turn on religious communities. The strict discipline imposed on nunneries' inhabitants in the decades preceding and following the 1563 Tridentine council decree, and the subsequent drastic ecclesiastical approach toward their female-gendered art have long obscured its transformation of monastic settings into splendid environments and the emergence of patrician cloistered women as sophisticated patrons of artworks that enriched their lives. Adopting interdisciplinary points of view, this book has recovered the messages of this monastic corpus, treating images as a system of actions and intentions.

As shown throughout the book, this courtly conventual visual culture, which was seen by ecclesiastical authorities as dangerously transgressing the boundaries of monastic decorum, taught nuns to use their eyes to gain insights about the secular world that lay beyond their walls. Poetic subjects rendered in alluring forms appear to have encouraged cultivated religious women to surrender to the doctrine of sensual and intellectual pleasure encoded in the images. This ensemble of works in diverse media, including frescoes, maiolica tiles, and wood intarsia inscriptions, encapsulates the ambiguous identity of aristocratic nuns occupying a liminal zone between the secluded and secular spheres, a world of paradoxes and contradictions mirrored in images intended to serve as stimuli to the inhabitants. Such courtly conventual art culminated in the celebrated chamber frescoed by Correggio in San Paolo in Parma, which links the history of Italian Renaissance art history to that of female monasticism in productive ways. Correggio's sensuous style and enigmatic representations impress viewers with unprecedented force, speaking of their female beholders' perception of the immanent world, and their journeys of the imagination. As the culmination of artistic, monastic, and cultural traditions, Correggio's frescoes presuppose a sequence of refined images and objects that expanded elite nuns' knowledge beyond the Christian interpretation of things and commented on conventions of internal and external surveyance aimed at suppressing their presence in cities. As a multidisciplinary study of this overlooked class of courtly monastic art and its unexpected negotiation of pagan learning and Christian piety – and its fluid dialectic

Facing page   detail of fig. 27c

between precepts and lifestyle – this book has investigated the dense imbrications between the works of art and female patrician religious viewers to fill a lacuna in current narratives of Italian Renaissance art. In doing so, it has also attempted to respond to larger questions including how the engagement among artists, works, and spectators can help to define the place of the profane within the sacred world; and how this conventual corpus and its makers' inventive approaches to compositions and subjects can more broadly enhance understanding of the art and culture of the period.

The narratives offered in this book are conversant with questions of social art history, vision, and gender studies. Additionally, recent critical rethinking of ideas of space has proven fruitful for reflecting on the perception of richly decorated monastic places, and the transfer of knowledge, emotions, and the imagining of the world that the images afforded. Artworks shifted religious women's invisibility into a tangible presence to elicit the beholder's empathetic reactions. My objective was to realign this conventual visual corpus with its historical viewers' modalities of living and viewing, bringing out forms of synaesthetic vision and phenomenological experience that the works unfolded. Throughout, I have suggested instances in which vision, conceived in the Renaissance as a receptive process, turned material objects into triggers of sophisticated contemplation and, at times, contestation of rigid religious norms.[1] Artworks therefore became vehicles for nuns to transmute sensory impressions into understanding. Poetic and unusual devotional subjects metamorphosed conventual spaces into sites of status, mediation, and productive thinking, mingling discourses of courtly culture with religious practices, learning with spiritual nourishment. Decorated monastic parlors, chapter houses, nuns' choirs, and abbatial apartments, among other places, are presented as deposits of memories, vectors of plural communication, and bearers of cultural density, affirming elite nuns' multilayered reality in the Renaissance's male-dominated society. Artists responded to the nuns' liminal status and desire for visibility with an awareness of the subversive claims that magnificent objects in strictly regulated settings would make, an agency that amounted to forms of disobedience in environments that were expected, in many cases, to be devoid of images. Equally, the resistance to linear signification of grotesques and hieroglyphs that fill some conventual spaces could be seen to negotiate the fluid intersections between pre-Christian and Christian knowledge, further refracting magic beliefs forbidden to nuns. The indeterminacy of the grotesque forms, in particular, signals interest in exploring what lies below the surface, the mys-

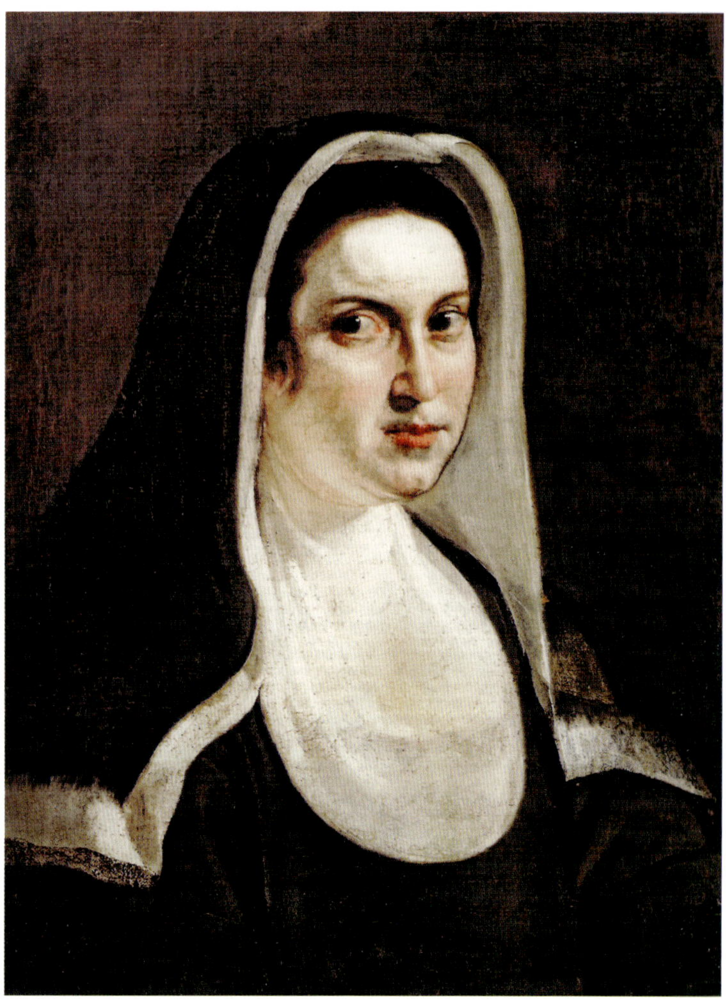

196   Artemisia Gentileschi, *Portrait of a Nun*, ca. 1613–18, oil on canvas, 70 × 52.5 cm (27^9/$_{16}$ × 20^{43}/$_{64}$ in), private collection

teries of religion, nature, and art to which religious women were meant to be privy. Difficult, literary images, which had long been considered the bases of meditation and creative thinking, were thus to provide consecrated women with sites of negotiation, constituting engines for introspection and emotional renewal.

As material traces of nuns' opposition to the strict regime of seclusion, as vehicles of expression for monastic lives spent with acute perceptions of boundaries to be bridged, this unconventional body of monastic artworks opens out sets of unexpected associations and relationships. While the colorful maiolica pavement from the convent of San Paolo representing, among other things, amorous stories comments on the rule that nuns should keep their eyes downcast while walking, the mythological themes and drolleries painted on ceilings and the upper portions of walls required nuns to break with the strictures of the lowered gaze to access the content of such imagery. This book reconstructs this lost conventual culture of viewing and imagining that could be at once serious, witty, challenging, and provocative. By researching and integrating into the history of the Italian Renaissance this little explored artistic tradition that developed in convents of "peripheral" cities like Parma and Brescia, this book has attempted to expand its narratives. It has further complicated the authority of the predominant artistic canon established by Giorgio Vasari in his *Lives* (1550 and 1568), which focused on the centers of Florence, Rome, and Venice, to enrich understanding of a periphery in which a neglected conventual corpus had a vital place; this, ultimately, may contribute to the rethinking of the Italian Renaissance in geographical terms. It has embraced a notion of "visual culture" to accommodate works of low aesthetic value or that have long been considered minor arts (as have maiolica tiles), showing how "high" art extended to decorative works. In addition, this book has focused on the arts of an elite female monastic group that, despite its status, held a marginalized position in contemporary society, working toward accounts that are representative of women and minorities.

Modern comprehension of the values of this courtly conventual corpus has up to now been affected by its physical displacement, concealment, and even destruction. Tridentine authorities implemented mechanisms of seclusion (from grated windows to high walls) and tactics of psychological domination that paternalistically treated nuns as an inferior class of Christians, and compiled lists of their "abuses," including the possession of fashionable clothing, luxurious artifacts, and portraits that were removed from convents. It is possible that Artemisia Gentileschi's *Portrait of a Nun* (ca. 1613–18; fig. 196) constitutes one such forbidden object. It presents a fascinating three-quarter image of a nun still in the bloom of youth and dressed in the habit of her religious order. She turns to look out at the viewer with a somewhat perturbed, sidelong expression, and pursed, sealed, red lips. The nun's intelligent and piercing dark eyes compel beholders to return her gaze, and to enter an intense dialogue with her. A transparent white collar barely covers her pale, radiant skin, while her brunette hair is not completely contained by or folded under the veil that frames her luminous face. Her expression speaks of firmness.[2] Surviving images like this portrait, along with frescoes, intarsia works, "curious" artifacts, and richly illustrated books, long enshrined conventual spaces and nuns' lives, blurring the distinction between the sacred and the profane.

As this book has demonstrated, any study of this artistic corpus and its conceptual reframing faces challenges intrinsic to both its fractured history and to a misogynist literature that has buried its existence, and that has much shaped our modern views of the female monastic world. But the findings presented here have revealed the development of an unconventional courtly visual culture with its own value, one which was interconnected with the leading strands of intellectual culture in the age of Erasmus. Despite its cyclical suppression, this female-gendered monastic art has continued to resurface in various forms and media across Europe and beyond throughout the early modern period, making the study of its compelling manifestations in Renaissance Italy just one chapter of a potential, larger art-historical narrative stretching across the globe. Although it was a corpus with a negated existence and whose genesis revolved around inequality and inconsistency, these intriguing images, once framed within their own critical parameters, can teach us how nuns used artworks to fashion and control their ambiguous liminal identities. In this book these narratives have centered on the remarkable artworks produced for the elite Benedictine community of San Paolo in Parma and a few other Northern Italian convents, but future investigations could fruitfully expand the inquiry to the arts of female religious communities in other regions. If nothing else, however, I hope that this book has served to illuminate the neglected node of Italian Renaissance courtly conventual art and its challenges, by reflecting on a singularly rich corpus within its artistic, monastic, and intellectual traditions, and that it can be a spur for explorations to come.

Notes

INTRODUCTION

1 H. J. Schroeder, ed., "Concerning Regulars and Nuns," in *Canons and Decrees of the Council of Trent* (St. Louis, Mo. 1960), 217–32.

2 Among Hamburger's compelling studies are Jeffrey F. Hamburger, *The Visual and the Visionary: Art and Female Spirituality in Late Medieval Germany* (New York 1998) and "The Medieval Work of Art: Wherein the 'Work'? Wherein the 'Art'?" in *The Mind's Eye: Art and Theological Argument in the Middle Ages*, ed. Jeffrey F. Hamburger and Anne-Marie Bouché (Princeton, N.J. 2006), 374–412.

3 Although limited to a few titles of Zarri, Lowe and Evangelisti's rich record of publications, the following covers their ground-breaking contributions to the history of female monasticism in Renaissance Italy: Gabriella Zarri, *Recinti: Donne, clausura e matrimonio nella prima età moderna* (Bologna 2000); K.J.P. Lowe, *Nuns' Chronicles and Convent Culture in Renaissance and Counter Reformation Italy* (Cambridge 2003); Silvia Evangelisti, *Nuns: A History of Convent Life 1450–1700* (Oxford 2007).

4 Helen Hills, *Invisible City: The Architecture of Devotion in Seventeenth-Century Neapolitan Convents* (Oxford 2004); "The Housing of Institutional Architecture: Searching for a Domestic Holy in Post-Tridentine Italian Convents," in *Domestic Institutional Interiors in Early Modern Europe*, ed. Sandra Cavallo and Silvia Evangelisti (Aldershot 2009), 120–50.

5 Venice, Biblioteca Marciana, Cod. Cicogna 2570, *Monache della Città e Diocesi di Venezia*, May 23, 1509, "Monache non escano da loro Mon[aste]rij, etc.," 151–2: "Per el tenor de la presente significheremo a Vui Venerabile Abbadesse dei Monasterij de la Città e Diocese nostra de Veniexia como per fidedigne relation habiamo inteso: et certam.te cum maximo dolore cordis et summa displicentia, che molte de le Monache vostre insino fuora del Mon.rio et vanno vagando per civitates in caxa de seculari, in piazza de San Marco et in altri luoghi vestide da secular ad libitum voluntatis sue cum maximo scandalo totius civitatis, infamia de Mon.rij vostri, et offesa de la Divina Maestà." All translations mine unless otherwise stated.

6 See esp. the misogynist report by the Venetian chronicler Girolamo Priuli, *I Diarii*, Rerum Italicarum Scriptores, vol. 24, part 4 (Città di Castello 1912), June–July 1509, 115: "Tuta la citade veramente mormorava et cridava che se dovesse fare provixione ali monasterii dele monache conventuale, che se atrovavanno in la citade veneta, che se chiamavanno monasterii apertii, quali heranno publici bordelli . . . Per il peccato gravissimo di queste monache meretrice se judichava fusse proceduto in gran parte la ruina del Statto Veneto" (Truly the whole city murmured and shouted that provisions should be made regarding the unreformed convents that were found in the city of Venice. They were called open convents, but were [really] public whore houses . . . It was considered that the nuns' grievous sin is responsible in

great part for the ruin of the State of Venice). And on nuns' adverse behaviors see also Mary Laven, *Virgins of Venice: Enclosed Lives and Broken Vows in the Renaissance Convent* (London 2002), 142, recording another Priuli entry referring to "noble girls, born of the foremost nobility and parentage of the city [who] had been transformed into public whores."

7   For Fra Timoteo's denunciation see Marino Sanuto, *Diarii*, ed. Rinaldo Fulin et al., 58 vols. (Venice 1879–1903; Bologna 1969–70), vol. 1, col. 836, December 24, 1497: "Signori, vui fate serar le chiesie per paura di la peste: fate prudentemente; ma se Dio vorrà, non vallerà a far serar le chiesie . . . Et pezo: quando vien qualche signor in questa terra, li mostrate li monasterii di monache, non monasterii ma prostibuli e bordeli pubblici."

8   Foucault argued that every advance of power and knowledge contains its counter-history and that there have always been forms of buried knowledge in past and present civilizations: Michel Foucault, "Questions on Geography," and "Two Lectures," in *Power/Knowledge: Selected Interviews and Other Writings 1972–1977*, ed. Colin Gordon (New York 1980), 63–77, esp. 70; 78–108, esp. 81–2.

9   On this complex interrelationship see the now-classic study by Mircea Eliade, *The Sacred and the Profane: The Nature of Religion*, trans. W. Track (New York 1987) and Jeffrey F. Hamburger, Petra Marx, and Susan Marti, "The Time of the Orders, 1200–1500: An Introduction," in *Crown and Veil: Female Monasticism from the Fifth to the Fifteenth Centuries*, trans. Dietlinde Hamburger, ed. Jeffrey F. Hamburger and Susan Marti (New York 2008), 41–74, esp. 46–7.

10   Michel Foucault, "Of Other Spaces," *Diacritics* (Spring 1986): 22–7.

11   Michel de Certeau, "Walking in the City," in *The Practice of Everyday Life*, trans. Steven F. Rendall (Berkeley 1984), 91–118 and Georges Didi-Huberman, *Confronting Images: Questioning the Ends of a Certain History of Art*, trans. John Goodman (University Park, Pa. 2005), 141–3.

CHAPTER I   COURTS OF ELITE VIRGINS

1   Throughout the book I use the word "convent" (and its rarer cognate "nunnery") in its modern English usage with reference to female religious communities. The English terms "monastery" and "convent" mainly denote male and female monastic institutions without specifying the regime of segregation of their inhabitants. Their Italian equivalent "monastero" and "convento" instead implied and imply their inhabitants' different seclusion regimes, for which see Agostino Pugliese, "Monastero," in *Enciclopedia cattolica*, 12 vols.

(Vatican City 1957), 8: 1270–75; Jean Nicholas Walty and Giovanni Odoari, "Convento," *Dizionario degli istituti di perfezione*, ed. Guerrino Pelliccia and Giancarlo Rocca, 9 vols. (Rome 1980), 2, 1698–1703.

2   The iconography, attribution, and chronology of Cosimo Rosselli's picture have been debated in the literature: Edith Gabrielli, *Cosimo Rosselli: catalogo ragionato* (Turin 2007), 151–3. For the painting date of 1490s: Anabel Thomas, *Art and Piety in the Female Religious Communities of Renaissance Italy: Iconography, Space, and the Religious Woman's Perspective* (Cambridge 2003), 254–79, esp. 259. For a discussion of Bosch's multilayered image see Lynn F. Jacobs, "The Triptychs by Hieronymus Bosch," *Sixteenth Century Journal* 31, 4 (2000): 1009–41, esp. 1015–16.

3   In the fifteenth and sixteenth centuries, the number of girls destined for convents increased steadily in Florence, Venice, Milan, and Bologna, among other Italian cities, due to the escalation of marriage dowries and the rigid terms of the feudal system designed to maintain families' patrimonies intact: Richard Trexler, "Le Célibat à la fin du moyen âge: les religieuses de Florence," *Annales* 27 (1972): 1337–53; Gabriella Zarri, "I monasteri femminili di Bologna tra il XIII e il XVII secolo," *Atti e memorie della Deputazione di storia patria per le province di Romagna*, n.s. 24 (1973): 133–234; Lucia Sebastiani, "Monasteri femminili milanesi tra medioevo ed età moderna," in *Florence and Milan: Comparisons and Relations*, Proceedings of two conferences at Villa I Tatti, ed. Craig Hugh Smyth and Gian Carlo Garfagnini, 2 vols. (Florence 1989), 2: 3–15; Jutta Gisela Sperling, *Convents and the Body Politic in Late Renaissance Venice* (Chicago 1999), 18–36.

4   BCA, MS B 778, Giovanni Boccadiferro, "Discorso sopra il Governo delle Monache," in Baldassare Carrati, *Miscellanea di notizie storiche bolognesi*, fols. 166r–198v, esp. 178v: "Come vogliono questi tali far legge che non si empiano li monasteri; se essi monasterii debbono esser il ridotto di quelle che maritar non puonsi? Vogliono forse essi che restino in Casa alli pericoli che io dico. O vogliono forse anche che vadino vagabonde per mille stalle e altri vitii, per essi luochi, con tanta infamia del sesso femminile?" On Boccadiferro's writing see Gabriella Zarri, *Recinti: Donne, clausura e matrimonio nella prima età moderna* (Bologna 2000), 46–8.

5   Gabriella Zarri, "Monasteri femminili e città (secoli XV–XVIII)," in *Storia d'Italia: Annali*, ed. Giorgio Chittolini and Giovanni Miccoli (Turin 1986), 9: 359–429; Silvia Evangelisti, "Wives, Widows, and Brides of Christ: Marriage and the Convent in the Historiography of Early Modern Italy," *The Historical Journal* 43, 1 (2000): 233–47; Merry Wiesner-Hanks, "Women's History and Social History: Are Structures Necessary?," in *Time, Space and Women's Lives in Early Modern*

Europe, ed. Anne Jacobson Schutte, Thomas Kuehn, Silvana Seidel Menchi (Kirksville, Mo. 2001), 3–16.

6   A Venetian Benedictine nun and a writer, Arcangela Tarabotti (d. 1652) was forced into the convent because she was disabled and with little prospect of marriage. She composed a pungent critique on coerced monachization, *Inferno monacale*: see Anne Jacobson Schutte, "Between Venice and Rome: The Dilemma of Involuntary Nuns," *Sixteenth Century Journal* 41, 2 (2010): 415–39.

7   Dante Alighieri, *Divine Comedy*, trans. Charles S. Singleton, 3 vols. (Princeton 1970), 3: 84–5. As noticed by Wood, Piccarda Donati is the embodiment of violated chastity: Jeryldene Wood, *Women, Art and Spirituality* (Cambridge 1996), 65.

8   Ippolita Gonzaga communicated to her brother her decision to take vows in 1516: Alessandro Luzio, "Isabella d'Este di fronte a Giulio II negli ultimi tre anni del suo pontificato," *Archivio storico lombardo*, 17 (1912): 245–334, esp. 331–3. Ippolita's artistic patronage has been the focus of Sally Anne Hickson, *Women, Art and Architectural Patronage in Renaissance Mantua* (Aldershot 2012), 90–94. On Cecilia Gonzaga's withdrawal to the convent of the Poor Clares see Wood, *Women*, 88–96 and on her program of studies see *Her Immaculate Hand: Selected Works by and about the Women Humanists of Quattrocento Italy*, trans. and ed. M. L. King and A. Rabil (Binghamton, N.Y. 1991), 91–105.

9   Eleonora Luciano, "Cecilia Gonzaga," in *The Renaissance Portrait from Bellini to Donatello*, ed. Keith Christiansen and Stefan Weppelmann, exh. cat. (New York 2011), 231–2 (with previous bibliography).

10   Elizabeth Makowski, *Canon Law and Cloistered Women: Periculoso and its Commentators 1298–1545* (Washington, D.C. 1999), 28; Francesca Medioli, "An Unequal Law: The Enforcement of *clausura* Before and After the Council of Trent," in *Women in Renaissance and Early Modern Europe*, ed. Christine Meek (Bodmin, Cornwall 2000), 136–52; Francesca Medioli, "Dimensions of the Cloister," in Schutte, Kuehn, and Menchi, *Time, Space and Women's Lives*, 165–80.

11   On the Tridentine decree and its effects see Jo Ann Kay McNamara, *Sisters in Arms: Catholic Nuns through Two Millennia* (Cambridge, Mass. and London 1996), 112–13; Francesca Medioli, Paola Vismara Chiappa, and Gabriella Zarri, "De Monialibus (secoli XVI–XVII–XVIII)," *Rivista di storia e letteratura religiosa* 33, 3 (1997): 643–715. Among the female communities segregated before the Tridentine decree was that of the sophisticated canonesses of Le Vergini in Venice. Despite their fierce resistance, as their chronicle attests, they were enclosed in the early sixteenth century; K. J. P. Lowe, *Nuns' Chronicles and Convent Culture in Renaissance and Counter Reformation Italy* (Cambridge 2003), 190–204. In Florence, the implementation of the Tridentine decree was preceded by tighter regulations imposed on nuns by the Grand Duke of Florence, Cosimo I, in the mid-sixteenth century; Silvia Evangelisti, "'We Do Not Have It and We Do Not Want It': Women, Power and Convent Reform in Florence," *Sixteenth Century Journal* 34, 3 (2003): 677–700.

12   Filarete, *Treatise on Architecture*, trans. John R. Spencer, 2 vols. (New Haven and London 1965), 1: x, 78r: "Do not doubt that in the execution it will be built in such a way that it will be convenient, beautiful, and decent as a monastery ought to be." On Filarete's model of the raised gallery for nuns see Liliana Grassi, "L'iconologia delle chiese monastiche femminili dall'alto medioevo ai secoli XVI–XVII," *Arte Lombarda* 9 (1964): 131–50, esp. 139.

13   Helen Hills, "The Housing of Institutional Architecture: Searching for a Domestic Holy in Post-Tridentine Italian Convents," in *Domestic Institutional Interiors in Early Modern Europe*, ed. Sandra Cavallo and Silvia Evangelisti (Aldershot 2009), 119–50, esp. 122–3, 140–41; Gaston Bachelard, *The Poetics of Space*, trans. Maria Jolas, foreword Etienne Gilson (Boston 1969), 320–21.

14   Anne Leader, *The Badia of Florence: Art and Observance in a Renaissance Monastery* (Bloomington and Indianapolis 2012), 108. On the function and typology of cloisters see Wolfgang Braunfels, *Monasteries of Western Europe: The Architecture of the Orders* (London 1972), 47–66; Caroline Bruzelius and Constance H. Berman, eds., "Monastic Architecture for Women," *Gesta* 31, 2 (1992): 73–134; Anna Elisabeth Werdehausen, "L'architettura monastica in Lombardia fra Quattrocento e Cinquecento: proposta per un metodo di ricerca," in *Giovanni Antonio Amadeo: Scultura e architettura del suo tempo*, ed. Janice Shell and Liana Castelfranchi Vegas (Milan 1993), 329–51, esp. 333.

15   Leon Battista Alberti, *On the Art of Building in Ten Books*, trans. Joseph Rykwert et al. (Cambridge 1988), Bk 6, x. Alberti related the fortified architecture of convents to prisons, for which see Helen Hills, *Invisible City: The Architecture of Devotion in Seventeenth-Century Neapolitan Convents* (Oxford 2004), 166–7.

16   Alberti, *On the Art of Building*, Bk 6, x.

17   Florence, Archivio di Stato, Miscellanea di Piante 283, fols. 7v–8r, "Prospettiva del Monastero di San Giuliano dalla parte dell'orto piccolo," 1717; Gabriella Zarri, "La Vita religiosa tra rinascimento e controriforma. *Sponsa Christi*: Nozze mistiche e professione monastica," in *Monaca, moglie, serva, cortigiana: Vita e immagine delle donne tra rinascimento e controriforma*, ed. Sara F. Matthews-Grieco (Florence 2001), 102–51, esp. 102–3, 150–51.

18   Georgia Clarke, *Roman House – Renaissance Palaces: Inventing Antiquity in Fifteenth-Century Italy* (Cambridge 2003), 102.

19 This notion of "monastic fun" has been advanced by Elissa Weaver, *Convent Theatre in Early Modern Italy: Spiritual Fun and Learning for Women* (Cambridge 2002), 49–95; "The Convent Muses: The Secular Writing of Italian Nuns, 1450–1650," in *Women and Faith: Catholic Religious Life in Italy from Late Antiquity to the Present*, ed. Lucetta Scaraffia and Gabriella Zarri (Cambridge 1999), 138. More recently on nuns and theatrical pieces see Christine Scippa Bhasin, "Nuns on Stage in Counter-Reformation Venice (1570–1750)," Ph.D. diss., Northwestern University 2012.

20 Bologna, Archivio Generale Arcivescovile, Miscellanee Vecchie, 804, filz. 23, Alcune regole et ordinat[io]ni utili per le visite et Riforme di Monasteri di Suore, December 9, 1576: "[Fanno] molti abusi del Carnevale come di [far] comedie, balli, canti, vestimenti da secolari da homo e da donna."

21 David Williams, *The Cistercians in the Early Middle Ages* (Leominster 1998), 243; Zarri, "Monasteri femminili e città," 391–4.

22 Marino Sanuto, *I Diarii (1496–1533)*, ed. Rinaldi Fulin et al., 58 vols. (Venice 1879–1903; Bologna 1969–70), 8: col. 307, May 25, 1509 records the infringements of rules at La Celestia convent and refers to young lovers of nuns as "munegini." See Tracy E. Cooper, *Palladio's Venice: Architecture and Society in a Renaissance Republic* (New Haven and London 2005), 175–9 on the art patronage in the convent. On banquets and musical matinées in parlors of Venetian monastic houses see Mary Laven, *Virgins of Venice: Enclosed Lives and Broken Vows in the Renaissance Convent* (London 2002), 90; Sperling, *Convents and the Body Politic*, 158–60.

23 In his 1576 report, the Bolognese apostolic visitor reproached nuns for having altered grates to be seen and have physical contact with outsiders visiting them: Bologna, Archivio Generale Arcivescovile, Miscellanee Vecchie, 804, filz. 25, Abusi delle Suore, December 9, 1576: "Alcuni conventi si trovano ch'hanno le bande delle grade che quando gli pare le possono levare via e restano le grade di ferro senza altro impedimento et la suora ch'è alla grada si vede tutta da quelli che sono di fuori et anco in alcuni luoghi per le grade si può toccare le mani . . . a chi gli piace." On instructions given to Parmese convents in the Tridentine period see Giovanni Battista Castelli, *Visitatio Civitatis Parmae 1578–79*, with notes by Enrico dall'Olio, 2 vols. (Parma 2000), 1: 350: "Le grati del parlatorio, dove sono quattro audienze, si ristrengano fra un mese secondo la forma data nelli decreti generali delle monache et tra tanto non sia lecito ad alcuna monacha dar'audienza à quelli parlatorij con i finestrini aperti sotto pena di escommunicazione da incorrersi subbito dalla monacha, che vi parlarà, e di non poter'andare à parlatorio, ò rota, ò porta per sei mesi, et alla Abbadessa della privatione del grado Abbatiale, e d'inhabilità a poter mai più esser creata Abbadessa."

24 Baldassar Castiglione, *The Book of the Courtier*, trans. Charles Singleton (Garden City, N.Y. 1959), II, 1. Castiglione's statement could be seen to echo a passage by the fourth-century St. Ambrose in his *De Virginibus* (On Virgins) stating that "a beauty that is heard of but not seen is all the more desirable" (2.4.22).

25 Tridentine authorities lamented the perpetual presence of merchants, shoemakers and other unauthorized workers at the gates of convents. Workers with permission to enter were said to access nunneries too "many times, unnecessarily": Bologna, Archivio Generale Arcivescovile, Miscellanee Vecchie, 804, filz. 25, Abusi delle Suore, December 9, 1576: "Vanno continuamente ogni giorno, et quando gli piace, Calzolari et Mercanti da saglie, e veli neri . . . et altri mercanti . . . se ne vano alle Porte et ivi con la Porta aperta mostrano le loro mercanzie et le loro robe alle suore . . . Li fattori, le fattore, li facchini . . . li falignami, li moradori, magnani, li quali tutti hanno licentia d'entrare in convento in caso di necessità aprobata da superiori . . . entra[no] assai volte senza bisogno."

26 ASPr, Diplomatico, Documenti Privati, no. 6794, June 8, 1509.

27 Katherine Gill, "Open Monasteries for Women in Late Medieval and Early Modern Italy," in *The Crannied Wall: Women, Religion, and the Arts in Early Modern Europe*, ed. Craig A. Monson (Ann Arbor, Mich. 1992), 16 and Sperling, *Convents and the Body Politic*, 126.

28 On adaptations and revisions of the Benedictine Rule for female religious communities see Jan Gerchow, Katrinette Bodarwé, Susan Marti, and Hedwig Röckelein, "Early Monasteries and Foundations (500–1200)," in *Crown & Veil: Female Monasticism from the Fifth to the Fifteenth Centuries*, ed. Jeffrey Hamburger and Susan Marti (New York 2008), esp. 28–9; Franca Ela Consolino, "Female Asceticism and Monasticism in Italy from the Fourth to the Eighth Centuries," in *Women and Faith: Catholic Religious Life in Italy from Late Antiquity to the Present*, ed. Lucetta Scaraffia and Gabriella Zarri (Cambridge, Mass. 1999), esp. 27–30; Lisa Cremaschi, ed., "Libretto estratto dalla regola di Benedetto," in *Regole monastiche femminili* (Turin 2003), 223–88. It is known, for example, that a few educated abbesses like the famous Eloïse d'Argenteuil (d. 1164) from the convent of the Paraclete, near Nogent-sur-Seine in Champagne, collaborated with her former lover, Abbot Peter Abelard, on a modified version of the Benedictine Rule: Patricia Ranft, *Women and the Religious Life in Pre-Modern Europe* (New York 1996), 48–9.

29 Lowe, *Nuns' Chronicles*, 189.

30 A finely colored copy of this incunabulum is kept in Ferrara, Biblioteca Ariostea (S.16.5.10), *Prologo de l'ordine del vivere neli monasteri de monache & temporale & spirituale. Excepta da*

diversi scripti de Hieronymo ad Eustochio sua Figliuola spirituale & ale sorelle (Ferrara 1497). On the attribution of the wood-cuts to the Pico Master (early 1470s–1494) see Lilian Armstrong, "Il Maestro di Pico: un miniatore veneziano del tardo Quattrocento," *Saggi e memorie di storia dell'arte* 17 (1990): 7–39, esp. 27–30. For a discussion of the *Prologo* and related comportment literature for Renaissance women see Gabriella Zarri, "Tra monache e confessori: la corte di Lucrezia Borgia," in *L'età di Alfonso I e la pittura del Dosso* (Modena 2004), 105–6.

31 Gabriella Zarri, "Christian Good Manners: Spiritual and Monastic Rules in the Quattro- and Cinquecento," in *Women in Italian Renaissance Culture and Society*, ed. Letizia Panizza (Oxford 2000), 76–91.

32 On female sexuality and mechanisms of repression the literature has greatly expanded in recent decades. Useful discussions remain Nicholas S. Davidson, "Sex, Religion, and the Law: Disciplining Desire," in *A Cultural History of Sexuality in the Renaissance*, ed. Bette Talvacchia, 6 vols. (Oxford 2011), 3: 95–111; Peter Stallybrass, "Patriarchal Territories: The Body Enclosed," in *Rewriting the Renaissance: The Discourses of Sexual Difference in Early Modern Europe*, ed. Margaret W. Ferguson, Maureen Quilligan, and Nancy J. Vickers (Chicago 1986), 123–42.

33 Erika Rummel, ed., *Erasmus on Women* (Toronto 1996), 23–38.

34 Desiderius Erasmus, "The Girl with no Interest in Marriage," in *Collected Works of Erasmus: Colloquies*, trans. and annot. Craigh R. Thompson, vol. 39 (Toronto 1997), 293.

35 Cherubino da Spoleto, *Regole della Vita Spirituale e della Vita Matrimoniale* (Parma 1487), aii v: "o anima christiana che persuo amore no[n] stenti un pocho di tempo abstenendoti da questi tali dilecti; e maxi[m]e pensando che per essi terreni piaceri liquali tu disprezi ti sono apparechiati i[n] paradiso piaceri e gaudii eterni. Stultizia granda e follia certamente si debbe existimare perdere ta[n]ti grandi beni p[er] chosi piccoli e transitorii e disonesti piaceri." On the disciplinary role of these texts see Zarri, "Christian Good Manners," 76–91, esp. 85 and Dilwyn Knox, "Civility, Courtesy and Women in the Italian Renaissance," in *Women in Italian Renaissance Culture and Society*, ed. Letizia Panizza (Oxford 2000), 3–19.

36 Mauss stresses the social construction of what he termed "bodily habit": Marcel Mauss, "Techniques of the Body," *Economy and Society* 2, 1 (1973): 70–87.

37 Bonaventura Gonzaga da Reggio, "Della buona disciplina da osservarsi," in *Alcuni avvertimenti nella vita monacale, utili e necessari a ciascheduna vergine di Christo* (Venice 1576), 34: "Non siate mai tanto sicura di non essere vista, che non procediate nel veder con prudenza, nel tatto con castità . . . come se fosse tutto il mondo à mirar le vostre actioni. Ci vede anco l'istesso Dio, Signore e Giudice nostro. Ci vede parimente la propria nostra coscienza."

38 Hills, *Invisible City*, 144.

39 Simona Braghetti, "La 'perfetta monaca': Creanza cristiana in convento tra letteratura, precettistica e iconografia," in *Vita artistica nel monastero femminile: Exempla*, ed. Vera Fortunati (Bologna 2002), 59.

40 For discussion of these issues as regards medieval monastic traditions see Christopher S. Wood, "'Curious Images' and the Art of Description," *Word and Image* 11, 4 (1995): 332–52; Mary Carruthers, *The Craft of Thought: Meditation, Rhetoric and the Making of Images, 400–1200* (Cambridge 1998), 97; Suzanne Conklin Akbari, *Seeing through the Veil: Optical Theory and Medieval Allegory* (Toronto 2004), 9, referring to the skepticism of some medieval authors about the identity of sight and knowledge.

41 Sharon Strocchia, *Nuns and Nunneries in Renaissance Florence* (Baltimore 2009), 84–91. Annuities are also known to have been invested in the renovation and decoration of monastic buildings: Gary M. Radke, "Nuns and their Art: The Case of San Zaccaria in Renaissance Venice," *Renaissance Quarterly*, 54, 2 (2001): 430–59, esp. 447–8. Although Tridentine authorities legislated against annuities, this practice was still followed in seventeenth-century Naples: Carla Russo, *I monasteri femminili di clausura a Napoli nel secolo XVII* (Naples 1970), 56.

42 On the Masaccio attribution see Jacqueline Marie Musacchio, *The Art and Ritual of Childbirth in Renaissance Italy* (New Haven and London 1999), 35–6. Carl Brandon Suehlke and Cecilia Frosinini, *The Panel Paintings of Masolino and Masaccio* (Milan 2002), 25–3, link the tray to the "circle of Masaccio."

43 On "bad" nuns and their mobility in Genoa see Giovanna Petti Balbi, *Genova medioevale vista dai contemporanei* (Genoa 1978), 117; Giovanni Soranzo, *Matteo Bossi di Verona (1427–1502): i suoi scritti ed il suo epistolario* (Padua 1965), 31–2, 234–5; Valeria Polonio, "Un affare di stato: la riforma delle monache a Genova nel xv secolo," in *Monastica et humanistica: Scritti in onore di Gregorio Penco*, ed. Francesco G. B. Trolese (Cesena 2003), 323–52.

44 Sperling, *Convents and the Body Politic*, 127.

45 Ibid., 129.

46 On Santa Patrizia and the absence of regulations governing its community before the Tridentine decree see Annamaria Facchiano, "Monasteri benedettini o capitoli di canonichesse," *Benedectina* 31, 1 (1991): 35–60; Annamaria Facchiano, *Monasteri femminili e nobiltà a Napoli tra medioevo ed età moderna: il necrologio di S. Patrizia (sec. XII–XVI)* (Altavilla Salentina 1992); Hills, *Invisible City*, 37.

47 Ambrogio Traversari, *Hodoeporicon*, ed. Vittorio Tamburini, intro. Eugenio Garin (Florence 1985), 115, 116, 204; Costanzo

Somigli and Tommaso Bargellini, *Ambrogio Traversari, monaco camaldolese* (Bologna 1986), 156.

48 On Santa Cristina as a center of music in Bologna see Craig A. Monson, *Disembodied Voices: Music and Culture in an Early Modern Italian Convent* (Berkeley 1995), 164.

49 Monson, *Disembodied Voices*, 166.

50 The antiphonary in the Biblioteca Estense in Modena was long attributed to Amico Aspertini. For its reattribution and chronology see Massimo Medica's entry in *Amico Aspertini*, ed. Andrea Emiliani and Daniela Scaglietti Kelescian, exh. cat. (Bologna 2008), 268–9. The noble-woman Bernardina Isolani was apparently also a gifted calligrapher: Craig A. Monson, "Elena Malvezzi's Keyboard Manuscript: A New Sixteenth-Century Source," *Early Music History* 9 (1989): 84 n. 30.

51 Strocchia, *Nuns*, 111–13, 125–6. In general, servant nuns constituted the labor force in textile and book production.

52 On the phenomenon of nun-artists in medieval and Renaissance times see e.g. Jeffrey F. Hamburger, *Nuns as Artists: The Visual Culture of a Medieval Convent* (Los Angeles and London, 1997); Norma Broude and Mary Garrard, *Reclaiming Female Agency: Feminist Art History after Postmodernism* (Berkeley 2005), 1–25. Plautilla Nelli's career has recently been discussed by Catherine Turrill, "Nuns' Stories: Suor Plautilla Nelli, Madre Pittora, and her Compagne in the Convent of Santa Caterina da Siena," in *Plautilla Nelli (1524 –1588): The Painter-Prioress of Renaissance Florence*, ed. Jonathan Nelson (Florence 2008), 9–27, esp. 13.

53 Victor Turner, "Betwixt and Between: The Liminal Period in Rites of Passage," in *Proceedings of the American Ethnological Society for 1964* (Seattle 1964), 4–20; Caroline Walker Bynum, "Women's Stories, Women's Symbols: A Critique of Victor Turner's Theory of Liminality," in *Anthropology and the Study of Religion*, ed. Robert L. Moore and Frank Reynolds (Chicago 1984), 105–25.

54 [Giovanni di Dio], *Decor Puellarum zoe Honore de le Donzelle la quale da Regola, Forma e Modo al Stato de le Honeste Donzelle* (Venice [1471]), ch. vi: "Lanima de le donzelle lievemente rimane atoxichata e morta; et per tanto ve priego fugite le fabule et historie, can[c]ione, libri, et parole che contegna materia de luxuria, de gola, et amor carnali, ni de noze ne di simel vani et sensuali parlari."

55 On the literacy of Le Vergini canonesses see Lowe, *Nuns' Chronicles*, 78–89. On nuns as writers of chronicles and histories of their convents see ibid. and Saundra Weddle, ed., *The Chronicle of Le Murate: Giustina Niccolini* (Toronto 2011).

56 On conventual libraries, see the seventeenth-century inventory of the library of the Corpus Domini in Bologna (a community founded by the mystic-painter Caterina Vigri), listing spiritual and humanist texts: Serena Spanò Martinelli, "La biblioteca del Corpus Domini bolognese: l'inconsueto spaccato di una cultura monastica femminile," *La Bibliofilia*, 88, 1 (1986): 1–21. On libraries of early modern Milanese convents, esp. lists of poetic texts, see Danilo Zardin, *Donna e religiosa di rara eccellenza: Prospera Corona Bascapè. I libri e la cultura nei monasteri milanesi del Cinque e Seicento* (Florence 1992), 74–96.

57 On female education in general see Paul Grendler, *Schooling in Renaissance Italy* (Baltimore 1989), 87–102; Margaret King, *Women of the Renaissance* (Chicago 1991), 157–239. On the role of convents in the education of Renaissance women see Gabriella Zarri, "Le Istituzioni dell'educazione femminile," in *Le Sedi della cultura nell'Emilia Romagna. I Secoli moderni: le istituzioni e il pensiero*, 5 vols. (Bologna 1987), 5: 84–109; Sharon Strocchia, "Learning the Virtues: Convent Schools and Female Culture in Renaissance Florence," in *Women's Education in Early Modern Europe: A History 1500–1600*, ed. Barbara J. Whitehead (London 1999), 3–46.

58 Bernardino Zambotti, *Diario Ferrarese dall'anno 1476 sino al 1504*, ed. Giuseppe Pardi, Rerum Italicarum Scriptores, 34 vols. (Bologna 1937), 24: vii, 99: "A dì 29, il sabbado [December 1481]. La illustrissima duchessa nostra acompagnò, insieme con lo signore messer Sigismondo da Este, doe soe donzelle vestide da spoxe, suxo la caretta soa, in lo monastero del Corpo de Christo, una de quelli de l'Avogaro, l'altra fiola de Carlo da San Zorzo."

59 Ibid., 83: "Adì 19, la domenega matina [November 1480]. Sore Eufroxina, mia sorella, fu acompagnata da più ziltin-donne a piedi insino al monastero de Sancto Agostino, con zoveni inanti, vestida de brochado d'arzento con li capili zoxo per spale, con l'anchona e uno bambino ornatissimo e con dupiero de cira bianca segondo il consueto de le spoxe."

60 The traveler's report is quoted in Evangelisti, *Nuns*, 50.

61 Gabriella Zarri, "Recinti sacri: Sito e forma dei monasteri femminili a Bologna tra '500 e '600," in *Luoghi sacri e spazi della santità*, ed. Sofia Boesch Gajano and Lucetta Scaraffia (Turin 1990), 385–6. On prints representing girls' entrances to Bolognese convents see Mariarosa Cesari, "'Per encomiar le donzelle ch'entrano nel chiostro': Pubblicazioni celebrative per monacazioni femminili tra Sei e Settecento nelle raccolte dell'Archiginnasio," *Il Carrobbio* 19/20 (1993–94): 203–22.

62 Zarri, "Vita religiosa," esp. 130–37.

63 Kate Lowe, "Secular Brides and Convent Brides: Wedding Ceremonies in Italy during the Renaissance and Counter-Reformation," in *Marriage in Italy*, ed. Trevor Dean and K.J.P. Lowe (Cambridge 1998), 56, recognizes that the illumination represents the "veiling and consecration (mislabelled vestition) of Suor Antonia." For a different interpretation of this image see Zarri, "Vita religiosa," 126. Dated ca. 1500, the Uffizi miniature has tentatively been

attributed to Antonia Uccello, the daughter of the painter Paolo Uccello (1397–1475) and a nun, whose skill at drawing was acknowledged by Vasari.

64 Lowe, "Secular Brides," 59.

65 Ibid., 51. On celebratory poems marking the profession rites of nuns, see Abigail Brundin, "On the Convent Threshold: Poetry for New Nuns in Early Modern Italy," *Renaissance Quarterly* 65 (2012): 1125–65.

66 On monastic dowries and their implications see Evangelisti, *Nuns*, 91–2.

67 Umberto Benassi, *Storia di Parma*, 5 vols. (Parma 1899–1906), 1: 151; Cristina Cecchinelli, "La riforma dei monasteri femminili a Parma nel primo Cinquecento: S. Paolo e S. Quintino," *Aurea Parma* 84, 1 (2005): 3–48, esp. 6 n. 8.

68 Adriano Franceschini, *Artisti a Ferrara in età umanistica e rinascimentale: testimonianze archivistiche*, 2 vols. (Ferrara and Rome 1999), 1: 394, doc. 705a, March 22, 1453; Luke Syson and Dora Thornton, *Objects of Virtue: Art in Renaissance Italy* (Los Angeles 2001), 38.

69 Parma, BP, Fondo Moreau de Saint Mery, cassetta 46, fasc. XXXI/1, *Nota di quanto ricercasi ad una Giovine, che voglia Monacarsi nel V[enerando]. Monastero di S. Paolo di Parma*. In 1598 Parma's Bishop Ferrante Farnese issued specifications concerning the dowry package necessary to be admitted to local convents: Giovanni Drei, "Le leggi suntuarie a Parma," in *Miscellanea di studi storici in onore di Giovanni Sforza* (Lucca 1920), 641–59, esp. 655, "Ordini circa li mobili, robbe et altre cose da darsi per le Monache, quando vestiranno, o faranno Professione nei Monasteri di questa città di Parma."

70 Benassi, *Storia*, 1: 151; David Ekserdjian, *Correggio* (New Haven and London 1997), 194.

71 Parma, BP, Fondo Moreau de Saint Mery, cassetta 46, fasc. XXXI/1, *Nota di quanto vi vuole per vestire, e professare una conversa in S. Paolo di Parma*. On the role of *converse* in Venetian nunneries see Sperling, *Convents and the Body Politic*, 116–17; Lowe, *Nuns' Chronicles*, 157–8.

72 Evangelisti, *Nuns*, 30–32.

73 Raffaella Sarti, *Europe at Home: Family and Material Culture 1500–1800*, trans. Allan Cameron (New Haven and London 2002), 29–38.

74 Isabella Campagnol, *Forbidden Fashions: Invisible Luxuries in Early Venetian Convents* (Lubbock, Tex. 2014), 82–5; Gabriella Zarri, "Il velo delle monache: Repertori di costume degli ordini religiosi (secoli XV–XVIII)," in *Il velo in area mediterranea tra storia e simbolo: Tardo medioevo–prima età moderna*, ed. Giuseppina Muzzarelli, Maria Grazia Nico Ottaviani, and Gabriella Zarri (Bologna 2014), 195–210, esp. 205–8.

75 Campagnol, *Forbidden Fashions*, 62–90; Janet Mayo, *A History of Ecclesiastical Dress* (London 1984), 36; Désiré Koslin, "The Dress of Monastic and Religious Women as Seen in Art from the Early Middle Ages to the Reformation," Ph.D. diss., New York University 1999, 81.

CHAPTER II ART FOR NUNS

1 On the different models of vision (intromissive and extramissive) and the fallacy of sight as constructed in Renaissance thought see David C. Lindberg, *Theories of Vision from Al-Kindi to Kepler* (Chicago 1976), 104–46; David Summers, *Vision, Reflection, and Desire in Western Painting* (Chapel Hill, N.C. 2007), 155–65; Robert S. Nelson, ed., "Introduction," in *Visuality Before and Beyond the Renaissance: Seeing as Others Saw* (Cambridge 2000), 1–21; John Shannon Hendrix and Charles H. Carman, eds., "Introduction," in *Renaissance Theories of Vision* (Farnham 2010), 1–9.

2 Augusta Ghidiglia Quintavalle and Lucia Fornari, *Arte in Emilia 4: Capolavori ritrovati e artisti inediti dal '300 al '700* (Parma 1971–2), 31; Maria Chiara Cavazzoni, entry in *Galleria Nazionale di Parma: Catalogo delle opere dall'antico al Cinquecento*, ed. Lucia Fornari Schianchi (Parma 1997), 84–5; Maria Chiara Cavazzoni, "Jacopo Loschi: Proposte per il catalogo e lo sviluppo stilistico," *Arte Cristiana* 86 (1998): 5–16, esp. 6–7.

3 This chapter expands on arguments discussed in Giancarla Periti, "Female Self-Commemoration, Spirituality and Lineage in Jacopo Loschi's Frescoes for the Convent of San Paolo in Parma," *I Tatti Studies* 13 (2010): 11–32.

4 Enrico Scarabelli Zunti, *Memorie e documenti di belle arti parmigiane (1050–1450)* (Parma 1911), 1: 40–41. Scholarship on Loschi includes Arturo Carlo Quintavalle, "Appunti per Jacopo Loschi," *Aurea Parma* 43, 1 (1959): 200–08; Giuseppa Z. Zanichelli, "Strutture della produzione artistica a Parma nel XV secolo," in *Parma: le tradizioni dell'immagine*, Quaderni di Storia dell'Arte 17 (Parma 1991), 13–62, esp. 26–30; Fabrizio Tonelli, "Loschi tra conti e frati: Date e committenti per l'ex oratorio di San Gerolamo," *Parma per l'arte*, n.s. 3, 1 (1997): 7–33.

5 Anabel Thomas demonstrates that conventual communities tended to hire local artists, in *Art and Piety in the Female Religious Communities of Renaissance Italy: Iconography, Space, and the Religious Woman's Perspective* (Cambridge 2003), 135–91, esp. 148–9, 182–3.

6 On Sigifredo's decree for the founding of the convent see Ireneo Affò, *Storia della città di Parma*, 4 vols. (Parma 1792), 1: 384–6; Laura Bandini, "Il monastero femminile di San Paolo Apostolo in Parma dalla fondazione al XV secolo," *Società, donne e storia* 2 (2004): 105–13. The community of San Paolo adhered to the Benedictine Rule until the dissolution of their house in 1810 under French revolutionary

legislation. However, the convent did not shut down completely: the nuns refused to leave and eventually regained control of the institution. Ultimately, they were replaced by nuns from another order (the Sacred Heart) in 1834.

7   In general, founders of convents reserved for themselves the right to choose the earliest abbesses: Alessandra Veronese, "Monasteri femminili in Italia settentrionale nell'alto medioevo: Confronto con i monasteri maschili attraverso un tentativo di analisi statistica," *Benedectina* 34, 2 (1987): 355–422; Bandini, "Monastero femminile," 156–7, discussing the lands that members of the Attonidi family, including Countess Matilda of Canossa (1046–1115), donated to San Paolo.

8   Bandini, "Monastero femminile," 114–15.

9   ASPr, Diplomatico, Documenti Privati, cassetta 3, doc. 48, 1187.

10 ASPr, Diplomatico, Documenti Imperiali, cassetta 5, doc. 87, 1210 and cassetta 9, doc. 93, June 23, 1226; Bandini, "Monastero femminile," 116–18.

11 Giovanni Mario Allodi, "Delfino della Pergola," in *Serie cronologica dei vescovi di Parma*, 2 vols. (Parma 1856), 1: 702–67; Michele Ansani, "La provvista dei benefici (1450–1466): Strumenti e limiti dell'intervento ducale," in *Gli Sforza, la chiesa lombarda, la corte di Roma: Strutture e pratiche beneficiarie nel ducato di Milano (1450–1535)*, ed. Giorgio Chittolini (Naples 1989), 1–113, esp. 67–8.

12 Agnese Benedetti's conventual life was full of scandal and drama. After having served as *priora* for three years (1425–8), Agnese, uncommonly, was not elected as abbess. In consequence, she did not recognize Caterina Castrobarco as the elected abbess. After Castrobarco's death in 1433, the majority of the nuns cast their votes for Agnese but some votes went to another nun, Selvaggia Arcimboldi. At the time, Agnese was not in residence in the convent, a key requisite for election as abbess: she was reported as living in her brother Ludovico's household. Given that Selvaggia was not of age, the Benedetti clan pushed through Agnese's election and obtained the papal confirmation: Laura Bandini, "La nomina delle badesse nel monastero di San Paolo: Maristella Aldighieri e Agnese Benedetti," *Aurea Parma* 88, 2 (2004): 245–56, esp. 250–54.

13 ASPr, Conventi Soppressi Serie IX, Benedettine di San Paolo, Pergamene, b. 1, December 4, 1431. See Roberto Greci, "Gli Stati minori della Padania: un anacronismo funzionale," in *Storia della società italiana*, ed. Giovanni Cherubini, 25 vols. (Milan 1988), 8: 203–32, esp. 229 n. 3.

14 Giorgio Chittolini, "Il particolarismo signorile e feudale in Emilia tra Quattro e Cinquecento," in *La formazione dello stato regionale e le istituzioni del contado* (Turin 1979), 254–91; Marco Gentile, *Fazioni al governo: Politica e società a Parma nel Quattrocento* (Rome 2009), 71–177. For the series of

benefits that the Sforza rulers gave San Paolo see ASPr, Conventi Soppressi, Serie IX, Benedettine di San Paolo, b. 1, May 21, 1456; Ansani, "Provvista dei benefici," 35–6; Gianluca Battioni, "La diocesi parmense durante l'episcopato di Sacromoro da Rimini (1467–1482)," in Chittolini, ed., *Gli Sforza*, 115–213, esp. 140–41.

15 Letizia Arcangeli, "Ragioni politiche della disciplina monastica: il caso di Parma tra Quattrocento e Cinquecento," in *Donna, disciplina, creanza cristiana dal XV al XVII secolo: Studi e testi a stampa*, ed. Gabriella Zarri (Rome 1996), 166 n. 3. In general, on the enforcement of seclusion in Italian Renaissance convents see Pio Paschini, "I monasteri femminili in Italia nel Cinquecento," in *Problemi di vita religiosa in Italia nel Cinquecento* (Padua 1960), 31–60; Katherine Gill, "Scandala: Controversies concerning Clausura and Women's Religious Communities in Late Medieval Italy," in *Christendom and its Discontents: Execution, Persecution and Rebellion 1000–1500*, ed. Scott Waugh and Peter Diehl (Cambridge 1995), 177–203.

16 Angelo Pezzana, *Storia della città di Parma*, 5 vols. (Parma 1837–59), 3: 190 n. 3, reports that: "due monache Giovanna Pallavicino e Masina Lalatta avevano in questo tempo ottenuto breve di Pio II che le autorizzava a passare nel monastero di S. Maria delle Grazie dell'Ordine di S. Chiara verso loro affermazione che in quello di S. Paolo non poteano utilmente servire a Dio, perchè non vi si praticavano quegli atti di penitenza e di mortificazione cristiana che credevano proprii del loro stato."

17 Caroline Walker Bynum, "Religious Women in the Later Middle Ages," in *Christian Spirituality: High Middle Ages and Reformation*, ed. Jill Raitt, Bernard McGinn, and John Meyendorff (New York 1987), 121–39.

18 Pezzana, *Storia*, 3: 190 n. 3: "Ma avendo la badessa [Selvaggia Arcimboldi] fatto aperto al Pontefice come la loro determinazione suscitata fosse piuttosto da *istigazione diabolica e da muliebre leggerezza* [original emphases] che da vero spirito di divozione, non essendo loro vietato di far opere di penitenza anche in S. Paolo, ove si attenessero alla regola di S. Benedetto, Pio II revocò la concessione a dì tre di novembre." On the Arcimboldi family, including Selvaggia and Cardinal Giovanni who held prominent ecclesiastical offices, see Roberto Greci, "Proprietà immobiliari, mobilità, carriera di una famiglia parmense del tardo medioevo: gli Arcimboldi," *Quaderni storici* 6, 1 (1988): 9–36, esp. 28 n. 22.

19 SBEAP, Enrico Scarabelli Zunti, "Materiale per una guida artistica e storica di Parma: Chiese e conventi," vol. II (M–V), MS III, fol. 121r.

20 Bandini, "Monastero femminile," 142 n. 123, referring to a record dating to 1433 naming the *conversus* Giacomo as a witness to nuns' litigations in the cloister of San Paolo.

21 Pier Maria Rossi commissioned a charming painted room in his Torrechiara castle with representations of love and his land holdings: Chad Coerver, "Donna/Dono: Chivalry and Adulterous Exchange in the Quattrocento," in *Picturing Women in Renaissance and Baroque Italy*, ed. Geraldine A. Johnson and Sara F. Matthews Grieco (Cambridge 1997), 197–221; Jean C. Campbell, "Pier Maria's Treasure: Love, Knowledge and the Invention of the Source in the Camera d'Oro at Torrechiara," in *Emilia e Marche nel Rinascimento: l'identità visiva della "periferia,"* ed. Giancarla Periti (Azzano [Bg], 2005), 63–88; Giuseppa Z. Zanichelli, "La committenza dei Rossi: Immagini di potere fra sacro e profano," in *Le Signorie dei Rossi di Parma tra XIV e XVI secolo*, ed. Letizia Arcangeli and Marco Gentile (Florence 2007), 196–212.

22 On Antonia Torelli's dowry and the Rossi couple's separation see ASPr, Notarile, Gaspare Zangrandi, filza 189, June 3, 1455; Pezzana, *Storia*, 2: 297. On Torelli's financial independence and artistic patronage see Gianni Capelli and Pier Paolo Mendogni, *Il Castello di Torrechiara: Storia. Architettura Dipinti* (Parma 1994), 29; Timothy McCall, "Visual Imagery and Historical Invisibility: Antonia Torelli, her Husband, and his Mistress in Fifteenth-Century Parma," *Renaissance Studies* 23, 3 (2009): 269–87.

23 Nadia Covini, "Le condotte dei Rossi di Parma. Tra conflitti interstatali e 'picciole guerre' locali (1447–1482)," in *Le Signorie dei Rossi di Parma*, 57–100, esp. 81–4.

24 The Torelli–Arcimboldi contract has been published, albeit partially, by Giuseppa Z. Zanichelli, *I Conti e il minio: Codici miniati dei Rossi 1325–1482* (Parma 1996), 85 n. 82.

25 ASPr, Notarile, Gherardo Mastagi, filza 37, October 2, 1455: "dederunt, concesserunt et locaverunt magnificae et potenti dominae Antoniae . . . seu casamenti dicti Monasterii praedicti, qui locus alia nuncupatur vulgariter La Infermeria, et qui locus minatur ruynam, incipiendo a ponte seu volta unius canalis labentis per ipsum locum et ipsam voltam claudendo in domo infrascripta et de qua infra fit mentio hedificanda per ipsam dominam Antoniam et veniendo versus Ecclesiam dicti Monasterii per tantum quantum durat ipsum locum . . . fondo, seu casamento et seu parte casamenti ut supra prefata domina Antonia construi et hedificari facere posset et valet unam domum pro usu et habitatione condecenti ipsius dominae Antoniae et in qua ipsa domina Antonia habet et habere debeat, et intelligat ut usum, usufructum et habitationem."

26 On the transformation of infirmaries into abbatial residences see Jackie Hall, "East of the Cloister: Infirmaries, Abbots' Lodgings, and Other Chambers," in *Perspectives for an Architecture of Solitude: Essays on Cistercians, Art, and Architecture in Honor of Peter Fergusson*, ed. Terryl N. Kinder (Turnhout 2004), 199–212; Paolo Piva, "San Benedetto in Polirone: lo sviluppo storico di un'edilizia monastica," *Civiltà mantovana* 20 (1988): 31–71, esp. 35–9; Paolo Piva, "Quel che sappiamo sulla *Domus Infirmorum* in un'abbazia benedettina: San Benedetto Po," *Postumia* 6 (1995): 79–88, esp. 81.

27 Franciscus Marius Grapaldus, *De Partibus Aedium* (Parma 1494; *Addita modo, verborum explicatione quae in eodem libro continentur*, 1516), 2.7. On Grapaldo's section on the *valetudinarium* see Georgia Clarke, *Roman House – Renaissance Palaces: Inventing Antiquity in Fifteenth-Century Italy* (Cambridge 2003), 102.

28 A record, drawn up on May 2, 1257, speaks of a hospital adjacent to San Paolo: BP, MS Parm. 1626, *Liber Ospitalis Rodulfi comunitatis Parmae*, fol. 16r; Allodi, *Serie cronologica*, 1: 713. For an overview of hospitals in fifteenth-century Parma see Marco Pellegri, *Gli Xenodochi di Parma e provincia dagli inizi al 1471* (Parma 1973).

29 On the multivalent functions of chapter houses and their decorations see Sheila Bonde and Clark Maines, "Monastic Struggle and Ritual Resolution: Centrality and Community in the Gothic Chapter Room," in *Saint-Jean-des-Vignes in Soissons: Approaches to its Architecture, Archeology, and History*, ed. Sheila Bonde and Clark Maines (Turnhout 2003), 262–302, esp. 293–6; Joanna Cannon, *Religious Poverty, Visual Riches: Art in the Dominican Churches of Central Italy in the Thirteenth and Fourteenth Centuries* (New Haven and London 2013), 186–99.

30 Redrawn from Gozzi's late eighteenth-century plan of the convent of San Paolo, this plan of the monastic spaces is intended as an aid to help visualize the buildings that constituted the nunnery in the 1470s.

31 BP, MS Parm. 922, Angelo Mario Edoari da Erba, *Compendio copiosissimo dell'Origine, Antichità, Successi e Nobiltà della Città di Parma, suo popolo, e Territorio estratto dal raccolto da varii Autori . . . l'anno 1572*, fol. 246: "ristorò con molta sollecitudine, e spese, di boniss. fabriche la Chiesa sua di S. Paolo."

32 SBEAP, Scarabelli Zunti, "Materiale," MS 111, fol. 109r.

33 Giovanni Battista Castelli, *Visitatio Civitatis Parmae 1578–79*, with notes by Enrico dall'Olio, 2 vols. (Parma 2000), 1: 259–64. On pastoral visits in the diocese of Parma see Adriano Prosperi, "Dall'investitura papale alla santificazione del potere: Appunti per una ricerca sui primi Farnese e le istituzioni ecclesiastiche a Parma," in *Le corti farnesiane di Parma e Piacenza (1545–1622): I, Potere e società nello stato farnesiano*, ed. Marzio A. Romani (Rome 1978), 161–88, esp. 172.

34 Giuseppina Longhi and Aldo Spina, "Il complesso monastico di San Paolo," 2 vols., thesis, Politecnico di Milano 1991–2, 1: 10.

35 ASPr, Inventario dei Beni dei Conventi Soppressi, September 13, 1810, no. 123. An overlooked statement in the notes of Scarabelli Zunti relates, albeit indirectly, that Loschi's frescoes

were in the chapter house: SBEAP, Scarabelli Zunti, "Materiale," MS III, fol. 106v: "L'antica torre era presso la fronte della Chiesa attuale alla destra di chi entra nella medesina. Ma tutto fu più tardi innovato, cosicchè non appartengono alla vecchia chiesa che que' frammenti di pitture scoperte nel 1859 dietro la cappella del monumento Neipperg."

36 ASPr, Mappe del Patrimonio dello Stato, vol. VI, no. 584, *Pianta icnografica* [sic] *dell'edifizio di San Paolo e sue dipendenze in Parma*, June 4, 1851.

37 Longhi and Spina, "Complesso monastico," 1: 63–7.

38 The phenomenon of girls *in serbanza*, that is, entering convents for educational purposes, has been discussed by Sharon Strocchia, "Taken into Custody: Girls and Convent Guardianship in Renaissance Florence," *Renaissance Studies* 17, 2 (2003): 177–200.

39 Bandini, "Monastero femminile," 130–33.

40 Ibid., 122. The Benedictine Rule does not indicate any age limit for the election of abbots. On the figure, role, and power of the abbess see Gregorio Penco, *Storia del monachesimo in Italia: dalle origini alla fine del medioevo* (Milan 1983), 335–55; Maria Teresa Medici, "Sulla giurisdizione temporale e spirituale dell'abbadessa," in *Il monachesimo femminile in Italia dall'alto medioevo a confronto con l'oggi*, ed. Gabriella Zarri (Negarine di San Pietro in Cariago [Ve] 1997), 75–86.

41 The correct date of Maria Benedetti's election comes from the documentation surveyed by Michele Ansani, *Camera Apostolica: Documenti relativi alla diocesi del ducato di Milano. I "Libri Annatarum" di Innocenzo VIII (1458–1471)* (Milan 1994), 362–3.

42 BP, Edoari da Erba, fol. 246. While the date of Abbess Benedetti's death is unknown, the election of her successor (see Chapter Three) took place in 1484. Within a monastic world structured by long-standing regulations and customs that year can be taken as the time of the abbess's death.

43 ASPr, Conventi Soppressi, Serie IX, Benedettine di San Paolo, busta 1, January 5, 1463; Pezzana, *Storia*, 3: 231 [1463]; 307 [1469] referring to Abbess Benedetti also conferring benefits to individuals of her choice.

44 On the genealogy of the Benedetti family see SBEAP, MS III, Scarabelli Zunti, "Materiale," fol. 121r.

45 Ibid., for this document summarized by Scarabelli Zunti. Another of Maria's sisters, Giacoma, entered the local convent of San Domenico. She commissioned a lavishly illuminated manuscript from the so-called Maestro delle Ore Sanvitale: Giuseppa Z. Zanichelli, "Il Maestro delle Ore Sanvitale e la bottega di Cristoforo Caselli: miniatura a Parma nella seconda metà del XV secolo," *Artes* 2 (1994): 38–61, esp. 47–8.

46 SBEAP, MS 101, Enrico Scarabelli Zunti, "Documenti e memorie di belle arti parmigiane," vol. II, fol. 44. Giberto Bajardi and Simona Benedetti had at least four children: Matteo, Gaspare, Palmia, and Francesco.

47 Anselmo Lentini, "Santa Scolastica," in *Bibliotheca Sanctorum*, 13 vols. (Rome 1968), 11: 742–50; Anna Maria Canopi, "Santa Scolastica," in *Monachesimo benedettino femminile* (Seregno [Mi] 1994), 17–27; Viktor Dammertz, ed., *San Benedetto: Il fondatore. L'Europa dal 480 al 1980* (Milan 1980), 88–100. According to St. Gregory's *Dialogues*, Scholastica had an annual meeting with her brother, and during their last encounter they ate and prayed together all night. This scene is represented in an illumination of the *Speculum Historiale* of Vincent de Beauvais and in the predella of Lorenzo Monaco's *Coronation of the Virgin* altarpiece (1414; Florence, Uffizi). As Anne Leader suggests in *The Badia of Florence: Art and Observance in a Renaissance Monastery* (Bloomington and Indianapolis 2012), 200, perhaps the mural of St. Scholastica's last meeting with St. Benedict was among the lost scenes painted on the walls of the cloister of the Badia in Florence (ca. 1435–9), a cycle now in ruinous condition.

48 *Indice generale degli incunaboli delle biblioteche d'Italia*, 6 vols. (Rome 1945), 3: 44–5 lists the Latin edition of St. Gregory's *Dialogues* printed in Paris in 1477–8 and the copies in the vernacular that had appeared in Venice two years earlier. In Modena, Domenico Rococciolo printed a copy of this text in 1481, when another edition was published in Milan.

49 Maria Laura Cristiani, "Gli affreschi del Sacro Speco," in *I monasteri benedettini di Subiaco*, ed. Claudio Giumelli (Milan 1982), 192–239; Antonio Ricci and Maria Antonietta Orlandi, eds., *Lo spazio del silenzio: Storia e restauri dei monasteri benedettini di Subiaco* (Subiaco 2004), 181–91. Alessandro Tomei has argued for the presence of two different masters, one influenced by northern models and the other nourished by local prototypes, working in both Santa Scolastica and Sacro Speco in the early fifteenth century: Tomei, "Tra Abruzzo e Lazio: Affreschi quattrocenteschi nel transetto di Santa Scolastica a Subiaco," in *L'Abruzzo in età angioina: Arte di frontiera tra medioevo e rinascimento*, ed. Daniele Benati and Alessandro Tomei (Milan 2006), 237–53.

50 Caroline Walker Bynum, *Holy Feast and Holy Fast: The Religious Significance of Food to Medieval Women* (Berkeley 1987), 190–93.

51 St. Gregory, *Dialogues*, ch. 33, describes St. Scholastica as a girl consecrated to God from her youth.

52 In 1471, the prior of Parma's Carthusian monastery praised the piety of the nuns of San Paolo, granting them "the spiritual benefices of the Carthusian order": ASPr, Pergamene Miniate, stanza 14, cassetta 17, doc. 5, May 12, 1471. The letter is mentioned in Pezzana, *Storia*, 3: 338.

53 Richard Goldthwaite, "The Economic and Social World of Italian Renaissance Maiolica," *Renaissance Quarterly* 42 (1989): 1–32; Luke Syson and Dora Thornton, *Objects of*

Virtue: Art in Renaissance Italy (Los Angeles 2001), 200–20; Marta Ajmar, "Talking Pots: Strategies for Producing Novelty and the Consumption of Painted Pottery in Renaissance Italy," in *The Art Market in Italy: 15th–17th Centuries*, ed. Marcello Fantoni, Louisa Matthew, and Sara F. Matthews-Grieco (Modena 2003), 55–64, esp. 58–9.

54 Timothy Wilson, *Ceramic Art of the Italian Renaissance* (London and Austin, Tex. 1987), 34–8; Timothy Wilson, ed., *Italian Renaissance Pottery: Papers written in Association with a Colloquium at the British Museum* (London 1991); John V. G. Mallet and Franz Adrian Dreier, *The Hockemeyer Collection: Maiolica and Glass* (Bremen 1998); Elisa P. Sani, "The Ornamental Language of Maiolica," in *Italian Renaissance Maiolica* (London 2012), 43–73; Carmen Ravanelli Guidotti, "Montelupo *Figurato*: An Historiographical Profile," in *The "Figurato" Maiolica of Montelupo* (Rome 2012), 35–54.

55 Laurie Fusco and Gino Corti, *Lorenzo de' Medici, Collector and Antiquarian* (Cambridge 2006), 79–80. Gifts of maiolica objects were often accompanied by sonnets; Augusto Campana, "Poesie umanistiche relative a ceramiche," *Faenza* 32 (1946): 59–68.

56 In addition to the maiolica floor, a now fragmentary sculpted tin-glazed maiolica frieze probably ornamented the main portal of the convent. It is kept in the storage room of Parma's SBEAP. From the top, it features rows of rosettes, lively putti, vine trellises, and purple grapes. According to Scarabelli Zunti, Abbess Benedetti commissioned it, which dates it to the late Quattrocento: SBEAP, Scarabelli Zunti, "Materiale," MS III, fols. 112r–112v; ASPr, Direzione del Patrimonio dello Stato, busta 138, March 22, 1849; Laudedeo Testi, *Parma* (Bergamo 1905), 110; Longhi and Spina, "Complesso monastico," I: 70. Given its fine quality, this frieze has been connected to a maiolica bust representing a bishop attributed to Galeotto Pavesi, a Modenese-born ceramist active in Parma until 1479: Aldo Galli, "Santa Redegonda e Santa Felicola: Due sculture del Quattrocento a Parma," in *Scritti per l'Istituto germanico di storia dell'arte di Firenze: Settanta studiosi italiani*, ed. Cristina Acidini Luchinat et al. (Florence 1997), 111–18, esp. n. 5. It remains unclear whether a recently rediscovered late Quattrocento polychrome terracotta polyptych representing the Nativity and scenes from the life of the Virgin, now on display in the San Paolo gallery, was or was not commissioned by the conventual community: Clelia Alessandrini, "San Paolo: dalla riscoperta della Camera all'attuale sistemazione museografica," *Aurea Parma* (2012): 47–56, esp. 54.

57 On the tin-glazed pavements for Ercole and Isabella d'Este see Giuseppe Campori, *Maiolica e porcellana di Ferrara nei secoli XV e XVI* (Pesaro 1879), 10–11; John V. G. Mallet, "Tiled Floors and Court Designers in Mantua and Northern Italy,"

in *La corte di Mantova nell'età di Andrea Mantegna*, ed. Cesare Mozzarelli, Robert Oresko, and Leandro Ventura (Rome 1997), 261; Chiara Forlani, "I pavimenti ceramici rinascimentali commissionati da Isabella d'Este: Storia di una dispersione," in *Atti XX Convegno Internazionale della Ceramica* I (1987): 223–32. On the Petrucci maiolica floor, the majority of whose tiles are in the Victoria and Albert Museum, London, see Elizabeth Miller and Alun Graves, "Rethinking the Petrucci Pavement," *Renaissance Studies* 24, 1 (2010): 94–118; Philippa Jackson, "The Patronage of Pandolfo the Magnificent," in *Renaissance Siena: Art for a City*, exh. cat., ed. Luke Syson (New Haven and London 2008), 64–7.

58 Leon Battista Alberti, *On the Art of Building in Ten Books*, trans. Joseph Rykwert et al. (Cambridge 1988), 7.x and 9.iv; Filarete [Antonio Averlino)], *Treatise on Architecture*, trans. John R. Spencer, 2 vols. (New Haven and London 1965), I: IX.67r; Angela Dressen, *Pavimenti decorati del Quattrocento in Italia* (Venice 2008), 229–41. In general on tiles and pavements in the early modern period see Francesco Quinterio, *Maiolica nell'architettura del rinascimento italiano (1440–1520)* (Florence 1990), 28–36, 68–71; Wolfgang Wolters, "Fussböden," in *Architektur und Ornament: Venezianischer Bauschmuck der Renaissance* (Munich 2000), 204–20.

59 Fabio Barry, "Walking on Water: Cosmic Floors in Antiquity and the Middle Ages," *Art Bulletin* 89, 4 (2007): 627–57.

60 Plinio [Pliny the Elder], *Istoria naturale tradotta di lingua latina in Fiorentino per me Cristoforo Landino* (Venice 1476), 35.xxv: "Elithostrati cominciarono ne' tempi di Sylla con piccole cruste. E ancora hoggi dura quello el quale lui fece a Preneste nel Tempio della Fortuna. Cacciati poi di terra e pavimenti passarono nelle volte chome prono vitio e questo certamente fu trovato da Agrippa nelle terme le quali fece a Roma e le cose di terra dipinse a fuocho." For Vasari's discussion of the maiolica technique see Giorgio Vasari, *Le vite de' più eccellenti pittori, scultori e architettori nelle redazioni del 1550 e 1568*, ed. Rosanna Bettarini and Paola Barocchi, 6 vols. (Florence 1966–87), I: 74: "Altri [moderni artefici] fanno alle più gentili pavimenti di terracotta a mattoncini con varii spartimenti et invetriati a fuoco, come in vasi di terra dipinti di varii colori e con fregi e fogliami dipinti; ma questa sorta di pavimenti più conviene alle stufe et a' bagni che alle fonti."

61 Niccolò Perotti, *Cornucopiae seu linguae latinae commentarii* (1489; Venice 1513), 154: "Huiusmodi pavimenta lapideis sive figulinis crustis constat vitro tectis atque encausto pictis, inventum Agrippae in Thermis, quas Romae aedificavit"; 893: "Item inuro, quod proprie significat adhibito ignii fingo, quod genus picturae encausticae dicitur. Et qui ita pingit encaustes, et opus ita pictum, encaustum." As noted by Collareta, Perotti conflated the terms *encaustum* and *inustum*, developing the

notion of *encaustum* as a "glowing genus picturae," referring to maiolica tiled floors: Marco Collareta, 'Encaustum Vulgo Smaltum': Note sulla percezione umanistica delle tecniche figurative," *Annali della Scuola normale superiore di Pisa*, ser. III, 14, 2 (1984): 759–69. A Latin eighteenth-century description of the maiolica tiles in Naples's Pontano chapel (ca. 1492) refers to them as an encaustic painting: Guido Donatone, "Inediti esemplari di maiolica napoletana di età rinascimentale," in *Centro Studi per la storia della ceramica meridionale – sezione Napoli* (1997), 27–34, esp. 30.

62 Grapaldus, *De Partibus Aedium*, 2.1.

63 Leon Battista Alberti, *On Painting*, trans. Cecil Grayson (London 1972), bk 2. On the system of linear perspective and its impact on the development of Renaissance art see Rebecca Zorach, *The Passionate Triangle* (Chicago 2011), esp. 29–34.

64 Rosalind E. Krauss, "Horizontality," in *Formless: A User's Guide*, ed. Yve-Alain Bois and Rosalind E. Krauss (Cambridge, Mass. 1997), 93–103, esp. 95–7.

65 For a brilliant discussion of ancient Roman pavements and the perception of them see Rebecca Molholt, "Roman Labyrinth Mosaics and the Experience of Motion," *Art Bulletin* 93, 3 (2011): 287–303. Arguing for a notion of mobile perceiving bodies, my discussion ultimately complicates and nuances the way "period people" interacted with images, as outlined by Michael Baxandall, *Painting and Experience in Fifteenth-Century Italy. A Primer in the Social History of Pictorial Style*, 2nd ed. (Oxford 1988), 86–108.

66 On the phenomenology of the touch and gaze see Georges Didi-Huberman, *Confronting Images: Questioning the Ends of a Certain History of Art*, trans. John Goodman (University Park, Pa. 2005), 30, 141–3.

67 Lucia Fornari Schianchi, *Ai piedi della badessa: un pavimento maiolicato per Maria de' Benedetti badessa di S. Paolo dal 1471 al 1482* (Parma 1988); Mitsumasa Takanashi, ed., *Parma: Grazia e affetti, natura e artificio. Protagonisti dell'arte da Correggio a Lanfranco*, exh. cat., 2 vols. (Tokyo 2007), 1: 48.

68 Including the three rectangular white and blue tiles, the total amounts to 346. Several tiles from the San Paolo corpus are also in major European museums, in London, Paris, and Berlin; Giorgio Monaco, "Le collezioni del R. Museo di antichità di Parma: Cenni storici," *Aurea Parma* 2 (1938): 174; Carola Fiocco and Gabriella Gherardi, "Il pavimento di S. Paolo a Parma," *Ceramica per l'edilizia international* 72 (1980): 11–13; Alessandrini, "San Paolo," esp. 53. See also Timothy Wilson's detailed entry for the Parmese tile in the British Museum: Dora Thornton and Timothy Wilson, eds., *Italian Renaissance Ceramics: A Catalogue of the British Museum Collection*, 2 vols. (London 2009), 2: 614–15, cat. 381. In comparison, the almost contemporary maiolica pavement of the Vaselli chapel in Bologna comprises 1,046 extant tiles of various geometric forms; Carmen Ravanelli Guidotti, *Il pavimento della cappella Vaselli in San Petronio a Bologna* (Bologna 1988), 93. The decorated floor formerly in the church of Santa Maria del Riposo in Fano (1501), probably of Pesaro manufacture, comprised ca. 1600 titles, while there are more than 400 tiles from the Petrucci pavement (see n. 57 above); Sani, "Floors," in *Italian Renaissance Maiolica*, 169–177, esp. 173, 175. In sum, the San Paolo tiles are relatively few but nonetheless impressive for their decoration and subjects.

69 There are 193 tiles measuring ca. 19 × 19 cm, 99 larger tiles (ca. 21 × 21 cm), and 51 unmeasured tiles. The exceptional thickness of the San Paolo tiles matches that of the tiles for Isabella d'Este (4.8 cm or 1⅞ in), indicating that there were practical reasons for having a thick tiled floor. Isabella d'Este ordered thick tiles to protect against rats nesting under the floorboards: Sani, *Italian Renaissance Maiolica*, 170.

70 Ibid., 175, reports that the Petrucci maiolica pavement comprises tiles of different shapes and sizes (triangular, two sizes of square and pentagonal tiles). The thickness of the Petrucci tiles is ca. 3.2 cm (ca. 1⅛ in).

71 Fornari Schianchi, *Ai piedi della badessa*, 22; Giuliana Gardelli, *Maiolica per l'architettura: Pavimenti e rivestimenti rinascimentali di Urbino e del suo territorio* (Urbino 1993), 131–7; Alessandro Bettini, "Le maioliche della discordia," *Ceramicantica* 2 (1991): 12–18, proposing that the Pesarese workshop of Almerico Fedeli di Ventura executed the tiles; Dressen, *Pavimenti decorati*, 357–8; Wilson, entry in Thornton and Wilson, eds., *Italian Renaissance Ceramics*, 2: 614–15. Guido Donatone has agreed with the Pesarese attribution and has proposed connections with Neapolitan maiolica: Guido Donatone, *La maiolica napoletana dagli Aragonesi* (Naples 2013), 23–30.

72 According to Sarah Cartwright, the Pesarese copy of Marcanova's antiquarian sylloge is now in Paris, Bibliothèque Nationale, MS Lat. 5825F: Sarah Cartwright, "Antiquarianism in Pesaro: Text and Image in MS Urb. Lat. 899," *Rivista di storia della miniatura* 13 (2009): 129–40.

73 Andrea Ciaroni, *Maioliche del Quattrocento a Pesaro: Frammenti di storia dell'arte ceramica dalla bottega dei Fedeli* (Florence 2004), app. VIII, 194, publishes a letter of 1480, in which the Duke of Milan, Galeazzo Sforza, thanks Costanzo Sforza for his gift of maiolica wares ("vasi"). Traffic in art objects between Parma and Pesaro is also documented in the Quattrocento, e.g. the Parmese goldsmith Gianfrancesco Enzola struck a medal of Costanzo Sforza in 1475: George Francis Hill, *A Corpus of Italian Medals of the Renaissance before Cellini*, 2 vols. (London 1930; repr. Florence 1984), 1: 72–3; 2: pl. 46. On Alessandro Sforza's artistic investments see Maria Grazia Albertini Ottolenghi, "L'altro 'centro': Alessandro Sforza e Pesaro," in Periti, ed., *Emilia e Marche*, 253–72. The fine quality of Pesarese maiolica is proudly proclaimed in a 1486

edict issued by Costanzo Sforza's son, Giovanni, asserting that the local maiolica was praised "by each *intendente* throughout Italy and abroad": Paride Berardi, *L'antica maiolica di Pesaro dal XIV al XVII secolo* (Florence 1984), 207–9; Alessandro Bettini, "La ceramica a Pesaro tra il XIV e il XVII secolo," in *Fatti di ceramica nelle Marche dal Trecento al Novecento*, ed. Gian Carlo Bojani (Macerata 1997), 31–95. Between 1476 and 1490, the first known Italian maiolica service was made for foreign royalty – the King of Hungary, Matthias Corvinus and his wife – and has been attributed to Pesarese potters, some of whom traveled to Buda in 1488.

74 Pezzana, *Storia*, 4: 20–21; Letizia Arcangeli, "'Come bosco et spelunca di latroni': Città e ordine pubblico a Parma e nello stato di Milano tra Quattrocento e Cinquecento," in *Le polizie informali*, ed. Livio Antonelli (Rubettino [CZ] 2010), 65–90.

75 BAV, MS Urb. Lat. 899, *Ordine delle nozze dello Illustrissimo Signore Meser Costantio Sfortia de Aragonia et della Illustrissima Madonna Camilla de Aragonia sua consorte nell'anno 1475*, fols. 97r, 119r; Jane Bridgeman, *A Renaissance Wedding: The Celebration at Pesaro for the Marriage of Costanzo Sforza and Camilla Marzano d'Aragona (26–30 May 1475)* (Brepols 2013), 108, 131. The Vatican manuscript (124 fols.) was probably written by Leonardo di Giovanni Tolosani del Colle at the Pesaro court either at the time of the wedding (1475) or some time before 1480, which is the date the colophon indicates. In addition to the illustrated manuscript, a printed edition of the wedding celebrations (albeit with no images) was published in Vicenza by Hermannus Liechtenstein in 1475. Pandolfo Collenuccio delivered the wedding oration for the Sforza couple: Anthony F. D'Elia, "Marriage, Sexual Pleasure, and Learned Brides in the Wedding Orations of Fifteenth-Century Italy," *Renaissance Quarterly* 55, 2 (2002): 379–433, esp. 391–3.

76 Cambridge, Corpus Christi College, Parker Library, *Cronica majora*, Part II, MS 16, fol. 151v. The Benedictine Matthew Paris (1200–1259) was an excellent calligrapher and manuscript illuminator.

77 Kathryn Blair Moore, "The Disappearance of an Author and the Emergence of a Genre: Niccolò da Poggibonsi and Pilgrimage Guidebooks between Manuscript and Print," *Renaissance Quarterly* 96, 2 (2013): 357–411, esp. 365–8.

78 Oxford, Bodleian Library, MS Canon. Lat. Misc. 280, fol. 69r. Different from contemporary renditions of the elephant, this drawing after Cyriacus was first published in Ludovico Bertalot and Augusto Campana, "Gli scritti di Iacopo Zeno ed il suo elogio di Ciriaco di Ancona," *Bibliofilia* 41 (1939): 367, later discussed by Phyllis Williams Lehmann, *Cyriacus of Ancona's Egyptian Visit and its Reflections in Gentile Bellini and Hieronymus Bosch* (Locust Valley, N.Y. 1971), 14; Brian Curran, *The Egyptian Renaissance: The Afterlife of Ancient Egypt in Early*

Modern Italy (Chicago 2007), 137–8, referring to a woodcut from the *Hypnerotomachia Poliphili* of 1499 featuring an elephant carrying an Egyptian obelisk passing through its body (a model possibly reworked by Gian Lorenzo Bernini in the sculpture in front of the church of Santa Maria della Minerva in Rome). However, other prints from the *Hypnerotomachia* depict elephants carrying triumphal chariots.

79 Millard Meiss, *Andrea Mantegna as Illuminator: An Episode in Renaissance Art, Humanism, and Diplomacy* (New York 1957), 9–12; Luciano Bellosi, entry in *Mantegna 1431–1506*, ed. Giovanni Agosti and Dominique Thiébaut, exh. cat. (Paris 2010), 119–20, for the contested attribution of the illumination and the discussion of engravings after Mantegna's *Triumph of Caesar* displaying elephants. On the elephant motif on the façade of Palazzo Fantuzzi in Bologna see Raffaella Rossi Manaresi, "Materiali e rifiniture nell'edilizia storica bolognese: Ipotesi sull'immagine della città," *Bollettino d'arte* 84–5 (1994): 167–82, esp. 171, pl. II. Schongauer's print has often been described as showing an elephant carrying a crenellated, turreted basket on a saddle. But crenellated baskets and castles motifs on the backs of elephants could be misconstrued and one turns into the other: Stephan Kemperdick, *Martin Schongauer. Eine Monografie* (Petersberg 2004), 151

80 BAV, MS Urb. Lat. 899, *Ordine delle nozze*, fol. 88r. On festivities and performances connected with royal weddings and esp. in Pesaro see Philine Helas, *Lebende Bilder in der Italienischen Festkultur des 15. Jahrhunderts* (Berlin 1999), 215–16.

81 BAV, MS Urb. Lat. 899, *Ordine delle nozze*, fols. 86r–87r: "in questo venne anche a presentare la universita delli giudei di Pesaro li quali ven[n]ero cum lainfrascripta livrea bella e ornatissima representando la regina Sabba quando venne á visitare e presentare a Salamone cum questo ordine . . . Eve[ni]na inprima alquanti giovani e putti a dui a dui [fol. 86v] cum novi habiti di persona e ditesta alla Arabesca cum palme ve[r]di datteri in mano. Poi veniva uno Elephante maggiore assai che uno grande bove col muso e colli denti si ben contrafatto che quasi pareva vero. Ne sivedea chil portasse anci dasi medesimo si vedea caminare si bene erano comp[ar]tite le gambe delli homini che erano dentro cum quelle dello elephante che impossibile saria a scrivere chi non l'avesse veduto el mirabile arteficio desso. Et sop[ra] questo elephante era una sedia doro coperta da una ombrella doro. Et in questa sedia sedea una donna ebrea coronata in forma di Regina vestita doro. E drieto allei venieno dui altri elephanti simili sopra li quali era uno castello cum torre e bandiere pieno di damiselle di quella Regina [f. 87r] cum gigli e bandiere in mano. E dietro a tutti questi veniva grande turba de essi hebrei de ogni eta vestiti pure alla Arabesca doro e de argento e turche di varii colori." On

the fascination for automata that attracted audiences in the Renaissance see Lorraine Daston and Katherine Park, *Wonders and the Order of Nature, 1150–1750* (New York 1998), 255–301.

82 Cartwright has argued for the common authorship of the Sforza wedding manuscript and the copy of Marcanova's antiquarian sylloge (see n. 72 above): Cartwright, "Antiquarianism in Pesaro," 129–40. Similarities between the representation of the Queen of Sheba bringing gifts to Solomon from the Sforza manuscript and an early fifteenth-century Byzantine illumination featuring a Turkish woman, identified as Mehmet II's hapless bride Sitt Hatun, were highlighted by Rosamond E. Mack, "Elephants Bearing Ladies in an Italian Renaissance Pageant and an Eastern Manuscript," National Gallery of Art, Work-in-Progress lecture series, Washington, D.C., October 17, 2005.

83 The iconographic richness of the San Paolo tiled floor has convinced scholars that its design was not left to the potters alone and that artists, ranging from Jacopo Loschi, Giovanni Santi, and Almerico Fedeli di Ventura, were conceivably involved in the project: Laudedeo Testi, "Pier Ilario e Michele Mazzola: Notizie sulla pittura parmigiana dal 1250 c. alla fine del XV secolo," *Bollettino d'arte* 3 (1910): 86; Luigi Bini, "Le lune della badessa," *Ceramica* 9 (1954): 28–32; Gardelli, *Maiolica*, 134; Dressen, *Pavimenti decorati*, 358; Bettini, "Maioliche della discordia," 12–18; Ciaroni, *Maioliche*, 65. Gaetano Ballardini has correctly proposed that multiple designers were responsible for the figures on the tile surfaces: Gaetano Ballardini, "Il pavimento maiolicato di San Paolo," *Rassegna della istruzione artistica* (1936): 33–8.

84 On Toschi's report see Fornari Schianchi, *Ai piedi della badessa*, 66 n. 7. For Scarabelli's description see SBEAP, Scarabelli Zunti, "Materiale," MS III, fol. 112r: "Rispetto alla Benedetti posso io aggiungere che essa fece venire da Faenza rari mattoni verniciati a smalto per lastricare alcune stanze del suo cenobio, e questo è provato essendo che parecchi di que' mattoni scampati dal cattivo genio della distruzione portano ancora colorate le insegne gentilizie della Benedetti, cioe' di tre bande azzurre in campo d'oro, con pastorale per cimiero, e le iniziali della splendida ordinatrice."

85 Campori, *Maiolica e porcellana*, 125–6.

86 Fornari Schianchi, *Ai piedi della badessa*, 90; Lucia Fornari Schianchi, "Grandi committenze delle badesse nelle arti minori," in Marzio Dall'Acqua, ed., *Il monastero di San Paolo* (Parma 1990), 43–50, esp. 45.

87 Marzio Dall'Acqua, "Il monastero di San Paolo," in *Il monastero di San Paolo*, 33; Longhi and Spina, "Complesso monastico," 1: 9, 44–5.

88 ASPr, Direzione del Patrimonio dello Stato, busta 149, June 13 and July 13, 1855.

89 My working hypothesis about the possible dual manufacture of the maiolica tiles and their installation in two distinct spaces is an effort to offer a plausible reconstruction based on seemingly contradictory available evidence.

90 It is indisputable that by the early sixteenth century maiolica tile floors consisted of tiles of different shapes and sizes arranged in various patterns, displaying decorative motifs such as grotesques, which are wholly absent in the San Paolo corpus. But there the new tiles could have replicated the typologies and style of old ones, so as not to create an obvious break. The fact that Giovanna Piacenza's own stemma does not appear on the tiles could be seen as another indication that she reused the maiolica corpus, which she identified with her ancestral predecessor. Another instance of reuse includes a few tiles from a now lost maiolica floor probably made for Pope Eugenius IV (r. 1431–47), originally laid in the Vatican palace and later installed in a corner of the chapel of St. Helen in Santa Croce in Gerusalemme in Rome. Possibly of Spanish manufacture, the small group of tiles constitutes a form of ornament that seems to emphasize the citizenship of the chapel patrons, the Spanish cardinals Mendoza and Carvajal; Dressen, *Pavimenti decorati*, 67, 185, 336–7.

91 ASPr, Notarile, Giovanni Ludovico Sacca, filza 280, November 28, 1482. Registering Sebastiano Bergonzi's will, this record indicates that his first wife was Giovanna Benedetti, buried in the family chapel in San Paolo. She gave birth to Agnese, Giovanna Piacenza's mother, on which more in Chapter Four.

92 On the power of the gaze seen within semiotic theory, see Norman Bryson, "The Gaze in the Expanded Field," in *Vision and Visuality*, ed. Hal Foster (Seattle 1988), 87–108, esp. 105.

93 Sheila Bonde and Clark Maines, "A Room of One's Own: Elite Spaces in Monasteries of the Reform Movement and an Abbot's Parlor at the Augustinian Saint-Jean-des-Vignes (Soissons), France," in *Religion and Belief in Medieval Europe*, ed. Guy de Boe and Frans Verhaeghe, 4 vols. (Zellik 1997), 4: 43–53, esp. 45.

94 As possible confirmation, during the renovation of the eastern convent zone to adapt it for use as a library (the Biblioteca Guanda), a fragment of a maiolica tile was found: Francesco Barocelli, "Il Correggio nel monastero di San Paolo e l'umanesimo monastico di Giovanna Piacenza," in *Il Correggio nella Camera di San Paolo* (Milan 2010), 230; Alessandrini, "San Paolo," 53.

95 In 1235 the Cistercians ordered the removal of a "pavimentum curiosum" from the monastic church of Le Gard in the diocese of Amiens and punished the abbot for having permitted its installation; Christopher S. Wood, "'Curious Images' and the Art of Description," *Word and Image* 11, 4 (1995): 338.

Another tin-glazed pavement dating to the early fifteenth century and decorated with heraldic and figural motifs was found in the ducal oratory at the Chartreuse of Champmol, Dijon: Sherry C. M. Lindquist, *Agency, Visuality and Society at the Chartreuse de Champmol* (Aldershot 2008), 36–40.

96 St. Bernard quoted in Conrad Rudolph, *The "Things of Greater Importance": Bernard of Clairvaux's Apologia and the Medieval Attitude toward Art* (Philadelphia 1990), 11. In his *On Praying to God* (1524) Erasmus, in contrast, lamented that floors in churches were uneven due to slabs and plaques making pavements "difficult to walk on": Desiderius Erasmus, "On Praying to God," in *Collected Works of Erasmus: Spiritualia and Pastoralia*, ed. John O'Malley, vol. 70 (Toronto 1998), 202.

97 Michel de Certeau, "Walking in the City," in *The Practice of Everyday Life*, trans. Steven F. Rendall (Berkeley 1984), 91–118, esp. 102–3.

98 On the phenomenological experience of motion and the viewer's kinaesthetic perception see Molholt, "Roman Labyrinth Mosaics," 287–303.

99 Certeau, "Walking in the City," 107, 109–10. On the practice of walking while keeping eyes cast down, as articulated in the critical literature see Brian Reynolds and Joseph Fitzpatrick, "The Transversality of Michel de Certeau: Foucault's Panoptic Discourse and the Cartographic Impulse," *Diacritics* 29, 3 (1999): 63–80; Martin Jay, *Downcast Eyes: The Denigration of Vision in Twentieth-Century French Thought* (Berkeley 1993), 263–318.

100 Eugene Y. Wang, "Watching the Steps: Peripatetic Vision in Medieval China," in *Visuality Before and Beyond the Renaissance*, 116–42, esp. 124. For a discussion of peripatetic viewers and their interactivity with works (not necessarily pavements) of medieval art see Jacqueline E. Jung, *The Gothic Screen: Space, Sculpture, and Community in the Cathedrals of France and Germany, ca. 1200–1400* (Cambridge 2013), 107–28, esp. 111; Nino Zchomelidse and Giovanni Freni, eds., "Introduction," in *Meaning in Motion: The Semantics of Movement in Medieval Art* (Princeton 2011), vi–x.

101 Certeau, "Walking in the City," 97.

102 *Regola di Sancto Benedecto nuovamente vulgarizata* (Florence after 1500), ch. 7, "Della Humilità": "El duodecimo grado della humilita essere el monacho non solamente col quore ma ancora co epso corpo se[m]p[re] dimostri humilita a chi lo vede: cio e che nel exercitio/nel monasterio/nel oratorio/ nel orto/nella via/nel campo/ & brevemente dovunq[ue] sara/sedendo/andando/stando stia sempre col capo inclinato/ cogli sguardi defixi in terra: stimandosi se[m]p[re] colpevole de sua peccati. Et pe[n]si di gia esser[e] s[pe]tato oltremedo iudicio di Dio: dice[n]do semp[re] nel suo quore/quello che dixe q[ue]l publichano dello evangelio cogli ochi fixi in terra:

Signore io peccatore non sono degno di levare gli ochi mia in verso elcielo. Et col propheta ancora: Sommi piegato & humiliato da ogni parte"; *The Rule of St. Benedict* (Ampleforth 2003), 32. On the prescription for lowered eyes see Pozzi's sensitive observations: Giovanni Pozzi, "Occhi bassi," in *Thematologie des Kleinen = Petits thèmes littéraires*, ed. Edgar Marsch and Giovanni Pozzi (Fribourg 1986), 163–4, 201.

103 Roberta Orsini Landini and Mary Westerman Bulgarella, "Costume in Fifteenth-Century Florentine Portraits of Women," in *Virtue and Beauty: Leonardo's Ginevra de' Benci and Renaissance Portraits of Women*, ed. David Alan Brown, exh. cat. (Washington, D.C. 2002), 89–97. See Carmen Ravanelli Guidotti, *Delle gentili donne di Faenza: Studio del "ritratto" sulla ceramica faentina del rinascimento* (Ferrara 2000), 74–82, for a discussion of *belle* as a subject common to other maiolica genres, esp. *belle* plates, which served as love gifts.

104 Ravanelli Guidotti, *Il pavimento*, 217–22, esp. 218–19.

105 Boccaccio's famous compilation of the biographies of historical and mythological heroines, *Concerning Famous Women* (1374), inspired a body of fifteenth-century writings on women by Antonio Cornazzano, Vespasiano da Bisticci, and Jacopo Filippo Foresti, among others. The praise of beauties from a particular city culminated in Giovanni Sabadino degli Arienti's eulogy of women from Bologna in his *Gynevera de le clare donne* (ca. 1489–92); Antonia Tissoni Benvenuti, *Il Quattrocento settentrionale* (Bari 1981), 190–97.

106 Luke Syson, "Belle: Picturing Beautiful Women," in *Art and Love in Renaissance Italy*, exh. cat., ed. Andrea Bayer (New York 2008), 248.

107 Marta Ajmar and Dora Thornton, "When is a Portrait not a Portrait? Belle Donne on Maiolica and the Renaissance Praise of Local Beauties," in *The Image of the Individual: Portraits in the Renaissance*, ed. Nicholas Mann and Luke Syson (London 1998), 138–53, esp. 148–9; Dressen, *Pavimenti decorati*, 198–9 stating that portraits of real individuals appear on maiolica tiles. Recent scholarship on portraits has also made clear that faces can transmit information beyond the sitter's identity: Georges Didi-Huberman, "The Portrait, the Individual and the Singular: Remarks on the Legacy of Aby Warburg," in *The Image of the Individual*, 165–88; Jodi Cranston, *The Poetics of Portraiture in the Italian Renaissance* (Cambridge 2000), 8; Maria H. Loh, "Faciality," *Oxford Art Journal* 32, 3 (2009): 341–63.

108 ASPr, Notarile, Gaspare Prati, filza 232, May 23, 1507; Umberto Benassi, *Storia di Parma*, 5 vols. (Parma 1899–1906), 1: 151; Barocelli, *Correggio*, 234.

109 The inscription reads: "Heu sub requia Lucreccia flumina cesa"; Fornari Schianchi, *Ai piedi della badessa*, 22.

110 On masquerade and masquerading and its multiple values in the early modern world see John Martin, "Inventing Sincer-

110 ity, Refashioning Prudence," *American Historical Review* 102, 5 (1997): 1309–42, esp. 1324–6; Charles Dempsey, "Portraits and Masks in the Art of Lorenzo de' Medici, Botticelli, and Politian's *Stanze per la Giostra*," *Renaissance Quarterly* 52, 1 (1999): 1–42.

111 Caroline Walker Bynum, *Metamorphosis and Identity* (New York 2001), 189. Real and imagined identities are complex sites of negotiation and relationships, on which see Louis Althusser, "Ideology and Ideological State Apparatuses (Notes Towards an Investigation)," in *Lenin and Philosophy, and Other Essays*, trans. Ben Brewster (New York 2001), 127–86.

112 On veils that can be used to transgress rules of decorum and the negotiation between secular and sacred values see Eugenia Paulicelli, "From the Sacred to the Secular: The Gendered Geography of Veils in Italian Cinquecento Fashion," in *Ornamentalism: The Art of Renaissance Accessories*, ed. Bella Mirabella (Ann Arbor 2011), 40–58; Isabella Campagnol, "Veli rivelatori: le donne veneziane e il significato simbolico del velo," in *Velo e velatio: Significato e rappresentazione nella cultura figurativa dei secoli XV–XVII*, ed. Gabriella Zarri (Rome 2014), 55–72, esp. 66–7.

113 For a careful transcription of Michiel's description of Jacometto's portraits see Rossella Lauber, "'Opera perfettissima': Marcantonio Michiel e la *Notizia d'opere di disegno*," in *Il Collezionismo a Venezia e nel Veneto ai tempi della Serenissima*, ed. Bernard Aikema, Rossella Lauber and Max Seidel (Venice 2005), 97: "Vi è un ritratto picolo de M[esser] Alvixe Contarini q[uondam] M[esser] . . . che morse già anni, et ne l'istesso quadretto un ritratto a l'incontro d'una monacha da San Segondo, et sopra la coperta de detti ritratti una cervetta in un paese, et nella coperta de cuoro de detto quadretto fogliami di oro maxenato, di mano di Iacometto, opera perfettissima." In 1565 the portraits were recorded in the Vendramin collection with an attribution to Giovanni Bellini.

114 John Pope-Hennessy, *The Robert Lehman Collection: I. Italian Painting* (Princeton 1987), cat. 96–7; Brown, *Virtue and Beauty*, 154–7; Nancy Edwards, in Bayer, *Art and Love*, 265–8. In a letter dating to 1497 written by the humanist Michele Placiola to Ermolao Barbaro, Jacometto is said to be already dead, and is recognized as "the first artist in the world ("el primo homo del mondo")": Lina Bolzoni, *Il Cuore di cristallo: ragionamenti d'amore, poesia e ritratto nel rinascimento* (Turin 2010), 267.

115 The reflectography of this much damaged image, which originally simulated gilt bronze, has revealed "a male figure seated with legs spread on a rocky outcrop with trees in the foreground. A body of water extends to the left and a gondola . . . is more near the shoreline": Andrea Bayer, in *The Renaissance Portrait from Donatello to Bellini*, exh. cat., ed. Keith Christiansen and Stefan Weppelmann (New York 2011), 346.

116 Brown, *Virtue and Beauty*, 154.

117 Bologna, Archivio Generale Arcivescovile, Miscellanee Vecchie 804, filza 23, Alcune regole et ordinat.ni utili per le visite et Riforme di Monasteri di Suore, December 9, 1576: "; [tengono] molta vanità nel habito . . . faza liscia . . . le giovani arditissime, senza alcuno rispetto . . . tengono ucilli, capeli . . . et altre vanità . . . [hanno] . . . panni per vestirsi da huomo, delle vesti di seta da spose, et altre loro vanità . . . che talvolta stanno per Carnevali . . . mesi."

118 Isabella Campagnol, *Fordidden Fashions: Invisible Luxuries in Early Venetian Convents* (Lubbock, Tex. 2014), 85–90.

119 Ferrara, Biblioteca Ariostea, *Prologo de l'ordine del vivere neli monasteri de monache & temporale & spirituale. Excepta da diversi scripti de Hieronymo ad Eustochio sua Figliuola spirituale & ale sorelle* (Ferrara 1497), Ch. 28: "[le femine] . . . in pietre p[re]ciose e orname[n]ti extrinseci po[n]gono la loro gloria. No[n] basta a loro la libidine de[n]tro nata d[ell]a natura: ma cerchano cagioni di p[rov]uocare la libidine. Desiderano senza dubio che gli ochii de gli homini co[n]te[m]planti loro & le ge[m]me: finalmente si fermio ne la faccia azioch[è] co ceni d[e] soi ochii più facilmente incitino a libidinoso i[n]ce[n]dio. Che ti glorii o publica meretrice ne le margaritte e gemme."

120 Andreas Cappellanus, "Loving Nuns," in *On Love*, trans. P. G. Welsh (London 1982), b.1, 8.

121 The diptych format was used to celebrate married couples, e.g. Nicolas Froment's *Matheron Diptych* (ca. 1475, Paris, Louvre); John Oliver Hand, Catherine A. Metzger, and Ron Spronk, *Prayers and Portraits: Unfolding the Netherlandish Diptych*, exh. cat. (Washington, D.C., New Haven and London 2006), 82–6.

122 Bayer, entry on Jacometto's portraits, in Christiansen and Weppelmann, *Renaissance Portrait from Donatello to Bellini*, 346.

123 Ibid., 347 for the description of how Jacometto's panels were mounted originally. On the small boxes exchanged by lovers see Syson and Thornton, *Objects of Virtue*, 62; Adrian W. B. Randolph, *Touching Objects. Intimate Experiences of Italian Fifteenth-Century Art* (New Haven and London 2014), 117–129.

124 Edwards in Bayer, *Art and Love*, 266. Indeed, widows founded and entered convents to find more comfortable and acceptable living conditions than in the outside world. But they did not necessarily take monastic vows, because they were afraid of losing their powers and property: Renée P. Baernstein, *A Convent Tale: A Century of Sisterhood in Spanish Milan* (New York and London 2002), 47–9.

125 Alessandro Angelini, "Jacometto Veneziano e gli umanisti: Proposta per il 'Ritratto di Luca Pacioli e di Guidubaldo da Montefeltro' del Museo di Capodimonte," *Prospettiva* 147–8

126 (2012): 126–49, esp. 137, arguing for a religious identity for Jacometto's female sitter.

126 Flaminio Cornelio, *Ecclesiae venetae, antiquis monumentis nunc etiam primum editis illustratae ac in decades distributae*, 15 vols. (Venice 1749), vol. 9, 1–49, esp. 11.

127 Lauber, "'Opera perfettissima,'" 97, 114.

128 Benjamin Paul, *Nuns and Reform Art in Early Modern Venice: The Architecture of Santi Cosma e Damiano and its Decoration from Tintoretto to Tiepolo* (Aldershot 2012), 46–7, reports that the lands pertaining to San Secondo were incorporated within the property of the local Benedictine reformed convent of SS. Cosma e Damiano in 1534.

129 Alessandro Spinelli, *Versi del 400 e del 600 attinenti a Pittori o a Cose d'Arte tratti dai Mss. Estensi* (Carpi 1892), 6; Arnaldo Segarizzi, "Ulisse Aleotti rimatore veneziano del secolo xv," *Giornale storico della letteratura italiana* 47 (1906): 41–66, esp. 66; Giovanni Agosti, "Intorno a Vasari," in *Su Mantegna I* (Milan 2005), 284–5 n. 28 doubts the authenticity of Aleotti's sonnet on the grounds that no religious woman could have sat for Mantegna.

130 Lowe, *Nuns' Chronicles*, 372.

131 Didi-Huberman, "The Portrait," esp. 183–5.

132 Maria Monica Donato, "Gli eroi romani tra storia ed 'exemplum': i primi cicli umanistici di Uomini Famosi," in *Memoria dell'antico nell'arte italiana*, ed. Salvatore Settis, 3 vols. (Turin 1985), 2: 97–152. On the male head motif on maiolica pavements and other vessels from the mid-fifteenth century see Carmen Ravanelli Guidotti, *Immagini, personaggi ed emblemi cavallereschi sulla maiolica italiana* (Faenza 1998), figs. 10, 23, 24.

133 Ciaroni, *Maioliche*, 58.

134 Niklas Luhmann, "Love as a Generalized Symbolic Medium of Communication," in *Love as Passion: The Codification of Intimacy*, trans. Jeremy Gaines and Doris L. Jones (Cambridge, Mass. 1986), 20.

135 Charles S. Ross, "Introduction," in Matteo Maria Boiardo, *Orlando innamorato* (Oxford and New York 1995), vii–xxvii.

136 Cecil Clough, "Chivalry and Magnificence in the Golden Age of Italian Renaissance," in *Chivalry in the Renaissance* (Rochester, N.Y. 1990), 25–48; Aldo Scaglione, *Knights at Court, Courtliness, Chivalry, and Courtesy from Ottonian Germany to Italian Renaissance* (Berkeley 1991), 212–21.

137 Andrea Bajardi, *Trattato Amoroso di Adriano e Narcisa intitolato Philogene* (Parma 1508), Hii, Nii, Niii, Niiii, Oii. On Bajardi's writings and influence on local arts see Antonia Tissoni Benvenuti, in *Letteratura italiana, il Quattrocento*, 2 vols. (Bari 1972), 2: 398–9, 422–3; Anna Ceruti Burgio, *Studi sul Quattrocento parmense* (Pisa 1988); Paola Medioli Masotti, "Letteratura e società a Parma nel Quattrocento," in *Parma e l'umanesimo italiano* (Padua 1986), 51–64; Mary Vaccaro, "Par-

migianino and Andrea Bajardi: Figuring Petrarchan Beauty in Renaissance Parma," *Word and Image* 17 (2001): 243–58.

138 Leone Smagliati, *Cronaca parmense (1494–1518)*, ed. Sergio di Noto (Parma 1970), 119.

139 Gabriella Zarri, *Recinti*, 316–46, esp. 327, 336, 339–40; Sharon Strocchia, "When the Bishop Married the Abbess: Masculinity and Power in Florentine Episcopal Entry Rites, 1300–1600," *Gender & History*, 19, 2 (2007): 346–68.

140 Detlef Hoffmann, Peter F. Kopp, and Fritz Koreny, eds., *Spielkarten, ihre Kunst und Geschichte in Mitteleuropa*, exh. cat. (Vienna 1974), 50–51; Giordano Berti and Andrea Vitali, eds., *Le carte di corte: i tarocchi. Gioco e magia alla corte degli Estensi* (Bologna 1988), 21–33.

141 Bologna, Archivio Generale Arcivescovile, Miscellanee Vecchie, 804, filza 23, "Alcune regole et ordinat.ni utili per le visite et Riforme di Monasteri di Suore," December 9, 1576: "In alcuni Mon.[asteri] per Natale giocano alle carte e dadi."

142 The emphasis on prayer and spiritual love had long been a component of monastic culture, structuring nuns' relationships with the divine as a sensual liaison between Christ and his spiritual brides: Jean Leclercq, *The Love of Learning and the Desire for God: A Study of Monastic Culture*, trans. Catharine Misrahi (New York 1982), 31–54; more recently, Erika Lauren Lindgren, *Sensual Encounters: Monastic Women and Spirituality in Medieval Germany* (New York 2009), 58–87.

143 Ciaroni, *Maioliche*, 157, pl. xxv. For this motif on later plates, ca.1510–20, see also Catherine Hess, *Italian Ceramics: Catalogue of the J. Paul Getty Museum Collection* (Los Angeles 2002), 128–33. On the Lando maiolica pavement, which was of Pesarese production, see Annalisa Torrini Perissa and Francesca Saccardo, eds., *Maiolica a Venezia: un pavimento rinascimentale nella chiesa di San Sebastiano* (Venice 2000), 45.

144 On these subjects depicting the cruelty of love see Erwin Panofsky, "Bound Cupid," in *Studies in Iconology: Humanistic Themes in the Art of the Renaissance* (New York 1962), 127; Ravanelli Guidotti, *Il pavimento*, 142–3; Bayer, *Art and Love*, 91–2.

145 For a tradition of medieval images with a potential for subversion and inversion see Michael Camille, *Image on the Edge: The Margins of Medieval Art* (Cambridge, Mass. 1992), 26–31.

146 Michael Camille, *The Medieval Art of Love: Objects and Subjects of Desire* (New York 1998), 47–9.

147 Bologna, Archivio Generale Arcivescovile, Miscellanee Vecchie 804, filza 23, "Alcune regole et ordinat.ni utili per le visite et Riforme di Monasteri di Suore," December 9, 1576: "Tengono e ligono libri vani, como Furioso, Petrarcha, Bochacio."

148 Publius Ovidius Naso, *Metamorphoseos* (Parma 1480); Ovid, *Metamorphoses*, trans. Frank Justus Miller, Loeb Edition (Cambridge, Mass. 1954), 4.55–166.

149 It is known that the Bolognese writer Sabadino degli Arienti had a vernacular translation of the story of Pyramus and Thisbe in 1471: Carolyn James, *Giovanni Sabadino degli Arienti: A Literary Career* (Florence 1996), 53, 69–92.

150 See, among other sources, Ovid, *Heroides: Amores*, trans. Grant Showerman, rev. G. P. Goold (Cambridge, Mass. 1977), 16.51; Virgil, *Aeneid*, trans. H. Rushton Fairclough, Loeb Edition, 2 vols. (Cambridge, Mass. 1960), 1. 26.

151 Patricia Collins, "Prints and the Development of *istoriato* Painting on Italian Renaissance Maiolica," *Print Quarterly* 4, 3 (1987): 223–35; Carmen Ravanelli Guidotti, "Le Metamorfosi 'vulgari' d'Ovidio sulla maiolica italiana," in *Die Rezeption der "Metamorphosen" des Ovid in der Neuzeit: Der Antike Mythos in Text und Bild*, ed. Hermann Walter and Hans-Jürgen Horn (Berlin 1995), 85–97; Julia C. Triolo, "The Armorial Maiolica of Francesco Xanto Avelli" (Ph.D. diss., Pennsylvania State University 1996), 156–61.

152 Ravanelli Guidotti, *Il pavimento*, 240–90.

153 Ann Moss, *Printed Commonplace-Books and the Structuring of Renaissance Thought* (Oxford 1996), 106–9.

154 The often repeated motif of clasped hands accompanied by the words "Fides Omnia" appears on a jar from Pesaro (1470–80; London, Victoria and Albert Museum): Ciaroni, *Maioliche*, 70–71. Several floor tiles in the Vaselli chapel and those from the Lando chapel show the same symbol and message: Ravanelli Guidotti, *Il pavimento*, 84; Torrini Perissa and Saccardo, *Maiolica a Venezia*, 20, 42.

CHAPTER III ART, CONTEMPLATION, AND SPLENDOR

1 Girolamo Savonarola, *Lettere e scritti apologetici*, ed. Roberto Ridolfi, Vincenzo Romano, and Armando F. Verde (Rome 1984), 44 (September 10, 1493): "Edificare conventi poveri e semplici, vestire di grosso panno e vecchio e ritoppato, mangiare e bere secondo la determinazione de li Santi, sobriamente, avere celle povere, senza alcuna superfluità, servare li silenzii e darsi a la contemplazione e solitudine, lassando la familiarità del seculo, non è novo modo di vivere religioso; ma bene è novo modo alla religione de' mendicanti edificare palazzi con le colonne di marmo, e farsi stanzie le quali seriano sufficiente a li signori; avere possessione contro la professione di tutto l'Ordine, non avendo fede in Christo, el quale dice: *Primum quaerite regnum Dei, et haec omnia adicientur vobis*; vestire non del panno più vile ma del più vano; poco orare; vagare in ogni loco; volere essere povero ma che non manchi niente; e fare altre simili novità in scandolo de le anime. Li Padri antiqui fecieno a un modo, li Padri novi fanno a un altro modo, cioè al contrario delli antiqui. Ora ciascuno elegga e seguiti quello che li pare."

2 Desiderius Erasmus, "A Pilgrimage for Religion's Sake," in *Collected Works of Erasmus: Colloquies*, trans. and annot. Craig R. Thompson, vol. 40 (Toronto 1997), 644. Erasmus had expressed the same criticism in his "On Praying to God," in *Collected Works of Erasmus: Spiritualia and Pastoralia*, ed. John O'Malley, vol. 70 (Toronto 1998), 202–3.

3 The notion of the aristocratization of monastic spaces has been conceptualized productively by Helen Hills, *Invisible City: The Architecture of Devotion in Seventeenth-Century Neapolitan Convents* (Oxford 2004), 139–60, esp. 155–6; Helen Hills, "The Housing of Institutional Architecture: Searching for a Domestic Holy in Post-Tridentine Italian Convents," in *Domestic Institutional Interiors in Early Modern Europe*, ed. Sandra Cavallo and Silvia Evangelisti (Aldershot 2009), 120–50, esp. 133–5.

4 Caroline Walker Bynum, *Christian Materiality: An Essay on Religion in Late Medieval Europe* (New York 2011), 25–36 has posited that nuns' piety was characterized by an increased awareness of the power of materials.

5 ASPr, Culto, "Controversie tra vescovo e comune di Parma," busta 2082: "Li Camini nelle Camere si possono tollerare per quelle vecchie solamente che l'hanno sin hora, ma per l'avenire non si doverà concedere a niuna, sia che si voglia, et morendo le monache ch'ora havevano i Camini, si levino in ogni modo guastandosi affato . . . l'Arme o insegne delle famiglie proprie ch'alle Monache si sono fatte fare nelle celle loro, per compatire all'imbecillità d'esse, si possono tollerare, ma che non se ne faria mai più altra sia che si voglia che simili vanità non convengano."

6 Relevant documentation on the layout of nuns' apartments comes from the convents of Santa Patrizia in Naples and Santa Cristina della Fondazza in Bologna (see Chapter One), but these buildings have been adapted to house universities and drastic alterations have compromised their original structures: Annamaria Facchiano, "Monachesimo femminile nel Mezzogiorno medievale e moderno," in *Il monachesimo femminile in Italia dall'alto medioevo al secolo XVII: a confronto con l'oggi*, ed. Gabriella Zarri (Negarine di San Pietro in Cariano [Vr] 1997), 187–8; Elisa Novi Chavarria, *Monache e gentildonne: un labile confine. Poteri politici e identità religiose nei monasteri napoletani secoli XVI–XVII* (Milan 2001), 120–27; Valeria Rubbi, "L'architettura del monastero femminile: Exempla," in *Vita artistica nel monastero femminile: Exempla*, ed. Vera Fortunati (Bologna 2002), 76–97, esp. 87–8.

7 On the traffic in nuns' cells see the excellent publications by Silvia Evangelisti, "'Farne quello che pare e piace . . .' L'uso e la trasmissione delle celle nel monastero di Santa Giulia di Brescia (1579–1688)," *Quaderni Storici* 88 (1995): 85–110; "Rooms to Share: Convent Cells and Social Relations in Early Modern Italy," *Past and Present* (2006): 55–71.

8 The literature on materiality and corporeality has grown exponentially in past decades. On materials as vehicles in complex networks of relations and exchanges, as well as on their vibrant qualities and effects, see, among others, Arjun Appadurai, ed., *The Social Life of Things: Commodities in Cultural Perspective* (Cambridge 1986), 3–63; Hans Belting, *An Anthropology of Images: Picture, Medium, Body*, trans. Thomas Dunlap (Princeton and Oxford 2011), 6–20.

9 Letizia Castelli, *Il monastero di S. Antonio in Polesine: un approccio storico artistico in età medievale* (Ferrara 1992), 19, 35, 46–7. Records attest that the Este continued to patronize works of art for this community well into the sixteenth century: Adolfo Venturi, "Pittori della corte ducale a Ferrara nella prima decade del secolo XVI," *Archivio storico dell'arte* 7 (1894): 297. The church of Sant'Antonio originally housed a monumental altarpiece signed by the local painter Benvenuto Tisi called Garofalo, representing the *Lamentation over Christ* (1527; now Milan, Brera): Emanuela Daffra, ed., *Benvenuto Tisi detto il Garofalo: il Compianto da Sant'Antonio in Polesine* (Milan 1998), 9–33.

10 Shown in an exhibition in 2006, this corpus is now kept in store at the Soprintendenza per i Beni Archeologici in Ferrara: Chiara Guarnieri, ed., *S. Antonio in Polesine: archeologia e storia di un monastero estense* (Florence 2006), 243–51, pls 47–8.

11 Jeffrey F. Hamburger, *The Visual and the Visionary: Art and Female Spirituality in Late Medieval Germany* (New York 1998), 81. Another example of precious possessions kept by nuns in their cells comes from the Dominican community of St. Katherine in Augsburg. In 1499 this community also commissioned for their chapter house images of the seven Roman pilgrimage churches from the most outstanding German painters, including Hans Holbein and Hans Burgkmair: Marie-Luise Ehrenschwendtner, "Virtual Pilgrimages? Enclosure and the Practice of Piety at St. Katherine's Convent, Augsburg," *Journal of Ecclesiastical History* 60, 1 (2009): 45–73, discussing nuns' experience of the works replacing their physical journeys to the holy sites in Rome. In other words, the artworks substituted for the real basilicas to be visited to gain indulgences connected to the pilgrimage to Rome. For an investigation of Burgkmair's image seen in the light of semiotic theories see Mitchell B. Merback, "Recognitions: Theme and Metatheme in Hans Burgkmair the Elder's Santa Croce in Gerusalemme of 1504," *Art Bulletin* 96, 3 (2014): 288–318.

12 Margaret L. King, "Book-Lined Cells: Women and Humanism in the Early Modern Italian Renaissance," in *Beyond Their Sex: Learned Women of the European Past* (New York and London 1980), 66–90; Paula Findlen, "Possessing the Past: The Material World of the Italian Renaissance," *The American Historical Review*, 103, 1 (1998): 83–104 on the meaningfulness of artifacts.

13 On Abbess Lucrezia Matina's inventory see Teresa Visuso, ed., *Vincenzo degli Azani da Pavia e la cultura figurativa in Sicilia nell'età di Carlo V*, exh. cat. (Syracuse, Sicily 1999), 195.

14 Bologna, Archivio Generale Arcivescovile, Miscellanee Vecchie 804, filza 25, "Abusi delle suore," December 9, 1576: "delle superfluità . . . che tengono in cella; delle molte vanità ch'hanno nelle loro casse; delle carte da gioco e dadi che tengono e si fano prestar per giocare; delle vanitadi alle lor pareti . . . de denari che tengono apresso; del tener in cella e cassa scritti e figure lascive; del leger libri profani e lascivi . . . delli vani colori, acque e spechi che tengono."

15 For a discussion and translation of Giulia Caracciolo's full response to the vicar see Hills, *Invisible City*, 117–18.

16 On the notion of a work of art and/or an object having intentions and presence see Alfred Gell, *Art and Agency: An Anthropological Theory* (Oxford 1988), 22–3, 28–50.

17 On the agency of objects that bring their own associations to different cultural contexts see Nile Green, "Ostrich Eggs and Peacock Feathers: Sacred Objects as Cultural Exchange between Christianity and Islam," *Al-Masāq* 18, 1 (2006): 27–66; Bynum, *Christian Materiality*, 267–86.

18 Giovanni Battista Armenini, *De' veri precetti della pittura* (Ravenna 1587; Turin 1980), 196: "Ma in quelle delle monache è bene a farle sul muro . . . non essendo esse sottoposte a le mutazioni, come i frati." For a brief discussion of Armenini's passage see Evangelisti, "Rooms to Share," 68.

19 Armenini, *De' veri precetti*, 196: "e perchè meglio nella mente si conservassero nella loro purità e divozione, non ci vorrei altre pitture, dopo i misteri del Crocifisso e della Madonna, che delle Sacre Scritture e delle vite di quelle sa[n]te verginelle, dalle quali tenessero essempi per i loro martirii. E perchè con piú forza se gli movessero gli affetti, non le vorrei dipinte se non per mano di valentissimi pittori, sì come per cosí vivaci opere, e per esser elle naturalmente pietose, si disponessero a patir maggiormente e si traessero infiammate nello ardore della carità e dell'amore divino."

20 Ibid., "E certo che quelle pitture, le quali sono fatte da' goffi, muovono alle volte la simplicità di quelle a riso et lascivia, dove le vivaci si trovano che le penetrano fino al vivo del cuore. Dipoi né in questi luoghi o siano a lor privati opur communi a tutte, vorrei che si dipingessero se non con gli abiti onestissimi e che fossero tutte l'invenzioni vestite di purità e di devozione, riserbando la grandezza della varietà e delle maniere per quei luoghi che sono magnifichi e superbi."

21 For an analysis of the intersections between art and the Tridentine devotional doctrine see Stuart Lingo, *Federico Barocci: Allure and Devotion in Late Renaissance Painting* (New Haven and London 2008), 90–121.

22 The Foucauldian notion of *dispositif* (a mechanism, an apparatus) connected to devotional works intended as presence and sign is used by Georges Didi-Huberman, *Fra Angelico: Dissemblance and Figuration*, trans. Jane Marie Todd (Chicago 1995), 60–101, esp. 87–9. Praise of monks' prayers in the solitude of their cells is found in the Dominican constitutions, among other texts. On the function and role of Fra Angelico's frescoes in San Marco see William Hood, *Fra Angelico at San Marco* (New Haven and London 1993), 195–236.

23 Francisco de Hollanda, *Four Dialogues on Painting*, trans. Aubrey F. G. Bell (London 1928), 15–16. On the development of the devout style in Italian Renaissance art, attracting admirers through its pleasing aesthetic language, see Alexander Nagel, *Michelangelo and the Reform of Art* (Cambridge 2000), 191–3; Charles Dempsey, "Introduction," in *Drawing Relationships in Northern Italian Renaissance Art. Patronage and Theories of Invention*, ed. Giancarla Periti (Aldershot 2004), 1–9.

24 Gabriella Zarri, "Tra monache e confessori: la corte di Lucrezia Borgia," in *L'età di Alfonso I e la pittura del Dosso* (Modena 2004), 103–18, esp. 104.

25 On the attribution, chronology, and meanings of the sibyl cycle in the Casa Romei, which now serves as a museum, see Matilde Gagliardo, "Le Sibille nel giardino: un ciclo di affreschi per Giovanni Romei a Ferrara," *Prospettiva* 64 (1991): 14–37.

26 Teodosio Lombardi, *Gli Estensi ed il monastero del Corpus Domini* (Ferrara 1980), 4, 153–7; Zarri, *Recinti*, 160. Now deteriorated, the sibyl murals were whitewashed in the past but exactly when remains difficult to establish: Carla di Francesco, ed., *Le sibille di Casa Romei: Storia e restauro* (Ravenna 1998), 65–72.

27 Cristiana Prestianni, "Un documento inedito sulla committenza di Giovanna da Piacenza nel monastero di San Paolo," *Aurea Parma* 93, 1 (2009): 103–32, esp. 122–6, for the payment to Mazzola. A record confirming the location of the nuns' dormitory above Correggio's painted room was transcribed by Luigi Pungileoni, *Memorie istoriche di Antonio Allegri detto il Correggio*, 3 vols. (Parma 1817–22), 2: 122, reporting a payment in 1522 to the local *scalpellino* (stonecarver) Giovan Francesco d'Agrate: "M. Jo. Francesco picapreda per la fabbrica del dormitorio verso il giardino grande che sta sopra la stanza dipinta." From the late sixteenth century on, the documentation repeatedly attests to stability and ventilation problems in the nuns' cells arranged around the cloister: BP, Smeraldo Smeraldi, "Diario delle visite per vie, canali, edifici dal feb. 1598 all'agosto 1600," MS Parm. 535, August 1, 1598, fols. 84r–85r; ASPr, Notarile, Presidenza dell'Interno, busta 189, March 12, 1827.

28 Francesco Barocelli, "Il Correggio nel monastero di San Paolo e l'umanesimo monastico di Giovanna Piacenza," in *Il Correggio nella Camera di San Paolo* (Milan 2010), 240. A heavily damaged fresco (now Parma, Pinacoteca Stuard) from the early sixteenth century, representing the head of St. Peter in a tondo, was recently discovered in the roof area, and has also been connected with the decoration of the nuns' dormitory.

29 Giovanni Battista Castelli, *Visitatio Civitatis Parmae 1578–79*, with notes by Enrico dall'Olio, 2 vols. (Parma 2000), 1: 349–50.

30 Judith C. Brown, *Immodest Acts: The Life of a Lesbian Nun in Renaissance Italy* (New York 1986); Jutta Gisela Sperling, *Convents and the Body Politic in Late Renaissance Venice* (Chicago 1999), 161–3.

31 It was believed, e.g., that the impregnation of nuns could generate monstrous babies. In 1512 the so-called "monster of Ravenna" was born supposedly from the relationship between a nun and a monk. Presented in popular prints as a deformed, hirsute creature, he is depicted with a horn, an eye on his leg, and evil feet. This baby was soon interpreted as an omen foreshadowing the battle that devastated Ravenna in April 1512, when the French bloodily defeated the papal army and then sacked the city: Ottavia Niccoli, "Il mostro di Ravenna: Teratologia e propaganda nei fogli volanti del primo Cinquecento," in *Ravenna in età veneziana*, ed. Dante Bolognesi (Ravenna 1986), 245–77.

32 Olga Zorzi Pugliese, *Castiglione's The Book of the Courtier (Libro del Cortegiano): A Classic in the Making* (Rome 2008), 225.

33 Pietro Aretino, *Dialoghi: Ragionamento della Nanna e dell'Antonia*, ed. Giulio Davico Bonino (Turin 1975), 36–7: "di modo che fra me stessa ringraziava l'ora e il punto del mio farmi suora, giudicando il vero paradiso quello delle suore."

34 Daffra, *Benvenuto Tisi*, 14 n. 27.

35 On Holbein's image and the multilayered role of music in convents see Mariagrazia Carlone, "Monache in immagini musicali," in *Soror mea, sponsa mea: Arte e musica nei conventi femminili in Italia tra Cinquecento e Seicento*, ed. Chiara Sirk and Candace Smith (Venice 2009), 117–45; Robert L. Kendrick, *Celestial Sirens: Nuns and their Music in Early Modern Milan* (Oxford 1996), 58–89.

36 Luciano Patetta, "La tipologia delle chiese doppie (dal medioevo alla controriforma)," in *Storia e tipologia: Cinque saggi sull'architettura del passato* (Milan 1989), 17–71.

37 Hamburger, "The Visual and the Visionary: The Image in Late Medieval Monastic Devotion" in *Visual and the Visionary*, 111–48,

38 For enlightening discussions on the role, efficacy, and function of the Christian image in sixteenth-century Europe see Joseph Leo Koerner, *The Reformation of the Image* (Chicago 2004), 19–37; Alexander Nagel, "Experiments in Art and Reform in Italy in the Early Sixteenth Century," in *The Pontificate of Clement VII: History, Politics, Culture*, ed. Sheryl

Reiss and Kenneth Gouwens (Aldershot 2005), 385–409; Stephen J. Campbell, "Renaissance Naturalism and the Jewish Bible: Ferrara, Brescia, Bergamo, 1520–1540," in *Judaism and Christian Art: Aesthetic Anxieties from the Catacombs to Colonialism*, ed. Herbert L. Kessler and David Nirenberg (Philadelphia and Oxford 2011), 291–327.

39 ASPr, Notarile, Giovan Battista Bistocchi, filza 529, May 28, 1505; Marzio Dall'Acqua, "Il Monastero di San Paolo," in *Il Monastero di San Paolo* (Parma 1990), 28.

40 Araldi received two payment installments in 1507 for a total of 118 *lire imperiali*: Augusta Ghidiglia Quintavalle, "Alessandro Araldi," *Rivista dell'Istituto di storia di archeologia e storia dell'arte* 7 (1958): 291–333, esp. 326.

41 ASPr, Notarile, Giovan Battista Bistocchi, filza 529, May 28, 1505: "Item che se la dita madona abatissa vorà che 'l dito M.ro Alexandro vada a Milano a vedere el Cenaculo che la dita madona sia obligata a darge una cavalcadura et far tuta la spesa che ge andarà andar e star là e tornar a casa et etiam se l' acadese andare in altro locho per la dita opera che la obliga a darme una bona cavalcatura." Albeit crossed out, this provision was probably first discussed among the parties and only later dismissed. Araldi seems to have traveled to Milan in 1516, when he probably executed a copy of Leonardo's *Last Supper*, which remained in his workshop until his death in 1528. It is now on display in the San Paolo museum: Mariangela Giusto, entry, in *Galleria Nazionale di Parma: Catalogo delle opere dall'antico al Cinquecento*, ed. Lucia Fornari Schianchi (Parma 1997), 128–9.

42 On "resemblance" among monastic works see Anne Dunlop, "Introduction: The Augustinians, the Mendicant Orders, and Early Renaissance Art," in *Art and the Augustinian Order in Renaissance Italy*, ed. Louise Bourda and Anne Dunlop (Aldershot 2007), 1–13, esp. 6.

43 My discussion of "accademia" contextualizes and develops one of Steinberg's intuitions with reference to Araldi's copy of Leonardo's *Last Supper*: Leo Steinberg, *Leonardo's Incessant Last Supper* (New York 2001), 239. It remains unclear whether or not it was known in early sixteenth-century Parma that Alessandro Carissimi, who was born into a local wealthy family, served as a model for "the hand of Christ" in Leonardo's *Last Supper*, as the artist reported in his notebook: Jean Paul Richter, ed., *The Literary Works of Leonardo da Vinci*, 2 vols. (London 1970), 2: 352.

44 Born ca. 1460 in Parma, Araldi was active for a wide spectrum of private and religious local patrons until his death in the late 1520s. Documentation confirms that in 1496, Araldi, then in Mantua, asked Jacopo d'Atri, the secretary of the marquis of Mantua, Francesco Gonzaga, for a letter of accreditation (*lettera di familiarità*) to visit Venice: Giovanni Agosti, *Su Mantegna I* (Milan 2005), 208 n. 5. On the Araldi-

Savoldo connection see Creighton Gilbert, "Savoldo, Cima, Parma, and the Pio Family," *Venezia Cinquecento* 4, 8 (1994): 113–25. In 1506 Savoldo visited Parma where he was Araldi's guest.

45 Araldi's close relationships with the Bergonzi family to which the abbesses belonged could be seen as another reason for his continued work in San Paolo. In 1503, e.g., Benedetto and Francesco Bergonzi, Abbess Cecilia's brothers, served as witnesses to a record drawn up in the convent establishing the dowry that Araldi was to pay for his daughter Orsolina: SBEAP, MS 101, Enrico Scarabelli Zunti, "Documenti e memorie di belle arti parmigiane," vol. II (1451–1509), fol. 22bis.

46 On the Monteluce altarpiece installed in 1525, which was meant to be modeled after Domenico Ghirlandaio's *Coronation of the Virgin* for the Franciscan community of Narni, see John Shearman, *Raphael in Early Modern Sources (1483–1602)*, 2 vols. (New Haven and London 2003), 1: 752–5; Alberto Maria Sartore, "'Begun by Master Raphael': The Monteluce 'Coronation of the Virgin,'" *Burlington Magazine* 153 June (2011): 387–91.

47 Jeffrey F. Hamburger, "'To make women weep': Ugly Art as 'Feminine' and the Origins of Modern Aesthetics," *Res* 31 (1997): 32 developing Hans Belting's paradigm shift from the pre-modern to the modern, autonomous image characterized by its emphasis on aesthetic values: Hans Belting, *Likeness and Presence: A History of the Image before the Era of Art*, trans. Edmund Jephcott (Chicago 1994), 458–89.

48 Ida Gianfranceschi, "Il Monastero di Santa Giulia dalla fondazione al XIV secolo," in Giampietro Belotti, ed., *San Salvatore e Santa Giulia: Storia di un monastero femminile dalla fondazione longobarda alla destinazione museale* (Brescia 2004), 11–35; Giampietro Belotti, "Il Monastero di Santa Giulia dal XIV secolo alla soppressione napoleonica," in ibid., 37–105.

49 Giorgio Vasari, "Proemio delle Vite," in *Le Vite de' più eccellenti pittori, scultori e architettori nelle redazioni del 1550 e 1568*, ed. Rosanna Bettarini and Paola Barocchi, 6 vols. (Florence 1966–87), 2: 24. Now exhibited in the museum of Santa Giulia that occupies the site of the convent, its treasury included precious medieval works like Desiderius' sumptuous cross and the *lipsanotheca*, an ivory reliquary casket with superbly carved figurative decoration. On Ferramola's frescoes dating to ca. 1513–24 in the upper-level nuns' choir of Santa Maria in Solario, then functioning as a treasury, see Massimiliano Capella, "I cicli pittorici di Floriano Ferramola," in *San Salvatore, Santa Giulia a Brescia: il monastero nella storia*, ed. Renata Stradiotti (Milan 2001), 201–9, esp. 201–5.

50 Ida Gianfranceschi Vettori, Elena Lucchesi Ragni, and Maurizio Mondini, eds., *Il coro delle monache: Cori e corali*, exh. cat. (Milan 2003), 60.

51   The affiliation of the nuns of Santa Giulia with the Cass-
     inese Congregation was a prolonged and multi-step process
     that first required winning over some recalcitrant nuns to
     adherence to strict cloister rules. A defamatory Latin inscrip-
     tion carved on a marble slab testifies to internal division
     within the community in the 1470s: Vasco Frati, "Un duro
     e lungo conflitto fra le monache di Santa Giulia: un'
     iscrizione infamante (1478) e un documento controverso
     (1498)," in Stradiotti, *San Salvatore, Santa Giulia a Brescia*,
     381–5. On reform in the convent see Giovanni Spinelli,
     "L'applicazione della riforma di Santa Giustina al monastero
     di Santa Giulia nel xv secolo," in ibid., 193–9.

52   Tommaso Leccisotti, *Congregationis S. Iustinae de Padua
     O.S.B. Ordinationes Capitulorum Generalium: Parte II (1475–
     1504)* (Montecassino 1970), 59. On the Congregation and its
     reformed agenda see Barry Collett, *Italian Benedictine Scholars
     and the Reformation: The Congregation of Santa Giustina of
     Padua* (Oxford 1985), 1–76; Massimo Zaggia, *Tra Mantova e
     la Sicilia nel Cinquecento. II: la congregazione benedettina cassinese
     nel Cinquecento* (Florence 2003), 401–526.

53   *Regola di Sancto Benedecto nuovamente vulgarizata* (Florence after
     1500), ch. 52: "Dello Oratorio del monastero": "Oratorio
     aquello solamente si adoperi/che suo nome significa: ne altra
     cosa visi faccia o visi riponga. Finita lopera di Dio tutti con
     sommo silentio escano fuora . . . accioche elfratello elquale
     privatamente vuole orare/ non sia impedito per indiscretione
     daltri."

54   Ludovico Barbo, "Forma Orationis et Meditationis Con-
     gregationi Monachorum S. Iustine," in *Ludovico Barbo
     (1381–1443)*, ed. Ildefonso Tassi (Rome 1952), esp. 143–
     56.

55   Ida Gianfranceschi Vettori, *Gli affreschi cinquecenteschi di Santa
     Giulia come documenti storici* (Brescia 1978), 28–35; Francesco
     de Leonardis, "Decorazione del coro delle monache nella
     chiesa di Santa Giulia," in Fiorella Frisoni, Francesco de
     Leonardis, and Rossana Prestini, *Paolo da Caylina il Giovane
     e la bottega dei da Caylina nel panorama artistico bresciano fra
     Quattrocento e Cinquecento* (Brescia 2003), 78–83.

56   Enrico Camisani, "Obizio," in *Bibliotheca Sanctorum*, 16 vols.
     (Rome 1967), 9: 1085–6.

57   For a discussion of this pictorial cycle see Alessandro Nova,
     Girolamo Romanino (Turin 1994), 259–60.

58   Leon Battista Alberti, *On Painting*, trans. John R. Spencer
     (London 1956), 63.

59   On the Christian image and its ambivalence (displaying not
     only the religious subject but also the manner of its own
     representation, that is, "not only the *what* but also the *how*")
     see Klaus Krüger, *Das Bild als Schleier des Unsichtbaren: Ästhe-
     tische Illusion in der Kunst der frühen Neuzeit in Italien* (Munich
     2001), esp. 95–106; Klaus Krüger, "Authenticity and Fiction:

On the Pictorial Construction of Inner Presence in Early
Modern Italy," in *Image and Imagination of the Religious Self
in Late Medieval and Early Modern Europe*, ed. Reindert L.
Falkenburg, Walter S. Melion, and Todd M. Richardson
(Turnhout 2007), 37–69, esp. 67. On images' conscious presentation of contents that orient, direct, and attract the viewer's gaze see also Victor I. Stoichita, *The Self-Aware Image:
An Insight into Early Modern Meta-Painting* (Cambridge 1997),
34–53.

60   On Romanino's unorthodox pictorial style and its intersec-
     tions with Folengo's maccheronic language see Alessandro
     Nova, "Folengo and Romanino: The Questione della
     Lingua and its Eccentric Trends," *Art Bulletin* 76, 4 (1994):
     664–79.

61   On Romanino's altarpiece (ca. 1513–14) and his *Last Supper*
     (1513) for the Cassinese monastery of Santa Giustina in
     Padua see Nova, *Romanino*, 217–21; Alexander Nagel, *The
     Controversy of Renaissance Art* (Chicago 2011), 153–6.

62   Giorgio Picasso, ed., "San Maurizio al Monastero Maggiore,"
     in *Monasteri benedettini in Lombardia* (Milan 1980), 67–79;
     Annamaria Ambrosioni, "Le abitanti del monastero: il medi-
     oevo," in *San Maurizio al Monastero Maggiore: Guida storico
     artistica* (Milan 1998), 12–18. Probably founded in the ninth
     century, the convent was erected on the Roman remains of
     the third-century wall and the polygonal tower of the circus
     built by Emperor Maximinus Herculius. Hence it is with
     good reason that today it houses the Archeological Museum
     of Milan, although the new use has entailed massive altera-
     tions to its monastic layout.

63   Giovanni Battista Sannazzaro and Grazioso Sironi, "Per la
     chiesa di S. Maurizio al Monastero Maggiore di Milano: gli
     antecedenti ed i primi decenni," *Raccolta vinciana* 30 (2003):
     239–65.

64   Hills, *Invisible City*, 149–50. On the first floor the nuns' choir
     also includes a walkway bordered by Serlian arches.

65   The exact date of the adherence of the San Maurizio nuns
     to the Cassinese Congregation is controversial. Ambrosioni,
     "Abitanti del monastero," 12, reports that it happened in
     1506. But documentation supplied by Roberta Mariani
     demonstrates that the local Cassinese monks of San Pietro
     in Gessate, albeit reluctantly, finally accepted responsibility
     for the nuns' care in 1480. The San Maurizio community
     had been admitted to the Cassinese Congregation as early
     as 1457: Roberta Mariani, "Monasteri benedettini a Milano
     prima della Riforma," in Zarri, *Monachesimo femminile*,
     219–47, esp. 226.

66   Vasari was the first to attribute the frescoes in San Maurizio
     to Luini: Vasari, *Vite*, 5; 435. Maria Teresa Binaghi Olivari,
     Bernardino Luini (Milan 2007), 26 has indicated an early
     chronology of Luini's frescoes (ca. 1517–19), arguing that the

Bentivoglio and not the nuns were probably the patrons. Marani, Bandera, and Quattrini have instead proposed a chronology of ca. 1521–4, which has been widely accepted: Pietro C. Marani, "Bernardino Luini's Frescoes in San Maurizio: Literary Circles, the Lombard Tradition, and Central-Italian Classicism," in *Bernardino Luini and Renaissance Painting in Milan: The Frescoes of San Maurizio al Monastero Maggiore*, ed. Sandrina Bandera and Maria Teresa Fiorio (Milan 2000), 53–74; Sandrina Bandera, "The Decoration Project" and "The First Phase of the Decoration in the Convent Section of the Church," in Bandera and Fiorio, *Luini and Renaissance Painting*, 45–52; Cristina Quattrini, *Brera mai vista. Lo Scherno di Cam: un dipinto riscoperto di Bernardino Luini* (Milan 2006), 41–4. Most recently, Dario Trento and Chiara Battezzati have postponed the chronology to ca. 1530–45, assigning the murals' execution to Luini's sons: Dario Trento, "Alessandro Bentivoglio, Bernardino Luini e la scuola di San Maurizio al Monastero Maggiore," *Ricerche di storia dell'arte* 77 (2002): 61–83, esp. 76; Chiara Battezzati, in *Bernardino Luini e i suoi figli: Itinerari*, ed. Giovanni Agosti, Rossana Sacchi, and Jacopo Stoppa (Milan 2014), 122–47, esp. 133–7.

67 The Bentivoglio coats of arms and the initials AL and HIP, standing for Alessandro Bentivoglio and Ippolita Sforza, Alessandra Bentivoglio's relatives, appear on the dividing wall facing the nuns: Rossana Sacchi, *Il disegno incompiuto: la politica artistica di Francesco II Sforza e di Massimiliano Stampa*, 2 vols. (Milan 2005), 1: 329.

68 *Regola di Sancto Benedecto*, ch. 52, "Et vole[n]do p[er] adve[n]tura a[n]cora uno altro secretame[n]te orare: semplicemente entri dentro [lo oratorio] & ori/no[n] con alta voce; ma con lachryme & inte[n]tione di quore."

69 Nuns circulating in their choir did not engage with the "pure landscape images" now visible in the chapels. Technical examination of the paint layers has confirmed that these landscape scenes were heavily restored, if not totally repainted, in the early twentieth century. Discussed as prime examples of "pure landscape pictures" in Renaissance Italy, and of the natural world framed within the monastic realm, these scenes, unfortunately, do not contribute anything to the history of Western landscape. Instead, they testify to how Renaissance values were rethought and remade in later times: Sandrina Bandera and Paola Zanolini, "Wall Painting Techniques and Restoration," in Bandera and Fiorio, *Luini and Renaissance Painting*, esp. 114–16. For an argument for the authenticity of the frescoes see Mary Ann Winkelmes, "Taking Part: Benedictine Nuns as Patrons of Art and Architecture," in Johnson and Matthews Grieco, *Picturing Women*, 99–100, n. 11.

70 Petrarch, *Secretum*, ed. and trans. Ugo Dotti (Rome 1993), 3.10.3–4; Petrarch, *The Life of Solitude*, trans. Jacob Zeitlin (Urbana, Ill. 1924), 2.1–18; Petrarch, *Rerum memorandarum libri*, ed. Giuseppe Billanovich (Florence 1945), 1.6. On the consolatory role of landscape painting see Frances Gage, "Exercise for Mind and Body: Giulio Mancini, Collecting, and the Beholding of Landscape Painting in the Seventeenth Century," *Renaissance Quarterly* 61, 4 (2008): 1167–207.

71 On the contested identification of the sitters in Luini's frescoes see Trento, "Alessandro Bentivoglio, Bernardino Luini," esp. 64–8, 71–2; Marani, "Bernardino Luini's Frescoes," 56, arguing for the Ippolita-Alessandro Bentivoglio couple; Binaghi Olivari, *Bernardino Luini*, 34; Sacchi, *Disegno incompiuto*, 1: 329–35, for the alternative sitters.

72 Bandello's book opens with a dedication to Ippolita Sforza Bentivoglio, who is mentioned in several novels. Alessandro Bentivoglio figures in several novels as well: Matteo Bandello, *Novelle*, ed. Giuseppe Guido Ferrero (Turin 1970).

73 For the Costa altarpiece see Emilio Negro and Nicosetta Roio, *Lorenzo Costa 1460–1535* (Modena 2001), 91–3. Francesco Francia is said to have painted Alessandro Bentivoglio as one of the shepherds in his *Nativity* (ca. 1499; Bologna, Pinacoteca Nazionale): Andrea Bacchi, "Vicende della pittura nell'età di Giovanni II Bentivoglio," in *Bentivolorum magnificentia: principe e cultura a Bologna nel rinascimento*, ed. Bruno Basile (Bologna 1984), 324. Alessandro Bentivoglio has recently been posited as the patron of a set of small-scale marble reliefs, executed ca. 1530 by Benedetto Cervi, a former collaborator of the sculptor Agostino Busti called Bambaia: Peter Lüdermann, "Agostino Busti detto il Bambaja e la sua cerchia: Temi all'antica nella scultura milanese del primo Cinquecento," *Studi di storia dell'arte* 24 (2013): 83–128, with previous bibliography on artworks that Alessandro collected in Milan.

74 Leccisotti, *Congregationis S. Iustinae de Padua*, 55–6.

75 Leone Smagliati, *Cronaca parmense (1494–1518)*, ed. Sergio di Noto (Parma 1970), 140: "A 25 genaro [1510], fu finito il choro di S. Paulo de dipingere, dove stava le sore a cantar: e lo comencið a far dipingere la reverenda badesa Orsina Bergoncia e fecelo finire la badesa Giovanna da Piasenza e lo dipinsi Alesandro di Araldi da Parma e così gli stalli gli fece Luchino Bianchino da Parma." Despite Smagliati's notation, the chronology of Bianchino's choirstalls has been debated. Angelo Pezzana first raised doubts, questioning the authenticity of an inscription painted on a small wood plaque attached to the frame of the choirstalls, arguing that "1510" replaced an original "1520": Angelo Pezzana, *Memorie degli scrittori e letterati parmigiani raccolte da Padre Ireneo Affò e continuate da Angelo Pezzana*, 7 vols. in 4 (Parma 1825–33), 6: 2.277; Lucia Fornari Schianchi, "Grandi committenze delle badesse nelle arti minori," in Dall'Acqua, *Monastero di*

San Paolo, 43–80, esp. 47. The restoration report dating to 2001 (see n. 95 below) confirms that the inscription was retouched, but not that its content was manipulated. Massimo Ferretti and Alessandra Talignani convincingly argued for the 1510 date, the latter based on a close study of the stylistic features of the stalls and their documentation: Massimo Ferretti, "I maestri della prospettiva," in *Storia dell'arte italiana* (Turin 1982), 11: 457–585, esp. 543–4; Alessandra Talignani, "Marc'Antonio Zucchi, non Luchino Bianchino: su un gruppo di tarsie parmensi con prospettive urbane," in *Forme del legno: Intagli e tarsie fra gotico e rinascimento*, ed. Gabriele Donati and Valeria E. Genovese (Pisa 2013), 195–212.

76 Alessandra Talignani, "Nuovi documenti sul coro ligneo di San Paolo," *Aurea Parma*, forthcoming.

77 James Elkins, *The Poetics of Perspective* (Ithaca, N.Y. and London 1994), 133, noted that "intarsia is a discipline that used perspective for part of its subject matter, and in a decidedly intellectual fashion."

78 BP, Fondo Moreau de Saint Mery, cassetta 46, fasc. XXXI/1, "Notificazione del Vener. Monastero di San Paolo in Parma presentata alla Real Giunta il di 15 Marzo 1767," for a description of the choir of San Paolo before its alteration. It is reported that Giovanna Piacenza's arms and initials filled the walls.

79 Patrizia Merati, ed., *Camera Apostolica: Documenti relativi alla Diocesi del ducato di Milano. I "Libri Annatarum" di Innocenzo VIII (1482–1492)*, vol. 3 (Milan 2000), 47. Conflicts in abbatial elections were not infrequent in early modern elite convents: K. J. P. Lowe, "Elections of Abbesses and Notions of Identity in Fifteenth- and Sixteenth-Century Italy, with Special Reference to Venice," *Renaissance Quarterly* 54, 2 (2001): 389–429.

80 The precious handwritten notes compiled by Scarabelli Zunti provide a summary of a now-lost record dating to October 5, 1484, attesting Caterina Bravi's nomination of relatives as representatives to oversee the convent's finances: SBEAP, Enrico Scarabelli Zunti, "Materiale per una guida artistica e storica di Parma: Chiese e conventi," MS 111, vol. II (M–V), fol. 131r.

81 Arcangeli, "Ragioni politiche," 170 n. 20.

82 ASPr, Notarile, Gaspare Prati, filza 227, February 10, 1487, on the settlement with Caterina Bravi. On Cecilia Bergonzi acting against usurpers of the convent's properties see Angelo Pezzana, *Storia della città di Parma*, 5 vols. (Parma 1837–59), 5: 74. Although usurpers are not specified in the papal bull of October 14, 1486, the unjust appropriation of lands, castles, and goods pertaining to San Paolo is condemned. Two abbots and an archbishop were entrusted with the convent's finances and were to assist Cecilia in regaining the properties. They were also requested to defend the com-

munity from "presumptuous molesters and offenders" of nuns' reputation.

83 BP, Fondo Moreau de Saint Mery, cassetta 46, fasc. XXXI/1, "Notificazione del Vener. Monastero di San Paolo in Parma presentata alla Real Giunta il di 15 Marzo 1767." One inscription includes the abbess's initials "CB" and her device with the words: "Revd.a D.a Cecilia de Bergonziis S. Pauli/Abbatiss. Hoc. mur . . . vetustate et/negligentia super . . . tempore colapsum/A fundamentis In pristinum facien . . ./Splendore reficiendos curavit MCCCCLXXXXIIII" (The reverend lady, Cecilia Bergonzi, Abbess of San Paolo, rebuilt this wall . . . from its foundations which had collapsed due to old age and neglect . . . over the years. And she took care that it was restored to its [original] splendor, 1494). On the eastern arm of the San Paolo cloister built with a double loggia ca. 1480–90 under Cecilia's tenure see Fabrizio Tonelli, "L'architettura parmense fra '400 e '500, il chiostro della Badia e il cortile del Castello di Torrechiara," in *L'Abbazia benedettina della Neve a Torrechiara*, ed. Fabrizio Tonelli and Barbara Zilocchi (Parma 2010), 83–108, esp. 90.

84 The Latin inscription reads: "Cecilia Antistes nulli virtute secunda/Fecit, Bergonzae gloria magna Domus." According to Ireneo Affò, this inscribed slab was reinserted into the pavement adjacent to the convent's seclusion door leading to the garden: *Ragionamento del Padre Ireneo Affò sopra una stanza dipinta dal celeberrimo Antonio Allegri da Correggio nel monistero di S. Paolo in Parma* (Parma 1794), 27.

85 Julia Haig Gaisser, *Pierio Valeriano and the Ill Fortune of Learned Men: A Renaissance Humanist and His World* (Ann Arbor, Mich. 1999), 185. On the foundation and development of printing in Renaissance Parma see Ireneo Affò, *Saggio di memorie su la tipografia parmense del secolo XV* (Parma 1791); Luigi Balsamo, "Editoria e umanesimo a Parma tra Quattro e Cinquecento," in *Parma e l'umanesimo italiano*, ed. Paola Medioli Masotti (Padua 1986), 77–95, esp. 86–93. A posthumous medal from the *Museo Mazzucchelliano*, an eighteenth-century collection of prints of ancient coins and Renaissance portrait medals, portrays Ugoleto's profile on the obverse; on the reverse a genius playing a lyre is shown with the motto: THADEUS UGOLETUS MUSARUM CULTOR (Taddeo Ugoleto, the worshipper of the Muses); Ireneo Affò, *Memorie di Taddeo Ugoleto parmigiano bibliotecario di Mattia Corvino re d'Ungheria* (Parma 1781), 10–11.

86 Reggio Emilia, Biblioteca Panizzi, Michele Fabrizio Ferrarini, "Antiquarium sive Divae Antiquitatis Sacrarium," MS C 398, fols. 93r–96v, esp. 94r. On the genesis of Ferrarini's sylloge, known in several copies, see Claudio Franzoni, "Gli studi antiquari di Michele Fabrizio Ferrarini," in *Il "Portico dei Marmi": le prime collezioni a Reggio Emilia e la*

nascita del Museo civico, exh. cat. (Reggio Emilia 1999), 25–37; Giancarla Periti, "Epigraphy and the Semiotics of the Line in Late Quattrocento Italy," in *LINEA I: Grafie di immagini tra Quattrocento e Cinquecento*, ed. Marzia Faietti and Gerhard Wolf (Venice 2008), 191–210. On *all'antica* inscriptions and stelae placed in gardens and courtyards that asserted the status of palace owners see Leonard Barkan, *Unearthing the Past: Archeology and Aesthetics in the Making of Renaissance Culture* (New Haven and London 1999), 27–8; Georgia Clarke, *Roman House – Renaissance Palaces: Inventing Antiquity in Fifteenth-Century Italy* (Cambridge 2003), 227–32.

87   For unpublished records on the Bergonzi see BP, MS Parm. 446, Carlo Vaghi, "Miscellanee Diverse," fol. 46r (1489). Francesco and Cecilia Bergonzi were descended from Ilario who resided in the district of the Cassinese church of San Giovanni Evangelista in Parma, for which see Alessandra Talignani, "Un disegno inedito e qualche appunto per la tomba di Marco Colla nella Cattedrale di Parma," *Aurea Parma* 87, 1 (2003): 9–30, n. 45.

88   Lowe, "Elections of Abbesses," 391.

89   ASPr, Diplomi Pontifici, cassetta 15, doc. 327, April 15, 1505. For discussion of this bull see Pezzana, *Storia*, 5: 74 n. 2; Umberto Benassi, *Storia di Parma*, 5 vols. (Parma 1899–1906), 1: 109–10; Dall'Acqua, "Il Monastero di San Paolo," in *Monastero di San Paolo*, 30. Over time, revisions were made to the minimum required age to be elected abbess in San Paolo, which is stated to be 28 years in the 1505 document.

90   Only in 1588 did the convent of San Paolo join the Cassinese Congregation: ASPr, Conventi Soppressi, Serie IX, Benedettine di San Paolo, busta 1, no. 15, 1588. It has been assumed that the female community of San Paolo adhered to the Congregation at an earlier date, but this assumption is not supported by documentary evidence. There were multiple attempts to reform the convent (see Chapter Four), which cannot be taken, however, for an actual affiliation to the Cassinese Congregation, for which a formal acceptance of the supervisory role by a local male monastic community was required. The community of Sant'Alessandro was the only Parmese female religious institution to join the Cassinese Congregation in the late Quattrocento: ASPr, Conventi e Confraternite, VIII, Sant'Alessandro, busta 33, "Relazione della Unione del Monist.o di S. Alessandro alla Congreg.ne di S.ta Giustina di Padova, e sua Riforma seguita l'anno 1486."

91   Smagliati, *Cronaca parmense*, 93: "A 25 aprile [1507], morì la badesa di San Polo, deta Orsina, fiola de Francesco Bergontio; e fu subito creata, con voce di tute le sore, una fiola de madona Agnese da Piasensa, la qual fu nominata madona Giovana."

92   As far as the altarpiece for the San Paolo church is concerned, David Ekserdjian has argued that a painting by Giulio Romano, *Christ the Redeemer between the Virgin and St. John the Baptist with Sts. Paul and Catherine of Alexandria* (Parma, Galleria Nazionale), with a traditional provenance of San Paolo, served as the main altarpiece. He further implies that Giovanna Piacenza commissioned it from Raphael before his death in 1520, and that the commission was then taken over by Giulio Romano: David Ekserdjian, *Correggio* (New Haven and London 1997), 78–9. In ca. 1526 the iconography of the glory of Christ was adapted to ornament St. Blaise's rich cope in Michelangelo Anselmi's altarpiece ordered by the Commune of Parma for the Cathedral: Elisabetta Fadda, *Michelangelo Anselmi* (Turin 2004), 165–6.

93   Ferretti, "Maestri della prospettiva," 543; Lucia Fornari Schianchi, *Il coro dell'oratorio della SS. Trinità dei Rossi in Parma* (Parma 1996), 9–19; Arturo Carlo Quintavalle, "Cristoforo da Lendinara: la città neoplatonica e quella storica," in *Basilica cattedrale di Parma: Novecento anni di arte, storia e fede*, ed. Arturo Carlo Quintavalle, Marco Pellegri, and Franco Maria Ricci, 3 vols. (Parma 2005), 1: 211–63, esp. 246–9.

94   SBEAP, Roberto Bergamaschi and Giovanna Menegazzi, "Relazione di Restauro," October 29, 2001, fol. 2.

95   Massimo Ferretti and Alessandra Talignani have recognized the richly ornate lectern as carved by Marco Antonio Zucchi (not by Bianchino) and executed ca. 1510: Ferretti, "Maestri della prospettiva," 546 n. 13; Talignani, "Marc'Antonio Zucchi," 195–212, esp. 201–02.

96   Ferretti, "Maestri della prospettiva," 484, on the Council of Trent ordering stalls to abut the walls of choirs.

97   Ferretti, "Maestri della prospettiva," 543. Also see Pier Luigi Bagatin, *Le pitture di Lorenzo e Cristoforo da Lendinara* (Treviso 2004), 496.

98   ASPr, Notarile, Antonio Maria Rainieri, filza, 688, May 27, 1507; SBEAP, Enrico Scarabelli Zunti, "Materiale," MS III, fol. 250r.

99   Marco Pellegri, "Il coro delle monache di Sant'Ulderico," in *Frammenti fugaci di un passato in Parma e provincia* (Parma 1999), 165–72. On the Mazzola altarpiece (ca. 1510s) set on the high altar of the church see Stefania Colla, "Michele and Pier Ilario Mazzola's Madonna and Child with Saints," in *Galleria Nazionale di Parma*, 120. For the foundation history see SBEAP, Scarabelli Zunti, "Materiale," MS III, fols. 249r–262v, and more recently Fabrizia Dalcò, "Monastero di Sant'Ulderico," in *Monasteri: alle radici della città e del territorio di Parma nel medioevo* (Parma 2007), 125–31.

100   ASPr, Notarile, Antonio Maria Rainieri, filza 687, April 4, 1505; Amadio Ronchini, "Intorno alla scoltura in legno:

Notizie storico-patrie," *Atti e memorie delle R.R. Deputazioni di storia patria per le provincie modenesi e parmensi* 8 (1876): 297–328, esp. 314.

101 ASPr, Notarile, Antonio Maria Rainieri, filza 687, April 4, 1505: "Il dicto magistro sia obligato a fare li stali del Coro di sancto odorico numero 24 videlicet 12 per lato a la fogia et facione de li stali de sancto francisco excepto che le prospective in loco de le quale elo debia fare grupi de tarsie varii et diversi cum boni et perfecti disegni tali che empiano il loco dove andariano le prospective, et che siano beli e laudevoli al giudicio de homini da bene et che intedano." For a discussion of Baruffi's choirstalls see Ferretti, "Maestri della prospettiva," 543; Massimo Ferretti, "Il coro di San Sisto," in *La Madonna per San Sisto di Raffaello e la cultura piacentina della prima metà del Cinquecento*, ed. Paola Ceschi Lavagetto (Parma 1985), 113–31, esp. 117–22.

102 See Luke Syson, entry in *Leonardo da Vinci: Painter at the Court of Milan*, ed. Luke Syson and Larry Keith, exh. cat. (London 2011), 217–18; Charles Nicholl, *Leonardo da Vinci: Flights of the Mind* (New York 2004), 305–7, pointing out that Leonardo recognized Bramante as the one who had devised the knot patterns or *groppi*. These interwoven patterns of cords have been explained either as a decorative motif applied in many media or as symbolic forms alluding to the various disciplines (painting, poetry, and music) cultivated in the "Academia Leonardi Vinci": Carmen Bambach Cappel, "Leonardo, Tagliente, and Dürer: 'la scienza del far di groppi,'" *Achademia Leonardi Vinci* 4 (1991): 72–98; Jill Pederson, "Henrico Boscano's *Isola Beata*: New Evidence for the Academia Leonardi Vinci in Renaissance Milan," *Renaissance Studies* 22, 4 (2008): 450–75, supplying a list of artists, poets, and humanists recorded in a newly found manuscript, Boscano's *Isola Beata* (ca. 1513), as members of Leonardo's Academy in Milan.

103 On the apotropaic values of knot-patterns in ancient civilizations see Gell, *Art and Agency*, 83–4.

104 ASPr, Notarile, Antonio Maria Rainieri, filza 687, April 4, 1505: "et dicto magistro sia obligato a fare una bela et bona prospectiva convenientemente granda in lo stalo de la Abatessa e a tutti quatri li cantoni del coro l'arma della Abatessa cum il fusse de conveniente grandeza."

105 Ibid: "item che la stessa madona li debia dare la Casa . . . dove stavino domino Johane hoc est la entrata cum la corte et uno redo de soto et una camera de sopra cum una letera et uno lecto cum li lencioli et coperta . . . et un'altera camera da sotto."

106 *Regola di Sancto Benedecto*, ch. 66, "El monasterio (se ei possibile) si debbe in talmodo ordinare: che habbi drento da se tutte lecose necessarie: cio e acqua/mulino/orto & forno . . . si che in epso sexercitino arte diverse."

107 Cristina Cecchinelli, "Il contratto della casa presa in affitto a Parma dal Correggio nel 1523 alla presenza del Rondani," *Aurea Parma* 93, 3 (2009): 347–68, esp. 349–51.

108 Zucchi later achieved fame for his choirstalls for San Giovanni Evangelista but he is certainly one of the major wood-carver-architects in early sixteenth-century Parma: Bruno Adorni, ed., *L'Abbazia benedettina di San Giovanni Evangelista a Parma* (Milan 1979), 162–71; Talignani, "Marc'Antonio Zucchi," 195–212.

109 On the foundation of San Quintino see BP, Fondo Moreau de Saint Mery, cassetta 46, fasc. XXXI/1, "Monache di San Quintino Benedettine"; Ireneo Affò, *Vita della Beata Orsolina da Parma* (Parma 1786), 6–70; Enrico Scarabelli Zunti, *Cenni storico-artistici intorno alla chiesa e al già monastero di San Quintino in Parma* (Parma 1846), 6–7; Dalcò, "Monastero di San Quintino," in *Monasteri*, 117–23. On this community's artistic commissions, including Marmitta's altarpiece and illuminated manuscripts, see Valeria Vecchi, "Tre donne Sanvitale nel primo Cinquecento a Parma: Susanna, Laura, Paola," *Aurea Parma* 80, 1 (1986): 57–79; Beatrice Bentivoglio-Ravasio, entry in *Francesco Marmitta*, ed. Andrea Bacchi et al., (Turin 1994), 329–33; Giuseppa Z. Zanichelli, "Il Maestro del Libro d'Ore Sanvitale e la bottega di Cristoforo Caselli: miniatura a Parma nella seconda metà del XV secolo," *Artes* 2 (1994): 39–68; Aldo Galli, "Miniature parmigiane nel rinascimento: due corali delle monache di San Quintino ritrovati a Genova," *Parma per l'arte* n.s. 8, 1 (2002): 25–42.

110 Franciscus Marius Grapaldus, *De Partibus Aedium* (Parma 1494; 1516), 2.1: "Emblemata . . . quae in lignis etiam fieri decenter videmus." See also Ferretti, "Maestri della prospettiva," 469; Marco Collareta, "'Encaustum Vulgo Smaltum': Note sulla percezione umanistica delle tecniche figurative," *Annali della Scuola normale superiore di Pisa*, ser. III, 14, 2 (1984): 759–69, esp. 768–9. Grapaldo's *De Partibus* is a philological lexicon rather than an architecture treatise, and this unusual feature made it a successful publication in its own time: twelve editions (including translations in French and German) were published in less than 40 years, including six Latin editions between 1501 and 1517. In 1512 Julius II appointed Grapaldo poet laureate in Rome, on which occasion he recited his poem "In deditione Patriae S. Julio II Pont. Max": Ireneo Affò, *Memorie degli scrittori e letterati parmigianini*, 5 vols. (Parma 1789–97), 3: 125–50, esp. 137–41; Pezzana, *Memorie*, 6: 2.392–3; Adorni, *L'Abbazia benedettina*, 47–9, on Grapaldo's funerary marble tablet in the church of San Giovanni Evangelista.

111 Denis L. Drysdall, "Préhistoire de l'emblème: commentaires et emplois du terme avant Alciati," *Nouvelle revue du seizième siècle* 6 (1988): 29–44.

112 Giorgio Vasari, *Vite*, 1: 155–7, esp. 157: "E perché tale professione consiste solo ne' disegni che siano atti a tale esercizio, pieni di casamenti e di cose che abbino i lineamenti quadrati e si possa per via di chiari e di scuri dare loro forza e rilievo, hannolo fatto sempre persone che hanno avuto più pacienza che disegno."

CHAPTER IV GIOVANNA PIACENZA'S ABBATIAL APARTMENT

1 On this tradition of abbots' dwellings see Terryl Kinder, *Cistercian Europe: Architecture of Contemplation* (Grand Rapids, Mich. 2002), 355–9; Jackie Hall, "East of the Cloister: Infirmaries, Abbots' Lodgings, and Other Chambers," in *Perspectives for an Architecture of Solitude: Essays on Cistercians, Art, and Architecture in Honor of Peter Fergusson*, ed. Terryl N. Kinder (Turnhout 2004), 199–212; Wolfgang Braunfels, *Monasteries of Western Europe: The Architecture of the Orders* (London 1972), 58–63 (on Cluny), 201–20 (Baroque princely abbeys); Andrea Calore, "'Il palatium abbatis' di S. Giustina: Sec. XII," in *I Benedettini a Padova e nel territorio padovano attraverso i secoli*, exh. cat. (Padua 1980), 45–54; Paolo Piva, "Quel che sappiamo sulla *Domus Infirmorum* in un'abbazia benedettina: San Benedetto Po," *Postumia* 6 (1995): 79–88.

2 On the medieval tradition of the bishop's ornate residence see Maureen C. Miller, *The Bishop's Palace: Architecture and Authority in Medieval Italy* (Ithaca, N.Y. 2000), 170–252.

3 Matilde Gagliardo, "Il verziere nella cappella: le sibille quattrocentesche del Palazzo Vescovile di Albenga," in *Scritti di storia dell'arte in onore di Sylvie Béguin*, ed. Mario di Giampaolo and Elisabetta Saccomani (Naples 2001), 53–67; Cecilia Prete, "Marcello Fogolino e gli affreschi di Palazzo Roverella ad Ascoli Piceno," in *Pittura veneta nelle Marche*, ed. Valter Curzi (Cinisello Balsamo 2000), 205–9.

4 An independent residence for the abbess is documented in the convent of Santa Giulia in Brescia, but nothing is known about its furnishings and decorations: Giampietro Belotti, "Il monastero di Santa Giulia dal XIV secolo alla soppressione napoleonica," in *San Salvatore e Santa Giulia: Storia di un monastero femminile dalla fondazione longobarda alla destinazione museale*, ed. Giampietro Belotti (Brescia 2004), 37–106, esp. 88. A sixteenth-century ground plan of the Dominican convent of San Jacopo in Florence includes an abbess's room: Anabel Thomas, *Art and Piety in the Female Religious Communities of Renaissance Italy: Iconography, Space, and the Religious Woman's Perspective* (Cambridge 2003), 97–8.

5 On this portrait see the entry in Jeffrey F. Hamburger and Robert Suckale, eds., *Krone und Schleier: Kunst aus Mittelalterlichen Frauenklöstern*, exh. cat. (Munich 2005), 339–40.

6 Andrea Pearson, "Images and the Ideal of Women's Monasticism: Two Paintings from the Cistercian Convent of Flines," *Renaissance Quarterly* 54 (2001): 1356–402; John Oliver Hand, Catherine A. Metzger, and Ron Spronk, eds., *Prayers and Portraits: Unfolding the Netherlandish Diptych*, exh. cat. (Washington, D.C., New Haven and London 2006), 30–35. Bellegambe's *Abbess Jeanne de Boubais* appears on the outer panel of a diptych, while the inner side depicts a Cistercian monk accompanied by St. Bernard holding the crosier. St. Bernard presents the monk to the Virgin Mary and Christ Child on the left wing. Bellegambe's diptych and his monumental *Cellier Altarpiece* (ca. 1509; New York, Metropolitan Museum of Art) seem to have been commissioned by Abbess Boubais for clerics who promoted the reform of her convent at Flines, near Douai (France).

7 The patronage, original location, and function of the Freiburg tapestry panel have been debated: James A. Rushing, "Iwein as Slave of Woman: The 'Maltererteppich' in Freiburg," *Zeitschrift für Kunstgeschichte* 55, 1 (1992): 124–35; Sebastian Bock, ed., *Bestandskataloge der weltlichen Ortsstiftungen der Stadt Freiburg i. Br. die Textilien*, 5 vols. (Freiburg 2001), 5: 87–94; Erika Lauren Lindgren, *Sensual Encounters: Monastic Women and Spirituality in Medieval Germany* (New York 2009), 75–6. On the topos of the power of women, and the possibility of the reversal of gender roles threatening authorities, see Susan L. Smith, *The Power of Women: A Topos in Medieval Art and Literature* (Philadelphia, Pa. 1995), 4–19. The Aristotle episode also appears in the painted chamber of ca. 1305–15 in the tower of the Palazzo Comunale in San Gimignano (Siena): Jean C. Campbell, *The Game of Courting and the Art of the Commune of San Gimignano, 1290–1320* (Princeton 1997), 124–6.

8 This notion of conventual ornate spaces as "other" is indebted to Michel Foucault, "Of Other Spaces," *Diacritics* (Spring 1986): 22–7.

9 Mary Carruthers, *The Craft of Thought: Meditation, Rhetoric, and the Making of Images, 400–1200* (Cambridge 1998), 122. On the notion that inscriptions were considered both texts and images in the Renaissance, producing meaning as written words (or *scriptura*), but also as visual forms to be absorbed at a glance see also Giancarla Periti, "Epigraphy and the Semiotics of the Line in Late Quattrocento Italy," in *LINEA I: Grafie di immagini tra Quattrocento e Cinquecento*, ed. Marzia Faietti and Gerhard Wolf (Venice 2008), 191–210.

10 Leone Smagliati, *Cronaca parmense (1494–1518)*, ed. Sergio di Noto (Parma 1970), 148 [June 18, 1510]. On street violence and political upheaval in Renaissance Parma see Letizia Arcangeli, "'Come bosco et spelunca di latroni': Città e ordine pubblico a Parma e nello stato di Milano tra Quattrocento e Cinquecento," in *Le polizie informali*, ed. Livio Antonelli (Rubettino [CZ] 2010), 65–90.

11 Smagliati, *Cronaca*, 161–2 [November 30, 1510]: "festa vituperosa . . . nè vi poterono andare la magior parte de mariti . . . o altri dela città. Fecesi mascari e giochi e durò fino a 6 ore." During the French occupation, some citizens had to flee Parma, including the humanist Giorgio Anselmi from 1499 to 1512: Fortunato Rizzi, "Giorgio Anselmi," *Aurea Parma* 37 (1953): 143–62, esp. 149–51.

12 Letizia Arcangeli, "Ragioni politiche della disciplina monastica: il caso di Parma tra Quattrocento e Cinquecento," in *Donna, disciplina, creanza cristiana dal XV al XVII secolo: Studi e testi a stampa*, ed. Gabriella Zarri (Rome 1996), 165–87, esp. 167–8, 177.

13 A certain Antonio Piacenza is mentioned in the 1413 merchant guild, and his initials A[ntonius] P[lacentia] were recorded on a now-lost building façade near the church of Santo Stefano. Apparently, this house was next to that of the famous poet Petrarch when he resided in Parma intermittently in 1341–51 and worked on his *De Remediis utriusque Fortunae*: SBEAP, Enrico Scarabelli Zunti, "Materiale per una guida artistica e storica di Parma: Chiese e conventi," MS III, vol. II (M–V), fol. 227r; Amadio Ronchini, "La dimora del Petrarca in Parma," *Atti e memorie delle RR. Deputazioni di storia patria per le provincie modenesi e parmensi* 7 (1874): 343–67. Other documentation also shows that Sebastiano Bergonzi (Giovanna's maternal grandfather) married twice and had at least four sons (Paolo, Sigismondo, Ludovico, and Ottaviano) and two daughters (Camilla and Agnese): ASPr, Notarile, Giovanni Ludovico Sacca, filza 280, November 28, 1482.

14 On the Bergonzi-Piacenza-Montini clan and its influence in early modern Parma see Letizia Arcangeli, "Sul linguaggio della politica nell'Italia del primo Cinquecento: le fonti della città di Parma," *Per Marino Berengo: Studi degli Allievi* (Milan 2000), 76–113; Letizia Arcangeli, "Tra Milano e Roma: Esperienze politiche nella Parma del primo Cinquecento," in *Emilia e Marche nel rinascimento: l'identità visiva della "Periferia,"* ed. Giancarla Periti (Azzano [Bg] 2005), 89–118. The sister of Canon Giacomo Colla and Giovanna Piacenza's aunt, Briseide Colla Bergonzi, commissioned Correggio's famous *Il Giorno* altarpiece: David Ekserdjian, *Correggio* (New Haven and London 1997), 193–204; Giancarla Periti, "Nota sulla 'maniera moderna' di Correggio a Parma," in *Parmigianino e il manierismo europeo*, ed. Lucia Fornari Schianchi (Cinisello Balsamo 2002), 298–303.

15 Giovanna's mother, Agnese Bergonzi, belonged to a different branch of the Bergonzi family from that of the previous abbesses, and their animosity predated Giovanna's election: Francesco Barocelli, "Il Correggio nel monastero di San Paolo e l'umanesimo monastico di Giovanna Piacenza," in *Il Correggio nella Camera di San Paolo* (Milan 2010), 234–5.

16 For documentation on Giovanna's election see ASPr, Diplomatico, Diplomi Pontifici, cass. 16, 332, April 27, 1507; 334, January 3, 1508 and Notarile, Gaspare Prati, filza 232, May 4, 1507. The loss of the baptismal registers covering the period 1470–85 makes it impossible to establish Giovanna Piacenza's exact birthdate, while it is known that she took her vows in 1498: Barocelli, *Correggio*, 244, n. 62.

17 For a brilliant interpretation of the decoration of Bartolomeo Montini's funerary chapel in the right transept of Parma Cathedral see Alessandra Talignani, "La cappella Montini nella cattedrale di Parma: un *unicum* di forme, colori ed epigrafi nella 'periferia,'" in Periti, *Emilia e Marche nel Rinascimento*, 119–80. On Bonzagni's medal of Scipione Montini Rosa, which has only the date MDXV on its reverse: Davide Gasparotto, entry in *Parmigianino e il manierismo europeo*, ed. Lucia Fornari Schianchi and Sylvia Ferino-Pagden, exh. cat. (Cinisello Balsamo 2003), 341. Scipione Montini Rosa is known to art historians for a reference in the 1534 correspondence between Federigo Gonzaga and the Governor of Parma, Alessandro Caccia, in which it is speculated that Scipione was the keeper of Correggio's cartoons of the *Loves of Jupiter*: Ekserdjian, *Correggio*, 291.

18 Umberto Benassi, *Storia di Parma*, 5 vols. (Parma 1899–1906), 1: 15, 3: 41, 128.

19 Smagliati, *Cronaca*, 149 [July 22, 1510]; 154 [October 12, 1510]. On the Garimberti–Rosa litigation in the context of the local political factions see Letizia Arcangeli, "Principi, homines e 'partesani' nel ritorno dei Rossi," in *Le signorie dei Rossi tra XIV e XVI secolo* (Florence 2007), 231–306, esp. 288–9.

20 For documents regarding the architect da Erba active in San Paolo see Luigi Pungileoni, *Memorie istoriche di Antonio Allegri detto il Correggio*, 3 vols. (Parma 1817–22), 2: 122 and Cristiana Prestianni, "Un documento inedito sulla committenza di Giovanna da Piacenza nel monastero di San Paolo," *Aurea Parma* 93, 1 (2009): 103–32, esp. 119–21. On the features of Giorgio da Erba's architecture see Mario Salmi, "Bernardino Zaccagni e l'architettura del rinascimento a Parma," *Bollettino d'arte* 12, 1–4 (1918): 85–169, esp 135–6; Bruno Adorni, ed. *L'Abbazia benedettina di San Giovanni Evangelista a Parma* (Milan 1979), 44–53.

21 Bruno Adorni and Mariarita Furlotti, "L'architettura a Parma all'epoca del Parmigianino," in Fornari Schianchi, *Parmigianino e il manierismo europeo*, 360–69; Fabrizio Tonelli, "Per Correggio, Parmigianino, Anselmi, Bedoli e l'architettura," in *Parmigianino e la scuola di Parma* (Viadana [Mn] 2004), 47–74.

22 Augusta Ghidiglia Quintavalle, "Alessandro Araldi," *Rivista dell'Istituto nazionale d'archeologia e storia dell'arte* 7 (1958):

291–333, esp. 293; Maria Cristina Chiusa, *Alessandro Araldi: la "maniera antico-moderna" a Parma* (Parma 1996), 16.

23 Barocelli, *Correggio*, 239, has interpreted the female saint as Santa Giustina, a leading figure within reformed institutions affiliated with the Benedictine Cassinese Congregation. As mentioned in Chapter Three, San Paolo adhered to the Cassinese Congregation only in the late sixteenth century. This iconographic identification therefore does not seem plausible in a convent that long resisted the reformed agenda of the Congregation.

24 Francesco Barocelli, *La Pinacoteca Stuard di Parma: gli ambienti storici, le sculture, le incisioni, gli arredi* (Milan 2005), 158–9.

25 Ireneo Affò, *Ragionamento del Padre Ireneo Affò sopra una stanza dipinta dal celeberrimo Antonio Allegri da Correggio nel monistero di S. Paolo in Parma* (Parma 1794), 30: "JOANNA PLACENTIA/ABB. INSTIT. OPTIMIS/ANTIQUIORA NON NE/GLIGENS AD PERPETUI/TATEM LUCULENTIOREM/APPARATU COE-NOBIUM/EREXIT NOVIS TECTIS/INDUCTIS AMPLISS."

26 Evelyn Welch, "Public Magnificence and Private Display: Giovanni Pontano's *De Splendore* (1498) and the Domestic Arts," *Journal of Design History* 15, 4 (2002): 211–21; Georgia Clarke, *Roman House – Renaissance Palaces: Inventing Antiquity in Fifteenth-Century Italy* (Cambridge 2003), 97–105.

27 Some instances of the reuse of ancient spolia in Renaissance conventual sites are known. According to Francesco Sansovino, the Venetian Benedictine nuns of San Zaccaria incorporated ninth-century capitals carved with eagles in their church: Francesco Sansovino, *Venetia città nobilissima et singolare: descritta in XIII libri* (Venice 1581), 1.26. As noted in Chapter Three, the nuns of San Maurizio in Milan adapted the Roman remains on which their convent was built, including a third-century polygonal tower, the walls of which are decorated with Christological scenes and saints dating to the early fourteenth century.

28 Flavio Biondo, "Roma Triumphans," in *Opera* (Basel 1531), 189–90 and Clarke, *Roman House*, 101–2.

29 ASPr, Notarile, Girolamo Balestra, filza 833, August 28, 1524: "infra[scriptae] habitationes et loca nova fabricata per ipsam dom[inam] abbatissam in dicto mon[asterio] videlicet: unus salonus seu sala magna a terreno super canipa cum duabus Cameris eidem salono adherentibus ac oratorio et lodia a terreno exytente ante dictum salonum Cameras et orato-rium ac camerino adherent[e] dictis Cameris; item unus alius locus superior et una cella, ac una coquina cum mas-saritiis dictae coquinae et cum canipa exytente de subtus dictas Cameras et oratorium reservata alia canipa maiori exytente de subtus dictum salonum dictis monialibus; item hortum minorem cum Curia adherente dicto horto respic-iente versus stratam publicam et domos illorum de Ferraria et locum audientiae parvae; item utinsilia et ornamenta dictorum locorum reservatorum ipsi dominae abbatissae videlicet ea quae videbantur ipsi dominae abbatissae pro eius usu et personarum eidem deserventium." On this document and the description of the abbatial quarters see Affò, *Ragiona-mento*, 30; Marzio Dall'Acqua, ed., *Il monastero di San Paolo* (Parma 1990), 33; Giuseppina Longhi and Aldo Spina, "Il complesso monastico di San Paolo," 2 vols., thesis, Politec-nico di Milano 1991–2, 1: 14.

30 It is unclear if Giovanna's residence remained available to her one-year successors. After the enforcement of strict seclusion (1524), the earliest mention of the apartment dates to 1598 when the local cartographer and engineer Smeraldo Smeraldi obtained permission to visit the convent because buildings were in need of repair. At that time the abbatial residence seems to have been inhabited by Princess Margherita Farnese (1567–1643) who was forced to retire to San Paolo after the annulment of her marriage to Vincenzo Gonzaga in 1584: BP, Smeraldo Smeraldi, "Diario delle visite per vie, canali, edifici dal feb. 1598 all'agosto 1600," MS Parm. 535, August 1, 1598, Visita al convento di San Paolo, fols. 82v–83r, for the description of the apartment.

31 The bibliography on the layout and settings of apartments in Italian Renaissance palaces has grown in recent decades. Useful references remain Brenda Preyer, "The Florentine Casa," in *At Home in Renaissance Italy*, ed. Marta Ajmar-Wollheim and Flora Dennis, exh. cat. (London 2006), 34–49; Patricia Fortini Brown, "Not having the Name of Palazzo," in *Private Lives in Renaissance Venice: Art, Architecture and the Family* (New Haven and London 2004), 23–51. Architectural treatises instructing Renaissance readers how to design their houses and what forms were appropriate for self-represen-tation have been discussed, among others, by Kathleen Weil-Garris and John F. D'Amico, *The Renaissance Cardinal's Ideal Palace: A Chapter from Cortesi's De Cardinalatu* (Rome 1980), 57–67; Peter Thornton, *The Italian Renaissance Interior 1400–1600* (London 1991), 284–320; Clarke, *Roman House*, 87–105.

32 Stephen J. Campbell, *The Cabinet of Eros: Renaissance Mytho-logical Painting and the Studiolo of Isabella d'Este* (New Haven and London 2004), 62.

33 Franciscus Marius Grapaldus, *De Partibus Aedium* (Parma 1494; 1516), 2.1; Weil-Garris and D'Amico *Renaissance Car-dinal's Ideal Palace*, 74–5.

34 Preyer, "Florentine Casa," 35–6.

35 Sheila Bonde and Clark Maines, "A Room of One's Own: Elite Spaces in Monasteries of the Reform Movement and an Abbot's Parlor at the Augustinian Saint-Jean-des-Vignes, Sois-sons (France)," in *Religion and Belief in Medieval Europe*, ed. Guy de Boe and Frans Verhaeghe, 4 vols. (Zellik 1997), 4: 45–6.

36 The Panopticon was designed by Jeremy Bentham in the late eighteenth century. It consisted of an annular building

with a central tower from which a watchman would monitor the inmates in the surrounding cells. Despite that, the watchman could not check on all the prisoners simultaneously, nor could they see him, and it is therefore expected that they would not misbehave. Foucault's main point is that surveillance and repression were carried out through the force of the gaze identified with a notion of power: Michel Foucault, *Discipline and Punish: The Birth of the Prison*, trans. Alan Sheridan (New York 1979), 195–228. See also Helen Hills, *Invisible City: The Architecture of Devotion in Seventeenth-Century Neapolitan Convents* (Oxford 2004), 145 on Foucault's inverted model of surveillance in monastic buildings.

37 ASPr, Notarile, Giovanni Antonio Del Monte, filza 539, September 6, 1507: "il lapicida Antonio Ferrari de Grate, oriundo del ducato di Milano, ora abitante a Parma in vicinia di San Sepolcro, promette a Giovanna da Piacenza Badessa di San Paolo di Parma di consegnarle 9 paia di colonne di lunghezza e grandezza di quelle esistenti ora in opera alla pergola . . . del monastero, cioè fusti e fulcimenti a 7 l.i. per ogni paio e per tutto il mese di marzo prossimo future a spese di Antonio eccetto la conduzione delle lapidi da Serravalle a casa di Antonio dove lavorerà le colonne . . ." As observed by Fabrizio Tonelli, the style of the columns of the east side of the cloister, which date to ca. 1480–90, is archaizing with respect to that of the most recently carved columns by D'Agrate. Clashes of styles in monastic buildings were common and generally accepted by their patrons: Fabrizio Tonelli, "L'architettura parmense fra '400 e '500, il chiostro della Badia e il cortile del Castello di Torrechiara," in *L'Abbazia benedettina della Neve a Torrechiara*, ed. Fabrizio Tonelli and Barbara Zilocchi (Parma 2010), 90, 99.

38 The cloister of San Paolo has been under renovation for several years, which has severely limited the possibility of an adequate photographic campaign. The present-day loggia of five arcades facing Giovanna Piacenza's apartment is what remains after the incorporation of the far east arcade into the eastern arm of the cloister, and the dismantling of three arcades. Longhi and Spina, "Il complesso," 1: 26 refer to early seventeenth-century records attesting that the west arm of the cloister (of seven arcades) was being built at the time. This cloister was ultimately completed only in the eighteenth century but previously the arm located along the abbatial residence was basically a garden loggia.

39 Longhi and Spina, 'Il complesso," 1: 45, for a brief reference to the meeting hall in a mid nineteenth-century document. Here it is described as a vaulted, open-air, brick space.

40 Marcus Terentius Varro, *On the Latin Language*, trans. Roland G. Kent (Cambridge, Mass. 1967), 5.155.

41 Jürgen Schulz, "The Houses of the Dandalo," *Journal of the Society of Architectural Historians* 52 (1993): 401 n. 43; Clarke, *Roman House*, 15, referring to the debate raised by a contemporary inscription carved on the Loggia del Consiglio in Verona, completed in 1492. It was said that the Loggia resembled Roman arches. Based on the authority of ancient authors, the inscription should be changed: the Loggia is called an "atrium" but should instead be called a "curia," that is, the place where a senate meets.

42 Leon Battista Alberti, *On the Art of Building in Ten Books*, trans. Joseph Rykwert et al. (Cambridge 1988), v.iii; Grapaldus, *De Partibus*, 1.1, 2.1.

43 Kathleen Wren Christian, *Empire Without End: Antiquities Collections in Renaissance Rome, c. 1350–1527* (New Haven and London 2010), 121–34, 152–87, on Roman gardens populated with sculptures and used as *academiae*.

44 Cortesi, *De Cardinalatu*, 83.

45 Amedeo Belluzzi, "La grotta di Palazzo Te a Mantua," in *Arte delle grotte*, ed. Cristina Acidini Luchinat et al. (Genoa 1987), 47; Michaela Marek, "La loggia di Psyche nella Farnesina: Per la ricostruzione ed il significato," in *Raffaello a Roma*, ed. Christoph Luitpold Frommel and Matthias Winner (Rome 1986), 209–16.

46 Talignani, "Cappella Montini," esp. 146–8.

47 Francesco Colonna, *Hypnerotomachia Poliphili*, ed. Giovanni Pozzi and Lucia A. Ciapponi, 2 vols. (Padua 1980), 1: 348–9.

48 Jacopo Caviceo, *Il Peregrino*, ed. Luigi Vignali (Rome 1993) and Anna Ceruti Burgio, "Strutture narrative e modelli culturali del "Peregrino" di Iacopo Caviceo," *Aurea Parma* 62 (1978): 42–54.

49 On the notion of court as a social setting and as a site of refinement and education see Stephen C. Jaeger, *The Origins of Courtliness: Civilizing Trends and the Formation of Courtly Ideals 939–1210* (Philadelphia, Pa. 1985), 80–82, 155–62; Aldo Scaglione, *Knights at Court, Courtliness, Chivalry, and Courtesy from Ottonian Germany to Italian Renaissance* (Berkeley 1991), 5–14, 426–41.

50 Dilwyn Knox, "Civility, Courtesy and Women in the Italian Renaissance," in *Women in Italian Renaissance Culture and Society*, ed. Letizia Panizza (Oxford 2000), 10.

51 Olga Zorzi Pugliese, *Castiglione's The Book of the Courtier (Il Libro del Cortegiano): A Classic in the Making* (Rome 2008), 72–138.

52 Desiderius Erasmus, "The Council of Women," in *Collected Works: Colloquies*, trans. and annot. Craig R. Thompson, vol. 40 (Toronto 1997), 906.

53 On the notion of "other" space and its real and fictional construct see Foucault, "Of Other Spaces," 27. Developing Foucault's view, my own reflections are based on literature treating courtly culture and decorations that exceed the

boundary of monastic decorum to engage viewers in affective ways. My interpretation further differs from Camilla Russell's sociological reading of convents as "third" monastic sites that "existed in the lives of some women, as they moved between marriage and convent": Camilla Russell, "Convent Culture in Early Modern Italy: Laywomen and Religious Subversiveness in a Neapolitan Convent," in *Practices of Gender in Late Medieval and Early Modern Europe*, ed. Megan Cassidy-Welch and Peter Sherlock (Turnhout 2008), 57–76, esp. 62.

54 Campbell, *Cabinet of Eros*, 150–51, 182–3 offers a sophisticated treatment of discourses of lightness and levity in the studiolo setting.

55 [Titus Maccius Plautus], *M. Actii Plauti Asinii. Comoediae viginti nuper emendatae et in eas Pyladae Brixiani Lucubrationes. Thadaei Ugoleti: et Grapaldi virorum illustrium Scholia. Anselmi Epiphyllides* (Parma 1510), ii.

56 Loredana Chines, "Ancora sull'autonomia della fabula: la fortuna di Plauto ed un nuovo paradigma ermeneutico," in *La parola degli antichi: Umanesimo emiliano tra scuola e poesia* (Rome 1998), 114–31.

57 Richard Hardin, "Encountering Plautus in the Renaissance: A Humanist Debate on Comedy," *Renaissance Quarterly* 60, 3 (2007): 789–818, esp. 796.

58 Jean Leclercq, *The Love of Learning and the Desire for God: A Study of Monastic Culture*, trans. Catharine Misrahi (New York 1974), 136–7.

59 Lucia Fornari Schianchi, *Ai piedi della badessa: un pavimento maiolicato per Maria de' Benedetti badessa di San Paolo dal 1471 al 1482* (Parma 1988), 36; Chiusa, *Alessandro Araldi*, 74–9. On the history of the so-called "cell of St. Catherine" and its renovations see Longhi and Spina, "Complesso monastico," 1: 9; 49–50. They noted that the north gate was used for the reception of goods into the convent in the seventeenth and eighteenth centuries. Although the "cell" is permanently closed, Araldi's frescoes are visible through a glass door installed in 2005. It should also be noted that the attribution of the murals to Araldi has been questioned in the scholarship, and that a recent contribution tentatively proposes that the architect and painter Cesare Cesariano executed them: Alessandro Rovetta, Elio Monducci, Corrado Caselli, *Cesare Cesariano e il rinascimento a Reggio Emilia* (Cinisello Balsamo 2008), 237–8.

60 *Regola di Sancto Benedecto nuovamente vulgarizata* (Florence after 1500), ch. 66: "Alla porta del monasterio si pongha uno vechio savio che sappi pigliare & rendere la risposta: la maturita del quale non lo lasci andare vagando. El quale portinario de[bba] havere la cella apresso la porta: siche quegli che vengono sempre lo truovino presente e dallui ricevino risposta . . . Et have[n]do decto portinario bisogno daiuto: gli sia dato uno fratello più giovane."

61 Quintavalle, "Alessandro Araldi," 20 has argued that Araldi derived his compositional structure from Pinturicchio's *Subjugation before Pope Eugenius IV* (1502–7; Siena, Piccolomini Library), but it is unclear how Araldi could have known Pinturicchio's model. Two preparatory drawings by Araldi (Fogg Museum, Harvard University, Cambridge, Mass.) document the artist's care in sketching the figures but also his shortcomings.

62 St. Jerome's letters addressed to Marcella are the most numerous. In Marcella's circle of women living a conventual life there were the patrician Paula and her daughter Eustochium (or Julia): *Select Letters of St. Jerome*. trans. F. A. Wright (London 1933), 483–97. For the diffusion of Jerome's letters among Renaissance female audiences see Gabriella Zarri, "Tra monache e confessori: la corte di Lucrezia Borgia," in *L'età di Alfonso I e la pittura del Dosso* (Modena 2004), 103–18, esp. 105–6.

63 Jérôme Labourt, ed., *St. Jérôme: Lettres*, 8 vols. (Paris 1949–63), 2: 100–14, Letter 46 to Paula, Eustochium, and Marcella. As St. Jerome put it (100), monks and virgins are the "flowers and most precious jewels among the ornaments of the Church."

64 On St. Catherine's hagiography and its development in Italian literature, see Giovanni B. Bronzini, "Caterina di Alessandria," in *Bibliotheca Sanctorum*, 16 vols. (Rome 1963), 3: 954–78; René Coursault, *Sainte Catherine d'Alexandrie: Le mythe et la tradition. Hagiographie et littérature chrétienne, iconographie et traditions populaires* (Paris 1984), 76–8; Cynthia Stollhans, "Saint Catherine of Alexandria and her Book in Italian Art," *Source* 26, 3 (2007): 23–9.

65 Petrus de Natalibus, *Catalogus Sanctorum et Gestorum eorum* (Venice 1493), bk x, ch. 105. Other Latin and vernacular accounts of St. Catherine's life include Domenico Rococciolo's *Legenda di Santa Caterina* (1490), Battista Spagnuoli Mantuanus's *Parthenicae Secundae Sanctae Catherinae* (1489, 1499, 1502).

66 Jacopo Philippo Bergomense [Jacopo Filippo Foresti], *De Plurimis Claris selectisque Mulieribus* (Ferrara 1497), fols. 88r–91r.

67 BNC, MS Pal. 726, Agostino Strozzi, "Defensione de le donne," fol. 54r: "fu excelle[n]te di mirabile eruditione di tutte le discipline."

68 Giovan Ludovico Vives, *De l'ufficio del marito come si debba portare verso la moglie. De l'Istitutione della femina Christiana, vergine, maritata, ò vedova. De lo ammaestrare i fanciulli ne le arti liberali* (Venice 1546), 74: "Che diro de le donne Christiane? . . . ò di Catharina d'Alessandria figliuola di Costo, laquale vinse disputando Filosofi dottissimi . . . [75] Quai lettere si debbono temere da la femina, et à quale debbe ella darsi? . . . Diasi à gli studi de la sapientia, che formano li costumi à la vertù, et mostrano la via di vivere santame[n]te.

Circa l'eloquenza la donna non ne ha bisogno, bastale che sia buona e savia, quando che non si biasima la don[n]a per tacere, ma si bene per essere ignorante e trista . . . Voglio che la donna si occupi ne la Filosofia morale, che forma li costumi, e impari per se stessa ò per li figliuoli e per le sorelle nel Signore . . . [76] Ma la femina da bene debbe piu tosto stare in casa, e non essere da gli altri conosciuta. Quando è ne la moltitudine, stia co gli occhi bassi, taccia vergognosamente, accioche quantunq. sia veduta da molti, niuno l'oda parlare . . . La donna impari con silentio, ma non voglio che la donna insegni, ne habbia sopra l'huomo l'autorità, anzi che stia in silentio."

69 According to St. Paul, 1 Corinthians 14.34: "In your congregation, as in all congregations of Christ's people, the women must keep silence; for they are not permitted to speak in public, but to show submission"; trans. W. J. Conybeare, *The Life and Epistles of St. Paul* (New York 1970).

70 Desiderius Erasmus, "The Abbot and the Learned Lady," in *Collected Works of Erasmus: Colloquies*, 39: 501, 503.

71 Stephen Kolsky, *The Ghost of Boccaccio: Writing on Famous Women in Renaissance Italy* (Turnhout 2005), 175–85; Virginia Cox, "Gender and Eloquence in Ercole de' Roberti's *Portia and Brutus*," *Renaissance Quarterly* 62 (2009): 61–101.

72 On women perceived as Amazonian and masculine see Margaret L. King, *Women of the Renaissance* (Chicago 1991), 175–207, esp. 189.

73 Marta Ajmar, "Exemplary Women in Renaissance Italy: Ambivalent Models of Behaviour?" in *Women in Italian Renaissance Culture and Society*, ed. Letizia Panizza (Oxford 2000), 257.

74 Clelia Alessandrini, "San Paolo: dalla riscoperta della Camera all'attuale sistemazione museografica," *Aurea Parma* (2012): 47–56, esp. 51 reports that late Quattrocentesque pictorial fragments were found on the wall of the square chamber facing onto Correggio's painted room.

75 Smeraldi, fol. 83r: "Siamo poi passati nel giardino, a vedere il loco ove vogliano mettere la fontana, che è ove erano i camarini da stillare per la sig.ra Principessa, et vi è una nichia."

76 Affò, *Ragionamento*, 29.

77 Grapaldus, *De Partibus Aedium*, 2.8.

78 Cortesi, *De Cardinalatu*, 93.

79 ASPr, Dipartimento di Grazia e Giustizia e Buongoverno, busta 642, November 15, 1856.

80 Affò, *Ragionamento*, 32: "[dal Gabinetto contiguo] si passa al Camerino, la cui soffitta egregiamente travagliata in legno, porta nel cornicione otto brevi detti metà greci, metà latini." Albeit without any persuasive argumentation, Remo Cattelani challenged Affò's historical description of the original placement of the abbess's *camerino* (the back room), instead proposing that the *camerino* lay adjacent to Correggio's painted room on the south: Remo Cattelani, "ΙΩΑΝΝΕ ΠΛΑΚΗΝΤΙΗ ΙΟΑΝΝΑ PLACENTIA ABB.," *Parma nell'arte* 7, 1 (1975): 7–20; Barocelli, *Correggio*, 322–4 for the attribution of the intarsia work to Zucchi.

81 For a discussion of the *studiolo*, its function, embellishments, and the ambiguous role of the artwork collected in such settings to nourish and cure afflicted individuals, and to cultivate them, see Dora Thornton, *The Scholar in his Study: Ownership and Experience in Renaissance Italy* (New Haven and London 1997), esp. 27–51; Campbell, *Cabinet of Eros*, 29–57, esp. 37–8 on the role of inscriptions and mottoes.

82 Grapaldus, *De Partibus Aedium*, 2.9; Jean-Louis Charlet, "La bibliothèque, le livre et le papier d'après Francesco Mario Grapaldo: De *Partibus Aedium*, 2.9.," in *Studi latini in ricordo di Rita Cappelletto* (Urbino 1996), 347–64.

83 Giancarla Periti, "About Parmigianino's Early Portraits," *Memoirs of the American Academy in Rome*, 59/60 (2014–2015), forthcoming.

84 The same merging of content and ornament has recently been described with reference to several pseudo-inscriptions in Renaissance images: Alexander Nagel, "Twenty-five Notes on Pseudo-script in Italian Art," *Res* 59–60 (2011): 229–48.

85 Angelo Pezzana, *Memorie degli scrittori e letterati parmigiani raccolte da Padre Ireneo Affò e continuate da Angelo Pezzana*, 7 vols. in 4 (Parma 1825–33), 6, pt 1: 320. Difficulties in visualizing Pezzana's description of the arrangement of the Greek and Latin inscriptions on the walls could also be the result of the early nineteenth-century alterations made to the layout of the apartment. For example, it seems that a doorway was opened between the oratory and the *camerino*. This alteration of the abbatial residence can best be seen in the Sanseverini plan (1800–04; see fig. 96).

86 The Greek sentences are not grammatically correct. Their transcriptions require adjustments to make some modicum of sense, and for the anagrams to work. Similarly to previous scholars who treated this intarsia corpus (mainly art historians, not philologists), I felt adjustments were necessary to try to make sense of what is very nearly nonsense. In other words, emendations allow us to read words of potential signification and not just assemblages of Greek syllables with no real meaning. There are several plausible scenarios (including misunderstanding of instructions by the woodcarver) that could explain the "incorrect" Greek sentences.

87 Given the obscurity of the Greek inscriptions, their translation should be intended as provisional, more doubtful than

certain. The translations proposed are consistent with those offered in the previous scholarship (especially by Charles Dempsey) that has tried to make sense of these almost impossible Greek sentences. For this research I benefited from the expertise of both Dr. Michael B. Sullivan and Prof. Soultana Mavromati-Katsougiannopoulou, whom I especially want to thank here. See Cattelani, "ΙΩΑΝΝΕ ΠΛΑΚΗΝΤΙΗ IOANNA PLACENTIA ABB.," 8–9; Erwin Panofsky, *The Iconography of Correggio's Camera di San Paolo* (London 1961), 10–11; Charles Dempsey, "*Sua cuique mihi mea*: The *mottos* in the Camerino of Giovanna da Piacenza in the Convent of San Paolo," *The Burlington Magazine* 132 (1990): 490–93.

88 Giulio Camillo Delminio, *Tutte l'Opere* (Venice 1580), 339–43.

89 Georgii Anselmi Nepotis, *Hecuba* (Parma 1506); Wolfgang Schmitt, "Zwei Lateinische *Hekabe*-Ubersetzungen vom Jahre 1506: Ein Beitrag zur Geschichte humanisticher Ubersetzungen in der Renaissance," in *Die gesellschaftliche Bedeutung des Antiken Dramas für seine und für unsere Zeit*, ed. Walter Hofmann and Heinrich Kuch (Berlin 1973), 239–74; Angelo Pertusi, "Il ritorno alle fonti del teatro greco classico," in *Dotti bizantini e libri greci nell'Italia del secolo XV*, ed. Mariarosa Cortesi and Enrico V. Maltese (Naples 1992), 407–8. Only a select number of humanists mastered Greek; more often scholars were not versed in it.

90 Vittore Branca, *Poliziano e l'umanesimo della parola* (Turin 1983), 125–33.

91 Carruthers, *Craft of Thought*, 161–5.

92 Baldassar Castiglione, *The Book of the Courtier*, trans. Charles S. Singleton (Garden City, N.Y. 1959), II.57–61.

93 Ibid., 61.

94 On puns and wordplay in early modern culture see Carlo Ossola, "Les devins de la lettre et les masques du double: la diffusion de l'anagrammisme à la Renaissance," in *Devins et charlatans au temps de la Renaissance*, ed. M. T. Jones-Davies (Paris 1979), 135; Ernst Robert Curtius, *European Literature and the Latin Middle Ages* (Princeton 1988), 419; Georges Didi-Huberman, *Confronting Images: Questioning the Ends of a Certain History of Art*, trans. Jodi Goodman (University Park, Pa. 2005), 145–50.

95 François Rigolot, "L'anagramme comme signe de l'idéologie du text," in *Poétique et onomastique: l'exemple de la Renaissance* (Geneva 1977), 86.

96 The ancient model of the *viri faceti* is discussed in Aelius Spartianus, "Vita Hadriani," in *Historiae Augustae Scriptores Sex* (Paris 1603), 14.11. The *Historia Augustae*, including Spartianus's text, was published in 1519 by Aldus's heirs. Erasmus alludes to the ideal of the *vir facetus* who is mentally acute and skillful with words in a few of his *Colloquia*: Erasmus, "Convivium Fabulosum" in *Colloquies*, 39: 571–89. See also Lawrence V. Ryan, "Erasmi *Convivia*: The Banquet Colloquies of Erasmus," *Medievalia et Humanistica* 8 (1977): 201–15.

97 On the apotropaic significance of the *ouroboros* sign in Byzantine culture see Eunice Dauterman Maguire and Henry Maguire, *Other Icons: Art and Power in Byzantine Secular Culture* (Princeton 2007), 74.

98 Herbert Stanley Sheppard, "The Ouroboros and the Unity of Matters in Alchemy: A Study in Origins," *Ambix* 10, 2 (1962): 83–96; *The Hieroglyphics of Horapollo*, trans. George Boas (New York 1950), 57.

99 Dempsey, "*Sua cuique mihi mea*," 490–93. Some of Giovanna's devices were remade in the mid-nineteenth century including those used as ornaments of the wooden lintels in the entrance hall (see fig. 104).

100 Lorenzo Cornigli, "Venerabili Mulieri D. Joannae Placentiae divina gratia monasterii Sancti Pauli Parmensis Antistiti, Filiae Suae Spirituali in Domino dilectissimae Laurentius Cornilius Civis ac Presbyter Parmensis Salutem perpetuam dicit," in Pezzana, *Memorie*, 6, pt 2: 275. Ann E. Matter, *The Voice of My Beloved: The Song of Songs in Western Medieval Christianity* (Philadelphia, Pa. 1992), Song of Songs, 1.2–3. As discussed by Matter, there are at least 100 commentaries and homilies on the Song of Songs composed between the sixth century and 1515. St. Bernard offered a spiritual interpretation of the Song of Songs as the love between Christ and the soul. But there were other more ambivalent readings about who spoke first (the bride or the bridegroom) in the opening verses. On interpretations that stress its sensual language and implications see Stephen D. Moore, "The Song of Songs in the History of Sexuality," *Church History* 69, 2 (2000): 328–49.

101 Michaelis Pselli, *Philosophica Minora: Opuscula Psychologica, Theologica, Daemonologica*, vol. 2, ed. D. J. O'Meara (Leipzig 1989), ch. 46; John Duffy, "Reactions of Two Byzantine Intellectuals to the Theory and Practice of Magic: Michael Psellos and Michael Italikos," *Byzantine Magic*, ed. Henry Maguire (Washington, D.C. 1995), 83–97, esp. 89.

102 *Regola di Sancto Benedecto*, ch. 48, "Della quotidiana opera delle mane": "Otiosita e inimica della anima: & pertanto a certi tempi si debbono occupare efrategli in lavorio di mano & acerti altri in lectione divine." See also Brian Vickers, "Leisure and Idleness in the Renaissance: The Ambivalence of Otium," *Renaissance Studies* 4, 1 (1990): 1–37; 4, 2: 107–54.

103 Desiderius Erasmus, "Suum cuique pulchrum/What is one's own is beautiful," in *Collected Works of Erasmus: Adages*, trans. Margaret Mann Philips, annot. R. A. B. Mynors, vol. 31 (Toronto 1982), 158–61, esp. 158, noticing that artists are blindly in love with their own creations: "A work is to the craftsman something like the offspring of the mind."

104 The notion of individuality has been discussed with particular sensitivity by Thomas Keller, Morton Sosna, and David Wellbery, eds., *Reconstructing Individualism: Autonomy, Individuality, and the Self in Western Thought* (Stanford 1986), 1–15; Carol Thomas Neely, "Constructing the Subject: Feminist Practice and the New Renaissance Discourses," *English Literary History* 18 (1988): 5–18

105 Publius Ovidius Naso, "Fastorum libri," *Opera* (Parma 1477); Ovid, *Fasti 1, A Commentary*, ed. Steven Green (Leiden 2004). See also Francesco Lo Monaco, "Dal commento medioevale al commento umanistico: il caso dei "Fasti" di Ovidio," *Studi Italiani di Filologia Classica* 10 (1992): 848–60.

106 Salmi, "Bernardino Zaccagni," 135 n. 2; Talignani, "Cappella Montini," esp. 138–40 n. 101 and n. 108. According to Anna Coliva, d'Agrate sculpted a lavabo (ca. 1507–14) for the nuns, now at the entrance of the sacristy in Santa Maria della Steccata in Parma: Anna Coliva, entry in *Santa Maria della Steccata a Parma*, ed. Bruno Adorni (Parma 1982), 223–4. Giovan Francesco d'Agrate may also have been responsible for the font now on display in San Paolo.

107 Affò, *Ragionamento*, 32. The extant *titulus* and Giovanna's device were restored in the nineteenth century. Among other alterations made, a second door to the apartment was opened on the east wall of Correggio's painted room, resulting in the two doors visible today. Gozzi's plan of the convent shows communication between the Araldi and Correggio painted chambers via one door.

108 Petrarch, *Remedies for Fortune Fair and Foul*, trans. and comment Conrad H. Rawski, 5 vols. (Bloomington and Indianapolis 1991), 2: bk 2, "Remedies for adversities."

109 Maria Ortensia Banzola, "Il Palazzo del vescovado," *Parma nell'arte* 14, 2 (1982): 25–51, esp. 42; Vincenzo Banzola, "I lavori di restauro al cortile del vescovado," in *Saggi e testimonianze in onore di Francesco Borri* (Parma 1982), 13–34, esp. 19.

110 Bishop of Parma from 1509, Cardinal Alessandro Farnese resided only briefly in the city in 1516 to promote reforms, including the obligation for clerics to wear religious habit, and the prohibition against carrying weapons and cohabitation with women: Cristina Cecchinelli, "Agli esordi del potere farnesiano a Parma: il cardinale Alessandro Farnese vescovo-amministratore della diocesi (1509–1534)," *Rivista di storia della chiesa in Italia* 1 (2009): 91–124, esp. 112.

111 Smagliati, *Cronaca*, 110. The bishop's palace incarnated male ecclesiastical leadership. It also served to house the governor, Francesco Guicciardini, in 1521 and was used for wedding banquets, university committee hearings, and for meetings of the Cathedral's canons: Nestore Pelicelli, *Il vescovado di Parma* (Parma 1922); Gianluca Battioni, "Sacromoro da Rimini ed il governo della diocesi parmense," in *Parma e l'umanesimo italiano*, ed. Paola Medioli Masotti (Padua 1986), 55–73.

112 Antonio Manfredi, "'Apud Alatrium, Campaniae Oppidum,' Giovanni Tortelli and the Abbey under Pope Nicholas v," in *Walls and Memory: The Abbey of San Sebastiano at Alatri (Lazio) from Late Roman Monastery to Renaissance Villa and Beyond*, ed. Elizabeth Fentress et al. (Turnhout 2005), 154–84, esp. 173–6; Stephanie Leone, "From Medieval Monastery to Early Renaissance Villa: The Patronage of Giovanni Tortelli," in ibid., 196–200. See also Antonfrancesco Doni, *Lettere* (Venice 1544), letter 47 addressed to Agostino Landi, illustrating the inscriptions on lintels in Paolo Giovio's villa built on Lake Como.

113 The lintel that corresponds to the one mentioned by Vasari was discovered in Viterbo in the 1940s: Enzo Bentivoglio, "Bramante e il geroglifico di Viterbo," *Mitteilungen des Kunsthistorischen Institutes in Florenz* 16 (1992): 167–74; Brian Curran, *The Egyptian Renaissance: The Afterlife of Ancient Egypt in Early Modern Italy* (Chicago 2007), 169.

114 Colonna, *Hypnerotomachia Poliphili*, 1: 127. Different interpretations have been proposed about the value that the women represent, and the etymology of their names: Pozzi, ibid., 2: 119. The Hebrew, Greek, and Latin captions on the doors are reversed (or misplaced) and do not correspond to the described realms behind the doors. Only the Arabic captions correlate with the description in the text.

115 On what the "correct" choice meant in the Renaissance world see J. B. Korolec, "Free Will and Free Choice," in *The Cambridge History of Later Medieval Philosophy: From the Rediscovery of Aristotle to the Disintegration of Scholasticism, 1100–1600*, ed. Norman Kretzmann, Anthony Kenny, and Jan Pinborg (Cambridge 1988), 629–41.

116 Colonna, *Hypnerotomachia*, 1: 131. Telemia tells Poliphilo that he is in the place (of Mater Amoris) where he can find "the thing you love most . . . the one thing in the world which your obstinate heart without pause thinks and hopes for" (Questo è quel loco . . . che troverai la cosa più amata da te . . . ch'è cosa del mundo della quale il tuo ostinato core senza intermissione pensa e opta).

117 Cecilia Davis-Weyer, *Early Medieval Art 300–1150: Sources and Documents* (Englewood Cliffs, N.J. 1971), 21; Carruthers, *Craft of Thought*, 179.

118 Persius, *Satires*, trans. J. R. Jenkinson (Warminster 1980), 1.7; Michael Coffey, *Roman Satire* (London 1976), 102–4.

119 Erasmus, "Extra quaerere sese/To seek outside oneself" in *Collected Works: Adages*, 33, 258.

120 Remigio Sabbadini, *Classici e umanisti da Codici Ambrosiani* (Florence 1933), 113–19; Marco Petoletti, "Ugolino Pisani, lettore di Aristotele e la sua polemica nascosta contro Leonardo Bruni traduttore dell'Etica Nicomachea," in *Margarita*

Amicorum: Studi di cultura europea per Agostino Sottili, ed. Fabio Forner et al., 2 vols. (Milan 2005), 2: 879–909.

121 Bartolomeo Fonzio, "Tadeus vel de locis Persianis," in *Opera Exquisitissima Bartholomei Fontii Florentini*, ed. Georgius Remus (Frankfurt 1621), 6–28. Fonzio's autographed manuscript (Wolfenbüttel, Herzog August Bibliothek) used for this German edition is a luxurious codex composed for presentation to Matthias Corvinus in ca. 1489: Wolfgang Milde, *Die Wolfenbütteler Corvinen* (Wolfenbüttel 1995), 18–19. For a later manuscript copy of Fonzio's "Tadeus," see Florence, Biblioteca Riccardiana, MS 1220 I, Bartolomeus Fontius, "De Locis Persianis," fols. 106v–114r; Stefano Caroti and Stefano Zamponi, *Lo scrittoio di Bartolomeo Fonzio umanista fiorentino* (Milan 1974), 113–14.

122 Georgia Clarke, "Vitruvian Paradigms," *Papers of the British School at Rome* 70 (2002): 319–46, esp. 328; Zita Pataki, "Rex Ductus – Rex Augustus: Herrscherbild und Herrscherrepräsentation am Hof des Königs Matthias Corvinus," *Ars: Journal of the Institute of Art History of Slovak Academy of Sciences* 41, 1 (2008): 29–54. Ancient and modern texts printed under Corvinus's aegis are discussed in Nicola Bono, ed., *Nel segno del Corvo: Libri e miniature della Biblioteca di Mattia Corvino re d'Ungheria (1433–1490)*, exh. cat. (Modena 2003).

123 ASPr, Notarile, Galeazzo Piazza, filza 937, June 7, 1518; Alberto del Prato, "Librai e biblioteche parmensi del secolo XV," *Archivio storico per le province parmensi* 4 (1904): 1–18, 36–56. On Ugoleto's life and cultural role in sixteenth-century Parma see Ireneo Affò, *Memorie di Taddeo Ugoleto parmigiano bibliotecario di Mattia Corvino re d'Ungheria* (Parma 1781), 27; Affò, "Taddeo Ugoleto," in *Memorie*, 3: 105–24; Pezzana, "Taddeo Ugoleto," in *Memorie*, 6, pt 2.: 382–7; Fortunato Rizzi, "Un umanista ignorato: Taddeo Ugoleto," *Aurea Parma* 37 (1953): 3–17, 79–91; Angelo Ciavarella, "Un editore e umanista filologo: Taddeo Ugoleto detto Della Rocca," *Archivio storico per le province parmensi* 9 (1957): 133–73.

124 Francis Cairns, *Tibullus: A Hellenistic Poet at Rome* (Cambridge 1979), 207–8; R. O. A. M. Lyne, *The Latin Love Poet* (Oxford 1980), 175–87; Robert Maltby, *Tibullus: Elegies. Text, Introduction and Commentary* (Cambridge 2002), 237; Gian Biagio Conte, *Latin Literature: A History*, trans. Joseph B. Solodow (Baltimore and London 1994), 321–31. One of the most detailed manuals of love published before Ovid, Tibullus's elegiac corpus was known to humanists thanks to Venetian editions, e.g. Albius Tibullus, Catullus, and Propertius, *Elegiae et Carmina* (Venice 1491).

125 [Plautus], *Comoediae viginti*, "Aulularia," 63v–76v.

126 The only copy of Moille's *Alphabetum* (36 leaves) that seems to exist is BP, Inc. Parm. 1229: Stanley Morison, ed., *A Newly Discovered Treatise on Classic Letter Design printed at Parma by*

Damianus de Moyllus (Paris 1927); Domenico Fava, "Le conquiste tecniche di un grande tipografo del Quattrocento," in *Gutenberg Jahrbuch: Festschrift zur Fünfhundert Jahrfeier der Erfindung der Buchdruckkunst* (Mainz 1940), 147–56; Lucia A. Ciapponi, "A Fragmentary Treatise on Epigraphic Alphabets by Fra Giocondo da Verona," *Renaissance Quarterly* 32, 1 (1979): 18–40, esp. 19; Periti, "Epigraphy and the Semiotics of the Line," 191–210.

127 Emile Chavin de Malan, *Histoire de Saint François d'Assise* (Paris 1841), CXXXIII. I wish to thank Dr. Michael B. Sullivan for this reference.

128 Ferrara, Biblioteca Ariostea, *Prologo de l'ordine del vivere neli monasteri de monache & temporale & spirituale. Excepta da diversi scripti de Hieronymo ad Eustochio sua Figliuola spirituale & ale sorelle* (Ferrara 1497), chs 19, 41.

129 On the office of bishop see Adriano Prosperi, "La figura del vescovo fra Quattro e Cinquecento: Persistenze, disagi e novità," in *Storia d'Italia: Annali*, ed. Giorgio Chittolini and Giovanni Miccoli (Turin 1986), 9: 218–63.

130 On the notion of "soft iconophobia" see Alexander Nagel, *The Controversy of Renaissance Art* (Chicago 2011), 197–8.

131 Filarete [Antonio Averlino], *Treatise on Architecture*, trans. John R. Spencer, 2 vols. (New Haven and London 1965), 1: IX, 66v.

132 On Cles' renovation and decoration of his palace see Laura Dal Prà, "Johannes Hinderback e Bernardo Cles: Funzionalità e decorazione nella sede dei principi vescovi di Trento. Spunti per una ricerca," in *Il Castello del Buonconsiglio*, ed. Enrico Castelnuovo, 2 vols. (Trent 1996), 2: 31–69; Laura Dal Prà, "Umanesimo e arti figurative nel principato vescovile di Trento: Note di lavoro," in *Rinascimento e passione per l'antico: Andrea Riccio e il suo tempo*, exh. cat. (Trent 2008), 179–201; Thomas Frangenberg, "Decorum in the Magno Palazzo in Trent," *Renaissance Studies* 7, 4 (1993): 352–78. There are also inscriptions over doors in Cles' palace. Albeit indirectly, recently rediscovered correspondence dated 1532 seems to suggest that Cardinal Cles wished to invite Correggio to work in Trent: Rossana Sacchi, *Il disegno incompiuto. La politica artistica di Francesco II Sforza e di Massimiliano Stampa,* 2 vols (Milan 2005), 1: 159–61.

133 Frangenberg, "Decorum," 364; Lia Camerlengo, "La loggia del principe. Temi mitologici negli affreschi di Romanino a Trento: fonti e motivi," in *Romanino: un pittore in rivolta nel Rinascimento italiano*, exh. cat. (Milan 2006), 258–71, esp. 274, for the publication of Mattioli's passage in defense of Romanino's art.

134 Transcribed in the eighteenth century, Cornigli's text was published by Pezzana, *Memorie*, 6, pt 2: 274–7. On Cornigli's profile as a scribe see Giuseppa Z. Zanichelli, ed., *Luminatum et ligatum fuit de manu mea. Codici miniati padani: scriptoria e committenza*, exh. cat. (Parma 1994), 17. In general, on cal-

ligraphers and illuminators involved in the making of gradu-als and books of hours in Renaissance Parma see Silvia Scipioni, "*Heures Me Fault de Notre Dame*. Il Libro d'Ore manoscritto: Strumento di devozione e segno di prestigio," in *Cum Picturis Ystoriatum: Codici devozionali e liturgici della Biblioteca Palatina*, exh. cat. (Modena 2001), 19–24.

135 On this 1515 document see Marzio Dall'Acqua, ed., *Correggio e il suo tempo*, exh. cat. (Parma 1984), 34.

136 Peter Howard, "Preaching Magnificence in Renaissance Florence," *Renaissance Quarterly* 61, 2 (2008): 325–69.

137 Cornigli, "Venerabili Mulieri D. Joannae Placentiae," 6, pt 2: 275: "Maximaque aedium claustralium parte instaurata, et reformata, ac novis conclavibus ad habitandum atque venus-tis ac utilibus a fundamentis ipsis extructis, atque dignissima supellectile instructis." For the transcription of Cornigli's text, see Giancarla Periti, "Correggio, Giovanna Piacenza, and the Tradition of Monastic Interiors," in *Artibus et Historiae*, forthcoming.

138 For a discussion of notions of utility, *magnificentia*, and decor in Renaissance architectural texts see Clarke, *Roman House*, 52–5.

139 In classical literature, usefulness was associated with sensory delight in the Horatian saying *utile dulci*: Flaccus Quintus Horatius, "De Arte Poetica," in *Opera* (Venice 1486), 107r–117r; Horace, "The Art of Poetry," in *Satires, Epistles, and Ars Poetica*, trans. H. Rushton Fairclough, Loeb Edition (Cam-bridge, Mass. 1991), II.333–35: "Poets aim either to benefit, or to amuse, or to utter words at once both pleasing and helpful to life." Castiglione added in his *Cortegiano*, I, 52 (*Book of the Courtier*, trans. Singleton): "It is fitting for our Courtier to have knowledge of painting also, since it is decorous and useful and was prized in those times when men were of greater worth than now."

140 Conrad Rudolph, "La resistenza all'arte nell'occidente," in *Arte e storia nel Medioevo*, ed. Enrico Castelnuovo and Giuseppe Sergi, 4 vols. (Turin 2004), 3: 49–84, esp. 68–79.

141 Conrad Rudolph, *Artistic Change at St-Denis: Abbot Suger's Program and the Early Twelfth-Century Controversy over Art* (Princeton 1990), 57.

142 Petrarch, *Remedies for Fortune*, 1.40, "Paintings."

CHAPTER V MONSTROSITIES,
FEMALE EXEMPLARITY,
REGENERATION

1 Nicole Dacos, *La découverte de la Domus Aurea et la formation des grotesques à la Renaissance* (London 1969), 5–50; Cristina Acidini Luchinat, "La grottesca," in *Storia dell'arte italiana*, vol. 11 (Turin 1982), 161–200.

2 Among recent studies on Araldi's painted room see Giuseppa Z. Zanichelli, *Iconologia della camera di Alessandro Araldi nel monastero di San Paolo in Parma*, intro. Arturo Carlo Quinta-valle (Parma 1979); Giuseppa Z. Zanichelli, "Alessandro Araldi e la camera di San Paolo," in *Il monastero di San Paolo*, ed. Marzio Dall'Acqua (Milan 1990), 81–111; Maria Cristina Chiusa, *Alessandro Araldi: la "maniera antico-moderna" a Parma* (Parma 1996); Francesco Barocelli, "Tra antico e moderno," in *Il Correggio nella Camera di San Paolo* (Milan 2010), 248–65.

3 Franciscus Marius Grapaldus, *De Partibus Aedium* (Parma 1494; *Addita modo, verborum explicatione quae in eodem libro continentur*, 1516), 2.2; Martine Furno, "Le lemme Basilica dans le *Partibus Aedium* de Grapaldo," in *Devenir roi: Essais sur la littérature adressée au Prince*, ed. Isabelle Cogitore and Francis Goyet (Grenoble 2006), 213–22, 274–9.

4 Ireneo Affò, *Ragionamento del Padre Ireneo Affò sopra una stanza dipinta dal celeberrimo Antonio Allegri da Correggio nel monistero di S. Paolo in Parma* (Parma 1794), 35–6: "Nessuno à fatto motto sin ora di questa Pittura, che per essere di mano antica e molto inferiore all'altra, onde siamo princi-palmente solleciti, non sembrò forse cosa da tenerne gran conto. A me però giova di mentovarlo . . . Questa prima Pittura parve al Signor Callani ed a me lavoro dell'Araldi, singolarmente nelle lunette, piene di rappresentazioni e figure simboliche trattate per quel tempo con amore ed eleganza."

5 ASPr, Notarile, Galeazzo Piazza, f. 935, June 23, 1514; June 26, 1514; see also Affò, *Ragionamento*, 68.

6 Benassi's text remains a goldmine of information on the complex historical reality of sixteenth-century Parma: Umberto Benassi, *Storia di Parma*, 5 vols. (Parma 1899–1906), 3: 41–5, 64.

7 On *spiritelli* as an artistic type in the Renaissance, see Charles Dempsey, *Inventing the Renaissance Putto* (Chapel Hill, N.C. 2001), 6–61, esp. 26–49. The role of classical marble reliefs with playful putti from Ravenna's Basilica of San Vitale, considered to be the prototype of Donatello's modern *spiri-telli*, has been discussed by Ulrich Pfisterer, *Donatello und die Entdeckung der Stile, 1430–1445* (Munich 2002), 206–16; Marc Bormand, "The *Spiritelli* of the Renaissance," in *The Spring-time of the Renaissance: Sculpture and the Arts in Florence 1400–1600*, ed. Beatrice Paolozzi Strozzi and Marc Bormand, exh. cat. (Florence 2013), 111–17.

8 Zanichelli, *Iconologia*, 54–5; Zanichelli, "Araldi," 105. See Marzio Dall'Acqua, ed., *Correggio e il suo tempo*, exh. cat. (Parma 1984), 84, for the contract that Araldi signed with the *fabbriceri* of Parma Cathedral. Araldi was not their first choice and was recruited only after a team of artists had already been hired; his work was "to be appraised by impar-tial experts."

9   Henri Lefebvre, *The Production of Space*, trans. Donald Nicholson-Smith (Oxford 1993), 14.

10 Suggestive reflections on the eyes' permeability in looking at Mantegna's painted room have been offered by Anne Dunlop, *Painted Palaces: The Rise of Secular Art in Early Renaissance Italy* (University Park, Pa. 2009), 211–17; Stephen J. Campbell, "Mantegna's *Camera Picta*: Visuality and Pathos," *Art History* 37, 2 (2014): 315–32, esp. 329.

11 See esp. Zanichelli, *Iconologia*, 28; Zanichelli, "Araldi," 87.

12 *The New Jerome Biblical Commentary*, ed. Raymond E. Brown, Joseph A. Fitzmyer, and Roland E. Murphy (London 1990), 536–7.

13 St. Augustine, *Expositions on the Book of Psalms*, trans. J. Tweed, 4 vols. (Oxford 1850), 4: 288–9.

14 On the pedagogical role of the Psalms see Paul Gehl, "Mystical Language Models in Monastic Educational Psychology," *Journal of Medieval and Renaissance Studies* 14 (1984): 219–43, esp. 220–26.

15 Psalms were learnt outside monasteries, as well. Abridged versions of the psalms began to circulate in the late fifteenth century, especially for use among the laity, along with translations of the seven penitential psalms, including those by Petrarch, Lefèvre d'Étaples, and Grapaldo. The last printed his *Libellus Psalmorum Poenitentialium una cum variis Orationibus, et Litaniis novae inventionis ad imitationem Regalis Psalmistae pro singulis hebdomadae diebus* in Parma in 1505.

16 Erasmus commented on only eleven psalms, but this writing has been seen to express his views on restoring authentic Christian beliefs: Desiderius Erasmus, "Introduction: Expositions of the Psalms," in *Collected Works of Erasmus: Expositions of the Psalms*, trans. and annot. Michael J. Heath, vol. 63 (Toronto 1997), xxx; Michael J. Heath, "Erasmus and the Psalms," in *The Bible in the Renaissance*, ed. Richard Griffiths (Aldershot 2001), 28–44.

17 Desiderius Erasmus, "The Handbook of the Christian Soldier," in *Collected Works of Erasmus: Spiritualia*, ed. John O'Malley, vol. 66 (Toronto 1988), 35.

18 Pietro Bembo, *Gli Asolani*, ed. Giorgio Dilemmi (Florence 1991), bk 1, xiv, 50–51 (p. 26).

19 Letizia A. Panizza, "Stoic Psychotherapy in the Middle Ages and Renaissance: Petrarch's *De remediis*," in *Atoms, Pneuma, and Tranquillity: Epicurean and Stoic Themes in European Thought*, ed. Margaret J. Osler (Cambridge 1991), 39–65, esp. 45.

20 On the candelabrum woodcut see Francesco Colonna, *Hypnerotomachia Poliphili*, ed. Giovanni Pozzi and Lucia A. Ciapponi, 2 vols. (Padua 1980), 1: 121; Brian Curran, *The Egyptian Renaissance: The Afterlife of Ancient Egypt in Early Modern Italy* (Chicago 2007), 140.

21 Philippe Morel, *Les grotesques: les figures de l'imaginaire dans la peinture italienne de la fin de la Renaissance* (Paris 1997), 111–12.

22 Dario Gamboni, *Potential Images: Ambiguity and Indeterminacy in Modern Art*, trans. Mark Treharne (London 2002), 37.

23 Within the growing literature on grotesque works and the margins of art, see André Chastel, *La grottesque: essai sur l' "ornement sans nom"* (Paris 1988), 19–38; Michael Camille, *Image on the Edge: The Margins of Medieval Art* (Cambridge, Mass. and London 1992), 11–55; Hellmut Wohl, "Ornament," in *The Aesthetics of Italian Renaissance Art: A Reconsideration of Style* (Cambridge 1999), 201–21; Claire Farago and Carol Komadina Parenteau, "The Grotesque Idol: Imaginary, Symbolic and Real," in *The Idol in the Age of Art: Objects, Devotion and the Early Modern World*, ed. Michael W. Cole and Rebecca Zorach (Aldershot 2009), 105–131; François Quiviger, *The Sensory World of Italian Renaissance Art* (London 2010), 70–87, esp. 76.

24 Vitruvius, *Ten Books on Architecture*, trans. Ingrid Rowland, commentary by Thomas Noble Howe (Cambridge 1999), VII.5.3–4.

25 Horace, "The Art of Poetry," in *Satires, Epistles, and Ars Poetica*, trans. H. Rushton Fairclough, Loeb Edition (Cambridge, Mass. 1991), 1–12: "If a painter chose to join a human head to the neck of a horse, and to spread feathers of many a hue over limbs picked up now here now there . . . could you my friends . . . refrain from laughing? Believe me . . . quite like such pictures will be a book, whose idle fancies shall be shaped like a sick man's dreams . . . Painters and poets . . . have always had an equal right in hazarding anything. We know it: this licence we poets claim and in our turn we grant the like; but not so far that savage should mate with tame."

26 Cennino Cennini, *Il libro d'arte*, ed. Franco Brunello (Vicenza 1971), 4; Martin Kemp, "From Mimesis to Fantasia: The Quattrocento Vocabulary of Creative Inspiration," *Viator* 8 (1977): 347–98. Kemp also discusses the organization and location of faculties of the soul (imagination, intellect, and memory).

27 Benvenuto Cellini, "Vita," in *Opere di Baldasare Castiglione, Giovanni della Casa, Benvenuto Cellini*, ed. Carlo Cordiè (Milan and Naples 1960), 561–2.

28 Gabriele Paleotti, *Discourse on Sacred and Profane Images*, trans. Willian McCuaig (Los Angeles 2012), 2.40–42; Morel, *Grotesques*, 119–22.

29 Bernard of Clairvaux, "Apologia ad Guillelmum Abbatem," in *The "Things of Greater Importance": Bernard of Clairvaux's Apologia and the Medieval Attitude toward Art*, ed. Conrad Rudolph (Philadelphia 1990), 29; John of Salisbury, *Policraticus: Of the Frivolities of Courtiers and the Footprints of Philosophers*, ed. and trans. Cary J. Nederman (Cambridge and New York 1990), bk 8, ch. 12.

30 Thomas A. Dale, "Monsters, Deformities, and Phantasmata in the Cloister of St-Michel-de-Cuxa," *Art Bulletin* 83, 3 (2001): 402–36.

31 Pinturicchio's Roman grotesque works in the vaulted ceilings of the palace of Giuliano della Rovere and in the Piccolomini Library in Siena have been mentioned as possible sources for Araldi, especially because they show grotesques imitating relief carvings set against dark grounds. But it remains to be proven that Araldi traveled to Rome or Siena (ca. 1510–12): Dacos, *Découverte*, 90–91; Chiusa, *Araldi*, 28.

32 On Nicoletto da Modena's print and Araldi's grotesques see Chiusa, *Araldi*, 24, 27. The role of these "ornamental" panels in the dissemination of antiquarian motifs has been discussed by Mark J. Zucker, ed., *The Illustrated Bartsch 25* [*Commentary: Early Italian Masters*] (New York 1984), 23–9, 227–38, esp. 230–31; Marzia Faietti and Konrad Oberhuber, eds., *Bologna e l'umanesimo 1490–1510*, exh. cat. (Bologna 1988), 250–51.

33 On the relationships between sculpted aquatic monsters in Renaissance art and the *Hypnerotomachia* models see Alison Luchs, *The Mermaids of Venice: Fantastic Sea Creatures in Venetian Renaissance Art* (London 2010), 54–9.

34 Alessandra Talignani, "La cappella Montini nella cattedrale di Parma: un *unicum* di forme, colori ed epigrafi nella 'periferia,'" in *Emilia e Marche nel Rinascimento: l'identità visiva della 'periferia,'* ed. Giancarla Periti (Azzano [Bg] 2005), 119–80. The fictive mosaic of the Montini chapel served as a model for the new decoration of the northern and eastern niches of the cathedral's apse commissioned from Correggio, Parmigianino, and other local artists from 1522 onward: David Ekserdjian, *Parmigianino* (New Haven and London 2006), 5.

35 Cesare Cesariano, *De Architectura libri dece traducti de latino in vulgare affigurati* (Como 1521), fol. 117v. Cesariano's works in San Giovanni Evangelista have been discussed by Bruno Adorni, ed., *L'Abbazia benedettina di San Giovanni Evangelista a Parma* (Milan 1979), 86–90; Davide Gasparotto, "Parma e la maniera 'antico-moderna' tra Quattro e Cinquecento," in *Il Libro d'Ore Durazzo: Volume di commento*, ed. Andrea de Marchi (Modena 2008), 67–102, esp. 89.

36 Zanichelli, *Iconologia*, 44; Innis H. Shoemaker, ed., *The Engravings of Marcantonio Raimondi*, exh. cat. (Lawrence, Kan. 1981), 100–01.

37 On the role of Marcantonio's prints in the development of Italian Renaissance art see David Lindau and Peter Parshall, *The Renaissance Print, 1470–1550* (New Haven and London 1994), 103–46; Lisa Pon, *Raphael, Dürer, and Marcantonio Raimondi: Copying and the Italian Renaissance Print* (New Haven and London 2004), 92–142.

38 Isotta Nogarola, "Dialogue of the Equal and Unequal Sin of Adam and Eve: Verona 1451," in *Complete Writings: Letterbook, Dialogue on Adam and Eve, Orations*, ed. and trans. Margaret L. King and Diana Robin (Chicago 2004), 145–58.

39 Margaret L. King and Albert Rabil Jr, eds., *Her Immaculate Hand: Selected Works by and about the Women Humanists of Quattrocento Italy* (Asheville 2000), 80, for a significant passage in Ceresa's text positing Adam and Eve's mutual responsibility: "For [woman's] nature is not immune to sin; nature produced our mother [Eve], not from earth or rock, but from Adam's humanity. To be human is, however, to incline sometimes to good, but sometimes to pleasure. We are quite an imperfect animal . . . [But] you great men, wielding such authority, commanding such success . . . be careful . . . For where there is greater wisdom, there lies greater guilt."

40 Agrippa's radical view on Original Sin and the role of the progenitors has been commented on by Marc van de Poel, *Cornelius Agrippa: The Humanist Theologian and his Declamations* (Leiden 1997), 225–45, esp. 235–6.

41 Zanichelli, *Iconologia*, 36. Francia's preparatory drawing, along with others of similar subject, is what survives as evidence for his lost mural paintings in the Bentivoglio palace in Bologna, which are mentioned in Vasari's life of the artist: Andrea Bacchi, "Vicende della pittura nell'età di Giovanni II Bentivoglio," in *Bentivolorum magnificentia: principe e cultura a Bologna nel rinascimento*, ed. Bruno Basile (Rome 1984), 285–335, esp. 326–7; Faietti and Oberhuber, *Bologna e l'umanesimo*, 260–61.

42 Zanichelli, *Iconologia*, 41; Shoemaker, *The Engravings*, 96–9.

43 On the practice and meaning of artistic imitation in Renaissance Italy see Enrico Castelnuovo and Carlo Ginzburg, "Center and Periphery," in *History of Italian Art*, trans. Ellen Bianchini and Claire Dorey, 2 vols. (Cambridge 1994), 1: 29–112, esp. 76–7; Alessandro Nova, "Centro, periferia, provincia: Tiziano e Romanino," in *Romanino: un pittore in rivolta nel rinascimento italiano*, exh. cat. (Cinisello Balsamo 2006), 48–67, esp. 56–7; and Stephen J. Campbell, "Renaissance Naturalism and the Jewish Bible: Ferrara, Brescia, Bergamo, 1520–1540," in *Judaism and Christian Art: Aesthetic Anxieties from the Catacombs to Colonialism*, ed. Herbert L. Kessler and David Nirenberg (Philadelphia, Pa. and Oxford 2011), 291–327, esp. 297–305.

44 As traced by Alexander Nagel, this complex dialectic between pre-Christian and Christian mysteries, the exploration of the secrets of nature to arouse wonder at God's creations, was further manifested in Andrea Riccio's unusual Moses statue with ram's horns (ca. 1513), once placed atop the fountain in the antechamber to the refectory of Santa Giustina in Padua: Alexander Nagel, *The Controversy of Renaissance Art* (Chicago 2011), 153–66.

45 Begun by Bernardino da Parenzo before 1500, the lost frescoes in the great cloister at Santa Giustina were recorded in

late eighteenth-century prints after designs by Francesco Mengardi. Sources for these murals including hieroglyphs and literary images have been discussed by Maria Pia Billanovich, "Una miniera di epigrafi e di antichità: il chiostro maggiore di Santa Giustina a Padova," *Italia medioevale e umanistica* 12 (1969): 197–293, esp. 224–52; Alberta de Nicolò Salmazo, *Bernardino da Parenzo: un pittore "antiquario" di fine Quattrocento* (Padua 1989), 56–9; Cristina Bragaglia, "Girolamo del Santo e gli affreschi del chiostro maggiore di Santa Giustina a Padova: Fonti iconografiche," *Bollettino del Museo civico di Padova* 82 (1993): 171–94.

46   Curran, *Egyptian Renaissance*, 231–2.

47   Philippe Morel, "Grotesques et hiéroglyphes: la bibliothèque de S. Giovanni Evangelista à Parme," in *Grotesques*, 49–61. In this context, it is worth mentioning the grotesque candelabra that surround an unusual series of portraits of Greek, Latin, and Arabic philosophers, mathematicians, and astronomers on the ceiling of a room in the Umiliati complex of Sant' Abbondio in Cremona. Attributed to the local artist Francesco Casella (ca. 1513) and commissioned by the general of the Umiliati order, Girolamo Landriani, these murals have been connected to interests in Arabic culture registered in early Cinquecento Cremona: Marika Leino and Charles Burnett, "Myth and Astronomy in the Frescoes at Sant'Abbondio in Cremona," *Journal of the Warburg and Courtauld Institutes* 66 (2003): 273–88; Marco Tanzi, *Brera mai vista: girovaghi, eccentrici, ponentini. Francesco Casella, Cremona 1517* (Milan 2004), 27–33.

48   St. Augustine, *On True Religion*, trans. J. H. S. Burleigh (Chicago 1959), XLIX, 94; Christopher S. Wood, "'Curious Images' and the Art of Description," *Word and Image* 11, 4 (1995): 332–52, esp. 337.

49   Representations of skeletons and like figures in Rosso Fiorentino's art have been suggestively connected to beliefs in necromancy and witchcraft by Stephen J. Campbell, "Fare una Cosa Morta Parer Viva": Michelangelo, Rosso Fiorentino, and the (Un)Divinity of Art," *Art Bulletin* 84, 4 (2002): 596–620; Eugenio Battisti, *L'Antirinascimento*, 2 vols. (Milan 1989), 1: 157–79.

50   Christopher S. Wood, "Countermagical Combinations by Dosso Dossi," *Res* 49/50 (2006): 151–70.

51   The crucial reading of Parmigianino's portrait remains that by Ute Davitt Asmus, "Fontanellato I. Sabatizzare il mondo, Parmigianino's Bildnis des Conte Galeazzo Sanvitale," *Mitteilungen des Kunsthistorischen Institutes in Florenz* 27 (1983): 2–40. Sensitive observations on the intersections between Parmigianino's art, alchemy, and esotericism have been made by Alessandro Nova, "Einleitung: Frühneuzeitliche Quellen und Moderne Interpretationen: Technik, Alchemie und Antikenrezeption im Werk Parmigianinos," in *Parmigianino:*

Zitat, Porträt, Mythos, ed. Alessandro Nova (Perugia 2006), 6–14. Parmigianino's works of the late 1530s, in particular his frescoes in Santa Maria della Steccata, have been explored in the light of local debate on magic, but my discussion covers texts that have not previously been explored by Elisabetta Fadda, "Da Parma a Casalmaggiore: Parmigianino ultimo atto," in *Parmigianino e la pratica dell'alchimia*, ed. Sylvia Ferino-Pagden et al. (Milan 2003), 39–49.

52   For a learned treatment of these doctrines see Curran, *Egyptian Renaissance*, 92–7. See also Chiara Cresciani, "Hermeticism and Alchemy: The Case of Ludovico Lazzarelli," *Early Science and Medicine* 5, 2 (2000): 145–59.

53   Marsilio Ficino, "Commentary on Plotinus' *Enneads*," in *Opera Omnia*, 2 vols. (Basel 1576; repr. Turin 1962), 2: 1768; Curran, *Egyptian Renaissance*, 97–8; Charles Dempsey, "Renaissance Hieroglyphic Studies and Gentile Bellini's *Saint Mark Preaching in Alexandria*," in *Hermeticism and the Renaissance: Intellectual History and the Occult in Early Modern Europe*, ed. Ingrid Merkel and Allen G. Debus (Toronto 1988), 342–65, esp. 346–7.

54   Marsilio Ficino, *Three Books on Life*, ed. Carol V. Kaske and John R. Clark (Binghamton, N.Y. 1989), 304–7 citing Hermes Trismegistus *Asclepius*, 37; Curran, *Egyptian Renaissance*, 98. Ficino's translation of *Iamblichus' Mysteries of the Egyptians and Assyrians*, a text dealing with rituals, often seen as magical in essence and performed to evoke the presence of one or more gods, is the subject of a letter addressed to the Parmese Taddeo Ugoleto, then the librarian at Buda. Ficino promises Ugoleto to make available this text for Corvinus's library: Valery Rees, "Marsilio Ficino and the Rise of Philosophic Interests in Buda," in *Italy and Hungary: Humanism and Art in the Early Renaissance*, ed. Péter Farbaky and Louis A. Waldman (Florence 2011), 127–48, esp. 136–7, 147.

55   Florence, Biblioteca Laurenziana, Plut. 44.35, Georgii Parmensis, *Divinum Opus de Magia Disciplina*. Anselmi junior composed a poem in honor of his ancestor's text: Georgii Anselmi, *Epigrammaton Libri Septem: Sosthyrides Peplum Palladis Aeglogae Quattor* (Venice 1528), bk 4, fols 48r–48v, "In Libros Astrologic. Institutionum Georgii Anselmi Avi."

56   On this peasant practice of divination see Charles Burnett, "The Scapulimancy of Giorgio Anselmi's *Divinum Opus de Magia Disciplina*," in *Magic and Divination in the Middle Ages* (Aldershot 1996), 63–79. On Giorgio Anselmi the Elder see Liliana Panella, "Anselmi Giorgio senior," in *Dizionario biografico degli italiani*, vol. 3 (Rome 1961), 377–8; Lynn Thorndike, *A History of Magic and Experimental Science*, 8 vols. (New York 1923–58), 4: 243–6, 677–9.

57   Paola Zambelli, "Continuity in the Definition of Natural Magic from Pico to Della Porta: Astrology and Magic in Italy and North of the Alps," in *White Magic, Black Magic in*

the European Renaissance (Leiden 2007), 9–27; Raffaella Castagnola, ed., *I Guicciardini e le scienze occulte* (Florence 1990), 50, 232, 235, 268–9. Castagnola published a letter of October 1523 from the Riminese Ramberto Malatesta (educated in Florence under Ficino) to the Florentine Luigi Guicciardini. Malatesta and Guicciardini's brother, Francesco (the former governor of Parma), had consulted Anselmi's manuscript on magic except for one missing book that Malatesta wanted to recover in order to print Anselmi's text.

58 For the intersections of Renaissance discourses on magic, artistic practices, and the artist/magus's agency in the creation of art see Michael Cole, "The Demonic Arts and the Origin of the Medium," *Art Bulletin* 84, 4 (2002): 621–40, esp. 625; Wood, "Countermagical Combinations," 151–70.

59 Agrippa von Nettesheim, *Three Books of Occult Philosophy*, ed. Donal Tyson (St. Paul, Minn. 1995), 1.40; Cole, "Demonic Arts," 633.

60 It has also been proposed that Giorgio Anselmi and the local painter Michelangelo Anselmi could have been related given their families' adjacent chapels in the Carmine church in Parma: Elisabetta Fadda, *Michelangelo Anselmi* (Turin 2004), 75–6.

61 Different interpretations of Parmigianino's portrait have been proposed by Carmen Bambach et al., eds., *Correggio and Parmigianino: Master Draughtsmen of the Renaissance*, exh. cat. (London 2000), 177; Michael Thimann, "*Fece senza ritrarlo l'immagine sua*: Mimesis, capriccio und invenzione in Parmigianinos Porträts," in Nova, *Parmigianino*, 65–77, esp. 66–7. On skulls as signifiers of the body see Hans Belting, "The Coat of Arms and the Portrait: Two Media of the Body," in *An Anthropology of Images: Picture, Medium, Body* (Princeton 2011), 62–83, esp. 77.

62 Georgii Anselmi, *In Cupidinem Captivum* (Parma 1506), 21; Curran, *Egyptian Renaissance*, 103–4; Giancarla Periti, "Epigraphy and the Semiotics of the Line in Late Quattrocento Italy," in *LINEA I: Grafie di immagini tra Quattrocento e Cinquecento*, ed. Marzia Faietti and Gerhard Wolf (Venice 2008), 208–9.

63 Nicolaus Cusanus, *Certi Tractatus et libri altissimae contemplationis et doctrinae a praeclarae memoriae praestantissimo doctissimoque viro Nicolao de Cusa* (Cortemaggiore 1502). This rare edition of Cusa's writings includes, among others, *De Docta ignorantia; Ydiotae; De Mente; De Visione Dei; De Mathematicis complementis; De Venatione Sapientiae; De Ludo Globi; De Mathematica Perfectione; De Berillo; De Coniecturis*. Cusa's text was published by the itinerant printer Benedetto Dolcibelli: Vito Ghizzoni, "Rolando II Pallavicino Princeps humanissimae humanitatis," *Archivio storico per le province parmensi* 31 (1979): 212–30; Alfonso Garuti, "Dolcibelli Benedetto," in *Dizionario biografico degli italiani*, vol. 40 (Rome 1991), 435–8.

64 Pallavicino's cousin, also Rolando (d. 1529), his wife, and their young daughter are represented in the lower register of an altarpiece by Francesco Zaganelli (1518), a family cameo confirming that the Pallavicinos wanted to be seen as cultivated rulers: Katherine A. McIver, "Music, Patrons and Politics: A Re-assessment of Zaganelli's Altarpiece for Rolando Pallavicino and Domitilla Gambara," in *Art and Music in the Early Modern Period: Essays in Honor of Franca Trinchieri Camiz*, ed. Katherine A. McIver (Aldershot 2003), 45–56.

65 Nicolaus Cusanus, "De Berillo," in *Tractatus*, fols II5v–LL3v; Nicholas of Cusa, "De Beryllo," in *Metaphysical Speculations: Six Latin Texts*, trans. Jasper Hopkins (Minneapolis 1998), 792–838. A recent thought-provoking linking of Cusa's writings on mathematics and perspective and Renaissance works of art is by Rebecca Zorach, *The Passionate Triangle* (Chicago 2011).

66 Nicholas of Cusa, "On Learned Ignorance," in *Selected Spiritual Writings*, trans. H. Lawrence (New York 1997), 87–213; David C. Lindberg, *Theories of Vision from Al-Kindi to Kepler* (Chicago 1976), 58–177.

67 Cusanus, "Ydiotae: De Mente," in *Tractatus*, fols Q1r–S4r; Nicholas of Cusa, "The Layman on Mind," in *On Wisdom and Knowledge*, ed. Jasper Hopkins (Minneapolis 1996), 159–317, esp. 204–5.

68 Nicholas of Cusa, "Layman on Mind," 231. See also Walter Page, "Medieval and Renaissance Contributions to Knowledge of the Brain and Its Functions," in *The History and Philosophy of Knowledge of the Brain and Its Functions*, ed. Frederick N. Poynter (Oxford 1958), 95–114; Michael Camille, "Before the Gaze: The Internal Senses and Late Medieval Practices of Seeing," in *Visuality Before and Beyond the Renaissance: Seeing as Others Saw*, ed. Robert S. Nelson (Cambridge 2000), 197–223.

69 Cusanus, "De Visione Dei," in *Tractatus*, fols AA1v–CC8v; Nicholas of Cusa, "On the Vision of God," in *Selected Spiritual Writings*, 235–89, esp. 288.

70 M. Führer, "The Consolation of Contemplation in Nicholas of Cusa's De Visione Dei," in *Nicholas of Cusa on Christ and the Church: Essays in Memory of Chandler McCuskey for the American Cusanus Society*, ed. Gerald Christianson and Thomas M. Izbicki (Leiden 1996), 221–40; Gerhard Wolf, *Schleier und Spiegel: Traditionen des Christusbildes und die Bildkonzepte der Renaissance* (Munich 2002), 201–72.

71 Michel de Certeau and Catherine Porter, "The Gaze in Nicholas of Cusa," *Diacritics* 17, 3 (1987): 18.

72 Rodolfo Signorini, *Opus Hoc Tenue: Lettura storica, iconografica, iconologica della camera dipinta di Andrea Mantegna*, intro. Eugenio Battisti (Parma 1985), 113–246; Randolph Starn and Loren Partridge, "A Room for a Renaissance Prince: The Camera Picta in Mantua 1465–1474," in *Arts of Power: Three*

Halls of State in Italy 1300–1600 (Berkeley 1992), 83–6, 90–126; Campbell, "Mantegna's *Camera Picta*," 315–32.

73 Ann E. Moyer, *The Philosophers' Game: Rithmomachia in Medieval and Renaissance Europe* (Ann Arbor, Mich. 2001), 80.

74 Claude V. Palisca, *Humanism in Italian Renaissance Musical Thought* (New Haven and London 1985), 164–78.

75 Giovanni Agosti, *Su Mantegna I* (Milan 2005), 384–5.

76 Pampurino's ceiling is now displayed at the Victoria and Albert Museum, London: Mina Gregori, "Alessandro Pampurino," in *I Campi e la cultura artistica cremonese del Cinquecento*, exh. cat. (Milan 1985), 42–5, esp. 43–4; Marcin Fabiański, "The Cremonese Ceiling Examined in Its Original Studiolo Setting," *Artibus et Historiae* 9, 17 (1988): 189–212.

77 The decorated chamber in Palazzo Costabili seems to be the result of a collaboration between Cesare Cesariano (painted architecture) and Garofalo (figures): Alessandra Pattanaro, "Garofalo e Cesariano in Palazzo Costabili a Ferrara," *Prospettiva* 73/74 (1994): 97–110; Anna Maria Fioravanti Baraldi, *Il Garofalo: Benvenuto Tisi pittore (c. 1476–1559)* (Ferrara 1993), 130–32, 138–42. On spectacles staged for viewers in painted chambers see Dunlop, *Painted Palaces*, 153–63.

78 W. J. Conybeare, *The Life and Epistles of St. Paul* (New York 1970), I Timothy 2.11–12; Henricus Cornelius Agrippa, *Declamation on the Nobility and Preeminence of the Female Sex*, trans. and ed. Albert Rabil Jr. (Chicago and London 1996), 79–80 ("Among the Jews Miriam, together with Moses, entered the sanctuary with Aaron and was considered a priestess"); 84 ("no more than the theologian Apollos blushed to be instructed by Priscilla").

79 Barbara Newman, "Renaissance Feminism and Esoteric Theology: The Case of Cornelius Agrippa," *Viator* 24 (1993): 338.

80 Roberto Guerrini, *Studi su Valerio Massimo (con un capitolo sulla fortuna nell'iconografia umanistica): Perugino, Beccafumi, Pordenone* (Pisa 1981). Valerius Maximus's *Memorable Deeds and Sayings* is listed in the 1491 inventory of books owned by Taddeo Ugoleto: Gianluca Battioni, "Per la storia della cultura parmense in età sforzesca: l'inventario catalogo di una libreria cittadina del 1491," *Archivio storico per le province parmensi* 38 (1986): 464.

81 Timothy Hampton, *Writing from History: The Rhetoric of Exemplarity in Renaissance Literature* (Ithaca, N.Y. and London 1990), 14.

82 Desiderius Erasmus, *Collected Works: Literary and Educational Writings 2, De Copia/De Ratione Studii*, ed. Craig R. Thompson, vol. 24 (Toronto 1978), 607. On the plural reading of *exempla* and their tension see John D. Lyons, *Exemplum: The Rhetoric of Example in Early Modern France and Italy* (Princeton 1989), 17; François Rigolot, "The Renaissance Crisis of Exemplarity," *Journal of the History of Ideas* 59 (1998): 557–63.

83 Lyons, *Exemplum*, 18. See also Karl-Heinz Stierle, "L'Histoire comme exemple: l'exemple comme histoire," *Poétique* 10 (1972): 176–98.

84 Lyons, *Exemplum*, 19.

85 Karl Giehlow, "Die Hieroglyphenkunde des Humanismus in der Allegorie der Renaissance, besonders der Ehrenpforte Kaisers Maximilian I," *Jahrbuch der Kunsthistorischen Sammlungen des Allerhöchsten Kaiserhauses* 32 (1915): 1–105, esp. 35–40; John Cunnally, *Images of the Illustrious: The Numismatic Presence in the Renaissance* (Princeton 1999); Federica Missere Fontana, "Raccolte numismatiche e scambi antiquari del Cinquecento: gli stati estensi," *Atti e memorie: Accademia nazionale di scienze, lettere e arti* 11 (1993/94): 213–56.

86 Celio Calcagnini, *Opera Aliquot* (Basel 1544), 173.

87 Maria Monica Donato, "*Historia Parens Patavum*: per una tradizione d'arte civica dal Medievo all'età moderna," in *Percorsi di parole e immagini (1400–1600)*, ed. Angela Guidotti and Massimiliano Rossi (Lucca 2000), 63.

88 Nicolaus Cusanus, "De Ludo Globi," in *Tractatus*, fols AA2r–DD3r, esp. DD1r–DD3r.

89 Francis Haskell, *History and Its Image* (New Haven and London 1993), 25.

90 Luke Syson, "Holes and Loops: The Display and Collection of Medals in Renaissance Italy," *Journal of Design History* 15, 4 (2002): 235.

91 ASPr, Notarile, Galeazzo Piazza, filza 937, June 7, 1518 (will and inventory of the properties of Taddeo Ugoleto). On the almost contemporary collection of antiques gathered by another prominent local figure, Francesco Bajardi, the patron of Parmigianino, see David Ekserdjian, "Parmigianino and the Antique," *Apollo* 154 (July 2001): 50.

92 On alchemical medals in Renaissance inventories see John Cunnally, "The Role of Greek and Roman Coins," Ph.D. diss., University of Pennsylvania 1984, 28.

93 For suggestive observations on the "intelligible dimensions" of small things see Claude Lévi-Strauss, *The Savage Mind* (London 1972), 22–33; John Mack, *The Art of Small Things* (Cambridge, Mass. 2007), 69–75. For Paleotti on coins see Paleotti, *Discourse on Sacred and Profane Images*, 1.14; Federica Missere Fontana, "Raccolte numismatiche e scambi antiquari a Bologna fra Quattrocento e Seicento: Parte I," *Bollettino di numismatica* 25 (1995): 172–3.

94 Richard V. Schofield, "Avoiding Rome: An Introduction to Lombard Sculptors and the Antique," *Arte lombarda* 100, 1 (1992): 29–44; Richard V. Schofield, "Amadeo's System," in *Giovanni Antonio Amadeo: Scultura e architettura del suo tempo*, ed. Janice Shell and Liana Castelfranchi (Milan 1993), 125–56.

95 In ca. 1522, in the nave of San Giovanni Evangelista, Correggio and his team painted scenes of pagan and Jewish sacrifice, with burning altars and Greek inscriptions, to great

effect: Adorni, *Abbazia benedettina*, 122–4; Mary Vaccaro, "A Drawing from the Circle of Correggio in the Uffizi," *Burlington Magazine* 149 (2007): 472–8.

96 Colonna, *Hypnerotomachia Poliphili*, 1: 186.

97 Jutta Gisela Sperling, *Convents and the Body Politic in Late Renaissance Venice* (Chicago 1999), 139.

98 Dempsey, *Inventing the Renaissance Putto*, 222. Informed viewers could have further linked Araldi's desperate mask to its ultimate source, Mantegna's bacchic mask emerging among grotesque ornaments in his Camera Picta and often interpreted as a self-portrait.

99 Erik Iversen, *The Myth of Egypt and its Hieroglyphs in European Tradition*, 2nd edn. (Princeton 1993), 57–87; Rudolf Wittkower, "Hieroglyphics in the Early Renaissance," in *Allegory and the Migration of Symbols* (London 1977), 113–28; Patrizia Castelli, *I geroglifici e il mito dell'Egitto nel Rinascimento* (Florence 1979); Dempsey, "Renaissance Hieroglyphic Studies," 348–55; Curran, *Egyptian Renaissance*, 107–87.

100 [Horapollo], *The Hieroglyphics of Horapollo*, trans. George Boas (New York 1950), 83: "To symbolize what cannot happen, they [the Egyptians] draw men walking on water. Or if they wish to show this otherwise they draw a headless man walking about. Since both are impossible, they may be logically used for that."

101 On this abridged *Hieroglyphica* (Naples, Biblioteca Nazionale, MS V.E.5), copied by a certain Thomas Scandianus, see Curran, *Egyptian Renaissance*, 103; Periti, "Epigraphy and the Semiotics of the Line," 208.

102 Leon Battista Alberti, *On the Art of Building in Ten Books*, trans. Joseph Rykwert et al. (Cambridge 1988), 8.iv.

103 For a discussion of the hieroglyphs in Carissimi's sepulcher sketch, which was ultimately used for another tomb, see Alessandra Talignani, "QUID EVADET: una traccia dell'*Hypnerotomachia Poliphili* a Parma nel sepolcro di Vincenzo Carissimi," *Artes* 5 (1997): 111–37.

104 On Dürer's *Triumphal Arch* see Wittkower, "Hieroglyphics in the Early Renaissance," esp. 122–5; Larry Silver, *Marketing Maximilian: The Visual Ideology of a Holy Roman Emperor* (Princeton 2008), 24–7. On Dürer's drawings of the hieroglyphs in the Latin translation of Horapollo's *Hieroglyphica*, which were presented to Maximilian in 1514, see Giehlow, "Hieroglyphenkunde," esp. 10–14, app. fig. 68.

105 Anthony Halliday, "The Literary Sources of Mantegna's *Triumphs of Caesar*," *Annali della Scuola normale superiore di Pisa*, s. III, 24, 1 (1994): 337–96; Stephen J. Campbell, "Mantegna's Triumph: The Cultural Politics of Imitation 'all'antica' at the Court of Mantua, 1490–1530," in *Artists at Court: Image-Making and Identity, 1300–1550* (Chicago 2004), 91–105; Caroline Elam, "Les *Triomphes* de Mantegna: la Forme et la Vie," in *Mantegna: 1431–1506*, ed. Giovanni Agosti and Dominique Thiébaut, exh. cat. (Paris 2010), 363–71, 386–7. As early as 1497–8 Giulio Campagnola engraved two of Mantegna's triumphs, and Giovanni Antonio da Brescia cut others in 1500–04: Jane Martineau et al., eds., *Andrea Mantegna*, exh. cat. (London 1992), 375–78, 383.

106 Zanichelli, *Iconologia*, 32–3.

107 Marianne Pade, *The Reception of Plutarch's Lives in Fifteenth-Century Italy*, 2 vols. (Copenhagen 2007), 1: 141–3, 385–8. For other commentaries on Aemilius's triumph see Francesco Albertini, *Opusculum de mirabilibus nouae & ueteris vrbis Romae* (Rome 1510), 73v–75r. Lomazzo recommends Aemilius's triumph as the exemplar of ancient triumphs: Giovanni Paolo Lomazzo, *Trattato dell'Arte de la Pittura* (Milan 1584), 6.42, esp. 396–7.

108 Plutarch, "Life of Aemilius Paulus," in *Lives*, trans. Bernardotte Perrin, Loeb Edition, 11 vols. (London and New York 1914–26), 6: XXXV.

109 Ibid., XXXVI.

110 Zanichelli has seen this figure as a citation from Raimondi's print of *God Appearing to Noah* (ca. 1513–15): Zanichelli, *Iconologia*, 33.

111 On the Borghese portrait and its debated attribution to Raphael see Pier Luigi de Vecchi, *Raffaello: la mimesi, l'armonia, e l'invenzione* (Florence 1995), 250. For a full technical report on the work, which has been repainted several times, see Hugo Chapman, Tom Henry, and Carol Plazzotta, *Raphael: From Urbino to Rome*, exh. cat. (London 2004), 174–5.

112 Zanichelli, "Araldi," 106.

113 Horace, *Art of Poetry*, 12.

114 Caresses and kisses had as much a sentimental as a sexual dimension in the Renaissance. In a monastic context they were related to the ambivalent understanding of the opening verses of the Song of Songs: "Let him kiss me with the kisses of his mouth." These verses have been interpreted both as a spiritual and a sexual manifestation of desire and love between the bride and bridegroom. Bernard of Clairvaux's spiritual commentary on the Song of Songs was published several times (1492, 1494, and 1500): Max Engammare, *Qu'il me baise des baisiers de sa bouche: le Cantique des Cantiques à la Renaissance* (Geneva 1993), 65–103. For an erotic reading of the text see Stephen D. Moore, "The Song of Songs in the History of Sexuality," *Church History* 69, 2 (2000): 328–49.

115 BNC, *Fiori di Virtù* (Venice 1500), cap. XXXIII, De la Inte[m]-perantia: "et puote . . . assimigliare el vitio della inte[m]-perantia allo liocorno ovvero unicorno che è una bestia che ha tanta delectatione de stare con donzelle vergine che cioè lui ne vede alcuna e va da lei e se le ado[r]menta in braccio . . . . e i cacciatori in tal modo lo pigliano . . . Et

per questa sua inte[m]perantia Plato dice che niuno vitio al mondo sia pegiore che la inte[m]perantia perchè da lei procedono tutti i mali."

116 Paris, Institut de France, MS H1, fol. 11r. On Leonardo's drawing and notes see Lise Gotfredsen, *The Unicorn* (New York 1999), 129, 132 and Carmen Bambach, *Leonardo da Vinci: Master Draftsman*, exh. cat. (New York 2003), 308.

117 Agosti and Thiébaut, *Mantegna*, 307–08, 310–11. On Giovanni Antonio da Brescia's print that is a reversed version of Mantegna's composition, see Zucker, *Illustrated Bartsch*, 258. It is unclear if this and another engraving, which is a copy of Mantegna's image, derive from the same or different drawings. Zucker distinguishes between a printmaker known as Zoan Andrea and Giovanni Antonio da Brescia, but more recent studies have determined that they are one and the same person: Suzanne Boorsch, "Mantegna and His Printmakers," in *Andrea Mantegna*, 56–66, 437–8, 443–4. For Girolamo Mocetto's engraving of *Judith with the Head of Holofernes* see Zucker, *Illustrated Bartsch*, 41–2.

118 Horst Woldemar Janson, *Apes and Ape Lore in the Middle Ages and the Renaissance* (London 1952), 73–99, 287–314.

119 Valerius Maximus, *Memorable Deeds and Sayings: One Thousand Tales from Ancient Rome*, trans. Henry John Walker (Indianapolis and Cambridge 2004), bk 5.4, ext. 1.

120 An early Cinquecento plaquette (London, Victoria and Albert Museum) with the story of Pero and Mycon was made for a Cremonese patron: John Pope-Hennessy, *Renaissance Bronze from the Samuel H. Kress Collection* (London 1965), 41 n. 132, fig. 122. In general on Caritas Romana in Italian Renaissance art and literature see W. Deonna, "La Légende de Pero et de Micon et l'allitement symbolique," *Latomus: Revue d'études latines* 13 (1954): 140–66, 356–75; Elfriede Regina Knauer, "Caritas Romana," *Jahrbuch der Berliner Museen* 6 (1954): 9–23; Lucia Köllner, *Die töchterliche Liebe: ein Mysteriumgeheimnis. Die sogenannte Caritas Romana* (Frankfurt 1997), 43–51, 95–104.

121 Valerius Maximus also narrates the story of a young "freeborn" woman who nourished her mother in prison: Valerius Maximus, *Memorable Deeds*, bk 5.4.7. See Brigitte Buettner, *Boccaccio's Des Cleres et nobles femmes: System of Signification in an Illuminated Manuscript* (Seattle 1996), 42; Christine de Pizan, *The Book of the City of Ladies*, trans. Earl Jeffrey Richards, foreword by Natalie Zemon Davis (New York 1998), 113–16, esp. 115; Sabadino degli Arienti, *Gynevera de le clare donne* (Bologna 1888), 52.

122 Jacopo Sannazaro, *Arcadia*, ed. Carlo Vecce (Rome 2013), XI.37–8; Dempsey, *Inventing the Renaissance Putto*, 96; Stephen J. Campbell, *The Cabinet of Eros: Renaissance Mythological Painting and the Studiolo of Isabella d'Este* (New Haven and London 2004), 152–4. Sannazaro's description of Mantegna's

representation of the playful satyrs reappears, albeit slightly modified, in Ascanio Botta's *Rurale*, a pastoral poem printed in 1521 and 1524 in Cremona. Botta's text probably had wide circulation in Parma's circles (even as a manuscript) because Botta was Giorgio Anselmi's brother-in-law: Ascanio Botta, *Il Rurale secondo le prime due edizioni del 1521 e 1524*, ed. Manuela Rossi (Cremona 1985), 38; Giovanni Agosti, "Scrittori che parlano di artisti, tra Quattro e Cinquecento in Lombardia," in *Quattro Pezzi Lombardi (per Maria Teresa Binaghi)* (Brescia 1998), 85.

123 Lucian, *Zeuxis, or, Antiochus*, trans. A. M. Harmon, 3 vols. (London 1919–67), 1: 6.157–9. Vecce has suggested that Sannazaro's reference could come from Lucian's *De Conscribenda Historia*, 25.23: Vecce in Sannazaro, *Arcadia*, 271.

124 On Peregrino da Cesena's fine print see Faietti and Oberhuber, *Bologna e l'umanesimo*, 338–9.

125 Servius, *Servii Grammatici qui feruntur in Vergilii carmina commentarii*, ed. G. Thilo and H. Hagen (1881–7), 4 vols. in 3 (Hildesheim 1986), 3: 532. See Charles C. Chiasson, "Myth, Ritual and Authorial Control in Herodotus' Story of Cleobis and Biton (Hist. 1.31)," *American Journal of Philology* 126 (2005): 41–64; Herodotus, *The Histories*, trans. Aubrey de Sélincourt (London 1996), 1.31; Valerius Maximus, *Memorable Deeds*, bk 5.4, ext. 4; Plutarch, "Solon," in *Lives*, 1.xxvii.5.

126 Carlo Falciani, "Francesco I ritratto a Fontainebleau," in *Il ritratto nell'Europa nel Cinquecento* (Florence 2007), 29–66, esp. 55–6; Rebecca Zorach, *Blood, Milk, Ink, Gold: Abundance and Excess in the French Renaissance* (Chicago 2005), 56–7.

127 Known for his frescoes at Santa Giustina, Bernardino da Parenzo sketched the Argive brothers as sleeping children in an allegorical drawing, the so-called *Hercules at the Crossroad* (now Oxford, Christ Church; ca. 1496): Salmazo, *Bernardino da Parenzo*, 50–52.

128 For a survey of representations see *Cléobis et Biton: une mythe oublié*, exh. cat. (Carcassonne 1995).

129 Pirro Ligorio, "Grottesche," in *Scritti d'arte del Cinquecento*, ed. Paola Barocchi, 3 vols. (Milan 1973), 3: 2683–4: "Quell'altri che significarono il fine della vita felice, vi dipinsero Cleobi e Bitone, fratelli giovinetti, che tirarono il carro al sacrificio, condussero la madre a celebrare nella solennità del tempio della Iunone Argiva. Et avendo questi recato gran contentezza all'Argivi, furono onorati e stimati senza peccato. Onde la madre e lo popolo pregavano la dea che gli donasse la felicità. E furono adormentati nel tempio, nè mai più si svegliarono."

CHAPTER VI CORREGGIO'S WIT, IRONY, AND THE ENIGMATIC IMAGE

1 Painted by indirect request of Francesco II Gonzaga to celebrate victory over the French troops at Fornovo near Parma, Mantegna's *Madonna of the Victory*, once in the church of Santa Maria della Vittoria in Mantua, was transferred to Paris after the Napoleonic invasion of Italy in 1798: Giovanni Agosti and Dominique Thiébaut, eds., *Mantegna 1431–1506*, exh. cat. (Paris 2010), 304–6.

2 Correggio's early training and relationship with Mantegna are debated questions in the literature. Seventeenth-century sources speak of Correggio's intervention in the decoration of Mantegna's funerary chapel in Sant'Andrea in Mantua and in the atrium of the church, but scholars have discordant views about attributing this work to the artist: David Ekserdjian, *Correggio* (New Haven and London 1997), 23–7. Whatever the opinions regarding this early corpus are, a recently discovered document dating to 1512 confirms a financial transaction between Francesco Mantegna, Andrea's son, and the young Correggio: Rodolfo Signorini, "Un inedito su Francesco Mantegna e il Correggio," *Quaderni di Palazzo Te* 3 (1996): 79–80; Giovanni Agosti, *Su Mantegna I* (Milan 2005), 198, 218, 224. Correggio's painted room in San Paolo reworks Mantegna's conception of the illusionistic decoration of the dome in his funerary chapel, a space that is recreated by vegetation, fruit, and trellis webbing.

3 Desiderius Erasmus, "Ignem ne gladio fodito/Stir not the fire with a sword," in *Collected Works of Erasmus: Adages*, trans. Margaret Mann Phillips, annot. R. A. B. Mynors, vol. 31 (Toronto 1982), 36.

4 Erwin Panofsky, *The Iconography of Correggio's Camera di San Paolo* (London 1961). Panofsky's iconographic approach has been the subject of much critical rethinking in the scholarship, among others, by Yve-Alain Bois, "Panofsky Early and Late," *Art in America* 73, 7 (1985): 9–15; Georges Didi-Huberman, *Confronting Images: Questioning the Ends of a Certain History of Art*, trans. John Goodman (University Park, Pa. 2005), 53–84 on Panofsky's ways to neutralize contrasting or ambiguous readings of Renaissance literary images.

5 Ernst Gombrich, *Topos and Topicality in Renaissance Art* (London 1975). Consistent with Panofsky's reading are instead Ghizzoni and Barocelli's contributions, which interpret Correggio's images within Neoplatonic philosophy: Vito Ghizzoni, "La Caccia della sapienza di Antonio Lieto," *Commentari* (1978): 104–15; Francesco Barocelli, "Umanesimo e cultura monastica: la Camera di Correggio nel monastero di San Paolo," in *Il Correggio nella camera di San Paolo* (Milan 2010), 276–365.

6 Maureen Pelta, "Form and Convent: Correggio and the Decoration of the Camera di San Paolo," Ph.D. diss., Bryn Mawr College 1989; Maurizio Calvesi, "Gli Inconsulti ed i virtuosi," *Art & Dossier* (1990): 23–36; Barry Collett, "Definition of Humanity in the Early Sixteenth Century: Correggio, Isidoro Clario, Zarlino, and the Restoration of 'Imago Dei,'" *Brixia Sacra. Isidoro Clario 1495ca–1555: Umanista, teologo tra Erasmo e la Controriforma* 11, 4 (2006): 109–24, esp. 118–19. Staring at Correggio's putti and being stared at, the literary critic Alberto Arbasino has written insightful remarks on the topic: Alberto Arbasino, *Su Correggio* (Milan 2008), 7–23.

7 Regina Stefaniak, "Correggio's *Camera di San Paolo*: An Archeology of the Gaze," *Art History*, 16, 2 (1993): 203–38, esp. 228.

8 Alessandro Nova, "Beobachten und Beobachtet werden: Die Metamorphose des Betrachters und des Betrachteten bei Correggio und Parmigianino," in *Imagination und Wirklichkeit zum Verhältnis von mentalen und realen Bildern in der Kunst der Frühen Neuzeit*, ed. Klaus Krüger and Alessandro Nova (Mainz 2000), 81–98, esp. 89–90.

9 On the value of grisaille painting in antiquity and its imitation in Mantegna's art in the context of the *paragone* with sculpture see Pliny the Elder, *Natural History*, trans. H. Rackham, Loeb Edition (Cambridge, Mass. 1968), 35, 36, 64: "[Zeuxis] also painted monochromes in white"; Sarah Blake McHam, *Pliny and the Artistic Culture of the Italian Renaissance: The Legacy of the Natural History* (New Haven and London 2013), 234–36.

10 On eroticized representations of Diana, including Correggio's image, and interpretations of the myth of the hunt in the Renaissance, see Stephen J. Campbell, *The Cabinet of Eros: Renaissance Mythological Painting and the Studiolo of Isabella d'Este* (New Haven and London 2004), 66–7.

11 Nicolaus Cusanus, "De Venatione Sapientiae," in *Certi Tractatus et libri altissimae contemplationis et doctrinae a praeclarae memoriae praestantissimo doctissimoque viro Nicolao de Cusa* (Cortemaggiore 1502), F6r–I9v; Clyde Lee Miller, "Possibility and Divine Prey: *De Venatione Sapientiae* (1463)," in *Reading Cusanus: Metaphor and Dialectic in a Conjectural Universe* (Washington, D.C. 2003), 206–40, esp. 233–5. On Caviceo's text see the modern critical edition: Jacopo Caviceo, *Il Peregrino*, ed. Luigi Vignali (Rome 1993), esp. bk 3, chs 62, 65–6, 68 on Peregrino's dealings with the abbess of the convent of Sant'Andrea in Ravenna who gave him permission to enter the monastic house to see Genevera, and who helped their marriage.

12 On the *serio-ludere* poetic in the early modern literature see Ernst Robert Curtius, "Jest and Earnest in Medieval Literature," in *European Literature and the Latin Middle Ages*, trans. Willard R. Trask, afterword Peter Godman (Princeton 1990),

417–35; Rosalie L. Colie, "Problems of Paradox," in *Paradoxica Epidemica: The Renaissance Tradition of Paradox* (Princeton 1966), 4–40; Dilwyn Knox, *Ironia: Medieval and Renaissance Ideas on Irony* (Leiden 1989), 19–37, 97–109. The therapeutic value of games and play has been discussed by Carlo Vecce, "Leonardo e il gioco," in *Passare il tempo: la letteratura del gioco e dell'intrattenimento dal XII al XVI secolo*, 2 vols. (Rome 1993), 1: 269–312; Lina Bolzoni, *Il Cuore di cristallo: ragionamenti d'amore, poesia e ritratto nel rinascimento* (Turin 2010), 103–6.

13 Giorgio Anselmi junior has been indicated as the possible adviser of Correggio's frescoes by Ireneo Affò, *Ragionamento del Padre Ireneo Affò sopra una stanza dipinta dal celeberrimo Antonio Allegri da Correggio nel monistero di S. Paolo in Parma* (Parma 1794), 46; Panofsky, *The Iconography*, 27. As these scholars have acknowledged, Anselmi's daughter Virginia took vows in San Paolo in 1519.

14 The concept of *ludus litterarum* is discussed in Plautus's *Rudens* (The Rope) 43, which was published in Parma in 1510: [Titus Maccius Plautus], "Rudens" in *M. Actii Plauti Asinii. Comoediae viginti nuper emendatae et in eas Pyladae Brixiani Lucubrationes. Thadaei Ugoleti: et Grapaldi virorum illustrium Scholia, Anselmi Epiphyllides* (Parma 1510), 267r–282v. Known to the Parmese literati, Cusa's *Ludo Globi* (1502) also refers to the notion of *ludus litterarum*. For Cusa's interest in pursuing ethical matters based on games see Ann E. Moyer, *The Philosophers' Game: Rithmomachia in Medieval and Renaissance Europe* (Ann Arbor, Mich. 2001), 53–5. In general, on the semantic richness of the term *ludus* see Andrea Nuti, *Ludus et iocus: Percorsi di ludicità nella lingua latina* (Treviso 1998), 82–94.

15 Elissa Weaver, "Spasso spirituale, ovvero il gioco delle monache," in *Passare il tempo*, 1: 351–71.

16 Leonard Barkan, *The Gods made Flesh: Metamorphosis and the Pursuit of Paganism* (New Haven and London 1986), 177.

17 Georgii Anselmi, "Stupori," in *Epigrammaton Libri Septem: Sosthyrides Peplum Palladis Aeglogae Quattor* (Parma 1526; Venice 1528), 7.90r–92r. See David A. Campbell, "Gallambic Poems of the 15th and 16th Centuries: Sources of the Bacchic Odes of the Pléiade School," *Bibliothèque d'humanisme et renaissance* 22 (1960): 490–510, esp. 496–500; Elisabeth Klecker, "Admiratio Initialis: Der Stuporhymnus des Giorgio Anselmi," *Studi umanistici piceni* 20 (2000): 4–20.

18 For a recent discussion of Agrippa's theories of binding and the power of the eyes to fasten onlookers see Thijs Weststeijn, "Seeing and the Transfer of Spirits in Early Modern Art Theory," in *Renaissance Theories of Vision*, ed. John Shannon Hendrix and Charles H. Carman (Farnham 2010), 149–69, esp. 151–2.

19 Panofsky, *The Iconography*, 48.

20 Filarete, *Treatise on Architecture*, ed. John R. Spencer, 2 vols. (New Haven and London 1965), 1: IX.70r. In general, on chimneypieces and their decoration see Peter Thornton, *The Italian Renaissance Interior, 1400–1600* (London 1991), 20–23; Brenda Preyer, "Chimney," in *At Home in Renaissance Italy*, ed. Marta Ajmar-Wollheim and Flora Dennis, exh. cat. (London 2006), 284–7. A red chalk sketch by Correggio of 1520–24 featuring a chimneypiece with unusually detailed moldings further attests his interest in fireplaces: Arthur E. Popham, *Correggio's Drawings* (London 1957), 199–200. It is unclear whether Correggio knew Mantegna's Camera Picta but, if he was familiar with it, he seems to have been determined to rework it.

21 On the debated chronology of this fresco (transferred to wood support, now Milan, Pinacoteca di Brera) and the related fragments from the Villa Pelucca's decoration, see Giovanni Agosti, Rossana Sacchi, and Jacopo Stoppa, entry in *Bernardino Luini e i suoi figli*, ed. Giovanni Agosti and Jacopo Stoppa, exh. cat. (Milan 2014), 101–35.

22 Caroline Walker Bynum, "Women's Stories, Women's Symbols: A Critique of Victor Turner's Theory of Liminality," in *Anthropology and the Study of Religion*, ed. Robert L. Moore and Frank Reynolds (Chicago 1984), 105–25, esp. 111–15.

23 Eugenio Battisti has correlated eroticized representations of Diana turning into Luna (the Moon) with necromantic peasant beliefs (the so-called "game of Diana"), in which the chaste goddess becomes a luxuriant figure presiding over magic rituals. While this reading is not plausible for Correggio's fully clothed, albeit voluptuous Diana, it is true that the semantic fluidity of the painter's representation teases out multiple associations: Eugenio Battisti, *L'Antirinascimento*, 2 vols. (Milan 1989), 1: 163.

24 Claudianus, "In Raptum Proserpinae," in *Opera* (Parma 1493), Rr–T5v; Claudian, *De Raptu Proserpinae*, trans. Maurice Platnauer, Loeb Edition (London 1963), 2.30–35: "Her shining arms were bare, her straying locks fluttered in the gentle breeze . . . Her Cretan tunic, gathered with girdles twain, flows down to her knees, and on her waving dress Delos wanders and stretches surrounded by a golden sea." See also Giancarla Periti, "Enigmatic Beauty: Correggio's Camera di San Paolo," in *Drawing Relationships in Northern Italian Renaissance Art: Patronage and Theories of Invention*, ed. Giancarla Periti, intro. Charles Dempsey (Aldershot 2004), 153–76, esp. 164–5.

25 Ricci went so far to identify this ancient sarcophagus from the Gonzaga collection in Mantua as Correggio's source: Corrado Ricci, *Correggio* (London 1930), 65, pl. 2.

26 Lilio Gregorio Giraldi, "Historiae Deorum Gentilium de Diana, Luna, Hecate, Iside," in *De Deis Gentium Varia et Multipla Historia* (Basel 1548), 491–9; Erika Simon and Gerhard

Bauchhess, "Artemis/Diana," in *Lexicon Iconographicum Mythologiae Classicae*, ed. Jean Ch. Balty et al. (Zürich 1981), 1: 900–11

27 Amended by Puteolano, the Parmese edition of Catullus's and Statius's writings (Corallus 1473) is an extremely rare text: Julia Haig Gaisser, *Catullus and his Renaissance Readers* (Oxford 1993), 32–5. On Catullus's key passages describing Diana-Luna see Catullus, *The Poems*, intro., rev. Kenneth Quinn (London 1970), 34.13–16: "Thee, Lucina, the travailing/Mother haileth, a sovereign/Juno; Trivia thou, the bright/Moon, a glory reflected."

28 Anselmi, *Epigrammaton Libri Septem*, 3.32r–33r.

29 Critical assessments of bedrooms in Renaissance Italy include Thornton, *Renaissance Interior*, 284–5; Richard Aste, "Bartolomeo Bettini and his Florentine 'Chamber' Decoration," in *Venus and Love: Michelangelo and the New Ideal of Beauty*, ed. Franca Falletti and Jonathan Katz Nelson, exh. cat. (Florence 2002), 3–25.

30 Mary Carruthers, *The Craft of Thought: Meditation, Rhetoric, and the Making of Images, 400–1200* (Cambridge 1998), 171.

31 Sardi's letter was published by Federica Missere Fontana, "Raccolte numismatiche e scambi antiquari del Cinquecento: gli stati estensi," *Atti e memorie: Accademia nazionale di scienze, lettere e arti* 11 (1993/94): 219.

32 On the multiple interpretations of arcane *symbola* in the Renaissance see Christopher S. Celenza, *Piety and Pythagoras in Renaissance Florence: The Symbolum Nesianum* (Leiden 2001), 52–67; Maria Frati, "Dal discorso narrativo al discorso proverbiale: i *Convelata* di Leon Battista Alberti ed Erasmo da Rotterdam," *Schede umanistiche* 2 (1999): 55–78.

33 Erasmus, "Ignem ne gladio fodito," in *Collected Works of Erasmus*, 31, 36. The San Paolo *Ignem gladio ne fodias* reworks the original Erasmian *Ignem ne gladio fodito*, showing the appropriation of this Pythagorean aphorism in the context of the room. Adaptations and reinventions of sayings were standard in the Renaissance.

34 Castiglione discusses aggressive prudence with reference to stories of ancient and modern courageous women: Baldassar Castiglione, *The Book of the Courtier*, trans. Charles S. Singleton (Garden City, N.Y. 1959), III.31–4.

35 John Martin, "Inventing Sincerity, Refashioning Prudence," *American Historical Review*, 102, 5 (1997): 1309–42, esp. 1324–6; Jon R. Snyder, *Dissimulation and the Culture of Secrecy in the Renaissance* (Berkeley, Cal. 2009), 1–27.

36 Popham, *Correggio's Drawings*, 14; Carmen Bambach et al., eds., *Correggio and Parmigianino: Master Draughtsmen of the Renaissance*, exh. cat. (London 2000), 37; Mario Di Giampaolo, *Correggio Disegnatore* (Milan 2001), "Entry 8," n.p.

37 Hugo Chapman, entry in Bambach et al., *Correggio and Parmigianino*, 37.

38 Panofsky, *The Iconography*, 92.

39 Ibid., 53, 80.

40 See Anthony Cutler's discussion in *The Glory of Byzantium: Art and Culture of the Middle Byzantine Era, A.D. 843–1261*, ed. Helen C. Evans and William D. Wixom, exh. cat. (New York 1997), 232–3 n. 155.

41 On the interpretation of Lotto's frescoes at Trescore see Francesca Cortesi Bosco, *Gli Affreschi dell'Oratorio Suardi a Trescore* (Milan 1997), 12–16; Charles Dempsey, *Inventing the Renaissance Putto* (Chapel Hill, N.C. 2001), 64–5.

42 For the putto as a bearer of the various spirits affecting the body and the mind through the window of the eye see Dempsey, *Inventing the Renaissance Putto*, 43–7.

43 Ibid., 63.

44 Annibale Carracci quoted in Giovanna Perini, *Gli scritti dei Carracci* (Bologna 1990), 150–51: "i puttini del Correggio spirano, vivono e ridono con una grazia e verità che bisogna con essi ridere e rallegrarsi."

45 On the linking of the beholder and painted spaces see Jean C. Campbell, "Pier Maria Rossi's Treasure: Love, Knowledge, and the Invention of the Source in the Camera d'oro at Torrechiara," in *Emilia e Marche nel Rinascimento: l'identità visiva della "periferia,"* ed. Giancarla Periti (Azzano [Bg] 2005), 63–88; Anne Dunlop, *Painted Palaces: The Rise of Secular Art in Early Renaissance Italy* (University Park, Pa. 2009), 153–63; Stephen J. Campbell, "Mantegna's *Camera Picta*: Visuality and Pathos," *Art History* 37, 2 (2014): 314–33.

46 On perspective problems when painting on curved surfaces with reference to Correggio's dome decorations in San Giovanna Evangelista and in Parma Cathedral see John Shearman, "Domes," in *Only Connect . . . Art and the Spectator in the Italian Renaissance* (Princeton 1988), 181–8; Carolyn Smyth, *Correggio's Frescoes in Parma Cathedral* (Princeton 1997), 13–95.

47 Stefaniak, "Correggio's *Camera*," 230–31 recognized the gazing putti and their power of fascination as representations of the evil eye, positing that the viewer is co-opted into the painted surface as if one turns into the other. Correggio's understanding of discourses of sensations and fascination was more poetic than dogmatic, however, and his staring, sensual putti are linked more than has previously been recognized to nuns gaining perception of the physical world from which they were meant to be severed.

48 At the top of the so-called Camera d'Oro in Torrechiara (a village just outside Parma) painted in ca. 1460 appears the IHS sign of God, an instance that Correggio could have known. See Campbell, "Pier Maria Rossi's Treasure," 68; Giuseppa Z. Zanichelli, "La committenza dei Rossi: Immagini di potere fra sacro e profano," in *Le Signorie dei Rossi di Parma tra XIV e XVI secolo*, ed. Letizia Arcangeli and Marco Gentile (Florence 2007), 196–208.

49 Stefaniak, "Correggio's *Camera*," 228.

50 Desiderius Erasmus, *Collected Works of Erasmus: Colloquies*, trans. and annot. Craig R. Thompson, vol. 39 (Toronto 1997), 279–301, "The Girl with No Interest in Marriage"; 302–5, "The Repentant Girl."

51 Alice E. Wilson, "Introduction," in Andrea Navagero, *Lusus* (Nieuwkoop 1973), 7–18. Anselmi dedicated one of his poems to his friend Navagero who came to Parma in 1523 in the role of orator of the Venetian Republic: Anselmi, "Ad Andream Navagerium," in *Epigrammaton Libri Septem*, 1.13v–14r. Navagero and Andrea Beazzano had a double portrait made by another possible friend, Raphael, in ca. 1516 (Rome, Doria Pamphilj Gallery).

52 Gaisser, *Catullus*, 255–6; Elizabeth M. Young, "Catullus's Phaselus (C.4): Mastering a New Wave of Poetic Speech," *Arethusa* 44, 1 (2011): 69–88.

53 Anselmi, "In P. Virgilii Opera," in *Epigrammaton Libri Septem*, 1.2r–2v. The literary intertexts of Anselmi's writings have been discussed by James Hutton, *The Greek Anthology in Italy to the Year 1800* (Ithaca, N.Y. 1935), 173–4; Leonard Grant, *Neo-Latin Literature and the Pastoral* (Chapel Hill, N.C. 1965), 235–6, 245–6; Gaisser, *Catullus*, 266–9; Franz Römer, "Martial in drei Monodistichen des Giorgio Anselmi," *Wiener Studien* 101 (1988): 339–50; Elisabeth Klecker, *Dichtung über Dichtung: Homer und Vergil in Lateinischen Italienischer Humanisten des 15. und 16. Jahrhunderts* (Vienna 1994), 146–63.

54 BP, Smeraldo Smeraldi, "Diario delle visite per vie, canali, edifici dal feb. 1598 all'agosto 1600," MS Parm. 535, August 1, 1598, 83r: "un volto fatto a spicco con luneti, ove gli ha finto un pergolato, con uva e frutti, et certi ovati ove sono molti puttini bellissimi, con varie et diverse attioni, et motti; nelli luneti poi vi sono alcune istoriete chiare e scure; et sotto vi è una cornice intorno alla quale sono attacati alcuni drapi con dentro vasi, tazze, boccali, et altri vasellami finti d'argento, ma bellissimi."

55 Augusta Ghidiglia Quintavalle, "Risultati del restauro," in Roberto Longhi, *Il Correggio nella Camera di San Paolo*, ed. Augusta Ghidiglia Quintavalle (Parma 1972), 117–30, esp. 122, on Correggio's modeling of his figures according to the actual sources of light in the room: "[Grazie ai restauri] nelle lunette . . . è riemersa chiaramente la fonte di luce prima illegibile, che rade dal basso le figure provenendo dalle due finestre poste nel lato nord, fonte della quale l'artista ha reso con perizia la proiezione nelle quattro pareti e, quindi, le diverse angolazioni, lasciando in ombra le lunette a nord e illuminando le altre in modo esatto." Against any intellectual implications in Correggio's frescoes, Longhi's interpretation emphasizes the artist's pictorial style as a form of antiquarianism originating with Mantegna.

56 Ausonius, "Mosella," in *Opera* (Parma 1499), lines 61–8. Lines 55–60 are especially suggestive: "Through still surface transparencies we see/Deep secrets; for the river can no more/ Hide what it holds than air and wind, cloud-free;/An arcane treasure-house, a limpid store/Of scattered shapes, sky-blue or water-blue."

57 The 1522 document is quoted in Marzio Dall'Acqua, ed., *Correggio e il suo tempo*, exh. cat. (Parma 1984), 50: "[ornar di pitura con quelle istorie. . . che imitano] e il vivo o il bronzo, o il marmo, secondo richiede ai suoi lochi e il dovere de la fa[b]rica et le ragioni e vageza de essa pittura." Cristina Cecchinelli, "Il pittore e i ponteggi: Nuovi documenti e nuove date per gli affreschi del Correggio nella cupola della Cattedrale di Parma," *Nuovi Studi* 14, 2009 (2010): 135–52, esp. 136–7, has noted the anomalies of this document, arguing that it should be considered an agreement to secure the artist for future work rather than a real contract. On sketches and drawings related to the Cathedral decoration made after Correggio's death (1534) see Mary Vaccaro, "After Correggio: Drawings by Giorgio Gandini del Grano for Parma Cathedral," *Master Drawings* 53, 1 (2015): 59–80.

58 Secundus Gaius Plinius, *Historia Naturalis*, with annotations by Philippus Beroaldus (Parma 1476) and Pliny, *Natural History*, 35, 36.74. For Anselmi's sonnet on Timanthes see Anselmi, "De Timante Pictore," in *Epigrammaton Libri Septem*, 4.46r.

59 Affò, *Ragionamento*, 44–5; Ricci, *Correggio*, 51–4.

60 Pietro Bembo, *Lettere*, ed. Ernesto Travi, 4 vols. (Bologna 1987–93), 3: 380, no. 1416, letter of October 8, 1532; Davide Gasparotto, "Il mito della collezione," in *Pietro Bembo e l'invenzione del Rinascimento*, ed. Guido Beltramini, Davide Gasparotto, Adolfo Tura, exh. cat. (Venice 2013), 48–65, esp. 60–61.

61 Claudio Franzoni, "Le raccolte del 'Teatro di Ombrone' ed il viaggio in Oriente del pittore: le *Epistole* di Giovanni Filoteo Achillini," *Rivista di letteratura italiana* 8, 2 (1990): 287–335, esp. 313. For additional significant studies on the topic see John Cunnally, *Images of the Illustrious: The Numismatic Presence in the Renaissance* (Princeton 1999), 35; Federica Missere Fontana, "Raccolte numismatiche e scambi antiquari a Bologna fra Quattrocento e Seicento: Parte I," *Bollettino di numismatica* 25 (1995): 161–209, esp. 173–4.

62 Amico's bizarre recordings of antiquities in both graphic and painted works piqued viewers, as noticed by Marzia Faietti and Arnold Nesselrath, "Bizar più che reverso di medaglia: un codex avec grotesques, monstres et ornaments du jeune Amico Aspertini," *Revue de l'art* 107, 1 (1995): 44–88; Ulrich Pfisterer, *Lysippus und seine Freunde. Liebesgaben und Gedächtnis im Rom der Renaissance oder: Das erste Jahrhundert der Medaille* (Berlin 2008), 106–24.

63 Lilio Gregorio Giraldi, *Libelli Duo, in quorum altero Aenigmata pleraque Antiquorum, in altero Pythagorae Symbola* (Basel 1551),

8–63. Giraldi's text was composed when he was in the service of Alberto III Pio. On the relationships between Alberto Pio, the ruler of a fiefdom in western Emilia, and Parmese families and artists, including Bernardino Loschi, who painted a cycle of Muses (ca. 1509) in Alberto's studiolo in Carpi, see Alessandra Sarchi, "The Studiolo of Alberto Pio da Carpi," in Periti, *Drawing Relationships*, 129–51.

64 Maia Wellington Gahtan, "Giraldi's Aenigmata," in *Acta Conventus Neo-Latini Bonnensis: Proceedings of the Twelfth International Congress of Neo-Latin Studies*, ed. Perrine Galand-Hallyn and Roda Schnur (Temple, Ariz. 2006), 315–23, esp. 319–20; Celenza, *Piety and Pythagoras*, 71–83.

65 On the notion of brevity in Renaissance literature see Rosalie Littell Colie, "Small Forms: Multo in Parvo," in *The Resources of Kind: Genre-Theory in the Renaissance*, ed. Barbara K. Lewalski (Berkeley, Cal. 1973), 32–75; Claudie Balavoine, "Bouquets de fleurs et colliers de perles: sur les recueils de formes brèves au XVI siècle," in *Les Formes brèves de la prose et le discours discontinu (XVI–XVII siècles)*, ed. Jean Lafond (Paris 1984), 51–71.

66 Sari Kivistö, "The Concept of Obscurity in Humanist Polemics of the Early Sixteenth Century," in *Acta Conventus Neo-Latini Bonnensis*, 430–38; Suzanne Conklin Akbari, *Seeing through the Veil: Optical Theory and Medieval Allegory* (Toronto 2004), 234–43.

67 For sensitive observations on the early sixteenth-century commentaries on Plautus's comedies see Loredana Chines, *La parola degli antichi: Umanesimo emiliano tra scuola e poesia* (Rome 1998), 120–24.

68 Francesco Petrarca, *Invective contra Medicum*, ed. Pier Giorgio Ricci (Rome 1978), 1187–217; Giovanni Boccaccio, *In Defense of Poetry: Genealogiae Deorum Gentilium Liber XIV*, ed. Jeremy Reedy (Toronto 1978), 14.7.

69 See Kathleen Weil-Garris and John F. D'Amico, *The Renaissance Cardinal's Ideal Palace: A Chapter from Cortesi's De Cardinalatu* (Rome 1980), 97.

70 Wittkower first suggested, briefly, that Correggio's pictorial language in the lunettes was "implicitly, though not explicitly, hieroglyphic": Rudolf Wittkower, "Hieroglyphics in the Early Renaissance," in *Allegory and the Migration of Symbols*, rep. ed. (London 1987), 127.

71 Dario Gamboni, *Potential Images: Ambiguity and Indeterminacy in Modern Art* (London 2002), 18–19.

72 For hieroglyphs remaining "all the stronger if the meaning is enigmatic or figurative or paradoxical" see Thomas Green, "Erasmus' *Festina Lente*: Vulnerabilities of the Humanistic Text," in *Mimesis, From Mirror to Method, Augustine to Descartes*, ed. John D. Lyons and Stephen G. Nichols (Hanover, N.H. 1982), 136–7.

73 Giovanni Romano, "Correggio in Mantua and San Benedetto Po," in *Dosso's Fate: Painting and Court Culture in Renaissance Italy*, ed. Luisa Ciammitti, Steven F. Ostrow, and Salvatore Settis (Los Angeles 1998), 15–16.

74 Luigi Pungileoni, *Memorie istoriche di Antonio Allegri detto il Correggio*, 3 vols. (Parma 1817–22), 2, 115.

75 Canon Bartolomeo Montini was the legal representative in Parma of the ruler and poet Niccolò da Correggio: Correggio, Archivio Comunale, Notaio Affaroso Affarosi, filza 2, October 1, 1502, no. 248. On Montini as a patron of art for his chapel in the Cathedral see Alessandra Talignani, "La cappella Montini nella cattedrale di Parma: un *unicum* di forme, colori ed epigrafi nella 'periferia,'" in Periti, *Emilia e Marche nel Rinascimento*, 119–80.

76 Giancarla Periti, "From Allegri to Laetus-Lieto: The Shaping of Correggio's Artistic Distinctiveness," *Art Bulletin* 86, 3 (2004): 459–76.

77 Annibale Carracci quoted in Anne Summerscale, *Malvasia's Life of the Carracci: Commentary and Translation* (University Park, Pa. 2000), 97–8: "perchè quelle del Coreggio sono stati suoi pensieri, suoi concetti, che si vede si è cavato lui di sua testa et inventato da sé, assicurandosi solo con l'originale. Gli altri sono tutti appoggiati a qualche cosa non sua, chi al modelo, chi alle statue, chi alle carte, tutte le opere de gli altri sono rappresentate come possono esser, queste di quest'homo come veramente sono." See also Perini, *Gli scritti*, 150–51.

78 Cecil Gould, *The Paintings of Correggio* (London 1976), 40–50, referring to a possible trip to Rome as early as 1513–14. Longhi, *Il Correggio*, 71–2, 82, argues for a trip ca. 1518 before the execution of the San Paolo decoration that made it possible for the artist to discover "a purity almost like a new Greece" (*purezza quasi di novella Grecia*).

79 Ricci, *Correggio*, 63. Correggio would obviously have known and studied Raphael's *Sistine Madonna* (ca. 1512–14) once in the Benedictine Cassinese church of San Sisto in Piacenza.

80 Desiderii Erasmi Roterodami, "Moriae Encomium," in *Opera Omnia*, vol. 4.3 (Amsterdam and Oxford 1979), 68 and Desiderius Erasmus, *The Praise of Folly*, trans. and ed. Clarence H. Miller (New Haven and London 1979), 3 ("if trifles lead to serious ideas"). A useful commentary remains Erasmus, *Collected Works: Adages*, 31: "Introduction," 3–28.

81 Erasmo da Rotterdam, "Convivium fabulosum," in *Colloquia*, ed. Cecilia Asso, intro. Adriano Prosperi (Turin 2002), 706: "Nihil iucundius, quam quum serio tractantur nugae."

82 Nino Zchomelidse and Giovanni Freni, eds., *Meaning in Motion: The Semantics of Movement in Medieval Art* (Princeton 2011), vi–x.

83 The lost, obscure Milanese painting that Cesare Cesariano describes as a "geroglifico" should be attributed to either

Bramante or Leonardo, according to Carlo Pedretti, "Giorgione e Leonardo," in *Giorgione e l'umanesimo veneziano II*, ed. Rodolfo Pallucchini (Florence 1981), 485–512. On "difficult" subjects and their need for interpretative flexibility see Alexander Nagel and Lorenzo Pericolo, "Unresolved Images: An Introduction to Aporia as an Analytical Category in the Interpretation of Early Modern Art," in *Subject as Aporia in Early Modern Art*, ed. Alexander Nagel and Lorenzo Pericolo (Aldershot 2010), 1–15, esp. 7–8; Stephen J. Campbell, "Naturalism and the Venetian 'Poesia': Grafting, Metaphor, and Embodiment in Giorgione, Titian, and the Campagnolas," in ibid., 115–42.

84 Gabriele Paleotti, "On Pictures that are Obscure and Difficult to Understand," in *Discourse on Sacred and Profane Images*, trans. William McCuaig (Los Angeles 2012), 2.33.

85 Paula Findlen, "Jokes of Nature and Jokes of Knowledge: The Playfulness of Scientific Discourse in Early Modern Europe," *Renaissance Quarterly* 43, 2 (1990): 303.

86 Calvo's translation reflects the early sixteenth-century debate on Vitruvius's canon of architectural orders and the documentary study of antiquity developed within Raphael's circle in Rome. Doubts about Calvo as the scribe of the vernacular translation of Vitruvius's text have been raised by John Shearman, *Raphael in Early Modern Sources: 1483–1602*, 2 vols. (New Haven and London 2003), 1: 401–4. Quoting Vitruvius, *De Architectura*, IV.i.7–8, on the origin of the Ionic order, see Calvo's translation in Vincenzo Fontana and Paolo Morachiello, *Vitruvio e Raffaello: il "De Architectura" di Vitruvio nella traduzione inedita di Fabio Calvo Ravennate* (Rome 1975), 170–71: "Poi anchora volendo loro constituire la ede di Diana di Nova forma over spezie, seguitando quelle medesime vestigie e principii, trasferirno questa Misura del corpo de l'homo alla gracilità e gentileza delle DONNE [in Raphael's hand] e fecero la colonna alta otto grosseze per haver una forma più excelsa et alta: e socto la basa, cioè la più bassa parte della colonna, messero la spira, cioè quel ornamento nella basa facto in forma d'un circulo di corda in luoco di scarpa, et al capitello aggionsero li voluti come capilamenti over capelli crespi et avolti e cincinati e anellati a destra et a sinixtra, con li cimazi e fructi in luoco di crini ornarno la fronte d'esso; et a tutto el tronco della colonna fecero le strie over canali tirate giù dritte come le falde delle veste a usanza di matrone. Così di doi defferenzie di colonne la invenzione, una virile senza alcuno ornamento e nuda di spezie e forma, l'altra di muliebre subtilità et ornata, con le lor simetrie e misure inmitarno. Ma li posteri, procedendo e di elegantia e di subtilità di iudizio e delletatosi di più gracili e subtili modoli e misure, fecero la colonna dorica alta septe grosseze e la ionica otto grosseze e meza, e quel che fecero prima li Jonici fu detto jonico." The form of an

Ionic volute reappears at the back of Diana's chariot over the fireplace, as if to reiterate her link with this quintessentially feminine architectural order.

87 BAV, Barb. Lat. 4424, Giuliano da Sangallo, *Libro di Molti Disegni*, "Basilica Aemilia," fol. 26r; Cristiano Huelsen, *Il Libro di Giuliano da Sangallo: Codice Barberiniano Latino 4424* (Leipzig 1919), 34–5; Stefano Borsi, *Giuliano da Sangallo: i disegni di architettura e dell'antico* (Rome 1985), 144–6.

88 Vicentino's letter is cited in Luke Syson and Dora Thornton, *Objects of Virtue: Art in Renaissance Italy* (Los Angeles 2001), 93.

89 Correggio's figure of Genius has been interpreted either as a prefiguration of positive outcomes heralding good fortune or as symbolizing the element of water: Ricci, *Correggio*, 53; Panofsky, *The Iconography*, 90–92.

90 Jane Chance, *The Genius Figure in Antiquity and the Middle Ages* (New York 1975), 7–41.

91 Erasmus, "Genius Malus/An Evil Genius," in *Collected Works: Adages*, 31: 116–18; "Bonae Fortunae, or Boni Genii/Here is to good luck or A blessing on it," ibid., 32: 38–9; D. T. Starnes, "The Figure of Genius in the Renaissance," *Studies in the Renaissance* 11 (1964): 234–44, esp. 237.

92 J. A. Maritz, "From Pompey to Plymouth: The Personification of Africa in the Art of Europe," *Scolia: Studies in Classical Antiquities* 11 (2002): 65–79; J. A. Maritz, "The Image of Africa: The Evidence of the Coinage," *Acta Classica: Proceedings of the Classical Association of South Africa* 41 (2001): 105–25. Maritz has proposed strong visual and textual evidence, revisiting the standard interpretation of Africa discussed by Marcel Le Glay, "Africa," in *Lexicon Iconographicum*, 1: 250–55.

93 Pliny, *Natural History*, 28, 5, 24; Pliny, *Epistles*, trans. Betty Radice, Loeb Edition (Cambridge, Mass. 1969), 7.27.2; Claudianus, "De Bello Gildonico," in *Opera* (Parma 1493), B7r–C6v; Claudian, *The War against Gildo* [*De Bello Gildonico*], trans. Maurice Platnauer, Loeb Edition, 2 vols. (Cambridge, Mass. 1976), 1: 135–9; J. A. Maritz, "The Classical Image of Africa: The Evidence from Claudian," *Acta Classica: Proceedings of the Classical Association of South Africa* 43 (2000): 81–99.

94 Two other lunettes, one featuring a young woman striding forward and carrying an infant in frontal view on the south wall (see fig. 159), the other presenting a handsome nude youth standing guard with a spear on the opposite wall (see fig. 160) have elicited divergent interpretations and still lack a convincing explanation. The latter image could be linked to Pliny's description of Polykleitos's *Doryphoros*, which means "spear-bearer." It was considered the ultimate model statue, therefore a powerful prototype for Renaissance sculpture: Richard Tobin, "The Pose of the Doryphoros," in *Polykleitos, the Doryphoros, and Tradition*, ed. Warren G. Moon

(Madison, Wis. 1995), 52–64. For a different interpretation see Maurizio Calvesi, "Giove Statore nella *Tempesta* e nella camera di San Paolo," *Storia dell'Arte* 86 (1996): 5–12.

95 Anselmi, *Epiphyllides*, 292: "Nos argenteus numisma habemus Thadaei Ugoleti, viri eruditissimi, et amicissimi nobis manus, in quo templi facies, et aquila fulmen gerens, cui inscriptio est Petillius Capitolinum."

96 L. Richardson Jr, *A New Topographical History of Ancient Rome* (Baltimore 1992), 221–4, on the temple of Jupiter Capitolinus.

97 Giambattista Giraldi quoted in Luke Syson and Larry Keith, eds., *Leonardo da Vinci: Painter at the Court of Milan*, exh. cat. (London 2011), 250.

98 Ricci, *Correggio*, 53, pl. II; Panofsky, *The Iconography*, 70–72. Ricci traced the artist's model to a Roman coin of Domitian showing the temple of Jupiter Capitolinus, and within it the enthroned god holding a scepter in his left hand. Panofsky pointed out instead the similarity between coins representing Jupiter Capitolinus and those illustrating Serapis, a Greco-Egyptian god shown enthroned with a scepter indicating his rule of the underworld.

99 For significant observations on the architectural orders shown in *all'antica* buildings painted by Renaissance Parmese artists see Fabrizio Tonelli, "Per Correggio, Parmigianino, Anselmi, Bedoli e l'architettura," in *Parmigianino e la scuola di Parma* (Viadana [Mn] 2004), 48–9. Tonelli has recently attributed to Correggio the design of the main cloister (the so-called "cloister of the columns") of the Cassinese monastery of San Pietro in Modena (ca. 1530–32), pushing an interpretation of Correggio as an artist-architect a step forward: Fabrizio Tonelli, "Il Chiostro ionico dei Cassinesi di San Pietro a Modena: una proposta per Correggio, una per Girolamo Bedoli e alcuni spunti per Cristoforo Solari," in *Su questa Pietra . . . Nuovi studi e ricerche sull'Abbazia benedettina di San Pietro in Modena*, ed. Sonia Cavicchioli and Vincenzo Vandelli (Modena 2014), 89–106.

100 Erika Simon, *Die Götter der Römer* (Munich 1990), 107–18; Robert Schilling, "A propos de l'expression 'Iupiter Optimus Maximus,'" *Societas Academica Dacoromana* 3 (1964): 343–8.

101 Anselmi, "Iovi et Diis Omnibus," in *Epigrammaton Libri Septem*, 2.22v–23r: "Maxime optime Juppiterque, vosque/ Omnes Dii Deaeque, quis agello/Sedem ex paupere dico dedicoque/Et solemnia rite sacra et aras/Hac re, legeque, dico dedicoque/Quae dixi monumenta, sacra atque aras."

102 Claudio Franzoni, "Tra Correggio e la Grecia: Antonio Allegri e l'arte classica," in *Correggio*, ed. Anna Coliva, exh. cat. (Milan 2008), 47–57, esp. 50.

103 Frederick Kiefer, "The Conflation of Fortuna and Occasio in Renaissance Thought and Iconography," *Journal of Medieval and Renaissance Studies* 9, 1 (1979): 1–28; Iiro Kajanto,

"Interpreting Fortuna Redux," in *Homenagem a Joseph M. Piel por ocasião do seu 85 aniversário* (Tübingen 1988), 35–50.

104 Erasmus, "Fortes Fortuna Adiuvat/Fortune favours the brave," in *Adages*, 31: 187–8.

105 Erasmus, "Manum admoventi fortuna est imploranda/Set your hand to the work before you appeal to Fortune," ibid., 33: 118–19.

106 Homer, *Iliad*, trans. A. Murray, Loeb Edition (London 1925), 15.14–18. On Probus see Panofsky, *The Iconography*, 85. On the publication of Homer see Kostantinos Staikos, "Manuscripts and Printed Editions of Homer during the Renaissance," *Pharos: Journal of the Netherlands Institute in Athens* 13 (2005): 159–71; Robin Sowerby, "Early Humanist Failure with Homer (I and II)," *Journal of the Classical Tradition* 4, 1 (1997): 37–63; ibid., 4, 2 (1997): 165–94.

107 Anselmi, "In Homeri Libros," in *Epigrammaton Libri Septem*, 2.15v–16r.

108 Panofsky, *The Iconography*, 84–8; Stefania Massari, ed., *Giulio Bonasone*, 2 vols. (Rome 1983), I: 115–16.

109 On ancient remains and modern drawings displaying the flayed Marsyas see Phyllis Bober Pray and Ruth Rubinstein, eds., *Renaissance Artists and Antique Sculpture* (London 1986), 72–3, 75; Fabrizio Paolucci, "Antiquities and Antiquarians in Florence in the First Half of the 15th Century," in *The Springtime of the Renaissance: Sculpture and the Arts in Florence 1400–1460*, ed. Beatrice Paolozzi Strozzi and Marc Bormand (Florence 2013), 39–43, esp. 43; Hérica Valladares, "The *Io* in Correggio: Ovid and the Metamorphosis of a Renaissance Painter," in John North and Peter Mack, eds., *The Afterlife of Ovid* (*Bulletin of the Institute of Classical Studies Supplement 130*) (London 2015), 137–58 for the regendering of Marsyas into Hera.

110 Jean-Joseph Goux, "Vesta, or the Place of Being," *Representations* 1 (1983), 95: "What is sacred is that which cannot be touched, approached, violated; and from this point of view is the incest taboo which radically underlines the sacred by setting up women as unapproachable."

111 Giraldi, "Vesta," in *De Deis Gentium*, 205. The fifteenth-century writer Vespasiano da Bisticci had stated that the temples of the vestal virgins were the earliest equivalents of nunneries: Vespasiano da Bisticci, "De le Vergini Vestali," in *Libro delle lodi delle donne*, ed. Giuseppe Lombardi (Rome 1999), cxiv.

112 Consistent with the image of Vesta standing for virginal nuns are two other lunettes on the western wall (see fig. 156) portraying charming girls in semitransparent gowns exposing their lower legs, probably to suggest their physical and spiritual intactness or chastity, the *sine qua non* of nuns' life. They have been associated with a coin struck by Claudius bearing the inscription *Spes Augusta*: Ricci, *Correggio*, 56, pl.

113 Erasmus, "Courtship," in *Colloquies*, 39: 256–78.

114 Panofsky suggested that for this image Correggio copied the sestertius of Emperor Antoninus Pius (138–61 CE) bearing the inscription "Pietati Aug.," and featuring a woman carrying a globe and a baby, with two other children, and that his torch and globe-bearing figure "seem to greet the new-born Jupiter [in the adjacent lunette] and, as it were, to offer him the rule of the world": Panofsky, *The Iconography*, 74. Calvesi, however, associated this figure with representations of *Venus Vincitrix*: Calvesi, "Gli inconsulti," 23–36.

115 Statius, *Thebaid*, trans. J. H. Mozley, Loeb Edition (Cambridge, Mass. 1989), 7.72–4: "with bloody hand dark Bellona guides the team and plies them hard with her long spear. The off-spring of Cyllene grew stiff with terror at the sight, and cast down his eyes"; Silius Italicus, *Punica* (Parma 1481); Silius Italicus, *Punica*, trans. J. D. Duff, Loeb Edition (Cambridge, Mass. 1989), 4.438–9: "Wrath accompanied by the Furies, and countless forms of bloody death; and Bellona, busy with the reins, urged on the four courses with her fatal scourge."

116 Vladimir Juřen, "*Pan Terrificus* de Politien," *Bibliothèque de l'humanisme et Renaissance* 33 (1971): 641–5.

117 On *Pan terrificus* see Panofsky, *The Iconography*, 39–45, discussing Dürer's engraving of the *Satyr Family* (1505) as a possible, albeit elusive, model; Dempsey, *Inventing the Renaissance Putto*, 122; Campbell, *Cabinet of Eros*, 150–51.

118 According to Stefano Pierguidi, the sculptural counterpart of Correggio's Pan is the almost contemporary, small bronze satyrs by the Paduan sculptor Andrea Riccio, either standing or seated carrying a conch shell and a tall vase: Stefano Pierguidi, "Pan terrificus a Padova: i satiri con conchiglia di Andrea Riccio e Severo da Ravenna," *Bibliothèque d'humanisme et Renaissance* 68, 2 (2006): 333–40. These *bronzetti* were probably unknown to Correggio, however, and they do not seem to rely on the same textual sources as Correggio's *Pan terrificus*.

119 On bedrooms as the sites of nightmares and visions, the *locus classicus* is Cicero, *Somnium Scipionis*, ed. Alessandro Ronconi (Florence 1961), 10.

120 Ute W. Gottschall, "Securitas," in *Lexicon Iconographicum*, 8: 2.1090–93.

121 On Campagnola's Saturn, an ancient gem, and a relief still *in situ* in the triumphal arch at Benevento see Agosti, *Su Mantegna*, 87–8; Vincenzo Farinella, "Saxl, Saturno e Benevento," *Prospettiva* 40 (1985): 68–71.

122 W. Deonna, "Le Groupe des Trois Graces nues et sa descendance," *Revue archéologique* 31, 1 (1930): 274–332; Pray Bober and Rubinstein, "Three Graces," in *Renaissance Artists*, 95–7.

123 Erasmus, "Nudae Gratiae/Naked are the Graces," in *Collected Works: Adages*, 34 : 25; Horace, *Carmina*, trans. C. E. Bennett, Loeb Edition (Cambridge, Mass. 1978), 1.30.6–7; 4.7.5–6; Seneca, *De Beneficiis*, trans. John W. Basore, Loeb Edition (London 1935), 1.3.2–5. Horace portrays the Graces as goddesses of the earth's liberality, while Seneca speaks of them as an example of the giving and receiving of benefits.

124 Erasmus's essay "Between Friends all is Common" opens his *Adages*: Kathy Eden, *Friends Hold All Things in Common: Tradition, Intellectual Property, and the Adages of Erasmus* (New Haven and London 2001).

125 Panofksy, *The Iconography*, 38.

126 Particularly significant is the notion of reciprocity between the painted space and the beholder as if their boundaries were blurred: Dunlop, *Painted Palaces*, 120; Campbell, "Mantegna's *Camera Picta*," 314–33.

127 Paolo Valesio, *Ascoltare il silenzio: la retorica come teoria* (Bologna 1986), 382: "Il silenzio che serve specificamente a sottolineare e, per così dire, magnificare le forme del dire che lo incorniciano: un tal silenzio copre l'intera gamma che va da figure retoriche come la reticenza . . . fino alla fenomenologia della punteggiatura, che possono essere veduti anche come modi di creare minuscoli spazi di silenzio tra le parole" (silence, which serves specifically to underline and, so to speak, to magnify the verbal forms that frame it; such a silence spans the entire series ranging from rhetorical figures like reticence . . . to the phenomenology of punctuation, which can also be seen as ways to create small intervals of silence between words).

CONCLUSION

1 On the dense dialectic between rules and lifestyle with reference to Franciscanism, a form of regulated monastic life that this book does not cover but that, nonetheless, had a strong impact on the perception of art, see Giorgio Agamben, *Altissima povertà: regole monastiche e forma di vita* (Vicenza 2011).

2 Roberto Contini and Francesco Solinas, *Artemisia Gentileschi: Storia di una passione*, exh. cat. (Milan 2011), 170.

ABBREVIATIONS

ASPr   Archivio di Stato, Parma
BAV   Biblioteca Apostolica Vaticana, Vatican City
BCA   Biblioteca Comunale dell'Archiginnasio, Bologna
BNC   Biblioteca Nazionale Centrale, Florence
BP   Biblioteca Palatina, Parma
SBEAP   Soprintendenza Belle Arti e Paesaggio per le
    Province di Parma e Piacenza, Parma

PRIMARY SOURCES

BCA, MS B 778, Giovanni Boccadiferro, "Discorso sopra il
    Governo delle Monache," in Baldassare Carrati, *Miscellanea
    di notizie storiche bolognesi*, fols. 166r–198v

Bologna, Archivio Generale Arcivescovile, Miscellanee Vecchie
    804

Cambridge, Corpus Christi College, Parker Library, MS 16,
    Cronica majora, Part II

Correggio, Archivio Comunale, Notaio Affaroso Affarosi

Ferrara, Biblioteca Ariostea, S.16.5.10, *Prologo de l'ordine del
    vivere neli monasteri de monache & temporale & spirituale. Excepta
    da diversi scripti de Hieronymo ad Eustochio sua Figliuola spiritu-
    ale & ale sorelle* (Ferrara 1497)

Florence
    Biblioteca Riccardiana, MS 1220 I, Bartolomeus Fontius,
        "De Locis Persianis"
    Biblioteca Laurenziana, Plut. 44.35, Georgii Parmensis,
        Divinum Opus de Magia Disciplina
    BNC, MS Pal. 726, Agostino Strozzi, "Defensione de le
        donne"
    Fiori di Virtù (Venice 1500)
Oxford, Bodleian Library, MS Canon. Lat. Misc. 280
Paris, Bibliothèque Nationale, MS Lat. 5825F.
Parma, ASPr
    Conventi Soppressi, Serie IX, Benedettine di San Paolo
    Conventi e Confraternite, VIII, Sant'Alessandro
    Culto, "Controversie tra vescovo e comune di Parma," busta
        2082
    Dipartimento di Grazia e Giustizia e Buongoverno
    Diplomi Pontifici
    Direzione del Patrimonio dello Stato
    Documenti Privati
    Documenti Imperiali
    Mappe del Patrimonio dello Stato, vol. VI, no. 584, June 4,
        1851, *Pianta icnografica* [sic] *dell'edifizio di San Paolo e sue
        dipendenze in Parma*
    Notarile, Girolamo Balestra
        Gherardo Mastagi
        Galeazzo Piazza
        Gaspare Prati

Antonio Maria Rainieri

Giovanni Ludovico Sacca

Pergamene Miniate

Presidenza dell'Interno

Parma, BP

MS Parm. 446, Carlo Vaghi, "Miscellanee Diverse"

Fondo Moreau de Saint Mery, cassetta 46, fasc. XXXI/I

MS Parm. 922, Angelo Mario di Edoari da Erba, *Compendio copiosissimo dell'Origine, Antichità, Successi e Nobiltà della Città di Parma, suo popolo, e Territorio estratto dal raccolto da varii Autori da Angelo de Edoari da Herba Parmiggiano l'anno 1572*

MS Parm. 535, Smeraldo Smeraldi, "Diario delle visite per vie, canali, edifici dal feb. 1598 all'agosto 1600"

Parma, SBEAP

Roberto Bergamaschi and Giovanna Menegazzi, "Relazione di Restauro"

MS 101, Enrico Scarabelli Zunti, "Documenti e memorie di belle arti parmigiane," vol. II (1451–1509)

MS 111, Enrico Scarabelli Zunti, "Materiale per una guida artistica e storica di Parma: Chiese e conventi," vol. II

Reggio Emilia, Biblioteca Panizzi, MS C 398, Michele Fabrizio Ferrarini, "Antiquarium"

Vatican City, BAV

Barb. Lat. 4424, Giuliano da Sangallo, *Libro di Molti Disegni*

MS Urb. Lat. 899, *Ordine delle nozze dello Illustrissimo Signore Meser Costantio Sfortia de Aragonia et della Illustrissima Madonna Camilla de Aragonia sua consorte nell'anno 1475*

Venice, Biblioteca Marciana, Cod. Cicogna 2570, *Monache della Città e Diocesi di Venezia*, 1509

PRINTED SOURCES

Acidini Luchinat, Cristina, "La grottesca," in *Storia dell'arte italiana*, vol. II (Turin 1982), 161–200.

Adorni, Bruno, ed., *L'Abbazia benedettina di San Giovanni Evangelista a Parma* (Milan 1979).

——, ed., *Santa Maria della Steccata a Parma* (Parma 1982).

——, and Mariarita Furlotti, "L'architettura a Parma all'epoca del Parmigianino," in *Parmigianino e il manierismo europeo*, ed. Lucia Fornari Schianchi (Milan 2002), 360–69.

Affò, Ireneo, *Memorie di Taddeo Ugoleto parmigiano bibliotecario di Mattia Corvino re d'Ungheria* (Parma 1781).

——, *Saggio di memorie su la tipografia parmense del secolo XV* (Parma 1791).

——, *Storia della città di Parma*, 4 vols. (Parma 1792).

——, *Ragionamento del Padre Ireneo Affò sopra una stanza dipinta dal celeberrimo Antonio Allegri da Correggio nel monistero di S. Paolo in Parma* (Parma 1794).

Agosti, Giovanni, *Bambaia e il classicismo lombardo* (Turin 1990).

——, *Su Mantegna I* (Milan 2005).

Agosti, Giovanni, and Dominique Thiébaut, eds., *Mantegna 1431–1506*, exh. cat. (Paris 2010).

Agosti, Giovanni, Rossana Sacchi, and Jacopo Stoppa, eds., *Bernardino Luini e i suoi figli. Itinerari* (Milan 2014).

Agrippa von Nettesheim, Henricus Cornelius, *Three Books of Occult Philosophy*, ed. Donal Tyson (St. Paul, Minn. 1995).

——, *Declamation on the Nobility and Preeminence of the Female Sex*, trans. and ed. Albert Rabil Jr. (Chicago and London 1996).

Ajmar, Marta, "Exemplary Women in Renaissance Italy: Ambivalent Models of Behaviour?" in *Women in Italian Renaissance Culture and Society*, ed. Letizia Panizza (Oxford 2000), 244–64.

——, "Talking Pots: Strategies for Producing Novelty and the Consumption of Painted Pottery in Renaissance Italy," in *The Art Market in Italy: 15th–17th Centuries*, ed. Marcello Fantoni, Louisa Matthew, and Sara F. Matthews Grieco (Modena 2003), 55–64.

——, and Dora Thornton, "When is a Portrait not a Portrait? Belle Donne on Maiolica and the Renaissance Praise of Local Beauties," in *The Image of the Individual: Portraits in the Renaissance*, ed. Nicholas Mann and Luke Syson (London 1998), 138–53.

Akbari, Suzanne Conklin, *Seeing through the Veil: Optical Theory and Medieval Allegory* (Toronto 2004).

Alberti, Leon Battista, *On Painting*, trans. Cecil Grayson (London 1972).

——, *On the Art of Building in Ten Books*, trans. Joseph Rykwert et al. (Cambridge 1988).

Albertini, Francesco, *Opusculum de mirabilibus nouae & ueteris vrbis Romae* (Rome 1510).

Albertini Ottolenghi, Maria Grazia, "L'altro 'centro': Alessandro Sforza e Pesaro," in *Emilia e Marche nel Rinascimento: l'identità visiva della "Periferia,"* ed. Giancarla Periti (Azzano [Bg] 2005), 253–72.

Alessandrini, Clelia, "San Paolo: dalla riscoperta della Camera all'attuale sistemazione museografica," *Aurea Parma* (2012): 47–56.

Alighieri, Dante, *Divine Comedy*, trans. Charles S. Singleton, 3 vols. (Princeton 1970).

Allen, Denise, and Peta Motture, eds., *Andrea Riccio: Renaissance Master of Bronze*, exh. cat. (New York 2008).

Allen, Don Cameron, *Mysteriously Meant: The Rediscovery of Pagan Symbolism and Allegorical Interpretation in the Renaissance* (Baltimore and London 1970).

Allodi, Giovanni Maria, *Serie cronologica dei vescovi di Parma*, 2 vols. (Parma 1856).

Althusser, Louis, "Ideology and Ideological State Apparatuses (Notes Towards an Investigation)," in *Lenin and Philosophy, and Other Essays*, trans. Ben Brewster (New York 2001), 127–86.

Angelini, Alessandro, "Jacometto Veneziano e gli umanisti: Proposta per il 'Ritratto di Luca Pacioli e di Guidubaldo da Montefeltro' del Museo di Capodimonte," *Prospettiva* 147–8 (2012): 126–49.

Ansani, Michele, "La provvista dei benefici (1450–1466): Strumenti e limiti dell'intervento ducale," in *Gli Sforza, la chiesa lombarda, la corte di Roma: Strutture e pratiche beneficiarie nel ducato di Milano (1450–1535)*, ed. Giorgio Chittolini (Naples 1989), 1–113.

——, *Camera Apostolica: Documenti relativi alla diocesi del ducato di Milano. I "Libri Annatarum" di Innocenzo VIII (1458–1471)* (Milan 1994).

Anselmi Nepotis, Georgii, *Hecuba* (Parma 1506).

Anselmi, Georgii *Epigrammaton Libri Septem: Sosthyrides Peplum Palladis Aeglogae Quattor* (Parma 1526; Venice 1528).

——, *In Cupidinem Captivum* (Parma 1506).

Arbasino, Alberto, *Su Correggio* (Milan 2008).

Arcangeli, Letizia, "Ragioni politiche della disciplina monastica: il caso di Parma tra Quattrocento e Cinquecento," in *Donna, disciplina, creanza cristiana dal XV al XVII secolo: Studi e testi a stampa*, ed. Gabriella Zarri (Rome 1996), 165–87.

——, "Sul linguaggio della politica nell'Italia del primo Cinquecento: le fonti della città di Parma," *Per Marino Berengo: Studi degli Allievi* (Milan 2000), 76–113.

——, "Tra Milano e Roma: Esperienze politiche nella Parma del primo Cinquecento," in *Emilia e Marche nel rinascimento: l'identità visiva della "Periferia,"* ed. Giancarla Periti (Azzano [Bg] 2005), 89–118.

——, "Principi, *homines* e 'partesani' nel ritorno dei Rossi," in *Le signorie dei Rossi tra XIV e XVI secolo* (Florence 2007), 231–306.

——, "'Come bosco et spelunca di latroni': Città e ordine pubblico a Parma e nello stato di Milano tra Quattrocento e Cinquecento," in *Le polizie informali*, ed. Livio Antonelli (Rubbettino [CZ] 2010), 65–90.

Aretino, Pietro, *Dialoghi: Ragionamento della Nanna e dell'Antonia*, ed. Giulio Davico Bonino (Turin 1975).

Armenini, Giovanni Battista, *De' veri precetti della pittura* (Ravenna 1587; Turin 1980).

Armstrong, Lilian, "Il Maestro di Pico: un miniatore veneziano del tardo Quattrocento," *Saggi e memorie di storia dell'arte* 17 (1990): 7–39.

Artioli, Angela, *Il monastero di S. Antonio in Polesine* (Ferrara 1996).

Aste, Richard, "Bartolomeo Bettini and his Florentine 'Chamber' Decoration," in *Venus and Love: Michelangelo and the New Ideal of Beauty*, ed. Franca Falletti and Jonathan Katz Nelson, exh. cat. (Florence 2002), 3–25.

Augustine, Saint, *Expositions on the Book of Psalms*, trans. J. Tweed, 4 vols. (Oxford 1850).

——, *De Civitate Dei* [*City of God*] (Stuttgart 1981).

——, *Confessions*, ed. Henry Chadwick (Oxford and New York 1991).

Ausonius, *Opera* (Parma 1499).

Averlino, Antonio *see under* Filarete.

Bacchi, Andrea, "Vicende della pittura nell'età di Giovanni II Bentivoglio," in *Bentivolorum magnificentia: principe e cultura a Bologna nel rinascimento*, ed. Bruno Basile (Bologna 1984), 285–335.

——, et al., *Francesco Marmitta* (Turin 1994).

Bachelard, Gaston, *The Poetics of Space*, trans. Maria Jolas, foreword Etienne Gilson (Boston 1969).

Baernstein, Renée P., *A Convent Tale: A Century of Sisterhood in Spanish Milan* (New York and London 2002).

Bagatin, Pier Luigi, *Le pitture di Lorenzo e Cristoforo da Lendinara* (Treviso 2004).

Bajardi, Andrea, *Trattato Amoroso di Adriano e Narcisa intitolato Philogene* (Parma 1508).

Balavoine, Claudie, "Bouquets de fleurs et colliers de perles: sur les recueils de formes brèves au XVI siècle," in *Les Formes brèves de la prose et le discours discontinu (XVI–XVII siècles)*, ed. Jean Lafond (Paris 1984), 51–72.

Ballardini, Gaetano, "Il pavimento maiolicato di San Paolo," *Rassegna della istruzione artistica* (1936): 33–8.

Balsamo, Luigi, "Editoria e umanesimo a Parma tra Quattro e Cinquecento," in *Parma e l'umanesimo italiano*, ed. Paola Medioli Masotti (Padua 1986), 77–95.

Bambach Cappel, Carmen, "Leonardo, Tagliente, and Dürer: 'la scienza del far di groppi,'" *Achademia Leonardi Vinci* 4 (1991): 72–98.

Bambach, Carmen, et al., eds., *Correggio and Parmigianino: Master Draughtsmen of the Renaissance*, exh. cat. (London 2000).

——, *Leonardo da Vinci: Master Draftsman*, exh. cat. (New York 2003).

Bandini, Laura, "Il monastero femminile di San Paolo Apostolo in Parma dalla fondazione al xv secolo," *Società, donne e storia* 2 (2004): 101–281.

——, "La nomina delle badesse nel monastero di San Paolo: Maristella Aldighieri e Agnese Benedetti," *Aurea Parma* 88, 2 (2004): 245–56.

Banzola, Maria Ortensia, "Il Palazzo del vescovado," *Parma nell'arte* 14, 2 (1982), 25–51.

Banzola, Vincenzo, "I lavori di restauro al cortile del vescovado," in *Saggi e testimonianze in onore di Francesco Borri* (Parma 1982), 13–34.

Barbo, Ludovico, "Forma Orationis et Meditationis Congregationi Monachorum S. Iustine," in *Ludovico Barbo (1381–1443)*, ed. Ildefonso Tassi (Rome 1952).

Barkan, Leonard, *The Gods made Flesh: Metamorphosis and the Pursuit of Paganism* (New Haven and London 1986).

——, *Unearthing the Past: Archeology and Aesthetics in the Making of Renaissance Culture* (New Haven and London 1999).

Barocelli, Francesco, *La Pinacoteca Stuard di Parma: gli ambienti storici, le sculture, le incisioni, gli arredi* (Milan 2005).

——, ed., *Il Correggio nella camera di San Paolo* (Milan 2010).

Barry, Fabio, "Walking on Water: Cosmic Floors in Antiquity and the Middle Ages," *Art Bulletin* 89, 4 (2007): 627–57.

Battioni, Gianluca, "Per la storia della cultura parmense in età sforzesca: l'inventario catalogo di una libreria cittadina del 1491," *Archivio storico per le province parmensi* 38 (1986): 432–68.

——, "Sacromoro da Rimini ed il governo della diocesi parmense," in *Parma e l'umanesimo italiano*, ed. Paola Medioli Masotti (Padua 1986), 55–73.

Battisti, Eugenio, *L'Antirinascimento*, 2 vols. (Milan 1989).

Baxandall, Michael, *Painting and Experience in Fifteenth-Century Italy. A Primer in the Social History of Pictorial Style*, 2nd ed. (Oxford 1988).

Bayer, Andrea, ed., *Art and Love in Renaissance Italy* (New York 2008).

Bell, Susan Groag, "Medieval Women Book Owners: Arbiters of Lay Piety and Ambassadors of Culture," *Signs* 7 (1982): 742–68.

Belotti, Giampietro, ed., *San Salvatore e Santa Giulia: Storia di un monastero femminile dalla fondazione longobarda alla destinazione museale* (Brescia 2004).

Belozerskaya, Marina, *Luxury Arts of the Renaissance* (Los Angeles 2005).

Belting, Hans, *Likeness and Presence: A History of the Image before the Era of Art*, trans. Edmund Jephcott (Chicago 1994).

——, *An Anthropology of Images: Picture, Medium, Body*, trans. Thomas Dunlap (Princeton and Oxford 2011).

Bembo, Pietro, *Gli Asolani*, ed. Giorgio Dilemmi (Florence 1991).

Benassi, Umberto, *Storia di Parma*, 5 vols. (Parma 1899–1906).

Regola di Sancto Benedecto nuovamente vulgarizata (Florence after 1500).

Bentivoglio, Enzo, "Bramante e il geroglifico di Viterbo," *Mitteilungen des Kunsthistorischen Institutes in Florenz* 16 (1992): 167–74.

Berardi, Paride, *L'antica maiolica di Pesaro dal XIV al XVII secolo* (Florence 1984).

Bergomense, Jacopo Philippo, *De Plurimis Claris selectisque Mulieribus* (Ferrara 1497).

Bernard of Clairvaux, *The "Things of Greater Importance": Bernard of Clairvaux's Apologia and the Medieval Attitude toward Art*, ed. Conrad Rudolph (Philadelphia 1990).

——, *On the Song of Songs I*, trans. Kilian Walsh (Kalamazoo 1981).

Bertalot, Ludovico, and Augusto Campana, "Gli Scritti di Iacopo Zeno ed il suo elogio di Ciriaco di Ancona," *Bibliofilia* 41 (1939): 356–76.

Berti, Giordano, and Andrea Vitali, eds., *Le carte di corte: i tarocchi. Gioco e magia alla corte degli Estensi* (Bologna 1988).

Bettini, Alessandro, "Le maioliche della discordia," *Ceramicantica* 2 (1991): 12–18.

——, "La ceramica a Pesaro tra il xiv e il xvii secolo," in *Fatti di ceramica nelle Marche dal Trecento al Novecento*, ed. Gian Carlo Bojani (Macerata 1997), 31–95.

Bettini, Maurizio, *Le Orecchie di Hermes: Studi di antropologia e letterature classiche* (Turin 2000).

Biblia Sacra Iuxta Vulgatam Versionem, ed. Robert Weber (Stuttgart 1994).

Billanovich, Maria Pia, "Una miniera di epigrafi e di antichità: il chiostro maggiore di Santa Giustina a Padova," *Italia medioevale e umanistica* 12 (1969): 197–293.

Binaghi Olivari, Maria Teresa, *Sacro e profano nella pittura di Bernardino Luini* (Milan 1975).

——, *Bernardino Luini* (Milan 2007).

Bini, Luigi, "Le lune della badessa," *Ceramica* 9 (1954): 28–32.

Biondo, Flavio, *Opera* (Basel 1531).

Bisticci, Vespasiano da, "De le Vergini Vestali," in *Libro delle lodi delle donne*, ed. Giuseppe Lombardi (Rome 1999).

Blake McHam, Sarah, *Pliny and the Artistic Culture of the Italian Renaissance: The Legacy of the Natural History* (New Haven and London 2013).

Bober, Phyllis Pray, and Ruth Rubinstein, eds., *Renaissance Artists and Antique Sculpture* (London 1986).

Boccaccio, Giovanni, *Genealogiae Deorum Gentilium Libri*, ed. Vincenzo Romano (Bari 1951).

——, *In Defense of Poetry: Genealogiae Deorum Gentilium Liber XIV*, ed. Jeremy Reedy (Toronto 1978).

——, *Corbaccio*, intro. and notes Francesco Erbani (Milan 1988).

——, *Decameron*, ed. Vittore Branca (Turin 1991).

Bock, Sebastian, ed., *Bestandskataloge der weltlichen Ortsstiftungen der Stadt Freiburg i. Br. die Textilien*, 5 vols. (Freiburg 2001).

Bois, Yve-Alain, review, "Panofsky Early and Late," *Art in America* 73, 7 (1985): 9–15.

Bolzoni, Lina, *Il Cuore di cristallo: ragionamenti d'amore, poesia e ritratto nel rinascimento* (Turin 2010).

Bonde, Sheila, and Clark Maines, "A Room of One's Own: Elite Spaces in Monasteries of the Reform Movement and an Abbot's Parlor at the Augustinian Saint-Jean-des-Vignes, Soissons (France)," in *Religion and Belief in Medieval Europe*, ed. Guy de Boe and Frans Verhaeghe, 4 vols. (Zellik 1997), 4: 43–53.

——, "Monastic Struggle and Ritual Resolution: Centrality and Community in the Gothic Chapter Room," in *Saint-Jean-des-Vignes in Soissons: Approaches to its Architecture, Archeology, and History*, ed. Sheila Bonde and Clark Maines (Turnhout 2003), 262–302.

Bonfini, Antonio, *La Latinizzazione del Trattato di Architettura di Filarete (1488–89)*, ed. Maria Beltramini (Pisa 2000).

Bormand, Marc, "The *Spiritelli* of the Renaissance," in *The Springtime of the Renaissance: Sculpture and the Arts in Florence 1400–1600*, ed. Beatrice Paolozzi Strozzi and Marc Bormand, exh. cat. (Florence 2013), 111–17.

Borsi, Stefano, *Giuliano da Sangallo: i disegni di architettura e dell'antico* (Rome 1985).

Bosco, Francesca Cortesi, *Gli affreschi dell'Oratorio Suardi a Trescore* (Milan 1997).

Botta, Ascanio, *Il Rurale secondo le prime due edizioni del 1521 e 1524*, ed. Manuela Rossi (Cremona 1985).

Bourda, Louise, and Anne Dunlop, eds., *Art and the Augustinian Order in Renaissance Italy* (Aldershot 2007).

Bragaglia, Cristina, "Girolamo del Santo e gli affreschi del Chiostro maggiore di Santa Giustina a Padova: Fonti iconografiche," *Bollettino del Museo civico di Padova* 82 (1993): 171–94.

Braghetti, Simona, "La 'perfetta monaca': Creanza cristiana in convento tra letteratura, precettistica e iconografia," in *Vita artistica nel monastero femminile: Exempla*, ed. Vera Fortunati (Bologna 2002), 43–76.

Branca, Vittore, *Poliziano e l'umanesimo della parola* (Turin 1983).

Braunfels, Wolfgang, *Monasteries of Western Europe: The Architecture of the Orders* (London 1972).

Bridgeman, Jane, "Condecenti et netti . . .": Beauty, Dress and Gender in Italian Renaissance Art," in *Concepts of Beauty in Renaissance Art*, ed. Francis Ames-Lewis and Mary Rogers (Aldershot 1998), 44–51.

——, *A Renaissance Wedding: The Celebration at Pesaro for the Marriage of Costanzo Sforza and Camilla Marzano d'Aragona (26–30 May 1475)* (Brepols 2013).

Broude, Norma, and Mary Garrard, *Reclaiming Female Agency: Feminist Art History after Postmodernism* (Berkeley 2005).

Brown, Malcom C., "The Palazzo di San Sebastiano (1506–1512) and the Art Patronage of Francesco II Gonzaga, Fourth Marquis of Mantova," *Gazette des beaux-arts* 139 (1997): 131–80.

Bruzelius, Caroline, and Constance H. Berman, eds., "Monastic Architecture for Women," *Gesta* 31, 2 (1992): 73–134.

Buettner, Brigitte, *Boccaccio's Des Cleres et nobles femmes: System of Signification in an Illuminated Manuscript* (Seattle 1996).

Buganza, Stefania, "Floriano Ferramola rivisitato," *Arte cristiana* 8 (1998): 121–38.

Bugge, John, *Virginitas: An Essay in the History of a Medieval Ideal* (The Hague 1975).

Burnett, Charles, "The Scapulimancy of Giorgio Anselmi's *Divinum Opus de Magia Disciplina*," in *Magic and Divination in the Middle Ages* (Aldershot 1996), 63–79.

Butler, Judith C., *Immodest Acts: The Life of a Lesbian Nun in Renaissance Italy* (New York 1986).

Bynum, Caroline Walker, "Women's Stories, Women's Symbols: A Critique of Victor Turner's Theory of Liminality," in *Anthropology and the Study of Religion*, ed. Robert L. Moore and Frank Reynolds (Chicago 1984), 105–25.

——, *Holy Feast and Holy Fast: The Religious Significance of Food to Medieval Women* (Berkeley 1987).

——, "Religious Women in the Later Middle Ages," in *Christian Spirituality: High Middle Ages and Reformation*, ed. Jill Raitt, Bernard McGinn, and John Meyendorff (New York 1987), 121–39.

——, *Metamorphosis and Identity* (New York 2001).

——, *Christian Materiality: An Essay on Religion in Late Medieval Europe* (New York 2011).

Cairns, Francis, *Tibullus: A Hellenistic Poet at Rome* (Cambridge 1979).

Callimachus, *Hymn to Zeus*, trans. A. W. Mair, Loeb Edition (Cambridge, Mass. 1969).

Calore, Andrea, "'Il palatium abbatis' di S. Giustina: Sec. XII," in *I Benedettini a Padova e nel territorio padovano attraverso i secoli*, exh. cat. (Padua 1980), 45–54.

Calvesi, Maurizio, "Gli inconsulti ed i virtuosi," *Art & Dossier* (1990): 23–36.

——, "Giove Statore nella *Tempesta* e nella camera di San Paolo," *Storia dell'arte* 86 (1996): 5–12.

Camerlengo, Lia, "La loggia del principe. Temi mitologici negli affreschi di Romanino a Trento: fonti e motivi," in *Romanino: un pittore in rivolta nel Rinascimento italiano*, exh. cat. (Milan 2006), 258–71.

Camille, Michael, *The Gothic Idol: Ideology and Image-Making in Medieval Art* (Cambridge 1989).

——, *Image on the Edge: The Margins of Medieval Art* (Cambridge, Mass. 1992).

——, *The Medieval Art of Love: Objects and Subjects of Desire* (New York 1998).

——, "Before the Gaze: The Internal Senses and Late Medieval Practices of Seeing," in *Visuality Before and Beyond the Renaissance: Seeing as Others Saw*, ed. Robert S. Nelson (Cambridge 2000), 197–223.

Camisani, Enrico, "Obizio," in *Bibliotheca Sanctorum*, 16 vols., (Rome 1967), 9: 1085–6.

Campagnol, Isabella, *Forbidden Fashions: Invisible Luxuries in Early Venetian Convents* (Lubbock, Tex. 2014).

——, "Veli rivelatori: le donne veneziane e il significato simbolico del velo," in *Velo e velatio: Significato e rappresentazione nella cultura figurativa dei secoli XV–XVII*, ed. Gabriella Zarri (Rome 2014), 55–72.

Campana, Augusto, "Poesie umanistiche relative a ceramiche," *Faenza* 32 (1946): 59–68.

Campbell, Jean C., *The Game of Courting and the Art of the Commune of San Gimignano, 1290–1320* (Princeton 1997).

——, "Pier Maria Rossi's Treasure: Love, Knowledge, and the Invention of the Source in the Camera d'oro at Torrechiara," in *Emilia e Marche nel Rinascimento: l'identità visiva della "periferia,"* ed. Giancarla Periti (Azzano San Paolo [Bg], 2005), 63–88

Campbell, Stephen J., *Cosmè Tura of Ferrara: Style, Politics and the Renaissance City, 1450–1495* (New Haven and London 1997).

——, "Fare una Cosa Morta Parer Viva": Michelangelo, Rosso Fiorentino, and the (Un)Divinity of Art," *The Art Bulletin* 84, 4 (2002): 596–620.

——, "Mantegna's Triumph: The Cultural Politics of Imitation 'all'antica' at the Court of Mantua, 1490–1530," in *Artists at Court: Image-Making and Identity, 1300–1550* (Chicago 2004), 91–105.

——, *The Cabinet of Eros: Renaissance Mythological Painting and the Studiolo of Isabella d'Este* (New Haven and London 2004).

——, "Naturalism and the Venetian 'Poesia': Grafting, Metaphor, and Embodiment in Giorgione, Titian, and the Campagnolas," in *Subject as Aporia in Early Modern Art*, ed. Alexander Nagel and Lorenzo Pericolo (Farnham 2010), 115–42.

——, "Renaissance Naturalism and the Jewish Bible: Ferrara, Brescia, Bergamo, 1520–1540," in *Judaism and Christian Art: Aesthetic Anxieties from the Catacombs to Colonialism*, ed. Herbert L. Kessler and David Nirenberg (Philadelphia, Pa. and Oxford 2011), 291–327.

——, "Mantegna's *Camera Picta*: Visuality and Pathos," *Art History* 37, 2 (2014): 314–33.

Campori, Giuseppe, *Maiolica e porcellana di Ferrara nei secoli XV e XVI* (Pesaro 1879).

Cannon, Joanna, *Religious Poverty, Visual Riches: Art in the Dominican Churches of Central Italy in the Thirteenth and Fourteenth Centuries* (New Haven and London 2013).

Canopi, Anna Maria, "Santa Scolastica," in *Monachesimo benedettino femminile* (Seregno [Mi] 1994), 17–27.

Capelli, Gianni, and Pier Paolo Mendogni, *Il Castello di Torrechiara: storia. Architettura dipinti* (Parma 1994).

Cappellanus, Andrea, *On Love*, trans. P. G. Welsh (London 1982).

Carlone, Mariagrazia, "Monache in immagini musicali," in *Soror mea, sponsa mea: Arte e musica nei conventi femminili in Italia tra Cinquecento e Seicento*, ed. Chiara Sirk and Candace Smith (Venice 2009), 117–145.

Caroti, Stefano, and Stefano Zamponi, *Lo scrittoio di Bartolomeo Fonzio umanista fiorentino* (Milan 1974).

Carpesani, Francesco, *Commentaria Suorum Temporum (1457–1527)*, ed. Giacomo Zarotti (Parma 1975).

Carruthers, Mary, *The Craft of Thought: Meditation, Rhetoric, and the Making of Images, 400–1200* (Cambridge 1998).

Cartwright, Sarah, "Antiquarianism in Pesaro: Text and Image in MS Urb. Lat. 899," *Rivista di storia della miniatura* 13 (2009): 129–40.

Castagnola, Raffaella, ed., *I Guicciardini e le scienze occulte* (Florence 1990).

Castelli, Giovanni Battista, *Visitatio civitatis Parmae 1578–79*, with notes by Enrico dall'Olio, 2 vols. (Parma 2000).

Castelli, Patrizia, *I geroglifici e il mito dell'Egitto nel Rinascimento* (Florence 1979).

Castelnuovo, Enrico, and Carlo Ginzburg, "Center and Periphery," in *History of Italian Art*, trans. Ellen Bianchini and Claire Dorey, 2 vols. (Cambridge 1994), 1: 29–112.

Castiglione, Baldassar, *The Book of the Courtier*, trans. Charles S. Singleton (Garden City, N.Y. 1959).

Cattelani, Remo, "ΙΩΑΝΝΕ ΠΛΑΚΗΝΤΙΗ IOANNA PLACENTIA ABB.," *Parma nell'arte* 7, 1 (1975): 7–20.

Cavazzoni, Maria Chiara, "Jacopo Loschi: Proposte per il catalogo e lo sviluppo stilistico," *Arte Cristiana* 86 (1998): 5–16.

Caviceo, Jacopo, *Il Peregrino*, ed. Luigi Vignali (Rome 1993).

Cecchinelli, Cristina, "La riforma dei monasteri femminili a Parma nel primo Cinquecento: S. Paolo e S. Quintino," *Aurea Parma* 84, 1 (2005): 3–48.

——, "Agli esordi del potere farnesiano a Parma: il cardinale Alessandro Farnese vescovo-amministratore della diocesi (1509–1534)," *Rivista di storia della chiesa in Italia* 1 (2009): 91–124.

——, "Il contratto della casa presa in affitto a Parma dal Correggio nel 1523 alla presenza del Rondani," *Aurea Parma*, 93, 3 (2009): 347–68.

Celenza, Christopher S., *Piety and Pythagoras in Renaissance Florence: The Symbolum Nesianum* (Leiden 2001).

Celio Calcagnini, *Opera Aliquot* (Basel 1544).

Cennini, Cennino, *Il libro d'arte*, ed. Franco Brunello (Vicenza 1971).

Certeau, Michel de, *The Practice of Everyday Life*, trans. Steven F. Rendall (Berkeley, Cal. 1984).

——, *Culture in the Plural*, ed. Luce Giand (London and Minneapolis, 1997).

——, and Catherine Porter, "The Gaze in Nicholas of Cusa," *Diacritics* 17, 3 (1987): 2–38.

Ceruti Burgio, Anna, "Strutture narrative e modelli culturali del "Peregrino" di Iacopo Caviceo," *Aurea Parma* 62 (1978): 42–54.

——, *Studi sul Quattrocento parmense* (Pisa 1988).

Cesari, Mariarosa, "'Per encomiar le donzelle ch'entrano nel chiostro': Pubblicazioni celebrative per monacazioni femminili tra Sei e Settecento nelle raccolte dell'Archiginnasio," *Il Carrobbio* 19/20 (1993–94): 203–22.

Cesariano, Cesare, *De Architectura libri dece traducti de latino in vulgare affigurati* (Como 1521).

Chance, Jane, *The Genius Figure in Antiquity and the Middle Ages* (New York 1975).

Chapman, Hugo, Tom Henry, and Carol Plazzotta, *Raphael: From Urbino to Rome*, exh. cat. (London 2004).

Charlet, Jean-Louis, "La bibliothèque, le livre et le papier d'après Francesco Mario Grapaldo: De *Partibus Aedium*, 2.9.," in *Studi latini in ricordo di Rita Cappelletto* (Urbino 1996), 347–64.

Chastel, André, *La grottesque: essai sur l' "ornement sans nom"* (Paris 1988).

——, and Cesare de Seta, "Musaici di legname, cioè tarsie," *FMR* 4 (1987): 76–104.

Chavin de Malan, Emile, *Histoire de Saint François d'Assise* (Paris 1841).

Cherubino da Spoleto, *Regole della Vita Spirituale e della Vita Matrimoniale* (Parma 1487).

Chiasson, Charles C., "Myth, Ritual and Authorial Control in Herodotus' Story of Cleobis and Biton (Hist. 1.31)," *American Journal of Philology* 126 (2005): 41–64.

Chines, Loredana, *La parola degli antichi: Umanesimo emiliano tra scuola e poesia* (Rome 1998).

Chittolini, Giorgio, "Il particolarismo signorile e feudale in Emilia tra Quattro e Cinquecento," in *La formazione dello stato regionale e le istituzioni del contado* (Turin 1979), 254–91.

Chiusa, Maria Cristina, *Alessandro Araldi: la "maniera antico-moderna"a Parma* (Parma 1996).

Christiansen, Keith, and Stefan Weppelmann, eds., *The Renaissance Portrait from Donatello to Bellini*, exh. cat. (New York 2011).

Ciaroni, Andrea, *Maioliche del Quattrocento a Pesaro: Frammenti di storia dell'arte ceramica dalla bottega dei Fedeli* (Florence 2004).

Cicero, *Orator*, trans. H. Hubbel, Loeb Edition (Cambridge, Mass. 1939).

——, *Somnium Scipionis*, ed. Alessandro Ronconi (Florence 1961).

Cirillo, Giuseppe, "Girolamo Bedoli per i Bergonzi in San Francesco del Prato e altre congiunture di catalogo," *Parma nell'arte* 11, 2 (2005): 7–50.

Clark, Mark Edward, "Spes in the Early Imperial Cult: The Hope of Augustus," *Numen* 30, 1 (1983): 80–105.

Clarke, Georgia, "Vitruvian Paradigms," *Papers of the British School at Rome* 70 (2002): 319–46.

——, *Roman House – Renaissance Palaces: Inventing Antiquity in Fifteenth-Century Italy* (Cambridge 2003).

Claudian, *De Raptu Proserpinae*, trans. Maurice Platnauer, Loeb Edition (London 1963).

——, *The War Against Gildo* [*De Bello Gildonico*], trans. Maurice Platnauer, Loeb Edition, 2 vols. (Cambridge, Mass. 1976).

Claudianus [Claudian], *Opera* (Parma 1493).

Clement of Alexandria, *Stromata*, intro. Alain de Boulluec (Paris 1997).

Cléobis et Biton: une mythe oublié, exh. cat. (Carcassonne 1995).

Clough, Cecil, "Chivalry and Magnificence in the Golden Age of Italian Renaissance," in *Chivalry in the Renaissance* (Rochester, N.Y. 1990).

Clucas, Stephen, "Regimen Animarum et Corporum: The Body and Spatial Practice in Medieval and Renaissance Magic," in *The Body in Late Medieval and Early Modern Culture* (Aldershot 2000).

Coerver, Chad, "Donna/Dono: Chivalry and Adulterous Exchange in the Quattrocento," in *Picturing Women in Renaissance and Baroque Italy*, ed. Geraldine A. Johnson and Sara F. Matthews Grieco (Cambridge 1997), 197–221.

Coffey, Michael, *Roman Satire* (London 1976).

Cole, Michael W., "The Demonic Arts and the Origin of the Medium," *The Art Bulletin* 84, 4 (2002): 621–40.

——, and Rebecca Zorach, eds., *The Idol in the Age of Art: Objects, Devotion and the Early Modern World* (Aldershot 2009).

Colie, Rosalie L., *Paradoxica Epidemica: The Renaissance Tradition of Paradox* (Princeton 1966).

——, "Small Forms: Multo in Parvo," in *The Resources of Kind: Genre-Theory in the Renaissance*, ed. Barbara K. Lewalski (Berkeley, Cal. 1973), 32–75.

Collareta, Marco, "'Encaustum Vulgo Smaltum': Note sulla percezione umanistica delle tecniche figurative," *Annali della Scuola normale superiore di Pisa*, ser. III, 14, 2 (1984): 759–69.

Collett, Barry, *Italian Benedictine Scholars and the Reformation: The Congregation of Santa Giustina of Padua* (Oxford 1985).

——, "Definition of Humanity in the Early Sixteenth Century: Correggio, Isidoro Clario, Zarlino, and the Restoration of 'Imago Dei,'" in *Brixia Sacra. Isidoro Clario 1495ca–1555: Umanista, teologo tra Erasmo e la Controriforma* 11, 4 (2006): 109–24.

Collins, Patricia, "Prints and the Development of *istoriato* Painting on Italian Renaissance Maiolica," *Print Quarterly* 4, 3 (1987): 223–35.

Colonna, Francesco, *Hypnerotomachia Poliphili*, ed. Giovanni Pozzi and Lucia A. Ciapponi, 2 vols. (Padua 1980).

Consolino, Franca Ela, "Female Ascetism and Monasticism in Italy from the Fourth to the Eighth Centuries," in *Women and Faith: Catholic Religious Life in Italy from Late Antiquity to the Present*, ed. Lucia Scaraffia and Gabriella Zarri (Cambridge, Mass. 1999), 8–30.

Conte, Gian Biagio, *Genres and Readers: Lucretius, Love Elegy, Pliny Encyclopedia*, trans. Glenn W. Most, foreword by Charles Segal (Baltimore 1994).

——, *Latin Literature: A History*, trans. Joseph B. Solodow (Baltimore and London 1994).

Contini, Roberto, and Francesco Solinas, *Artemisia Gentileschi: Storia di una passione*, exh. cat. (Milan 2011).

Cooper, Tracy E., *Palladio's Venice: Architecture and Society in a Renaissance Republic* (New Haven and London 2005).

Cornelio, Flaminio, *Ecclesiae venetae, antiquis monumentis nunc etiam primum editis illustratae ac in decades distributae*, 15 vols. (Venice 1749), vol. 9.

Coursault, René, *Sainte Catherine d'Alexandrie: Le mythe et la tradition. Hagiographie et littérature chrétienne, iconographie et traditions populaires* (Paris 1984).

Cox, Virginia, "Gender and Eloquence in Ercole de' Roberti's Portia and Brutus," *Renaissance Quarterly* 62 (2009): 61–101.

Cranston, Jodi, *The Poetics of Portraiture in the Italian Renaissance* (Cambridge 2000).

Cremaschi, Lisa, ed., *Regole monastiche femminili* (Turin 2003).

Cresciani, Chiara, "Hermeticism and Alchemy: The Case of Ludovico Lazzarelli," *Early Science and Medicine* 5, 2 (2000): 145–59.

Cristiani, Maria Laura, "Gli affreschi del Sacro Speco," in *I Monasteri benedettini di Subiaco*, ed. Claudio Giumelli (Milan 1982), 192–239.

Cunnally, John, "The Role of Greek and Roman Coins," Ph.D. diss., University of Pennsylvania 1984.

——, *Images of the Illustrious: The Numismatic Presence in the Renaissance* (Princeton 1999).

Curran, Brian, *The Egyptian Renaissance: The Afterlife of Ancient Egypt in Early Modern Italy* (Chicago 2007).

Curtius, Ernst Robert, *European Literature and the Latin Middle Ages*, trans. Willard R. Trask, afterword Peter Godman (Princeton 1988 and 1990).

Cusa, Nicholas of, *On Wisdom and Knowledge*, ed. Jasper Hopkins (Minneapolis 1996).

——, *Selected Spiritual Writings*, trans. H. Lawrence (New York 1997).

——, "De Beryllo," in *Metaphysical Speculations: Six Latin Texts*, trans. Jasper Hopkins (Minneapolis 1998), 792–838.

Cusanus, Nicolaus [Nicolas of Cusa], *Certi Tractatus et libri altissimae contemplationis et doctrinae a praeclarae memoriae praestantissimo doctissimoque viro Nicolao de Cusa* (Cortemaggiore 1502).

Dacos, Nicole, *La découverte de la Domus Aurea et la formation des grotesques à la Renaissance* (London 1969).

Daffra, Emanuela, ed., *Benvenuto Tisi detto il Garofalo: il Compianto da Sant'Antonio in Polesine* (Milan 1998).

Dalcò, Fabrizia, *Monasteri: alle radici della città e del territorio di Parma nel medioevo* (Parma 2007).

Dale, A. Thomas, "Monsters, Deformities, and Phantasmata in the Cloister of St-Michel-de-Cuxa," *The Art Bulletin* 83, 3 (2001): 402–36.

Dall'Acqua, Marzio, ed., *Correggio e il suo tempo*, exh. cat. (Parma 1984).

——, *Il monastero di San Paolo* (Parma 1990).

Daston, Lorraine, and Katherine Park, *Wonders and the Order of Nature, 1150–1750* (New York 1998).

Dauterman Maguire, Eunice, and Henry Maguire, *Other Icons: Art and Power in Byzantine Secular Culture* (Princeton 2007).

Davidson, Nicholas S. "Sex, Religion, and the Law: Disciplining Desire," in *A Cultural History of Sexuality in the Renaissance*, ed. Bette Talvacchia, 6 vols. (Oxford 2011), 3: 95–111.

D'Elia, Anthony F., "Marriage, Sexual Pleasure, and Learned Brides in the Wedding Orations of Fifteenth-Century Italy," *Renaissance Quarterly* 55, 2 (2002): 379–433.

De Vecchi, Pier Luigi, *Raffaello: la mimesi, l'armonia, e l'invenzione* (Florence 1995).

——, and Giancarla Periti, "Introduction," in *Emilia e Marche nel Rinascimento: l'identità visiva della "periferia,"* ed. Giancarla Periti (Azzano [Bg], 2005), 7–11.

Dempsey, Charles, "Renaissance Hieroglyphic Studies and Gentile Bellini's *Saint Mark Preaching in Alexandria*," in *Hermeticism and the Renaissance: Intellectual History and the Occult in Early Modern Europe*, ed. Ingrid Merkel and Allen G. Debus (Toronto 1988), 342–65.

——, "*Sua cuique mihi mea*: The *mottos* in the Camerino of Giovanna da Piacenza in the Convent of San Paolo," *The Burlington Magazine* 132 (1990): 490–93.

——, "Portraits and Masks in the Art of Lorenzo de' Medici, Botticelli, and Politian's *Stanze per la Giostra*," *Renaissance Quarterly* 52, 1 (1999): 1–42.

——, *Inventing the Renaissance Putto* (Chapel Hill, N.C. 2001).

——, "Introduction," in *Drawing Relationships in Northern Italian Renaissance Art: Patronage and Theories of Invention*, ed. Giancarla Periti (Aldershot 2004), 1–9.

Deonna, W. "Le Groupe des Trois Graces nues et sa descendance," *Revue archéologique* 31, 1 (1930): 274–332.

Di Giampaolo, Mario, *Correggio disegnatore* (Milan 2001).

Didi-Huberman, Georges, *Fra Angelico: Dissemblance and Figuration*, trans. Jane Marie Todd (Chicago 1995).

——, "The Portrait, the Individual and the Singular: Remarks on the Legacy of Aby Warburg," in *The Image of the Individual: Portraits in the Renaissance*, ed. Nicholas Mann and Luke Syson (London 1998), 165–88.

——, *Confronting Images: Questioning the Ends of a Certain History of Art*, trans. John Goodman (University Park, Pa. 2005).

[Dio, Giovanni di], *Decor Puellarum zoe Honore de le Donzelle la quale da Regola, Forma e Modo al Stato de le Honeste Donzelle* (Venice [1471]).

Dionisotti, Carlo, *Geografia e storia della letteratura italiana* (Turin 1976).

Donato, Maria Monica, "Gli eroi romani tra storia ed 'exemplum': i primi cicli umanistici di Uomini Famosi," in *Memoria dell'antico nell'arte italiana*, ed. Salvatore Settis, 3 vols. (Turin 1985), 2: 97–152.

——, "*Historia Parens Patavum*: per una tradizione d'arte civica dal Medievo all'età moderna," in *Percorsi di parole e immagini (1400–1600)*, ed. Angela Guidotti and Massimiliano Rossi (Lucca 2000), 51–74.

Donatone, Guido, *La maiolica napoletana dagli Aragonesi* (Naples 2013).

Dressen, Angela, *Pavimenti decorati del Quattrocento in Italia* (Venice 2008).

Drysdall, Denis L., "Préhistoire de l'emblème: commentaires et emplois du terme avant Alciati," *Nouvelle revue du seizième siècle* 6 (1988): 29–44.

——, "A Note on the Relationships of the Latin and the Vernacular Translations of Horapollo from Fasanini to Caussin," *Emblematica* 4, 2 (1989): 225–41.

Duffy, John, "Reactions of Two Byzantine Intellectuals to the Theory and Practice of Magic: Michael Psellos and Michael Italikos," *Byzantine Magic*, ed. Henry Maguire (Washington, D.C. 1995), 83–97.

Dunlop, Anne, *Painted Palaces: The Rise of Secular Art in Early Renaissance Italy* (University Park, Pa. 2009).

Ebreo, Leone, *Dialoghi della Natura di Amore* (Venice 1545).

Eco, Umberto, "Intentio Lectoris: The State of the Art," in *The Limits of Interpretation* (Bloomington, Ind. 1990).

Eden, Kathy, *Friends Hold All Things in Common: Tradition, Intellectual Property, and the Adages of Erasmus* (New Haven and London 2001).

Ehrenschwendtner, Marie-Luise, "Virtual Pilgrimages? Enclosure and the Practice of Piety at St. Katherine's Convent, Augsburg," *Journal of Ecclesiastical History* 60, 1 (2009): 45–73.

Ekserdjian, David, *Correggio* (New Haven and London 1997).

——, "Parmigianino and the Antique," *Apollo* 154 (July 2001): 42–50.

——, *Parmigianino* (New Haven and London 2006).

Eliade, Mircea, *The Sacred and the Profane: The Nature of Religion*, trans. W. Track (New York 1987).

Elkins, James, *The Poetics of Perspective* (Ithaca, N.Y. and London 1994).

——, *Why are our Pictures Puzzles? On the Modern Origins of Pictorial Complexity* (London 1998).

Ellinger, Georg, *Geschichte der Neulateinischen Literatur im 16 Jahrhundert* (Berlin 1929).

Emiliani, Andrea, and Daniela Scaglietti Kelescian, eds., *Amico Aspertini*, exh. cat. (Bologna 2008).

Engammare, Max, *Qu'il me baise des baisiers de sa bouche: le Cantique des Cantiques à la Renaissance* (Geneva 1993).

Erasmus, Desiderius, *Collected Works: Literary and Educational Writings 2, De Copia/De Ratione Studii*, ed. Craig R. Thompson, vol. 24 (Toronto 1978).

——, *Collected Works of Erasmus: Adages*, trans. Margaret Mann Phillips, annot. R. A. B. Mynors, vols. 30–34 (Toronto 1982).

——, *Collected Works of Erasmus: Spiritualia*, ed. John O' Malley, vol. 66 (Toronto 1988).

——, *Erasmus on Women*, ed. Erika Rummel (Toronto 1996).

——, *Collected Works of Erasmus: Colloquies*, trans. and annot. Craig R. Thompson, vols. 39 and 40 (Toronto 1997).

——, *Collected Works of Erasmus: Expositions of the Psalms*, trans. and annot. Michael J. Heath, vol. 63 (Toronto 1997).

——, *Collected Works of Erasmus: Spiritualia and Pastoralia*, ed. John O'Malley, vol. 70 (Toronto 1998).

Evangelisti, Silvia, "'Farne quello che pare e piace . . .' L'uso e la trasmissione delle celle nel monastero di Santa Giulia di Brescia (1579–1688)," *Quaderni storici* 88 (1995): 85–140

——, "Moral Virtues and Personal Goods: The Double Representation of Female Monastic Identity (Florence, 16th and 17th centuries)," in *Women in the Religious Life*, ed. Olwen Hufton (Florence 1996), 35–60.

——, "Wives, Widows, and Brides of Christ: Marriage and the Convent in the Historiography of Early Modern Italy," *The Historical Journal* 43, 1 (2000): 233–47.

——, "'We Do Not Have It and We Do Not Want It': Women, Power, and Convent Reform in Florence," *The Sixteenth Century Journal* 34, 3 (2003): 677–700.

——, "Rooms to Share: Convent Cells and Social Relations in Early Modern Italy," *Past and Present* (2006): 55–71.

——, *Nuns: A History of Convent Life 1450–1700* (Oxford 2007).

Evans, Helen C., and William D. Wixom, eds., *The Glory of Byzantium: Art and Culture of the Middle Byzantine Era, A.D. 843–1261*, exh. cat. (New York 1997).

Fabiański, Marcin, "The Cremonese Ceiling Examined in Its Original Studiolo Setting," *Artibus et Historiae* 9, 17 (1988): 189–212.

Facchiano, Annamaria, "Monasteri benedettini o capitoli di canonichesse," *Benedectina* 31, 1 (1991): 35–60.

——, *Monasteri femminili e nobiltà a Napoli tra medioevo ed età moderna: il necrologio di S. Patrizia (sec. XII–XVI)* (Altavilla Salentina 1992).

Fadda, Elisabetta, "Da Parma a Casalmaggiore: Parmigianino ultimo atto," in *Parmigianino e la pratica dell'alchimia*, ed. Sylvia Ferino Pagden et al. (Milan 2003), 39–49.

——, *Michelangelo Anselmi* (Turin 2004).

Faietti, Marzia, and Arnold Nesselrath, "Bizar più che reverso di medaglia: un codex avec grotesques, monstres et ornaments du jeune Amico Aspertini," *Revue de l'art* 107, 1 (1995): 44–88.

Faietti, Marzia, and Konrad Oberhuber, eds., *Bologna e l'umanesimo 1490–1510*, exh. cat. (Bologna 1988).

Farago, Claire, and Carol Komadina Parenteau, "The Grotesque Idol: Imaginary, Symbolic and Real," in *The Idol in the Age of Art: Objects, Devotion and the Early Modern World*, ed. Michael W. Cole and Rebecca Zorach (Aldershot 2009), 105–131.

Farinella, Vincenzo, "Saxl, Saturno e Benevento," *Prospettiva* 40 (1985): 68–71.

Ferino Pagden, Sylvia, ed., *La prima donna pittrice: Sofonisba Anguissola. Die Malerin der Renaissance (um 1535–1625)*, exh. cat. (Vienna 1995).

Ferretti, Massimo, "I maestri della prospettiva," in *Storia dell'arte italiana* (Turin 1982), 11: 457–585.

——, "Il coro di San Sisto," in *La Madonna per San Sisto di Raffaello e la cultura piacentina della prima metà del Cinquecento*, ed. Paola Ceschi Lavagetto (Parma 1985), 113–31.

Ficino, Marsilio, *Three Books on Life*, ed. Carol V. Kaske and John R. Clark (Binghamton, N.Y. 1989).

Filarete [Antonio Averlino], *Treatise on Architecture*, trans. John R. Spencer, 2 vols. (New Haven and London 1965).

——, *Trattato di Architettura*, ed. A. Maria Finoli and Liliana Grassi (Milan 1972).

Findlen, Paula, "Jokes of Nature and Jokes of Knowledge: The Playfulness of Scientific Discourse in Early Modern Europe," *Renaissance Quarterly* 43, 2 (1990): 292–331.

——, "Possessing the Past: The Material World of the Italian Renaissance," *The American Historical Review* 103, 1 (1998): 83–104.

Finocchi Ghersi, Lorenzo, "Dalla maiolica al marmo: Modelli antiquari in alcuni pavimenti veneziani del Cinquecento," in

Pavimenti lapidei del Rinascimento a Venezia, ed. Lorenzo Lazzarini and Wolfgang Wolters (Venice 2010).

Fiocco, Carola, and Gabriella Gherardi, "Il pavimento di S. Paolo a Parma," *Ceramica per l'edilizia international* 72 (1980): 11–13.

Fioravanti Baraldi, Anna Maria, *Il Garofalo: Benvenuto Tisi Pittore (c. 1476–1559)* (Ferrara 1993).

Fiori di Virtù (Venice 1500).

Fontana, Vincenzo, and Paolo Morachiello, *Vitruvio e Raffaello: il "De Architectura" di Vitruvio nella traduzione inedita di Fabio Calvo Ravennate* (Rome 1975).

Forlani, Chiara, "I pavimenti ceramici rinascimentali commissionati da Isabella d'Este: Storia di una dispersione," in *Atti XX Convegno Internazionale della Ceramica* 1 (1987): 223–32.

Fornari Schianchi, Lucia, *Ai piedi della badessa: un pavimento maiolicato per Maria de' Benedetti badessa di San Paolo dal 1471 al 1482* (Parma 1988).

——, *Il coro dell'oratorio della SS. Trinità dei Rossi in Parma* (Parma 1996).

——, ed., *Galleria Nazionale di Parma: Catalogo delle opere dall'antico al Cinquecento* (Parma 1997).

——, and Sylvia Ferino-Pagden, eds., *Parmigianino e il manierismo europeo*, exh. cat. (Cinisello Balsamo 2003).

Fortini Brown, Patricia, "The Antiquarianism of Jacopo Bellini," *Artibus et Historiae* 13, 26 (1992): 65–84.

——, *Private Lives in Renaissance Venice: Art, Architecture and the Family* (New Haven and London 2004).

Foucault, Michel, *Discipline and Punish: The Birth of the Prison*, trans. Alan Sheridan (New York 1979).

——, *Power/Knowledge: Selected Interviews and Other Writings, 1972–1977*, ed. Colin Gordon (New York 1980).

——, "Of Other Spaces," *Diacritics* (Spring 1986): 22–7.

Franceschini, Adriano, *Artisti a Ferrara in età umanistica e rinascimentale: Testimonianze archivistiche*, 2 vols. (Ferrara and Rome 1999).

Francesco, Carla di, ed., *Le sibille di Casa Romei: Storia e restauro* (Ravenna 1998).

Frangenberg, Thomas, "Decorum in the Magno Palazzo in Trent," *Renaissance Studies* 7, 4 (1993): 352–78.

Franzoni, Claudio, "Le raccolte del 'Teatro di Ombrone' ed il viaggio in Oriente del pittore: le *Epistole* di Giovanni Filoteo Achillini," *Rivista di letteratura italiana* 8, 2 (1990): 287–335.

——, "Gli studi antiquari di Michele Fabrizio Ferrarini," in *Il "Portico dei Marmi": le prime collezioni a Reggio Emilia e la nascita del Museo civico*, exh. cat. (Reggio Emilia 1999), 25–37.

——, "Tra Correggio e la Grecia: Antonio Allegri e l'arte classica," in *Correggio*, ed. Anna Coliva, exh. cat. (Milan 2008), 47–57.

Freyhan, R. "The Evolution of the Caritas Figure in the Thirteenth and Fourteenth Centuries," *Journal of the Warburg and Courtauld Institutes* 11 (1948): 68–86.

Frisoni, Fiorella, Francesco de Leonardis, and Rossana Prestini, *Paolo da Caylina il Giovane e la bottega dei da Caylina nel panorama artistico bresciano fra Quattrocento e Cinquecento* (Brescia 2003).

Froidmont, Thomas de, "De modo bene vivendi," in *Patrologia Latina*, vol. 184 (Paris 1854).

Führer, M., "The Consolation of Contemplation in Nicholas of Cusa's De Visione Dei," in *Nicholas of Cusa on Christ and the Church: Essays in Memory of Chandler McCuskey for the American Cusanus Society*, ed. Gerald Christianson and Thomas M. Izbicki (Leiden 1996), 221–40.

Furno, Martine, "Le lemme Basilica dans le *Partibus Aedium* de Grapaldo," in *Devenir roi: Essais sur la littérature adressée au Prince*, ed. Isabelle Cogitore and Francis Goyet (Grenoble 2006), 213–22, 274–9.

Fusco, Laurie, and Gino Corti, *Lorenzo de' Medici, Collector and Antiquarian* (Cambridge 2006).

Gabrielli, Edith, *Cosimo Rosselli: catalogo ragionato* (Turin 2007).

Gage, Frances, "Exercise for Mind and Body: Giulio Mancini, Collecting, and the Beholding of Landscape Painting in the Seventeenth Century," *Renaissance Quarterly* 61, 4 (2008): 1167–207.

Gagliardo, Matilde, "Le Sibille nel giardino: un ciclo di affreschi per Giovanni Romei a Ferrara," *Prospettiva* 64 (1991): 14–37.

——, "Il verziere nella cappella: le sibille quattrocentesche del Palazzo Vescovile di Albenga," in *Scritti di storia dell'arte in onore di Sylvie Béguin*, ed. Mario di Giampaolo and Elisabetta Saccomani (Naples 2001), 53–67.

Gahtan, Maia Wellington "Giraldi's Aenigmata," in *Acta Conventus Neo-Latini Bonnensis: Proceedings of the Twelfth International Congress of Neo-Latin Studies*, ed. Perrine Galand-Hallyn and Roda Schnur (Temple, Ariz. 2006), 315–23.

Gaisser, Julia Haig, *Catullus and his Renaissance Readers* (Oxford 1993).

——, *Pierio Valeriano and the Ill Fortune of Learned Men: A Renaissance Humanist and His World* (Ann Arbor, Mich. 1999).

Galli, Aldo, "Santa Redegonda e Santa Felicola: Due sculture del Quattrocento a Parma," in *Scritti per l'Istituto germanico di storia dell'arte di Firenze: Settanta studiosi italiani*, ed. Cristina Acidini Luchinat et al. (Florence 1997), 111–18.

——, "Miniature parmigiane nel rinascimento: due corali delle monache di San Quintino ritrovati a Genova," *Parma per l'arte* n.s. 8, 1 (2002): 25–42.

Gamboni, Dario, *Potential Images: Ambiguity and Indeterminacy in Modern Art*, trans. Mark Treharne (London 2002).

Gardelli, Giuliana, *Maiolica per l'architettura: Pavimenti e rivestimenti rinascimentali di Urbino e del suo territorio* (Urbino 1993).

Gasparotto, Davide, "Parma e la maniera 'antico-moderna' tra Quattro e Cinquecento," in *Il Libro d'Ore Durazzo: Volume di commento*, ed. Andrea de Marchi (Modena 2008), 67–102.

——, "Il mito della collezione," in *Pietro Bembo e l'invenzione del Rinascimento*, ed. Guido Beltramini, Davide Gasparotto, Adolfo Tura, exh. cat. (Venice 2013), 48–65.

Gaudioso, Filippa Aliberti, ed., *Gli affreschi di Paolo III Farnese a Castel Sant'Angelo: Progetto ed esecuzione, 1543–1548*, exh. cat., 2 vols. (Rome 1981).

Gehl, Paul, "Mystical Language Models in Monastic Educational Psychology," *Journal of Medieval and Renaissance Studies* 14 (1984): 219–43.

Gell, Alfred, *Art and Agency: An Anthropological Theory* (Oxford 1988).

Gentile, Marco, *Fazioni al governo: Politica e società a Parma nel Quattrocento* (Rome 2009).

Gerchow, Jan, Katrinette Bodarwé, Susan Marti, and Hedwig Röckelein, "Early Monasteries and Foundations (500–1200)," in *Crown and Veil: Female Monasticism from the Fifth to the Fifteenth Centuries*, ed. Jeffrey Hamburger and Susan Marti (New York 2008), 13–40.

Ghidiglia Quintavalle, Augusta, "Alessandro Araldi," *Rivista dell'Istituto nazionale d'archeologia e storia dell'arte* 7 (1958): 291–333.

——, "Risultati del restauro," in Roberto Longhi, *Il Correggio nella Camera di San Paolo*, ed. Augusta Ghidiglia Quintavalle (Parma 1972), 117–30.

——, and Lucia Fornari, *Arte in Emilia 4: Capolavori ritrovati e artisti inediti dal '300 al '700* (Parma 1971–2).

Ghini, Enzo, and Francesca de Gramatica, eds., *Il "Magno Palazzo" di Bernardo Cles principe vescovo di Trento* (Trento 1988).

Gianfranceschi Vettori, Ida, *Gli affreschi cinquecenteschi di Santa Giulia come documenti storici* (Brescia 1978).

——, Elena Lucchesi Ragni, and Maurizio Mondini, eds., *Il coro delle monache: Cori e corali*, exh. cat. (Milan 2003).

Giehlow, Karl, "Die Hieroglyphenkunde des Humanismus in der Allegorie der Renaissance, besonders der Ehrenpforte Kaisers Maximilian I," *Jahrbuch der Kunsthistorischen Sammlungen des Allerhöchsten Kaiserhauses* 32 (1915): 1–232.

Gilbert, Creighton, "Savoldo, Cima, Parma, and the Pio Family," *Venezia Cinquecento* 4, 8 (1994): 113–25.

Gill, Katherine, "Open Monasteries for Women in Late Medieval and Early Modern Italy," in *The Crannied Wall: Women, Religion, and the Arts in Early Modern Europe*, ed. Craig A. Monson (Ann Arbor, Mich. 1992), 15–47.

——, "Scandala: Controversies concerning Clausura and Women's Religious Communities in Late Medieval Italy," in *Christendom and its Discontents: Execution, Persecution and Rebellion 1000–1500*, ed. Scott Waugh and Peter Diehl (Cambridge 1995), 177–203.

Giraldi, Lilio Gregorio, *Libelli Duo, in quorum altero Aenigmata pleraque Antiquorum, in altero Pythagorae Symbola* (Basel 1551).

Goldthwaite, Richard, "The Economic and Social World of Italian Renaissance Maiolica," *Renaissance Quarterly* 42 (1989): 1–32.

Gombrich, Ernst, *Topos and Topicality in Renaissance Art* (London 1975).

——, *The Sense of Order: A Study in the Psychology of Decorative Art* (Oxford 1979).

Gonzaga da Reggio, Bonaventura, *Alcuni avvertimenti nella vita monacale, utili e necessari a ciascheduna vergine di Christo* (Venice 1576).

Gotfredsen, Lise, *The Unicorn* (New York 1999).

Goux, Jean-Joseph, "Vesta, or the Place of Being," *Representations* 1 (1983): 91–107.

Grapaldus, Franciscus Marius, *De Partibus Aedium* (Parma 1494; *Addita modo, verborum explicatione quae in eodem libro continentur*, 1516).

——, *Libellus Psalmorum Poenitentialium una cum variis Orationibus, et Litaniis novae inventionis ad imitationem Regaliis Psalmistae pro singulis hedbomadae diebus* (Parma 1505).

Grassi, Liliana, "L'iconologia delle chiese monastiche femminili dall'alto medioevo ai secoli XVI–XVII," *Arte Lombarda* 9 (1964): 131–50.

Greco, Gaetano, *La Chiesa in Italia nell'età moderna* (Bari 1999).

Green, Nile, "Ostrich Eggs and Peacock Feathers: Sacred Objects as Cultural Exchange between Christianity and Islam," *Al-Masāq* 18, 1 (2006): 27–66.

Gregori, Mina, "Alessandro Pampurino," in *I Campi e la cultura artistica cremonese del Cinquecento*, exh. cat. (Milan 1985), 42–5.

Grendler, Paul, *Schooling in Renaissance Italy* (Baltimore 1989).

Guarnieri, Chiara, ed., *S. Antonio in Polesine: archeologia e storia di un monastero estense* (Florence 2006).

Guerrini, Roberto, *Studi su Valerio Massimo (con un capitolo sulla fortuna nell'iconografia umanistica): Perugino, Beccafumi, Pordenone* (Pisa 1981).

——, "Dal testo all'immagine: la 'pittura di storia' nel Rinascimento," in *Memoria dell'antico nell'arte italiana*, 3 vols. (Turin 1985), 2: 45–93.

Hall, Jackie, "East of the Cloister: Infirmaries, Abbots' Lodgings, and Other Chambers," in *Perspectives for an Architecture of Solitude: Essays on Cistercians, Art, and Architecture in Honor of Peter Fergusson*, ed. Terryl N. Kinder (Turnhout 2004), 199–212.

Hall, Marcia, "The Tramezzo in the Italian Renaissance, Revised," in *Thresholds of the Sacred: Architectural, Art Historical, Liturgical, and Theological Perspectives on Religious Screens, East and West*, ed. Sharon E. J. Gerstel (Washington, D.C. 2006), 215–32.

Halliday, Anthony, "The Literary Sources of Mantegna's *Triumphs of Caesar*," *Annali della Scuola normale superiore di Pisa*, s. III, 24, 1 (1994): 337–96.

Hamburger, Jeffrey F., *Nuns as Artists: The Visual Culture of a Medieval Convent* (Los Angeles and London 1997).

——, "'To make women weep': Ugly Art as 'Feminine' and the Origins of Modern Aesthetics," *Res* 31 (1997): 9–33.

——, *The Visual and the Visionary: Art and Female Spirituality in Late Medieval Germany* (New York 1998).

——, and Robert Suckale, eds., *Krone und Schleier: Kunst aus Mittelalterlichen Frauenklöstern*, exh. cat. (Munich 2005).

Hamburger, Jeffrey F., and Anne-Marie Bouché, eds., *The Mind's Eye: Art and Theological Argument in the Middle Ages* (Princeton 2006).

Hamburger, Jeffrey F., and Susan Marti, eds., *Crown and Veil: Female Monasticism from the Fifth to the Fifteenth Centuries*, trans. Dietlinde Hamburger (New York 2008).

Hampton, Timothy, *Writing from History: The Rhetoric of Exemplarity in Renaissance Literature* (Ithaca, N.Y. and London 1990).

Hand, John Oliver, Catherine A. Metzger, and Ron Spronk, eds., *Prayers and Portraits: Unfolding the Netherlandish Diptych*, exh. cat. (Washington, D.C., New Haven and London 2006).

Hardin, Richard, "Encountering Plautus in the Renaissance: A Humanist Debate on Comedy," *Renaissance Quarterly* 60, 3 (2007): 789–818.

Haskell, Francis, *History and Its Image* (New Haven and London 1993).

Heath, Michael J., "Erasmus and the Psalms," in *The Bible in the Renaissance*, ed. Richard Griffiths (Aldershot 2001), 28–44.

Helas, Philine, *Lebende Bilder in der Italienischen Festkultur des 15. Jahrhunderts* (Berlin 1999).

Hendrix, John Shannon, and Charles H. Carman, eds., *Renaissance Theories of Vision* (Farnham 2010).

Herodotus, *The Histories*, trans. Aubrey de Sélincourt (London 1996).

Hess, Catherine, *Italian Ceramics: Catalogue of the J. Paul Getty Museum Collection* (Los Angeles 2002).

Hill, George Francis, *A Corpus of Italian Medals of the Renaissance before Cellini*, 2 vols. (London 1930; repr. Florence 1984).

Hills, Helen, *Invisible City: The Architecture of Devotion in Seventeenth-Century Neapolitan Convents* (Oxford 2004).

——, "The Housing of Institutional Architecture: Searching for a Domestic Holy in Post-Tridentine Italian Convents," in *Domestic Institutional Interiors in Early Modern Europe*, ed. Sandra Cavallo and Silvia Evangelisti (Aldershot 2009), 131–50.

Hoffmann, Detlef, Peter F. Kopp, and Fritz Koreny, eds., *Spielkarten: ihre Kunst und Geschichte in Mitteleuropa*, exh. cat. (Vienna 1974).

Hollanda, Francisco de, *Four Dialogues on Painting*, trans. Aubrey F. G. Bell (London 1928).

Holly, Michael Ann, *Panofsky and the Foundations of Art History* (Ithaca, N.Y. 1984).

Hood, William, *Fra Angelico at San Marco* (New Haven and London 1993).

Horace, *Satires, Epistles, and Ars Poetica*, trans. H. Rushton Fairclough, Loeb Edition (Cambridge, Mass. 1991).

——, *Carmina*, trans. C. E. Bennett, Loeb Edition (Cambridge, Mass. 1978).

[Horapollo], *The Hieroglyphics of Horapollo*, trans. George Boas (New York 1950).

Howard, Peter, "Preaching Magnificence in Renaissance Florence," *Renaissance Quarterly* 61, 2 (2008): 325–69.

Huelsen, Cristiano, *Il Libro di Giuliano da Sangallo: Codice Barberiniano Latino 4424* (Leipzig 1919).

Hutton, James, *The Greek Anthology in Italy to the Year 1800* (Ithaca, N.Y. 1935).

Iversen, Erik, *The Myth of Egypt and Its Hieroglyphs in European Tradition*, 2nd ed. (Princeton 1993).

Jacobs, Lynn F., "The Triptychs by Hieronymus Bosch," *Sixteenth Century Journal* 31, 4 (2000): 1009–41.

Jacobson Schutte, Anne, "Between Venice and Rome: The Dilemma of Involuntary Nuns," *Sixteenth Century Journal* 41, 2 (2010): 415–39.

Jaeger, Bertrand, "La Loggia delle Muse nel Palazzo Te e la revivescenza dell'Egitto antico nel Rinascimento," in *Mantova e l'antico Egitto: da Giulio Romano a Giuseppe Acerbi* (Florence 1994).

Jaeger, Stephen C., *The Origins of Courtliness: Civilizing Trends and the Formation of Courtly Ideals 939–1210* (Philadelphia, Pa. 1985).

Jäggi, Carola, "Eastern Choir or Western Gallery? The Problem of the Place of the Nuns' Choir in Königsfelden and other Early Mendicant Nunneries," *Gesta* 40, 1 (2001): 79–93.

James, Carolyn, *Giovanni Sabadino degli Arienti: A Literary Career* (Florence 1996).

Janson, Horst Woldemar, *Apes and Ape Lore in the Middle Ages and the Renaissance* (London 1952).

Jauss, Hans Robert, "Literary History as a Challenge to Literary Theory," *New Literary History* 2 (1970): 7–37.

Jay, Martin, *Downcast Eyes: The Denigration of Vision in Twentieth-Century French Thought* (Berkeley, Calif. 1993).

Jordan, Constance, "Renaissance Women Defending Women: Arguments against Patriarchy," in *Italian Women Writers from the Renaissance to the Present: Revising the Canon*, ed. Maria Ornella Marotti (University Park, Pa. 1996), 55–67.

Juřen, Vladimir, "*Pan Terrificus* de Politien," *Bibliothèque de l'humanisme et Renaissance* 33 (1971): 641–5.

Kajanto, Iiro, "Interpreting Fortuna Redux," in *Homenagem a Joseph M. Piel por ocasião do seu 85 aniversário* (Tübingen 1988), 35–50.

Kay McNamara, Jo Ann, *Sisters in Arms: Catholic Nuns through Two Millennia* (Cambridge, Mass. and London 1996).

Keller, Thomas, Morton Sosna, and David Wellbery, eds., *Reconstructing Individualism: Autonomy, Individuality, and the Self in Western Thought* (Stanford 1986).

Kemp, Martin, 'From Mimesis to Fantasia: The Quattrocento Vocabulary of Creative Inspiration,' *Viator* 8 (1977): 347–98.

——, *The Marvelous Works of Nature and Man* (Cambridge, Mass. 1981).

Kendrick, Robert L., *Celestial Sirens: Nuns and their Music in Early Modern Milan* (Oxford 1996).

Kiefer, Frederick, "The Conflation of Fortuna and Occasio in Renaissance Thought and Iconography," *Journal of Medieval and Renaissance Studies* 9, 1 (1979): 1–28.

Kinder, Terryl, *Cistercian Europe: Architecture of Contemplation* (Grand Rapids, Mich. 2002).

King, Margaret L., "Book-Lined Cells: Women and Humanism in the Early Modern Italian Renaissance," in *Beyond Their Sex: Learned Women of the European Past* (New York and London 1980), 66–90.

——, *Women of the Renaissance* (Chicago 1991).

——, and Albert Rabil Jr, trans. and ed., *Her Immaculate Hand: Selected Works by and about the Women Humanists of Quattrocento Italy* (Asheville 2000).

Kivistö, Sari, "The Concept of Obscurity in Humanist Polemics of the Early Sixteenth Century," in *Acta Conventus Neo-Latini Bonnensis: Proceedings of the Twelfth International Congress of Neo-Latin Studies*, ed. Perrine Galand-Hallyn and Roda Schnur (Temple, Ariz. 2006), 430–38.

Klecker, Elisabeth, *Dichtung über Dichtung: Homer und Vergil in Lateinischen Italienischer Humanisten des 15. und 16. Jahrhunderts* (Vienna 1994).

——, "Admiratio Initialis: Der Stuporhymnus des Giorgio Anselmi," *Studi umanistici piceni* 20 (2000): 4–20.

Klibansky, Raymond, Erwin Panofsky, and Fritz Saxl, *Saturn and Melancholy: Studies in the History of Natural Philosophy, Religion, and Art* (New York 1964).

Knauer, Elfriede Regina, "Caritas Romana," *Jahrbuch der Berliner Museen* 6 (1954): 9–23.

Knox, Dilwyn, *Ironia: Medieval and Renaissance Ideas on Irony* (Leiden 1989).

——, "'Disciplina': le origini monastiche e clericali della civiltà delle buone maniere in Europa," *Annali dell'Istituto storico di Trento* 18 (1992): 335–70.

——, "Civility, Courtesy and Women in the Italian Renaissance," in *Women in Italian Renaissance Culture and Society*, ed. Letizia Panizza (Oxford 2000), 3–19.

Koerner, Joseph Leo, *The Reformation of the Image* (Chicago 2004).

Köllner, Lucia, *Die töchterliche Liebe: ein Mysteriumgeheimnis. Die sogenannte Caritas Romana* (Frankfurt 1997).

Kolsky, Stephen, *The Ghost of Boccaccio: Writing on Famous Women in Renaissance Italy* (Turnhout 2005).

Korolec, J. B., "Free Will and Free Choice," in *The Cambridge History of Later Medieval Philosophy: From the Rediscovery of Aristotle to the Disintegration of Scholasticism, 1100–1600*, ed. Norman Kretzmann, Anthony Kenny, and Jan Pinborg (Cambridge 1988), 629–41.

Krauss, Rosalind E., "Horizontality," in *Formless: A User's Guide*, ed. Yve-Alain Bois and Rosalind E. Krauss (Cambridge, Mass. 1997), 93–103.

Krüger, Klaus, *Das Bild als Schleier des Untsichtbaren: Ästhetische Illusion in der Kunst der frühen Neuzeit in Italien* (Munich 2001).

——, "Authenticity and Fiction: On the Pictorial Construction of Inner Presence in Early Modern Italy," in *Image and Imagination of the Religious Self in Late Medieval and Early Modern Europe*, ed. Reindert L. Falkenburg, Walter S. Melion, and Todd M. Richardson (Turnhout 2007), 37–69.

Labourt, Jérôme, ed., *St. Jérôme: Lettres*, 8 vols. (Paris 1949–63).

Lauber, Rossella, "'Opera perfettissima': Marcantonio Michiel e la *Notizia d'opere di disegno*," in *Il Collezionismo a Venezia e nel Veneto ai tempi della Serenissima*, ed. Bernard Aikema, Rossella Lauber, and Max Seidel (Venice 2005), 77–116.

Laven, Mary, *Virgins of Venice: Enclosed Lives and Broken Vows in the Renaissance Convent* (London 2002).

Leader, Anne, *The Badia of Florence: Art and Observance in a Renaissance Monastery* (Bloomington and Indianapolis 2012).

Leccisotti, Tommaso, *Congregationis S. Iustinae de Padua O.S.B. Ordinationes Capitulorum Generalium, Parte II (1475–1504)* (Montecassino 1970).

Leclercq, Jean, *The Love of Learning and the Desire for God: A Study of Monastic Culture*, trans. Catharine Misrahi (New York 1974 and 1982).

Leclercq-Marx, Jacqueline, *La Sirène dans la pensée et dans l'art de l'Antiquité et du Moyen Âge: du mythe païen au symbole Chrétien* (Brussels 1983).

Leglù, Catherine, and Stephen Milner, eds., "Introduction: Encountering Consolation," in *The Erotics of Consolation: Desire and Distance in the Late Middle Ages* (New York 2008).

Lehmann, Phyllis Williams, *Cyriacus of Ancona's Egyptian Visit and its Reflections in Gentile Bellini and Hieronymus Bosch* (Locust Valley, N.Y. 1971).

Lenzi, Maria Ludovica, *Donne e Madonne: l'educazione femminile nel primo Rinascimento* (Turin 1982).

Lévi-Strauss, Claude, *The Savage Mind* (London 1972).

Lexikon Iconographicum Mythologiae Classicae (Zürich 1981–2009)

Ligorio, Pirro, "Grottesche," in *Scritti d'arte del Cinquecento*, ed. Paola Barocchi, 3 vols. (Milan 1973).

Lindau, David, and Peter Parshall, *The Renaissance Print, 1470–1550* (New Haven and London 1994).

Lindberg, David C., *Theories of Vision from Al-Kindi to Kepler* (Chicago 1976).

Lindgren, Erika Lauren, *Sensual Encounters: Monastic Women and Spirituality in Medieval Germany* (New York 2009).

Lindquist, Sherry C. M., *Agency, Visuality and Society at the Chartreuse de Champmol* (Aldershot 2008).

Lingo, Stuart, *Federico Barocci: Allure and Devotion in Late Renaissance Painting* (New Haven and London 2008).

Loh, Maria H., "Faciality," *Oxford Art Journal* 32, 3 (2009): 341–63.

Lomazzo, Giovanni Paolo, *Trattato dell'Arte de la Pittura* (Milan 1584).

Lombardi, Teodosio, *Gli Estensi ed il monastero del Corpus Domini*, 4 vols. (Ferrara 1980).

——, *I Francescani a Ferrara*, 4 vols. (Bologna 1974).

Longhi, Giuseppina, and Aldo Spina, "Il complesso monastico di San Paolo," 2 vols., thesis, Politecnico di Milano 1991–2.

Longhi, Roberto, *Officina Ferrarese* (Florence 1956).

———, *Il Correggio nella Camera di San Paolo*, ed. Augusta Ghidiglia Quintavalle (Parma 1972).

Lowe, Kate, "Secular Brides and Convent Brides: Wedding Ceremonies in Italy during the Renaissance and Counter-Reformation," in *Marriage in Italy*, ed. Trevor Dean and K. J. P. Lowe (Cambridge 1998), 41–65.

Lowe, K. J. P., "History Writings from within the Convent in Cinquecento Italy: The Nuns' Version," in *Women in Italian Renaissance Culture and Society*, ed. Letizia Panizza (Oxford 2000), 105–21.

———, "Elections of Abbesses and Notions of Identity in Fifteenth- and Sixteenth-Century Italy, with Special Reference to Venice," *Renaissance Quarterly* 54, 2 (2001): 389–429.

———, *Nuns' Chronicles and Convent Culture in Renaissance and Counter Reformation Italy* (Cambridge 2003).

Luchs, Alison, *The Mermaids of Venice: Fantastic Sea Creatures in Venetian Renaissance Art* (London 2010).

Lucian, *Zeuxis, or, Antiochus*, trans. A. M. Harmon, 3 vols. (London 1919–67).

———, *Dialogues of the Gods*, trans. M. D. Macleod, Loeb Edition (Cambridge, Mass. 1961).

Luhmann, Niklas, *Love as Passion: The Codification of Intimacy*, trans. Jeremy Gaines and Doris L. Jones (Cambridge, Mass. 1986).

Lyons, John D., *Exemplum: The Rhetoric of Example in Early Modern France and Italy* (Princeton 1989).

Mack, John, *The Art of Small Things* (Cambridge, Mass. 2007).

Makowski, Elizabeth, *Canon Law and Cloistered Women: Periculoso and its Commentators 1298–1545* (Washington, D.C. 1999).

Mallet, John V. G., "Tiled Floors and Court Designers in Mantua and Northern Italy," in *La corte di Mantova nell'età di Andrea Mantegna*, ed. Cesare Mozzarelli, Robert Oresko, and Leandro Ventura (Rome 1997), 253–72.

Manaresi, Raffaella Rossi, "Materiali e rifiniture nell'edilizia storica bolognese: Ipotesi sull'immagine della città," *Bolletino d'arte* 84–5 (1994): 167–82.

Manfredi, Antonio, "'Apud Alatrium, Campaniae Oppidum,' Giovanni Tortelli and the Abbey under Pope Nicholas V," in *Walls and Memory: The Abbey of San Sebastiano at Alatri (Lazio) from Late Roman Monastery to Renaissance Villa and Beyond*, ed. Elizabeth Fentress et al. (Turnhout 2005).

Manni, Graziano, *I signori della prospettiva: le tarsie dei Canozi e dei canoziani, 1460–1520*, 2 vols. (Mirandola 2001).

Marani, Pietro C., "Bernardino Luini's Frescoes in San Maurizio: Literary Circles, the Lombard Tradition, and Central Italian Classicism," in *Bernardino Luini and Renaissance Painting in Milan: The Frescoes of San Maurizio al Monastero Maggiore*, ed. Sandrina Bandera and Maria Teresa Fiorio (Milan 2000), 53–74.

Marek, Michaela, "La loggia di Psyche nella Farnesina: Per la ricostruzione ed il significato," in *Raffaello a Roma*, ed. Christoph Luitpold Frommel and Matthias Winner (Rome 1986), 209–16.

Mariani, Roberta, "Monasteri Benedettini a Milano prima della Riforma," in *Il monachesimo femminile in Italia dall'alto Medioevo al secolo XVII: a confronto con l'oggi*, ed. Gabriella Zarri (Negarine di San Pietro in Cariano [Vr] 1997), 219–47.

Marinis, Tommaso de, *Le nozze di Costanzo Sforza e Camilla d'Aragona celebrate a Pesaro nel 1475* (Rome 1946).

Maritz, J. A., "The Classical Image of Africa: The Evidence from Claudian," *Acta Classica: Proceedings of the Classical Association of South Africa* 43 (2000): 81–99.

———, "The Image of Africa: The Evidence of the Coinage," *Acta Classica: Proceedings of the Classical Association of South Africa* 41 (2001): 105–25.

Marrow, H. James, "Inventing the Passion in the Late Middle Ages," in *The Passion Story: From Visual Representation to Social Drama*, ed. Marcia Kupfer (University Park, Pa. 2008).

Martin, John, "Inventing Sincerity, Refashioning Prudence," *American Historical Review* 102, 5 (1997): 1309–42.

Massari, Stefania, ed., *Giulio Bonasone*, 2 vols. (Rome 1983).

Matter, Ann E., *The Voice of My Beloved: The Song of Songs in Western Medieval Christianity* (Philadelphia, Pa. 1992).

Mauss, Marcel, "Techniques of the Body," *Economy and Society* 2, 1 (1973): 70–87.

Medici, Maria Teresa, "Sulla giurisdizione temporale e spirituale dell'abbadessa," in *Il monachesimo femminile in Italia dall'alto medioevo a confronto con l'oggi*, ed. Gabriella Zarri (Negarine di San Pietro in Cariago [Ve] 1997), 75–86.

Medioli, Francesca, "An Unequal Law: The Enforcement of *clausura* Before and After the Council of Trent," in *Women in Renaissance and Early Modern Europe*, ed. Christine Meek (Bodmin, Cornwall 2000), 136–52.

———, Paola Vismara Chiappa, and Gabriella Zarri, "De Monialibus (secoli XVI–XVII–XVIII)," *Rivista di storia e letteratura religiosa* 33, 3 (1997): 643–715.

Meiss, Millard, *Andrea Mantegna as Illuminator: An Episode in Renaissance Art, Humanism, and Diplomacy* (New York 1957).

Merati, Patrizia, ed., *Camera Apostolica: Documenti relativi alla Diocesi del ducato di Milano. I "Libri Annatarum" di Innocenzo VIII (1482–1492)*, (Milan 2000).

Merback, Mitchell B., "Recognitions: Theme and Metatheme in Hans Burgkmair the Elder's Santa Croce in Gerusalemme of 1504," *The Art Bulletin* 96, 3 (2014): 288–318.

Merleau-Ponty, Maurice, *The Merleau-Ponty Aesthetics Reader: Philosophy and Painting*, ed. Galen A. Johnson (Chicago 1993).

Miller, Clyde Lee, "Possibility and Divine Prey: *De Venatione Sapientiae* (1463)," in *Reading Cusanus: Metaphor and Dialectic in a Conjectural Universe* (Washington, D.C. 2003), 206–40.

Miller, Elizabeth, and Alun Graves, "Rethinking the Petrucci Pavement," *Renaissance Studies* 24, 1 (2010): 94–118.

Miller, Maureen, *The Bishop's Palace: Architecture and Authority in Medieval Italy* (Ithaca, N.Y. 2000).

Missere Fontana, Federica, "Raccolte numismatiche e scambi antiquari del Cinquecento: gli stati estensi," *Atti e memorie: Accademia nazionale di scienze, lettere e arti* 11 (1993/94): 213–56.

——, "Raccolte numismatiche e scambi antiquari a Bologna fra Quattrocento e Seicento: Parte I," *Bollettino di numismatica* 25 (1995): 161–209.

Molholt, Rebecca, "Roman Labyrinth Mosaics and the Experience of Motion," *The Art Bulletin* 93, 3 (2011): 287–303.

Monson, Craig A., "Elena Malvezzi's Keyboard Manuscript: A New Sixteenth-Century Source," *Early Music History* 9 (1989): 73–128.

——, *Disembodied Voices: Music and Culture in an Early Modern Italian Convent* (Berkeley, Cal. 1995).

——, "The Perilous Enchanting Allure of Convent Singing," in *Structures and Subjectivities: Attending to Early Modern Women*, ed. Joan E. Hartman and A. Seeff (Newark 2007).

Moore, Stephen D., "The Song of Songs in the History of Sexuality," *Church History* 69, 2 (2000): 328–49.

Morel, Philippe, *Les grotesques: les figures de l'imaginaire dans la peinture italienne de la fin de la Renaissance* (Paris 1997).

Moss, Ann, *Printed Commonplace-Books and the Structuring of Renaissance Thought* (Oxford 1996).

Moyer, Ann E., *The Philosophers' Game: Rithmomachia in Medieval and Renaissance Europe* (Ann Arbor, Mich. 2001).

Musacchio, Jacqueline Marie, *The Art and Ritual of Childbirth in Renaissance Italy* (New Haven and London 1999).

Nagel, Alexander, *Michelangelo and the Reform of Art* (Cambridge 2000).

——, *The Controversy of Renaissance Art* (Chicago 2011).

——, "Twenty-five Notes on Pseudo-script in Italian Art," *Res* 59–60 (2011): 229–48.

——, and Lorenzo Pericolo, "Unresolved Images: An Introduction to Aporia as an Analytical Category in the Interpretation of Early Modern Art," in *Subject as Aporia in Early Modern Art*, ed. Alexander Nagel and Lorenzo Pericolo (Aldershot 2010), 1–15.

——, and Christopher Wood, *Anachronic Renaissance* (New York 2010).

Natalibus, Petrus de, *Catalogus Sanctorum et Gestorum eorum* (Venice 1493).

Neely, Carol Thomas, "Constructing the Subject: Feminist Practice and the New Renaissance Discourses," *English Literary History* 18 (1988): 5–18.

Negro, Emilio, and Nicosetta Roio, *Lorenzo Costa 1460–1535* (Modena 2001).

Nelson, Robert S., ed., *Visuality Before and Beyond the Renaissance: Seeing as Others Saw* (Cambridge 2000).

Newby, Zahra, "Absorption and Erudition in Philostratus' Imagines," in *Philostratus*, ed. Ewen Bowie and Jaś Elsner (Cambridge 2009).

Newman, Barbara, "Renaissance Feminism and Esoteric Theology: The Case of Cornelius Agrippa," *Viator* 24 (1993): 337–56.

Niccoli, Ottavia, "Il mostro di Ravenna: Teratologia e propaganda nei fogli volanti del primo Cinquecento," in *Ravenna in età veneziana*, ed. Dante Bolognesi (Ravenna 1986), 245–77.

Nicholl, Charles, *Leonardo da Vinci: Flights of the Mind* (New York 2004).

Nicolò Salmazo, Alberta de, *Bernardino da Parenzo: un pittore "antiquario" di fine Quattrocento* (Padua 1989).

Nogarola, Isotta, "Dialogue of the Equal and Unequal Sin of Adam and Eve: Verona 1451," in *Complete Writings: Letterbook, Dialogue on Adam and Eve, Orations*, ed. and trans. Margaret L. King and Diana Robin (Chicago 2004), 145–58.

Nova, Alessandro, *Girolamo Romanino* (Turin 1994).

——, "Folengo and Romanino: The Questione della Lingua and its Eccentric Trends," *The Art Bulletin* 76, 4 (1994): 664–79.

——, "Beobachten und Beobachtet werden: Die Metamorphose des Betrachters und des Betrachteten bei Correggio und Parmigianino," in *Imagination und Wirklichkeit zum Verhältnis von mentalen und realen Bildern in der Kunst der Frühen Neuzeit*, ed. Klaus Krüger and Alessandro Nova (Mainz 2000), 81–98.

——, "Centro, periferia, provincia: Tiziano e Romanino," in *Romanino: un pittore in rivolta nel rinascimento italiano*, exh. cat. (Cinisello Balsamo 2006), 48–67.

——, ed., *Parmigianino: Zitat, Porträt, Mythos* (Perugia 2006).

Novi Chavarria, Elisa, *Monache e gentildonne: un labile confine. Poteri politici e identità religiose nei monasteri napoletani secoli XVI–XVII* (Milan 2001).

Orsini Landini, Roberta, and Mary Westerman Bulgarella, "Costume in Fifteenth-Century Florentine Portraits of Women," in *Virtue and Beauty: Leonardo's Ginevra de' Benci and Renaissance Portraits of Women*, ed. David Alan Brown, exh. cat. (Washington, D.C. 2002), 89–97.

Ossola, Carlo, "Les devins de la lettre et les masques du double: la diffusion de l'anagrammisme à la Renaissance," in *Devins et charlatans au temps de la Renaissance*, ed. M. T. Jones-Davies (Paris 1979).

Ovid, *Metamorphoses*, trans. Frank Justus Miller, Loeb Edition (Cambridge, Mass. 1954).

——, *Heroides: Amores*, trans. Grant Showerman, rev. G. P. Goold (Cambridge, Mass. 1977).

——, *Fasti 1, A Commentary*, ed. Steven Green (Leiden 2004).

Pade, Marianne, *The Reception of Plutarch's Lives in Fifteenth-Century Italy*, 2 vols. (Copenhagen 2007).

Page, Walter, "Medieval and Renaissance Contributions to Knowledge of the Brain and Its Functions," in *The History and Philosophy of Knowledge of the Brain and Its Functions*, ed. Frederick N. Poynter (Oxford 1958), 95–114.

Paleotti, Gabriele, *Discourse on Sacred and Profane Images*, trans. William McCuaig (Los Angeles 2012).

Palisca, Claude V., *Humanism in Italian Renaissance Musical Thought* (New Haven and London 1985).

Panizza, Letizia A., "Stoic Psychotherapy in the Middle Ages and Renaissance: Petrarch's *De remediis*," in *Atoms, Pneuma, and Tranquillity: Epicurean and Stoic Themes in European Thought*, ed. Margaret J. Osler (Cambridge 1991), 39–65.

Panofsky, Erwin, *The Iconography of Correggio's Camera di San Paolo* (London 1961).

Paolucci, Fabrizio, "Antiquities and Antiquarians in Florence in the First Half of the 15th Century," in *The Springtime of the Renaissance: Sculpture and the Arts in Florence 1400–1460*, ed. Beatrice Paolozzi Strozzi and Marc Bormand (Florence 2013), 39–43.

Paschini, Pio, "I monasteri femminili in Italia nel Cinquecento," in *Problemi di vita religiosa in Italia nel Cinquecento* (Padua 1960), 31–60.

Pasini, Amilcare, *Applicazione del concilio di Trento in diocesi di Parma nella visita apostolica di mons. G. B. Castelli* (Parma 1953).

Pataki, Zita, "Rex Ductus – Rex Augustus: Herrscherbild und Herrscherrepräsentation am Hof des Königs Matthias Corvinus," *Ars: Journal of the Institute of Art History of Slovak Academy of Sciences* 41, 1 (2008): 29–54.

Patetta, Luciano, "La tipologia delle chiese doppie (dal medioevo alla controriforma)," in *Storia e tipologia: Cinque saggi sull'architettura del passato* (Milan 1989), 17–71.

Pattanaro, Alessandra, "Garofalo e Cesariano in Palazzo Costabili a Ferrara," *Prospettiva* 73/74 (1994): 97–110.

Paul, Benjamin, *Nuns and Reform Art in Early Modern Venice: The Architecture of Santi Cosma e Damiano and its Decoration from Tintoretto to Tiepolo* (Aldershot 2012).

Paulicelli, Eugenia, "From the Sacred to the Secular: The Gendered Geography of Veils in Italian Cinquecento Fashion," in *Ornamentalism: The Art of Renaissance Accessories*, ed. Bella Mirabella (Ann Arbor, Mich. 2011), 40–58.

Payne, Alina, "Materiality, Crafting, and Scale in Renaissance Architecture," *Oxford Art Journal* 32, 3 (2009): 365–86.

Pearson, Andrea, "Images and the Ideal of Women's Monasticism: Two Paintings from the Cistercian Convent of Flines," *Renaissance Quarterly* 54 (2001): 1356–402.

Pederson, Jill, "Henrico Boscano's *Isola Beata*: New Evidence for the Academia Leonardi Vinci in Renaissance Milan," *Renaissance Studies* 22, 4 (2008): 450–75.

Pelicelli, Nestore, *Il vescovado di Parma* (Parma 1922).

——, *I vescovi della chiesa parmense*, 2 vols. (Parma 1936).

Pellegri, Marco, "Il coro delle monache di Sant'Ulderico," in *Frammenti fugaci di un passato in Parma e provincia* (Parma 1999), 165–72.

Penco, Gregorio, *Storia del monachesimo in Italia: dalle origini alla fine del medioevo* (Milan 1983).

Pentcheva, Bissera V., *The Sensual Icon: Space, Ritual, and the Senses in Byzantium* (University Park, Pa. 2010).

Perini, Giovanna, *Gli scritti dei Carracci* (Bologna 1990).

Periti, Giancarla, "Nota sulla 'maniera moderna' di Correggio a Parma," in *Parmigianino e il manierismo europeo*, ed. Lucia Fornari Schianchi (Cinisello Balsamo 2002), 298–303.

——, "Enigmatic Beauty: Correggio's Camera di San Paolo," in *Drawing Relationships in Northern Italian Renaissance Art: Patronage and Theories of Invention*, ed. Giancarla Periti, intro. Charles Dempsey (Aldershot 2004), 153–76.

——, "From Allegri to Laetus-Lieto: The Shaping of Correggio's Artistic Distinctiveness," *The Art Bulletin* 86, 3 (2004): 459–76.

——, "Art and Reform: Correggio's *Mystic Marriage of St. Catherine with St. Sebastian*," *The Sixteenth Century Journal* 38, 3 (2007): 683–703.

——, "Epigraphy and the Semiotics of the Line in Late Quattrocento Italy," in *LINEA I: Grafie di immagini tra Quattrocento e Cinquecento*, ed. Marzia Faietti and Gerhard Wolf (Venice 2008), 191–210.

——, "Female Self-Commemoration, Spirituality and Lineage in Jacopo Loschi's Frescoes for the Convent of San Paolo in Parma," *I Tatti Studies* 13 (2010): 11–32.

——, "About Parmigianino's Early Portraits," *Memoirs of the American Academy in Rome*, 59/60 (2014–15), forthcoming.

Perotti, Niccolò, *Cornucopiae seu linguae latinae commentarii* (Venice 1489; 1513).

Persius, *Satires*, trans. J. R. Jenkinson (Warminster 1980).

Petoletti, Marco, "Ugolino Pisani, lettore di Aristotele e la sua polemica nascosta contro Leonardo Bruni traduttore dell'Etica Nicomachea," in *Margarita Amicorum: Studi di cultura europea per Agostino Sottili*, ed. Fabio Forner et al., 2 vols. (Milan 2005), 2: 879–909.

Petrarch [Francesco Petrarca], *The Life of Solitude*, trans. Jacob Zeitlin (Urbana, Ill. 1924).

——, *Rerum memorandarum libri*, ed. Giuseppe Billanovich (Florence 1945).

——, *Invective contra Medicum*, ed. Pier Giorgio Ricci (Rome 1978).

——, *Remedies for Fortune Fair and Foul*, trans. and comment. Conrad H. Rawski, 5 vols. (Bloomington and Indianapolis 1991).

——, *Secretum*, ed. and trans. Ugo Dotti (Rome 1993).

Petti Balbi, Giovanna, *Genova medioevale vista dai contemporanei* (Genoa 1978).

Peverada, Enrico, "Il palazzo vescovile nel Quattrocento," in *Palazzo arcivescovile: il Cardinale Tommaso Ruffo a Ferrara*, ed. Carla di Francesco and Carlo Samaritani (Ferrara 1994), 45–59.

Pezzana, Angelo, *Memorie degli scrittori e letterati parmigiani raccolte da Padre Ireneo Affò, e continuate da Angelo Pezzana*, 7 vols. in 4 (Parma 1825–33).

——, *Storia della città di Parma*, 5 vols. (Parma 1837–59).

Pfisterer, Ulrich, *Donatello und die Entdeckung der Stile, 1430–1445* (Munich 2002).

———, *Lysippus und seine Freunde: Liebesgaben und Gedächtnis im Rom der Renaissance oder: Das erste Jahrhundert der Medaille* (Berlin 2008).

Philostratus, *Imagines*, trans. Arthur Fairbanks (London 1979).

Picasso, Giorgio, ed., "San Maurizio al Monastero Maggiore," in *Monasteri Benedettini in Lombardia* (Milan 1980).

Picone, Michelangelo, *Passare il tempo: la letteratura del gioco e dell'intrattenimento dal XII al XVI secolo*, 2 vols. (Rome 1993).

Piva, Paolo, "San Benedetto in Polirone: lo sviluppo storico di una edilizia monastica," *Civiltà mantovana* 20 (1988): 31–71.

———, "Quel che sappiamo sulla *Domus Infirmorum* in un'abbazia benedettina: San Benedetto Po," *Postumia* 6 (1995): 79–88.

Pizan, Christine de, *The Book of the City of Ladies*, trans. Earl Jeffrey Richards, foreword by Natalie Zemon Davis (New York 1998).

[Plautus, Titus Maccius] *M. Actii Plauti Asinii. Comoediae viginti nuper emendatae et in eas Pyladae Brixiani Lucubrationes. Thadaei Ugoleti: et Grapaldi virorum illustrium Scholia, Anselmi Epiphyllides* (Parma 1510).

Plinio [Pliny the Elder], *Istoria naturale tradotta di lingua latina in Fiorentino per me Cristoforo Landino* (Venice 1476).

Plinius, Secundus Gaius [Pliny the Elder], *Historia Naturalis*, with annotations by Philippus Beroaldus (Parma 1476).

Pliny the Elder, *Natural History*, trans. H. Rackham, Loeb Edition (Cambridge, Mass. 1968).

Plutarch, *Lives*, trans. Bernadotte Perrin, Loeb Edition, 11 vols. (London and New York 1914–26).

———, "Isis and Osiris," in *Moralia*, trans. Frank Cole Rabbit, Loeb Edition (Cambridge, Mass. 1986).

Poel, Marc van de, *Cornelius Agrippa: The Humanist Theologian and his Declamations* (Leiden 1997).

Polonio, Valeria, "Un affare di stato: la riforma delle monache a Genova nel xv secolo," in *Monastica et Humanistica: Scritti in Onore di Gregorio Penco*, ed. Francesco G. B. Trolese (Cesena 2003), 323–52.

Pon, Lisa, *Raphael, Dürer, and Marcantonio Raimondi: Copying and the Italian Renaissance Print* (New Haven and London 2004).

Pope-Hennessy, John, *Renaissance Bronze from the Samuel H. Kress Collection* (London 1965).

———, *The Robert Lehman Collection: I. Italian Painting* (Princeton 1987).

Popham, Arthur E., *Correggio's Drawings* (London 1957).

Pozzi, Giovanni, "Occhi bassi," in *Thematologie des Kleinen = Petits thèmes littéraires*, ed. Edgar Marsch and Giovanni Pozzi (Fribourg 1986).

Prà, Laura Dal, "Johannes Hinderback e Bernardo Cles: Funzionalità e decorazione nella sede dei principi vescovi di Trento. Spunti per una ricerca," in *Il Castello del Buonconsiglio*, ed. Enrico Castelnuovo, 2 vols. (Trent 1996), 2: 31–69.

———, "Umanesimo e arti figurative nel principato vescovile di Trento: Note di lavoro," in *Rinascimento e passione per l'antico: Andrea Riccio e il suo tempo*, exh. cat. (Trent 2008), 179–201.

Prato, Alberto del, "Librai e biblioteche parmensi del secolo xv," *Archivio storico per le province parmensi* 4 (1904): 1–18, 36–56.

Prestianni, Cristiana, "Un documento inedito sulla committenza di Giovanna da Piacenza nel monastero di San Paolo," *Aurea Parma* 93, 1 (2009): 103–32.

Prete, Cecilia, "Marcello Fogolino e gli affreschi di Palazzo Roverella ad Ascoli Piceno," in *Pittura veneta nelle Marche*, ed. Valter Curzi (Cinisello Balsamo 2000), 205–9.

Preyer, Brenda, "The Florentine Casa," in *At Home in Renaissance Italy*, ed. Marta Ajmar-Wollheim and Flora Dennis, exh. cat. (London 2006), 34–49.

Priuli, Girolamo, *I Diarii*, Rerum Italicarum Scriptores, vol. 24, part 4 (Città di Castello 1912).

Prosperi, Adriano, "Dall'investitura papale alla santificazione del potere: Appunti per una ricerca sui primi Farnese e le istituzioni ecclesiastiche a Parma," in *Le corti farnesiane di Parma e Piacenza (1545–1622): I, potere e società nello stato farnesiano*, ed. Marzio A. Romani (Rome 1978), 161–88.

Pselli, Michaelis, *Philosophica Minora: Opuscula Psychologica, Theologica, Daemonologica*, vol. 2, ed. D. J. O'Meara (Leipzig 1989).

Pungileoni, Luigi, *Memorie istoriche di Antonio Allegri detto il Correggio*, 3 vols. (Parma 1817–22).

Quattrini, Cristina, *Brera mai vista. Lo Scherno di Cam: un dipinto riscoperto di Bernardino Luini* (Milan 2006).

Quintavalle, Arturo Carlo, "Appunti per Jacopo Loschi," *Aurea Parma* 43, 1 (1959): 200–08.

———, "Luchino Bianchino," *Critica d'arte* 50 (1962): 36–54.

———, "Cristoforo da Lendinara: la città neoplatonica e quella storica," in *La Basilica cattedrale di Parma: Novecento anni di arte, storia e fede*, ed. Arturo Carlo Quintavalle, Marco Pellegri, and Franco Maria Ricci, 3 vols. (Parma 2005).

Quinterio, Francesco, *Maiolica nell'architettura del rinascimento italiano (1440–1520)* (Florence 1990).

Quintilian, *Institutio Oratoria*, trans. H. E. Butler, Loeb Edition (Cambridge, Mass. 1920).

Quiviger, François, *The Sensory World of Italian Renaissance Art* (London 2010), 70–87.

Radke, Gary, "Nuns and their Art: The Case of San Zaccaria in Renaissance Venice," *Renaissance Quarterly* 54, 2 (2001): 430–59.

Randolph, Adrian, "Regarding Women in Sacred Spaces," in *Picturing Women in Renaissance and Baroque Italy*, ed. Geraldine A. Johnson and Sara F. Matthews Grieco (Cambridge 1997), 17–41.

Ranft, Patricia, *Women and the Religious Life in Pre-Modern Europe* (New York 1996).

Ravanelli Guidotti, Carmen, *Il pavimento della cappella Vaselli in San Petronio a Bologna* (Bologna 1988).

———, "Le Metamorfosi 'vulgari' d'Ovidio sulla maiolica italiana," in *Die Rezeption der "Metamorphosen" des Ovid in der*

Neuzeit: Der Antike Mythos in Text und Bild, ed. Hermann Walter and Hans-Jürgen Horn (Berlin 1995), 85–97.

——, "Montelupo *Figurato*: An Historiographical Profile," in *The "Figurato" Maiolica of Montelupo*, trans. Julia C. Triolo (Rome 2012), 35–54.

Rees, Valery, "Marsilio Ficino and the Rise of Philosophic Interests in Buda," in *Italy and Hungary: Humanism and Art in the Early Renaissance*, ed. Péter Farbaky and Louis A. Waldman (Florence 2011), 127–48.

Reynolds, Brian, and Joseph Fitzpatrick, "The Transversality of Michel de Certeau: Foucault's Panoptic Discourse and the Cartographic Impulse," *Diacritics* 29, 3 (1999): 63–80.

Ricci, Antonio, and Maria Antonietta Orlandi, eds., *Lo spazio del silenzio: Storia e restauri dei monasteri benedettini di Subiaco* (Subiaco 2004).

Ricci, Corrado, *Jacopo Bellini e i suoi Libri di Disegni* (Florence 1908).

——, *Correggio* (London 1930).

Rice, F. Eugene, *Saint Jerome in the Renaissance* (Baltimore 1985).

Rigolot, François, "L'anagramme comme signe de l'idéologie du text," in *Poétique et onomastique: l'exemple de la Renaissance* (Geneva 1977).

——, "The Renaissance Crisis of Exemplarity," *Journal of the History of Ideas* 59 (1998): 557–63.

Rizzi, Fortunato, "Un umanista ignorato: Taddeo Ugoleto," *Aurea Parma* 37 (1953): 3–17, 79–91.

——, "Giorgio Anselmi," *Aurea Parma* 37 (1953): 143–62.

Romano, Giovanni, "Correggio in Mantua and San Benedetto Po," in *Dosso's Fate: Painting and Court Culture in Renaissance Italy*, ed. Luisa Ciammitti, Steven F. Ostrow, and Salvatore Settis (Los Angeles 1998), 15–40.

Römer, Franz, "Martial in drei Monodistichen des Giorgio Anselmi," *Wiener Studien* 101 (1988): 339–50.

Ronchini, Amadio, "La dimora del Petrarca in Parma," *Atti e memorie delle RR. Deputazioni di storia patria per le provincie modenesi e parmensi* 7 (1874): 343–67.

Rossi, Ismaele, *La Chiesa di San Maurizio in Milano: il Monastero Maggiore e le sue due torri* (Milan 1914).

Rovetta, Alessandro, Elio Monducci, and Corrado Caselli, *Cesare Cesariano e il Rinascimento a Reggio Emilia* (Reggio Emilia 2008).

Rubbi, Valeria, "L'architettura del monastero femminile: Exempla," in *Vita artistica nel monastero femminile: Exempla*, ed. Vera Fortunati (Bologna 2002), 76–97.

Rubin, Patricia, *Portraits by the Artist as a Young Man: Parmigianino ca. 1524* (Groningen 2007).

Rudolph, Conrad, *Artistic Change at St-Denis: Abbot Suger's Program and the Early Twelfth-Century Controversy over Art* (Princeton 1990).

——, ed., *The "Things of Greater Importance": Bernard of Clairvaux's Apologia and the Medieval Attitude toward Art* (Philadelphia 1990).

——, "La resistenza all'arte nell'occidente," in *Arte e storia nel Medioevo*, ed. Enrico Castelnuovo and Giuseppe Sergi, 4 vols. (Turin 2004), 3: 49–84.

Russell, Camilla, "Convent Culture in Early Modern Italy: Laywomen and Religious Subversiveness in a Neapolitan Convent," in *Practices of Gender in Late Medieval and Early Modern Europe*, ed. Megan Cassidy-Welch and Peter Sherlock (Turnhout 2008), 57–76.

Russo, Carla, *I monasteri femminili di clausura a Napoli nel secolo XVII* (Naples 1970).

Ryan, Lawrence V., "Erasmi *Convivia*: The Banquet Colloquies of Erasmus," *Medievalia et Humanistica* 8 (1977): 201–15.

Sabbadini, Remigio, *Classici e umanisti da Codici Ambrosiani* (Florence 1933).

Sacchi, Rossana, *Il disegno incompiuto: la politica artistica di Francesco II Sforza e di Massimiliano Stampa*, 2 vols. (Milan 2005).

Salmazo, Alberta de Nicolò, *Bernardino da Parenzo: un pittore "antiquario" di fine Quattrocento* (Padua 1989).

Salmi, Mario, "Bernardino Zaccagni e l'architettura del rinascimento a Parma," *Bollettino d'arte* 12, 1–4 (1918): 85–169.

Sani, Elisa P., *Italian Renaissance Maiolica* (London 2012).

Sannazzaro, Giovanni Battista, and Grazioso Sironi, "Per la chiesa di S. Maurizio al Monastero Maggiore di Milano: gli antecedenti ed i primi decenni," *Raccolta vinciana* 30 (2003): 239–65.

Sansovino, Francesco, *Venetia città nobilissima et singolare: descritta in XIII libri* (Venice 1581).

Santoro, Mario, *Fortuna, ragione e prudenza nella civiltà letteraria del Cinquecento* (Naples 1978).

Sanuto, Marino, *I Diarii* (1496–1533), ed. Rinaldo Fulin et al., 58 vols. (Venice 1879–1903; Bologna 1969–70).

Sarchi, Alessandra, "The Studiolo of Alberto Pio da Carpi," in *Drawing Relationships in Northern Italian Renaissance Art: Patronage and Theories of Invention*, ed. Giancarla Periti, intro. Charles Dempsey (Aldershot 2004), 129–51.

Sarti, Raffaella, *Europe at Home: Family and Material Culture 1500–1800*, trans. Allan Cameron (New Haven and London 2002).

Sartore, Alberto Maria, "'Begun by Master Raphael': The Monteluce 'Coronation of the Virgin,'" *Burlington Magazine* 153 June (2011): 387–91.

Savonarola, Girolamo, *Lettere e scritti apologetici*, ed. Roberto Ridolfi, Vincenzo Romano, and Armando F. Verde (Rome 1984).

Saxl, Fritz, "Pagan Sacrifice in the Italian Renaissance," *Journal of the Warburg and Courtauld Institutes* 2, 4 (1939): 346–67.

Scaglione, Aldo, *Knights at Court, Courtliness, Chivalry, and Courtesy from Ottonian Germany to Italian Renaissance* (Berkeley, Cal. 1991).

Scarabelli Zunti, Enrico, *Cenni storico-artistici intorno alla chiesa e al già monastero di San Quintino in Parma* (Parma 1846).

——, *Memorie e documenti di belle arti parmigiane (1050–1450)* (Parma 1911).

Scarpellini, Pietro, and Maria Rita Silvestrelli, *Pinturicchio* (Milan 2003).

Schilling, Robert, "A propos de l'expression 'Iupiter Optimus Maximus,'" *Societas Academica Dacoromana* 3 (1964): 343–8.

Schmitt, Wolfgang, "Zwei lateinische *Hekabe*-Ubersetzungen vom Jahre 1506: Ein Beitrag zur Geschichte humanisticher Ubersetzungen in der Renaissance," in *Die gesellschaftliche Bedeutung des Antiken Dramas für seine und für unsere Zeit*, ed. Walter Hofmann and Heinrich Kuch (Berlin 1973), 239–74.

Schofield, Richard V., "Avoiding Rome: An Introduction to Lombard Sculptors and the Antique," *Arte lombarda* 100, 1 (1992): 29–44.

——, "Amadeo's System," in *Giovanni Antonio Amadeo: Scultura e architettura del suo tempo*, ed. Janice Shell and Liana Castelfranchi (Milan 1993), 125–56.

Schroeder, H. J., ed., "Concerning Regulars and Nuns," in *Canons and Decrees of the Council of Trent* (St. Louis, Mo. 1960).

Schulz, Jürgen, "The Houses of the Dandalo," *Journal of the Society of Architectural Historians* 52 (1993): 391–415.

Schutt Brown, Cheryl A., "The Portrait of an Abbess: Lucrezia Agliardi Vertova," *The Rutgers Art Review* 14 (1994/96): 43–51.

Scipioni, Silvia, "*Heures Me Fault de Notre Dame*. Il Libro d'Ore manoscritto: Strumento di devozione e segno di prestigio," in *Cum Picturis Ystoriatum: Codici devozionali e liturgici della Biblioteca Palatina*, exh. cat. (Modena 2001), 19–24.

Sebastiani, Lucia, "Monasteri femminili milanesi tra medioevo ed età moderna," in *Florence and Milan: Comparisons and Relations*, ed. Craig Hugh Smyth and Gian Carlo Garfagnini, 2 vols. (Florence 1989), 2: 3–15.

Segala, Franco, *I ritratti dei Vescovi di Verona nelle sale del Palazzo Vescovile* (Verona 1993).

Segarizzi, Arnaldo, "Ulisse Aleotti rimatore veneziano del secolo xv," *Giornale storico della letteratura italiana* 47 (1906): 41–66.

Seneca, *De Beneficiis*, trans. John W. Basore, Loeb Edition (London 1935).

Servius, *Servii Grammatici qui feruntur in Vergilii carmina commentarii*, ed. G. Thilo and H. Hagen (1881–7), 4 vols. in 3 (Hildesheim 1986).

Shearman, John, "Domes," in *Only Connect . . . Art and the Spectator in the Italian Renaissance* (Princeton 1988), 149–91.

——, *Raphael in Early Modern Sources: 1483–1602*, 2 vols. (New Haven and London 2003).

Sheppard, Herbert Stanley, "The Ouroboros and the Unity of Matters in Alchemy: A Study in Origins," *Ambix* 10, 2 (1962): 83–96.

Shoemaker, Innis H., ed., *The Engravings of Marcantonio Raimondi*, exh. cat. (Lawrence, Kan. 1981).

Signorini, Rodolfo, *Opus Hoc Tenue: Lettura storica, iconografica, iconologica della camera dipinta di Andrea Mantegna*, intro. Eugenio Battisti (Parma 1985).

——, "AENIGMATA. 'Disegni d'arme e d'amore' ossia imprese e motti su medaglie e monete di principi Gonzaga e di tre personaggi coevi," in *Monete e medaglie di Mantova e dei Gonzaga dal XII al XIX secolo*, 2 vols. (Milan 1996).

——, "Un inedito su Francesco Mantegna e il Correggio," *Quaderni di Palazzo Te* 3 (1996): 79–80.

Silius Italicus, *Punica* (Parma 1481).

——, *Punica*, trans. J. D. Duff, Loeb Edition (Cambridge, Mass. 1989).

Silver, Larry, *Marketing Maximilian: The Visual Ideology of a Holy Roman Emperor* (Princeton 2008).

Simon, Erika, *Die Götter der Römer* (Munich 1990).

Sissa, Giulia, "Subtle Bodies," in *Fragments of a History of the Human Body*, ed. Michel Feher, Ramona Naddaff, and Nadia Tazi, 3 vols. (New York 1989), 1: 133–56.

Smagliati, Leone, *Cronaca parmense (1494–1518)*, ed. Sergio di Noto (Parma 1970).

Smith, Jonathan, *To Take Place: Toward Theory in Ritual* (Chicago 1987).

Smith, Susan L., *The Power of Women: A Topos in Medieval Art and Literature* (Philadelphia, Pa. 1995).

Smyth, Carolyn, *Correggio's Frescoes in Parma Cathedral* (Princeton 1997).

Snyder, Jon R., *Dissimulation and the Culture of Secrecy in the Renaissance* (Berkeley, Cal. 2009).

Somigli, Costanzo, and Tommaso Bargellini, *Ambrogio Traversari, monaco camaldolese* (Bologna 1986).

Soranzo, Giovanni, *Matteo Bossi di Verona (1427–1502): i suoi scritti ed il suo epistolario* (Padua 1965).

Sowerby, Robin, "Early Humanist Failure with Homer (I and II)," *Journal of the Classical Tradition* 4, 1 (1997): 37–63; ibid., 4, 2 (1997): 165–94.

Spanò Martinelli, Serena, "La biblioteca del Corpus Domini bolognese: l'inconsueto spaccato di una cultura monastica femminile," *La Bibliofilia*, 88, 1 (1986): 1–21.

Sperling, Jutta Gisela, *Convents and the Body Politic in Late Renaissance Venice* (Chicago 1999).

Speroni, Charles, *Wit and Wisdom in the Italian Renaissance* (Berkeley, Cal. 1964).

Spinelli, Alessandro, *Versi del 400 e del 600 attinenti a Pittori o a Cose d'Arte tratti dai Mss. Estensi* (Carpi 1892).

Spinelli, Giovanni, "La storiografia sul monastero nell'età moderna e contemporanea," in *S. Giulia di Brescia: Archeologia, arte, storia di un monastero regio dai Longobardi al Barbarossa* (Brescia 1992), 21–38.

Staikos, Kostantinos, "Manuscripts and Printed Editions of Homer during the Renaissance," *Pharos: Journal of the Netherlands Institute in Athens* 13 (2005): 159–71.

Stallybrass, Peter, "Patriarchal Territories: The Body Enclosed," in *Rewriting the Renaissance: The Discourses of Sexual Difference in Early Modern Europe*, ed. Margaret W. Ferguson, Maureen Quilligan, and Nancy J. Vickers (Chicago 1986), 123–42.

Starn, Randolph, and Loren Partridge, "A Room for a Renaissance Prince: The Camera Picta in Mantua 1465–1474," in *Arts of Power: Three Halls of State in Italy 1300–1600* (Berkeley, Cal. 1992), 83–126.

Starnes, D. T., "The Figure of Genius in the Renaissance," *Studies in the Renaissance* 11 (1964): 234–44.

Statius, *Thebaid*, trans. J. H. Mozley, Loeb Edition (Cambridge, Mass. 1989).

Stefaniak, Regina, "Correggio's *Camera di San Paolo*: An Archeology of the Gaze," *Art History*, 16, 2 (1993): 203–38.

Steinberg, Leo, *Leonardo's Incessant Last Supper* (New York 2001).

Stierle, Karl-Heinz, "L'Histoire comme exemple: l'exemple comme histoire," *Poétique* 10 (1972): 176–98.

Stoichita, Victor, *The Self-Aware Image: An Insight into Early Modern Meta-Painting* (Cambridge 1997).

Stollhans, Cynthia, "Saint Catherine of Alexandria and her Book in Italian Art," *Source* 26, 3 (2007): 23–9.

Stradiotti, Renata, ed., *San Salvatore, Santa Giulia a Brescia: il monastero nella storia* (Milan 2001).

Strauss, Walter L., ed., *Illustrated Bartsch: The Works of Marcantonio Raimondi and of His School* (New York 1978).

Strehlke, Carl B., and Cecilia Frosinini, *The Panel Paintings of Masolino and Masaccio* (Milan 2002).

Strocchia, Sharon, "Learning the Virtues: Convent Schools and Female Culture in Renaissance Florence," in *Women's Education in Early Modern Europe: A History 1500–1600*, ed. Barbara J. Whitehead (London 1999), 3–46.

——, "Taken into Custody: Girls and Convent Guardianship in Renaissance Florence," *Renaissance Studies* 17, 2 (2003): 177–200.

——, "When the Bishop Married the Abbess: Masculinity and Power in Florentine Episcopal Entry Rites, 1300–1600," *Gender & History*, 19, 2 (2007): 346–68.

——, *Nuns and Nunneries in Renaissance Florence* (Baltimore 2009).

Summerscale, Anne, *Malvasia's Life of the Carracci: Commentary and Translation* (University Park, Pa. 2000).

Syson, Luke, "Holes and Loops: The Display and Collection of Medals in Renaissance Italy," *Journal of Design History* 15, 4 (2002): 229–44.

——, "Belle: Picturing Beautiful Women," in *Art and Love in Renaissance Italy*, ed. Andrea Bayer, exh. cat. (New York 2008), 246–54.

——, and Larry Keith, eds., *Leonardo da Vinci: Painter at the Court of Milan*, exh. cat. (London 2011).

——, and Dora Thornton, *Objects of Virtue: Art in Renaissance Italy* (Los Angeles 2001).

Takanashi, Mitsumasa, ed., *Parma: Grazia e affetti, natura e artificio. Protagonisti dell'arte da Correggio a Lanfranco*, exh. cat., 2 vols. (Tokyo 2007).

Talignani, Alessandra, "QUID EVADET: una traccia dell'*Hypnerotomachia Poliphili* a Parma nel sepolcro di Vincenzo Carissimi," *Artes* 5 (1997): 111–37.

——, "Un disegno inedito e qualche appunto per la tomba di Marco Colla nella Cattedrale di Parma," *Aurea Parma* 87, 1 (2003): 9–30.

——, "Un polittico di Filippo Mazzola per Busseto," in *Parmigianino e la scuola di Parma* (Viadana [Mn] 2004), 11–28.

——, "La cappella Montini nella cattedrale di Parma: un *unicum* di forme, colori ed epigrafi nella 'periferia,'" in *Emilia e Marche nel Rinascimento: l'identità visiva della "periferia,"* ed. Giancarla Periti (Azzano [Bg], 2005), 119–80.

——, "Marc'Antonio Zucchi, non Luchino Bianchino: su un gruppo di tarsie parmensi con prospettive urbane," in *Forme del legno: Intagli e tarsie fra gotico e rinascimento*, ed. Gabriele Donati and Valeria E. Genovese (Pisa 2013), 195–212.

——, "Nuovi documenti sul coro ligneo di San Paolo," *Aurea Parma*, forthcoming.

Tamburini, Filippo, *Santi e peccatori: Confessioni e suppliche dai Registri della penitenziaria dell'Archivio segreto vaticano (1451–1586)* (Milan 1995).

Tarabotti, Arcangela, *Inferno monacale*, ed. Francesca Medioli (Turin 1990).

Testi, Laudedeo, *Parma* (Bergamo 1905).

——, "Pier Ilario e Michele Mazzola: Notizie sulla pittura parmigiana dal 1250 c. alla fine del xv secolo," *Bollettino d'arte* 3 (1910): 49–67, 81–104.

——, "Il Palazzo vescovile di Parma e i suoi restauri," *Aurea Parma* 4, 6 (1920): 325–35.

Thomas, Anabel, *Art and Piety in the Female Religious Communities of Renaissance Italy: Iconography, Space, and the Religious Woman's Perspective* (Cambridge 2003).

Thorndike, Lynn, *A History of Magic and Experimental Science*, 8 vols. (New York 1923–58).

Thornton, Dora, *The Scholar in his Study: Ownership and Experience in Renaissance Italy* (New Haven and London 1997).

——, and Timothy Wilson, eds., *Italian Renaissance Ceramics: A Catalogue of the British Museum Collection*, 2 vols. (London 2009).

Thornton, Peter, *The Italian Renaissance Interior 1400–1600* (London 1991).

Tibbeus Schulenburg, Jane, "Strict Active Enclosure and its Effects on the Female Monastic Experience (ca. 500–1000)," in *Distant Echoes: Medieval Religious Women*, ed. John A. Nichols and Lilian T. Shank (Kalamazoo 1984), 51–86.

Tibullus, *Elegies*, trans. and intro. Guy Lee (Leeds 1990).

——, *Il Quattrocento settentrionale* (Bari 1981).

Tobin, Richard, "The Pose of the Doryphoros," *Polykleitos, the Doryphoros, and Tradition*, ed. Warren G. Moon (Madison, Wis. 1995), 52–64.

Tomei, Alessandro, "Tra Abruzzo e Lazio: Affreschi quattrocenteschi nel transetto di Santa Scolastica a Subiaco," in *L'Abruzzo in età angioina: Arte di frontiera tra medioevo e rinascimento*, ed. Daniele Benati and Alessandro Tomei (Milan 2006), 237–53.

Tonelli, Fabrizio, "Loschi tra conti e frati: Date e committenti per l'ex oratorio di San Gerolamo," *Parma per l'arte*, n.s. 3, 1 (1997): 7–33.

———, "Per Correggio, Parmigianino, Anselmi, Bedoli e l'architettura," in *Parmigianino e la scuola di Parma* (Viadana [Mn] 2004), 47–74.

———, "L'architettura parmense fra '400 e '500, il chiostro della Badia e il cortile del Castello di Torrechiara," in *L'Abbazia Benedettina della Neve a Torrechiara*, ed. Fabrizio Tonelli and Barbara Zilocchi (Parma 2010), 83–108.

———, "Il Chiostro ionico dei Cassinesi di San Pietro a Modena: una proposta per Correggio, una per Girolamo Bedoli e alcuni spunti per Cristoforo Solari," in *Su questa Pietra . . . Nuovi studi e ricerche sull'Abbazia benedettina di San Pietro in Modena*, ed. Sonia Cavicchioli and Vincenzo Vandelli (Modena 2014), 89–106.

Torrini Perissa, Annalisa, and Francesca Saccardo, eds., *Maiolica a Venezia: un pavimento rinascimentale nella chiesa di San Sebastiano* (Venice 2000).

Trento, Dario, "Alessandro Bentivoglio, Bernardino Luini e la scuola di San Maurizio al Monastero Maggiore," *Ricerche di storia dell'arte* 77 (2002): 61–83.

Trexler, Richard, "Le Célibat à la fin du moyen âge: les religieuses de Florence," *Annales* 27 (1972): 1337–53.

Triolo, Julia C., "The Armorial Maiolica of Francesco Xanto Avelli" (Ph.D. diss., Pennsylvania State University 1996).

Turner, Victor, "Betwixt and Between: The Liminal Period in Rites of Passage," in *Proceedings of the American Ethnological Society for 1964* (Seattle 1964), 4–20.

———, *Dramas, Fields and Metaphors: Symbolic Action in Human Society* (Cornell 1974).

Vaccaro, Mary, "Parmigianino and Andrea Bajardi: Figuring Petrarchan Beauty in Renaissance Parma," *Word and Image* 17 (2001): 243–58.

———, *Parmigianino: i dipinti* (Turin 2002).

———, "A Drawing from the Circle of Correggio in the Uffizi," *Burlington Magazine* 149 (2007): 472–8.

———, "After Correggio: Drawings by Giorgio Gandini del Grano for Parma Cathedral," *Master Drawings* 53, 1 (2015): 59–80.

Valerius Maximus, *Memorable Deeds and Sayings*, trans. Henry John Walker (Indianapolis and Cambridge 2004).

Valesio, Paolo, *Ascoltare il silenzio: la retorica come teoria* (Bologna 1986).

Valladares, Hérica, "The *Io* in Correggio: Ovid and the Metamorphosis of a Renaissance Painter," in John North and Peter Mack, eds., *The Afterlife of Ovid* (*Bulletin of the Institute of Classical Studies Supplement 130*) (London 2015), 137–58.

Vannutelli, Carla, "Intorno a Leonardo Vidolenghi: Problemi di pittura pavese di secondo Quattrocento," *Paragone* 541 (1995): 3–29.

Varro, Marcus Terentius, *On the Latin Language*, trans. Roland G. Kent (Cambridge, Mass. 1967).

Vasari, Giorgio, *Le vite de' più eccellenti pittori, scultori e architettori nelle redazioni del 1550 e 1568*, ed. Rosanna Bettarini and Paola Barocchi, 6 vols. (Florence 1966–87).

Vecce, Carlo, "Leonardo e il gioco," in *Passare il tempo: la letteratura del gioco e dell'intrattenimento dal XII al XVI secolo*, 2 vols. (Rome 1993), 1: 269–312.

Venturi, Adolfo, "Pittori della corte ducale a Ferrara nella prima decade del secolo XVI," *Archivio storico dell'arte* 7 (1894): 296–306.

Vickers, Brian, "Leisure and Idleness in the Renaissance: The Ambivalence of Otium," *Renaissance Studies* 4, 1 (1990): 1–37; and 4, 2: 107–54.

Victor, Turner, "Betwixt and Between: The Liminal Period in Rites of Passage," in *Proceedings of the American Ethnological Society for 1964* (Seattle 1964), 4–20.

Vignali, Luigi, *Il Lessico "Neoterico" del De Partibus Aedium di Francesco Mario Grapaldo* (Parma 2005).

Virgil, *Aeneid*, trans. H. Rushton Fairclough, Loeb Edition, 2 vols. (Cambridge, Mass. 1960).

Visuso, Teresa, ed., *Vincenzo degli Azani da Pavia e la cultura figurativa in Sicilia nell'età di Carlo V*, exh. cat. (Syracuse, Sicily 1999).

Vitruvius, *Ten Books on Architecture*, trans. Ingrid Rowland, commentary by Thomas Noble Howe (Cambridge 1999).

Vives, Giovan Ludovico, *De l'ufficio del marito come si debba portare verso la mogli. De l'istitutione della femina Christiana, vergine, maritata, ò vedova. De lo ammaestrare i fanciulli ne le arti liberali* (Venice 1546).

Wang, Y. Eugene, "Watching the Steps: Peripatetic Vision in Medieval China," in *Beyond Visuality before and beyond the Renaissance: Seeing as Others Saw*, ed. Robert S. Nelson (Cambridge 2000), 116–42.

Watt, Diane, ed., *Medieval Women in their Communities* (Toronto 1997).

Weaver, Elissa, "The Convent Muses: The Secular Writing of Italian Nuns, 1450–1650," in *Women and Faith: Catholic Religious Life in Italy from Late Antiquity to the Present*, ed. Lucetta Scaraffia and Gabriella Zarri (Cambridge 1999), 129–43.

———, *Convent Theatre in Early Modern Italy: Spiritual Fun and Learning for Women* (Cambridge 2002).

Webbe, L. Nancy, "The Three Graces in Renaissance Art: Origins and Transformations of a Theme," 2 vols. (Ph.D. diss., Boston University 1986).

Weddle, Saundra, ed., *The Chronicle of Le Murate: Giustina Niccolini* (Toronto 2011).

Weil-Garris, Kathleen, and John F. D'Amico, *The Renaissance Cardinal's Ideal Palace: A Chapter from Cortesi's De Cardinalatu* (Rome 1980).

Welch, Evelyn, "Public Magnificence and Private Display: Giovanni Pontano's *De Splendore* (1498) and the Domestic Arts," *Journal of Design History* 15, 4 (2002): 211–21.

Werdehausen, Anna Elisabeth, "L'architettura monastica in Lombardia fra Quattrocento e Cinquecento: Proposta per un metodo di ricerca," in *Giovanni Antonio Amadeo: Scultura e architettura del suo tempo*, ed. Janice Shell and Liana Castelfranchi Vegas (Milan 1993), 329–51.

Weststeijn, Thijs, "Seeing and the Transfer of Spirits in Early Modern Art Theory," in *Renaissance Theories of Vision*, ed. John Shannon Hendrix and Charles H. Carman (Farnham 2010), 149–69.

Wiesner-Hanks, Merry, *Christianity and Sexuality in the Early Modern World: Regulating Desire, Reforming Practices* (London 2000).

——, "Women's History and Social History: Are Structures Necessary?," in *Time, Space and Women's Lives in Early Modern Europe*, ed. Anne Jacobson Schutte, Thomas Kuehn, and Silvana Seidel Menchi (Kirksville, Mo. 2001), 3–16.

Wilson, Timothy, *Ceramic Art of the Italian Renaissance* (London and Austin, Tex. 1987).

——, "Italian Maiolica around 1500: Some Considerations on the Background to Antwerp Maiolica," in *Maiolica in the North: The Archeology of Tin-Glazed Earthenware in North-West Europe c. 1500–1600* (London 1999), 5–21.

Winkelmes, Mary Ann, "Taking Part: Benedictine Nuns as Patrons of Art and Architecture," in *Picturing Women in Renaissance and Baroque Italy*, ed. Geraldine A. Johnson and Sara F. Matthews Grieco (Cambridge 1997), 91–110.

Wittkower, Rudolf, "Hieroglyphics in the Early Renaissance," in *Allegory and the Migration of Symbols*, rep. ed. (London 1987), 113–28.

Wolf, Gerhard, *Schleier und Spiegel: Traditionen des Christusbildes und die Bildkonzepte der Renaissance* (Munich 2002).

Wolters, Wolfang, "Fussböden," in *Architektur und Ornament: Venezianischer Bauschmuck der Renaissance* (Munich 2000), 204–20.

Wood, Christopher S., "'Curious Images' and the Art of Description," *Word and Image* 11, 4 (1995): 332–52.

——, "Countermagical Combinations by Dosso Dossi," *Res* 49/50 (2006): 151–70.

Wood, Jeryldene, *Women, Art and Spirituality* (Cambridge 1996).

Wren Christian, Kathleen, *Empire Without End: Antiquities Collections in Renaissance Rome, c. 1350–1527* (New Haven and London 2010).

Young, Elizabeth M., "Catullus's Phaselus (C.4): Mastering a New Wave of Poetic Speech," *Arethusa* 44, 1 (2011): 69–88.

Zaggia, Massimo, *Tra Mantova e la Sicilia nel Cinquecento. II: la congregazione benedettina cassinese nel Cinquecento* (Florence 2003).

Zambelli, Paola, *Una Reincarnazione di Pico ai tempi di Pomponazzi* (Venice 1994).

——, "Continuity in the Definition of Natural Magic from Pico to Della Porta: Astrology and Magic in Italy and North of the Alps," in *White Magic, Black Magic in the European Renaissance* (Leiden 2007), 9–27.

Zambotti, Bernardino, *Diario Ferrarese dall'anno 1476 sino al 1504*, ed. Giuseppe Pardi, Rerum Italicarum Scriptores 24 (Bologna 1937).

Zanichelli, Giuseppa Z., *Iconologia della camera di Alessandro Araldi nel monastero di San Paolo in Parma*, intro. Arturo Carlo Quintavalle (Parma 1979).

——, "Alessandro Araldi e la camera di San Paolo," in *Il monastero di San Paolo*, ed. Marzio Dall'Acqua (Parma 1990), 81–111.

——, *Luminatum et ligatum fuit de mano mea. Codici miniati padani: scriptoria e committenza*, exh. cat. (Parma 1994).

——, "Il Maestro del Libro d'Ore Sanvitale e la bottega di Cristoforo Caselli: miniatura a Parma nella seconda metà del XV secolo," *Artes* 2 (1994): 39–68.

——, *I Conti e il minio: Codici miniati dei Rossi 1325–1482* (Parma 1996).

——, "La committenza dei Rossi: Immagini di potere fra sacro e profano," in *Le Signorie dei Rossi di Parma tra XIV e XVI secolo*, ed. Letizia Arcangeli and Marco Gentile (Florence 2007), 187–212.

Zardin, Danilo, *Donna e religiosa di rara eccellenza: Prospera Corona Bascapè. I libri e la cultura nei monasteri milanesi del Cinque e Seicento* (Florence 1992).

Zarri, Gabriella, "I monasteri femminili di Bologna tra il XIII e il XVII secolo," *Atti e memorie della Deputazione di storia patria per le province di Romagna*, n.s. 24 (1973): 133–234.

——, "Monasteri femminili e città (secoli XV–XVIII)," in *Storia d'Italia: Annali*, ed. Giorgio Chittolini and Giovanni Miccoli (Turin 1986), 9: 359–429.

——, "Le Istituzioni dell'educazione femminile," in *Le Sedi della cultura nell'Emilia Romagna. I Secoli moderni: le istituzioni e il pensiero*, 5 vols. (Bologna 1987), 5: 84–109.

——, "Recinti sacri: Sito e forma dei monasteri femminili a Bologna tra '500 e '600," in *Luoghi sacri e spazi della santità*, ed. Sofia Boesch Gajano and Lucetta Scaraffia (Turin 1990), 381–96.

——, ed., *Il monachesimo femminile in Italia dall'alto medioevo al secolo XVII: a confronto con l'oggi* (Negarine di San Pietro in Cariano [Vr] 1997).

——, "Gender, Religious Institutions and Social Discipline: The Reform of the Regulars," in *Gender and Society in Renaissance Italy*, ed. Judith Brown and Robert Davis (London 1998).

——, *Recinti: Donne, clausura e matrimonio nella prima età moderna* (Bologna 2000).

——, "Christian Good Manners: Spiritual and Monastic Rules in the Quattro- and Cinquecento," in *Women in Italian Renaissance Culture and Society*, ed. Letizia Panizza (Oxford 2000), 76–91.

——, "Tra monache e confessori: la corte di Lucrezia Borgia," in *L'età di Alfonso I e la pittura del Dosso* (Modena 2004), 103–18.

——, "Il velo delle monache: Repertori di costume degli ordini religiosi (secoli XV–XVIII)," in *Il velo in area mediterranea tra storia e simbolo: Tardo medioevo–prima età moderna*, ed.

Giuseppina Muzzarelli, Maria Grazia Nico Ottaviani, and Gabriella Zarri (Bologna 2014), 195–210.

Zchomelidse, Nino, and Giovanni Freni, eds., *Meaning in Motion: The Semantics of Movement in Medieval Art* (Princeton 2011).

Zemon Davis, Natalie, "Boundaries and the Sense of Self in Sixteenth-Century France," in *Reconstructing Individualism: Autonomy, Individuality, and the Self in Western Thought*, ed. Thomas Heller, Morton Sosna, and David Wellbery (Stanford 1986).

Zorach, Rebecca, *Blood, Milk, Ink, Gold: Abundance and Excess in the French Renaissance* (Chicago 2005).

——, *The Passionate Triangle* (Chicago 2011).

Zorzi Pugliese, Olga, *Castiglione's The Book of the Courtier (Il Libro del Cortegiano): A Classic in the Making* (Rome 2008).

Photographic Credits

Index

286

Medusa imagery, 179, *179*, *181*, 182
punishment themes, *190*, 194, 196–97
reclining figural imagery, 200
Stupor incarnations in, 173–74
war and aggressive action personifications, *198*, 198–99

names, 26, 45, *46*, 116, 117–18
Natalibus, Petrus de (bishop), 113
Natural History (Pliny), 42, 193
nature
    invention *vs.* imitation of, 141
    jokes of, 190
    outdoor contemplation and power of, 109
    sacred mysteries and studies of, 151–52
Navagero, Andrea, 185
Nelli, Plautilla: *Last Supper*, 21
Nero (emperor), coins of, 193, 200, *200*
Niccolò da Poggibonsi, 48
Niccolò' Fiorentino, 201
Nogarola, Isotta, 114, 145
Nova, Alessandro, 170
nudes (*ignudi*), 127, *127*
numerology, 149, 153–54
nuns. *See also* abbesses; clothing and accessories;
    comportment codes; patrician nuns; rules and
    regulations
    artisan activities, 3, 21, *22*
    ecclesiastic hierarchy and status of, 4, 5, 38, 99, 154
    fresco depictions of, *30*, 32, *72*, *73*, 80–85, *84*, 88, *88*,
        159–60, *160*
    living quarters of, 74–79
    manual labor of, *8*, *9*, *10*, 21, 22, 24, 83, 120
    medieval author characterizations of, 175
    misogynist criticism of, 4–5, 58–59
    monastic lifestyle descriptions, 1, 4, 16–17, 185
    paintings featuring, *8*, *9*, *10*, 18–20, *19*, *206*, 207
    portrait paintings of, 5, *28*, 31, 57–60, *58*, *61*
    rites of passage, 23–24, *24*, *25*
    roles of, 9–10, 20, 83, 114
    scholarship studies on, 3
    sexual relations of, 4–5, 58–59, 78–79, 185
    social status comparisons of, 24, 34
    vestal virgin associations, 197–98
    vows of, 16, 17–18, 23, 185, 198
nun's cells, 34, 35, 36, 38, 74–79, *75*, *78*
nuns' choirs
    altarpieces in, 80, 91, 97
    artwork purpose in, 79
    choirstalls in, *93*, 93–97, *94*, *95*, *96*
    description and function, 34, 79
    San Maurizio frescoes, 85–93, *86*, *87*, *88*, *89*
    San Paolo frescos, 79–80
    San Paolo renovations of, 34, 94
    Santa Giulia frescoes, 80–85, *81*, *82*, *83*, *84*
Nutricia (Politian), 173

obedience
    behaviours contradictory to, 11, 20
    behaviours indicating, 52
    didiactic text illustrations of, 17, *17*
    fresco imagery with themes of duty and, 138, 156,
        157, 162, 163–65
    as ladders of spiritual perfection rung, 16
    manual labor and artisan work as, 21
    ornamentation as defiance of, 6, 50, 51, 127
    vows of, 16
Obizio, St., 84, *84*, 84–85
obscurity
    concealed portraits, 64, 119
    controversy of, 188, 190
    fresco interpretations and indeterminacy, 106, 148,
        155, 172, 188–90

inscriptions as word games, 116–19
motifs symbolizing, 190
occult. *See* magic
Occulta Philosophia (Trithemius), 150
Ombrone, 187
On [Intellectual] Eyeglasses (Cusa), 151
On Learned Ignorance (Cusa), 152
On the Vision of God (Cusa), 152
opposites, coincidence of, 1, 4, 74, 76, 138, 151–52, 169
*Ordine delle nozze dello Illustrissimo Signore Meser
    Costantio Sfortia*, 48–49, *49*
Ordinum Religiosorum in Ecclesia Militanti Catalogus
    (Buonanni), 26, *26*
Orlando innamorato (Bioardo), 63
"other" spaces, concept of, 102, 110–11, 173
otium (leisure), 52, 74, 108, 120–21, 176. *See also*
    recreation
ouroboros signs, 119, *119*, 194
Ovid, 69, 121, 187
ownership pride, *118*, 121
oxen skull imagery (*bucrania*), 191, 194

paganism. *See also* mythology
    censorship and restriction of, 22, 128
    fresco imagery with themes of, 127, *127*, 147–48, 189
    grotesque associations with, 141–42
    and idolatry, 128–29, 147–48, 150
    traits associated with, 120
paintings. *See also* frescoes
    admittance dowries including, 24
    floor tile ornamentation comparisons, 43
    fresco illusionistic imagery as transported, 145–47,
        146, *147*
    function of appropriate and skillful, 128
    of nude figures, 75, 127
    nun-artist production of, 21
    nun portraits, 5, 31, 57–60, *58*, *61*
    restrictions on ownership of, 59
    viewing experiences and roles of, 43
palaces. *See also* episcopal palaces
    architectural design requirements for, 128
    ecclesiastical design recommendations, 108, 109, 116,
        188
    monastic *vs.* secular comparisons, 108, 111, 109
Palazzo Costabili (Ferrara), 154
Palazzo Ducale. *See* Camera Picta, Palazzo Ducale,
    Mantua (Mantegna)
Palazzo Fantuzzi (Bologna), 48
Palazzo Roverella (Ascoli Piceno), 99
Palazzo Te (Mantua), 109
Palazzo Vescovile (Ferrara), 154
Paleotti, Gabriele (bishop), 125, 141, 155, 190
Pallavicino, Giovanna (nun), 33
Pallavicino, Rolando II, 151
Pampurino, Alessandro, 154
Pan (mythological character), 182, *182*, 194, *199*, 199–200
panic, feelings of, 199–200
Panizza, Letizia, 139
Panofsky, Erwin
    Correggio's arrow interpretations, 182
    Correggio's Fates, 202
    Correggio's frescoes and decoding starting point, 174
    Correggio's gemstone identifications, 179
    Correggio's humanist tradition, 169, 171
    Correggio's punishment of Hera, 196
    Correggio study contributions, 100, 138
papal privilege, 32–34, 125
Paradise, from *Divine Comedy* (Dante Alighieri), 10–11
paragone of materials, 145, *186*, 186–87
Paris (mythological figure), 70, *70*
Paris, Matthew, 48
parlors, 12, 13–15, *15*, 108, 115

Parma (Italy)
    artistic patronage in, 32
    artists from, 32, 80, 96
    convents in, 16, *96*, 96–97 (*see also* San Paolo convent)
    ecclesiastic jurisdiction conflicts, 33
    maiolica pottery production in, 46
    monasteries in, 97, 135, 143, 148
    political instability in, 46, 102–3
    public bonfires of the vanities, 103
    public festivities in, 63–64
Parma Cathedral, 137, 143, *143*, 182, 187, *187*
Parmigianino
    artistic style, 80
    Head of Giorgio Anselmi, 150–51, *151*
    Portrait of a Collector (Marco Garbazza?), 116, *117*
    Portrait of Galeazzo Sanvitale, 149, *149*
    Rocca Sanvitale frescoes, 182 (detail), *183*, 187
parodies, 162, 165, 173, 185, 187
Passio Mauritii et sotiorum eius (Marcello), 48
Passion of Christ, 76, *82*, 83, 86–88, *87*
patrician laywomen
    clothing and accessories of, *30*, 38, 58
    conventual residency of, 34, 35, 36, 38
    floor tile portraits of, 56, *56*
    fresco portraits of, 36–37, 38
patrician nuns. *See also* abbesses; nuns
    admittance dowries, 24
    claustration obligations and observations, 11, 12
    clothing and accessories, 11, 18, 20, 26, 26–27, *28*, 57,
        58
    conventual admission, 10–11
    conventual regulations opposed by, 20
    finances of, 18
    lifestyle descriptions, 1, 3, 4, 5
    living quarters of, 74–79, *75*, *78* (*see also* furnishings;
        possessions)
    mobility restrictions and circulation freedom, 18–20
    monastic lifestyle descriptions, 1, 22, 26
    parlor entertainment depictions, 14, *15*
    portraits of, 5, 31, 54–55, *56*, 56–57, 57–60, *58*, *61*
    rites of passage of, 23–24, *24*, *25*
    social status and special treatment of, 20, 22, 24, 26
    surname retention, 26
Patrizi, Francesco, 111
patronage
    conventual rivalry and, 73–74, 96–97
    conventual sponsorship, 14, 20
    donor portraits, 91–92
    markers as signs of, 43, 64, 123
    pictorial planning process and, 137–38
Paul, St., 105, 154
Paulinus of Nola (bishop), 123
Paulus, Aemilius, 157, 158, *159*
peacocks, 70, *71*
Pelta, Maureen, 169
Penni, Gianfrancesco: Santa Maria di Monteluce
    altarpiece, with Romano and Raphael, 80
Peregrino, Il (Caviceo), 110, 172
perfume metaphors, 119–20, 184
Periculoso (Boniface VIII), 12
Pero (mythological character), 162, *162*
Perotti, Niccolò, 42–43
Perseus of Macedon (king), 158
Persius, 123–24, 200
personal devices, 116, *119*, 119–20
Pesaro (Italy), 45–46, 49, 60
Petillius Capitolinus coin, 194, *195*
Petrarch
    art as idolatry, 128–29
    coin/medal collections, 155
    contemplation for spiritual transcendence, 90–91
    excessive love remedies as reading, 139–40

Sanvitale, Galeazzo, 149, *149*
Sanvitale, Giovanna (abbess), 97
San Zaccaria convent (Venice), 14, *15*, 23
sarcophagi, 157, *158*, 176, *176*
Sardi, Gaspare, 177
Sarti, Raffaella, 26
Satires (Persius), 124
Saturn (god), 200
satyrs
    breastfeeding imagery, 163, *163*
    as fresco subjects, 134, *134*, 136, 142–43, 153, 165
    with masks, 157
    punishment themes and myths of, 197
Savonarola, Girolamo, 59, 73, 128
scala perfectionis, 16
scapulimancy, 150
Scarabelli Zunti, Enrico, 33, 49
Schianchi, Lucia Fornari, 44–45, 46, 49–50
Scholastica, St.
    as role model for nuns, 39
    Sacro Speco frescoes featuring, 38–39, *39*
    San Maurizio frescoes featuring, 88, *91*, 92
    San Paolo frescoes featuring, 31, *31*, 38, 39
Schongauer, Martin: *Elephant, The*, 48, *48*
scorpions, *192*, 193, *193*
seclusion. *See* claustration
self-glory, 124
self-identity, 116, 118–20, *119*, 128
self-knowledge, 121
self-love, 121, 122
self-reflection, 52–53, 56–57, *69*
self-reimagination, 57–60, *58*, *61*
self-reliance, 123–24, 200
self-restraint, 7, 18, 52, 66, 158, 160, 177
sella, 53, *53*
Seneca, 201
sententiae, 122, 139–40
serio-ludere, 173, 189
Servius, 163, 164
sexuality. *See also* chastity
    conventual vows and restrictions of, criticism, 185
    floor tile themes, 67, *67*
    fresco imagery, 78
    nuns and accusations of, criticism, 4–5, 58–59
    rooms associated with, 79, 176, 185
    sexual relations, 78–79, 185
    virgin and unicorn eroticism, 158–60, *160*
Sforza, Alessandro, 46, 66
Sforza, Camilla of Aragon, 47, 48–49, *49*
Sforza, Costanzo, 46–47, 48–49, *49*
Sforza, Ippolita, 91, *91*
Sforza castle, 167, *169*, 189–90
Sforza family, 38, 102
Sforza wedding manuscript, 48–49, *49*
sharing themes, 201–2
shells, scallop, 190, *190*
Sigifredo II (bishop), 32
Sigismondo d'Este, 23
signatures of artists, 21, 123, 154, 189
silence, 114, 176, 184, 203
Silius Italicus, 198
Sixtus IV (pope), 20
sloth (idleness), 68, 120, 128
Smagliati, Leone, 64, 93, 103, 122–23
Smeraldi, Smeraldo, 115–16, 185–86
snakes, tail-eating (*ouroboros*), 119, *119*, 194
social status
    architecture and art as manifestations of, 106, 127–28
    conventual life as marker of, 113
    ecclesiastical gender comparisons, 5, 38, 99, 154
    possessions as manifestations of, 76

property management for, 33
religious community portraits illustrating, 38
rivalry and competition, 93, 96–97
symbols of, 1, 32, 38, 124
Solomon's Temple (Jerusalem), 13
Song of Songs, 176
sphinxes, 131, *137*, 146, *148*
Spina, Aldo, 50; *109*
spiritelli. See putti
spirits. *See also* demons/demonic spirits
    body penetration methods, 150, 174, 183
    fire evoking, 140
    personal, *192*, 193
    vital, 136, 151, 183
    wind, 137
spiritual perfection
    conventual lifestyles and goals of, 1, 11, 16
    deterrents to, 29
    devotional objects and meditation for, 79
    grotesque imagery for inner struggle contemplation,
    142
    virtues assisting in, 18, 198
spiritual renewal. *See* regeneration
spiritual transcendence, 90–91
SS. Trinità dei Rossi (*now* Santa Teresa del Bambin
    Gesù, Parma), 93, 93–96, *94*, *95*
St. Florian Abbey (Austria), 99
St. Katherine (Freiburg), 100
stag heads, 179, *181*
Statius, 198
Stefaniak, Regina, 170, 184
stemma. See arms, coats of
stones, semiprecious, 150, 152, 179, *181*, 182
Strocchia, Sharon, 18, 21
Strozzi, Agostino (abbot), 113
stupor, 173–74
Stupori (Anselmi the Younger), 173–74
Suardi oratory, 182, *183*
Suger (abbot), 128
surveillance and supervision, 108
swords
    floor tile imagery, 66, 69, *70*
    fresco imagery, 161, *161*, 162
    inscriptions and symbolism of, 168, 177
symbola, 155, 177, 187
Symbola Pythagorae Moraliter Explicata (Beroaldo), 177
Syson, Luke, 42, 54, 155

tableware, 24, 67, *67*, 74
Tadeus vel de locis Persianis (Fonzio), 124
tapestries, 1, 100, *102–3*
Tarabotti, Arcangela, 10
tarot cards, 66, *66*
temples, 13, 190–91, *191*, 193, 194, *195*
Terence, 111, 124
terror, 199–200
textile production, 21, *22*, 23
theatrical performances, 13–14, 109, 173
theatrum Sapientiae (theater of wisdom), 148
Thebaid (Statius), 198
Thisbe (mythological character), 69–70, *70*
Thornton, Dora, 42, 54
Three Graces, The, 127, *127*, 194, 196, 201, *201*
Tibullus, 124
Timanthes, 187
Timoteo, 4–5
tituli (one-line inscriptions), 121–25, *122*, *123*, 168–69
Tonelli, Fabrizio, 194
tonsure, 23, 31, 56
torches, 197, 198, *198*
Torelli, Antonia, *30*, 34, 35, 36, 38
Torelli, Costanza (abbess), 34

Tornabuoni, Giovanna, 201
Tortelli, Giovanni, villa of, 123
Toschi, Paolo, 49, 50
tournaments, 63
Tractatus et Libri (Cusa), 151
transformation, as viewer experience, 51, 52, 57, 138
transvestism, 14
Trattato di Architettura (Filarete), 12, *13*, 124, *125*, 125–26, 174
Traversari, Ambrogio, 21
Trithemius, Johannes (abbot), 150
triumphs, Roman, 131, 157, 158, *159*, 194
trust, 68, 70, *71*, 123–24
Turner, Victor, 22
Tusculan Disputations (*Tusculanæ Disputationes*) (Cicero),
    121, 139

Ugoleto, Taddeo
    anagrams, 117, 118
    biographical information, 95
    coin/medal collections of, 155, 196
    Filarete text translations, 174
    inscription usage, 95
    levity, 111
    manuscript studies and collections, 124
    Plautus comedies, commentaries on, 188
    Plautus plays reprinted by, 124
    republications of, 193
    San Paolo associations, 95, 124
unicorns, 11, *11*, 68, 77, 158–60, *160*
Ursula, St., 74, *75*
utility, as architectural value, 108, 128

Valeriano, Pierio, 95
Valerius Maximus, 155, 162, 163
Valerius Probus, 196
Van der Aa, Petrus, 14
vanity, 26, 68, 103, 128, 162
Vasari, Giorgio, 21, 42, 71, 81, 97, 123, 207
veiling (rite of passage), 23–24, *24*, *25*
Velázquez, Diego: *Portrait of the Venerable Mother Jerónima
    de la Fuente*, 58
Veneziano, Jacometto
    Portrait of Alvise Contarini, 57, *57*–58, *59*
    Portrait of a Nun from San Secondo, 4, 5, 28 (detail), 31,
        57–58, 59–60, 159
    Portrait of a Woman, possibly a Novice of San Secondo,
        60, *61*
Venus (goddess), 70, *70*, 174, *174*
Verde (nun), 24
Vergil, Polydor, 193
Verrocchio, 63
Vespasian (emperor), coins of, 194
vestals, *197*, 197–98
Vicentino (Vincenzo de Grandi), 191
Vicenza, Andrea, 24
Villa Farnesina (Rome), 109
Villa Pelucca (Milan), 174, *174*, 187
Villa Schifanoia (Ferrara), 42
Virgil, 69, 119, 163, 185, 194, 196
Virgin Mary
    altarpiece frescoes featuring, 167, *169*
    cathedral dome frescoes featuring, 182, 187, *187*
    convent frescoes featuring, *30*, 31, 32, 36–37, 38, 56
    subject suitability for nuns, 76
virgins. *See also* chastity
    intercessory roles of, 9, 83
    Roman vestal, *197*, 197–98
    with unicorns, 11, *11*, 68, 158–60, *160*
Viridario (Achillini), 187
virtue(s), female
    architectural designs contributing to, 128
    architectural investments symbolizing, 94–95